ThomsonNOW™

for *The Essence of Anthropology*

Just what you need to learn NOW!

Take charge of your learning with **ThomsonNOW**™ for *The Essence of Anthropology*, the first assessment-centered student learning tool for anthropology. This powerful and interactive resource will help you gauge your own unique study needs. Then, it gives you a personalized study plan that helps you focus your study time on the concepts you most need to master. This unmatched resource enhances the text, providing you with a seamless, integrated learning system. Which means you'll spend less time flipping through pages or navigating websites and more time learning the material.

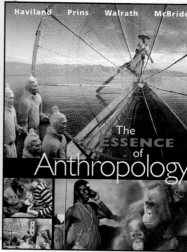

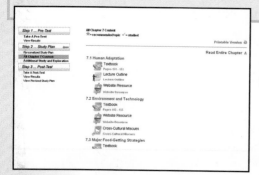

How Does It Work?

Just log on to **ThomsonNOW for *The Essence of Anthropology*** by using the access code packaged with your text.* You will immediately notice the system's simple, browser-based format—as easy to use as surfing the web. Just a click of the mouse gives you the freedom to enter and explore the system at any point. You can build a complete, personalized learning plan for yourself by taking advantage of all three of **ThomsonNOW's** powerful components.

What I Know

A *Pre-Test* is the first step. *Pre-Test* questions are designed to help you identify what you need to study more—you receive your score automatically. Once you've completed the *Pre-Test*, a detailed *Personalized Study* plan (based on your test results) outlines the concepts you need to review and presents links to specific pages in your textbook that discuss that concept.

What I Need to Learn

Working from your *Personalized Study* plan, you will be guided to media-enhanced activities such as map exercises, learning modules, and video exercises to help you master the material. This section helps you gain a full understanding of the chapter material.

What I've Learned

An optional *Post-Test* ensures that you've mastered the concepts in each chapter. As with the *Pre-Test*, your individual results may be e-mailed to your instructor to help you both assess your progress. If you need to improve your score, **ThomsonNOW for *The Essence of Anthropology*** will work with you as you continue to build your knowledge.

Instructors

ThomsonNOW for *The Essence of Anthropology* gives you access to comprehensive course management and presentation materials that will enhance your teaching and your students' learning. Contact your Thomson representative about packaging access with new copies of the text at no additional cost to your students, and visit **www.thomsonedu.com/thomsonnow** for a tour.

*Access to **ThomsonNOW** for *The Essence of Anthropology* is web based. **Your instructor may have chosen to package the access code card with your new text.** In this case, you'll find the access card within this text, which contains your free four-month pass code, allowing you anytime access to **ThomsonNOW**. If your instructor did not order the free access code card to be packaged with your text—or if you have a used copy of the text—you can still obtain an access code for a nominal fee. Just visit the Thomson Wadsworth E-Commerce site at www. thomsonedu.com/anthropology, where easy-to-follow instructions help you purchase your access code.

Log on to **ThomsonNOW for *The Essence of Anthropology*** and get one step closer to success!

Take a tour online at **www.thomsonedu.com/anthropology**

W9-CXU-136

The Essence
of Anthropology

WILLIAM A. HAVILAND
Professor Emeritus
University of Vermont

HARALD E. L. PRINS
Kansas State University

DANA WALRATH
University of Vermont

BUNNY McBRIDE
Kansas State University

high>

THOMSON
™
WADSWORTH

Australia • Brazil • Canada • Mexico • Singapore • Spain • United Kingdom • United States

THE ESSENCE OF ANTHROPOLOGY: William A. Haviland, Harald E. L. Prins, Dana Walrath, Bunny McBride

Anthropology Editor: Lin Marshall
Development Editor: Julie Cheng
Assistant Editor: Leata Holloway
Editorial Assistant: Danielle Yumol
Technology Project Manager: Dee Dee Zobian
Marketing Manager: Caroline Concilla
Marketing Assistant: Teresa Jessen
Marketing Communications Manager: Linda Yip
Project Manager, Editorial Production: Emily Smith
Creative Director: Rob Hugel
Art Director: Maria Epes
Print Buyer: Barbara Britton
Permissions Editor: Sarah D'Stair
Production Service: Robin C. Hood
Text Designer: Lisa Buckley

Photo Researcher: Billie L. Porter
Copy Editor: Jennifer Gordon
Illustrator: Carol Zuber-Mallison
Compositor: Pre-Press Company, Inc.
Cover Designer: Larry Didona
Cover Images: Fisherman with Fishing Weir: © Bob Krist/CORBIS; Maasai Moran Warrior on Cell Phone, Kenya: © Joseph Van Os / Getty Images; Terracotta Army Xian China: © Geoffrey Morgan / Alamy; Orangutan: © STOCK IMAGE / Alamy; Student teacher Joyce Butler of Columbia University and famous chimpanzee (Pan troglodytes), Nim Chimpsky: © Susan Kuklin / Photo Researchers, Inc.; Mesa Verde National Park, Colorado: Tower House, Anasazi ruins. © Larry Kolvoord/The Image Works
Text and Cover Printer: Courier Corporation/Kendallville

© 2007 Thomson Wadsworth, a part of The Thomson Corporation. Thomson, the Star logo, and Wadsworth are trademarks used herein under license.

ALL RIGHTS RESERVED. No part of this work covered by the copyright hereon may be reproduced or used in any form or by any means— graphic, electronic, or mechanical, including photocopying, recording, taping, Web distribution, information storage and retrieval systems, or in any other manner—without the written permission of the publisher.

Printed in the United States of America
2 3 4 5 6 7 10 09 08 07 06

For more information about our products, contact us at:
Thomson Learning Academic Resource Center
1-800-423-0563
For permission to use material from this text or product, submit a request online at **http://www.thomsonrights.com.**
Any additional questions about permissions can be submitted by email to **thomsonrights@thomson.com.**

ExamView® and ExamView Pro® are registered trademarks of FSCreations, Inc. Windows is a registered trademark of the Microsoft Corporation used herein under license. Macintosh and Power Macintosh are registered trademarks of Apple Computer, Inc. Used herein under license.

© 2007 Thomson Learning, Inc. All Rights Reserved. Thomson Learning WebTutor™ is a trademark of Thomson Learning, Inc.

Thomson Higher Education
10 Davis Drive
Belmont, CA 94002-3098
USA

Library of Congress Control Number: 2006925021

ISBN-13: 978-0-534-62371-5
ISBN-10: 0-534-62371-9

We dedicate this book to the memory of our mutual friend and colleague Jim Petersen, a warm-hearted and generous-spirited scholar who personified the ideal anthropologist.

ABOUT THE AUTHORS

The Essence of Anthropology authors, Bunny McBride, Dana Walrath, Harald Prins, and William Haviland.

While distinct from one another, all four members of this author team share overlapping research interests and a similar vision of what anthropology is (and should be) about. For example, all are "true believers" in the four-field approach to anthropology and all have some involvement in applied work.

Dr. William A. Haviland is Professor Emeritus at the University of Vermont, where he has taught since 1965. He holds a Ph.D. in Anthropology from the University of Pennsylvania and has published widely on archaeological, ethnological, and physical anthropological research carried out in Guatemala, Maine, and Vermont. Dr. Haviland is a member of many professional societies, including the American Anthropological Association and the American Association for the Advancement of Science, and he has participated in many projects, including "Gender and the Anthropological Curriculum," sponsored by the American Anthropological Association in 1988. Dr. Haviland has always loved teaching and writing for anthropology students and he has a passionate interest in indigenous rights, having worked with the Maya for years. He continues to work with Native Americans in the northeastern United States.

Harald E. L. Prins (Ph.D. New School 1988) is a University Distinguished Professor of Anthropology at Kansas State University and guest curator at the National Museum of Natural History, Smithsonian Institution. Born in The Netherlands, he studied at universities in Europe and the United States. He has done extensive fieldwork among indigenous peoples in South and North America, published dozens of articles in five languages, co-edited some books, and authored "The Mi'kmaq: Resistance, Accommodation, and Cultural Survival" (1996). He also made award-winning documentaries and served as president of the Society for Visual Anthropology and visual anthropology editor of the *American Anthropologist*. Dr. Prins has won his university's most prestigious undergraduate teaching awards and held the Coffman Chair for University Distinguished Teaching Scholars (2004–05). Active in human rights, he served as expert witness in Native rights cases in the U.S. Senate and various Canadian courts, and was instrumental in the successful federal recognition and land claims of the Aroostook band of Micmacs (1991).

Dr. Dana Walrath is Assistant Professor of Family Medicine at the University of Vermont and a Women's Studies affiliated faculty member. She earned her Ph.D. from the University of Pennsylvania and is a medical and biological anthropologist with principal interests in biocultural aspects of reproduction, health and disease, sex differences, genetics, and evolutionary medicine. She directs an innovative educational program at the University of Vermont's College of Medicine that brings anthropological theory and practice to first-year medical students. Dr. Walrath received pre-doctoral fellowships from the National Science Foundation, Foreign Languages Area Studies, and the University of Pennsylvania. Before joining the

faculty at the University of Vermont in 2000, she taught at the University of Pennsylvania and Temple University. Her recent research has been supported by the Health Resources and Services Administration and the Centers for Disease Control. Dr. Walrath's publications have appeared in *Current Anthropology, American Anthropologist,* and *American Journal of Physical Anthropology.* She is an active member of the Council on the Anthropology of Reproduction and the Society of Medical Anthropology. She served on the national committee that developed women's health-care learning objectives for undergraduate medical education sponsored by the Association of Professors of Obstetrics and Gynecology.

Bunny McBride is an award-winning author with an M.A. degree in Anthropology from Columbia University. She is an adjunct lecturer of anthropology at Kansas State University and taught as a regular visiting lecturer at Principia College in Illinois, 1981–2003. She has also taught at the Salt Institute for Documentary Field Studies in Portland, Maine, and given dozens of guest lectures in public and academic venues. Her books include *Women of the Dawn* (University of Nebraska Press, 1999), *Molly Spotted Elk: A Penobscot in Paris* (University of Oklahoma Press, 1995), and *Our Lives in Our Hands: Micmac Indian Basketmakers* (Nimbus and Tilbury House, 1990). Working in close collaboration with Native

American communities, she has served as curator of museum exhibits based on these books. From 1981–1991 McBride did historical research and community development work for the Aroostook band of Micmacs in Maine, contributing to their successful efforts to gain federal status, establish a land base, and revitalize cultural traditions. In 1999 the Maine state legislature gave McBride a special commendation for her research and writing on the history of Native women in the state—an honor initiated by elected tribal representatives in the legislature. Currently, she serves as co-principal investigator for a National Parks Service ethnographic research project, oral history advisor for the Kansas Humanities Council, and board member of the Women's World Summit Foundation, based in Geneva, Switzerland.

Brief Contents

Contents

Features Contents

Original Studies

Anthropology Applied

Biocultural Connections

Preface

For some time now we have been contemplating how to present anthropology to undergraduates in a textbook that is reader-friendly and to-the-point, while doing justice to the breadth and depth of the discipline. With the publication of *The Essence of Anthropology,* we think we have done just that.

The Essence is a concise, reader-friendly text for introductory courses in four-field anthropology—or, as we prefer to think of it, *holistic anthropology.* It stands on the substantial shoulders of our *Anthropology: The Human Challenge* (the discipline's leading introductory textbook for three decades), but has its own fresh and less weighty character. As we wrote these pages, the word "essence" served as our guiding force—alerting us to reach for content that covers anthropology's classical foundations and modern ramifications without getting carried away by too many details or examples. We aimed for an engaging, quick-moving narrative that gives anthropology majors a solid basis for more advanced coursework while sowing seeds of awareness in all students concerning cultural and biological diversity.

OUR MISSION

It is common for students to enter an introductory anthropology class intrigued by the general subject but with little more than a vague sense of what it is all about. Thus, the first and most obvious task of our text is to provide a thorough introduction to the discipline—its foundations as a domain of knowledge and its major insights into the rich diversity of humans as a culture-making species. In doing this, we draw from the research and ideas of a number of traditions of anthropological thought, exposing students to a mix of theoretical perspectives and methodologies. Such inclusiveness reflects our conviction that different approaches offer distinctly important insights about human biology, behavior, and beliefs.

If most students start out with only a vague sense of what anthropology is, they often have less clear—and potentially more problematical—views of the superiority of their own culture and its place in the world. A secondary task for this text, then, is to prod students to appreciate the rich complexity and breadth of human behavior. Along with this is the task of helping them understand why there are so many differences and similarities in the human condition, past and present. Debates regarding globalization and notions of progress, the "naturalness" of the mother/father/child(ren) nuclear family, new genetic technologies, and how gender roles relate to biological variation all

benefit greatly from the fresh and often fascinating insights gained through anthropology. This probing aspect of our discipline is perhaps the most valuable gift we can pass on to those who take our classes. If we, as teachers (and textbook authors), do our jobs well, students will gain a wider and more open-minded outlook on the world and a critical but constructive perspective on their own cultures. To paraphrase the famous poet T.S. Eliot: After all our explorations, they will come home and know the place for the first time.

If ever there were a time when students needed anthropological tools to step out of culture-bound ways of thinking and acting and to gain a more tolerant view of humanity in which respect for other ways of life grows out of actual understanding and appreciation, it is now. Thus, we have written this text, in large part, as a tool to help students make sense of our increasingly complex world and to navigate through its interrelated biological and cultural networks with knowledge and skill, whatever professional path they take. We see it as a guide for people entering the often bewildering maze of global crossroads in the 21st century.

A DISTINCTIVE APPROACH

Two key factors distinguish *The Essence* from other introductory anthropology texts: Our integrative presentation of the discipline's four fields and a trio of unifying themes that tie the book together and keep students from feeling lost.

Integration of the Four Fields

Unlike traditional texts that present anthropology's four "fields"—archaeology, linguistics, cultural, and physical anthropology—as if they were relatively separate or independent, our book takes an integrative approach. This reflects the comprehensive character of our discipline, a domain of knowledge where members of our species are studied in their totality—as social creatures biologically evolved with the inherent capacity of learning and sharing culture by means of symbolic communication. This approach also reflects our collective experience as practicing anthropologists who recognize that we cannot fully understand humanity in all its fascinating complexity unless we see the systemic interplay between environmental, physiological, material, social, ideological, psychological, and symbolic factors, both past and present.

For analytical purposes, of course, we have no choice but to discuss physical anthropology as distinct from archaeology, linguistics, and sociocultural anthropology. Accordingly, there are separate chapters that focus primarily on each field, but the links between them are shown repeatedly. Among many examples of this integrative approach, Chapter 8 on Race and Human Diversity discusses the social context of "race" and recent cultural practices that have impacted the human genome. Similarly, material concerning linguistics appears not only in the chapter on Language and Communication (10), but also in the chapters on Living Primates (3), Human Evolution (5), and the Emergence of Cities and States (7). These chapters include material on the linguistic capabilities of apes, the emergence of human language, and the origin of writing. In addition, every chapter includes a "biocultural connection" box to further illustrate the interplay of biological and cultural processes in shaping the human experience.

Unifying Themes

In our own teaching, we have come to recognize the value of marking out unifying themes that help students see the big picture as they grapple with the great array of concepts and information encountered in the study of human beings. In *The Essence* we employ three such themes.

1) We present anthropology as a study of humankind's responses through time to the fundamental **challenges of survival**. Each chapter is framed by this theme, opening with a Challenge Issue paragraph and photograph and ending with Questions for Reflection tied to that particular challenge.

2) We emphasize the integration of human culture and biology in the steps humans take to meet these challenges. This **biocultural connection** theme appears throughout the text—as a thread in the main narrative and in a boxed feature that highlights this connection with a topical example for each chapter.

3) We track the emergence of **globalization and its disparate impact on various peoples and cultures around the world**. While European colonization was a global force for centuries, leaving a significant—often devastating—footprint on the affected peoples in Asia, Africa, and the Americas, decolonization began about 200 years ago and became a worldwide wave in the mid-1900s. Since the 1960s, however, political-economic hegemony has taken a new and fast-paced form, namely globalization (in many ways a concept that expands or builds on imperialism). Both forms of global domination—colonialism and globalization—run through *Essence,* culminating in the final chapter where we apply the concept of structural power to globalization, discussing it in terms of hard and soft power and linking it to structural violence.

PEDAGOGY

The Essence of Anthropology features a range of learning aids, in addition to the three unifying themes described above. Each pedagogical piece plays an important role in the learning process—from clarifying and enlivening the material, to revealing relevancy and aiding recall.

Accessible Language and a Cross-Cultural Voice

What could be more basic in pedagogy than clear communication? In addition to our standing as professional anthropologists, all four co-authors have made a specialty of speaking to audiences outside of our profession. Using that experience in the writing of this text, we made a point of cutting through a lot of unnecessary jargon to speak directly to students. Manuscript reviewers recognized this, noting that even the most difficult concepts are presented in prose that is straightforward and easy for today's first- and second-year college students to understand, without feeling they are being "spoken down to." Where technical terms are necessary, they appear in bold-faced type, are carefully defined in the narrative, and defined again in the running glossary in simple, clear language.

Accessibility involves not only clear writing but also an engaging voice or style. The voice of *The Essence* is distinct among introductory texts in the discipline, for it has been written from a cross-cultural perspective. This means we strove to avoid the typical Western "we/they" voice in favor of a more inclusive one that will resonate with both Western and non-Western students and professors. Moreover, the book highlights the theories and work of anthropologists from all over the world. Finally, its cultural examples come from industrial and postindustrial societies as well as nonindustral ones.

Challenge Issues and Questions for Reflection

Each chapter opens with a Challenge Issue, which frames the book's theme of humankind's responses through time to the fundamental challenges of survival within the context of the particular chapter. And each chapter closes with Questions for Reflection, which relate back to the Challenge Issue presented on the chapter's opening page. These questions are designed to stimulate and deepen thought, trigger class discussion, and link the material to the students' own lives.

Chapter Outlines and Closing Summaries

At the beginning of each chapter, we also include an outline of key topics that sets up a mental framework for the material covered. And at the end of each chapter, we also provide a bulleted summary that recaps the more important ideas presented in the chapter. These summaries provide handy study points for students without giving the impression that one can get by without reading the chapter itself.

Visuals

Like the other Haviland *et al* textbooks, *The Essence* is richly illustrated, featuring a notable array of maps, photographs, and figures. This is important since humans—like all primates—are visually oriented, and a well-chosen image may serve to "fix" key information in a student's mind. Unlike some competing texts, all of our visuals are in color, enhancing their appeal and impact.

Original Studies

Selected from ethnographies and other original works by anthropologists, these studies present concrete examples that bring specific concepts to life and convey the passion of the authors. Each study sheds additional light on an important anthropological concept or subject area found in the chapter where it appears. Notably, each one is integrated within the flow of a chapter narrative, signaling students that their content is not extraneous or supplemental.

Featured in 11 of the chapters, these studies cover a range of topics: "Fighting HIV/AIDS in Africa: Traditional Healers on the Front Line," by Suzanne Leclerc-Madlala; "Ninety-Eight Percent Alike: What Our Similarity to Apes Tells Us about Our Understanding of Genetics," by Jonathan Marks; "Reconciliation and Its Cultural Modification in Primates," by Franz de Waal; "Whispers from the Ice," by S. Simpson; "The Real Dirt on Rain Forest Fertility," by Charles C. Mann; "A Feckless Quest for the Basketball Gene," by Jonathan Marks; "Intellectual Abilities of Orangutans," by H. Lyn White Miles; "The Blessed Curse: Spirituality and Sexual Difference as Viewed by Euro-American and Native American Cultures," by R. K. Williamson; "Gardens of the Mekranoti Kayapo," by D. Werner; "Arranging Marriage in India," by Serena Nanda; and "Standardizing the Body: The Question of Choice," by Laura Nader.

Anthropology Applied

These succinct and compelling profiles illustrate anthropology's wide-ranging relevance in today's world and give students a glimpse into a variety of the careers anthropologists enjoy. Featured in eight of the chapters,

they include: "Forensic Anthropology: Voices for the Dead," "Stone Tools for Modern Surgeons," "Action Archaeology and the Community at El Pilar," "New Houses for Apache Indians," "Resolving a Native American Tribal Membership Dispute," "Dispute Resolution and the Anthropologist," "Reconciling Modern Medicine with Traditional Beliefs in Swaziland," and "Development Anthropology and Dams."

Biocultural Connections

Appearing in every chapter, this feature illustrates how cultural and biological processes interact to shape human biology, beliefs, and behavior. It reflects the integrated biocultural approach central to the field of anthropology today. The eighteen topics include "The Anthropology of Organ Transplantation," "The Social Impact of Genetics on Reproduction," "Nonhuman Primates and Human Diseases," "Kennewick Man," "Evolution and Human Birth," "Breastfeeding, Fertility, and Beliefs," "Social Stratification and Diseases of Civilization: Tuberculosis," "Paleolithic Prescriptions for Today's Diseases," "Adult Human Stature and the Effects of Culture: An Archaeological Example," "The Biology of Human Speech," "Down's Syndrome Across Cultures," "The Cultural and Political Ecology of Disease," "Marriage Prohibitions in the United States," "African Burial Ground Project," "Gender, Sex, and Human Violence," "Altered States, Art, and Archaeology," "Studying the Emergence of New Diseases," and "Picturing Pesticides."

Barrel Model of Culture

Every culture, past and present, is an integrated and dynamic system of adaptation that responds to a combination of internal and external factors. This is illustrated by what we refer to as the "barrel model" of culture, depicted in a simple, but telling, drawing (Figure 9.2) showing the interrelatedness of social, ideological, and economic factors within a cultural system along with outside influences of environment, climate, and other societies. Throughout the book examples are linked back to this point.

Integrated Gender Coverage

In contrast to many introductory texts, *The Essence* integrates rather than separates gender coverage. Thus, material on gender-related issues is included in *every* chapter. The result of this approach is a measure of gender-related material that far exceeds the single chapter that most books contain.

Why is the gender-related material integrated? Because concepts and issues surrounding gender are almost always too complicated to remove from their context.

Moreover, spreading this material through all of the chapters emphasizes how considerations of gender enter into virtually everything people do. Further, integration of gender into the book's "biological" chapters allows students to grasp the analytic distinction between sex and gender, illustrating the subtle influence of gender norms on biological theories about sex difference. Gender-related material ranges from discussions of gender roles in evolutionary discourse and studies of nonhuman primates, to intersexuality, homosexual identity, same-sex marriage, and female genital mutilation. Through a steady drumbeat of such coverage, this edition avoids ghettoizing gender to a single chapter that is preceded and followed by resounding silence.

Glossary

The running glossary is designed to catch the student's eye, reinforcing the meaning of each newly introduced term. It is also useful for chapter review, as the student may readily isolate the new terms from those introduced in earlier chapters. A complete glossary is also included at the back of the book. In the glossaries each term is defined in clear, understandable language. As a result, less class time is required for going over terms, leaving instructors free to pursue matters of great interest.

CHAPTER HIGHLIGHTS

The pedagogical features described above strengthen each of the eighteen chapters in *The Essence of Anthropology* by serving as threads that tie the text together and help students feel the holistic nature of the discipline. In addition, the engaging presentation of the concepts, themselves, provide students with a solid foundation in the principles and practices of anthropology today. The chapter highlights presented below offer a preview.

Chapter 1: The Essence of Anthropology
The book's opening chapter introduces students to the holistic discipline of anthropology, the unique focus of each of its sub-disciplines, and the common philosophical and methodological approaches they share. We discuss fieldwork and the comparative method, along with ethical issues and examples of applied anthropology in each of the sub-disciplines. Two boxed features help illustrate the interconnection of biology and culture in the human experience: Suzanne Leclerc-Madlala's compelling Original Study, "Fighting HIV/AIDS in Africa: Traditional Healers on the Front Line," and a Biocultural Connection highlighting Margaret Lock's work on the anthropology of organ transplantation. An Anthropology Applied box on forensic anthropology and archaeology illustrates the importance of forensics in the investigations of international

human rights abuses. The chapter closes with a section titled "Anthropology and Globalization," in which we show the relevance of anthropology to several of today's most significant social and political issues.

Chapter 2: Biology and Evolution
This chapter provides clear but simple explanations of evolutionary processes at the population, individual, and molecular levels. We integrate cultural and biological approaches through the historical exploration of the genetics revolution. The chapter's Biocultural Connection, "The Social Impact of Genetics on Reproduction," features the work of cultural anthropologist Rayna Rapp and provides students with concrete examples of the influence of genetics on people's lives. Similarly, the Original Study "Ninety-Eight Percent Alike: What Our Similarity to Apes Tells Us about Our Understanding of Genetics" by biological anthropologist Jonathan Marks illustrates that scientific data are interpreted within human contexts. This Original Study is tied into our discussion of the alternative classificatory schemes (hominin versus hominid), allowing students to see that the schemes differ depending upon whether classification is based on genetic criteria or morphology. We include this discussion for two reasons: First, in the popular press students will see both "hominid" (*New York Times*) and "hominin" (*National Geographic*) used. Second, practicing anthropologists such as their professors may prefer one term over the other. Having this discussion in the book makes the text compatible with both classificatory approaches. A simple, elegant table defining the various taxonomic levels accompanies this discussion.

Chapter 3: Living Primates
Here we survey the amazing diversity found in the biology and behavior of the major living primate groups. While we focus particularly on the African ape species since they are most closely related to humans, students will gain a broad understanding of the mammalian primate pattern of adaptation and the distinctions among the five major primate groups. For simplicity we employ the traditional grade distinction between prosimians and anthropoid primates (rather than strepsirhine/haplorhine dichotomy) in our survey of diversity among living primates. Content-rich figures help convey a great deal of material without excessive length. Gender issues are featured through the important perspectives of female primatologists and a balanced focus on both male and female primates in contemporary field studies. Primatologist Frans de Waal's fascinating Original Study "Reconciliation and Its Cultural Modification in Primates" offers an excellent example of how primatologists have reworked older theories—in this case, the emphasis on aggression and male dominance hierarchies. The

pioneering contributions of Japanese primatologist Kinji Imanishi and his students to field methods and theory are included in the text. Jane Goodall's work to protect the rights of chimpanzees used in biomedical research is featured in the chapter's Biocultural Connection.

Chapter 4: Field Methods in Archaeology and Paleoanthropology

This chapter on archaeological and paleoanthropological methods provides a thorough introduction to shared excavation and dating techniques as the book shifts its focus to the study of the distant past. The chapter touches on the basics of site discovery, mapping, and artifact and fossil recovery, illustrating the importance of documentation and analysis of physical and material remains. A table summarizes dating methods describing the application and limitations of each method. Genetic techniques, such as the extraction of DNA from fossils, are also described. The growing specialization of bioarchaeology is introduced including a discussion of how gender roles and the status of women in the past can be examined through bioarchaeological analyses. The chapter also features a Biocultural Connection on the controversy surrounding Kennewick Man. The chapter's Original Study, "Whispers from the Ice," provides an excellent example of successful collaboration among researchers and the community in which they work in the sensitive handling of newly discovered skeletal remains.

Chapter 5: Human Evolution

This chapter begins with a discussion of the general principles and theories of macroevolution and a picture of how paleoanthropologists go about reconstructing evolutionary relationships and behavior in the past. Our overview of mammalian primate evolution concentrates on the "essence" of the fossil record during the last 5–8 million years. We provide a good overview of bipedalism and of the diversity among the australopithecines without getting bogged down in nomenclature. We explain that paleoanthropologists can take either a "lumping" or "splitting" approach to the fossil record. Examining the genus *Homo,* we show the increasing importance of culture as a means of solving the challenges of existence as seen in the remains of ancient stone tools, hearths, dwellings, and art, and in the spread of humans from Africa to Asia and Europe. We provide students with an overview of the two major competing theories (recent African origins and multiregional continuity) for modern human origins exploring the disputed place of the Neandertals in the process. Our goal here is to show how paleoanthropologists engage in debate as they reconstruct the past rather than come out in favor of one of these hypotheses. The chapter's Biocultural Connection, "Evolution and Human Birth," discusses the influence of contemporary gender roles and associated biomedical birth practices on theories about the evolution of the human birth pattern. The Anthropology Applied feature, "Stone Tools for Modern Surgeons," demonstrates the sophistication of ancient technology through their contemporary use in operating rooms.

Chapter 6: The Neolithic Revolution: The Domestication of Plants and Animals

This chapter focuses on the major cultural changes of the Neolithic transition, the domestication of plants and animals along with settlements into villages. Theories accounting for these cultural changes are presented along with a survey of the independent changes throughout the globe. A discussion of differences in the rates of biological and cultural change provides students with a framework for thinking about human health past, present, and future. The Biocultural Connection featuring the work of Melvin Konner and Carol Worthman on ovulation and breastfeeding practices among the Ju/'hoansi provides a concrete example of the interaction of cultural practice and human biology relevant to the Neolithic. A compelling Original Study, "The Real Dirt on Rain Forest Fertility," describes the work in the Amazon by an international team of archaeologists that is making significant contributions to our understanding of farming practices in the past and to increasing the productivity of rain forest soil today.

Chapter 7: The Emergence of Cities and States

Presenting the ancient monuments most readily associated with the field of archaeology, this chapter surveys the emergence of cities and states throughout the world, along with the theories that account for their development. Cities and states are not presented as a more advanced phase of cultural development, but rather as an emerging social system with its own positive and negative features. The chapter explores how the various vocational specializations characteristic of cities and states foster technological and other developments while also producing stratified societies in which some classes of people have a greater share of resources than others. A case study on the great Maya city, Tikal, provides perspective on how archaeologists use the data they recover to reconstruct past behavior and beliefs. The practical knowledge that can be derived from archaeological study is emphasized in the Anthropology Applied feature, "Action Archaeology and the Community at El Pilar." This box features Anabel Ford's work to establish an international preserve (spanning Belize and Guatemala) and sustainable ecotourism surrounding the great Maya city of El Pilar, the Maya site she discovered. A Biocultural Connection illustrates the relationship between poverty and disease that began with the earliest socially stratified societies and continues today.

Chapter 8: Modern Human Diversity: Race and Racism

The interplay of biology and culture is emphasized in a discussion of biological variation seen throughout the world. We use a historical approach to help students understand human biological variation and particularly to demonstrate why race is not a valid biological category when applied to humans. The work of Linnaeus, Blumenbach, and Samuel Morton form part of our discussion of the intellectual history of the classification of humans into a series of racial types. Revealing the role of 19th- and early 20th-century physical anthropology in maintaining false racial hierarchies, we show that discrete human races do not exist. Global variation in skin pigmentation due to variation in UV radiation is presented as an example of adaptation to a specific environment. This discussion helps students see the difference between the legitimate study of human biological variation and the ways that social beliefs about biological difference can turn into racism. Jonathan Marks' Original Study, "The Feckless Quest for the Basketball Gene," reinforces these concepts. Closing the chapter, we examine the effects of the human-made environment on human biological variation through several examples of micro-evolutionary change related to human health. A Biocultural Connection, "Paleolithic Prescriptions for Today's Diseases," introduces students to the perspective of evolutionary medicine, which takes lessons from human evolutionary history and applies them to health problems today.

Chapter 9: The Characteristics of Culture

Here we address anthropology's core concept of culture, exploring the term and its significance for human individuals and societies. Elaborating on culture as the medium through which humans handle the problems of existence, we mark out its characteristics as something that is learned, shared, based on symbols, integrated, and dynamic. This chapter includes discussions on fieldwork and the comparative method; culture and adaptation; the functions of culture; culture, society and the individual; and culture and change. Special features include a Biocultural Connection titled "Adult Human Stature and the Effects of Culture: An Archaeological Example," and an Anthropology Applied box, "New Houses for Apache Indians," profiling anthropologist George Esber's role in designing culturally appropriate homes for a Native American community. Also in this chapter is an original illustration we call the "barrel model," which conveys the integrative and dynamic nature of culture and introduces the concepts of infrastructure/social structure/superstructure.

Chapter 10: Language and Communication

One of humankind's most distinctive characteristics is language, a sophisticated means of communication through which culture is transmitted from one generation to the next. In this chapter we investigate the nature of language and the three branches of linguistic anthropology—descriptive linguistics, historical linguistics, and the study of language in its social and cultural settings (ethnolinguistics and sociolinguistics). We look at language and gender, as well as processes of language divergence and language loss and revival. This chapter also includes sections on body language (proxemics and kinesics), paralanguage, and tonal languages (which comprise 70 percent of the world's languages), plus a historical sketch about the emergence of writing. The latter takes readers from traditional speech performatives and memory devices to Egyptian hieroglyphics to the conception and spread of the alphabet to the 2003–2012 Literacy Decade established by the United Nations. Finally, Chapter 10 presents two features—a lively Original Study on "Language and the Intellectual Ability of Orangutans" by L.W. Miles, and an illustrated Biocultural Connection box on "The Biology of Human Speech."

Chapter 11: Social Identity, Personality, and Gender

Every culture has developed reliable ways to teach children the behavior that is expected of them as members of their community—a social structure that ensures that individuals growing up in a society will contribute to its survival. Since adult personality is in large part the product of life experiences, the ways children are raised and educated play major roles in the shaping of their later selves. Looking at individual identity within a sociocultural context, we survey a range of issues: the concept of "self," enculturation and the behavioral environment, social identity through personal naming, the development of personality, the concepts of group and modal personality, and the idea of national character. A substantial section titled "Alternative Gender Models from a Cross-Cultural Perspective" provides a thought-provoking historical overview of intersexuality, transsexuality, and transgendering, including current statistics on the incidence of intersexuality worldwide. Boxed features include the Biocultural Connection "Down's Syndrome Across Cultures," and on R. K. Williamson's stirring Original Study on intersexuality, "The Blessed Curse."

Chapter 12: Subsistence and Exchange

Here we investigate the various ways humans meet their basic needs and how societies adapt through culture to the environment. This connects to the subject matter of economic systems—the production, distribution, and consumption of goods—also covered in this chapter. We begin with a discussion of adaptation, followed by profiles on modes of subsistence in which we look at food-foraging and food-producing societies—pastoralism, crop cultivation, and industrialization. Under the heading "Subsistence and Economics," we delve into such matters as the control of resources (natural, technological, labor) and types of labor division (gender, age, cooperative labor, craft specialization). A section on distribution and exchange defines various forms of reciprocity (with a detailed, illustrated description of the Kula ring), along with redistribution (including a potlatch account), and market exchange. We also touch on leveling mechanisms and feature two special boxes: a Biocultural Connection on "The Cultural and Political Ecology of Disease" and Dennis Werner's Original Study on "Gardens of the Mekranoti Kayapo," which analyzes the productivity of a slash-and-burn gardening community in the central Amazon basin in Brazil.

Chapter 13: Sex, Marriage, and Family

This chapter looks at marriage and family in their various forms and the roles they play in meeting the challenges of human existence—from creating alliances that help ensure survival to regulating sexual activity in order to balance sexual desires with the need for stability and security. Exploring the close interconnection among sexual reproductive practices, marriage, family, and household, we discuss the household as the basic building block in a culture's social structure, the center where child rearing, as well as shelter, economic production, consumption, and inheritance are commonly organized. And we explain that the core of the household usually consists of some form of family—people who are married to one another and/or a group of relatives stemming from the parent-child bond and the interdependence of men and women. Particulars addressed in this chapter include the incest taboo, endogamy and exogamy, dowry and bride-price, cousin marriage, same-sex marriage, divorce, residence patterns, and non-family households. Of special note: a discussion contrasting past and present Christian and Muslim Shariah laws concerning the regulation of sexual relations; a passage on how new reproductive technologies (NRTs) are impacting the ways humans think about and form families; and definitions of marriage, family, nuclear family, and extended family that have been updated to encompass current real-life situations around the world. Also noteworthy are Serena Nanda's Original Study, "Arranging Marriage in India," and Martin Ottenheimer's Biocultural Connection box on "Marriage Prohibitions in the United States."

Chapter 14: Kinship and Other Methods of Grouping

This chapter elaborates on the fact that in most cultural systems solutions to many organizational challenges (such as defense, resource allocation, and labor) are beyond the scope of family and household and require broader cooperative efforts based on kinship and other forms of grouping that help ensure material and emotional security.

We look at the various forms of descent groups and the roles descent plays as an integrated feature in a cultural system. Details and examples are presented concerning lineages, clans, phratries, and moieties (highlighting Hopi Indian matriclans and Scottish highland patriclans), followed by illustrated examples of a representative range of kinship systems and their kinship terminologies. A substantial section on grouping beyond kinship includes discussions of grouping by gender, age, common interest, and social rank—with examples including the Mundurucu of Brazil, the Tiriki of East Africa, and common interests groups ranging from labor unions to religious organizations. Our narrative on caste explores its historical context and role in India's Hindu culture and also presents examples of caste-like situations from other parts of the world. An Anthropology Applied box relays the role descent played in "Resolving a Native American Tribal Membership Dispute," and Michael Blakey's Biocultural Connection box on "African Burial Ground Project" tells how this archaeological dig revealed the physical wear and tear of an entire community brought on by the social institution of slavery.

Chapter 15: Politics, Power, and Violence

Inevitably, social living entails friction, which can escalate to violent conflict and create an uncertainty that works against humankind's deep-seated psychological need for structure and security. Thus, every society requires some means for resolving conflicts and preventing the breakdown of social order. This chapter investigates these issues as they present themselves within a range of uncentralized and centralized political systems—from kin-ordered bands and tribes, to chiefdoms and states. We explore the question of power, the intersection of politics and religion, and issues of political leadership and gender. Discussing the maintenance of order, we look at internalized and externalized controls, along with social control through witchcraft and through law. We mark the functions of law and the ways different societies deal with crime—including new sentencing laws in Canada based on traditional Native American restorative justice techniques such as the Talking Circle. Then, shifting our focus from maintaining order within a society to political organization and external affairs, we discuss warfare and offer a 5000-year overview of armed conflicts among humans. Special features in this chapter include a Biocultural Connection box, "Gender, Sex, and Human Violence," and an Anthropology Applied box, "Dispute Resolution and the Anthropologist."

Chapter 16: Spirituality, Religion, and the Supernatural

Opening with a description of the anthropological approach to religion and noting current distinctions between religion and spirituality, this chapter goes on to discuss beliefs concerning supernatural beings and forces (gods and goddesses, ancestral spirits, animism, and animatism), types of religious specialists (priests and priestesses, as well as shamans), and also rituals and ceremonies (rites of passage and rites of intensification). A section on shamanism explores the origins of the term and presents our "shamanic complex" model of how shamanic healings take place. A substantial section on religion, magic, and witchcraft highlights Ibibio witchcraft, while a passage about the functions of religion marks out its psychological and social functions. This last section also makes the point that people often turn to religion or spirituality in the hope of reaching a specific goal, such as the healing of physical, emotional, and social ills. Touching on religion and cultural change, this chapter introduces revitalization movements. Also, it delves into the relationship between art and religion, showing how much of what we call art has been created in the service of religion, spirituality, and the supernatural: myths to explain ritual practices, objects to portray important deities, music and dances for ceremonial use, pictorial art to record supernatural experiences and/or to serve as objects of supernatural power in their own right. Special features here include a Biocultural Connection box on "Altered States, Art, and Archaeology," as well as an Anthropology Applied box titled "Reconciling Modern Medicine with Traditional Beliefs in Swaziland," which illustrates the importance of understanding a cultural group's metaphysical beliefs about the cause of illness in order to treat a problem effectively.

Chapter 17: Processes of Change

The themes and terminology of globalization are woven through this chapter, which includes definitions that distinguish progress from modernization, rebellion from revolution, and acculturation from enculturation. Here, we discuss mechanisms of change—innovation, diffusion, and cultural loss, as well as repressive change. Our exploration of the latter covers acculturation, ethnocide, and genocide, citing a range of the all-too-many repressive-change examples from around the world. This chapter also looks at reactions to such change, including revitalization movements, rebellions, and revolutions. A discussion on modernization touches on the issue of self-determination among indigenous peoples and highlights two contrasting cases: Skolt Lapp reindeer herders in Finland and Shuar Indians of Ecuador. Also featured is a historical profile of applied or practical anthropology and the emergence of action or advocacy anthropology in collaboration with indigenous societies, ethnic minorities, and other besieged or repressed groups. The chapter's last pages discuss globalization as a worldwide process of accelerated modernization in which all parts of the earth are becoming interconnected in one vast interrelated and all-encompassing system. Also featured is a Biocultural

Connection on "Studying the Emergence of New Diseases," and an Anthropology Applied piece, "Development Anthropology and Dams," about the work of Michael Horowitz at the Institute for Development Anthropology.

Chapter 18: Global Challenges, Local Responses, and the Role of Anthropology

Our final chapter zeroes in on numerous global challenges confronting the human species today—and prods students to use the anthropological tools they have learned to think critically about these issues and take informed steps to help bring about a future in which humans live in harmony with each other and the nature that sustains us all. Sections on global culture and ethnic resurgence look at Westernization and its counterforce of growing nationalism and the breakup of multi-ethnic states. We present examples of resistance to globalization, and discuss pluralism and multiculturalism. A substantial section about the rise of global corporations places this phenomenon in historical context and highlights the largest corporations (making particular note of media corporations and the emergence of the "global mediascape"). Under the heading "Structural Power in the Age of Globalization," we recount the ever-widening gap between those who have wealth and power and those who do not. We define and illustrate the term *structural power* and its two branches—hard power (military and economic might) and soft power (media might that gains control through ideological influence). We then address "Problems of Structural Violence"—from pollution to epidemics of hunger and obesity. We also touch on "the culture of discontent," including the psychological problems born of powerful marketing messages that shape cultural standards concerning the ideal human body. Tied to this is Laura Nader's Original Study "Standardizing the Body: The Question of Choice." Also featured is a Biocultural Connection, "Picturing Pesticides." The chapter closes on an encouraging note about anthropology's potential for helping to solve practical problems on local and global levels—accompanied by a photo montage of anthropologically informed organizations involved in such efforts.

SUPPLEMENTS

The Essence of Anthropology comes with a strong supplements program to help instructors create an effective learning environment both inside and outside the classroom and to aid students in mastering the material.

Supplements for Instructors

Online Instructor's Manual with Test Bank

The Instructor's Manual offers detailed chapter outlines, lecture suggestions, key terms, and student activities such as *InfoTrac College Edition* exercises and Internet exercises. In addition, there are over 75 chapter test questions including multiple choice, true/false, fill-in-the-blank, short answer, and essay.

ExamView Computerized and Online Testing

Create, deliver, and customize tests and study guides (both print and online) in minutes with this easy to use assessment and tutorial system. ExamView offers both a Quick Test Wizard and an Online Test Wizard that guide you step-by-step throughout the process of creating tests, while its unique "WYSWYG" capability allows you to see the test you are creating onscreen exactly as it will print or display online. You can build tests of up to 250 questions using up to 12 question types. Using ExamView's complete word processing capabilities, you can enter an unlimited number of new questions or edit existing questions.

Multimedia Manager for Anthropology: A Microsoft PowerPoint Link Tool

This new CD-ROM contains digital media and Microsoft PowerPoint presentations for all of Wadsworth's 2007 introductory anthropology texts, placing images, lectures, and video clips at your fingertips. This CD-ROM includes preassembled Microsoft PowerPoint presentations, and charts, graphs, maps, and line art from all Wadsworth anthropology texts. You can add your own lecture notes and images to create a customized lecture presentation. Also, an Earthwatch Institute Research Expedition feature offers even more images.

Wadsworth Anthropology Video Library

Qualified adopters may select full-length videos from an extensive library of offerings drawn from such excellent educational video sources as *Films for the Humanities and Sciences.*

ABC Anthropology Video Series

This exclusive video series was created jointly by Wadsworth and ABC for the anthropology course. Each video contains approximately 60 minutes of footage originally broadcast on ABC within the past several years. The videos are broken into short two- to seven-minute segments, perfect for classroom use as lecture launchers or to illustrate key anthropological concepts. An annotated table of contents accompanies each video, providing descriptions of the segments and suggestions for their possible use within the course.

A Guide to Visual Anthropology

Prepared by Jayasinhji Jhala of Temple University, this guide provides a compendium of fifty of the most outstanding classic and contemporary anthropological films. The guide describes the films, tells why they are important, and gives suggestions for their use in the classroom.

AIDS in Africa DVD

Southern Africa has been overcome by a pandemic of unparalleled proportions. This documentary series focuses on the new democracy of Namibia and the many actions that are being taken to control HIV/AIDS. Included in this series are four documentary films created by the Periclean Scholars at Elon University: 1) *Young Struggles, Eternal Faith,* which focuses on caregivers in the faith community; 2) *The Shining Lights of Opuwo,* which shows how young people share their messages of hope through song and dance; 3) *A Measure of Our Humanity,* which describes HIV/AIDS as an issue related to gender, poverty, stigma, education, and justice; and 4) *You Wake Me Up,* a story of 2 HIV + women and their acts of courage helping other women learn to survive. Thomson/Wadsworth is excited to offer these award-winning films to instructors for use in class. When presenting topics such as gender, faith, culture, poverty, and so on, the films will be enlightening for students and will expand their global perspective of HIV/AIDS.

JoinIn on TurningPoint

The Anthropology discipline at Thomson Wadsworth is pleased to offer **JoinIn**™ (clicker) content for Audience Response Systems tailored to this text. Use the program by posing your own questions and display students' answers instantly within the Microsoft® PowerPoint® slides of your existing lecture. Or, utilize any or all of the following content that will be included with your Anthropology JoinIn product:

- **Opinion polls** on issues important to each Anthropology chapter (five questions per chapter). Students may feel uncomfortable talking about sensitive subjects such as sexuality or religion. JoinIn gives students complete anonymity and helps students feel connected to the issues.
- **Conceptual quiz questions** for each chapter. Give students a quick quiz during or after the chapter lecture and determine if they have understood the material.
- **Plus, pre-assembled PowerPoint lecture slides** for each chapter of your book are included with the material above integrated into the slides. All of the work integrating clicker questions into the chapter lecture slides has been done for you!

The program can be used to simply take role, or it can assess your students' progress and opinions with in-class questions. Enhance how your students interact with you, your lecture, and each other. For college and university adopters only. *Contact your local Thomson representative to learn more.*

Online Resources for Instructors and Students

ThomsonNOW for the Essence of Anthropology

Instructors can empower students with ThomsonNOW, the online assessment-centered student tutorial system for *The Essence of Anthropology*. Seamlessly tied to the text, this Web-based learning tool comes at no additional cost with every new copy of the book. This powerful and interactive resource helps students gauge their unique study needs for each chapter with a pretest, then gives them a personalized study plan that focuses their study time on the concepts they most need to master. Included in students' personalized study plans are learning modules, animations, map exercises, videos, and many more resources to help students better understand the chapter material. They then take a posttest to see if they are ready to move onto the next chapter. To get started with ThomsonNOW, students are directed to www.thomsonedu.com where they can create an account through 1Pass.

Anthropology Online: Book Companion Website

Go to http://thomsonedu.com/anthropology and click on *The Essence of Anthropology* to reach the website that accompanies this book. This website offers many study aids, including self-quizzes for each chapter and a practice final exam, crossword puzzles, flashcards, as well as links to anthropology websites and information on the latest theories and discoveries in the field.

Anthropology Resource Center

This online center offers a wealth of information and useful tools for both instructors and students in all four fields of anthropology. It includes interactive maps, learning modules, video exercises, and breaking news in anthropology. For instructors, the Resource Center includes a gateway to time-saving teaching tools, such as image banks, sample syllabi, and more. To get started with the Anthropology Resource Center, students and instructors are directed to http://thomsonedu.com where they can create an account through 1Pass.

Thomson InSite for Writing and Research with Turnitin Originality Checker

InSite features a full suite of writing, peer review, online grading, and e-portfolio applications. It is an all-in-one tool that helps instructors manage the flow of papers electronically and allows students to submit papers and peer reviews online. Also included in the suite is Turnitin, an original check that offers a simple solution for instructors who want a strong deterrent against plagiarism, as well as encouragement for students to employ proper research techniques. Access is available for packaging with each copy of this book. For more information, visit http://insite.thomson.com

InfoTrac College Edition

InfoTrac College Edition is an online library that offers full-length articles from thousands of scholarly and popular publications. Among the journals available are *American Anthropologist, Current Anthropology*, and *Canadian Review of Sociology and Anthropology*. To get started with InfoTrac, students are directed to http://thomsonedu.com where they can create an account through 1pass.

Supplements for Students

Study Guide

The Study Guide includes learning objectives, detailed chapter outlines and key terms to aid in student study; activities such as InfoTrac College Edition exercises and Internet exercises to help students apply their knowledge; and over fifty practice test questions per chapter including multiple choice, true/false, fill-in-the-blank, short answer, and essay questions.

Basic Genetics for Anthropology CD-ROM: Principles and Applications (Stand-Alone Version), by Jurmain and Kilgore

This student CD-ROM expands on such biological concepts as biological inheritance (genes, DNA sequencing, etc.) and applications of that to modern human populations at the molecular level (human variation and adaptation, i.e., to disease, diet, growth, and development). Interactive animations and simulations bring these important concepts to life for students so they can fully understand the essential biological principles required for physical anthropology. Also available are quizzes and interactive flashcards for further study.

Hominid Fossils CD-ROM: An Interactive Atlas, by James Ahern

The interactive atlas CD-ROM includes over seventy five key fossils important for a clear understanding of human evolution. The QuickTime Virtual Reality (QTVR) "object" movie format for each fossil enables students to have a near-authentic experience of working with these important finds, by allowing them to rotate the fossil 360 degrees. Unlike some VR media, QTVR objects are made using actual photographs of the real objects and thus better preserve details of color and texture. The fossils used are high-quality research casts and real fossils. The organization of the atlas is non-linear, with three levels and multiple paths, enabling students to see how the fossil fits into the map of human evolution in terms of geography, time, and evolution. The CD-ROM offers students an inviting, authentic learning environment, one that also contains a dynamic quizzing feature that will allow students to test their knowledge of fossil and species identification, as well as provide more detailed information about the fossil record.

Virtual Laboratories for Physical Anthropology CD-ROM, 4th edition, by John Kappelman
The new edition of this full color, interactive CD-ROM provides students with a hands-on computer component for completing lab assignments at school or at home. Through the use of video clips, 3-D animations, sound, and digital images, students can actively participate in twelve labs as part of their physical anthropology and archaeology course. The labs and assignments teach students how to formulate and test hypotheses with exercises that include how to measure, plot, interpret, and evaluate a variety of data drawn from osteological, behavioral, and fossil materials. Also available online.

Readings and Case Studies

Globalization and Change in Fifteen Cultures: Born in One World, Living in Another, edited by George Spindler and Janice E. Stockard
In this volume, fifteen case study authors write about culture change in today's diverse settings around the world. Each original article provides insight into the dynamics and meanings of change, as well as the effects of globalization at the local level.

Case Studies in Cultural Anthropology, edited by George Spindler and Janice E. Stockard
Select from more than sixty classic and contemporary ethnographies representing geographic and topical diversity. Newer case studies focus on culture change and culture continuity, reflecting the globalization of the world.

Case Studies in Contemporary Social Issues, edited by John A. Young
Framed around social issues, these new contemporary case studies are globally comparative and represent the cutting-edge work of anthropologists today.

Case Studies in Archaeology, edited by Jeffrey Quilter
These engaging accounts of cutting-edge archaeological techniques, issues, and solutions—as well as studies discussing the collection of material remains—range from site-specific excavations to types of archaeology practiced.

Modules in Physical Anthropology
Each free-standing module is actually a complete text chapter, featuring the same quality of pedagogy and illustration that are contained in Thomson Wadsworth's physical anthropology texts.

Primate Evolution Module, by Robert Jurmain
Robert Jurmain examines primate evolution as it has developed over the last 60 million years, helping students understand the ecological adaptations and evolutionary relationships of fossil forms to each other and to contemporary primates. Using what they know about primate anatomy and social behavior, students will learn to "flesh out" the bones and teeth that make up the evolutionary record of primate origins.

Forensics Anthropology Module: A Brief Review, by Diane France
Diane France explores the myths and realities of the search for human remains in crime scenes, what should be expected from a forensic anthropology expert in the courtroom, some of the special challenges in mass fatality incident responses (such as plane crashes and terrorist acts), and what students should consider if they want to purse a career in forensic anthropology.

Molecular Anthropology Module, by Leslie Knapp
Leslie Knapp explores how molecular genetic methods are used to understand the organization and expression of genetic information in humans and nonhuman primates. Students will learn about the common laboratory methods used to study genetic variation and evolution in molecular anthropology. Examples are drawn from up-to-date research on human evolutionary origins and comparative primate genomics to demonstrate that scientific research is an ongoing process with theories frequently being questioned and re-evaluated.

Acknowledgments

Mark Twain once apologized for writing a long letter, explaining that he didn't have time to write a short one. We can identify. It took more time and effort than we anticipated to come up with a concise four-field anthropology textbook that zeroes in on the essence of our discipline. And it took collaboration—not only among the four members of our author team, but among numerous other colleagues. We are particularly grateful for the remarkable group of manuscript reviewers listed below. They provided unusually detailed and thoughtful feedback that helped us to hone and re-hone our narrative into this economical text.

Randal Allison, Blinn College
Jeffery A. Behm, University of Wisconsin–Oshkosh
Andrew Buckser, Purdue University
Garrett W. Cook, Baylor University
Lorenzo Covarrubias, California State University, Monterey Bay
Marie Elaine Danforth, University of Southern Mississippi
Katherine Dettwyler, Millersville University
Paul B. Gordiejew, Youngstown State University
Gregory Stephen Gullette, Georgia State University
Christine Hanson, University of Alaska, Anchorage
Les W. Field, University of New Mexico
Gloria Gozdzik, West Virginia University
Charles W. Houck, University of North Carolina, Charlotte
Loren R. Lease, Youngstown State University
Michael Love, California State University, Northridge
Katherine C. MacKinnon, Saint Louis University
J. Alan May, University of North Carolina, Charlotte
James H. McDonald, University of Texas–San Antonio
Mike McDonald, Florida Gulf Coast University
H. Lyn Miles, University of Tennessee, Chattanooga
Laura Putsche, University of Idaho
John Rhoades, St. John Fisher College
Robert Rhoades, University of Georgia
Ronald C. Schirmer, Minnesota State University, Mankato
Mark Tromans, Broward Community College
Michael Wesch, Kansas State University

We carefully considered and made use of the wide range of comments provided by these individuals. Our decisions on how to utilize their suggestions were influenced by our own perspectives on anthropology and teaching, combined with the priorities and page limits of this text. Thus, neither our reviewers, nor any of the other anthropologists mentioned here should be held responsible for any shortcomings in this book. They should, however, be credited as contributors to many of the book's strengths.

Thanks, too, go to colleagues who provided material for some of the Original Study, Biocultural Connection, and Anthropology Applied boxes in this text: Michael Blakey, Katherine A. Dettwyler, George Esber, Anabel Ford, Edward C. Green, Suzanne LeClerc-Madlala, Charles C. Mann, Jonathan Marks, H. Lyn Miles, Laura Nader, Serena Nanda, Martin Ottenheimer, Sherry Simpson, Frans B. M. de Waal, Dennis Werner, and R. K. Williamson. Among these individuals we particularly want to acknowledge our admiration and affection for our friend and colleague Jim Petersen whose life came to an abrupt and tragic end while conducting the field work in the Brazilian Amazon that is featured in Charles C. Mann's piece in Chapter 6.

We have debts of gratitude to office workers in our departments for their cheerful help in clerical matters: Debbie Hedrick, Karen Rundquist, Emira Smailagic, and Laurie McCrea. And to colleagues Yvette Pigeon, John Fogarty, Lewis First, Martin Ottenheimer, Harriet Ottenheimer, and Michael Wesch for engaging in lively discussions of anthropological and pedagogical approaches. Also worthy of note here are the introductory anthropology teaching assistants who, through the years, have shed light for us on effective ways to reach new generations of students.

Our thanksgiving inventory would be incomplete without mentioning individuals at Wadsworth Publishing who helped conceive this text and bring it to fruition. Special gratitude goes to Senior Acquisitions Editor Lin Marshall for her vision, vigor, and anthropological knowledge and to Developmental Editor Julie Cheng for her calming influence and attention to detail. Our thanks also go out to Wadsworth's skilled and enthusiastic editorial, design, and production team: Eve Howard (Vice President and Editor-in-Chief), Dee Dee Zobian (Technology Project Manager), Caroline Concilla (Executive Marketing Manager, Social Sciences), as well as Assistant Editor Leata Holloway, Editorial Assistant Danielle M. Yumol, and Marketing Assistant Teresa Jessen.

In addition to all of the above, we have had the invaluable aid of several most able freelancers, including Christine Davis of Two Chicks Advertising & Marketing. We are especially thankful to have had the opportunity to work once again with copyeditor Jennifer Gordon and production coordinator Robin Hood. The visuals of the text were greatly enhanced by the excellent work of photo researcher Billie Porter and illustrator Carol Zuber-Mallison.

And finally, all of us are indebted to family members who have not only put up with our textbook preoccupation, but cheered us on in the endeavor. Dana had the tireless support and keen eye of husband Peter Bingham—along with the varied contributions of their three sons Nishan, Tavid, and Aram Bingham. As co-author spouses under the same roof, Harald and Bunny have picked up the slack for each other on every front to help this project move along smoothly. But the biggest debt of gratitude may be in Bill's corner: for more than three decades he has had invaluable input and support in his textbook tasks from his spouse Anita de Laguna Haviland.

© Sandi Fellman

CHALLENGE ISSUE

Part of being human is our fascination with ourselves. Where did we come from? Why do we act in certain ways? What makes us tick? While some answer these challenging questions with biological mechanisms and others with social or spiritual explanations, the discipline of anthropology addresses them through a holistic integrated approach. Anthropology considers human culture and biology, in all times and places, as inextricably intertwined, each affecting the other in important ways. Our biocultural nature is evident in the photograph of the famous Japanese tattoo artist Horiyoshi III, holding his newborn son. Every one of us comes into the world in a natural state with a biological profile, but over time we acquire a cultural identity, etched into our minds and sometimes into our very skin.

1

The Essence of Anthropology

THE ANTHROPOLOGICAL PERSPECTIVE

Anthropology is the study of humankind in all times and places. Of course many other research disciplines are concerned in one way or another with humans. For example, anatomy and physiology focus on our species as biological organisms. The social sciences are concerned with human relationships, while the humanities examine artistic and philosophical achievements in human cultures. Anthropology is distinct because of its focus on the interconnections and interdependence of all aspects of the human experience in all places, in the present and deep into the past, well before written history. It is this unique, broad **holistic perspective** that equips anthropologists so well to address that elusive thing we call human nature.

Anthropologists welcome the contributions of researchers from other disciplines and in return offer their own findings for the benefit of these other disciplines. Anthropologists do not expect, for example, to know as much about the structure of the human eye as anatomists or as much about the perception of color as psychologists. As synthesizers, however, anthropologists are prepared to understand how these bodies of knowledge relate to color-naming practices in different

anthropology The study of humankind in all times and places.

holistic perspective A fundamental principle of anthropology, that the various parts of human culture and biology must be viewed in the broadest possible context in order to understand their interconnections and interdependence.

human societies. Because they look for the broad basis of human ideas and practices without limiting themselves to any single social or biological aspect, anthropologists can acquire an especially expansive and inclusive overview of the complex biological and cultural organism that is the human being.

The holistic perspective also helps anthropologists stay keenly aware of ways that their own cultural ideas and values may impact upon their research. As the old saying goes, people often see what they believe, rather than what appears before their eyes. By maintaining a critical awareness of their own assumptions about human nature—checking and rechecking the ways their beliefs and actions might be shaping their research—anthropologists strive to gain objective knowledge about people. Equipped with this awareness, anthropologists have contributed uniquely to our understanding of diversity in human thought, biology, and behavior, as well as to our understanding of the many things humans have in common.

While other social sciences have predominantly concentrated on contemporary peoples living in North American and European (Western) societies, anthropologists have traditionally focused on non-Western peoples and cultures. Anthropologists believe that to fully understand the complexities of human ideas, behavior, and biology, all humans, wherever and whenever, must be studied. A cross-cultural and long-term evolutionary perspective distinguishes anthropology from other social sciences. This approach guards against the danger that theories of human behavior will be **culture-bound:** that is, based on assumptions about the world and reality that come from the researcher's own particular culture.

As a case in point, consider the fact that infants in the United States typically sleep apart from their parents. To most North Americans, this may seem quite normal, but cross-cultural research shows that "co-sleeping," of mother and baby in particular, is the rule. Only in the past 200 years, generally in Western industrialized societies, has it been considered proper for parents to sleep apart from their infants. In a way, this practice amounts to a cultural experiment in child rearing.

Recent studies have shown that separation of mother and infant in Western societies has important biological and cultural consequences. For one thing, it increases the length of the infant's crying bouts. Some mothers incorrectly interpret the cause as a deficiency in breast milk and switch to less healthy bottle formulas, and in extreme cases, the crying may provoke physical abuse. But the benefits of co-sleeping go beyond significant reductions in crying: Infants also nurse more often

and three times as long per feeding; they receive more stimulation (important for brain development); and they are apparently less susceptible to sudden infant death syndrome (SIDS or "crib death"). There are benefits to the mother as well: Frequent nursing prevents early ovulation after childbirth, and she gets at least as much sleep as mothers who sleep without their infants.[1]

These benefits may lead one to ask: Why do so many mothers continue to sleep apart from their infants?

© Documentary Educational Resources

Anthropologists come from many corners of the world and carry out research in a huge variety of cultures all around the globe. Dr. Jayasinhji Jhala hails from the old city of Dhrangadhra in Gujarat, northeast India. A member of the Jhala clan of Rajputs, an aristocratic caste of warriors, he grew up in the royal palace of his father, the maharaja. After earning a bachelor of arts degree in India, he came to the United States and earned a master's degree in visual studies from the Massachusetts Institute of Technology, followed by a Ph.D. in anthropology from Harvard. Currently a professor and director of the Visual Anthropology program and laboratory at Temple University, he returns regularly to India with students to film cultural traditions in his own caste-stratified society.

culture-bound Theories about the world and reality based on the assumptions and values of one's own culture

[1]Barr, R. G. (1997, October). The crying game. *Natural History,* 47. Also, McKenna, J. J. (2002, September-October). Breastfeeding and bedsharing. *Mothering,* 28–37.

In North America the cultural values of independence and consumerism come into play. To begin building individual identities, babies are provided with rooms (or at least space) of their own. This room of one's own also provides parents with a place for the toys, furniture, and other paraphernalia associated with "good" and "caring" parenting in North America.

ANTHROPOLOGY AND ITS FIELDS

Individual anthropologists tend to specialize in one of four fields or subdisciplines: physical anthropology, archaeology, linguistic anthropology, or cultural anthropology (Figure 1.1). Some anthropologists consider archaeology and linguistics as part of the broader study of human cultures, but, archaeology and linguistics also have close ties to biological anthropology. For example, while linguistic anthropology focuses on the cultural aspects of language, it has deep connections to the evolution of human language and the biological basis of speech and language studied within physical anthropology. Each of anthropology's fields may take a distinct approach to the study of humans, but all gather and analyze data that are essential to explaining similarities and differences among humans, across time and space. Moreover, all of them generate knowledge that has numerous practical applications. Within the four fields are individuals who practice **applied anthropology,** which entails the use of anthropological knowledge and methods to solve practical problems. Applied anthropologists do not offer their perspectives from the sidelines. Instead, they actively

Figure 1.1 **The Four Fields of Anthropology**
Note that the divisions between the fields are not sharp, indicating that their boundaries overlap.

applied anthropology The use of anthropological knowledge and methods to solve practical problems, often for a specific client.

collaborate with the communities in which they work—setting goals, solving problems, and conducting research together. In this book, examples of how anthropology contributes to solving a wide range of the challenges humans face appear in Anthropology Applied features.

Physical Anthropology

Physical anthropology, also called *biological anthropology,* focuses on humans as biological organisms. Traditionally, biological anthropologists concentrated on human evolution, primatology, growth and development, human adaptation, and forensics. Today, **molecular anthropology,** or the anthropological study of genes and genetic relationships, is another vital component of biological anthropology. Comparisons among groups separated by time, geography, or the frequency of a particular gene can reveal how humans have adapted and where they have migrated. As experts in the anatomy of human bones and tissues, physical anthropologists lend their knowledge about the body to applied areas such as gross anatomy laboratories, public health, and criminal investigations.

Paleoanthropology

Human evolutionary studies (known as **paleoanthropology**) focus on biological changes through time to understand how, when, and why we became the kind of organisms we are today. In biological terms, we humans are primates, one of the many kinds of mammals. Because we share a common ancestry with other primates, most specifically apes, paleoanthropologists look back to the earliest primates (65 or so million years ago), or even the earliest mammals (225 million years ago), to reconstruct the complex path of human evolution. Paleoanthropology, unlike other evolutionary studies, takes a **biocultural** approach focusing on the interaction of biology and culture.

The fossilized skeletons of our ancestors allow paleoanthropologists to reconstruct the course of human evolutionary history. They compare the size and shape of these fossils to one another and to the bones of living species. With each new fossil discovery, paleoanthropologists have another piece to add to human evolutionary history. Biochemical and genetic

physical anthropology Also known as biological anthropology. The systematic study of humans as biological organisms.
molecular anthropology A branch of biological anthropology that uses genetic and biochemical techniques to test hypotheses about human evolution, adaptation, and variation.
paleoanthropology The study of the origins and predecessors of the present human species.
biocultural Focusing on the interaction of biology and culture.

studies add considerably to the fossil evidence. As we will see in later chapters, genetic evidence establishes the close relationship between humans and ape species—chimpanzees, bonobos, and gorillas. Genetic analyses indicate that the human line originated 5 to 8 million years ago. Physical anthropology therefore deals with much greater time spans than archaeology or other branches of anthropology.

Primatology

Studying the anatomy and behavior of the other primates helps us understand what we share with our closest living relatives and what makes humans unique. Therefore, **primatology,** or the study of living and fossil primates, is a vital part of physical anthropology. Primates include the Asian and African apes, as well as monkeys, lemurs, lorises, and tarsiers. Biologically, humans are apes—large-bodied, broad-shouldered primates with no tail. Detailed studies of ape behavior in the wild indicate that the sharing of learned behavior is a significant part of their social life. Increasingly, primatologists designate the shared, learned behavior of nonhuman apes as culture. For example, tool use and communication systems indicate the elementary basis of language in some ape societies. Primate studies offer scientifically grounded perspectives on the behavior of our ancestors, as well as greater appreciation and respect for the abilities of our closest living relatives. As human activity encroaches on all parts of the world, many primate species are endangered. Primatologists often advocate for the preservation of primate habitats so

© 1998 Jim Leachman

Monkeys and apes have long fascinated humans, owing to our many shared anatomical and behavioral characteristics. The study of other primates provides us with important clues as to what life may have been like for our own ancestors.

primatology   The study of living and fossil primates.

that these remarkable animals will be able to continue to inhabit the earth with us.

Human Growth, Adaptation, and Variation

Another specialty of physical anthropologists is the study of human growth and development. Anthropologists examine biological mechanisms of growth as well as the impact of the environment on the growth process. Franz Boas, a pioneer of anthropology of the early 20th century, compared the heights of European immigrants who spent their childhood in "the old country" to the increased heights obtained by their children who grew up in the United States. Today, physical anthropologists study the impacts of disease, pollution, and poverty on growth. Comparisons between human and nonhuman primate growth patterns can provide clues to the evolutionary history of humans. Detailed anthropological studies of the hormonal, genetic, and physiological basis of healthy growth in living humans also contribute significantly to the health of children today.

Studies of human adaptation focus on the capacity of humans to adapt or adjust to their material environment—biologically and culturally. This branch of physical anthropology takes a comparative approach to humans living today in a variety of environments. Humans are remarkable among the primates in that they now inhabit the entire earth. Though cultural adaptations make it possible for humans to live in some environmental extremes, biological adaptations also contribute to survival in extreme cold, heat, and high altitude.

Some of these biological adaptations are built into the genetic makeup of populations. The long period of human growth and development provides ample opportunity for the environment to shape the human body. *Developmental adaptations* are responsible for some features of human variation such as the enlargement of the right ventricle of the heart to help push blood to the lungs among the Quechua Indians of highland Peru. *Physiological adaptations* are short-term changes in response to a particular environmental stimulus. For example, a person who normally lives at sea level will undergo a series of physiological responses if she suddenly moves to a high altitude. All of these kinds of biological adaptation contribute to present-day human variation.

Human differences include visible traits such as height, body build, and skin color, as well as biochemical factors such as blood type and susceptibility to certain diseases. Still, we remain members of a single species. Physical anthropology applies all the techniques of modern biology to achieve fuller understanding of human variation and its relationship to the different environments in which people have lived. Research in physical anthropology on human variation has debunked false notions of biologically defined races, a notion based on widespread misinterpretation of human variation.

Forensic Anthropology

One of the many practical applications of physical anthropology is **forensic anthropology:** the identification of human skeletal remains for legal purposes. Although they are called upon by law enforcement authorities to identify murder victims, forensic anthropologists also investigate human rights abuses such as systematic genocides, terrorism, and war crimes. These specialists use details of skeletal anatomy to establish the age, sex, population affiliation, and stature of the deceased; often forensic anthropologists can also determine whether the person was right- or left-handed, exhibited any physical abnormalities, or had experienced trauma. While forensics relies upon differing frequencies of certain skeletal characteristics to establish population affiliation, it is nevertheless false to say that all people from a given population have a particular type of skeleton. (See the Anthropology Applied feature to read about the work of several forensic anthropologists and forensic archaeologists.)

Archaeology

Archaeology is the branch of anthropology that studies human cultures through the recovery and analysis of material remains and environmental data. Such material products include tools, pottery, hearths, and enclosures that remain as traces of cultural practices in the past, as well as human, plant, and marine remains, some of which date back 2.5 million years. The details of exactly how these traces were arranged when they were found reflect specific human ideas and behavior. For example, shallow, restricted concentrations of charcoal that include oxidized earth, bone fragments, and charred plant remains, located near pieces of fire-cracked rock, pottery, and tools suitable for food preparation, indicate cooking and food processing. Such remains can reveal much about a people's diet and subsistence practices. Together with skeletal remains, these material remains help archaeologists reconstruct the biocultural context of human life in the past.

Archaeologists can reach back for clues to human behavior far beyond the mere 5,000 years to which historians are confined by their reliance on written records. Calling this time period "prehistoric" does not mean that these societies were less interested in their history or that they did not have ways of recording and transmitting history. It simply means that written records do not exist. That said, archaeologists are not limited to the study of societies with no written records; they may also study those for which historic documents are available to supplement the material remains. In most literate societies, written records are associated with governing elites rather than with farmers, fishers, laborers, or slaves. Although written records can tell archaeologists much that might not be known from archaeological evidence alone, it is equally true that material remains can tell historians much about a society that is not apparent from its written documents.

Although most archaeologists concentrate on the human past, some of them study material objects in contemporary settings. One example is the Garbage Project, founded by William Rathje at the University of Arizona in 1973. This carefully controlled study of household waste continues to produce thought-provoking information about contemporary social issues. Among its accomplishments, the project has tested the validity of survey techniques, upon which sociologists, economists, other social scientists and policymakers rely heavily. The tests show a significant difference between what people *say* they do and what the garbage analysis shows they *actually* do. Ideas about human behavior based on simple survey techniques may therefore be seriously in error.

Cultural Resource Management

While archaeology may conjure up images of ancient pyramids and the like, much archaeological fieldwork is carried out as **cultural resource management.** What distinguishes this work from traditional archaeological research is that it is part of activities legislated to preserve important aspects of a country's prehistoric and historic heritage. For example, in the United States, if the transportation department of a state government plans to replace an inadequate highway bridge, steps have to be taken to identify and protect any significant prehistoric or historic resources that might be affected by this new construction. Since passage of the Historic Preservation Act of 1966, the National Environmental Policy Act of 1969, and the Archaeological and Historical Preservation Act

forensic anthropology Subfield of applied physical anthropology that specializes in the identification of human skeletal remains for legal purposes.

archaeology The study of human cultures through the recovery and analysis of material remains and environmental data.

cultural resource management A branch of archaeology that is concerned with survey and/or excavation of archaeological and historical remains threatened by construction or development and policy surrounding protection of cultural resources.

Anthropology Applied

Forensic Anthropology: Voices for the Dead

Forensic anthropology is the identification of skeletal remains for legal purposes. Law enforcement authorities call upon forensic anthropologists to use skeletal remains to identify murder victims, missing persons, or people who have died in disasters, such as plane crashes. Forensic anthropologists have also contributed substantially to the investigation of human rights abuses in all parts of the world by identifying victims and documenting the cause of their death.

Among the best-known forensic anthropologists is Clyde C. Snow. He has been practicing in this field for 40 years, first for the Federal Aviation Administration and more recently as a freelance consultant. In addition to the usual police work, Snow has studied the remains of General George Armstrong Custer and his men from the 1876 battlefield at Little Big Horn, and in 1985, he went to Brazil, where he identified the remains of

Physical anthropologists do not just study fossil skulls. Here Clyde Snow holds the skull of a Kurd who was executed by Iraqi security forces. Snow specializes in forensic anthropology and is widely known for his work identifying victims of state-sponsored terrorism.

the notorious Nazi war criminal Josef Mengele.

He was also instrumental in establishing the first forensic team devoted to documenting cases of human rights abuses around the world. This began in 1984 when he went to Argentina at the request of a newly elected civilian government to help with the identification of remains of the *desaparecidos,* or "disappeared ones," the 9,000 or more people who were eliminated by government death squads during seven years of military rule. A year later, he returned to give expert testimony at the trial of nine junta members and to teach Argentineans how to recover, clean, repair, preserve, photograph, x-ray, and analyze bones. Besides providing factual accounts of the fate of victims to their surviving kin and refuting the assertions of "revisionists" that the massacres never happened, the work of Snow and his Argentinean associates was crucial in convicting several military officers of kidnapping, torture, and murder.

Since Snow's pioneering work, forensic anthropologists have become increasingly involved in the investigation of human rights abuses in all parts of the world, from Chile to Guatemala, Haiti, the Philippines, Rwanda, Iraq, Bosnia, and Kosovo. Meanwhile, they continue to do important work for more typical clients. In the United States these clients include the Federal Bureau of Investigation and city, state, and county medical examiners' offices.

Forensic anthropologists specializing in skeletal remains commonly work closely with forensic archaeologists. The relation between them is rather like that between a forensic pathologist, who examines a corpse to establish time and manner of death, and a crime scene investigator, who searches the site for clues. While the forensic anthropologist deals with the human remains—often only bones and teeth—the forensic archaeologist controls the site, recording the position of all relevant finds and recovering any clues associated with the

remains. In Rwanda, for example, a team assembled in 1995 to investigate a mass atrocity for the United Nations included archaeologists from the U.S. National Park Service's Midwest Archaeological Center. They performed the standard archaeological procedures of mapping the site, determining its boundaries, photographing and recording all surface finds, and excavating, photographing, and recording buried skeletons and associated materials in mass graves.[a]

In another example, Karen Burns of the University of Georgia was part of a team sent to northern Iraq after the 1991 Gulf War to investigate alleged atrocities. On a military base where there had been many executions, she excavated the remains of a man's body found lying on its side facing Mecca, conforming to Islamic practice. Although there was no intact clothing, two threads of polyester used to sew clothing were found along the sides of both legs. Although the threads survived, the clothing, because it was made of natural fiber, had decayed. "Those two threads at each side of the leg just shouted that his family didn't bury him," says Burns.[b] Proper though his position was, no Islamic family would bury their own in a garment sewn with polyester thread; proper ritual would require a simple shroud.

In recent years two major anthropological analyses of skeletal remains have occurred in New York City dealing with both past and present atrocities. Amy Zelson Mundorff, a forensic anthropologist for New York City's Office of the Chief Medical Examiner, was injured in the September 11, 2001, terrorist attack on the World Trade Center. Two days later she returned to work to supervise and coordinate the management, treatment, and cataloging of people who lost their lives in the attack.

Just a short walk away, construction workers in lower Manhattan discovered a 17th- and 18th-century African burial ground in 1991 (see Chapter 15).

© Susan Meiselas/Magnum Photos

Archaeological investigation of the burial ground revealed the horror of slavery in North America, showing that even young children were worked so far beyond their ability to endure that their spines were fractured. Biological archaeologist Michael Blakey, who led the research team, notes: "Although bioarchaeology and forensics are often confused, when skeletal biologists use the population as the unit of analysis (rather than the individual), and incorporate cultural and historical context (rather than simply ascribing biological characteristics), and report on the lifeways of a past community (rather than on a crime for the police and courts), it is bioarchaeology rather than forensics."[c]

Thus, several kinds of anthropologists analyze human remains for a variety of purposes contributing to the documentation and correction of atrocities committed by humans of the past and present. ■ ■ ■

[a]Conner, M. (1996). The archaeology of contemporary mass graves. *SAA Bulletin, 14*(4), 6, 31.
[b]Cornwell, T. (1995, November 10). Skeleton staff. *Times Higher Education*, 20.
[c]Blakey, M. Personal communication, October 29, 2003.

of 1974, cultural resource management is required for any building project that is partially funded or licensed by the U.S. government. As a result, the field of cultural resource management has flourished. Many archaeologists are employed by such agencies as the Army Corps of Engineers, the National Park Service, the U.S. Forest Service, and the U.S. Soil and Conservation Service to assist in the preservation, restoration, and salvage of archaeological resources.

Archaeologists are also employed by state historic preservation agencies. Finally, they consult for engineering firms to help them prepare environmental impact statements. Some of these archaeologists operate out of universities and colleges, while others are on the staffs of independent consulting firms.

Linguistic Anthropology

Perhaps the most distinctive feature of the human species is language. Although the sounds and gestures made by some other animals—especially by apes—may serve functions comparable to those of human language, no other animal has developed a system of symbolic communication as complex as that of humans. Language allows people to preserve and transmit countless details of their culture from generation to generation.

The branch of anthropology that studies human languages is called **linguistic anthropology.** Linguists may deal with the description of a language (the way a sentence is formed, or a verb conjugated), the history of languages (the way languages develop and change with the passage of time), or with the relation between language and culture. All three approaches yield valuable information about how people communicate and how they understand the world around them. The everyday language of English-speaking North Americans, for example, includes a number of slang words, such as *dough, greenback, dust, loot, bucks, change,* and *bread,* to identify what an indigenous inhabitant of Papua New Guinea would recognize only as "money." The profusion of names helps to identify a thing of special importance to a culture.

Anthropological linguists also make a significant contribution to our understanding of the human past. By working out relationships among languages and examining their spatial distributions, they may estimate how long the speakers of those languages have lived where they do. By identifying those words in related languages that have survived from an ancient ancestral tongue, anthropological linguists can also suggest not only where, but how, the speakers of the ancestral language lived. Such work shows linguistic ties between geographically distant groups such as the people of Finland and Turkey.

Linguistic anthropology is practiced in a number of applied settings. For example, linguistic anthropologists have collaborated with ethnic minorities in the revival of languages suppressed or lost during periods of oppression by another ethnic group. Anthropologists have helped to create written forms of some languages that previously existed only in an oral form. These examples of applied linguistic anthropology represent the kind of true collaboration that is characteristic of anthropological fieldwork today.

Cultural Anthropology

Cultural anthropology (also called *social* or *sociocultural anthropology*) is the study of customary patterns in human behavior, thought, and feelings. It focuses on humans as culture-producing and culture-reproducing creatures.

linguistic anthropology The study of human languages.

cultural anthropology Also known as social or sociocultural anthropology. The study of customary patterns in human behavior, thought, and feelings. It focuses on humans as culture-producing and culture-reproducing creatures.

Thus, in order to understand the work of the cultural anthropologist, we must clarify what we mean by "culture." The concept is discussed in detail in Chapter 9, but for our purposes here, we may think of **culture** as the (often unconscious) standards by which societies—structured groups of people—operate. These standards are socially learned, rather than acquired through biological inheritance. Because they determine, or at least guide, normal day-to-day behavior, thought, and emotional patterns of the members of a society, human activities, ideas, and feelings are above all culturally acquired and influenced. The manifestations of culture may vary considerably from place to place, but no person is "more cultured" in the anthropological sense than any other.

Cultural anthropology has two main components: ethnography and ethnology. An **ethnography** is a detailed description of a particular culture primarily based on **fieldwork,** which is the term anthropologists use for on-location research. Because the hallmark of ethnographic fieldwork is a combination of social participation and personal observation within the community being studied, as well as interviews and discussions with individual members of a group, the ethnographic method is commonly referred to as **participant observation.** Today, participant observation research has grown to become active collaboration between anthropologists and the communities in which they work.

Ethnographies provide the information used to make systematic comparisons among cultures all across the world. Known as **ethnology,** such cross-cultural research allows anthropologists to develop anthropological theories that help explain why certain important differences or similarities occur among groups.

culture The (often unconscious) standards by which societies—structured groups of people—operate. These standards are socially learned, rather than acquired through biological inheritance.

ethnography A detailed description of a particular culture primarily based on fieldwork.

fieldwork The term anthropologists use for on-location research.

participant observation In ethnography, the technique of learning a people's culture through social participation and personal observation within the community being studied, as well as interviews and discussion with individual members of the group over an extended period of time.

ethnology The study and analysis of different cultures from a comparative or historical point of view, utilizing ethnographic accounts and developing anthropological theories that help explain why certain important differences or similarities occur among groups.

Ethnography

Through participant observation—eating a people's food, sleeping under their roof, learning how to speak and behave acceptably, and personally experiencing the habits and customs—the ethnographer is able to understand the culture of the society in which he or she is doing fieldwork more fully than a nonparticipant researcher ever could. Being a participant observer does not mean that the anthropologist must join in a people's battles in order to study a culture in which warfare is prominent; but by living among a warlike people, the ethnographer should be able to understand how warfare fits into the overall cultural framework. She or he must observe carefully to gain an overview without placing too much emphasis on one part at the expense of another. Only by discovering how all aspects of a culture—its social, political, economic, and religious practices and institutions—relate to one another can the ethnographer begin to understand the cultural system. An ethnographer's most essential tools are notebooks, pen/pencil, camera, tape recorder, and, increasingly, a laptop computer. Most important of all, he or she needs flexible social skills.

The popular image of ethnographic fieldwork is that it occurs among people who live in far-off, isolated places. To be sure, much ethnographic work has been done in the remote villages of Africa or South America, the islands of the Pacific Ocean, the Indian reservations of North America, the deserts of Australia, and so on. However, as the discipline of anthropology developed, Western cultures also became a legitimate focus of anthropological study. Some of this shift occurred as scholars from non-Western cultures became anthropologists. Ethnographic fieldwork has transformed from expert Western anthropologists studying people in "other" places to collaborations among anthropologists from all parts of the world and the varied communities in which they work. Today, anthropologists from all around the globe employ the same research techniques that were used in the study of non-Western peoples to explore such diverse subjects as religious movements, street gangs, land rights, schools, marriage practices, conflict resolution, corporate bureaucracies, and health-care systems in Western cultures.

Ethnology

Although ethnographic fieldwork is basic to cultural anthropology, it is not the sole occupation of the cultural anthropologist. Largely descriptive in nature, ethnography provides the raw data needed for ethnology—the branch of cultural anthropology that involves cross-cultural comparisons and theories that explain differences or similarities among groups. Intriguing insights into one's own beliefs and practices may come from cross-cultural comparisons. Consider, for example, the amount of time spent on domestic chores by industrialized peoples and traditional food foragers (people who rely on wild plant and animal resources for subsistence). Anthropological research among food foragers has shown that they work far less at domestic tasks, and indeed less at all subsistence pursuits, than do people in industrialized societies. Urban women in the United States who were not working for wages outside their homes put 55 hours a week into their housework—this despite all the "labor-saving" dishwashers, washing machines, clothes dryers, vacuum cleaners, food processors, and microwave ovens; in contrast, aboriginal women in Australia devoted 20 hours a week to their chores.[2] Nevertheless, consumer appliances have become important indicators of a high standard of living in the United States due to the widespread belief that household appliances reduce housework and increase leisure time.

Considering such cross-cultural comparisons, one may think of ethnology as the study of alternative ways of doing things. But more than that, by making systematic comparisons, ethnologists seek to arrive at scientific conclusions concerning the function and operation of cultural practices in all times and places.

Today cultural anthropologists contribute to applied anthropology in a variety of contexts ranging from business to education to governmental interventions to humanitarian aid. One of the earliest contexts in which knowledge from cultural anthropology was applied to a practical problem was the international public health movement that began in the 1920s, marking the beginning of the subdiscipline of medical anthropology.

Medical Anthropology

While medical anthropology is centered within cultural anthropology, it is a specialization that cross-cuts all the traditional anthropological fields. Some of the earliest medical anthropologists were individuals trained as physicians and ethnographers who investigated health beliefs and practices of people in exotic places while also providing them with "Western" medicine. Medical anthropologists during this early period translated local experiences of sickness into the scientific language of Western biomedicine. Following a re-evaluation of this ethnocentric

approach in the 1970s, **medical anthropology** emerged as a specialization that brings theoretical and applied approaches from cultural and biological anthropology to the study of human health and disease. Medical anthropologists study medical systems as cultural systems similar to any other social institution. They also examine healing traditions and practices cross-culturally and use scientific models drawn from biological anthropology to understand and improve human health. Medical anthropologists have also turned their attention toward biomedicine, focusing on the social and cultural aspects of health care in their own societies. Their work sheds light on the connections between human health and political and economic forces, both globally and locally. Many of the Biocultural Connections featured throughout this text present the work of medical anthropologists, as does "The Anthropology of Organ Transplantation."

ANTHROPOLOGY, SCIENCE, AND THE HUMANITIES

Anthropology has sometimes been called the most humane of the sciences and the most scientific of the humanities—a designation that most anthropologists accept with pride. Given their intense involvement with people of all times and places, it should come as no surprise that anthropology has amassed considerable information about human failure and success, weakness and greatness—the real stuff of the humanities. While anthropologists steer clear of a "cold" impersonal scientific approach that reduces people and the things they do and think to mere numbers, their quantitative studies have contributed substantially to the scientific study of the human condition. But even the most scientific anthropologists always keep in mind that human societies are made up of individuals with rich assortments of emotions and aspirations that demand respect. Beyond this, anthropologists remain committed to the proposition that one cannot fully understand another culture by simply observing it; as the term *participant observation* implies, one must *experience* it as well. This same commitment to fieldwork and to the systematic collection of data, whether it is qualitative or quantitative, is also evidence of the scientific side of anthropology. Anthropology is

---

[2]Bodley, J. H. (1985). *Anthropology and contemporary human problems* (2nd ed., p. 69). Palo Alto, CA: Mayfield.

medical anthropology A specialization in anthropology that brings theoretical and applied approaches from cultural and biological anthropology to the study of human health and disease.

Biocultural Connection

The Anthropology of Organ Transplantation

In 1954, the first organ transplant occurred in Boston when surgeons removed a kidney from one identical twin to place it inside his sick brother. Though some transplants rely upon living donors, routine organ transplantation depends largely upon the availability of organs obtained from individuals who have died.

From an anthropological perspective, the meanings of death and the body vary cross-culturally. While death could be said to represent a particular biological state, social agreement about this state's significance is of paramount importance. Anthropologist Margaret Lock has explored differences between Japanese and North American acceptance of the biological state of "brain death" and how it affects the practice of organ transplants.

Brain death relies upon the absence of measurable electrical currents in the brain and the inability to breathe without technological assistance. The brain-dead individual, though attached to machines, still seems alive with a beating heart and pink cheeks. North Americans find brain death acceptable, in part, because personhood and individuality are culturally located in the brain. North American comfort with brain death has allowed for the "gift of life" through organ donation and subsequent transplantation.

By contrast, in Japan, the concept of brain death is hotly contested and organ transplants are rarely performed. The Japanese do not incorporate a mind-body split into their models of themselves and locate personhood through-

out the body rather than in the brain. They resist accepting a warm pink body as a corpse from which organs can be "harvested." Further, organs cannot be transformed into "gifts" because anonymous donation is not compatible with Japanese social patterns of reciprocal exchange.

Organ transplantation carries far greater social meaning than the purely biological movement of an organ from one individual to another. Cultural and biological processes are tightly woven into every aspect of this new social practice. *(Based on M. Lock (2001). Twice dead: Organ transplants and the reinvention of death. Berkeley: University of California Press.)* ■ ■ ■

---

an **empirical** social science based on observations about humans. But anthropology is distinguished from other sciences by the diverse ways in which scientific research is conducted within this discipline.

Science, a carefully honed way of producing knowledge, aims to reveal and explain the underlying logic, the structural processes that make the world "tick." It is a creative endeavor that seeks testable explanations for observed phenomena, ideally in terms of the workings of hidden but unchanging principles, or laws. Two basic ingredients are essential for this: imagination and skepticism. Imagination, though capable of leading us astray, is required to help us recognize unexpected ways phenomena might be ordered and to think of old things in new ways. Without it, there can be no science. Skepticism is what allows us to distinguish fact (an observation verified by others) from fancy, to test our speculations, and to prevent our imaginations from running away with us.

In their search for explanations, scientists do not assume that things are always as they appear on the surface. After all, what could be more obvious than that the earth is a stable entity, around which the sun travels every day? And yet, it isn't so.

Like other scientists, anthropologists often begin their research with a **hypothesis** (a tentative explanation or hunch) about the possible relationships between certain observed facts or events. By gathering various kinds of data that seem to ground such suggested explanations on evidence, anthropologists come up with a **theory**—an explanation supported by a reliable body of data. In their effort to demonstrate linkages between *known* facts or events, anthropologists may discover *unexpected* facts, events, or relationships. An important function of theory is that it guides us in our explorations and may result in new knowledge. Equally important, the newly discovered facts may provide evidence that certain explanations, however popular or firmly believed to be true, are unfounded. When the evidence is lacking or fails to support the suggested explanations, anthropologists are forced to drop promising hypotheses or attractive hunches. In other words, anthropology relies on empirical evidence. Moreover, no scientific theory, no matter how widely accepted by the international community of scholars, is beyond challenge.

---

empirical Based on observations of the world rather than on intuition or faith.

hypothesis A tentative explanation of the relation between certain phenomena.

theory In science, an explanation of natural phenomena, supported by a reliable body of data.

Straightforward though the scientific approach may seem, its application is not always easy. For instance, once a hypothesis has been proposed, the person who suggested it is strongly motivated to verify it, and this can cause one to unwittingly overlook negative evidence and unanticipated findings. This is a familiar problem in all science as noted by paleontologist Stephen Jay Gould: "The greatest impediment to scientific innovation is usually a conceptual lock, not a factual lock."[3] Because culture provides humans with their concepts and shapes our very thoughts, it can be challenging to frame hypotheses or develop interpretations that are not culture-bound. By encompassing both humanism and science, the discipline of anthropology can draw on its internal diversity to overcome conceptual locks.

Fieldwork

All anthropologists think about whether their culture may have shaped the scientific questions they are asking. In so doing, they rely heavily on a technique that has proved successful in other disciplines: They immerse themselves in the data to the fullest extent possible. In the process, anthropologists become so thoroughly familiar with even the smallest details that they can begin to recognize underlying patterns in the data, many of which might have been overlooked. Recognition of such patterns enables the anthropologist to frame meaningful hypotheses, which then may be subjected to further testing in the field. Within anthropology, fieldwork provides additional rigor to the concept of total immersion in the data.

While fieldwork was introduced above in connection with cultural anthropology, it is characteristic of all the anthropological subdisciplines. Archaeologists and paleoanthropologists excavate in the field. A biological anthropologist interested in the effects of globalization on nutrition and growth will live in the field among a community of people to study this question. A primatologist might live among a group of chimpanzees or baboons just as a linguist will study the language of a community by living in that community. Fieldwork, being immersed in another culture, challenges the anthropologist to be constantly aware of the ways that cultural factors influence the research questions.

Fieldwork requires the researcher to step out of his or her cultural comfort zone into a world that is unfamiliar and sometimes unsettling. Anthropologists in the field are likely to face a host of challenges—physical, social, mental, political, and ethical. They may have to deal with the physical challenge of adjusting to unaccustomed food, climate, and hygiene conditions. Typically, anthropologists in the field struggle with such mental challenges as loneliness, feeling like a perpetual outsider, being socially clumsy and clueless in their new cultural setting, and having to be alert around the clock because anything that is happening or being said may be significant to their research. Political challenges include the possibility of unwittingly letting oneself be used by factions within the community, or being viewed with suspicion by government authorities who may suspect the anthropologist is a spy. And there are ethical dilemmas: what to do if faced with a cultural practice one finds troubling, such as female circumcision; how to deal with demands for food supplies and/or medicine; the temptation to use deception to gain vital information; and so on.

At the same time, fieldwork often leads to tangible and meaningful personal, professional, and social rewards, ranging from lasting friendships to vital knowledge and insights concerning the human condition that make positive contributions to people's lives. Something of the meaning of anthropological fieldwork—its usefulness and its impact on researcher and subject—is conveyed in the following Original Study by Suzanne Leclerc-Madlala, an anthropologist who left her familiar New England surroundings 20 years ago to do AIDS research among Zulu-speaking people in South Africa. Her research interest has changed the course of her own life, not to mention the lives of individuals who have AIDS/HIV and the type of treatment they receive.

---

[3]Gould, S. J. (1989). *Wonderful life* (p. 226). New York: Norton.

Original Study

Fighting HIV/AIDS in Africa: Traditional Healers on the Front Line

In the 1980s, as a North American anthropology graduate student at George Washington University in Washington D.C., I met and married a Zulu-speaking student from South Africa. It was the height of apartheid,

[continued]

[continued]

and upon moving to that country I was classified as "honorary black" and forced to live in a segregated township with my husband. The AIDS epidemic was in its infancy, but it was clear from the start that an anthropological understanding of how people perceive and engage with this disease would be crucial for developing interventions. I wanted to learn all that I could to make a difference, and this culminated in earning a Ph.D. from the University of Natal on the cultural construction of AIDS among the Zulu. The HIV/AIDS pandemic in Africa became my professional passion.

Faced with overwhelming global health-care needs, the World Health Organization passed a series of resolutions in the 1970s promoting collaboration between traditional and modern medicine. Such moves held a special relevance for Africa where traditional healers typically outnumber practitioners of modern medicine by a ratio of 100 to 1 or more. Given Africa's disproportionate burden of disease, supporting partnership efforts with traditional healers makes sense. But what sounds sensible today was once considered absurd, even heretical. For centuries Westerners generally viewed traditional healing as a whole lot of primitive mumbo jumbo practiced by witchdoctors with demonic powers who perpetuated superstition. Yet, its practice survived. Today, as the African continent grapples with an HIV/AIDS epidemic of crisis proportion, millions of sick people who are either too poor or too distant to access modern health care are proving that traditional healers are an invaluable resource in the fight against AIDS.

Of the world's estimated 40 million people currently infected by HIV, 70 percent live in sub-Saharan Africa, and the vast majority of children left orphaned by AIDS are African. From the 1980s onward, as Africa became synonymous with the rapid spread of HIV/AIDS, a number of prevention programs involved traditional healers. My initial research in South Africa's KwaZulu-Natal province—where it is estimated that 36 percent of the population is HIV infected—revealed that

traditional Zulu healers were regularly consulted for the treatment of sexually transmitted disease (STD). I found that such diseases, along with HIV/AIDS, were usually attributed to transgressions of taboos related to birth, pregnancy, marriage, and death. Moreover, these diseases were often understood within a framework of pollution and contagion, and like most serious illnesses, ultimately believed to have their causal roots in witchcraft.

In the course of my research, I investigated a pioneer program in STD and HIV education for traditional healers in the province. The program aimed to provide basic biomedical knowledge about the various modes of disease transmission, the means available for prevention, the diagnosing of symptoms, the keeping of records, and the making of patient referrals to local clinics and hospitals.

Interviews with the healers showed that many maintained a deep suspicion of modern medicine. They perceived AIDS education as a one-way street intended to press them into formal health structures and convince them of the superiority of modern medicine. Yet, today, few of the 6,000-plus KwaZulu-Natal healers who have been trained in AIDS education say they would opt for less collaboration; most want to have more.

Treatments by Zulu healers for HIV/AIDS often take the form of infusions of bitter herbs to "cleanse" the body, strengthen the blood, and remove misfortune and "pollution."

Medical anthropologist Suzanne Leclerc-Madlala visits with "Doctor" Koloko in KwaZulu-Natal, South Africa. This Zulu traditional healer proudly displays her official AIDS training certificate.

Some treatments provide effective relief from common ailments associated with AIDS such as itchy skin rashes, oral thrush, persistent diarrhea, and general debility. Indigenous plants such as *unwele (Sutherlandia frutescens)* and African potato *(Hypoxis hemerocallidea)* are well-known traditional medicines that have proven immuno-boosting properties.

Both have recently become available in modern pharmacies packaged in tablet form. With modern anti-retroviral treatments still well beyond the reach of most South Africans, indigenous medicines that can delay or alleviate some of the suffering caused by AIDS are proving to be valuable and popular treatments.

Knowledge about potentially infectious bodily fluids has led healers to change some of their practices. Where porcupine quills were once used to give a type of indigenous injection, patients are now advised to bring their own sewing needles to consultations. Patients provide their own individual razor blades for making incisions on their skin, where previously healers reused the same razor on many clients. Some healers claim they have given up the practice of biting clients' skin to remove foreign objects from the body. It is not uncommon today, especially in urban centers like Durban, to find healers proudly displaying AIDS training certificates in their inner-city "surgeries" where they don white jackets and wear protective latex gloves.

Politics and controversy have dogged South Africa's official response to HIV/AIDS. But back home in the waddle-and-daub, animal-skin-draped herbariums and divining huts of traditional healers, the politics of AIDS holds little relevance. Here the sick and dying are coming in droves to be treated by healers who have been part and parcel of community life (and death) since time immemorial. In many cases traditional healers have transformed their homes into hospices for AIDS patients. Because of the strong stigma that still plagues the disease, those with AIDS symptoms are often abandoned or sometimes chased away from their homes by family members. They seek refuge with healers who provide them with comfort in their final days. Healers' homes are also becoming orphanages as healers respond to what has been called the "third wave" of AIDS destruction: the growing legions of orphaned children.

The practice of traditional healing in Africa is adapting to the changing face of health and illness in the context of HIV/AIDS. But those who are suffering go to traditional healers not only in search of relief for physical symptoms. They go to learn about the ultimate cause of their disease—something other than the immediate cause of a sexually transmitted "germ" or "virus." They go to find answers to the "why me and not him" questions, the

"why now" and "why this." As with most traditional healing systems worldwide, healing among the Zulu and most all African ethnic groups cannot be separated from the spiritual concerns of the individual and the cosmological beliefs of the community at large. Traditional healers help to restore a sense of balance between the individual and the community, on one hand, and between the individual and the cosmos, or ancestors, on the other hand. They provide health care that is personalized, culturally appropriate, holistic, and tailored to meet the needs and expectations of the patient. In many ways it is a far more satisfactory form of healing than that offered by modern medicine.

Traditional healing in Africa is flourishing in the era of AIDS, and understanding why this is so requires a shift in the conceptual framework by which we understand, explain, and interpret health. Anthropological methods and its comparative and holistic perspective can facilitate, like no other discipline, the type of understanding that is urgently needed to address the AIDS crisis. *(By Suzanne Leclerc-Madlala. Adapted in part from S. Leclerc-Madlala (2002). Bodies and politics: Healing rituals in the democratic South Africa. In V. Faure (Ed.), Les cahiers de 'l'IFAS, No. 2. Johannesburg: The French Institute.)* ■ ■ ■

Unlike many other social scientists, anthropologists usually do not go into the field armed with prefigured questionnaires. Though they head into the field having completed considerable background research and some tentative hypotheses, they still recognize that many of the best discoveries are made by maintaining an open mind. As fieldwork proceeds, anthropologists sort out their observations, sometimes by formulating and testing limited or low-level hypotheses, or by intuition. The anthropologist works closely with the community so that the research process can become a collaborative effort. The results are constantly checked for consistency, for if the parts fail to fit together in a manner that is consistent, then the anthropologist knows that a mistake may have been made and that further inquiry is necessary.

Another issue in scientific fieldwork is validity. In the natural sciences, the reliability of a researcher's conclusions is established through the replication of observations and/or experiments by another researcher. Thus, it becomes obvious if one's colleague has "gotten it right." In anthropology, some researchers self-monitor through constantly checking their own biases and assumptions as they work and presenting these self-reflections along with their observations, a practice known as *reflexivity*.

Traditional validation by others is uniquely challenging in anthropology because observational access is often limited. Access to a particular research site can be constrained by a number of factors. Difficulties of travel, obtaining permits, insufficient funding, or social, political, and environmental conditions can hamper the process, and what may be observed in a certain context at a certain time may not be at others, and so on. Once an archaeological site has been excavated for the first time, the site is forever changed. Thus, one researcher cannot easily confirm the reliability or completeness of another's account. For this reason, anthropologists bear a special responsibility for accurate reporting. In the final research report, she or he must be clear about several basic things: Why was a particular location selected as a research site? What were the research objectives? What were the local conditions during fieldwork? Which local individuals provided the key information and major insights? How were the data collected and recorded? How did the researcher check his/her own biases? Without such background information, it is difficult for others to judge the validity of the account and the soundness of the researcher's conclusions.

ANTHROPOLOGY'S COMPARATIVE METHOD

The end product of anthropological research, if properly carried out, is a coherent statement about a people that provides an explanatory framework for understanding the beliefs, behavior, or biology of those who have been studied. And this, in turn, is what permits the anthropologist to frame broader hypotheses about human beliefs, behavior, and biology. A single instance of any phenomenon is generally insufficient for supporting a plausible hypothesis. Without some basis for comparison, the hypothesis grounded in a single case may be no more than a particular historical coincidence. On the other hand, a single case may be enough to cast doubt on, if not refute, a theory that had previously been held to be valid. For example, the discovery in 1948 that aborigines living in Australia's northern Arnhem Land put in an average workday of less than 6 hours, while living well above a level of bare sufficiency, was enough to call into question the widely accepted notion that food-foraging peoples are so preoccupied with finding scarce food that they lack time for any of life's more pleasurable activities. The observations made in the Arnhem Land study have since been confirmed many times over in various parts of the world.

Hypothetical explanations of cultural and biological phenomena may be tested through comparison of archaeological, biological, linguistic, historical, and/or ethnographic data for several societies found in a particular region. Carefully controlled comparison provides a broader basis for drawing general conclusions about humans than does the study of a single culture or population.

Ideally, theories in anthropology are generated from worldwide comparisons or comparisons across species or through time. The cross-cultural researcher examines a global sample of societies in order to discover whether or not hypotheses proposed to explain cultural phenomena or biological variation are universally applicable. However, the cross-cultural researcher depends upon data gathered by other scholars as well as his or her own. Similarly, archaeologists and biological anthropologists rely on artifacts and skeletal collections housed in museums, as well as published descriptions of these collections.

QUESTIONS OF ETHICS

The kinds of research carried out by anthropologists, and the settings within which they work, raise a number of important moral questions about the potential uses and abuses of our knowledge. While some of these questions are now incorporated into laws designed to protect human research subjects, anthropologists have been grappling with these issues for many years. Who will utilize our findings and for what purposes? Who decides what research questions are asked? Who, if anyone, will profit from the research? For example, in the case of research on an ethnic or religious minority whose values may be at odds with dominant mainstream society, will governmental or corporate interests use anthropological data to suppress that group? And what of traditional communities around the world? Who is to decide what changes should, or should not, be introduced for community "betterment"? And who defines what constitutes betterment—the community, a national government, or an international agency like the World Health Organization? What are the limits of cultural relativism when a traditional practice is considered a human rights abuse globally?

Then there is the problem of privacy. Anthropologists deal with matters that are private and sensitive, including things that individuals would prefer not to have generally known about them. How does one write about such important but delicate issues and at the same time

protect the privacy of the individuals who have shared their stories? The American Anthropological Association (AAA) maintains a Statement of Ethics, which is regularly examined and modified to reflect the practice of anthropology in a changing world. The AAA ethics statement is an educational document that lays out the rules and ideals applicable to anthropologists in all the subdisciplines. While the AAA has no legal authority, it does issue policy statements on research ethics questions as they come up. For example, recently the AAA recommended that field notes from medical settings should be protected and not subject to subpoena in malpractice lawsuits. This honors the ethical imperative to protect the privacy of individuals who have shared their stories with anthropologists.

Anthropologists recognize that they have special obligations to three sets of people: those whom they study, those who fund the research, and those in the profession who expect us to publish our findings so that they may be used to further our collective knowledge. Because fieldwork requires a relationship of trust between fieldworker and the community in which they work, the anthropologist's first responsibility clearly is to the people who have shared their stories and the greater community. Everything possible must be done to protect their physical, social, and psychological welfare and to honor their dignity and privacy. This task is frequently complex. For example, telling the story of a group of people gives information both to relief agencies who might help these people and to others who might take advantage of them. While anthropologists regard as basic a people's right to maintain their own culture, any connections with outsiders can endanger the cultural identity of the community being studied. To surmount these obstacles, anthropologists frequently collaborate with and contribute to the communities in which they are working, allowing the people being studied to have some say about how their stories are told.

ANTHROPOLOGY AND GLOBALIZATION

A holistic perspective and a long-term commitment to understanding the human species in all its variety is the essence of anthropology. Thus, anthropology is well equipped to grapple with an issue that has overriding importance for all of us at the beginning of the 21st century: **globalization.** This term refers to worldwide inter-

---

globalization Worldwide interconnectedness, evidenced in global movements of natural resources, trade goods, human labor, finance capital, information, and infectious diseases.

connectedness, evidenced in global movements of natural resources, trade goods, human labor, finance capital, information, and infectious diseases. Although worldwide travel, trade relations, and information flow have existed for several centuries, the pace and magnitude of these long-distance exchanges has picked up enormously in recent decades; the Internet, in particular, has greatly expanded information exchange capacities.

The powerful forces driving globalization are technological innovations, lower transportation and communication costs, faster knowledge transfers, and increased trade and financial integration among countries. Touching almost everybody's life on the planet, globalization is about economics as much as politics, and it changes human relations and ideas as well as our natural environments. Even geographically remote communities are quickly becoming more interdependent through globalization.

Doing research in all corners of the world, anthropologists are confronted with the impact of globalization on human communities wherever they are located. As participant observers, they describe and try to explain how individuals and organizations respond to the massive changes confronting them. Anthropologists may also find out how local responses sometimes change the global flows directed at them. Dramatically increasing every year, globalization can be a two-edged sword. It may generate economic growth and prosperity, but it also undermines long-established institutions. Generally, globalization has brought significant gains to higher-educated groups in wealthier countries, while doing little to boost developing countries and actually contributing to the erosion of traditional cultures. Upheavals born of globalization are key causes for rising levels of ethnic and religious conflict throughout the world.

Obviously, since all of us now live in a global village, we can no longer afford the luxury of ignoring our neighbors, no matter how distant they may seem to most of us. In this age of globalization, anthropology may not only provide humanity with useful insights concerning diversity, but it may also assist us in avoiding or overcoming significant problems born of that diversity. In countless social arenas, from schools to businesses to hospitals, anthropologists have done cross-cultural research that makes it possible for educators, businesspeople, and doctors to do their work more effectively.

For example, in the United States today, discrimination based on notions of race continues to be a serious issue affecting economic, political, and social relations. Far from being the biological reality it is supposed to be, anthropologists have shown that the concept of race (and the classification of human groups into higher and lower racial types) emerged in the 18th century as an ideological vehicle for justifying European dominance over Africans and American Indians. In fact, differences of skin color are simply surface adaptations to different climactic zones and have nothing to do with physical or mental capabilities. Indeed, geneticists find far more biological variation *within* any given human population than *among* them. In short, human "races" are divisive categories based on prejudice, false ideas of differences, and erroneous notions of the superiority of one's own group. Given the importance of this issue, race will be discussed further in Chapter 8.

A second example involves the issue of same-sex marriage. In 1989, Denmark became the first country to enact a comprehensive set of legal protections for same-sex couples, known as the Registered Partnership Act. At this writing, more than a half-dozen other countries and some individual states within the United States have passed similar laws, variously named, and numerous countries around the world are considering or have passed legislation providing people in homosexual unions the benefits and protections afforded by marriage.[4] In some societies, including Spain, Canada, Belgium, and

This boy, from an East African cattle-herding family, has the genetically based ability to digest milk, something that sets populations with dairying traditions apart from the majority of the world's inhabitants, regardless of their skin color. Because genetic traits are inherited independently, humans cannot be classified into races having any biological validity.

© Gordon Gahan/National Geographic Image Collection

the Netherlands, same-sex marriages are considered socially acceptable and allowed by law, even though opposite-sex marriages are far more common. As individuals, countries, and states struggle to define the boundaries of legal protections they will grant to same-sex couples, the anthropological perspective on marriage is useful. Anthropologists have documented same-sex marriages in human societies in various parts of the world, where they are regarded as acceptable under appropriate circumstances. Homosexual behavior occurs in the animal world just as it does among humans.[5] The key difference between people and other animals is that human societies possess beliefs regarding homosexual behavior, just as they do for heterosexual behavior. An understanding of global variation in marriage patterns and sexual behavior does not dictate that one pattern is more right than another. It simply illustrates that all human societies define the boundaries for social relationships.

---

[4]Merin, Y. (2002). *Equality for same-sex couples: The legal recognition of gay partnerships in Europe and the United States.* Chicago: University of Chicago Press. "Court says same-sex marriage is a right." *San Francisco Chronicle.* Feb. 5, 2004. Up-to-date overviews and breaking news on the global status of same-sex marriage is posted on the Internet by the Partners Task Force for Gay & Lesbian Couples at www.buddybuddy.com.

---

[5]Kirkpatrick, R. C. (2000). The evolution of human homosexual behavior. *Current Anthropology, 41,* 384.

A final example relates to the common confusion of *nation* with *state*. Anthropology makes an important distinction between these two: States are politically organized territories that are internationally recognized, whereas nations are socially organized bodies of people, who share ethnicity—a common origin, language, and cultural heritage. For example, the Kurds constitute a nation, but their homeland is divided among several states: Iran, Iraq, Turkey, and Syria. The modern boundaries among these states were drawn up after World War I, with little regard for the region's ethnic groups or nations. Similar processes have taken place throughout the world, especially in Asia and Africa, often making political conditions in these countries inherently unstable. As we will see in later chapters, states and nations rarely coincide, nations being split among different states, and states typically being controlled by members of one nation who commonly use their control to gain access to the land, resources, and labor of other nationalities within the state. Most of the armed conflicts in the world today, such as the many-layered conflicts among the peoples of the former Yugoslavia, are of this sort and are not mere acts of "tribalism" or "terrorism," as commonly asserted.

As these examples show, ignorance about other peoples and their ways is a cause of serious problems throughout the world. Anthropology offers a way of looking at and understanding the world's peoples— insights that are nothing less than basic skills for survival in this age of globalization.

Chapter Summary

■ Anthropology is the study of humankind. In employing a scientific approach, anthropologists seek to produce a reasonably objective understanding of both human diversity and those things all humans have in common.

■ Anthropology contains four major fields: physical anthropology, archaeology, linguistic anthropology, and cultural anthropology. Physical anthropology focuses on humans as biological organisms. Particular emphasis is given by physical anthropologists to tracing the evolutionary development of the human animal and studying biological variation within the species today. Forensics is an example of applied physical anthropology. Archaeologists study human cultures through the recovery and analysis of material remains and environmental data. Linguists, who study human languages, may deal with the description of a language, with the history of languages, or how languages are used in particular social settings. Cultural anthropologists study humans in terms of their cultures, the often-unconscious standards by which social groups operate. Medical anthropology is a growing specialization that cuts across all the subdisciplines.

■ Within all of anthropology's subdisciplines, one can find applied anthropologists who utilize the discipline's unique research methodology toward solving practical problems.

■ Some cultural anthropologists are ethnographers, who do a particular kind of hands-on fieldwork known as participant observation. They produce a detailed record of a specific culture in writing (and/or visual imagery) known as an ethnography. Other cultural anthropologists are also ethnologists, who study and analyze cultures from a comparative or historical point of view, utilizing ethnographic accounts. Often, they focus on a particular aspect of culture, such as religious or economic practices.

■ Unique among the sciences and humanities, anthropology has long emphasized the study of non-Western societies and a holistic approach, which aims to formulate theoretically valid explanations and interpretations of human diversity based on detailed studies of all aspects of human biology, behavior, and beliefs in all known societies, past and present.

■ Anthropologists are concerned with the objective and systematic study of humankind. The comparative method is key to all branches of anthropology. Anthropologists make broad comparisons among peoples and cultures past and present, related species, and fossil groups.

■ In anthropology, the humanities, social sciences, and natural sciences come together into a genuinely humanistic science. Anthropology's link with the humanities can be seen in its concern with people's beliefs, values, languages, arts, and literature—oral as well as written—but above all in its attempt to convey the experience of living in different cultures. As both science and humanity, anthropology has essential insights to offer the modern world, particularly in this era of globalization when understanding our neighbors in the global village has become a matter of survival for all.

Questions for Reflection

1. Anthropology uses a holistic approach to explain all aspects of human beliefs, behavior and biology. How might anthropology challenge your personal perspective on the following questions: Where did we come from? Why do we act in certain ways? What makes us tick?

2. From the holistic anthropological perspective, humans have one leg in culture and the other in nature. Are there examples from your life that illustrate the interconnectedness of human biology and culture?

3. Globalization can be described as a two-edged sword. How does it foster growth and destruction simultaneously?

4. The textbook definitions of *state* and *nation* are based on scientific distinctions between both organizational types. However, this distinction is commonly lost in everyday language. Consider, for instance, the names *United States of America* and the *United Nations*.

5. The Biocultural Connection in this chapter contrasts different cultural perspectives on "brain death," while the Original Study features a discussion about traditional Zulu healers and their role in dealing with AIDS victims. What do these two accounts suggest about the role of applied anthropology in dealing with cross-cultural health issues around the world?

Key Terms

anthropology	linguistic anthropology
holistic perspective	cultural anthropology
culture-bound	culture
applied anthropology	ethnography
physical anthropology	fieldwork
molecular anthropology	participant observation
paleoanthropology	ethnology
biocultural	medical anthropology
primatology	empirical
forensic anthropology	hypothesis
archaeology	theory
cultural resource management	globalization

Multimedia Review Tools

Make the Grade in Anthropology with ThomsonNOW

Thomson NOW! This powerful online study tool provides you with a *personalized study plan* based on your responses to a diagnostic pretest. Once you have mastered the material with the help of interactive learning tools, an integrated e-book, and more, you can take a post-test to confirm you are ready to move on to the next chapter. To get started with ThomsonNOW, check the card packaged with your book for the access code. Then go to http://www.thomsonedu.com to create an account through 1pass(tm). If there is no card in your book, go to http://www.thomsonedu.com to purchase an access code.

Companion Website and Anthropology Resource Center

Go to http://anthropology.wadsworth.com to reach the companion website for your text. This offers many study aids, including self quizzes for each chapter and a practice final exam, as well as links to anthropology websites and information on the latest theories and discoveries in the field.

Also, check out the Anthropology Resource Center for a wealth of learning materials that include interactive maps, video exercises, simulations, and breaking news in anthropology. Be sure to explore InfoTrac College Edition®, your online library that offers full-length articles from thousands of scholarly and popular publications. To reach the Anthropology Resource Center and InfoTrac College Edition, check the card packaged with your book for the access code. Then go to http://www.thomsonedu.com to create an account through 1pass™. If there is no card in your book, go to http://www.thomsonedu.com to purchase an access code.

© Chris Benton

Monumental sculptures of DNA, the molecule that contains the human genetic code, grace a variety of public spaces today. They illustrate the molecular structure of DNA as well as its profound social meaning. Through sculptures like this one, from the Lawrence Hall of Science, a public science museum and research center at the University of California, Berkeley, the structure of DNA becomes internalized as a normal part of daily life. Will scientific understanding of the human genetic code fundamentally reshape our conception of what it means to be human? How much of our lives are dictated by the structure of DNA? And what will be the social consequences of depicting humans as entities programmed by their DNA? Individuals and societies can answer these challenging questions using an anthropological perspective that emphasizes the connections between human biology and culture.

Biology and Evolution

2

EVOLUTION AND CREATION STORIES

A common part of the mythology of most peoples is a story explaining the appearance of humans on earth. The accounts of creation recorded in the Bible's Book of Genesis, for example, explain human origins. A vastly different example, serving the same function, is the traditional belief of the Nez Perce, a people native to eastern Oregon and Idaho. For the Nez Perce, humanity is the creation of Coyote, a trickster-transformer inhabiting the earth before humans. Coyote chased the giant beaver monster, Wishpoosh, over the earth leaving a trail to form the Columbia River. When Coyote caught Wishpoosh, he killed him, dragged his body to the riverbank and cut it into pieces, each body part transforming into one of the various peoples of this region. The Nez Perce were made from Wishpoosh's head, thus conferring on them great intelligence and horsemanship.[1]

Creation stories depict the relationship between humans and the rest of the natural world, sometimes reflecting a deep connection among people, other animals, and the earth. In the traditional Nez Perce creation story, groups of people derive from specific body parts—each possessing a special talent and relationship with a particular animal. By contrast, the story of creation depicted in the Book of Genesis emphasizes human uniqueness and the concept of time. Creation is depicted as a series of actions occurring over the course of 6 days. God's final act of creation is to fashion the first human from the earth in his own image before the seventh day of rest.

---

[1]Clark, E. E. (1966). *Indian legends of the Pacific Northwest* (p. 174). Berkeley: University of California Press.

Evolution, a major organizing principle of the biological sciences, also accounts for the diversity of life on earth. Theories of evolution provide explanations for how it works and for how the variety of organisms, both in the past and today, came into being. However, evolution differs from creation stories in that it explains the diversity of life in consistent scientific language, using testable ideas (hypotheses). Contemporary scientists make comparisons among living organisms to test hypotheses drawn from evolutionary theory. Through their research, scientists have deciphered the molecular basis of evolution and the mechanisms through which evolutionary forces work on populations of organisms. Though scientific theories of evolution treat humans as biological organisms, at the same time, historical and cultural processes also shape evolutionary theory and our understanding of it.

THE CLASSIFICATION OF LIVING THINGS

The development of biology and its central concept, evolution, provide an excellent example of the ways that historical and cultural processes can shape scientific thought. As the exploitation of foreign lands by European explorers, including Columbus, changed the prevailing European approach to the natural world, new life forms challenged the previously held notion of fixed unchanging life on earth.

Before this time, Europeans organized living things and inanimate objects alike into a ladder or hierarchy known as the Great Chain of Being, an approach to nature first developed by Aristotle in ancient Greece over 2,000 years ago. The categories were based upon visible similarities, and one member of each category was considered its "primate" (from the Latin *primus*), meaning the first or best of the group. For example, the primate of rocks was the diamond, and the primate of birds was the eagle, and so forth. Humans were at the very top of the ladder, just below the angels.

This classificatory system was in place until Carl von Linné, writing with a Latin pen name Carolus Linnaeus, developed the *Systema Naturae* or system of nature, in the 18th century, to classify all living things. A professor of medicine and botany in Sweden, von Linné prepared and prescribed medicinal plants as did other physicians of the time. He arranged for his students to join the major European voyages such as Captain James Cook's circumnavigation of the globe so they could bring back new medicinal plants and other life forms. Von Linné's compendium reflected a new understanding of life on earth and of the place of humanity among the animals.

Linnaeus noted the similarity among humans, monkeys, and apes, classifying them together as **primates.** But instead of being the first or the best of the animals on earth, primates are just one of several kinds of **mammal,** animals having body hair or fur who suckle or nurse their young. In other words, Linnaeus classified living things into a series of categories that are progressively more inclusive on the basis of internal and external visual similarities. **Species** are the smallest working units in biological classificatory systems. Species are defined as reproductively isolated populations or groups of populations capable of interbreeding to produce fertile offspring. Species are subdivisions of larger, more inclusive groups, called **genera** (singular, **genus**). Humans, for example, are classified in the genus *Homo* and species *sapiens*.

Linnaeus based his classificatory system on the following criteria:

1. *Body structure:* A Guernsey cow and a Holstein cow are the same species because they have identical body structure. A cow and a horse do not.
2. *Body function:* Cows and horses give birth to live young. Although they are different species, they are closer than either cows or horses are to chickens, which lay eggs and have no mammary glands.
3. *Sequence of bodily growth:* At the time of birth—or hatching out of the egg—young cows and chickens resemble their parents in their body plan. They are therefore more closely related to each other than either one is to the frog, whose tadpoles undergo a series of changes before attaining the basic adult form.

Modern **taxonomy,** or the science of classification (from the Greek for naming divisions), while retaining the structure of the Linnaean system, is based on more than body structure, function, and growth. Today, scientists also compare protein structure and genetic material

primates   The group of mammals that includes lemurs, lorises, tarsiers, monkeys, apes, and humans.

mammals   The class of vertebrate animals distinguished by bodies covered with fur, self-regulating temperature, and in females milk-producing mammary glands.

species   The smallest working unit in the system of classification. Among living organisms, species are populations or groups of populations capable of interbreeding and producing fertile viable offspring.

genus, genera (pl.)   In the system of plant and animal classification, a group of like species.

taxonomy   The science of classification.

to construct the relationship among living things. Such molecular comparisons can even be aimed at parasites, bacteria, and viruses, allowing scientists to classify or trace the origins of particular diseases, such as the recent outbreak of SARS (sudden acute respiratory syndrome) or HIV (human immunodeficiency virus).

In addition, cross-species comparisons identify anatomical features of similar function as **analogies,** while anatomical features that have evolved from a common ancestral feature are called **homologies.** For

> **analogies** In biology, structures possessed by different organisms that are superficially similar due to similar function; without sharing a common developmental pathway or structure.
>
> **homologies** In biology, structures possessed by two different organisms that arise in similar fashion and pass through similar stages during embryonic development though they may possess different functions.

example, the hand of a human and the wing of a bat evolved from the forelimb of a common ancestor, though they have acquired different functions: The human hand and bat wing are homologous structures. During their early embryonic development, homologous structures arise in a similar fashion and pass through similar stages before differentiating. The wings of birds and butterflies look similar and have a similar function (flying): These are analogous, but not homologous, structures because they do not follow the same developmental sequence.

Through careful comparison and analysis of organisms, Linnaeus and his successors have grouped species into genera and also into even larger groups such as families, orders, classes, phyla, and kingdoms. Each taxonomic level is distinguished by characteristics shared by all the organisms in the group. Table 2.1 presents the main categories of contemporary taxonomy applied to the classification of the human species, with a few of

TABLE 2.1   CLASSIFICATION OF HUMANS

Taxonomic Category	Category to Which Humans Belong	Biological Features Used to Define and Place Humans in this Category
Kingdom	Animalia	Humans are animals. We do not make our own food (as plants do) but depend upon intake of living food.
Phylum	Chordata	Humans are chordates. We have a notochord (a rodlike structure of cartilage) and nerve chord running along the back of the body as well as gill slits in the embryonic stage of our life cycle.
Subphylum*	Vertebrata	Humans are vertebrates possessing an internal backbone, with a segmented spinal column.
Class	Mammalia	Humans are mammals, warm-blooded animals covered with fur, possessing mammary glands for nourishing their young after birth.
Order	Primates	Humans are primates, a kind of mammal with a generalized anatomy, relatively large brains, and grasping hands and feet.
Suborder	Anthropoidea	Humans are anthropoids, social, daylight-active primates.
Superfamily	Hominoid	Humans are hominoids with broad flexible shoulders and no tail. Chimps, bonobos, gorillas, orangutans, gibbons, and siamangs are also hominoids.
Family Subfamily	Hominid Hominin	Humans are hominids. We are hominoids from Africa, genetically more closely related to chimps, bonobos, and gorillas than to hominoids from Asia. Some scientists use hominid to refer only to humans and their ancestors. Others include chimps and gorillas in this category, using the subfamily hominin to distinguish humans and their ancestors from chimps and gorillas and their ancestors.
Genus Species	*Homo* *sapiens*	Humans have large brains and rely on cultural adaptations to survive. Ancestral fossils are placed in this genus and species depending upon details of the skull shape and interpretations of their cultural capabilities. Genus and species names are always italicized.

*Most categories can be expanded or narrowed by adding the prefix "sub" or "super." A family could thus be part of a superfamily and in turn contain two or more subfamilies.

the more important distinguishing features noted for each category.

THE DISCOVERY OF EVOLUTION

Just as European seafaring and exploitation brought about an awareness of the diversity of life across the earth, construction and mining, which came with the onset of industrialization in Europe, brought about an awareness of change in life forms through time. Through cutting a railway line or some other work moving the earth, all sorts of fossils, or preserved remains, of past life forms were brought into the light.

At first, the fossilized remains of elephants and giant saber-toothed tigers in Europe were interpreted according to religious doctrine. For example, the early 19th-century theory of "catastrophism" invoked natural events like the Great Flood of the Book of Genesis to account for the disappearance of these species in European lands. With industrialization, however, Europeans became more comfortable with the ideas of change and progress. In hindsight, it seems inevitable that someone would hit upon the idea of evolution. So it was that, by the start of the 19th century, many naturalists had come to accept the idea that life had evolved, even though they were not clear about how it happened. It remained for Charles Darwin (1809–1882) to formulate a theory that has withstood the test of time.

Grandson of Erasmus Darwin (a physician, scientist, poet, and originator of a theory of evolution himself), Charles Darwin began the study of medicine at the University of Edinburgh, Scotland. Finding himself unfit for this profession, he went to Christ's College, Cambridge, to study theology. He then left Cambridge to take the position of companion to Captain Fitzroy on the *H.M.S. Beagle,* which was about to embark on an expedition to various poorly mapped parts of the world. The voyage lasted for almost 5 years, taking Darwin along the coasts of South America, to the Galapagos Islands, across the Pacific to Australia, and then across the Indian and Atlantic oceans to South America before returning to England in 1836. Observing the tremendous diversity of living creatures as well as the astounding fossils of extinct animals, Darwin began to note that species varied according to the environments they inhabited. The observations he made on this voyage, his readings of Sir Charles Lyell's *Principles of Geology* (1830), and the arguments he had with the orthodox and dogmatic Fitzroy all contributed to the ideas culminating in Darwin's most famous book, *On the Origin of Species.* This book, published in 1859, over 20 years after he returned from his voyage, described a theory of evolution accounting for change within species and for the emergence of new species in purely naturalistic terms.

Darwin added observations from English farm life and intellectual thought to the ideas he began to develop on the *Beagle.* He paid particular attention to domesticated animals and farmers' practice of breeding their stock to select for specific traits. Darwin's theoretical breakthrough derived partly from an essay by economist Thomas Malthus (1766–1834), which warned of the potential consequences of increased human population. Malthus observed that animal populations, unlike human populations, remained stable, due to a large proportion of animal offspring not surviving to maturity.

Darwin combined his observations into the theory of **natural selection** as follows: All species display a range of variation, and all have the ability to expand beyond their means of subsistence. It follows that, in their "struggle for existence," organisms with variations that help them to survive in a particular environment will reproduce with greater success than those without them. Thus, as generation succeeds generation, nature selects the most advantageous variations, and species evolve. So obvious did the idea seem in hindsight that Thomas Henry Huxley, one of the era's most prominent scientists, remarked, "How extremely stupid of me not to have thought of that."[2]

However straightforward the idea of evolution by natural selection may appear, the theory was (and has continued to be) a source of considerable controversy. Two problems plagued Darwin's theory throughout his career. First, how did variation arise in the first place? Second, what was the mechanism of heredity by which variable traits could be passed from one generation to the next? Ironically, some of the information Darwin needed, the basic laws of heredity, were available by 1866, through the experimental work of Gregor Mendel (1822–1884), an obscure monk, working in the monastery gardens in Brno, a city in the southeast of today's Czech Republic.

Mendel, who was raised on a farm, possessed two particular talents: a flair for mathematics and a passion for gardening. As with all farmers of his time, Mendel had an intuitive understanding of biological inheritance. He went a step farther, though, in that he recognized the need for a more systematic understanding. Thus, at age 34, he began careful breeding experiments in the monastery garden, starting with pea plants.

---

natural selection The evolutionary process through which factors in the environment exert pressure, favoring some individuals over others to produce the next generation.

---

[2]Quoted in Durant, J. C. (2000, April 23). Everybody into the gene pool. *New York Times Book Review,* p. 11.

Over 8 years, Mendel planted over 30,000 plants, controlling their pollination, observing the results, and figuring out the mathematics behind it all. This allowed him to predict the outcome of hybridization, or breeding that combined distinct varieties of the same species, over successive generations, in terms of basic laws of heredity. Though his findings were published in 1866 in a respected scientific journal, no one seemed to recognize the importance of Mendel's work during his lifetime. In 1900, cell biology had advanced to the point where rediscovery of Mendel's laws was inevitable, and in that year three European botanists, working independently of one another, rediscovered not only the laws but also Mendel's original paper. With this rediscovery, the science of genetics began. Still, it would be another 53 years before the molecular mechanisms of heredity, and the discrete units of inheritance, would be discovered. Today, a comprehensive understanding of heredity, molecular genetics, and population genetics support Darwinian evolutionary theory.

HEREDITY

In order to understand how evolution works, one has to have some understanding of the mechanics of heredity, because heritable variation constitutes the raw material for evolution. Our knowledge of the mechanisms of heredity is fairly recent; most of the fruitful research into the molecular level of inheritance has taken place in the past five decades. Although some aspects remain puzzling, the outlines by now are clear.

The Transmission of Genes

While today we define a **gene** as a portion of the DNA molecule containing a sequence of base pairs that encodes a particular protein, the molecular basis of the gene was not known at the turn of the 20th century when biologists coined the term from the Greek word for "birth." Mendel had deduced the presence and activity of genes by experimenting with garden peas to determine how various traits are passed from one generation to the next. Specifically, he discovered that inheritance was particulate, rather than blending, as Darwin and many others thought. That is, the units controlling the expression of visible traits come in pairs, one from each parent, and retain their separate identities over the generations rather than blending into a combination of parental traits in offspring. This was the basis of

genes Portions of DNA molecules that direct the synthesis of specific proteins.

Mendel's first **law of segregation,** which states that pairs of genes separate and keep their individuality and are passed on to the next generation, unaltered. Another of his laws—that of **independent assortment**—states that different traits (under the control of distinct genes) are inherited independently of one another.

Mendel's laws were abstract formulations based on statistical frequencies of observed characteristics, such as color and texture in generations of plants. His inferences about the mechanisms of inheritance were confirmed through the discovery of the cellular and molecular basis of inheritance in the first half of the 20th century. When **chromosomes,** the cellular structures containing the genetic information, were discovered at the start of the 20th century, they provided a visible vehicle for transmission of traits proposed in Mendel's laws.

It was not until 1953 that James Watson and Francis Crick found that genes are actually portions of molecules of deoxyribonucleic acid (**DNA**)—long strands of which form chromosomes. DNA is a complex molecule with an unusual shape, rather like two strands of a rope twisted around each other with ladderlike steps between the two strands. Alternating sugar and phosphate molecules form the backbone of these strands connected to each other by four base pairs: adenine, thymine, guanine, and cytosine (usually written as A, T, G, and C). Connections between the strands occur between so-called complementary pairs of bases (A to T, G to C; see Figure 2.1). Sequences of three complementary bases specify the sequence of amino acids in protein synthesis. This arrangement also confers upon genes the unique property of being able to replicate or make exact copies of themselves.

Genes and Alleles

A sequence of chemical bases on a molecule of DNA (a gene) constitutes a recipe for making proteins. As science writer Matt Ridley puts it, "Proteins . . . do almost every chemical, structural, and regulatory thing that is done in the body: they generate energy, fight infection,

law of segregation The Mendelian principle that variants of genes for a particular trait retain their separate identities through the generations.

law of independent assortment The Mendelian principle that genes controlling different traits are inherited independently of one another.

chromosomes In the cell nucleus, the structures visible during cellular division containing long strands of DNA combined with a protein.

DNA Deoxyribonucleic acid. The genetic material consisting of a complex molecule whose base structure directs the synthesis of proteins.

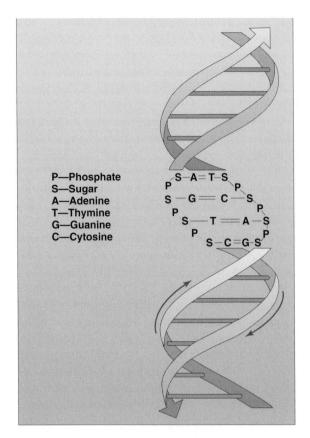

Figure 2.1
This diagrammatic representation of a portion of deoxyribonucleic acid (DNA) illustrates its twisted ladderlike structure. Alternating sugar and phosphate groups form the structural sides of the ladder. The connecting "rungs" are formed by pairings between complementary bases—adenine with thymine and cytosine with guanine.

P—Phosphate
S—Sugar
A—Adenine
T—Thymine
G—Guanine
C—Cytosine

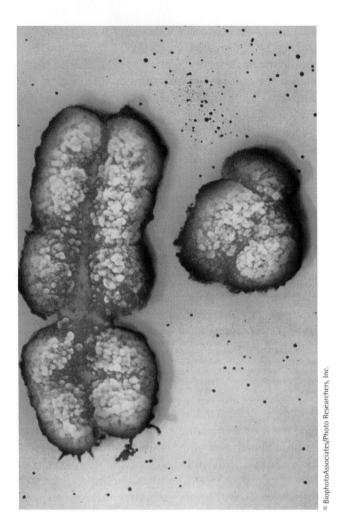

© BiophotoAssociates/Photo Researchers, Inc.

In addition to the twenty-two pairs of somatic or body chromosomes, humans possess one pair of sex chromosomes. Pictured here is the pair found in the normal male phenotype: a larger X chromosome (left) and smaller Y. The female phenotype is determined by the presence of two X chromosomes. Offspring inherit an X chromosome from their mothers but either an X or a Y from their fathers, resulting in approximately equal numbers of male and female offspring in subsequent generations. Though the Y chromosome is critical for differentiation into a male phenotype, compared to other chromosomes the Y is tiny and carries little genetic information.

digest food, form hair, carry oxygen, and so on and on."[3] Almost everything in the body is made *of* or *by* proteins.

Alternate forms of genes, known as **alleles,** exist. For example, the gene for a human blood type in the A-B-O system refers to a specific portion of a DNA molecule, and alleles correspond to alternate forms of this gene that determine the specific blood type (the A allele and B allele). Genes, then, are not really separate structures, as had once been imagined, but locations, like dots on a map. These genes provide the recipe for the many proteins that keep us alive and healthy.

The human **genome**—the complete sequence of human DNA—contains 3 billion chemical bases, with about 20,000–25,000 functioning genes, a number similar to that found in most mammals. Of the 3 billion

alleles Alternate forms of a single gene.
genome The complete structure sequence of DNA for a species.

[3]Ridley, M. (1999). *Genome: The autobiography of a species in 23 chapters* (p. 40). New York: HarperCollins.

bases, humans and mice are about 90 percent identical. Both species have a mere three times as many genes as in the fruit fly, but half the number of genes found in the rice plant. In other words the number of genes or base pairs does not explain every difference among organisms. At the same time, those 20,000 to 25,000 human genes account for only 1 to 1.5 percent of the entire genome, indicating that scientists still have far more to learn about how genes work. Frequently, genes themselves are split by long stretches of DNA that is not part of the known protein code. The 1,062 bases of the A-B-O blood group gene, for example, are interrupted by five such stretches. In the course of producing proteins, these stretches of DNA are metaphorically snipped out and left on the cutting room floor.

Cell Division

In order to grow and maintain good health, the body cells of an organism must divide and produce new cells. Cell division is initiated when the chromosomes replicate, forming a second pair that duplicates the original pair of chromosomes in the nucleus. To do this, the DNA "unzips" between the base pairs—adenine from thymine and guanine from cytosine—following which each base on each now-single strand attracts its complementary base, reconstituting the second half of the double helix. Each new pair is surrounded by a membrane and becomes the nucleus that directs the activities of a new cell. This kind of cell division is called **mitosis.** As long as no errors are made in this replication process, cells within organisms can divide to form daughter cells that are exact genetic copies of the parent cell.

Like most animals, humans reproduce sexually. One reason sex is so "popular," from an evolutionary perspective, is that it provides opportunity for genetic variation. All animals contain two copies of each chromosome, having inherited one from each parent. In humans this involves twenty-three pairs of chromosomes. Sexual reproduction can bring beneficial alleles together, purge the genome of harmful ones, and allow beneficial alleles to spread without being held back by the baggage of disadvantageous variants of other genes. While human societies have always regulated sexual reproduction in some ways, the science of genetics has had a tremendous impact on social aspects of reproduction as seen in this chapter's Biocultural Connection.

Sexual reproduction increases genetic diversity, which in turn has contributed to a multitude of adaptations among sexually reproducing species such as humans. When new individuals are produced through sexual reproduction, the process involves the merging of two cells, one from each parent. If two regular body cells, each containing twenty-three pairs of chromosomes, were to merge, the result would be a new individual with forty-six pairs of chromosomes; such an individual surely could not survive. But this increase in chromosome number does not occur, because the sex cells that join to form a new individual are the product of a different kind of cell division, called **meiosis.**

mitosis A kind of cell division that produces new cells having exactly the same number of chromosome pairs, and hence copies of genes, as the parent cell.

meiosis A kind of cell division that produces the sex cells, each of which has half the number of chromosomes found in other cells of the organism.

Biocultural Connection

The Social Impact of Genetics on Reproduction

While pregnancy and childbirth have been traditional subjects for cultural anthropological study, the genetics revolution has raised new questions for the biocultural study of reproduction. At first glance, the genetics revolution has simply expanded biological knowledge. Individuals today, compared to a hundred years ago, can now see their own genetic makeup even to the level of base pair sequence. A deeper look illustrates that this new biological knowledge has the capacity to profoundly transform cultures. In many cultures, the social experience of pregnancy and childbirth has changed dramatically as a result of the genetic revolution. New reproductive technologies allow for the genetic assessment of fertilized eggs and embryos (the earliest stage of animal development), with far-reaching social consequences.

These new reproductive technologies have also become the object of anthropological study as cultural anthropologists study the social impact of biological knowledge. Over the past 20 years, anthropologist Rayna Rapp has studied the social impact of prenatal (before birth) genetic testing in North America. Her work illustrates how biological knowledge is generated and interpreted by humans every step of the way.

Prenatal genetic testing is conducted most frequently through amniocentesis, a technique developed in the 1960s through which fluid, containing cells from the developing embryo, is drawn from the womb of a pregnant woman. The chromosomes and specific genes are then analyzed for abnormalities. Rapp traces the development of amniocentesis from an experimental procedure to one routinely used in pregnancy in North America. For example, today pregnant women over the age of 35 routinely undergo this test because certain genetic conditions are associated with older maternal age. Trisomy 21 or Down's syndrome, in which individuals have an extra 21st chromosome, can be easily identified through amniocentesis. Through ethnographic study, Rapp shows that a biological fact (such as an extra 21st chromosome) is open to diverse interpretation and reproductive choices by "potential parents." She also illustrates how genetic testing may lead to the labeling of disabled people as undesirable. Rapp's anthropological investigation of the social impact of amniocentesis illustrates the complex interplay between biological knowledge and cultural practices. ■ ■ ■

Although meiosis begins like mitosis, with the replication and doubling of the original genes in chromosomes, it proceeds to divide that number into four new cells rather than two (Figure 2.2). Thus each new cell has only half the number of chromosomes compared to the parent cell. Human eggs and sperm, for example, have only twenty-three single chromosomes (half of a pair), whereas body cells have twenty-three pairs, or forty-six chromosomes.

The process of meiotic division has important implications for genetics. Because paired chromosomes are separated, two different types of new cells will be formed; two of the four new cells will have one-half of a pair of chromosomes, and the other two will have the second half of the original chromosome pair. At the same time, corresponding portions of one chromosome may "cross over" to the other one, somewhat scrambling the genetic material compared to the original chromosomes. Sometimes, the original pair is **homozygous,** possessing identical alleles for a specific gene. For example, if in both

homozygous Refers to a chromosome pair that bears identical alleles for a single gene.

chromosomes of the original pair the gene for A-B-O blood type is represented by the allele for type A blood, then all new cells will have the "A" allele. But if the original pair is **heterozygous,** with the "A" allele on one chromosome and the allele for type B blood on the other, then half of the new cells will contain only the "B" allele; the offspring have a 50-50 chance of getting either one. It is impossible to predict any single individual's **genotype,** or genetic composition, but (as Mendel originally discovered) statistical probabilities can be established.

What happens when a child inherits the allele for type O blood from one parent and that for type A from the other? Will the child have blood of type A, O, or some mixture of the two? Many of these questions were answered by Mendel's original experiments.

Mendel discovered that certain alleles are able to mask the presence of others; one allele is dominant, whereas the other is recessive. Actually, it is the traits that are dominant or recessive, rather than the alleles

heterozygous Refers to a chromosome pair that bears different alleles for a single gene.

genotype The alleles possessed for a particular trait.

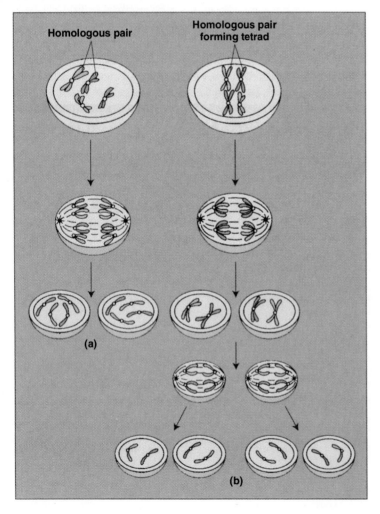

(a)

(b)

Figure 2.2

In cell division both mitosis (a) and meiosis (b) create new cells. However, in mitosis new cells are exact copies of the parent cell, whereas in meiosis "daughter" cells contain half of the parental number of chromosomes. Chromosomes in yellow originally came from one parent, those in blue from the other.

Homologous pair

Homologous pair forming tetrad

themselves; geneticists merely speak of dominant and recessive alleles for the sake of convenience. Thus, one might speak of the allele for type A blood as being dominant to the one for type O. An individual whose blood type genes are heterozygous, with one "A" and one "O" allele, will have type A blood. In other words, the heterozygous condition (AO) will show exactly the same physical characteristic, or **phenotype**, as the homozygous (AA), even though the two have a somewhat different genetic composition, or genotype. Only the homozygous recessive genotype (OO) will show the phenotype of type O blood.

The **dominance** of one allele does not mean that the **recessive** one is lost or in some way blended. A type A heterozygous parent (AO) will produce sex cells containing both "A" and "O" alleles. (This is an example of Mendel's law of segregation, that alleles retain their separate identities.) Recessive alleles can be handed down for generations before they are matched with another recessive allele in the process of sexual reproduction and show up in the phenotype. The presence of the dominant allele simply masks the expression of the recessive allele.

All of the traits Mendel studied in garden peas showed this dominant-recessive relationship, and so for some years it was believed that this was the only relationship possible. Later studies, however, have indicated that patterns of inheritance are not always so simple. In some cases, neither allele is dominant; they are both co-dominant. An example of co-dominance in human heredity can be seen also in the inheritance of blood types.

phenotype The observable or testable appearance of an organism that may or may not reflect a particular genotype due to the variable expression of dominant and recessive alleles.
dominance The ability of one allele for a trait to mask the presence of another allele.
recessive An allele for a trait whose expression is masked by the presence of a dominant allele.

Type A is produced by one allele; type B by another. A heterozygous individual will have a phenotype of AB, because neither allele can dominate the other.

The inheritance of blood types points out another complexity of heredity. Although each of us has at most two alleles for any given gene, the number of possible alleles for that gene that may be found in a population is by no means limited to two. Certain traits have three or more allelic forms. For example, over one hundred alleles exist for **hemoglobin**, the blood protein that carries oxygen. Only one allele can appear on each of the two homologous chromosomes, so each individual is limited to two genetic alleles.

Polygenetic Inheritance

So far, we have spoken as if the traits of organisms are determined by just one gene. However, most physical traits—such as height, skin color, or liability to disease—are controlled by multiple genes. In such cases, we speak of **polygenetic inheritance,** where the respective alleles of two or more genes influence phenotype. Because so many genes are involved, each of which may have alternative alleles, it is difficult to unravel the genetic underpinnings of any continuous trait. For this reason, characteristics subject to polygenetic inheritance exhibit a continuous range of variation in their phenotype expression and illustrate difficulties inherent with reconciling visible traits with their underlying genetic bases. As biological anthropologist Jonathan Marks demonstrates in the following Original Study, the relationship between genetics and continuous traits is a mystery still to be unraveled.

hemoglobin The protein that carries oxygen in the red blood cells.
polygenetic inheritance When two or more genes contribute to the phenotypic expression of single character.

Original Study

Ninety-Eight Percent Alike: What Our Similarity to Apes Tells Us about Our Understanding of Genetics

It's not too hard to tell Jane Goodall from a chimpanzee. Goodall is the one with long legs and short arms, a prominent forehead, and whites in her eyes. She's the one with a significant amount of hair only on her head, not all over her body. She's the one who walks, talks, and wears clothing.

A few decades ago, however, the nascent field of molecular genetics recognized an apparent paradox: However easy it may be to tell Jane Goodall from a chimpanzee on the basis of physical characteristics, it is considerably harder to tell them apart according to their genes.

More recently, geneticists have been able to determine with precision that humans and chimpanzees are over 98 percent identical genetically, and that figure has become one of the most well-known factoids in the popular scientific literature. It has been invoked to argue that we are simply a third kind of

[continued]

[continued]

chimpanzee, together with the common chimp and the rarer bonobo; to claim human rights for nonhuman apes; and to explain the roots of male aggression.

Using the figure in those ways, however, ignores the context necessary to make sense of it. Actually, our amazing genetic similarity to chimpanzees is a scientific fact constructed from two rather more mundane facts: our familiarity with the apes and our unfamiliarity with genetic comparisons.

To begin with, it is unfair to juxtapose the differences between the bodies of people and apes with the similarities in their genes. After all, we have been comparing the bodies of humans and chimpanzees for 300 years, and we have been comparing DNA sequences for less than 20 years. Now that we are familiar with chimpanzees, we quickly see how different they look from us. But when the chimpanzee was a novelty, in the 18th century, scholars were struck by the overwhelming similarity of human and ape bodies. And why not? Bone for bone, muscle for muscle, organ for organ, the bodies of humans and apes differ only in subtle ways. And yet, it is impossible to say just how physically similar they are. Forty percent? Sixty percent? Ninety-eight percent? Three-dimensional beings that develop over their lifetime don't lend themselves to a simple scale of similarity.

Genetics brings something different to the comparison. A DNA sequence is a one-dimensional entity, a long series of A, G, C, and T subunits. Align two sequences from different species and you can simply tabulate their similarities; if they match 98 out of 100 times, then the species are 98 percent genetically identical.

But is that more or less than their bodies match? We have no easy way to tell, for making sense of the question "How similar are a human and a chimp?" requires a frame of reference. In other words, we should be asking: "How similar are a human and a chimp, compared to what?" Let's try and answer the question. How similar are a human and a chimp, compared to, say, a sea urchin? The human and chimpanzee have limbs, skeletons, bilateral symmetry, a central nervous system; each bone, muscle, and organ matches. For all intents and purposes, the human and chimpanzee aren't 98 percent identical, they're 100 percent identical.

On the other hand, when we compare the DNA of humans and chimps, what does the percentage of similarity mean? We conceptualize it on a linear scale, on which 100 percent is perfectly identical, and 0 percent is totally different. But the structure of DNA gives the scale a statistical idiosyncrasy. Because DNA is a linear array of those four bases—A, G, C, and T—only four possibilities exist at any specific point in a DNA sequence. The laws of chance tell us that two random sequences from species that have no ancestry in common will match at about one in every four sites.

Thus, even two unrelated DNA sequences will be 25 percent identical, not 0 percent identical. (You can, of course, generate sequences more different than that, but greater differences would not occur randomly.) The most different two DNA sequences can be, then, is 75 percent different. Now consider that all multicellular life on earth is related. A human, a chimpanzee, and the banana the chimpanzee is eating share a remote common ancestry, but a common ancestry nevertheless. Therefore, if we compare any particular DNA sequence in a human and a banana, the sequence would have to be more than 25 percent identical. For the sake of argument, let's say 35 percent. In other words, your DNA is over one-third the same as a banana's. Yet, of course, there are few ways other than genetically in which a human could be shown to be one-third identical to a banana.

That context may help us to assess the 98 percent DNA similarity of humans and chimpanzees. The fact that our DNA is 98 percent identical to that of a chimp is not a transcendent statement about our natures but merely a decontextualized and culturally interpreted datum.

Moreover, the genetic comparison is misleading because it ignores qualitative differences among genomes. Genetic evolution involves much more than simply replacing one base with another. Thus, even among such close relatives as human and chimpanzee, we find that the chimp's genome is estimated to be about 10 percent larger than the human's; that one human chromosome contains a fusion of two small chimpanzee chromosomes; and that the tips of each chimpanzee chromosome contain a DNA sequence that is not present in humans.

In other words, the pattern we encounter genetically is actually quite close to the pattern we encounter anatomically. In spite of the shock the figure of 98 percent may give us, humans are obviously identifiably different from, as well as very similar to, chimpanzees. The apparent paradox is simply a result of how mundane the apes have become, and how exotic DNA still is. *(By Jonathan Marks (2000). 98% alike (what our similarity to apes tells us about our understanding of genetics). The Chronicle of Higher Education, May 12, B7. Reprinted by permission.)* ■ ■ ■

EVOLUTION, INDIVIDUALS, AND POPULATIONS

At the level of the individual, the study of genetics shows how traits are transmitted from parent to offspring, enabling a prediction about the chances that any given individual will display some phenotypic characteristic. At the level of the group, the study of genetics takes on additional significance, revealing how evolutionary processes account for the diversity of life on earth.

A key concept in genetics is that of the **population,** or a group of individuals within which breeding

population In biology, a group of similar individuals that can and do interbreed.

takes place. **Gene pool** refers to all the genetic variants possessed by members of a population. It is within populations that natural selection takes place, as some members contribute a disproportionate share of the next generation. Over generations, the relative proportions of alleles in a population changes (biological evolution) according to the varying reproductive success of individuals within that population. In other words, at the level of population genetics, **evolution** can be defined as changes in allele frequencies in populations. This is also known as microevolution. Four evolutionary forces—mutation, gene flow, genetic drift, and natural selection—are responsible for the genetic changes that underlie the biological variation present in species today. As we shall see, variation is at the heart of evolution. These evolutionary forces create and pattern diversity.

Mutation

The ultimate source of evolutionary change is **mutation** of genes because mutation constantly introduces new variation. Although some mutations may be harmful or beneficial to individuals, most mutations are neutral. But in an evolutionary sense, random mutation is inherently positive, as it provides the ultimate source of new genetic variation. New body plans—such as walking on two legs compared to knuckle walking like our closest relatives, chimpanzees and gorillas—ultimately depended on genetic mutation. A random mutation might create a new allele that creates a modified protein that makes a new biological task possible. Without the variation brought in through random mutations, populations cannot change over time in response to changing environments.

For sexually reproducing species like humans, the only mutations of any *evolutionary* consequence are those occurring in sex cells, since these cells form future generations. Mutations may arise whenever copying mistakes are made during cell division. This may involve a change in a single base of a DNA sequence, or at the other extreme, relocation of large segments of DNA, including entire chromosomes. As you read this page, the DNA in each cell of your body is being damaged.[4] Fortunately,

DNA repair enzymes constantly scan DNA for mistakes, slicing out damaged segments and patching up gaps. These repair mechanisms prevent diseases like cancer and ensure that we get a faithful copy of our parental inheritance. Genes controlling DNA repair therefore form a critical part of any species' genetic makeup.

Because no species has perfect DNA repair, new mutations arise continuously, so that all species continue to evolve. Geneticists have calculated the rate at which various types of mutant genes appear. In human populations, they run from a low of about five mutations per million sex cells formed, in the case of a gene abnormality that leads to the absence of an iris in the eye, to a high of about a hundred per million, in the case of a gene involved in a form of muscular dystrophy. The average is

'X-MEN' © Twentieth Century Fox. All rights reserved.

Mutagens—such as pollutants, preservatives, cigarette smoke, radiation, and even some medicines—threaten people in industrial societies. While the mutations from these environmental hazards are generally negative, mutation is overall a positive force in evolutionary terms as the ultimate source of all new genetic variation. The positive side of mutation is fictionalized in the special talents of the X-Men.

---

gene pool All the genetic variants possessed by members of a population.

evolution Changes in allele frequencies in populations. Also known as microevolution.

mutation Chance alteration of genetic material that produces new variation.

---

[4]Culotta, E., & Koshland, D. E., Jr. (1994). DNA repair works its way to the top. *Science, 266,* 1,926.

about thirty mutants per million. Environmental factors may increase the rate at which mutations occur. These include certain dyes, antibiotics, and chemicals used in the preservation of food. Radiation, whether of industrial or solar origin, represents another important cause of mutations. There is even evidence that stress can increase mutation rates, increasing the diversity necessary for selection if successful adaptation is to occur.[5]

In humans, as in all multicellular animals, the very nature of genetic material ensures that mutations will occur. For instance, the fact that genes are split by stretches of DNA that are not a part of that gene increases the chances that a simple "editing" mistake in the process of copying DNA will cause mutations. To cite one example, no fewer than fifty such segments of DNA fragment the gene for collagen—the main structural protein of the skin, bones, and teeth. One result of this seemingly inefficient situation is that it becomes possible to shuffle the gene segments themselves like a deck of cards, putting together new proteins with new functions. Although individuals may suffer as a result, mutations also confer versatility at the population level, making it possible for an evolving species to adapt more quickly to environmental changes. It is important to realize that mutations occur randomly and thus do not arise out of need for some new adaptation.

Genetic Drift

Genetic drift refers to chance fluctuations of allele frequencies of the gene pool of a population. These changes at the population level come about due to random events at the individual level. Over the course of their lifetime, each individual is subject to a number of random events affecting their survival. For example, an individual squirrel in good health and possessed of a number of advantageous traits may be killed in a forest fire; a genetically well-adapted baby cougar may not live longer than a day if its mother gets caught in an avalanche, whereas the weaker offspring of a mother that does not die may survive. In a large population, such accidents of nature are unimportant; the accidents that preserve individuals with certain alleles will be balanced out by the accidents that destroy them. However, in small populations, such averaging out may not be possible. Because human populations today are so large, we might suppose that human beings are unaffected by chance events. Although it is true that a rock slide that kills five campers whose home community has a total population of 100,000 is not statistically significant, a rock slide that kills five hunters from a small group of food foragers could significantly alter frequencies of alleles in the local gene pool. The group size of typical food foragers (people who hunt, fish, and gather other wild foods for subsistence) varies between about twenty-five and fifty.

These random events ultimately result in changes in frequencies of gene variants in a population, defined as the evolutionary force of genetic drift. The effects of genetic drift are most powerful in small populations. A particular kind of genetic drift, known as **founder effects,** may occur when an existing population splits up into two or more new ones, especially if one of these new populations is founded by a particularly small number of individuals. In such cases, it is unlikely that the gene frequencies of the smaller population will be representative of those of the larger one. Isolated island populations may possess limited variability due to founder effects. For example, in 1790, nine British sailors from the *H.M.S. Bounty*, six Tahitian men, and eight or nine Tahitian women settled on Pitcairn Island in the South Pacific. These individuals possessed only a small fraction of the total genetic variation in either Great Britain or Tahiti. After a conflict between the Tahitians and the British, the population was further reduced to one British man, Alexander Smith, the women, and some children. Thus today's population descended from a small number of individuals with a very narrow gene pool. The narrow gene pool results in high frequency of some genetic traits. Genetic drift is likely to have been an important factor in human evolution, because until 10,000 years ago all humans were food foragers who probably lived in relatively small, self-contained populations. Whenever biological variation is observed, whether it is the distant past or the present, it is always possible that chance events of genetic drift can account for the presence of this variation.

Gene Flow

Another factor that brings change to the gene pool of a population is **gene flow,** or the introduction of new alleles from nearby populations. Interbreeding allows "road-tested" genes to flow in and out of populations, thus increasing the total amount of variation present within the population. Migration of individuals or groups into the territory occupied by others may lead to

---

genetic drift Chance fluctuations of allele frequencies in the gene pool of a population.

founder effects A particular form of genetic drift deriving from a small founding population not possessing all the alleles present in the original population.

gene flow The introduction of alleles from the gene pool of one population into that of another.

---

[5]Chicurel, M. (2001). Can organisms speed their own evolution? *Science, 292*, 1,824–1,827.

gene flow. Geographical factors also affect gene flow. For example, if a river separates two populations of small mammals preventing interbreeding, these populations will begin to accrue random genetic differences from their isolation. If the river changes course and the two populations can interbreed freely again, new alleles that may have been present in only one population will now be present in both populations due to gene flow.

Among humans, social factors such as mating rules, intergroup conflict, and our ability to travel great distances affect gene flow. For example, the last 500 years have seen the introduction of alleles into Central and South American populations from both the Spanish colonists and the Africans whom Europeans imported as slaves. More recent migrations of people from East Asia have added to this mix. When gene flow is present, variation within populations increases. Throughout the history of human life on earth, gene flow has been important because it keeps populations from developing into separate species.

Natural Selection

Although gene flow and genetic drift may produce changes in the allele frequency of a population, that change would not necessarily make the population better adapted to its biological and social environment. Natural selection, the evolutionary force described by Darwin, accounts for *adaptive* change. **Adaptation** is a series of beneficial adjustments to the environment. As we will explore throughout this textbook, humans can adapt to their environment through culture as well as biology. When biological adaptation occurs at a genetic level, natural selection is at work.

Natural selection refers to the evolutionary process through which genetic variation at the population level is shaped to fit local environmental conditions. In other words, instead of a completely random selection of individuals whose traits will be passed on to the next generation, there is selection by the forces of nature. In the process, the frequency of genetic variants for harmful or nonadaptive traits within the population is reduced while the frequency of genetic variants for adaptive traits is increased. Over time, changes in the genetic structure of the population are visible in the biology or behavior of a population, and such genetic changes can result in the formation of new species.

The adaptability of organic structures and functions, no matter how much a source of wonder and fascination,

nevertheless falls short of perfection. This is so because natural selection can only work with what the existing store of genetic variation provides; it cannot create something entirely new. Variation protects populations from dying out or species from going extinct in changing environments. In the words of one evolutionary biologist, evolution is a process of tinkering, rather than design. Often tinkering involves balancing beneficial and harmful effects of a specific allele, as the case of sickle-cell anemia illustrates.

The Case of Sickle-Cell Anemia

Among human beings, a particularly well-studied case of an adaptation paid for by the misery of many individuals brings us to the example of **sickle-cell anemia,** a painful disease in which the oxygen-carrying red blood cells change shape (sickle) and clog the finest parts of the circulatory system. This disorder first came to the attention of geneticists in Chicago when it was observed that most North Americans who suffer from it are of African ancestry. Investigation traced the abnormality to populations that live in a clearly defined belt across cen-

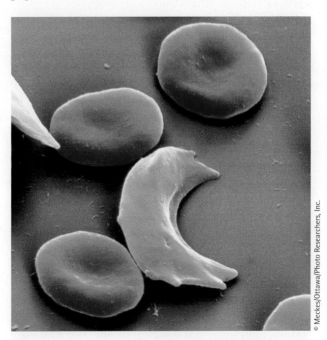

© Meckes/Ottawa/Photo Researchers, Inc.

Sickle-cell anemia is caused by a genetic mutation in a single base of the hemoglobin gene resulting in abnormal hemoglobin, called hemoglobin S. Those afflicted by the disease are homozygous for the allele "S," and all their red blood cells "sickle." Co-dominance is observable with the sickle and normal alleles. Heterozygotes make 50 percent normal hemoglobin and 50 percent sickle hemoglobin. Shown here is a sickle hemoglobin red blood cell among normal red blood cells.

---

adaptation A series of beneficial adjustments to the environment.

sickle-cell anemia An inherited form of anemia caused by a mutation in the hemoglobin protein that causes the red blood cells to assume a sickle shape.

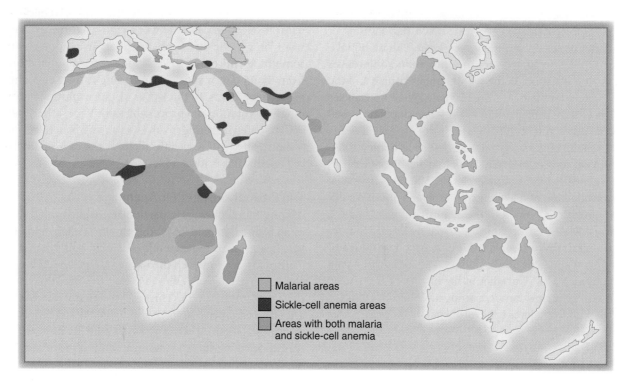

Figure 2.3
The allele that, in homozygotes, causes sickle-cell anemia makes heterozygotes resistant to falciparum malaria. Thus, the allele is most common in populations native to regions where this strain of malaria is common.

Legend:
- Malarial areas
- Sickle-cell anemia areas
- Areas with both malaria and sickle-cell anemia

tral Africa where the sickle-cell allele is found at surprisingly high frequencies. Geneticists were curious to know why such a harmful hereditary disability persisted in these populations. According to the theory of natural selection, any alleles that are harmful will tend to disappear from the group, because the individuals who are homozygous for the abnormality generally die—are "selected out"—before they are able to reproduce. Why, then, had this seemingly harmful condition remained in populations from central Africa?

The answer to this mystery began to emerge when it was noticed that the areas with high rates of sickle-cell anemia are also areas in which a particularly deadly form of malaria is common (Figure 2.3). This severe form of malaria causes many deaths or, in those who survive, high fevers that significantly interfere with their reproductive abilities. Moreover, it was discovered that hemoglobin abnormalities are also found in people living in parts of the Arabian Peninsula, Greece, Algeria, Syria, and India, all regions where malaria is (or was) common. Further research established that while individuals with hemoglobin abnormalities can still contract malaria, hemoglobin abnormalities are associated with an increased ability to survive the effects of the malarial parasite; it seems that the effects of the abnormal hemoglobin in limited amounts were less injurious than the effects of the malarial parasite. Thus, selection favored

heterozygous individuals with normal and sickling hemoglobin. The mutation that causes hemoglobin to sickle consists of a change in a single base of DNA so it can arise readily by chance. The loss of alleles for abnormal hemoglobin caused by the death of those homozygous for it (from sickle-cell anemia) was balanced out by the loss of alleles for normal hemoglobin, as those homozygous for normal hemoglobin were more likely to die from malaria.

This example also points out how adaptations tend to be specific; the abnormal hemoglobin was an adaptation to environments in which the malarial parasite flourished. When individuals adapted to malarial regions came to regions relatively free of malaria, what had been an adaptive characteristic became an injurious one. Without malaria, the abnormal hemoglobin becomes comparatively disadvantageous. Although the rates of sickle-cell trait are still relatively high among African Americans—about 9 percent show the sickling trait—this represents a significant decline from the approximately 22 percent who are estimated to have shown the trait when the first slaves were brought from Africa. A further decline over the next several generations is to be expected, as selection relaxes for the frequency of the sickle-cell allele.

This example also illustrates the important role culture may play even with respect to biological adaptation.

In Africa, the severe form of malaria was not a significant problem until humans abandoned food foraging for farming a few thousand years ago. In order to farm, people had to clear areas of the natural forest cover. In the forest, decaying vegetation on the forest floor had imparted an absorbent quality to the ground so that the heavy rainfall of the region rapidly soaked into the soil. But once stripped of its natural vegetation, the soil lost this quality.

Furthermore, the forest canopy was no longer there to break the force of the rainfall, and so the impact of the heavy rains tended to compact the soil further. The result was that stagnant puddles commonly formed after rains, providing the perfect breeding environment for the type of mosquito that is the host to the malarial parasite. These mosquitoes then began to flourish and transmit the malarial parasite to humans. Thus, humans unwittingly created the kind of environment that made a hitherto disadvantageous trait, the abnormal hemoglobin associated with sickle-cell anemia, advantageous. While the biological process of evolution accounts for the frequency of the sickle-cell allele, cultural processes shape the environment to which humans adapt.

ADAPTATION AND PHYSICAL VARIATION

While the relationship between sickle-cell disease and malaria provides us with a neat example of a genetic adaptation to a particular environment, continuous traits controlled by many genes can be studied in terms of adaptation to a particular environment as well. However, this tends to be more complex. Because specific examples of adaptation can be difficult to prove at times, scientists sometimes suggest that their colleagues' scenarios about adaptation are "Just So" stories.

Anthropologists study biological diversity in terms of **clines,** or the continuous gradation over space in the form or frequency of a trait. The spatial distribution or cline for the sickle-cell allele allowed anthropologists to identify the adaptive function of this gene in a malarial environment. Clinal analysis of a continuous trait such as body shape, which is controlled by a series of genes, allows anthropologists to interpret human global variation in body build as an adaptation to climate. Generally, people long native to regions with cold climates tend to have greater body bulk (not to be equated with fat) relative to their extremities (arms and legs) than do people native to regions with hot climates, who tend to be

clines Gradual changes in the frequency of an allele or trait over space.

relatively tall and slender. Interestingly, tall slender bodies show up in human evolution as early as 2 million years ago. A person with larger body bulk and relatively shorter extremities may suffer more from summer heat than someone whose extremities are relatively long and whose body is slender. But the person will conserve needed body heat under cold conditions. A bulky body tends to conserve more heat than a less bulky one, because it has less surface area relative to volume. In hot, open country, by contrast, people benefit from a long slender body that can get rid of excess heat quickly. A small slender body can also promote heat loss due to a high surface area to volume ratio.

In addition to these sorts of very long-term effects that climate may have imposed on human variation, climate can also contribute to human variation through its impact on the process of growth and development (developmental adaptation). For example, some of the physiological mechanisms for withstanding cold or dissipating heat have been shown to vary depending upon the climate an individual experiences as a child. Individuals spending their youth in very cold climates develop circulatory system modifications that allow them to remain comfortable at temperatures people from warmer climates cannot tolerate. Similarly, hot climate promotes the development of a higher density of sweat glands, creating a more efficient system for sweating to keep the body cool.

Cultural processes complicate studies of body build and climatic adaptation. For example, dietary differences particularly during childhood will cause variation in body shape through their effect on the growth process. Another complicating factor is clothing. Much of the way people adapt to cold is cultural, rather than biological. For example, Inuit peoples of northern Canada live in a region where much of the year is very cold. To cope with this, they long ago developed efficient clothing to keep the body warm. Because of this, the Inuit are provided with what amount to artificial tropical environments inside their clothing. Such cultural adaptations allow humans to inhabit the entire globe.

Some anthropologists have suggested that variation in such features as face and eye shape relate to climate. For example, biological anthropologists once proposed that the flat facial profile and round head, common in populations native to East and Central Asia, as well as Arctic North America, derive from adaptation to very cold environments. Though these features are common in Asian and Native American populations, considerable physical variation exists within each population. Some individuals who spread to North America from Asia have a more "European" head shape. Such variation lies at the heart of the Kennewick Man controversy described in the Biocultural Connection in Chapter 4.

In biological terms, evolution is responsible for all that humans share as well as the broad array of human diversity. Evolution is also responsible for the creation of new species over time. Primatologist Frans de Waal has said, "Evolution is a magnificent idea that has won over essentially everyone in the world willing to listen to scientific arguments."[6] We will return to the topic of human evolution in chapters that follow, but first we will look at the other living primates in order to understand the kinds of animals they are, what they have in common with humans, and what distinguishes the various forms.

_____

[6]de Waal, F. (2001). Sing the song of evolution. *Natural History, 110* (8), 77.

Chapter Summary

■ In the 18th century, Carolus Linnaeus (Carl von Linné) devised a system to classify the great variety of living things then known. On the basis of similarities in body structure, body function, and sequence of bodily growth, he grouped organisms into small groups, or species. Modern taxonomy still uses his basic system but now looks at such characteristics as chemical reactions of blood, protein structure, and the makeup of the genetic material itself. Although Linnaeus regarded species as fixed and unchangeable, this idea was challenged by the finding of fossils, the idea of progress, and the many continuities among different species.

■ Charles Darwin formulated a theory of evolution in 1859 as descent with modification occurring as a population adapts to its environment through natural selection. A population is a group of interbreeding individuals. While natural selection works upon individuals, evolution occurs at the population level as changes occur in frequency of certain alleles or traits.

■ Genes, the units of heredity, are segments of molecules of DNA (deoxyribonucleic acid), and the entire sequence of DNA is known as the genome. DNA is a complex molecule resembling two strands of rope twisted around each other with ladderlike rungs connecting the two strands. The sequence of bases along the DNA molecule directs the production of proteins. Proteins, in turn, constitute specific identifiable traits such as blood type. Just about everything in the human body is made of or by proteins, and human DNA provides the instructions for the thousands of proteins that keep us alive and healthy. DNA molecules have the unique property of being able to produce exact copies of themselves. As long as no errors are made in the process of replication, new daughter cells will be exact genetic copies of the parent cell.

■ DNA molecules are located on chromosomes, structures found in the nucleus of each cell. Each kind of organism has a characteristic number of chromosomes, which are usually found in pairs in sexually reproducing organisms. Humans have twenty-three pairs. Different versions or alternate forms of a gene for a given trait are called alleles. The total number of different alleles of genes available to a population is called its gene pool.

■ Mitosis, one kind of cell division that results in new cells, begins when the chromosomes (hence the genes) replicate, forming a duplicate of the original pair of chromosomes in the nucleus. Meiosis is related to sexual reproduction; it begins with the replication of original chromosomes, but these are divided into four cells, in humans each containing twenty-three single chromosomes. The normal human number of twenty-three pairs of chromosomes is re-established when an egg and sperm unite in the fertilization process.

■ In the late 19th century Gregor Mendel discovered the particulate nature of heredity and that some dominant alleles are able to mask the presence of recessive alleles. The allele for type A blood in humans, for example, is dominant to the allele for type O blood. Alleles that are both expressed when present are termed co-dominant. For example, an individual with the alleles for type A and type B blood has the AB blood type.

■ Phenotype refers to the physical characteristics of an organism, whereas genotype refers to its genetic composition. Two organisms may have different genotypes but the same phenotype. An individual with type A blood phenotype may possess either the AO or the AA genotype.

■ Four evolutionary forces—mutation, genetic drift, gene flow, and natural selection—affect the genetic structures of populations. Evolution at the level of population genetics is change in allele frequencies, which is also known as microevolution. The ultimate source of genetic variation is mutation, changes in DNA that may be helpful or harmful to the organism. Although mutations are inevitable given the nature of cellular chemistry, environmental factors—such as heat, chemicals, or radiation—can increase the mutation rate. The effect of random events on the gene pool of a small population is called genetic drift. Genetic drift may have been an important factor in human evolution because until 10,000 years ago humans lived in small isolated populations. Gene flow, the introduction of new variants of genes from nearby populations, distributes new variation to all populations and serves to prevent speciation.

■ Natural selection is the evolutionary force involved in adaptation. It reduces the frequency of alleles for harmful or maladaptive traits within a population and increases the frequency of alleles for adaptive traits. A well-studied example of adaptation through natural selection in humans is inheritance of the trait for sickling red blood cells. The sickle-cell trait, caused by the inheritance of an abnormal form of hemoglobin, is an adaptation

to life in regions in which malaria is common. In these regions, the sickle-cell trait plays a beneficial role, but in other parts of the world, the sickling trait is no longer advantageous, while the associated sickle-cell anemia remains injurious. Geneticists predict that as malaria is brought under control, within several generations, there will be a decline in the number of individuals who carry the allele responsible for sickle-cell anemia.

■ Physical anthropologists have determined that some human physical variation appears related to climatic adaptation. People native to cold climates tend to have greater body bulk relative to their extremities than individuals from hot climates; the latter tend to be relatively tall and slender. Studies involving body build and climate are complicated by other factors such as the effects on physique of diet and of clothing.

Questions for Reflection

1. The discovery of the structure and function of the DNA molecule impacts individuals and societies in many ways. Has the scientific understanding of the human genetic code challenged your conception of what it means to be human? How much of your life is dictated by the structure of DNA? And what will be the social consequences of depicting humans as entities programmed by their DNA?

2. The social meanings of science can challenge the place of other belief systems. Is it possible for spiritual and scientific models of human nature to coexist? How do you personally reconcile science and religion?

3. The four evolutionary forces—mutation, genetic drift, gene flow, and natural selection—all exert effects on biological variation. Some are at work in individuals while others function at the population level. Compare and contrast these evolutionary forces, outlining their contributions to biological variation.

4. The frequency of the sickle-cell allele in populations provides a classic example of adaptation on a genetic level. Describe the benefits of this deadly allele. Are mutations good or bad?

5. Why is the evolution of continuous traits more difficult to study than the evolution of a trait controlled by a single gene?

Key Terms

primates
mammals
species
genus, genera (pl.)
taxonomy
analogies

homologies
natural selection
genes
law of segregation
law of independent
    assortment

chromosomes
DNA
alleles
genome
mitosis
meiosis
homozygous
heterozygous
genotype
phenotype
dominance
recessive

hemoglobin
polygenetic inheritance
population
gene pool
evolution
mutation
genetic drift
founder effects
gene flow
adaptation
sickle-cell anemia
cline

Multimedia Review Tools

Make the Grade in Anthropology with ThomsonNOW

Thomson NOW! This powerful online study tool provides you with a *personalized study plan* based on your responses to a diagnostic pretest. Once you have mastered the material with the help of interactive learning tools, an integrated e-book, and more, you can take a post-test to confirm you are ready to move on to the next chapter. To get started with ThomsonNOW, check the card packaged with your book for the access code. Then go to http://www.thomsonedu.com to create an account through 1pass™. If there is no card in your book, go to http://www.thomsonedu.com to purchase an access code.

Companion Web Site and Anthropology Resource Center

Go to http://anthropology.wadsworth.com to reach the companion web site for your text. This offers many study aids, including self quizzes for each chapter and a practice final exam, as well as links to anthropology websites and information on the latest theories and discoveries in the field.

Also, check out the Anthropology Resource Center for a wealth of learning materials that include interactive maps, video exercises, simulations, and breaking news in anthropology. Be sure to explore InfoTrac College Edition®, your online library that offers full-length articles from thousands of scholarly and popular publications. To reach the Anthropology Resource Center and InfoTrac College Edition, check the card packaged with your book for the access code. Then go to http://www.thomsonedu.com to create an account through 1pass™. If there is no card in your book, go to http://www.thomsonedu.com to purchase an access code.

© Jodi Cobb/National Geographic Image Collectio

CHALLENGE ISSUE

Other primates have long fascinated humans owing to our many shared anatomical and behavioral characteristics. These temple monkeys in Thailand taking part in the annual monkey feast demonstrate our similarities. Our differences have had devastating consequences for our closest living relatives in the animal world. As a result of human destruction of primate habitats and hunting of primates for bush-meat or souvenirs, seventy-six primate species are now recognized as being in danger of extinction. In the 21st century humans face the challenge of making sure that the other primates do not go extinct due to human actions.

Living Primates

3

The diversity of life on earth attests to the fact that the challenge of survival can be solved in many ways. In evolutionary terms, survival means continued existence of the species beyond one individual's lifespan. It includes reproducing subsequent generations or avoiding extinction. Over the course of countless generations, each species has followed its own unique journey, an evolutionary history including random turns as well as patterned adaptation to the environment. Because new species are formed as populations diverge from one another, closely related species resemble one another due to recent common ancestry. In other words, closely related species have shared part of their evolutionary journey together. With each step living creatures can only build on what already exists, making today's diversity a product of tinkering with ancestral body plans, behaviors, and physiology.

In this chapter we will look at the biology and behavior of the primates, the group of animals to which humans belong. By doing so, we will gain a firmer understanding of those characteristics we share with other primates, as well as those that distinguish us from them and make us distinctively human. By studying communication and tool use among our primate cousins today, we may draw closer to an understanding of how and why humans developed as they did.

METHODS AND ETHICS IN PRIMATOLOGY

Just as anthropologists employ diverse methods to study humans, primatologists today use a variety of methods to study the biology, behavior, and evolutionary history of our closest living relatives. Some primatologists concentrate on the comparative anatomy of ancient skeletons while others trace evolutionary relationships by studying the comparative physiology and genetics of living species. Primatologists study the biology and behavior of living primates both in their natural habitats and in captivity in zoos, primate research colonies, or learning laboratories.

The classic image of a primatologist is someone like Jane Goodall, a world renowned British researcher who has devoted her career to in-depth observation of chimpanzees in their natural habitat in Tanzania. While documenting the range and nuance of chimpanzee behavior, she has also championed primate habitat conservation and humane treatment of primates in captivity. This philosophy of conservation and preservation is basic to primatology and has led to further innovations in research methods. For example, primatologists have developed a number of noninvasive methods that allow them to link primate biology and behavior in the field while minimizing physical disruption. Primatologists gather shedded hair, feces, or other body secretions left by the primates in the environment for later analysis in the laboratory. These analyses provide invaluable information about characteristics such as diet or genetic relatedness among a group of individuals.

Work with captive animals provides more than knowledge about the basic biology of primates. It has also allowed primatologists to document the humanity of our closest living relatives. Many of the amazing linguistic and conceptual abilities of primates became known through captive animal studies. Individual primatologists have devoted their careers to working with one or several primates in captivity, teaching the primate to communicate through pictures on a computer screen or American Sign Language. While it is recognized that even compassionate captivity imposes stress on primates, it is hoped that the knowledge gained through these studies will contribute ultimately to primate conservation and survival as human understanding of our closest living relatives increases.

At first glance it might seem that work with captive animals is inherently less "humane" when compared to field studies. However, field studies also raise important ethical issues for primatologists to consider. Primatologists must maintain an awareness of how their presence affects the behavior of the group. For example, does becoming tolerant of human observers make the primates more vulnerable? Primates habituated to humans commonly range beyond established preserves and come in close contact with other humans who may be more interested in hunting than observation. Contact between primates and humans can also expose endangered primates to infectious diseases carried by humans.

Whether working with primates in captivity or in the field, primatologists seriously consider the well-being of the primates they study.

PRIMATES AS MAMMALS

Biologists classify humans within the primate order, a subgroup of the class Mammalia. The other primates include lemurs, lorises, tarsiers, monkeys, and apes. Humans—together with chimpanzees, bonobos, gorillas, orangutans, gibbons, and siamangs—form the hominoids, colloquially known as apes, a superfamily within the primate order. As hominoids, humans are a kind of ape!

The primates are only one of several kinds of mammals, such as rodents, carnivores, ungulates (hoofed mammals), and so on. Primates, like other mammals, are intelligent animals, having more in the way of brains than reptiles or other kinds of vertebrates. This increased "brain power," along with the mammalian pattern of growth and development, forms the biological basis of the flexible behavior patterns typical of mammals. In most species, the young are born live, the egg being retained within the womb of the female until the embryo achieves an advanced state of growth. Once born, the young receive milk from their mothers' mammary glands, the structure from which the class Mammalia gets its name. During this period of infant dependency, young mammals are able to learn some of the things they will need for survival as adults.

Relative to other members of the animal kingdom, mammals are highly active. This activity is made possible by a relatively constant body temperature, an efficient respiratory system featuring a separation between the nasal (nose) and mouth cavities (allowing them to breathe while they eat), a diaphragm to assist in drawing in and letting out breath, and an efficient four-chambered heart that prevents mixing of oxygenated and deoxygenated blood. Primates possess a skeleton in which the limbs are positioned beneath the body, rather than out at the sides, for easy flexible movement. The bones of the limbs have joints constructed to permit growth in the young while simultaneously providing strong, hard joint surfaces that will stand up to the stresses of sustained activity. Mammals stop growing when they reach adulthood while reptiles continue to grow through their lives.

Mammals and reptiles also differ in terms of their teeth. Reptiles possess identical, pointed, peglike teeth while mammals have teeth specialized for particular purposes: incisors for nipping, gnawing, and cutting; canines for ripping, tearing, killing, and fighting; premolars that may either slice and tear or crush and grind (depending on the kind of animal); and molars for

Providing milk to young via mammary glands distinguishes mammals from other animals. Nursing young individuals is an important part of the general mammalian tendency to invest high amounts of energy into rearing relatively few young at a time. The pattern in reptiles is to lay many eggs that hatch independently, with the young fending for themselves.

crushing and grinding (Figure 3.1). This enables mammals to eat a wide variety of food—an advantage to them, since they require more food than reptiles to sustain their high activity level. But they pay a price: reptiles have unlimited tooth replacement throughout their lives, whereas mammals are limited to two sets. The first set serves the immature animal and is replaced by the "permanent" or adult teeth. The specializations of mammalian teeth allow species and evolutionary relationships to be identified through dental comparisons.

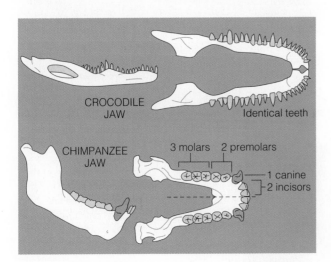

Figure 3.1
The crocodile jaw, like all reptiles, contains a series of identical teeth. If a tooth breaks or falls out, a new tooth will emerge in its place. Mammals, by contrast, possess precise numbers of specialized teeth, each with a particular shape characteristic of the group, as indicated on the chimpanzee jaw: Incisors in front are shown in blue, canines behind in red, followed by two premolars and three molars in yellow (the last being the "wisdom teeth" in humans).

Evidence from ancient skeletons indicates the first mammals appeared over 200 million years ago as small **nocturnal** (active at night) creatures. The earliest primatelike creatures came into being about 65 million years ago when a new mild climate favored the spread of dense tropical and subtropical forests over much of the earth. The change in climate and habitat, combined with the sudden extinction of dinosaurs, favored mammal diversification, including the evolutionary development of **arboreal** (tree-living) mammals from which primates evolved.

The ancestral primates possessed biological characteristics that allowed them to adapt to life in the forests. Their relatively small size enabled them to use tree branches not accessible to larger competitors and predators. Arboreal life opened up an abundant new food supply. The primates were able to gather leaves, flowers, fruits, insects, birds' eggs, and even nesting birds, rather than having to wait for them to fall to the ground. Natural selection favored those who judged depth correctly and gripped the branches tightly. Those individuals who survived life in the trees passed on their genes to the succeeding generations. Although the earliest primates were nocturnal, today most primate species are **diurnal** (active in the day). The transition to diurnal life in the trees involved important biological adjustments that helped shape the biology and behavior of humans today.

nocturnal Active at night and at rest during the day.
arboreal Living in the trees.
diurnal Active during the day and at rest at night.

PRIMATE CHARACTERISTICS

While the living primates are a varied group of animals, they do share a number of features. We humans, for example, can grasp, throw things, and see in three dimensions because of shared primate characteristics. Compared to other mammals, primates possess a relatively unspecialized anatomy while their behavioral patterns are diverse and flexible. Many primate characteristics are useful in one way or another to arboreal, or tree-dwelling, animals, although (as any squirrel knows) they are not essential to life in the trees. For animals preying upon the many insects living on the fruit and flowers of trees and shrubs, however, primate characteristics such as manipulative hands and keen vision would have been enormously adaptive. Life in the trees along with the visual predation of insects played a role in the evolution of primate biology.

Primate Dentition

The varied diet available to arboreal primates—shoots, leaves, insects, and fruits—required relatively unspecialized teeth, compared to those found in other mammals. The evolutionary trend for primate dentition has been toward a reduction in the number and size of the teeth. The earliest mammals as well as many living species of mammals today possess more incisors, premolars, and molar teeth than primates. The canines of most of the primates, especially males, are daggerlike and useful for ripping into tough foods. Canine teeth also serve well in social communication. All an adult male gorilla or baboon needs to do to get a youngster to be submissive is to raise his upper lip to display his sharp canines.

Sensory Organs

The primates' adaptation to arboreal life involved changes in the form and function of their sensory organs. The sense of smell was vital for the earliest ground-dwelling, night-active mammals. It enabled them to operate in the dark, to sniff out their food, and to detect hidden predators. However, for active tree life during daylight, good vision is a better guide than smell in judging the location of the next branch or tasty morsel. Accordingly, the sense of smell declined in primates, while vision became highly developed.

Travel through the trees demands judgments concerning depth, direction, distance, and the relationships of objects hanging in space, such as vines or branches. Monkeys, apes, and humans achieved this through binocular stereoscopic color vision (Figure 3.2), the ability to see the world in the three dimensions of height, width, and depth. **Binocular vision** (in which two eyes sit next to each other on the same plane so that their visual fields overlap) together with nerve connections that run from each eye to both sides of the brain confer complete depth perception characteristic of three-dimensional or **stereoscopic vision.** This arrangement allows nerve cells to integrate the images derived from each eye. Increased brain size in the visual area in primates and a greater

binocular vision   Vision with increased depth perception from two eyes set next to each other allowing their visual fields to overlap.

stereoscopic vision   Complete three-dimensional vision (or depth perception) from binocular vision and nerve connections that run from each eye to both sides of the brain allowing nerve cells to integrate the images derived from each eye.

Though the massive canine teeth of some male primates such as this baboon are serious weapons, they are more often used to communicate rather than to draw blood. Raising his lip to "flash" his canines to young members of the group will get them in line right away. Over the course of human evolution, overall canine size reduced as did differences in canine size between males and females.

© I. DeVore/Anthro-Photo

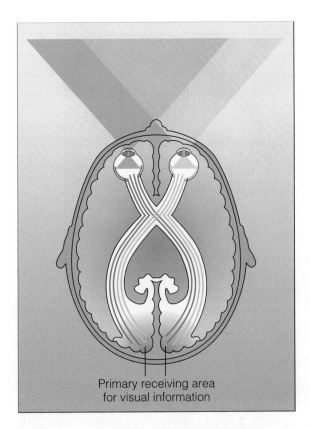

Primary receiving area
for visual information

Figure 3.2
Monkeys, apes, and humans possess binocular stereoscopic vision. Binocular vision refers to overlapping visual fields due to forward-facing eyes. Three-dimensional or stereoscopic vision comes from binocular vision and the transmission of information from each eye to both sides of the brain.

complexity of nerve connections also contributes to stereoscopic color vision.

Tree-living primates also possess an acute sense of touch. An effective feeling and grasping mechanism helps keep them from falling and tumbling while speeding through the trees. The early mammals from which primates evolved possessed tiny touch-sensitive hairs at the tips of their hands and feet. In primates, sensitive pads backed up by nails on the tips of the animals' fingers and toes replaced these hairs.

The Primate Brain

An increase in brain size, particularly in the cerebral hemispheres—the areas supporting conscious thought—occurred in the course of primate evolution. In monkeys, apes, and humans, the cerebral hemispheres completely cover the cerebellum, the part of the brain that coordinates the muscles and maintains body balance. One of the most significant outcomes of this development is the flexibility seen in primate behavior. Rather than relying on reflexes controlled by the cerebellum,

primates constantly react to a variety of features in the environment. Messages from the hands and feet, eyes and ears, as well as from the sensors of balance, movement, heat, touch, and pain, are simultaneously relayed to the cerebral cortex. Obviously the cortex had to evolve considerably in order to receive, analyze, and coordinate these impressions and transmit the appropriate response back down to the motor nerves. The enlarged, responsive, cerebral cortex provides the biological basis for flexible behavior patterns found in all primates, including humans.

The Primate Skeleton

The skeleton gives vertebrates—animals with internal backbones—their basic shape or silhouette, supports the soft tissues, and helps protect vital internal organs (Figure 3.3). Some evolutionary trends are evident in the primate skeleton. For example, as primates relied increasingly on vision rather than smell, the eyes rotated forward to become enclosed in a protective layer of bone. Simultaneously, the snout reduced in size. The opening at the base of the skull for the spinal cord to pass assumed a more forward position, reflecting some degree of upright posture rather than a constant four-footed stance.

The limbs of the primate skeleton follow the same basic ancestral plan seen in the earliest vertebrates. The upper portion of each arm or leg has a single long bone, the lower portion has two bones, and then hands or feet with five radiating digits. Other animals possess limbs specialized to optimize a particular behavior, such as running. In nearly all of the primates, the big toe and thumb are **opposable,** making it possible to grasp and manipulate objects such as sticks and stones with both the hands and feet. Humans and their direct ancestors are the only exceptions, having lost the opposable big toe.

The generalized limb pattern allows for flexible movements by primates. For example, the shape of the collarbone (clavicle) varies among primate groups depending upon their pattern of locomotion. Monkeys move about on all fours and so have narrow bodies with short collarbones. In the apes, a long collarbone orients the arms at the side rather than at the front of the body, allowing for heightened flexibility. With their broad flexible shoulder joints, apes can hang suspended from tree branches and swing from tree to tree. The retention of

opposable Able to bring the thumb or big toe in contact with the tips of the other digits on the same hand or foot in order to grasp objects.

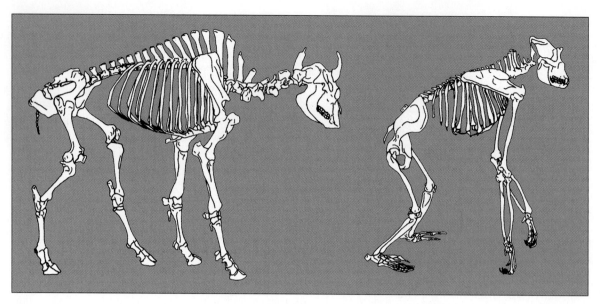

Figure 3.3
All primates possess the same ancestral vertebrate limb pattern as seen in reptiles and amphibians, consisting of a single upper long bone, two lower long bones, and five radiating digits (fingers and toes), as seen in this gorilla (right) skeleton. Other mammals such as bison (left) have a modified version of this pattern. In the course of evolution bison have lost all but two of their digits, which form their hooves. The second long bone in the lower part of the limb is reduced. Note also the joining of the skull and vertebral column in these skeletons. In bison (as in most mammals) the skull projects forward from the vertebral column, but in semi-erect gorillas, the vertebral column is further beneath the skull.

the flexible vertebrate limb pattern in primates was a valuable asset to evolving humans. It was, in part, having hands capable of grasping that enabled our own ancestors to manufacture and use tools and thus alter the course of their evolution. Today our ape anatomy allows humans to do things as varied as throw a baseball at lightning speed or weave intricate patterns from threads suspended on wide looms.

LIVING PRIMATES

Except for a few species of monkeys who live in temperate climates and humans who inhabit the entire globe, the living primates inhabit warm areas of the world. We will briefly explore the diversity of the five natural groupings of contemporary primates: (1) lemurs and lorises, (2) tarsiers, (3) New World monkeys (monkeys native to Central and South America), (4) Old World monkeys (monkeys native to Africa and Eurasia), and (5) apes. While lemurs, lorises, and tarsiers are grouped together by some primatologists as **prosimians** (from the Latin for "before monkeys") because they possess more of the traits common to the most ancient primates, molecular evidence has

shown that tarsiers are more closely related to monkeys, apes, and humans. Monkeys, apes, and humans are grouped together as **anthropoids** (from the Greek for "humanlike"). Dividing the primates into these two groupings makes sense in terms of their entire adaptive package. Many prosimian features correspond to the nocturnal behavioral pattern of smaller ancestral primates. The anthropoid primates tend to be larger, active in the daytime, and live in large social groups. The anthropoids out-competed diurnal prosimians in regions where both kinds of primate co-exist.

Lemurs and Lorises

Lemurs and lorises are the living primates whose anatomy and behavior most closely resemble those of the earliest primates. Lemurs are restricted to the island of Madagascar (off the east coast of Africa), while lorises range from Africa to southern and eastern Asia. The lorises, like the ancestral primates, are all nocturnal, or active at night, and arboreal. On Madagascar, where there was no competition from anthropoid primates until humans arrived, lemurs diversified substantially, with

prosimians A subdivision within the primate order that includes lemurs, lorises, and tarsiers.

anthropoids A subdivision within the primate order that includes New World Monkeys, Old World monkeys, and apes (including humans).

Over the course of their evolutionary history, primates came to rely more on their vision than on their sense of smell. Prosimians, who were the earliest group of primates to appear, maintain their reliance on smell primarily. On the island of Madagascar, home to many species of diurnal ground-dwelling lemurs, such as the ring-tailed lemur, the prosimians mark their territory and communicate through "smelly" messages left for others with a squirt from glands located on their wrists. Though prosimians appeared before the anthropoids in primate evolution, and retain many ancestral features such as their dependence on smell, they are no less evolved. Outside of Madagascar, prosimians remained arboreal and nocturnal due to competition from monkeys and apes.

© Dani/Jeske/Animals Animals–Earth Scenes. All rights reserved.

many lemur species becoming ground dwelling and diurnal, or active during the day. The fossil evidence from Madagascar shows that some lemurs even reached very large sizes.

All living prosimian species are small, with none larger than a good-sized dog. In general body outline, they resemble rodents and insect-eating animals, with short pointed snouts, large pointed ears, and big eyes. In the anatomy of the upper lip and snout, lemurs and lorises resemble nonprimate mammals, in that the upper lip is bound down to the gum, and the naked skin on the nose around the nostrils is moist and split. They also have long tails. The striped tail of a ring-tailed lemur is somewhat like the tail of a raccoon.

Lemurs and lorises have typical primate "hands," although they use them in pairs, rather than one at a time. Sensitive pads and flattened nails are located at the tips of the fingers and toes, although they retain a claw on their second toe, sometimes called a "grooming claw," which they use for scratching and cleaning. Lemurs and lorises possess another unique structure for grooming: a dental comb made up of the lower incisors and canines that projects forward from the jaw and that can be run through their fur. Though lemurs and lorises have retained a number of ancestral characteristics typical of the earliest fossil primates and the insectivores from which primates evolved, it is incorrect to think of them as "less evolved"; they have simply taken a unique evolutionary path since their divergence from the other primates.

Tarsiers

Outwardly, and in their nocturnal habit, tarsiers resemble the lemurs and lorises. Genetically, however, they are more closely related to monkeys and apes. In the structure of the nose and lips, and the part of the brain governing vision, tarsiers resemble monkeys.

Tarsiers are mainly nocturnal insect eaters. The head, eyes, and ears of these kitten-sized arboreal creatures are huge in proportion to the body, making them well adapted for nocturnal life. If human faces had eyes with the same proportions as tarsiers, our eyes would be approximately the size of oranges. Tarsiers have the remark-

© Michael Dick/Animals Animals–Earth Scenes. All rights reserved.

With their large eyes, tarsiers are well adapted for nocturnal life. If human faces had eyes with the same proportions as tarsiers, our eyes would be approximately the size of oranges. In their nocturnal habit and outward appearance, tarsiers resemble lemurs and lorises. Genetically, however, they are more closely related to monkeys and apes, causing scientists to rework the suborder divisions in primate taxonomy to reflect this evolutionary relationship.

able ability to turn their heads 180 degrees, so they can see where they have been as well as where they are going.

Tarsiers, like some lemurs and lorises, possess longer hind limbs than their front limbs, allowing them to move from tree to tree by vertical clinging and leaping. First they hang onto the trunk of one tree in an upright position, with their long legs curled up tightly like springs and their heads twisted to look in the direction they are moving. They propel themselves into the air, do a "180," and land facing the trunk on their tree of choice. Tarsiers are named for the elongated tarsal, or foot bone, that provides these tiny animals leverage for jumps of 6 feet or more.

Anthropoids: Monkeys and Apes

Monkeys and apes (including humans) resemble each other more than any of these groups resemble lemurs, lorises, and tarsiers. Humans are remarkably like monkeys but even more like the other apes in their appearance.

New World monkeys live in tropical forests of South and Central America. All are arboreal with long tails. Some groups of New World monkeys possess **prehensile** or grasping tails, which they use as a fifth limb. The naked skin on the undersides of their tails resembles the sensitive skin found at the tips of our fingers and is even covered with whorls like fingerprints. These and other features distinguish the New World monkeys from the Old World monkeys, apes, and humans. Old World monkeys and apes, including humans, have a 40-million-year shared evolutionary history in Africa that is distinct from the course taken by anthropoid primates in the tropical Americas.

The Old World monkeys, divided from the apes at the taxonomic level of superfamily, possess nonprehensile tails. They may live on the ground or in the trees, using a quadrupedal or four-footed pattern of locomotion on the ground or a palms-down position in the trees. Their bodies are narrow with hind limbs and forelimbs of equal length and relatively fixed and sturdy shoulder, elbow, and wrist joints. Old World monkey species range from tropical Africa and Asia to Gibraltar on the southern coast of Spain to Japan.

Some species of baboon, a kind of Old World monkey, have been of particular interest to paleoanthropologists because they live in environments similar to those in which humans may have originated. These baboons have abandoned trees (except for sleeping and refuge) and are largely terrestrial, living in the savannahs, deserts, and highlands of Africa. They have long, fierce faces and eat a diet consisting of leaves, seeds, insects, and lizards. They live in large, well-organized troops comprised of related females and adult males that have transferred out of other troops. Other species of baboons live in different environments.

Small and Great Apes

The other apes (the hominoid superfamily) are the closest living relatives we humans have in the animal world. They include gibbons, siamangs, orangutans, gorillas, chimpanzees, and bonobos. Apes are large, wide-bodied primates with no tails. All apes possess a shoulder anatomy specialized for hanging suspended below tree branches, although among apes only gibbons and talented gymnasts swing from branch to branch in the pattern known as **brachiation.** At the opposite extreme are gorillas, which generally climb trees, using their hands

prehensile Having the ability to grasp.

brachiation Using the arms to move from branch to branch, with the body hanging suspended beneath the arms.

Courtesy Dana Walrath

Grasping hands and three-dimensional vision enable primates like these South American monkeys to effectively lead active lives in the trees. In some New World monkey species, a grasping or prehensile tail makes life in the trees even easier. The naked skin on the undersides of their tails resembles the sensitive skin found at the tips of our fingers and is even covered with whorls like fingerprints. This sensory skin allows New World monkeys to use their tails as a fifth limb.

and feet to grip the trunks and branches. While smaller gorillas may swing from branch to branch, in larger individuals swinging is limited to leaning outward while reaching for fruit and clasping a limb for support. Still most of their time is spent on the ground. All apes except humans and their immediate ancestors possess arms that are longer than their legs.

In moving on the ground, the African apes "knuckle-walk" on the backs of their hands, resting their weight on the middle joints of the fingers. They stand erect when reaching for fruit, looking over tall grass, or in any activity where they find an erect position advantageous. Though apes can walk on two legs (bipedally) for short periods of time, the structure of the ape pelvis is not well suited to support the weight of the torso and limbs for more than several minutes.

Gibbons and siamangs, the small apes that are native to Southeast Asia and Malaya, have compact, slim bodies with extraordinarily long arms compared to their short legs, and stand about 3 feet high. Although their usual form of locomotion is brachiation, they can run erect, holding their arms out for balance. Gibbon and siamang males and females are similar in size, living in social groups of two adults and offspring.

Orangutans are found in Borneo and Sumatra. They are considerably taller than gibbons and siamangs and are much heavier, with the bulk characteristic of the great apes. In the closeness of the eyes and facial prominence, an orangutan looks humanlike. The people of Sumatra gave orangutans their name, "man of the forest," using the Malay term *orang*, which means "man." On the ground, orangutans walk with their forelimbs in a fists-sideways or a palms-down position. They are,

however, more arboreal than the African apes. Although sociable by nature, the orangutans of upland Borneo spend most of their time alone (except in the case of females with young), as they have to forage over a wide area to obtain sufficient food. By contrast, fruits and insects are sufficiently abundant in the swamps of Sumatra to sustain groups of adults and permit coordinated group travel. Thus, gregariousness is a function of the richness of their habitat.[1]

Gorillas, found in equatorial Africa, are the largest of the apes; an adult male can weigh over 450 pounds, with females about half that size. The body is covered with a thick coat of glossy black hair, and mature males have a silvery gray upper back. There is a strikingly human look about the face, and like humans, gorillas focus on things in their field of vision by directing the eyes rather than moving the head. Gorillas are mostly ground dwellers, but the lighter females and young may sleep in trees in carefully constructed nests. Because of their weight, adult males spend less time in the trees but raise and lower themselves among the tree branches when searching for fruit. Gorillas knuckle-walk, using all four limbs with the fingers of the hand flexed, placing the knuckles instead of the palm of the hand on the ground. They stand erect to reach for fruit, to see something more easily, or to threaten perceived sources of danger with their famous chest-beating displays. Though known for these displays to protect the members of their troop, adult male "silverback" gorillas are the gentle giants of the forest. As vegetarians, gorillas

---

[1]Normile, D. (1998). Habitat seen as playing larger role in shaping behavior. *Science, 279,* 1,454.

All apes, including humans, possess widely spaced flexible shoulder joints for hanging suspended below the branches or swinging from branch to branch. Gibbons are the masters of the swinging form of locomotion called brachiation (from the Latin for "arm motion"). Large apes, such as this orangutan, move slowly through the lower branches using their long arms to span great distances.

© Peter Drowne/Color-Pic, Inc.

devote a major portion of each day eating volumes of plant matter to sustain their massive bodies. Although gorillas are gentle and tolerant, bluffing is an important part of their behavioral repertoire.

Chimpanzees and bonobos are two closely related species of the same genus (*Pan*), bonobos being the least known and restricted in their distribution to the rainforests of the Democratic Republic of Congo. Common chimpanzees, by contrast, are widely distributed in the forested portions of sub-Saharan Africa. Long-time favorites in zoos and circuses, chimpanzees are regarded as particularly quick and clever. Nevertheless, all four great apes are of equal intelligence, despite some differences in cognitive styles. More arboreal than gorillas, but less so than orangutans, chimpanzees and bonobos forage on the ground much of the day, knuckle-walking like gorillas. At sunset, they return to the trees, where they build their nests. Chimps build their nests over a wide area, whereas bonobos prefer to build their nests close to one another.

BEHAVIORAL ADAPTATION

Primates adapt to their environments not only anatomically but also through a wide variety of behaviors. Primates are social animals, living and traveling in groups that vary in size from species to species. In many primate species, including humans, adolescence is a time during which individuals change the relationships they have had with the group they have known since birth. Among primates this change takes the form of migration of either males or females to new social groups.

Young apes spend more time reaching adulthood than do most other mammals. During this lengthy period of growth and development, they learn the behaviors of their social group. While biological factors play a role in the duration of primate dependency, many of the specific behaviors learned during childhood derive solely from the traditions of the group. The behavior of primates, particularly apes, provides anthropologists with clues about the earliest development of human cultural behavior.

Primatologists have carried out many studies of ape behavior in the animals' natural habitat, seeking models to help reconstruct the behavior of evolving humans. While no living primate lives exactly as our ancestors did, these studies have revealed remarkable variation and sophistication in ape behavior. Primatologists increasingly interpret these variations as cultural because they are learned rather than genetically programmed or instinctive. We shall concentrate on the behavior of two closely related African species of chimpanzee: common chimpanzees and bonobos.

Chimpanzee and Bonobo Behavior

Like nearly all primates, chimpanzees and bonobos are highly social animals. Among chimps, the largest social organizational unit is the **community,** usually composed of fifty or more individuals who collectively inhabit a large geographical area. Rarely, however, are all of these animals together at one time. Instead, they are usually found ranging singly or in small subgroups consisting of adult males, or females with their young, or males and females together with their young. In the course of their travels, subgroups may join forces and forage together, but sooner or later these will break up again into smaller units. Typically, when some individuals split off others join, so the composition of subunits shifts frequently.

Relationships among individuals within some of the ape communities studied are relatively harmonious. In the past, primatologists believed that male **dominance hierarchies,** in which some animals outrank and can dominate others, formed the basis of primate social structures. They noted that physical strength and size play a role in determining an animal's rank. By this measure males generally outrank females. However, the male-biased cultures of many primatologists may have contributed to this theoretical perspective with its emphasis on domination through superior size and strength. Male dominance hierarchies seemed "natural" to these early researchers.

With the benefit of detailed field studies over the last 40 years, including cutting-edge research by female primatologists such as Jane Goodall, the nuances of primate social behavior and the importance of female primates have been documented. High-ranking female chimpanzees may dominate low-ranking males. And among bonobos, female rank determines the social order of the group far more than male rank. While greater strength and size do contribute to an animal's higher rank, several other factors also come into play in determining its social position. These include the rank of its mother, which is largely determined through her cooperative social behavior and how effective each individual animal is at creating alliances with others.

On the whole, bonobo females form stronger bonds with one another than do chimpanzee females. Moreover, the strength of the bond between mother and son interferes with bonds among males. Not only do bonobo males defer to females in feeding, but alpha

community A unit of primate social organization composed of fifty or more individuals who inhabit a large geographical area together.

dominance hierarchies An observed ranking system in primate societies ordering individuals from high (alpha) to low standing corresponding to predictable behavioral interactions including domination.

(high-ranking) females have been observed chasing alpha males; such males may even yield to low-ranking females, particularly when groups of females form alliances.[2]

The emphasis on social ranking, competition, and attack behavior by Western primatologists may have derived in part from the values of Western cultures. By contrast, Japanese primatologist Kinji Imanishi, who initiated field studies of bonobos in the early 20th century, investigated and demonstrated the importance of social cooperation rather than competition. Likewise, Dutch primatologist Frans de Waal's research, highlighted in the following Original Study, shows that reconciliation after an attack may be even more important from an evolutionary perspective than the actual attacks.

[2]de Waal, F., Kano, T., & Parish, A. R. (1998). Comments. *Current Anthropology, 39*, 408, 410, 413.

Original Study

Reconciliation and Its Cultural Modification in Primates

Despite the continuing popularity of the struggle-for-life metaphor, it is increasingly recognized that there are drawbacks to open competition, hence that there are sound evolutionary reasons for curbing it. The dependency of social animals on group life and co-operation makes aggression a socially costly strategy. The basic dilemma facing many animals, including humans, is that they sometimes cannot win a fight without losing a friend.

This photo shows what may happen after a conflict—in this case between two female bonobos. About 10 minutes after their fight, the two females approach each other, with one clinging to the other and both rubbing their clitorises and genital swellings together in a pattern known as genito-genital (or GG) rubbing. This sexual contact, typical of bonobos, constitutes a so-called reconciliation. Chimpanzees, which are closely related to bonobos (and to us: bonobos and chimpanzees are our closest animal relatives), usually reconcile in a less sexual fashion, with an embrace and mouth-to-mouth kiss.

There is now evidence for reconciliation in more than twenty-five different primate species, not just in apes but also in many monkeys. The same sorts of studies have been conducted on human children in the schoolyard, and of course children show reconciliation as well. Researchers have even found reconciliation in dolphins, spotted hyenas, and some other nonprimates. Reconciliation seems widespread: a common mechanism found whenever relationships need to be maintained despite occasional conflict. [a, b]

The definition of reconciliation used in animal research is a friendly reunion between former opponents not long after a conflict. This is somewhat different from definitions in the dictionary, primarily because we look for an empirical definition that is useful in observational studies—in our case, the stipulation that the reunion happen not long after the conflict. There is no intrinsic reason that a reconciliation

Two adult female bonobos engage in so-called GG rubbing, a sexual form of reconciliation typical of this species.

© Amy Parish/Anthro-Photo

[continued]

[continued]

could not occur after hours or days, or, in the case of humans, generations.

Let me describe two interesting elaborations on the mechanism of reconciliation. One is *mediation*. Chimpanzees are the only animals to use mediators in conflict resolution. In order to be able to mediate conflict, one needs to understand relationships outside of oneself, which may be the reason why other animals fail to show this aspect of conflict resolution. For example, if two male chimpanzees have been involved in a fight, even on a very large island as where I did my studies, they can easily avoid each other, but instead they will sit opposite from each other, not too far apart, and avoid eye contact. They can sit like this for a long time. In this situation, a third party, such as an older female, may move in and try to solve the issue. The female will approach one of the males and groom him for a brief while. She then gets up and walks slowly to the other male, and the first male walks right behind her.

We have seen situations in which, if the first male failed to follow, the female turned around to grab his arm and make him follow. So the process of getting the two males in proximity seems intentional on the part of the female. She then begins grooming the other male, and the first male grooms her. Before long, the female disappears from the scene, and the males continue grooming: She has in effect brought the two parties together.

There exists a limited anthropological literature on the role of conflict resolution, a process absolutely crucial for the maintenance of the human social fabric in the same way that it is crucial for our primate relatives. In human society, mediation is often done by high-ranking or senior members of the community, sometimes culminating in feasts in which the restoration of harmony is celebrated.[c]

The second elaboration on the reconciliation concept is that it is not purely instinctive, not even in our animal relatives. It is a learned social skill subject to what primatologists now increasingly call "culture" (meaning that the behavior is subject to learning from others as opposed to genetic transmission[d]). To test the learnability of reconciliation, I conducted an experiment with young rhesus and stumptail monkeys.

Not nearly as conciliatory as stumptail monkeys, rhesus monkeys have the reputation of being rather aggressive and despotic. Stumptails are considered more laid-back and tolerant. We housed members of the two species together for 5 months. By the end of this period, they were a fully integrated group: They slept, played, and groomed together. After 5 months, we separated them again, and measured the effect of their time together on conciliatory behavior. The research controls—rhesus monkeys who had lived with one another, without any stumptails—showed absolutely no change in the tendency to reconcile. Stumptails showed a high rate of reconciliation, which was also expected, because they also do so if living together. The most interesting group was the experimental rhesus monkeys, those who had lived with stumptails.

These monkeys started out at the same low level of reconciliation as the rhesus controls, but after they had lived with the stumptails, and after we had segregated them again so that they were now housed only with other rhesus monkeys who had gone through the same experience, these rhesus monkeys reconciled as much as stumptails do. This means that we created a "new and improved" rhesus monkey, one that made up with its opponents far more easily than a regular rhesus monkey.[e]

This was in effect an experiment on social culture: We changed the culture of a group of rhesus monkeys and made it more similar to that of stumptail monkeys by exposing them to the practices of this other species. This experiment also shows that there exists a great deal of flexibility in primate behavior. We humans come from a long lineage of primates with great social sophistication and a well-developed potential for behavioral modification and learning from others. *(By Frans B. M. de Waal, Living Links, Yerkes National Primate Research Center, Emory University.)* ■ ■ ■

[a]de Waal, F. B. M. (2000). Primates—A natural heritage of conflict resolution. *Science, 28*, 586–590.
[b]Aureli, F., & de Waal, F. B. M. (2000). *Natural conflict resolution.* Berkeley: University of California Press.
[c]Reviewed by Frye, D. P. (2000). Conflict management in cross-cultural perspective. In F. Aureli & F. B. M. de Waal, *Natural conflict resolution* (pp. 334–351). Berkeley: University of California Press.
[d]See de Waal, F. B. M. (2001). *The ape and the sushi master.* New York: Basic Books, for a discussion of the animal culture concept.
[e]de Waal, F. B. M., & Johanowicz, D. L. (1993). Modification of reconciliation behavior through social experience: An experiment with two macaque species. *Child Development, 64*, 897–908.

The social sophistication characteristic of primates is evident in behaviors that at first glance might seem wholly practical. For example, **grooming,** the ritual cleaning of another animal to remove parasites and other matter from its skin or coat, is a common pastime for both chimpanzees and bonobos. Besides serving hygienic purposes, it can be a gesture of friendliness, closeness, appeasement, reconciliation, or even submission. Bonobos and chimpanzees have favorite grooming partners. Group sociability, an important behavioral trait undoubtedly also found among human ancestors, is further expressed in embracing, touching, and the joyous welcoming of other members of the ape community. Group protection and coordination of group efforts are facilitated by visual and vocal communication, including special calls for warnings, threats, and gathering. Unique

grooming The ritual cleaning of another animal's skin and fur to remove parasites and other matter.

to bonobos is the use of large leaves as trail signs to indicate their whereabouts to others not immediately present.[3]

Prior to the 1980s most primates were thought to be vegetarian while humans alone were considered meat-eating hunters. Pioneering research by British primatologist Jane Goodall, among others, revealed that the diets of monkeys and apes were extremely varied. Goodall's fieldwork among chimpanzees in their natural habitat at Gombe, a wildlife reserve on the eastern shores of Lake Tanganyika in Tanzania, revealed that these apes supplement their primary diet of fruits and other plant foods with insects and meat. Even more surprising, she found that in addition to killing small invertebrate animals for food, they also hunted and ate monkeys. Goodall observed chimpanzees grabbing adult red colobus monkeys and flailing them to death.[4] Since her pioneering work, other primatologists have documented hunting behavior in baboons and capuchin monkeys, among others.

Chimpanzee females sometimes hunt, but males do so far more frequently. When on the hunt, they may spend up to 2 hours watching, following, and chasing intended prey. Moreover, in contrast to the usual primate practice of each animal finding its own food, hunting frequently involves teamwork to trap and kill prey, particularly when hunting for baboons. Once a potential victim has been isolated from its troop, three or more adult chimps will carefully position themselves so as to block off escape routes while another pursues the prey. Following the kill, most who are present get a share of the meat, either by grabbing a piece as chance affords or by begging for it.

Whatever the nutritional value of meat, hunting is not done purely for dietary purposes, but for social and sexual reasons as well. U.S. anthropologist Craig Stanford, who has done fieldwork among the chimpanzees of Gombe since the early 1990s, found that these sizable apes (100-pound males are common) frequently kill animals weighing up to 25 pounds and eat much more meat than previously believed. Their preferred prey is the red colobus monkey that shares their forested habitat. Annually, chimpanzee hunting parties at Gombe kill about 20 percent of these monkeys, many of them babies, often shaking them out of the tops of 30-foot trees. They may capture and kill as many as seven victims in a raid. These hunts usually take place during the dry season when plant foods are less readily available and when females display genital swelling, which signals that they are ready to mate. On average, each chimp at Gombe eats about a quarter-pound of meat per day during the dry season, about the same amount consumed by contemporary human foragers in the region. For female chimps, a supply of protein-rich food helps support the increased nutritional requirements of pregnancy and lactation.

Somewhat different chimpanzee hunting practices have been observed in West Africa. At Tai National Park in the Ivory Coast, for instance, chimpanzees engage in highly coordinated team efforts to chase monkeys hiding in very tall trees in the dense tropical forest. Individuals who have especially distinguished themselves in a successful hunt see their contributions rewarded with more meat. Recent research shows that bonobos in Congo's rainforest also supplement their diet with meat obtained by means of hunting. Although their behavior resembles that of the chimpanzees, there are crucial differences.

Among bonobos hunting is primarily a female activity. Also, female hunters regularly share carcasses with other females, but less often with males. Even when the most dominant male throws a tantrum nearby, he may still be denied a share of meat.[5] Such discriminatory sharing among female bonobos is also evident when it comes to other foods such as fruits.

Chimpanzees and bonobos have not only developed different hunting strategies but also different sexual practices. For chimps, sexual activity—initiated by either the male or the female—occurs primarily during the periods when females signal their fertility through genital swelling. By most human standards, chimp sexual behavior is promiscuous. A dozen or so males have been observed to have as many as fifty copulations in one day with a single female. Dominant males try to monopolize females when the latter are most receptive sexually, although cooperation from the female is usually required for this to succeed. In addition, an individual female and a lower-ranking male sometimes form a temporary bond, leaving the group together for a few private days during the female's fertile period. Thus, dominant males do not necessarily father all (or even most) of the offspring in a social group. Social success, achieving alpha male status, does not translate neatly into the evolutionary currency of reproductive success.

In contrast to chimpanzees, bonobos (like humans) do not limit their sexual behavior to times of female fertility. Whereas the genitals of chimpanzee females are swollen only at times of fertility, female bonobo genitals are perpetually swollen. The constant swelling, in effect, conceals the females' **ovulation,** or moment when an

---

[3]Recer, P. (1998, February 16). Apes are shown to communicate in the wild. *Burlington Free Press*, p. 12A.

[4]Goodall J. (1986). *The chimpanzees of Gombe: Patterns of behavior.* Cambridge, MA: Belknap Press.

ovulation Moment when an egg released from the ovaries into the womb is receptive for fertilization.

---

[5]Ingmanson, E. J. (1998). Comment. *Current Anthropology, 39,* 409.

egg released into the womb is receptive for fertilization. Ovulation is also concealed in humans, by the absence of genital swelling at all times.

Concealed ovulation in humans and bonobos may play a role in the separation of sexual activity for social reasons and pleasure from the purely biological task of reproduction. In fact, among bonobos (as among humans) sexuality goes far beyond male–female mating for purposes of biological reproduction. Primatologists have observed virtually every possible combination of ages and sexes engaging in a remarkable array of sexual activities, including oral sex, tongue-kissing, and massaging each other's genitals. Male bonobos may mount each other, or one may rub his scrotum against that of the other. They have also been observed "penis fencing"—hanging face to face from a branch and rubbing their erect penises together as if crossing swords. Among females, genital rubbing is particularly common. As described in this chapter's Original Study, the primary function of most of this sex, both hetero- and homosexual, is to reduce tensions and resolve social conflicts. Since the documentation of a variety of sexual activities among bonobos, field studies by primatologists working with other species are now recording a variety of sexual behaviors among these species as well.

Reproduction and Care of Young

Most mammals mate only during specified breeding seasons occurring once or twice a year, but many primate species are able to breed at any time during the course of the year. The average adult female monkey or ape spends most of her adult life either pregnant or nursing her young, times at which she is not sexually receptive. Apes generally nurse each of their young for about 4 years. After her infant is weaned, she will become pregnant again. Many human societies modify the succession and timing of pregnancy and lactation by a variety of cultural means.

Among most (but not all) primates, females generally give birth to one infant at a time. Natural selection may have favored single births among primate tree dwellers because the primate infant, which has a highly developed grasping ability (the grasping reflex can also be seen in human infants), must be transported about by its mother, and more than one clinging infant would seriously encumber her as she moved about the trees.

Primates follow a pattern of bearing few young but devoting more time and effort to the care of each individual offspring. Compared to other mammals such as mice, which pass from birth to adulthood in a matter of weeks, primates spend a great deal of time growing up. As a general rule, the more closely related to humans the primate species is, the longer the period of infant and childhood

dependency. For example, a lemur is dependent upon its mother for only a few months after birth, while an ape is dependent for 4 or 5 years. A chimpanzee infant cannot survive if its mother dies before it reaches the age of 4 at the very least. During the juvenile period, young primates are still dependent upon the larger social group rather than on their mothers alone, using this period for learning and refining a variety of behaviors. If a juvenile primate's mother dies, he or she may be "adopted" by an older male or female member of the social group.

The long interval between births, particularly among the apes, results in small population sizes among our closest relatives. A female chimpanzee, for example, does not reach sexual maturity until about the age of 10, and once she produces her first live offspring, there is a period of 5 or 6 (on average 5.6) years before she will bear another. Thus, assuming that none of her offspring die before adulthood, a female chimpanzee must survive for at least 20 or 21 years just to maintain the size of chimpanzee populations at existing levels. In fact, chimpanzee infants and juveniles do die from time to time, and not all females live full reproductive lives. These chance events, combined with the long intervals between births, help explain why apes are far less abundant in the world today than are monkeys. Habitat destruction and hunting contributes further to declining ape populations.

A long slow period of growth and development, particularly among the hominoids, also provides opportunities. For example, bonobo and chimpanzee dependence on learned social behavior is related to their extended period of childhood development. Born without built-in responses dictating specific behavior in complex situations, the young chimp or bonobo, like the young human, learns how to strategically interact with others and even manipulate them for his or her own benefit—by trial and error, observation, imitation, and practice. Young primates make mistakes along the way, learning to modify their behavior based on the reactions of other members of the group. Each member of the community has a unique physical appearance and personality. Youngsters learn to match their interactive behaviors according to each individual's social position and temperament. Anatomical features such as a free upper lip (unlike lemurs or cats, for example) allow monkeys and apes varied facial expression, contributing to greater communication among individuals.

Communication

Primates, like many animals, vocalize. They have a great range of calls that are often used together with movements of the face or body to convey a message. Observers have not yet established the meaning of all the sounds, but a good number have been distinguished, such as warning calls, threat calls, defense calls, and gathering calls. The behavioral reactions of other animals hearing the call have also been studied. Among bonobos and chimpanzees, vocalizations are emotional. Much of these species' communication takes place by the use of specific gestures and postures. Indeed, a number of these, such as kissing and embracing, are in virtually universal use today among humans, as well as apes.

Primatologists have classified numerous kinds of chimpanzee vocalization and visual communication signals. Facial expressions convey emotional states such as distress, fear, or excitement. Numerous distinct vocalizations or calls have been associated with a variety of sensations. For example, chimps will smack their lips or clack their teeth to express pleasure with sociable body contact. Calls labeled "pant-hoots" can be differentiated into specific types used for arrival of individuals or inquiring. Together, these facilitate group protection, coordination of group efforts, and social interaction in general. One form of communication appears to be unique to bonobos: the use of trail markers. When foraging, the community breaks up into smaller groups, rejoining again in the evening to nest together. To keep track of each party's whereabouts, those in the lead will, at the intersections of trails or where downed trees obscure trails, deliberately stomp down the vegetation so as to indicate their direction, or rip off large leaves and place them carefully for the same purpose. Thus, they all know where to come together at the end of the day.[6]

Experiments with captive apes, carried out over several decades, reveal that their communicative abilities exceed what they make use of in the wild. In some of these experiments, bonobos and chimpanzees have been taught to communicate using symbols, as in the case of Kanzi, a bonobo who uses a keyboard. Other chimpanzees, gorillas, and orangutans have been taught American Sign Language. Although this research provoked controversy, in part because it challenged notions of human uniqueness, it has become evident that apes are capable of understanding language quite well, even using rudimentary grammar. They are able to generate original utterances, ask questions, distinguish naming something from asking for it, develop original ways to tell lies, coordinate their actions, and even spontaneously teach language to others. Even though they cannot literally *speak,* it is now clear that all of the great ape

species can develop *language skills* to the level of a 2- to 3-year-old human child.[7] From such knowledge, we may learn something about the origin of human language.

Use of Objects as Tools

Young chimpanzees also learn other functional behaviors from adults, such as how to make and use tools. A **tool** may be defined as an object used to facilitate some task or activity. Beyond deliberately modifying objects to make them suitable for particular purposes, chimps can to some extent modify them to regular patterns and may even prepare objects at one location in anticipation of future use at another place. For example, chimps have been observed selecting a long, slender branch, stripping off

© Martin Harvey/Peter Arnold, Inc.

Chimps use a variety of tools in the wild. Here a chimp is using a long stick stripped of its side branches to fish for termites. Chimps will select a stick when still quite far from a termite mound and modify its shape on their way to the snacking spot.

tool An object used to facilitate some task or activity.

[6]Recer, P. (1998, February 16). Apes shown to communicate in the wild. *Burlington Free Press,* p. 12A.

[7]Lestel, D. (1998). How chimpanzees have domesticated humans. *Anthropology Today, 12*(3); Miles, H. L. W. (1993). Language and the orangutan: The "old person" of the forest. In P. Cavalieri & P. Singer (Eds.), *The great ape project* (pp. 45–50). New York: St. Martin's Press.

its leaves, and carrying it on a "fishing" expedition to a termite nest. Reaching their destination, they insert the stick into the nest, wait a few minutes, and then pull it out to eat the insects clinging to it. Other examples of chimpanzee use of tools involve leaves, used as wipes or as sponges, to get drinking water out of a hollow. Large sticks may serve as clubs or as missiles (as may stones) in aggressive or defensive displays. Stones are used as hammers and anvils to crack open certain kinds of nuts. Twigs are used as toothpicks to clean teeth as well as to extract loose baby teeth. They use these dental tools not just on themselves but on other individuals as well.[8]

Bonobos in the wild have not been observed making and using tools to the extent that chimpanzees do. However, their use of large leaves as trail markers may be considered a form of tool use. Tool-making capabilities have also been demonstrated by a captive bonobo who independently made stone tools remarkably similar to the earliest tools made by our own ancestors.

As researchers uncover increasing evidence of the remarkable behavioral sophistication and intelligence of chimpanzees and other apes—including a capacity for conceptual thought previously unsuspected by most scientists—the widespread practice of caging our primate "cousins" and exploiting them for entertainment or medical experimentation becomes increasingly controversial. The Biocultural Connection discusses this complex issue.

THE QUESTION OF CULTURE

The more we learn of the behavior of our nearest primate relatives, the more we become aware of the importance to chimps of learned, socially shared practices and knowledge. This raises the question: Do chimpanzees, bonobos, and the other apes have culture? The answer appears to be yes. The detailed study of ape behavior has revealed variation among groups in use of tools and patterns of social engagement that seem to derive from the traditions of the group rather than a biologically determined script. Humans share with the other apes an ability to learn the complex but flexible patterns of behavior particular to a social group during a long period of childhood dependency.

Primate Behavior and Human Evolution

In Western societies there has been an unfortunate tendency to erect what paleontologist Stephen Jay Gould referred to as "golden barriers" that set us apart from the rest of the animal kingdom.[9] It is unfortunate, for it blinds us to the fact that a continuum exists between "us" and "them" (other animals). We have already seen that the physical differences between humans and apes are largely differences of degree, rather than kind.

It now appears that the same is true with respect to behavior. As primatologist Richard Wrangham once put it,

> Like humans, [chimpanzees] laugh, make up after a quarrel, support each other in times of trouble, medicate themselves with chemical and physical remedies, stop each other from eating poisonous foods, collaborate in the hunt, help each other over physical obstacles, raid neighboring groups, lose their tempers, get excited by dramatic weather, invent ways to show off, have family traditions and group traditions, make tools, devise plans, deceive, play tricks, grieve, and are cruel and are kind.[10]

This is not to say that we are "just" another ape; obviously, "degree" does make a difference. While the continuities between us and our primate kin reflect a common evolutionary heritage, our more recent evolution has taken us in a somewhat different direction. By looking at the range of behaviors displayed by contemporary apes and other primates, we may find clues to the practices and capabilities possessed by our own ancestors as their evolutionary path diverged from those of the other African apes. Human intellectual capacity for compassion has roots in our mammalian primate heritage. If it is granted that our closest living relatives, among other co-inhabitants of our planet, have an inherent right to survive, then it is imperative that humanity applies our compassion and intelligence toward ensuring their survival.

Primate Conservation

At present, no fewer than seventy-six species of primates are recognized as being in danger of extinction. Included among them are all of the great apes, as well as such formerly widespread and adaptable species as rhesus macaques. In the wild these animals are threatened by habitat destruction caused by economic development (farming, lumbering, cattle ranching, rubber tapping), as well as by hunters and trappers that are after them for food, trophies, research, or as exotic pets. Because

---

[8]McGrew, W.C. (2000). Dental care in chimps. *Science 288*, 1,747.

[9]Quoted in de Waal, F. (2001). *The ape and the sushi master* (p. 235). New York: Basic Books.

[10]Quoted in Mydens, S. (2001, August 12). He's not hairy, he's my brother. *New York Times,* sec. 4, p. 5.

Biocultural
Connection

Nonhuman Primates and Human Disease

Biological similarities among humans, apes, and Old World monkeys have led to the extensive use of these nonhuman primate species in biomedical research aimed at preventing or curing disease in humans. A cultural perspective that separates humans from our closest living relatives is necessary for this research to occur. Those who fully support these research efforts state that biomedical research in a limited number of chimpanzees or rhesus macaques lessens human suffering and spares human lives. The successful development of a vaccine for hepatitis B and hepatitis C through testing with chimpanzees, and current work on vaccines for HIV, are often cited as examples of a positive balance between vast human benefits and minimal chimpanzee suffering. Others, such as primatologist Jane Goodall, vehemently disagree with this approach. Goodall emphasizes that cultural processes determine the place of

animals within biomedical research. She advocates elimination of the cultural distinction between humans and our closest relatives for purposes of biomedical research.

Some biomedical research disturbs animals minimally. For example, DNA can be extracted from the hair naturally shed by living primates, allowing for cross-species comparisons of disease genes. To facilitate this process, primate cell repositories have been established for researchers to obtain samples of primate DNA. Other biomedical research is far more invasive to the individual primate. For example, to document the infectious nature of kuru, a disease closely related to mad cow disease, the extract from the brains of sick humans was injected into the brains of living chimpanzees. A year and a half later, the chimpanzees began to sicken. They had the same classic features of kuru—uncontrollable spasticity, seizures, dementia, and ultimately death.

The biological similarities of humans and other primates leading to such research practices derive from a long shared evolutionary history. By comparison, the cultural rules that allow our closest relatives to be the subjects of biomedical research are relatively short lived. As Jane Goodall has said, "Surely it should be a matter of moral responsibility that we humans, differing from other animals mainly by virtue of our more highly developed intellect and, with it, our greater capacity for understanding and compassion, ensure that the medical progress slowly detaches its roots from the manure of non-human animal suffering and despair. Particularly when this involves the servitude of our closest relatives."[a] ■ ■ ■

[a]Goodall, Jane. (1990). *Through a window: My thirty years with the chimpanzees of Gombe*. Boston: Houghton Mifflin.

monkeys and apes are so closely related to humans, they are regarded as essential for biomedical research in which humans cannot be used (see the Biocultural Connection). While most primates in laboratories are captive bred, an active trade in live primates continues to contribute to their local extinction.

Because of their vulnerability, the conservation of primates has become a matter of urgency. Both of the existing approaches to solving this problem apply knowledge gained from studies of free-ranging animals. The first approach is to maintain some populations in the wild, either by establishing preserves where animals are already living or by moving populations to places where suitable habitat exists. This approach requires constant monitoring and management

to ensure that sufficient space and resources remain available. The other approach is to maintain breeding colonies in captivity, in which case we must carefully provide the kind of physical and social environment that will encourage psychological and physical well-being, as well as reproductive success. Primates in zoos and laboratories do not successfully reproduce when deprived of such amenities as opportunities for climbing, materials to use for nest building, others with whom to socialize, and places for privacy. While such amenities contribute to the success of breeding colonies in captivity, ensuring the survival of our closest living relatives in suitable natural habitats is a far greater challenge that humans must meet in the years to come.

Chapter Summary

■ Primates, like most mammals, are intelligent animals whose young are born live and nourished with milk from their mothers. Like other mammals, they maintain constant body temperature and have respiratory and circulatory systems that will sustain high activity levels. Their skeleton and

teeth also resemble those of other mammals, although there are differences of detail.

■ Primates can be divided into five natural groupings: (1) lemurs and lorises, (2) tarsiers, (3) New World monkeys, (4) Old World monkeys, and (5) apes, including humans.

Lemurs, lorises, and tarsiers are sometimes grouped together as prosimians because they share a series of anatomical characteristics, while monkeys, apes, and humans are considered anthropoid or humanlike primates. Tarsiers are, however, more closely related to the monkeys and apes on a genetic level. Prosimians are more dependent on the sense of smell than anthropoids, and where competition from anthropoids is present, they are nocturnal arboreal creatures. Nearly all anthropoids are diurnal, exploiting a wide range of habitats and expressing considerable behavioral flexibility and variation.

■ Primates show a number of characteristics that developed as adaptations to insect predation and life in the trees. These adaptive characteristics include a generalized set of teeth, suited to insect eating but also a variety of fruits and leaves. These teeth are fewer in number and set in a smaller jaw than in most mammals. Other adaptations that developed in the course of primate evolution include binocular stereoscopic vision, or depth perception, and an intensified sense of touch particularly in the hands. This combination of developments had an effect upon the primate brain, resulting in larger size and greater complexity in later-appearing species. There were also changes in the primate skeleton: in particular, a reduction of the snout, an enlargement of the braincase, and numerous adaptations for upright posture and flexibility of limb movement.

■ The primate reproductive pattern can be characterized by fewer offspring born to each female and a longer period of infant dependency compared to most mammals. This period of dependency allows young primates to learn the behaviors of its group.

■ The apes are humans' closest relatives. Apes include gibbons, siamangs, orangutans, gorillas, bonobos, and chimpanzees. In their outward appearance, the apes seem to resemble one another more than they do humans, but their genetic structure and biochemistry reveal that the African apes, bonobos, chimpanzees, and gorillas are closer to humans than are orangutans, gibbons, and siamangs.

■ The social life of primates is complex. Primates are social animals, and most species live and travel in groups. Frequently individuals transfer to new groups at adolescence. In many primate species, both males and females can be organized into dominance hierarchies. In the case of females, high rank is associated with enhanced reproductive success. In males however, high rank does not necessarily confer a reproductive advantage.

■ A characteristic primate activity is grooming, which is a sign of closeness between individuals. Among chimpanzees, sexual interaction between adults of opposite sex generally takes place only when a female is in estrus. In bonobos, however, constant swelling of the female's genitals suggests constant estrus, whether or not she is actually fertile. A consequence of this concealed ovulation in bonobos is a separation of sexual activity from the biological task of reproduction. Among bonobos, sex between both opposite and same-sex individuals serves as a means of reducing tensions, as in the genital rubbing that frequently takes place between females.

■ Primates have elaborate systems of communication based on vocalizations and gestures. In addition, bonobos employ trail signs to communicate their whereabouts to others.

■ The diet of most primates is made up of a variety of fruits, leaves, and insects, but bonobos and chimpanzees sometimes hunt, kill, and eat animals as well. Among chimps, most hunting is done by males and may require considerable teamwork. By contrast, it is usually bonobo females that hunt. Once a kill is made, the meat is generally shared with other animals.

■ Among chimpanzees and the other apes, learned behavior is especially important. From adults, juveniles learn to use a variety of tools and substances for various purposes. Innovations made by one individual may be adopted by other animals, standardized, and passed on to succeeding generations. Because practices are learned, socially shared, and often differ from one group to another, we may speak of chimpanzee culture.

Questions for Reflection

1. In the 21st century humans face the challenge of making sure that other primate species do not go extinct. Why is this so important?

2. Considering some of the trends seen among the primates, such as increased brain size or reduced tooth number, why can't we say that some primates are more evolved than others? Are humans more evolved than chimpanzees?

3. Given the variation seen in the specific behaviors of chimp, bonobo, and gorilla groups, is it fair to say that our close relatives possess culture?

4. Many primate species, particularly apes, are endangered today. Though some features of ape biology may be responsible for apes' limited population size, humans, with ever-expanding population sizes, share these same biological features. Besides life cycle biology, what factors are causing endangerment of primates, and how can humans work to prevent the extinction of our closest living relatives?

Key Terms

nocturnal	prehensile
arboreal	brachiation
diurnal	community
binocular vision	dominance hierarchies
stereoscopic vision	grooming.
opposable	ovulation
prosimians	tool
anthropoids	

Multimedia Review Tools

Make the Grade in Anthropology with ThomsonNOW

Thomson NOW! This powerful online study tool provides you with a *personalized study plan* based on your responses to a diagnostic pretest. Once you have mastered the material with the help of interactive learning tools, an integrated e-book, and more, you can take a post-test to confirm you are ready to move on to the next chapter. To get started with ThomsonNOW, check the card packaged with your book for the access code. Then go to http://www.thomsonedu.com to create an account through 1pass™. If there is no card in your book, go to http://www. thomsonedu.com to purchase an access code.

Companion Web Site and Anthropology Resource Center

Go to http://anthropology.wadsworth.com to reach the companion website for your text. This offers many study aids, including self quizzes for each chapter and a practice final exam, as well as links to anthropology websites and information on the latest theories and discoveries in the field.

Also, check out the Anthropology Resource Center for a wealth of learning materials that include interactive maps, video exercises, simulations, and breaking news in anthropology. Be sure to explore InfoTrac College Edition®, your online library that offers full-length articles from thousands of scholarly and popular publications. To reach the Anthropology Resource Center and InfoTrac College Edition, check the card packaged with your book for the access code. Then go to http://www.thomsonedu.com to create an account through 1pass™. If there is no card in your book, go to http://www. thomsonedu.com to purchase an access code.

© Javier Trueba/Madrid Scientific Films

CHALLENGE ISSUE

Given the radical changes taking place in the world today, a scientific understanding of the past has never been more important. But scientific investigation of ancient remains challenges us to answer the complex question of who owns the past. Paleo-anthropologist Juan Luis Arsuaga and his team spent nearly an hour each day climbing underground through a narrow passage to a small enclosed space to excavate the Stone Age site Sima de los Huesos or Pit of Bones in Spain. After such efforts, do the ancient remains belong to the scientists, to the people living in the region under scientific investigation, or to whoever happens to have possession of them? Market forces convert these remains into very expensive collectibles and lead to systematic commercial mining of archaeological and fossil sites. Collaborations between local people and scientists not only preserves the ancient remains from market forces but also honors the connections of indigenous people to the places and remains under study.

Field Methods in Archaeology and Paleoanthropology

4

While the focus of anthropology is on peoples of all places and times, paleoanthropology and archaeology are the specialties most concerned with our past. Paleoanthropology and archaeology share a focus on **prehistory,** a conventional term used to refer to the period of time before written records. For some people, the term prehistoric might conjure up images of "primitive" cavemen and women, but it does not imply a lack of history or any inferiority, merely a lack of written history. Since the next three chapters of this book focus upon the past, this chapter will look at the methods archaeologists and paleoanthropologists use to study the past.

Most of us are familiar with some kind of archaeological material: the coin dug out of the earth, the fragment of an ancient pot, the spear point used by some ancient hunter. Finding and cataloguing such objects is often thought to be the chief goal of archaeology. While this was true in the 19th and early 20th century, when professional and amateur archaeologists alike collected cultural treasures, the situation changed by the mid-20th century. Today, the aim is to use archaeological remains to reconstruct the culture and worldview of past human societies. Archaeologists examine every recoverable detail from past societies, including all kinds of structures (not just palaces and temples), hearths, garbage dumps, bones, and plant remains. Although it may appear that archaeologists are digging up things, they are really digging up human biology, behavior, and beliefs.

> **prehistory** A conventional term used to refer to the period of time before the appearance of written records. Does not deny the existence of history, merely of written history.

Similarly, paleoanthropologists who study the physical remains of our ancestors and other ancient primates do more than find and catalogue old bones. Paleoanthropologists recover, describe, and organize these remains to see what they can tell us about human biological evolution. It is not so much a case of finding the ancient bones but finding out what the bones mean.

RECOVERING CULTURAL AND BIOLOGICAL REMAINS

Archaeologists and paleoanthropologists face a dilemma. The only way to thoroughly investigate our past is to excavate sites where biological and cultural remains are found. Unfortunately, excavation results in the site's destruction. Thus, every attempt is made to excavate in such a way that the location and context of everything recovered, no matter how small, is precisely recorded. These records help scientists make sense of the data and enhance our knowledge of the past. Knowledge that can be derived from physical and cultural remains diminishes dramatically if accurate and detailed records of the excavation are not kept. As the U.S. anthropologist Brian Fagan has put it:

> The fundamental premise of excavation is that all digging is destructive, even that done by experts. The archaeologist's primary responsibility, therefore, is to record a site for posterity as it is dug because there are no second chances.[1]

Archaeologists work with **artifacts,** any object fashioned or altered by humans—a flint scraper, a basket, an axe, or such things as house ruins or walls. An artifact expresses a facet of human culture. Because it is something that someone made, archaeologists like to say that an artifact is a product or representation of human behavior and beliefs or, in more technical terms, artifacts are **material culture.**

Artifacts are not considered in isolation; rather, they are integrated with biological and ecological remains. And just as important as the artifacts or physical

---

artifact Any object fashioned or altered by humans.

material culture The durable aspects of culture such as tools, structures, and art.

---

[1]Fagan, B. M. (1995). *People of the earth* (8th ed., p. 19). New York: HarperCollins.

remains themselves is the way they were left in the ground. For example, what people do with the things they have made, how they dispose of them, and how they lose them reflect important aspects of human culture. In other words, context allows archaeologists to understand the cultures of the past.

Similarly, context provides important information about biological remains. It provides information about which fossils are earlier or later in time than other fossils. Also, by noting the association of ancient human fossils with the remains of other species, the paleoanthropologist may make significant progress in reconstructing environmental settings of the past.

While cultural and physical remains represent distinct kinds of data, the fullest interpretations of the human past require the integration of ancient human biology and culture. Often paleoanthropologists and archaeologists work together to systematically excavate and analyze fragmentary remains, placing scraps of bone, shattered pottery, and scattered campsites into broad interpretive contexts.

The Nature of Fossils

Broadly defined, a **fossil** is any mineralized trace or impression of an organism that has been preserved in the earth's crust from past geologic time. Fossilization typically involves the hard parts of an organism. Bones, teeth, shells, horns, and the woody tissues of plants are the most successfully fossilized materials. Although the soft parts of an organism are rarely fossilized, the casts or impressions of footprints, brains, and even whole bodies, have sometimes been found. Because dead animals quickly attract meat-eating scavengers and bacteria that cause decomposition, they rarely survive long enough to become fossilized. For an organism to become a fossil, it must be covered by some protective substance soon after death.

An organism or part of an organism may be preserved in a number of ways. The whole animal may be frozen in ice, like the famous mammoths found in Siberia, safe from the actions of predators, weathering, and bacteria. Or it may be enclosed in a natural resin exuding from evergreen trees, later becoming hardened and fossilized as amber. Specimens of spiders and insects dating back millions of years have been preserved in the Baltic Sea area, which is rich in resin-producing evergreens such as pine, spruce, or fir trees.

---

fossil The preserved remains of plants and animals that lived in the past.

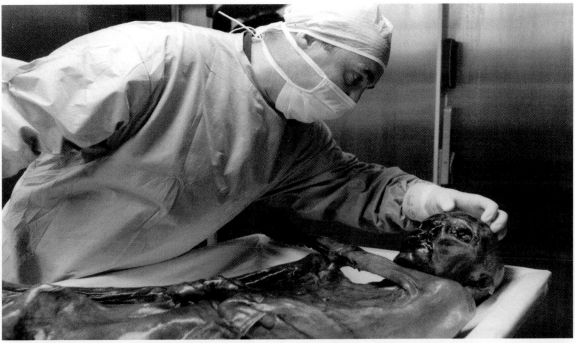

In rare circumstances, human bodies are so well preserved that they could be mistaken for recent corpses. Such is the case of the "Ice Man," exposed by the melting of an alpine glacier in northern Italy in 1991. The mummified body of a man who lived 5,200 years ago was found in the Tyrolean Alps, where it had been released by glacial melting. Both the Italian and the Austrian governments felt they had legitimate claims on this rare find, and they mounted legal and scientific arguments for housing the skeleton in their countries. These arguments continued as the specimen, just released from the ice, began to thaw.

An organism may be preserved in the bottoms of lakes and sea basins, where the body or body part may be quickly covered with sediment. An entire organism may also be mummified or preserved in tar pits, peat, oil, or asphalt bogs, in which the chemical environment prevents the growth of decay-producing bacteria. To become a fossil, the materials surrounding the physical remains gradually harden, forming a protective shell around the skeleton of the organism. The internal cavities of bones or teeth and other parts of the skeleton fill in with mineral deposits from the sediment immediately surrounding the specimen. Then the external walls of the bone decay and are replaced by calcium carbonate or silica.

Burial of the Dead

Entirely preserved fossil skeletons dating before the cultural practice of burial about 100,000 years ago are exceedingly rare. The human fossil record from this period consists of fragmentary remains. The fossil record for many other primates is even poorer, because organic materials decay rapidly in the tropical forests where they lived. The records are much more complete for primates such as evolving humans that lived on the grassy plains, or savannah environments, where conditions were far more favorable to the formation of fossils. This was particularly true in places where ash deposited from volcanic eruptions or waterborne sediments along lakes and streams could quickly cover organisms dying in these environments. At several localities in Ethiopia, Kenya, and Tanzania in East Africa, numerous fossils important for our understanding of human evolution have been found near ancient lakes and streams, often sandwiched between layers of volcanic ash.

In more recent times, such complete remains, although not common, are often quite spectacular and may be particularly informative. As an example, consider the recovery in 1994 of an Eskimo girl's remains in Point Barrow, Alaska, described in the Original Study. As seen in this case study, successful exploration of the past depends upon cooperation and respect between anthropologists and the living people with ancestral connections to the physical and cultural remains being studied.

Original Study

Whispers from the Ice

People grew excited when a summer rainstorm softened the bluff known as Ukkuqsi, sloughing off huge chunks of earth containing remains of historic and prehistoric houses, part of the old village that predates the modern community of Barrow. Left protruding from the slope was a human head. Archaeologist Anne Jensen happened to be in Barrow buying strapping tape when the body appeared. Her firm, SJS Archaeological Services, Inc., was closing a field season at nearby Point Franklin, and Jensen offered the team's help in a kind of archaeological triage to remove the body before it eroded completely from the earth. The North Slope Borough hired her and Glenn Sheehan, both associated with Pennsylvania's Bryn Mawr College, to conduct the work. The National Science Foundation, which supported the 3-year Point Franklin project, agreed to fund the autopsy and subsequent analysis of the body and artifacts.

The Ukkuqsi excavation quickly became a community event. In remarkably sunny and calm weather, volunteers troweled and picked through the thawing soil, finding trade beads, animal bones, and other items. Teenage boys worked alongside grandmothers. The smell of sea mammal oil, sweet at first then corrupt, mingled with ancient organic odors of decomposed vegetation. One man searched the beach for artifacts that had eroded from the bluff, discovering such treasures as two feather parkas. Elder Silas Negovanna, originally of Wainwright, visited several times, "more or less out of curiosity to see what they have in mind," he says. George Leavitt, who lives in a house on the bluff, stopped by one day while carrying home groceries and suggested a way to spray water to thaw the soil without washing away valuable artifacts. Tour groups added the excavation to their rounds.

"This community has a great interest in archaeology up here just because it's so recent to their experience," says oral historian Karen Brewster, a tall young woman who interviews elders as part of her work with the North Slope Borough's division of Inupiat History, Language, and Culture. "The site's right in town, and everybody was really fascinated by it."

Slowly, as the workers scraped and shoveled, the earth surrendered its historical hoard: carved wooden bowls, ladles, and such clothing as a mitten made from polar bear hide, birdskin parkas, and mukluks. The items spanned prehistoric times, dated in Barrow to before explorers first arrived in 1826.

The work prompted visiting elders to recall when they or their parents lived in traditional sod houses and relied wholly on the land and sea for sustenance. Some remembered sliding down the hill as children, before the sea gnawed away the slope. Others described the site's use as a lookout for whales or ships. For the archaeologists, having elders stand beside them and identify items and historical context is like hearing the past whispering in their ears. Elders often know from experience, or from stories, the answers to the scientists' questions about how items were used or made. "In this instance, usually the only puzzled people are the archaeologists," jokes archaeologist Sheehan.

A modern town of 4,000, Barrow exists in a cultural continuum, where history is not detached or remote but still pulses through contemporary life. People live, hunt, and fish where their ancestors did, but they can also buy fresh vegetables at the store and jet to other places. Elementary school classes include computer and Inupiaq language studies. Caribou skins, still ruddy with blood, and black brant carcasses hang near late-model cars outside homes equipped with television antennas. A man uses power tools to work on his whaling boat. And those who appear from the earth are not just bodies, but relatives. "We're not a people frozen in time," says Jana Harcharek, an Inupiat Eskimo who teaches Inupiaq and nurtures her culture among young people. "There will always be that connection between us [and our ancestors]. They're not a separate entity."

The past drew still closer as the archaeologists neared the body. After several days of digging through thawed soil, they used water supplied by the local fire station's tanker truck to melt through permafrost until they reached the remains, about 3 feet below the surface. A shell of clear ice encased the body, which rested in what appeared to be a former meat cellar. With the low-pressure play of water from the tanker, the archaeologists teased the icy casket from the frozen earth, exposing a tiny foot. Only then did they realize they had uncovered a child. "That was kind of sad, because she was about my daughter's size," says archaeologist Jensen.

The girl was curled up beneath a baleen toboggan and part of a covering that Inupiat elder Bertha Leavitt identified as a kayak skin by its stitching. The child, who appeared to be 5 or 6, remained remarkably intact after her dark passage through time. Her face was cloaked by a covering that puzzled some onlookers. It didn't look like human hair, or even fur, but something with a feathery residue. Finally they concluded it was a hood from a feather parka made of bird skins. The rest of her body was delineated muscle that had freeze-dried into a dark brick-red color. Her hands rested on her knees, which were drawn up to her chin. Frost particles coated the bends of her arms and legs.

"We decided we needed to go talk to the elders and see what they wanted, to get some kind of feeling as to whether they wanted to bury her right away, or whether they were willing to allow some studies in a respectful manner—

studies that would be of some use to residents of the North Slope," Jensen says. Working with community elders is not a radical idea to Jensen or Sheehan, whose previous work in the Arctic has earned them high regard from local officials who appreciate their sensitivity. The researchers feel obligated not only to follow community wishes but to invite villagers to sites and to share all information through public presentations. In fact, Jensen is reluctant to discuss findings with the press before the townspeople themselves hear it.

"It seems like it's a matter of simple common courtesy," she says. Such consideration can only help researchers, she points out. "If people don't get along with you, they're not going to talk to you, and they're liable to throw you out on your ear." In the past, scientists were not terribly sensitive about such matters, generally regarding human remains—and sometimes living Natives—as artifacts themselves. Once, the girl's body would have been hauled off to the catacombs of some university or museum, and relics would have disappeared into exhibit drawers in what Sheehan describes as "hit-and-run archaeology."

"Grave robbers" is how Inupiat Jana Harcharek refers to early Arctic researchers. "They took human remains and their burial goods. It's pretty gruesome. But, of course, at the time they thought they were doing science a big favor. Thank goodness attitudes have changed."

Today, not only scientists but municipal officials confer with the Barrow Elders Council when local people find skeletons from traditional platform burials out on the tundra, or when bodies appear in the house mounds. The elders appreciate such consultations, says Samuel Simmonds, a tall, dignified man known for his carving. A retired Presbyterian minister, he presided at burial ceremonies of the famous "frozen family," ancient Inupiats discovered in Barrow 13 years ago. "They were part of us, we know that," he says simply, as if the connection between old bones and bodies and living relatives is self-evident. In the case of the newly discovered body, he says, "We were concerned that it was reburied in a

respectful manner. They were nice enough to come over and ask us."

The elders also wanted to restrict media attention and prevent photographs of the body except for a few showing her position at the site. They approved a limited autopsy to help answer questions about the body's sex, age, and state of health. She was placed in an orange plastic body bag in a stainless steel morgue with the temperature turned down to below freezing.

With the help of staff at the Indian Health Service Hospital, Jensen sent the girl's still-frozen body to Anchorage's Providence Hospital. There she assisted with an autopsy performed by Dr. Michael Zimmerman of New York City's Mount Sinai Hospital. Zimmerman, an expert on prehistoric frozen bodies, had autopsied Barrow's frozen family in 1982, and was on his way to work on the prehistoric man recently discovered in the Alps.

The findings suggest the girl's life was very hard. She ultimately died of starvation, but also had emphysema caused by a rare congenital disease—the lack of an enzyme that protects the lungs. She probably was sickly and needed extra care all her brief life. The autopsy also found soot in her lungs from the family's sea mammal oil lamps, and she had osteoporosis, which was caused by a diet exclusively of meat from marine mammals.

The girl's stomach was empty, but her intestinal tract contained dirt and animal fur. That remains a mystery and raises questions about the condition of the rest of the family. "It's not likely that she would be hungry and everyone else well fed," Jensen says.

That the girl appears to have been placed deliberately in the cellar provokes further questions about precontact burial practices, which the researchers hope Barrow elders can help answer. Historic accounts indicate the dead often were wrapped in skins and laid out on the tundra on wooden platforms, rather than buried in the frozen earth. But perhaps the entire family was starving and too weak to remove the dead girl from the house, Jensen speculates. "We probably won't ever be able to say, 'This is the way it was,'" she adds. "For that you need a time machine."

The scientific team reported to the elders that radiocarbon dating places the girl's death in about A.D. 1200. If correct—for dating is technically tricky in the Arctic—the date would set the girl's life about 100 years before her people formed settled whaling villages, Sheehan says.

Following the autopsy and the body's return to Barrow in August, one last request by the elders was honored. The little girl, wrapped in her feather parka, was placed in a casket and buried in a small Christian ceremony next to the grave of the other prehistoric bodies. Hundreds of years after her death, an Inupiat daughter was welcomed back into the midst of her community.

The "rescue" of the little girl's body from the raw forces of time and nature means researchers and the Inupiat people will continue to learn still more about the region's culture. Sheehan and Jensen returned to Barrow in winter 1994 to explain their findings to townspeople. "We expect to learn just as much from them," Sheehan said before the trip. A North Slope Cultural Center scheduled for completion in 1996 will store and display artifacts from the dig sites.

Laboratory tests and analysis also will contribute information. The archaeologists hope measurements of heavy metals in the girl's body will allow comparisons with modern-day pollution contaminating the sea mammals that Inupiats eat today. The soot damage in her lungs might offer health implications for Third World people who rely on oil lamps, dung fires, and charcoal for heat and light. Genetic tests could illuminate early population movements of Inupiats. The project also serves as a model for good relations between archaeologists and Native people. "The larger overall message from this work is that scientists and communities don't have to be at odds," Sheehan says. "In fact, there are mutual interests that we all have. Scientists have obligations to communities. And when more scientists realize that, and when more communities hold scientists to those standards, then everybody will be happier." *(Adapted from Simpson S. (1995, April). Whispers from the ice. Alaska Magazine, p. 23–28. Reprinted by permission.)* ■ ■ ■

SEARCHING FOR ARTIFACTS AND FOSSILS

Where are artifacts and fossils found? Places containing archaeological remains of previous human activity are known as sites. There are many kinds of sites, and sometimes it is difficult to define their boundaries, for remains may be strewn over large areas. Sites are even found underwater. Some examples of sites identified by archaeologists and paleoanthropologists are hunting campsites, from which hunters went out to hunt game; kill sites, in which game was killed and butchered; village sites, in which domestic activities took place; and cemeteries, in which the dead, and sometimes their belongings, were buried.

While skeletons of recent peoples are frequently associated with their cultural remains, archaeological sites may or may not contain any physical remains. As we go back in time, the association of physical and cultural remains becomes less likely. Physical remains dating from before 2.5 million years ago are found in isolation. This is not proof of the absence of material culture but rather that the earliest forms of material culture were not preserved in the archaeological record. It is likely that the earliest tools were made of organic materials (such as the termiting sticks used by chimpanzees) that were much less likely to be preserved in the archaeological record. Similarly, fossils are found only in geological contexts where conditions are known to have been right for fossilization. By contrast, archaeological sites may be found just about anywhere, perhaps because many date from more recent periods.

Sometimes archaeological sites are marked by dramatic ruins, such as this Temple from the ancient Maya city of Tikal. Built by piling up rubble and facing it with stone blocks held together with mortar, it towers above the trees. While the scaffolding provides the opportunity for tourists to appreciate the grandeur of its full height, the benefits of learning about the ancient Maya through the experience of such a climb must be balanced with preserving these archaeological remains.

Site Identification

The first task for the archaeologist is actually finding sites to investigate. Archaeological sites, particularly very old ones, frequently lie buried underground covered by layers of sediment deposited since the site was in use. Most sites are revealed by the presence of artifacts. Chance may play a crucial role in the site's discovery, as in the previously discussed case of the site at Barrow, Alaska. Usually, however, the archaeologist will have to survey a region in order to plot the sites available for excavation. A survey can be made from the ground, but more and more use is made of remote sensing techniques, many of them byproducts of space-age technology. Aerial photographs have been used by archaeologists since the 1920s and are widely used today. Among other things, such photographs were used for the discovery and interpretation of the huge geometric and zoomorphic (from Latin for "animal-shaped") markings on the coastal desert of Peru.

More obvious sites, such as the human-made mounds or "tells" of the Middle East, are easier to spot from the ground, for the country is open. But it is more difficult to locate ruins, even those that are well above ground, where there is a heavy forest cover. Thus, the discovery of archaeological sites is strongly affected by local geography and climate.

Some sites may be spotted by changes in vegetation. For example, the topsoil of ancient storage and refuse pits is often richer in organic matter than that of the surrounding areas, and so it grows distinctive vegetation. At Tikal, an ancient Maya site in Guatemala, breadnut trees usually grow near the remains of ancient houses, so that archaeologists looking for the remains of houses at this site can use these trees as guideposts.

Courtesy Dana Walrath

Some archaeological features are best seen from the air, such as this figure of a hummingbird made in prehistoric times on the Nazca Desert of Peru.

On the ground, sites can be spotted by **soil marks,** or stains, showing up on the surface of recently plowed fields. From soil marks, many Bronze Age burial mounds were discovered in northern Hertfordshire and southwestern Cambridgeshire, England. The mounds hardly rose out of the ground, yet each was circled at its core by chalky soil marks. Sometimes the very presence of certain chalky rock is significant.

Documents, maps, and folklore are also useful to the archaeologist. Heinrich Schliemann, the famous and controversial 19th-century German archaeologist, was led to the discovery of Troy after a reading of Homer's *Iliad*. He assumed that the city described by Homer as Ilium was really Troy. Place names and local lore often are an indication that an archaeological site is to be found in the area. Archaeological surveys therefore often depend upon amateur collectors and local people who are usually familiar with history of the land.

Sometimes natural processes, such as soil erosion or droughts, expose sites or fossils. For example, in eastern North America and other areas where shellfish consumption was common, prehistoric refuse mounds, known as **middens,** filled with shells have been exposed by erosion along coastlines or river banks. Though natural forces sometimes expose fossils and sites, human physical and cultural remains are more often accidentally discovered in the course of some other human activity

such as construction. So frequently do construction projects uncover archaeological remains that in many countries, including the United States, construction projects require government approval in order to ensure the identification and protection of archaeological remains. Archaeological work known as cultural resource management (see Chapter 1) is now routinely carried out as part of the environmental review process for federally funded or licensed construction projects in the United States as it is in Europe.

Excavation

Once an investigator identifies a site likely to contribute to the research agenda, the next step is to plan and carry out excavation. To begin, the land is cleared, and the places to be excavated are plotted as a **grid system.** The surface of the site is divided into squares of equal size, and each square is numbered and marked with stakes. Each object found may then be located precisely in the square from which it came. (Remember, context is everything!) The starting point of a grid system may be a large rock, the edge of a stone wall, or an iron rod sunk into the ground. The starting point, one located precisely in three dimensions, is also known as the reference or **datum point.** At a large site covering several square miles, the plotting may be done in terms of

soil marks Stains that show up on the surface of recently plowed fields that reveal an archaeological site.

middens A refuse or garbage disposal area in an archaeological site.

grid system A system for recording data in three dimensions from an archaeological excavation.

datum point The starting, or reference, point for a grid system.

To recover very small objects easily missed in excavation, archaeologists routinely process the earth they remove.

individual structures, numbered according to the square of a "giant grid" in which they are found. In a gridded site, each square is dug separately with great care. Trowels are used to scrape the soil, and screens are used to sift all the loose soils so that even the smallest artifacts, such as flint chips or beads, are recovered.

A technique employed when looking for very fine objects, such as fish scales or very small bones, is called **flotation.** Flotation consists of immersing soil in water, causing the particles to separate. Some will float, others will sink to the bottom, and the remains can be easily retrieved. If the site is **stratified**—that is, if the remains lie in layers one upon the other—each layer, or stratum, will be dug separately. Each layer, having been laid down during a particular span of time, will contain artifacts deposited at the same time and belonging to the same culture. Culture change can be traced through the order in which artifacts were deposited—deeper layers reveal older artifacts. But, archaeologists Frank Hole and Robert F. Heizer suggest,

> because of difficulties in analyzing stratigraphy, archaeologists must use the greatest caution in drawing conclusions. Almost all interpretations of time, space, and culture contexts depend on stratigraphy. The refinements of lab-

flotation An archeological technique employed to recover very tiny objects by immersion of soil samples in water to separate heavy from light particles.

stratified Layered; said of archaeological sites where the remains lie in layers, one upon another.

oratory techniques for analysis are wasted if archaeologists cannot specify the stratigraphic position of their artifacts.[2]

If no stratification is present, then the archaeologist digs by arbitrary levels. Each square must be dug so that its edges and profiles are straight; walls between squares are often left standing to serve as visual correlates of the grid system.

Excavation of Fossils

Although fossil excavating is similar to archaeological excavation, some key differences exist. The paleoanthropologist must be particularly skilled in the techniques of geology, or have ready access to geological expertise, because a fossil is of little value unless its place in the sequence of rocks that contain it can be determined. In order to provide all the necessary expertise, paleoanthropological expeditions these days generally are made up of teams of experts in various fields in addition to physical anthropology. Surgical skill and caution are required to remove a fossil from its burial place without damage. An unusual combination of tools and materials is usually contained in the kit of the paleoanthropologist—pickaxes, enamel coating, burlap for bandages, and sculpting plaster.

To remove newly discovered bones, the paleoanthropologist begins uncovering the specimen, using

---

[2]Hole, F., & Heizer, R. F. (1969). *An introduction to prehistoric archeology* (p. 113). New York: Holt, Rinehart & Winston.

This photo shows a section excavated through a building at the ancient Maya site of Tikal and illustrates stratigraphy. Inside the building's base are the remains of walls and floors for earlier buildings. Oldest are the innermost and deepest walls and floors. As time wore on, the Maya periodically demolished upper portions of older buildings, the remains of which were buried beneath new construction.

©William A. Haviland

pick and shovel for initial excavation, then small camel-hair brushes and dental picks to remove loose and easily detachable debris surrounding the bones. Once the entire specimen has been uncovered (a process that may take days of back-breaking, patient labor), the bones are covered with shellac and tissue paper to prevent cracking and damage during further excavation and handling.

Both the fossil and the earth immediately surrounding it, or the matrix, are prepared for removal as a single block. The bones and matrix are cut out of the earth (but not removed), and more shellac is applied to the entire block to harden it. The bones are covered with burlap bandages dipped in plaster. Then the entire block is enclosed in more plaster and burlap bandages, perhaps splinted with tree branches, and allowed to dry overnight. After it has hardened, the entire block is carefully removed from the earth, ready for packing and transport to a laboratory. Before leaving the discovery area, the investigator makes a thorough sketch map of the terrain and pinpoints the find on geological maps to aid future investigators.

State of Preservation of Archaeological and Fossil Evidence

The results of excavation depend upon the nature of the remains as much as upon the excavator's digging skills. Inorganic materials such as stone and metal are more resistant to decay than organic ones such as wood and bone. Sometimes the anthropologist discovers an assemblage—a collection of artifacts—made of durable inorganic materials, such as stone tools, and traces of organic ones long since decomposed, such as woodwork (Figure 4.1), textiles, or food.

Climate, local geological conditions, and cultural practices also play a role in the state of preservation. For example, our knowledge of ancient Egyptian culture stems not only from their burial practices but from the effects of climate and soil on the state of preservation. The ancient Egyptians believed that eternal life could be achieved only if the dead person were buried with his or her worldly possessions. Hence, their tombs are usually filled with a wealth of artifacts even including the skele-

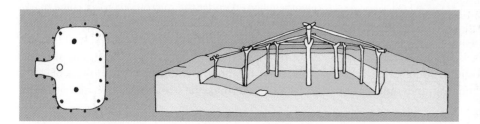

Figure 4.1
Although the wooden posts of a house may have long since decayed, their positions may still be marked by discoloration of the soil. The plan shown on the left, of an ancient posthole pattern and depression at Snaketown, Arizona, permits the hypothetical house reconstruction on the right.

tons of other humans owned by dynastic rulers. Under favorable climatic conditions, even the most perishable objects may survive over vast periods of time. Even the earliest Egyptian burials consisting of shallow pits in the sand often yield well-preserved corpses. Because these bodies were buried long before mummification was ever practiced, their preservation can only be the result of rapid desiccation, or complete drying out, in the warm desert climate. The elaborate tombs of the rulers of dynastic Egypt often contain wooden furniture, textiles, flowers, and written scrolls on paper made from papyrus reeds, barely touched by time, seemingly as fresh-looking as they were when deposited in the tomb as much as 5,000 years ago—a consequence of the region's arid climatic conditions. Of course, the ancient Egyptian burial practices selectively preserved more information about the elite members of society than the average individual.

The dryness of certain caves is also a factor in the preservation of **coprolites,** the scientific term for fossilized human or animal feces. Coprolites provide information on prehistoric diet and health. From the analysis of elements preserved in coprolites such as seeds, insect skeletons, and tiny bones from fish or amphibians, archaeologists and paleoanthropologists can directly determine what the inhabitants ate. This information, in turn, can shed light on overall health. Because many sources of food are available only in certain seasons, it is even possible to tell the time of year in which the food was eaten.

Certain climates can obliterate all evidence of organic remains. Maya ruins found in the tropical rainforests of Mesoamerica (the geographical area including southern Mexico and northern Central America) are often in a state of collapse—notwithstanding that many are massive structures of stone—as a result of the pressure exerted upon them by the heavy forest vegetation. The rain and humidity soon destroy almost all traces of woodwork, textiles, or basketry. Fortunately, impressions of these artifacts can sometimes be preserved in plaster, and some objects made of wood or plant fibers are depicted in stone carvings and pottery figurines. Thus, even in the face of substantial decay of organic substances, something may still be learned about them.

SORTING OUT THE EVIDENCE

Excavation records include a scale map of all the features, the stratification of each excavated square, a description of the exact location and depth of every artifact or bone unearthed, and photographs and scale

At the Maya site of Tikal, these manikin scepter figures originally made of wood were recovered from a king's tomb by pouring plaster into a cavity in the soil, left when the original organic material decayed.

©University of Pennsylvania Museum, Philadelphia 1967

drawings of the objects. This is the only way archaeological evidence can later be pieced together so as to arrive at a plausible reconstruction of a culture. Although the archaeologist or paleoanthropologist may be interested only in certain kinds of remains, every aspect of the site must be recorded, whether it is relevant to the particular investigation or not, because such evidence may be useful to others and would otherwise be permanently lost. In sum, archaeological sites are nonrenewable resources. The disturbance of the arrangement of artifacts, even by proper excavation, is permanent.

Looting of sites for personal profit can also cause permanent loss not only of artifacts but of the sites that held them. Looting has long been a threat to the archaeological record. But today, looting has become a high-tech endeavor. Avid collectors and fans of archaeological sites unwittingly aid looting activity through sharing detailed knowledge about site and artifact location over the Internet. The Internet has also provided a market for artifacts.

Once the artifact or fossil has been freed from the surrounding matrix, a variety of other laboratory methods come into play. For example, dental specimens are frequently analyzed under the microscope to examine markings on teeth that might provide clues about diet in the past. Specimens are now regularly scanned using computed tomography (CT scans) to analyze structural details of the bone. Imprints or **endocasts** of the insides of skulls are taken to determine the size and shape of ancient brains.

---

coprolites Preserved fecal material providing evidence of the diet and health of past organisms.

endocast A cast of the inside of a skull; helps determine the size and shape of the brain.

Though these 160,000-year-old fossil specimens of two adults and one child were first unearthed in Ethiopia in 1997, their discovery was not announced until 2003. Scientists completed the excavation, reconstructed, and analyzed the remains in the laboratory during the interim.

©2001 David L. Brill\Brill Atlanta

The genetics revolution has carried over even to ancient human remains. Anthropologists extract genetic material from skeletal remains in order to perform DNA comparisons between the specimen, other fossils, and living people. Small fragments of DNA are amplified or copied repeatedly using **polymerase chain reaction (PCR)** technology to provide a sufficient amount of material to perform these analyses. However, unless DNA is preserved in a stable material such as amber, it will decay over time. Therefore, analyses of DNA extracted from specimens older than about 50,000 years ago become increasingly unreliable due to the decay of DNA. Archaeologists and paleoanthropologists, as a rule of thumb, plan on at least 3 hours of laboratory work for each hour of fieldwork. In the lab, artifacts that have been recovered must first be cleaned and catalogued—often a tedious and time-consuming job—before they are ready for analysis.

Bioarchaeology, which seeks to understand past cultures through analysis of skeletal remains, is a growing area within anthropology. It combines the biological anthropologists' expertise in skeletal biology with the archaeological reconstruction of human cultures. Analysis of human skeletal material provides important insights into ancient peoples' diets, gender roles, social status, and patterns of activity. For example, analysis of human skeletons showed that elite members of society had access to better diets than lower ranking members of society, allowing them to reach their full growth potential. Gender roles in a given society can be assessed through skeletons as well. In fully preserved adult skeletons, the sex of the deceased individual can be assessed with a high accuracy, allowing for comparisons of male and female life expectancy, mortality, and health status. These analyses can help establish the social roles of men and women in past societies.

Recently, skeletal analyses have become more difficult to carry out, especially in the United States, where Native American communities now often request the return of skeletons from archaeological excavations for reburial as required by federal law. Anthropologists find themselves in a quandary over this requirement: As scientists, anthropologists know the importance of the information that can be gleaned from studies of human skeletons, but as scholars subject to ethical principles, they are bound to respect the feelings of those whose ancestors those skeletons represent. New techniques, such as 3D digital images of Native American skeletons, help to resolve this conflict as they allow for both rapid repatriation and continued study of skeletal remains. This chapter's Original Study provides an excellent example of archaeologists consulting with representatives of Native American communities to work out procedures agreeable to both parties. By contrast, scientists and American Indians have been unable to move beyond their conflicting views as seen with "Kennewick Man," the 9,300–year-old skeleton that was dislodged by the Columbia River in Washington State in 1996. This chapter's Biocultural Connection focuses on how this controversy is playing out in the federal courts.

polymerase chain reaction (PCR) A technique for amplifying or creating multiple copies of fragments of DNA so that it can be studied in the laboratory.

bioarchaeology The archaeological study of human remains emphasizing the preservation of cultural and social processes in the skeleton.

Biocultural Connection

Kennewick Man

"The Ancient One," or the "Kennewick Man," both refer to the 9,300-year-old skeletal remains that were found in 1996 below the surface of Lake Wallula, part of the Columbia River, in Kennewick, Washington State. This discovery has been the center of continuing controversy since it was made: Who owns these human remains? Who can determine what shall be done with them? Do the biological characteristics preserved in these remains play a role in determining their fate?

This particular conflict involves three major parties. Because the skeleton was found on a location for which the United States Army Corps of Engineers is responsible, this federal agency first took possession of the remains. Appealing to a new federal law, the Native American Graves Protection and Repatriation Act of 1990, a nearby American Indian group named the Confederated Tribes of the Umatilla Indian Reservation (representing the region's Umatilla, Cayuse, and Walla Walla nations) claimed the remains. Because Kennewick Man was found within their ancestral homeland, they argue that they are "culturally affil-

iated" with the individual they refer to as "The Ancient One." Viewing these human bones as belonging to an ancestor, they wish to return them to the earth in a respectful ceremony.

This claim was challenged in federal court by a group of scientists, including some archaeologists and biological anthropologists. They view these human remains, among the oldest ever discovered in the Western hemisphere, as scientifically precious, with potential to shed light on the earliest population movements in the Americas. The scientists do not want to "own" the remains but want the opportunity to study them. By means of DNA analysis, for instance, these scientists expect to determine possible prehistoric linkages between this individual and ancient human remains found elsewhere, including Asia. Moreover, scientific analysis may determine whether there actually exists any biological connection between these remains and currently living Native peoples, including individuals residing on the Umatilla Indian Reservation. Fearing the loss of a unique scientific specimen, they have filed a lawsuit in federal court to prevent rebur-

ial before these bones are researched and analyzed. Their legal challenge is not based on "cultural affiliation," which is a very difficult concept when it concerns such ancient human remains, but focuses on the fact that the region's Native peoples cannot prove they are direct lineal descendants. Unless such ties have been objectively established, they argue, Kennewick Man should be released for scientific study.

In 2004 federal court rulings allowed for initial scientific investigations. Just as these investigations were wrapping up in July 2005, the Senate Indian Affairs Committee heard testimony on a proposal by Arizona Senator John McCain to expand the Native American Graves Protection and Repatriation Act so that remains such as these would once again be unavailable for study. In the meantime, Doug Owsley, the forensic anthropologist from the Smithsonian Institution who is leading the research team has said that scientific investigation is yielding even more information than expected.

Because conflicting world views are at the center of this controversy, it is unlikely that it will be easily resolved. ■ ■ ■

DATING THE PAST

With accurate and detailed records of their excavations in hand, archaeologists and paleoanthropologists are able to deal with a crucial research issue: the question of age. As we have seen, analysis of physical and cultural remains is dependent on knowledge about the age of the artifacts or specimens. How, then, are the materials retrieved from excavations reliably dated? Calculating the age of physical and cultural remains is an important aspect of interpreting the past. Because archaeologists and paleoanthropologists deal so often with peoples and events in times far removed from our own, the calendar of historic times is of little use to them.

Remains can be dated by noting their position in the earth, by measuring the amount of chemicals contained in fossil bones, or through association with other plant, animal, or cultural remains. These methods are known as **relative dating** techniques because they do not establish precise dates for remains but rather the relationship among a series of remains. **Absolute dating** or **chronometric dat-**

ing (from the Latin for "measuring time") methods provide actual dates calculated in years "before the present" (BP). These methods rely upon advances in the disciplines of chemistry and physics that use properties such as rates of decay of radioactive elements. These elements may be present in the remains themselves or in the surrounding soil. Absolute dating methods scientifically establish actual dates for the major events of geological and evolutionary history. By comparing dates and remains across a variety of sites, anthropologists can reconstruct human origins, migrations, and technological developments.

Many relative and chronometric techniques are available. However, most of these techniques are applicable only for certain time spans and in certain environmental

relative dating In archaeology and paleoanthropology, designating an event, object, or fossil as being older or younger than another.

absolute or chronometric dating In archaeology and paleoanthropology, dates for archaeological materials based on solar years, centuries, or other units of absolute time.

contexts. Bear in mind also, that each of the chronometric dating techniques also has a margin of error. Ideally, archaeologists and paleoanthropologists try to utilize as many methods as are appropriate, given the materials available and the funds at their disposal. By doing so, they significantly reduce the risk of error. Several of the most frequently employed dating techniques are presented in Table 4.1.

TABLE 4.1	ABSOLUTE AND RELATIVE DATING METHODS USED BY ARCHAEOLOGISTS AND PALEOANTHROPOLOGISTS		
Dating Method	**Time Period**	**Method's Process**	**Drawbacks**
Stratigraphy	Relative only	Based on the law of superposition, which states that lower layers or strata are older than a higher stratum	Site specific; natural forces, such as earthquakes, and human activity, such as burials, disturb stratigraphic relationships
Fluorine analysis	Relative only	Compares the amount of fluorine from surrounding soil absorbed by specimens after deposition	Site specific
Faunal and floral series	Relative only	Sequencing remains into relative chronological order based on an evolutionary sequence established in another region with reliable absolute dates; called palynology when done with pollen grains	Dependent upon known relationships established elsewhere
Seriation	Relative only	Sequencing cultural remains into relative chronological order based on stylistic features	Dependent upon known relationships established elsewhere
Dendrochronology	About 3,000 years before present (BP) maximum	Compares tree growth rings preserved in a site with a tree of known age	Requires ancient trees of known age
Radiocarbon	Accurate < 50,000 BP	Compares the ratio of radioactive ^{14}C (with a half-life of 5,730 years) to stable ^{12}C in organic material	Increasingly inaccurate when assessing remains from greater than 50,000 years ago
Potassium argon (K-Ar)	> 200,000 BP	Compares the amount of radioactive potassium (^{40}K with a half-life of 1.25 billion years) to stable argon (^{40}Ar)	Requires volcanic ash; requires cross-checking due to contamination from atmospheric argon
Amino acid racemization	40,000–180,000 BP	Compares the change in the number of proteins in a right- vs. left-sided three-dimensional structure	Amino acids leached out from soil invariably cause error
Thermoluminescence	Possibly up to 200,000 BP	Measures the amount of light given off due to radioactivity when sample is heated to high temperatures	Technique developed for recent materials such as Greek pottery; not clear how accurate the dates will be for older remains
Electron spin resonance	Possibly up to about 200,000 BP	Measures the resonance of trapped electrons in a magnetic field	Works with tooth enamel, not yet developed for bone; problems with accuracy
Fission track	Wide range of times	Measures the tracks left in crystals by uranium as it decays; good cross-check for K-Ar technique	Useful for dating crystals only
Paleomagnetic reversals	Wide range of times	Measures orientation of magnetic particles in stones and links them to whether magnetic field of earth pulled toward the north or south during their formation	Large periods of normal or reversed magnetic orientation require dating by some other method; smaller events are known to interrupt the sequence
Uranium series	40,000–180,000	Measures the amount of uranium decaying in cave sites	Large error range

Establishment of dates for human physical and cultural remains is a vital part of understanding our past. For example, as paleoanthropologists reconstruct human evolutionary history and the movement of the genus *Homo* out of Africa, dates determine the story told by the bones. In the next chapter we will see that many of the theories about human origins are dependent upon dates. Similarly, as archaeologists dig up material culture, interpretations of the movement and interactions of past peoples depend on dating methods providing a sequence to the cultural remains.

Chance and the Study of the Past

The archaeological and fossil records are imperfect. Chance circumstances of preservation have determined what has and what has not survived the ravages of time. Thus, the biology and culture of our ancestors are reconstructed on the basis of incomplete and, possibly, unrepresentative samples of physical and cultural remains. The problems are further compounded by the role that chance continues to play in the discovery of prehistoric remains. Remains may come to light due to factors ranging from changing sea level, vegetation, or even a local government's decision to build a highway. In addition, past cultural processes have also shaped the archaeological and fossil record. We know more about the past due to the cultural practice of deliberate burial. We know more about the elite segments of past societies because they have left more material culture behind. However, as archaeologists have shifted their focus from gathering treasures to the reconstruction of human behavior, they now reconstruct a more complete picture of past societies. Similarly, paleoanthropologists no longer simply catalogue fossils; they interpret data about our ancestors in order to reconstruct the biological processes responsible for who we are today. The challenge of reconstructing our past will be met by a continual process of re-examination and modification as anthropologists discover new evidence in the earth, among living people, and in the laboratory leading to new understanding of human origins and past cultures.

Chapter Summary

■ Archaeology and physical anthropology are the two branches of anthropology most involved in the study of the human past. Archaeologists study material physical and ecological remains to describe and explain past human cultures; physical anthropologists called paleoanthropologists study fossil remains to understand the processes at work in human biological evolution. Each specialty contributes to the other's objectives, as well as its own, and the two share many methods of data recovery.

■ Artifacts are objects fashioned or altered by humans, such as a flint chip, a pottery vessel, or even a house. A fossil is any trace of an organism of past geological time that has been preserved in the earth's crust. Fossilization typically involves the hard parts of an organism and may involve preservation in bogs or tar pits, immersion in water, or inclusion in rock deposits. Fossilization is most apt to occur among animals and other organisms that live in or near water because of the likelihood that their corpses will be buried and preserved on sea, lake, and river bottoms. On land, conditions in caves or near active volcanic activity may be conducive to fossilization.

■ Material culture likely existed earlier than indicated by the archaeological record. The cultural practice of burial of the dead improved the fossil record. Sometimes both fossils and archaeological remains are discovered accidentally, for example, in plowing, quarrying, or in building construction; physical and cultural remains are not always found together.

■ Irregularities of the ground surface, unusual soil discoloration, and unexpected variations in vegetation type and coloring may indicate the location of a site. Maps, documents, and folklore may also provide further clues to the location of archaeological sites.

■ Once a site or locality has been selected for excavation, the area is divided and carefully marked with a grid system; the starting point of the dig is called the datum point. Each square within the grid is carefully excavated, and any archaeological or fossil remains are recovered through employment of various tools and screens; for very fine objects, the method of flotation is employed. The location of each artifact must be carefully noted. Once excavated, artifacts and fossils undergo further cleaning and preservation in the laboratory with the use of specialized tools and chemicals.

■ The durability of archaeological evidence depends upon climate and the nature of the artifacts. Inorganic materials are more resistant to decay than organic ones. However, given a very dry climate, even organic materials may be well preserved. Warm, moist climates as well as thick vegetation act to decompose organic material quickly, and even inorganic material may suffer from the effects of humidity and vegetation growth. The durability of archaeological evidence is also dependent upon the social customs of ancient people.

■ Because excavation in fact destroys a site, the archaeologist must maintain a thorough record in the form of maps, descriptions, scale drawings, and photographs of every aspect of the excavation. All artifacts must be cleaned and classified before being sent to the laboratory for analysis. Often the shape and markings of artifacts can determine their function, and the analysis of vegetable and animal remains may provide information.

■ There are two general approaches to dating archaeological and fossil remains. Relative dating methods determine the age of objects relative to one another. Absolute or chronometric dating methods rely on advances in the disciplines of chemistry and physics that use properties such as rates of decay of radioactive elements. Due to the margin of error present with many dating methods, archaeologists and paleoanthropologists combine several methods of dating to estimate the age of physical and cultural remains.

Questions for Reflection

1. While a scientific understanding of the past can contribute to solving challenges humans face today, the global community must first decide who owns the past. Do ancient remains belong to scientists, to people connected to the remains, or to whoever happens to have possession of the remains? For the common good of humanity, how can this question be resolved? What is the role of local and global values, markets, and politics in scientific study of the past?

2. The cultural practice of burial of the dead altered the fossil record and provided valuable insight into the beliefs and practices of past cultures. The same is true today. What beliefs are reflected in the traditions for treatment of the dead in your culture?

3. Controversy has surrounded Kennewick Man since this skeleton eroded from the banks of the Columbia River in Washington State in 1996. Scientists and Native American people both feel they have a right to these remains. What kinds of evidence support these differing perspectives? How should this controversy be resolved?

4. Why is dating so important for paleoanthropologists and archaeologists? Would an interpretation of physical or cultural remains change depending upon the date assigned to the remains?

5. How have random events as well as deliberate cultural practices shaped both the fossil and archaeological records? Why do we know more about some places and peoples than others?

Key Terms

prehistory	stratified
artifact	coprolites
material culture	endocast
fossil	polymerase chain reaction (PCR)
soil marks	
middens	bioarchaeology
grid system	relative dating
datum point	absolute or chronometric dating
flotation	

Multimedia Review Tools

Make the Grade in Anthropology with ThomsonNOW

Thomson NOW! This powerful online study tool provides you with a *personalized study plan* based on your responses to a diagnostic pretest. Once you have mastered the material with the help of interactive learning tools, an integrated e-book, and more, you can take a post-test to confirm you are ready to move on to the next chapter. To get started with ThomsonNOW, check the card packaged with your book for the access code. Then go to http://www.thomsonedu.com to create an account through 1pass™. If there is no card in your book, go to http://www.thomsonedu.com to purchase an access code.

Companion Website and Anthropology Resource Center

Go to http://anthropology.wadsworth.com to reach the companion website for your text. This offers many study aids, including self quizzes for each chapter and a practice final exam, as well as links to anthropology websites and information on the latest theories and discoveries in the field.

Also, check out the Anthropology Resource Center for a wealth of learning materials that include interactive maps, video exercises, simulations, and breaking news in anthropology. Be sure to explore InfoTrac College Edition®, your online library that offers full-length articles from thousands of scholarly and popular publications. To reach the Anthropology Resource Center and InfoTrac College Edition, check the card packaged with your book for the access code. Then go to http://www.thomsonedu.com to create an account through 1pass™. If there is no card in your book, go to http://www.thomsonedu.com to purchase an access code.

© AP/WideWorld Photos

CHALLENGE ISSUE

Over the past 5 million years, humans evolved from a small-brained African ape species able to walk on two legs to a species with complex culture inhabiting the entire globe. As humans came to rely on culture to meet the challenges of survival, they left behind spectacular evidence of their creativity and knowledge, such as these images of bison, panthers, and rhinoceroses painted 32,000 years ago in the Chauvet cave in France. These ancient paintings reflect a fundamental need to communicate, to record and share observations. Yet the ability to make these ancient paintings, like contemporary expressions of culture, is rooted in the biology of the human hand, eye, and brain.

Human Evolution

As well as being scholars, anthropologists attempting to piece together the puzzle of human evolution must be detectives, publicists, and creative thinkers, for the available evidence is often scant or full of misleading and even contradictory clues. The quest for the origins of humans from more ancient species has elements of a detective story; it involves mysteries concerning the emergence of humanity, none of which have been completely resolved to this day. These unanswered questions include, Which ancestors were the first to walk on two legs? Which were the first with human-sized brains? Who were the first to use tools, the first to use fire, the first to actually use sounds to produce what we call language?

Because each new discovery contributes to resolving the puzzle of human evolution, the order of discovery is important. Each new fossil, stone tool, painted cave wall, or laboratory result has the potential to reconfigure our understanding of human evolutionary history. Although all discoveries impact evolutionary studies, the role of culture in human evolution makes unraveling our past particularly complex.

Differences in the rates of biological and culture change account for some of the complications and debates relating to human evolutionary history. Cultural equipment and techniques can change rapidly with innovations occurring during the lifetime of individuals. By contrast, because it depends upon heritable traits, biological change requires many generations. Paleoanthropologists try to decipher whether an evident culture change in the past corresponds to a major biological change, such as the appearance of a new species. The biological evidence for new species often consists of small changes in the shape or size of the skull. When we take into account the variation present today within the species *Homo sapiens*, we can see why reconciling the relation between differences in skulls and culture change is often a source of debate within paleoanthropology.

U.S. anthropologist Misia Landau has noted that human evolutionary history follows the narrative form of a heroic epic because of the role culture plays in human evolution. The hero, or evolving human, is faced with a series of natural challenges that cannot be overcome from a strictly biological standpoint. Endowed with the gift of intelligence, the hero can meet these challenges and become fully human. In this narrative culture separates humans from other evolving animals. Tracing the major events in human evolution through the millions of years that led up to today may unintentionally imply a notion of progress. While it is true that the evolution of culture was critical to our becoming the kind of species we are today, we must bear in mind that many other species have followed their own evolutionary course, progressing through time in their own directions. We continue to share this planet with some of them, while others who were biologically successful for a time, surviving for millions of years, have since gone extinct.

MACROEVOLUTION AND THE PROCESS OF SPECIATION

While microevolution refers to changes in the allele frequencies of populations, **macroevolution** focuses upon the formation of new species (**speciation**) and on the evolutionary relationships between groups of species. The term *species* is usually defined as a population or group of populations that is capable of interbreeding and producing viable, fertile offspring. In other words, species are reproductively isolated. The bullfrogs in a farmer's pond are the same species as those in a neighboring pond, even though the two populations may never actually interbreed; in theory, they are capable of doing so if they are brought together. This definition, however, is not altogether satisfactory because isolated populations may be in the process of evolving into different species, and it is hard to tell exactly when they become biologically distinct. The microevolutionary forces of mutation, gene flow, genetic drift, and natural selection can lead to macroevolutionary change as species diverge.

Certain factors, known as isolating mechanisms, can separate breeding populations and lead to the appearance of new species. Because isolation prevents

gene flow, changes that affect the gene pool of one population cannot be introduced into the gene pool of the other. Random mutation may introduce new alleles in one of the isolated populations but not in the other. Genetic drift and natural selection may affect the two populations in different ways. Over time, as the two populations come to differ from each other, speciation occurs in a branching fashion known as **cladogenesis**. Speciation can also occur without branching, as a single population accumulates sufficient new mutations over time to be considered a separate species. This process is known as **anagenesis**. Speciation is inferred in the fossil record when a group of organisms takes on a different appearance over time.

Because speciation is a process, it can occur at various rates. Speciation through the process of adaptive change to the environment as proposed in Darwin's *Origin of Species* is generally considered to occur at a slow rate. In this model, speciation may occur as organisms become more adapted to their environments. Sometimes, however, speciation can occur quite rapidly. For example, a genetic mutation such as one involving a key regulatory gene can lead to the formation of a new body plan. Such genetic accidents may involve material that is broken off, transposed, or transferred from one chromosome to another. Genes that regulate the growth and development of an organism may have a major effect on its adult form. Scientists have discovered certain key genes called *homeobox genes* that are responsible for large-scale effects on the growth and development of the organism. If a new body plan happens to be adaptive, natural selection will maintain this new form during long periods of time rather than promoting change.

Paleontologists Stephen Jay Gould and Niles Eldred proposed that speciation occurs in a pattern of **punctuated equilibria** or the alternation between periods of rapid speciation and times of stability. Often, this conception of evolutionary change is contrasted with speciation through adaptation sometimes referred to as *Darwinian gradualism*. A close look at the genetics and the fossil record indicates that both models of evolutionary change are important.

It may be difficult to determine whether variation preserved in the fossil record presents evidence of

macroevolution Evolution above the species level.
speciation The process of forming new species.

cladogenesis Speciation through a branching mechanism whereby an ancestral population gives rise to two or more descendant populations.
anagenesis A sustained directional shift in a population's average characteristics.
punctuated equilibria A model of macroevolutionary change that suggests evolution occurs via long periods of stability or stasis punctuated by periods of rapid change.

© Oliver Meckes/Photo Researchers

Sometimes mutations in a single gene can cause reorganization of an organism's body plan. Here the "antennepedia" homeobox gene has caused legs to develop in the place of antennae on the heads of fruit flies.

separate species. How can we tell whether two sets of fossilized bones represent species that were capable of interbreeding and producing viable offspring? To approximate an answer to this question, paleoanthropologists use as many sources of data as possible to check the proposed evolutionary relationships. Paleoanthropologists use genetic and biochemical data, along with observations about the biology and behavior of living groups, to support theories about speciation in the past. Thus, reconstructing evolutionary relationships draws on much more than bones alone. Even with this rich array of scientific knowledge to draw upon, prevailing beliefs and biases can also impact the interpretation of fossil finds. Fortunately the self-correcting nature of scientific investigation allows evolutionary lineages to be redrawn in light of all new discoveries.

MAMMALIAN PRIMATE EVOLUTION

Humans have a long evolutionary history as mammals and primates that set the stage for the cultural beings we are today. Evidence from ancient skeletons indicates the first mammals appeared over 200 million years ago as small nocturnal creatures.

In the time since the appearance of the first mammals, the earth itself has changed considerably. During the past 200 million years, the position of the continents has changed through a process called **continental drift.** This process accounts for the re-arrangement of the adjacent land masses through the theory of plate tectonics (Figure 5.1). According to this theory, the continents, embedded in platelike segments of the earth, move their positions as the edges of the underlying plates are created or destroyed. Plate movements are also responsible for geological phenomena such as earthquakes, volcanic activity, and mountain formation. Continental drift is important for understanding the distribution of fossil primate groups whose history we will now explore. The shifting orientation of the earth's continents is also responsible for the climatic changes in the environment that affected the course of evolution for primates and other living things.

The earliest primatelike mammals came into being about 65 million years ago when a new, mild climate favored the spread of dense tropical and subtropical forests over much of the earth. The change in climate and habitat, combined with the sudden extinction of dinosaurs, favored mammal diversification, including the evolutionary development of arboreal mammals from which primates evolved. Fossil evidence indicates that the earliest primates began to develop around 65 million years ago, when the mass extinction of the dinosaurs opened new ecological niches for mammals. By 60 million years ago, primates inhabited North America and Eurasia (Europe and Asia), which at that time were joined together as the "supercontinent" Laurasia and separated from Africa. The earliest primates were small nocturnal insect eaters adapted to life in the trees.

By about 40 million years ago, diurnal anthropoid primates appeared, and fossil evidence indicates that Old World and New World species had separated by about this time. Many of the Old World anthropoid species became ground dwellers. By about 23 million years ago, at the start of the geological epoch known as the Miocene (Figure 5.2), the first fossil apes or hominoids began to appear in Asia, Africa, and Europe; hominoids are the broad-shouldered tailless primates that include all living and extinct apes and humans. The word *hominoid* comes from the Latin roots *Homo* and *Homin* (meaning "human being") and the suffix *oïdes* ("resembling"). As a group, hominoids get their name from their resemblance to humans. While some of these ancient primates were relatively small, others were larger than present-day gorillas.

continental drift According to the theory of plate tectonics, the movement of continents embedded in underlying plates on the earth's surface in relation to one another over the history of life on earth.

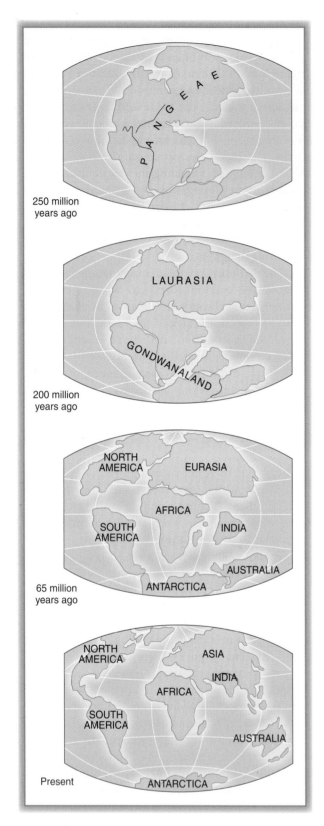

Figure 5.1
Continental drift is illustrated by the position of the continents during several geological periods. At the time of the extinction of the dinosaurs, 65 million years ago, the seas opened up by continental drift, creating isolating barriers between major land masses. About 23 million years ago, at the start of the geologic time period known as the Miocene epoch, African and Eurasian land masses reconnected.

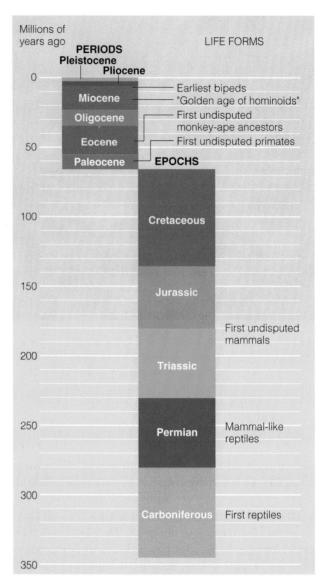

Figure 5.2
This timeline highlights the major milestones in the course of mammalian primate evolution that ultimately led to humans and their ancestors.

It was also during the Miocene that the African and Eurasian land masses made direct contact. For most of the preceding 100 million years, the Tethys Sea—a continuous body of water that joined what are now the Mediterranean and Black Seas to the Indian Ocean—barred migration between Africa and Eurasia. Connection of these land masses through what is now the Middle East allowed Old World primate groups such as African apes to expand their ranges into Eurasia. Miocene fossil remains of apes from this time period have been found from the caves of China, to the forests of France, to eastern Africa where the earliest fossil remains of bipeds have been found. So varied and ubiquitous were the fossil apes of this period that some primatologists have labeled the Miocene the "golden age of the hominoids."

HUMAN EVOLUTION

Humans and their ancestors are distinct among the hominoids for **bipedalism**—a special form of locomotion on two feet. Larger brains and bipedal locomotion constitute the most striking differences between contemporary humans and our closest primate relatives. Although we might like to think that it is our larger brains that make us special among fellow primates, it is now clear that bipedalism appeared at the beginning of the ancestral line leading to humans and played a pivotal role in setting us apart from the apes. Brain expansion came later.

In the past 30 years, genetic and biochemical studies have confirmed that the African apes—chimpanzees, bonobos, and gorillas—are our closest living relatives (Figure 5.3). By comparing genes and proteins among all the apes, scientists have estimated that gibbons, followed by orangutans, were the first to diverge from a very ancient common ancestral line. At some time between 8 and 5 million years ago, humans, chimpanzees, and gorillas began to follow separate evolutionary courses. Chimpanzees later diverged into two separate species: the common chimpanzee and the bonobo.

The First Bipeds

Between 15 and 5 million years ago, various kinds of hominoids lived throughout Africa and Eurasia. One of these apes living in Africa between 8 and 5 million years ago was a direct ancestor to the human line. Climatic change was characteristic of this time period and may have played a role in the success of bipedalism once it originated. In recent years spectacular discoveries have begun to fill in the fossil record from this critical time period, such as the 6-million-year-old *Orrorin*—meaning "original man"—fossils discovered in Kenya in 2001.[1] Also, a beautifully preserved 7- to 6-million-year-old skull nicknamed Toumai—meaning "hope for life"—was discovered in Chad, Central Africa, in 2002.[2]

For a hominoid fossil to be definitively classified as part of the human evolutionary line, certain evidence of bipedalism is required. Bipedalism is associated with anatomical changes literally from head to toe (Figure 5.4). Evidence of walking on two feet is preserved in the skull because balancing the skull above the spinal column in an upright posture requires a skull position relatively centered above the spinal column. The spinal

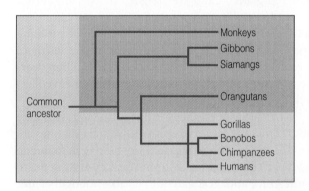

Figure 5.3
The relationship among monkeys, apes, and humans can be established by molecular similarities and differences. Although chimpanzees, gorillas, and orangutans physically resemble one another more than any of them resemble humans, molecular evidence indicates that humans are most closely related to the African ape species. Using a "molecular clock," scientists date the split between the human and African ape lines to between 8 and 5 million years ago. Over the past few years, several important fossil finds dating from between 7 to 5 million years ago have been discovered that support the molecular evidence.

> **bipedalism** A special form of locomotion on two feet found in humans and their ancestors.

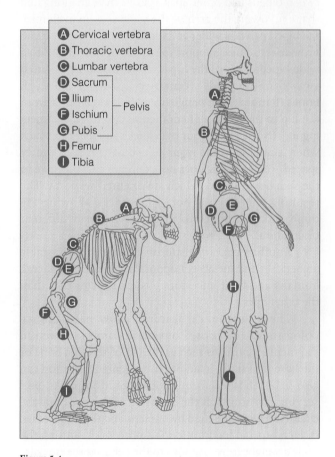

Figure 5.4
Changes in anatomy associated with bipedalism are evident in this comparison between a chimp and human skeleton.

[1]Senut, B., et al. (2001). First hominid from the Miocene (Lukeino formation, Kenya). *C. R. Academy of Science, Paris, 332*,137–144.
[2]Brunett, M., et al. (2002). A new hominid from the Upper Miocene of Chad, Central Africa. *Nature, 418,* 145–151.

cord leaves the skull at its base through an opening called the *foramen magnum* (Latin for "big opening"). In a knuckle-walker like a chimp, the foramen magnum is placed more toward the back of the skull while in a biped it is in a more forward position.

Extending down from the skull of a biped, the spinal column makes a series of convex and concave curves that together maintain the body in an upright posture by positioning the body's center of gravity above the legs rather than forward. The curves correspond to the neck (cervical), chest (thoracic), lower back (lumbar), and pelvic (sacral) regions of the spine, respectively. In a chimp, the shape of the spine follows a single arching curve. Interestingly, at birth the spines of human babies have a single arching curve as seen in adult apes. As they mature the curves characteristic of bipedalism appear, the cervical curve at about 3 months on average and the lumbar curve at around 12 months—a time when many babies begin to walk.

The shape of the pelvis also differs considerably between bipeds and other apes. Rather than an elongated shape following the arch of the spine as seen in chimps, the biped pelvis is wider and foreshortened so that it can provide structural support for the upright body. With a wide bipedal pelvis, the lower limbs would be oriented away from the body's center of gravity if the thigh bones (femora) didn't angle in toward each other from the hip to the knee, a phenomenon described as "knee-ing-in." (Notice how your own knees and feet can touch when standing while your hip joints remain widely spaced.) This angling does not continue past the knee to the shin bones (tibia), which are oriented vertically. The resulting knee joint is not symmetrical, allowing the thigh and shin bones to meet despite their different orientations.

Another characteristic of bipeds is their stable arched feet and the absent opposable big toe. In general, humans and their ancestors possess shorter toes than the other apes.

These anatomical features allow paleoanthropologists to "diagnose" bipedal locomotion even in fragmentary remains such as the top of the shin bone or the base of a skull. In addition, bipedal locomotion can also be established through fossilized footprints, preserving not so much the shape of foot bones but the characteristic stride used by humans and their ancestors. In fact, bipedal locomotion is a process of shifting the body's weight from one foot to the other as the nonsupporting foot swings forward.

The most dramatic confirmation of walking ability in early human ancestors comes from Laetoli, Tanzania, in East Africa, where 3.6 million years ago three individuals walked across newly fallen volcanic ash. Because it was damp, the ash took the impressions of their feet,

and these were sealed beneath subsequent ash falls until discovered in 1978. The shape of the footprints and the linear distance between each step are quite human.

All early bipeds are not necessarily direct ancestors to later humans. Consider, for example, fossils of the genus *Ardipithecus* (literally, "floor ape") that lived between 5.8 and 4.4 million years ago. Found in Ethiopia, East Africa, this genus was much smaller than a modern chimpanzee, but it was chimpanzeelike in other features, such as the shape and enamel thickness of its teeth. On the other hand, a partially complete skeleton of one *Ardipithecus* individual suggests that unlike chimpanzees, and like all other species in the human line, this creature was bipedal. Given the combination of bipedalism and chimpanzeelike characteristics, many paleoanthropologists consider it a side branch of the human evolutionary tree. Fossil evidence shows that over the next several million years, many bipedal species inhabited Africa—making it more accurate to refer to an evolutionary bush rather than a tree.

Australopithecines

Between 5 and 4 million years ago, the environment of eastern and southern Africa was a mosaic of open country with pockets of closed woodland. Scholars believe that some early bipeds inhabited some of the woodland pockets. Later human ancestors inhabited more open country known as *savannah*—grasslands with scattered trees and groves—and are assigned to one or another species of the genus **Australopithecus** (from Latin *australis,* meaning "southern," and Greek *pithekos,* meaning "ape"). Opinions vary on just how many species there were in Africa between about 4.3 and 1.1 million years ago. For our purposes, it suffices to refer to them collectively as "australopithecines."

The earliest definite australopithecine fossils date back 4.2 million years,[3] whereas the most recent ones are only about 1 million years old. They have been found up and down the length of eastern Africa from Ethiopia to South Africa and westward into Chad. Among the later australopithecines, a number of species had particularly large back teeth and correspondingly large muscles and bones associated with chewing. Collectively these species

Australopithecus The genus including several species of early bipeds from southern and eastern Africa living between about 4.3 and 1.1 million years ago, one of whom was directly ancestral to humans.

---

[3] Wolpoff, M. (1996). *Australopithecus:* A new look at an old ancestor. *General Anthropology, 3*(1), 2.

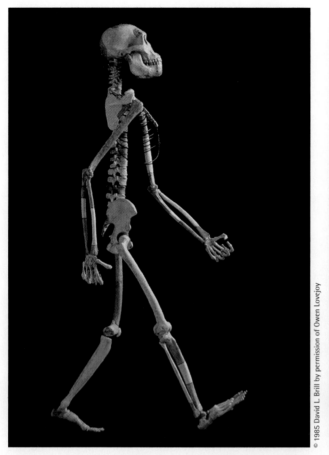

© 1985 David L Brill by permission of Owen Lovejoy

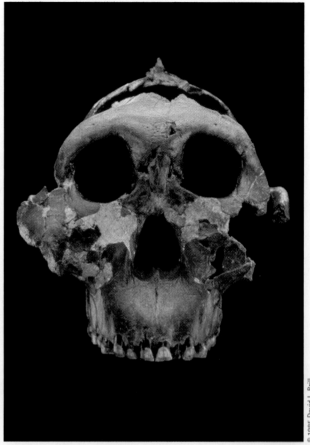

© 1985 David L Brill

A 40 percent complete skeleton, "Lucy" (named after the Beatles' song "Lucy in the Sky with Diamonds"—popular at the time of discovery) indicates that these australopithecine ancestors were bipedal. This adult female *Australopithecus* was only 3½ feet tall, typical of the small size of female australopithecines. By understanding the shapes of bones, paleoanthropologists have reconstructed an entire skeleton from the fragmentary remains that were discovered. (Note the darker color of the actual fossil remains, as opposed to the lighter reconstructed portions.)

Robust australopithecines had extremely large cheek teeth (molars) compared to the size of their front teeth. They also had large chewing muscles and a bony ridge on the top of their skulls for the attachment of those large muscles. If you place your own hands on the sides of your skull above your ears while opening and closing your jaw, you can feel where your chewing muscles attach to your skull. By moving your hands toward the top of your skull you can feel where these muscles end in humans.

are considered **robust australopithecines** because of the rugged nature of their chewing apparatus (large back teeth, large chewing muscles, and modifications on the skull for the insertion of these large muscles). The robust australopithecines inhabited both eastern and southern Africa until about 1 million years ago when they appear to have gone extinct. Based on their teeth and the chemicals preserved in their bones, the robust australopithecines appear to have had diets that included considerable vegetable matter. They are contrasted with

the **gracile australopithecines,** which possessed a more delicate chewing apparatus and were likely to have had a diet that included more meat. The proliferation of bipedal species indicates that this new mode of locomotion was very successful.

None of the australopithecines were as large as most modern humans, although all were much more muscular for their size. Males seem to have been significantly larger than females, with size differences between the sexes less than those found in living apes such as gorillas and orangutans but greater than those among living humans. Taking their relative body size into consideration, australopithecines possessed brains comparable to those of

robust australopithecines Several species within the genus *Australopithecus*, who lived from 2.5 and 1.1 million years ago in eastern and southern Africa; known for the rugged nature of their chewing apparatus (large back teeth, large chewing muscles, and bony ridge on their skull tops for the insertion of these large muscles).

gracile australopithecines Members of the genus *Australopithecus* possessing a more lightly built chewing apparatus; likely had a diet that included more meat than that of the robust australopithecines.

modern African apes. However, the shape of the jaw and some aspects of the teeth were more like those of modern humans than they were like those of apes.

Bipedalism is considered an important adaptive feature in the savannah environment for many reasons.[4] A biped could not run as fast as a quadruped but could keep up a steady pace over long distances in search of food and water without tiring. With free hands, a biped could take food to places where it could be eaten in relative safety and could carry infants rather than relying on the babies hanging on for themselves. As bipeds, australopithecines could use their hands to wield sticks or other objects in threat displays and to protect themselves against predators. (Other apes can do this but only for short bursts of time.) Also, erect posture is better suited for endurance running, as it exposes a smaller area of the body to the direct heat of the sun than a quadrupedal position, helping to prevent overheating on the open savannah. Furthermore, a biped with its head held high could see further, spotting food as well as predators from a distance.

Although adapted fully to bipedalism, curved toe bones and relatively long arms indicate australopithecines had not given up tree climbing altogether. One reason may be that sparsely distributed trees continued to be important places of refuge on the African savannah, a land teeming with dangerous predatory animals. Chimpanzees today build their night nests in trees, suggesting a habit that may have been part of the australopithecine pattern as well. In addition, trees provide rich sources of food such as fruits, seeds, and nuts. However, to survive in their savannah environment, early bipeds may have tried out supplementary sources of food on the ground, as they likely did around the time when the first members of the genus *Homo* appeared about 2.5 million years ago. In addition to plant foods, the major new source was animal protein. This was not protein from monkey meat obtained as a result of coordinated hunting parties like those of the chimpanzees and bonobos of today, but rather the fatty marrow and leftover edible flesh that remained in and on the bones of dead animals.

Homo habilis

Increased meat consumption by our early ancestors was important for human evolution. On the savannah, it is difficult for a primate with a humanlike digestive system to satisfy its protein requirements from available plant resources. Moreover, failure to do so has serious consequences: stunted growth, malnutrition, starvation, and death. Leaves and legumes (nitrogen-fixing plants, familiar modern examples being beans and peas) provide the

most readily accessible plant sources of protein. The problem is that these are hard for primates like us to digest unless they are cooked. The leaves and legumes available contain substances causing the proteins to pass right through the gut without being absorbed.

Chimpanzees have a similar problem today when out on the savannah. In this environment, they spend more than a third of their time going after insects like ants and termites while also searching for eggs and small vertebrate animals. Not only are such animal foods easily digestible, but they provide high-quality proteins that contain all the essential amino acids, the building blocks of protein, in just the right percentages. No single plant food does this by itself. Only the right combination of plants can supply the balance of amino acids provided by meat alone.

Our ancestors probably solved their dietary problems in much the same way that chimps on the savannah do today but with one key difference. For more efficient utilization of animal protein, our ancestors probably used sharp tools rather than daggerlike teeth for scavenging meat and later for butchering carcasses.

The earliest identifiable tools consist of a number of stone implements made by striking sharp-edged flakes from the surface of a stone core. In the process, cores were transformed into choppers. These flakes and choppers, first discovered in Olduvai Gorge in Tanzania, are

The oldest stone tools, dated to between 2.6 and 2.5 million years ago, were discovered in Gona, Ethiopia, by Ethiopian paleoanthropologist Sileshi Semaw.

© 1999 David L. Brill

---

[4]Lewin, R. (1987). Four legs bad, two legs good. *Science, 235,* 969.

known as implements in the **Oldowan** tool tradition. They mark the beginning of the **Lower Paleolithic,** or Old Stone Age, which lasted from about 2.5 million until approximately 250,000 or 200,000 years ago. The earliest tools of this sort, which were recently found in Ethiopia, are perhaps even 2.6 million years old.

Before this time, australopithecines probably used tools such as heavy sticks to dig up roots or ward off animals, unmodified stones to hurl as weapons or to crack open nuts and bones, and simple carrying devices made of hollow gourds or knotted plant fibers. These tools, however, are not traceable in the archaeological record.

Since the late 1960s, a number of sites in southern and eastern Africa have been discovered with fossil remains of a lightly built biped with a body all but indistinguishable from that of the earlier australopithecines, except that the teeth are smaller and the brain is significantly larger relative to body size. Furthermore, the inside of the skull shows a pattern in the left cerebral hemisphere that in contemporary humans is associated with language. While this does not prove that these bipeds used language, it suggests a marked advance in information-processing capacity over that of australopithecines. Since major brain-size increase and tooth-size reduction are important trends in the evolution of the genus *Homo,* paleoanthropologists designated these fossils as a new species: ***Homo habilis*** ("handy man").[5] Significantly, the earliest fossils to exhibit these trends appeared around 2.5 million years ago, coincident with the earliest evidence of stone tool making.

When paleoanthropologists from the 1960s and 1970s depicted the lifeways of early *Homo,* they concentrated on "man the hunter," a tough guy with a killer instinct wielding tools on a savannah teeming with meat, while the female members of the species stayed at home tending their young. However, this theoretical reconstruction of ancient human life is seriously flawed. There is insufficient evidence to support this view, and it reflects a male-centered bias in both the discipline's earlier accounts and in the ethnographic record of still-existing foraging cultures used for comparative purposes.

Until the 1960s, most anthropologists doing fieldwork among foragers stressed the role of male hunters and underreported the significance of female gatherers in providing food for the community. As anthropologists became aware of their own biases, they began to set the record straight, documenting the vital role of "woman the gatherer" in provisioning the social group in foraging cultures, past and present. (See this chapter's Biocultural Connection for another example of gender and paleoanthropological interpretation.) Moreover, new evidence suggests that early humans depended more on scavenging than on hunting. Indeed, microscopic analysis of cut marks on fossil bones, which commonly overlie marks made by the teeth of carnivores, suggest that the lightly built *Homo habilis* may have been a *tertiary scavenger:* third in line to feed off an animal killed by a predator. Recently, it has been suggested that evolving humans may even have been prey themselves and that the selective pressure imposed by predators played a role in brain expansion.[6]

Fortunately, tool-wielding ancestors could break open the shafts of long bones to get at the fat and protein-rich marrow inside. Although this scavenging hypothesis regarding our earliest human ancestors has attracted considerable attention and endorsement among a majority of experts, some have questioned it on the basis of evidence from recent research among wild chimpanzees at Gombe, Tanzania. This work suggests that our closest primate "cousins" have little interest in dead animals as food, but when scavenging actually does take place, female chimpanzees show more interest in it than do males. That *Homo habilis* (*H. habilis*) behaved similarly seems unlikely, however, in view of the evidence just noted on the fossil animal bones, as well as the fact that *H. habilis* was a different kind of primate, living in a different environment from chimpanzees.

Tools, Food, and Brain Expansion

Paleoanthropologists debate whether the evolution of the genus *Homo* from australopithecine ancestors was a gradual or sudden process or some combination of the two. Recently, researchers at the University of Pennsylvania announced discovery of a genetic mutation, shared by all humans but absent in apes, that acts to prevent growth of powerful jaw muscles.

Applying the theory of punctuated equilibria or sudden evolutionary transformation (discussed earlier in this chapter), they calculate that the mutation arose between 2.7 and 2.1 million years ago, the period when *H. habilis* first appeared. They argue that, without heavy jaw muscles attached to the outside of the brain case, a significant constraint to brain growth was removed. In other words, humans may have developed large brains

---

Oldowan The first stone tool industry, beginning between 2.6 and 2.5 million years ago.

Lower Paleolithic Old Stone Age beginning with the earliest Oldowan tools spanning from about 2.6 million to 250,000 or 200,000 years ago.

Homo habilis "Handy man." The first fossil members of the genus *Homo* appearing 2.5 million years ago, with larger brains and smaller faces than australopithecines.

---

[5] Leakey, L. S. B., Tobias, P. B., & Napier, J. R., (1964). A new species of the genus *Homo* from Olduvai Gorge. *Nature, 202,* 7–9. (Some have argued that *H. habilis* was too varied to be considered a single species.)

[6] Hart, D., & Sussman, R. W. (2005). *Man the hunted: Primates, predators, and human evolution.* Boulder, CO: Westview Press.

Biocultural Connection

Evolution and Human Birth

Because biology and culture have always shaped human experience, it can be a challenge to separate the influences of each of these factors on human practices. For example, in the 1950s, paleoanthropologists developed the theory that human childbirth is particularly difficult compared to birth in other mammals. This theory was based in part on the observation of a "tight fit" between the human mother's birth canal and the baby's head, though several other primates also possess similarly tight fits between the newborn's head or shoulders and the birth canal. Nevertheless, changes in the birth canal associated with bipedalism were held responsible for difficult birth in humans.

At the same historical moment, North American childbirth practices were changing. In one generation from the 1920s to the 1950s, birth shifted from the home to the hospital. In the process childbirth was transformed from something a woman normally accomplished at home, perhaps with the help of a midwife or relatives, into the high-tech delivery of a neonate (the medical term for a newborn) with the assistance of medically trained personnel. During the 1950s women were generally fully anesthetized during the birth process. Paleoanthropological theories mirrored the cultural norms, providing a scientific explanation for the change in North American childbirth practices.

As a scientific theory, the idea of especially difficult human birth stands on shaky ground. No fossil neonates have ever been recovered, and only a handful of complete pelves (the bones forming the birth canal) exist. Instead, scientists must examine the birth process in living humans and nonhuman primates to reconstruct the evolution of the human birth pattern. Cultural beliefs and practices, however, shape every aspect of birth. Cultural factors determine where a birth occurs, the actions of the individuals present, and beliefs about the nature of the experience.

When paleoanthropologists of the 1950s and 1960s asserted that human childbirth is more difficult than birth in other mammals, they may have been drawing upon their own North American cultural beliefs that childbirth is dangerous and belongs in a hospital. A quick look at global neonatal mortality statistics indicates that in countries such as the Netherlands and Sweden, healthy well-nourished women give birth successfully outside of hospitals as they did throughout human evolutionary history. In other countries, deaths related to childbirth reflect malnutrition, infectious disease, and the low social status of women, rather than an inherently faulty biology. ■ ■ ■

---

as an accidental byproduct of jaw-size reduction.[7] Natural selection added to the effects of the sudden change of the jaw through the gradual brain expansion that continued in the genus *Homo* until some 200,000 years ago. By then, brain size had approximately tripled and reached the levels of today's humans.

Many scenarios proposed for the adaptation of early *Homo*—such as the relationship among tools, food, and brain expansion—rely upon a feedback loop between brain size and behavior. The behaviors made possible by larger brains confer advantages to large-brained individuals, contributing to their increased reproductive success. Over time, gene frequencies shift such that variants with larger brains become more common in successive generations, and the population gradually evolves to acquiring a larger-brained form. In the case of tool making, the archaeological record provides us with tangible data concerning our ancestors' cultural abilities fitting with the simultaneous biological expansion of the brain.

Tool making itself puts a premium on manual dexterity over manual strength. In addition, the patterns of stone tools and fossilized animal bones at Oldowan sites in Africa suggest improved organization of the nervous system. The sources for stone used to make cutting and chopping tools were often far from the sites where tools were used to process parts of animal carcasses. Also, the high density of fossil bones at some Oldowan sites and patterns of seasonal weathering indicate such sites were repeatedly used over a period of years. It appears that the Oldowan sites were places where tools and the raw materials for making them were stockpiled for later use in butchering. This implies advanced preparation for meat processing and thereby attests to the growing importance of foresight and the ability to plan ahead.

Beginning with *H. habilis* in Africa by 2.5 million years ago, human evolution followed a sure course of increasing brain size relative to body size and increasing cultural development, each acting upon and thereby promoting the other.

Homo erectus

Shortly after 2 million years ago, by which time *Homo habilis* and Oldowan tools had become widespread in

[7]Stedman, H. H., et al.(2004). Myosin gene mutation correlates with anatomical changes in the human lineage. *Nature, 428*,415–418.

Africa, a new species, **Homo erectus** ("upright man") appeared on that continent. Unlike *H. habilis,* however, *H. erectus* did not remain confined to Africa. In fact, evidence of *H. erectus* fossils almost as old as those discovered in Africa have been found in the Caucasus Mountains of Georgia (between Turkey and Russia), south-central China, and on the island of Java, Indonesia. These fossils indicate that it was not long before members of the genus *Homo* spread widely throughout much of Asia and eventually Europe as well.

The emergence of *H. erectus* as a new species in the long course of human evolution coincided with the beginning of the Pleistocene epoch, which spanned from 1.8 million to 10,000 years ago. During this time of periodic global cooling, Arctic cold conditions and abundant snowfall in the earth's northern hemisphere created vast ice sheets that temporarily covered much of Eurasia and North America. These fluctuating major glacial periods often lasted tens of thousands of years, separated by intervening warm periods. During interglacial periods, the world warmed up to the point that the ice sheets melted and sea levels rose, but sea levels were generally much lower than today, exposing large surfaces of low-lying lands now under water.

Of all the epochs in the earth's 4.6 *billion*-year history, the Pleistocene is particularly significant for our species, for this era of dramatic climatic shifts is the period in which humans—from *H. erectus* to *H. sapiens*—evolved and spread all across the globe. Confronted by environmental changes due to climatic fluctuations or movements into different geographic areas, our early human ancestors

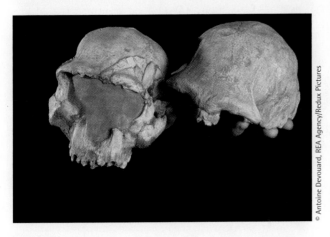

Compared to earlier species, *Homo erectus* skulls are characterized by a larger brain size, thick bones, and a pronounced bony ridge over the eye sockets, known as a brow ridge. *Homo erectus* first appeared in Africa about 2 million years ago; these two specimens from Dmanisi, Georgia (in the Caucasus Mountains between Turkey and Russia), are nearly as old.

© Antoine Devouard, REA Agency/Redux Pictures

Homo erectus "Upright man." A species within the genus *Homo* first appearing just after 2 million years ago in Africa and ultimately spreading throughout the Old World.

were constantly challenged to make biological and, more especially, cultural adaptations in order to survive and successfully reproduce. In the course of this long evolutionary process, random mutations introduced new characteristics into evolving populations in different regions of the world. As we shall see below, whether one or all of these populations contributed to modern humanity is one of the great debates of paleoanthropology.

The principle of natural selection was at work on humans as it was on all forms of life, favoring the perpetuation of certain characteristics within particular environmental conditions. At the same time, other characteristics that conferred no particular advantage or disadvantage also appeared by random mutation in geographically removed populations. The end result was a gradually growing physical variation in the genus *Homo.* In this context, it is not surprising that *H. erectus* fossils found in Africa, Asia, and Europe reveal levels of physical variation not unlike those seen in modern human populations living across the globe today. Many paleoanthropologists believe that the physical variation in the genus *Homo* was too great to consider all these specimens a single species, instead splitting *H. erectus* into a variety of distinct species.

Available fossil evidence indicates that *H. erectus* had body size and proportions similar to modern humans, though with heavier musculature. Differences in body size between the sexes diminished considerably compared to earlier bipeds, perhaps to facilitate successful childbirth.[8] Based on fossil skull evidence, *H. erectus* average brain size fell within the higher range of *H. habilis* and within the lower range of modern human brains. The dentition was fully human, though relatively large by modern standards. As one might expect, given its larger brain, *H. erectus* outstripped its predecessors in cultural abilities.

In Africa and most of Eurasia, the Oldowan chopper was replaced by the more sophisticated hand axe. At first the hand axes—shaped by regular blows giving them a larger and finer cutting edge than chopper tools—were probably all-purpose implements for food procurement and processing, and defense. But *H. erectus* also developed cleavers (like hand axes but without points) and various scrapers to process animal hides for bedding and clothing. In addition, this early human relied on flake tools used "as is" to cut meat and process vegetables, or refined by "retouching" into points and borers for drilling or punching holes in materials. Improved technological efficiency is also evident in *H. erectus'* use of raw materials.

Instead of making a few large tools out of big pieces of stone, *Homo erectus* placed a new emphasis on smaller tools, thus economizing their raw materials. Some of these raw materials continue even today to have practical value, as the Anthropology Applied feature illustrates.

[8]Hager, L. (1989). The evolution of sex differences in the hominid bony pelvis. Ph.D. dissertation, University of California, Berkeley.

Stone Tools for Modern Surgeons

When anthropologist Irven DeVore of Harvard University was to have some minor melanomas removed from his face, he did not leave it up to the surgeon to supply his own scalpels. Instead, he had graduate student John Shea make a scalpel. Making a blade of obsidian (a naturally occurring volcanic "glass") by the same techniques used by Upper Paleolithic people to make blades, he then hafted this in a wooden handle, using melted pine resin as glue and then lashing it with sinew. After the procedure, the surgeon reported that the obsidian scalpel was superior to metal ones.[a]

DeVore was not the first to undergo surgery in which stone scalpels were used. In 1975, Don Crabtree, then at Idaho State University, prepared the scalpels that his surgeon would use in Crabtree's heart surgery. In 1980, Payson Sheets at the University of Colorado prepared obsidian scalpels that were used successfully in eye surgery. And in 1986, David Pokotylo of the Museum of Anthropology at the University of British Columbia underwent reconstructive surgery on his hand with blades he himself had made (the hafting was done by his museum colleague, Len McFarlane).

The reason for these uses of scalpels modeled on ancient stone tools is that the anthropologists realized that obsidian is superior in almost every way to materials normally used to make scalpels: It is 210 to 1,050 times sharper than surgical steel, 100 to 500 times sharper than a razor blade, and 3 times sharper than a diamond blade (which not only costs much more, but cannot be made with more than 3 mm of cutting edge). Obsidian blades are easier to cut with and do less damage in the process (under a microscope, incisions made with the sharpest steel blades show torn ragged edges and are littered with bits of displaced flesh).[b] As a consequence, the surgeon has better control over what she or he is doing, and the incisions heal faster with less scarring and pain. Because of the superiority of obsidian scalpels, Sheets went so far as to form a corporation in partnership with Boulder, Colorado, eye surgeon Dr. Firmon Hardenbergh. Together, they developed a means of producing cores of uniform size from molten glass, as well as a machine to detach blades from the cores.

■ ■ ■

[a]Shreeve, J. (1995). *The Neandertal enigma: Solving the mystery of modern human origins* (p. 134). New York: William Morrow.
[b]Sheets, P. D. (1987). Dawn of a New Stone Age in eye surgery. In R. J. Sharer & W. Ashmore (Eds.), *Archaeology: Discovering our past* (p. 231). Palo Alto, CA: Mayfield.

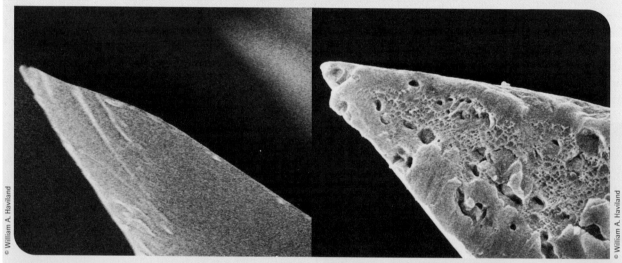

© William A. Haviland

These electron micrographs of the tips of an obsidian blade (left) and a modern steel scalpel illustrate the superiority of the obsidian.

Remains found in southern Africa also suggest that *H. erectus* may have learned to use fire by 1 million years ago. Fire gave our human ancestors more control over their environment. It permitted them to continue activities after dark and provided a means to frighten away predators. It supplied them with the warmth and light needed for cave dwelling, and it enabled them to cook their food. The ability to modify food culturally through cooking may have played a role in the reduction of the tooth size and jaws of later fossil groups since raw food is tougher and requires more chewing. However, cooking does more than this. It detoxifies a number of otherwise poisonous plants. In addition, it alters substances in plants, allowing important vitamins, minerals, and proteins to be absorbed from the gut rather than passing unused through the intestines. And, finally, it makes high-energy complex carbohydrates, such as starch, digestible.

In addition, without controlled use of fire, it is unlikely that early humans could have moved successfully into regions where winter temperatures regularly dropped below that point—as they must have in northern China or the mountain highlands of central Asia, or most of Europe, where the genus *Homo* spread some 780,000 years ago. Although considerable variation exists, studies of modern humans indicate that most people can remain reasonably comfortable down to 50 degrees Fahrenheit (10 degrees Celsius) with minimal clothing so long as they keep active. Below that temperature, hands and feet cool to the point of pain. In short, when our human ancestors learned to employ fire to warm and protect themselves and to cook their food, they dramatically increased their geographical range and nutritional options.

With *H. erectus* we also begin to have evidence of organized hunting as the means for procuring meat, animal hides, horn, bone, and sinew. Early evidence demonstrating the hunting technology of these ancestors includes 400,000-year-old wooden spears discovered in a peat bog (what was originally marsh or swamp land) in northern Germany, although it is likely that evolving humans had begun to hunt before then. Increased organizational ability may also be indicated in prehistoric sites such as Ambrona in Spain where it has been proposed that fires were used to drive a variety of large animals (including elephants) into a swamp for killing,[9] though grass fires have been proposed as an alternative explanation.

With *H. erectus,* then, we find a clearer manifestation than before of the complex interplay of biological, cultural, and ecological factors. Changes in social organization and technology paralleled an increase in brain size and complexity and a reduction in tooth and jaw size. The appearance of cultural adaptations such as controlled use of fire, cooking, and more complex tool kits may have facilitated language development. Analysis of Oldowan tools reveals *Homo habilis* to have been overwhelmingly right handed, handedness being a trait associated with language abilities. So, too, was *Homo erectus.* Moreover, the size of the opening for the nerve that controls tongue movement, so important for spoken language, is comparable to that of modern humans. Improvements in communication and social organization brought about by language undoubtedly contributed to better methods for food gathering and hunting, to a population increase, and to territorial expansion. Continuous biological and culture change through natural selection in the course of hundreds of thousands of years gradually transformed *H. erectus* into the next emerging species: *Homo sapiens.*

---

[9]Freeman, L. G. (1992). *Ambrona and Torralba: New evidence and interpretation.* Paper presented at the 91st Annual Meeting, American Anthropological Association.

Lumpers or Splitters

At various sites in Africa, Asia, and Europe, a number of fossils have been found that date to between roughly 400,000 and 200,000 years ago. The best population sample, bones of about thirty individuals of both sexes and all ages (but none older than about 40) comes from Atapuerca, a 400,000-year-old site in Spain (shown in the opening photograph for Chapter 4). Overall, these bones depict a mixture of characteristics of *Homo erectus* with those of early *Homo sapiens,* exactly what one would expect of fossil remains transitional between the two. For example, brain size overlaps the upper end of the *H. erectus* range and the lower end of the range for *H. sapiens.*

Whether one chooses to call these or any other contemporary fossils early *H. sapiens,* late *H. erectus,* or *Homo antecessor,* as did the Spanish anthropologists who discovered them, is more than a name game. Fossil names indicate researchers' perspectives about evolutionary relationships among groups. When specimens are given separate species names, it signifies that they form part of a reproductively isolated group.

Some paleoanthropologists approach the fossil record with the perspective that making such detailed biological determinations is arbitrary. Arguing that it is impossible to prove whether or not a collection of ancient bones and teeth represents a distinctive species, they tend to be "lumpers," placing more or less similar-looking fossil specimens together in more inclusive groups. "Splitters," by contrast, focus on the variation in the fossil record, interpreting minor differences in the shape of skeletons or skulls as evidence of distinctive biological species with corresponding cultural capacities. Referring to the variable shape of the bony ridge above ancient eyes, South African paleoanthropologist Philip Tobias has quipped, "Splitters will create a new species at the drop of a brow ridge." Splitting has the advantage of specificity while lumping has the advantage of simplicity.

The Neandertal Debate

Closer to the present, the fossil record provides us with many more human specimens compared to earlier periods. The record is particularly rich when it comes to **Neandertals,** perhaps the most controversial ancient members of the genus *Homo.* Typically, they are represented as the classic "cave men," stereotyped in Western popular media and even in museum displays as wild and hairy club-wielding brutes.

Neandertals A distinct group within the genus *Homo* inhabiting Europe and Southwest Asia from approximately 125,000 to 30,000 years ago.

Based on abundant fossil evidence, we now know that Neandertals were extremely muscular members of the genus *Homo* living from about 125,000 to approximately 30,000 years ago in Europe and parts of Asia. Although they had modern-sized brains, Neandertal faces and skulls were quite different from those of later fossilized remains, which are referred to as anatomically modern humans. Their large noses and teeth projected forward more than is the case with modern humans.

Neandertals generally had a sloping forehead and prominent bony brow ridges over their eyes; on the back of the skull a bony mass provided for attachment of powerful neck muscles. These features, while not exactly in line with modern ideals of European beauty, are also common in Norwegian and Danish skulls dating to about 1,000 years ago—the time of the Vikings.[10] Nevertheless, these anatomical similarities do little to negate the popular image of Neandertals as cave-dwelling brutes. Their rude reputation may also derive from the time of their discovery, as the first widely publicized Neandertal skull was found in 1856, well before scientific theories to account for human origins had gained acceptance.

This odd-looking old skull, happened upon near Düsseldorf in Germany's Neander "Valley" (*Tal* in German), took German scientists by surprise. Initially, they ex-

---

[10]Ferrie, H. (1997) An interview with C. Loring Brace. *Current Anthropology, 38,* 861.

plained its extraordinary features as evidence of some disfiguring disease in an invading "barbarian" from the east who had crawled into a deep cave to die. Although we now know that many aspects of the Neandertals' unique skull shape and body form represent their biological adaptation to an extremely cold climate, and that their brain size and capacity for cultural adaptation were noticeably superior to those of earlier members of the genus *Homo,* Neandertals are still surrounded by controversy.

Were Neandertals a separate species that became extinct about 30,000 years ago? Or were they a subspecies of *Homo sapiens*? And if they were not a dead-end, an unsuccessful side branch in human evolution, did they actually contribute to our modern human gene pool? In that case, so the argument goes, their direct descendants walk the earth now. The place of Neandertals in human evolutionary history is one of the most hotly debated arguments in paleoanthropology today.

The capacity for cultural adaptation in Neandertals was predictably superior to what it had been in earlier species. Neandertals' extensive use of fire, for example, was essential to survival in a cold climate like that of Europe during the various glacial periods. They lived in small bands or single-family units, both in the open and in caves, probably communicating through language. Evidence of deliberate burials of the deceased among Neandertals reflects a measure of ritual behavior in their communities.

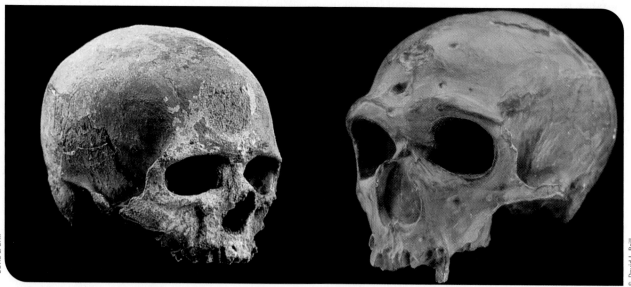

© David L Brill

At the same time that Neandertals were first discovered in the late 19th century, other fossil specimens known as Cro-Magnons were found near Neandertal sites in southwestern France. At the time of their discovery, they were thought to be two distinct ancient forms of a similar age. The invention of dating techniques allowed scientists to learn that Neandertals and Cro-Magnons did not co-exist. With a high forehead, the more recent Cro-Magnon skull (left) is more like contemporary Europeans than the older Neanderthal skull (right) with its prominent brow ridge and sloping forehead. In addition, some have proposed that cultural continuity in diet can be inferred between Cro-Magnons and contemporary French people. The Cro-Magnon skull has evidence of a fungal infection, perhaps from eating tainted mushrooms. Mushrooms are a delicacy in this region to this day. While Cro-Magnons are clearly the ancestors of contemporary humans, the exact relationship between Neandertals and living people today is one of the great debates of paleoanthropology.

Moreover, the fossil remains of an amputee discovered in Iraq and an arthritic man excavated in France imply that Neandertals cared for the disabled, something not seen previously in the human fossil record. The tool-making tradition of all but the latest Neandertals is called the **Mousterian** tradition after a site (Le Moustier) in the Dordogne region of southern France. *Mousterian* refers to a tradition of the Middle Paleolithic or Middle Stone Age tool industries of Europe and southwestern Asia, generally dating from about 125,000 until about 40,000 years ago.

Although considerable variability exists, Mousterian tools are generally lighter and smaller than those of earlier traditions. While previous industries obtained only two or three flakes from an entire stone core, Mousterian toolmakers obtained many smaller flakes, which they skillfully retouched and sharpened. Their tool kits also contained a greater variety of tool types than the earlier ones: hand axes, flakes, scrapers, borers, notched flakes for shaving wood, and many types of points that could be attached to wooden shafts to make spears. This variety of tools facilitated more effective use of food resources and enhanced the quality of clothing and shelter. These stone tools were used by *all* people, Neandertals and their contemporaries elsewhere, including Europe, western Asia, and North Africa, during this time period. By the time that classic Neandertals were disappearing between 40,000 and 30,000 years ago, their technology was comparable to the tool complexes used by anatomically modern *H. sapiens* during that same period.[11]

The Genus *Homo* Elsewhere

Meanwhile, archaic *H. sapiens* variants without the midfacial projection and massive muscle attachments on the back of the skull common among Neandertals inhabited other parts of the world. Human fossil skulls found near the Solo River in Java are a prime example. Dates for these specimens range from about 200,000 to 27,000 years ago. The fossils, with their modern-sized brains, display certain features of *H. erectus* combined with those of archaic as well as more modern *H. sapiens.*

Further, a spectacular new discovery on the Indonesian island of Flores illustrates that geographic isolation can account for an unusual amount of variation in morphology for members of the genus *Homo.* A small-bodied adult specimen—dated to between 38,000 and

18,000 years ago, no more than 1 meter (3 feet) tall with humanlike skull and teeth—was designated as the new species *Homo floresiensis* in 2004.[12]

The paleoanthropologists who discovered this specimen, along with discoveries of stone tools and the bones of other animal species dated back to 90,000 years ago, suggest that *Homo floresiensis* is "the end product of a long period of evolution on a comparatively small island where environmental conditions placed small body size at a selective advantage."[13] While some paleoanthropologists argue that the skeleton represents a diseased or abnormal individual, recent studies indicate that the ratio of brain size to body size in this specimen is like an australopithecine while the shape of the brain, as preserved on the inside of the skull, is like *Homo erectus.*[14]

Fossils from various parts of Africa, the most famous being a skull from Kabwe in Zambia, also show a combination of ancient and modern traits. Finally, similar remains have been found at several places in China. For these members of the genus *Homo,* improved cultural adaptive abilities relate to the fact that the brain had achieved modern size.

Such a brain made possible not only sophisticated technology but also conceptual thought of considerable intellectual complexity. Decorative pendants and objects with carved and engraved markings also appear in the archaeological record from this period. Objects were also commonly colored with pigments such as manganese dioxide and red or yellow ocher. The ceremonial burial of the dead and nonutilitarian, decorative objects provide additional evidence supporting theoretical arguments in favor of symbolic thinking and language use in these ancient populations.

Beginning around 200,000 years ago (see Figure 5.5), individuals with a somewhat more anatomically modern human appearance began to appear in Africa and southwestern Asia. While the earliest of these fossils are associated with the Mousterian tool industries used by the Neandertals, over time new tool industries and other forms of cultural expression appeared.

ANATOMICALLY MODERN PEOPLES AND THE UPPER PALEOLITHIC

A veritable explosion of tool types and other forms of cultural expression beginning about 40,000 years ago

---

Mousterian The tool industry of the Neandertals and their contemporaries of Europe, Southwest Asia, and northern Africa from 125,000 to 40,000 years ago.

---

[11]Mellars, P. (1989). Major issues in the emergence of modern humans. *Current Anthropology, 30,* 356–357.

[12]Brown, P., et al. (2004). A new small bodied hominin from the Late Pleistocene of Flores, Indonesia. *Nature, 431,* 1,055–1,061.

[13]Brown, et al., p. 1060.

[14]Falk, D., et al. (2005). The brain of LB1, *Homo floresiensis. Science, 308,* 242–245.

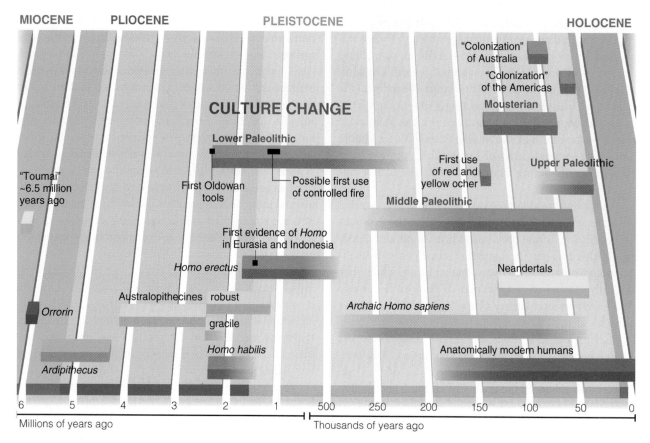

Figure 5.5
Paleoanthropologists debate the exact relationship among the bipedal species along with the number of species that existed over the past 8 to 5 million years. This timeline takes a "lumping" approach, limiting the number of fossil groups presented. Note also that the time spans for the Lower, Middle, and Upper Paleolithic vary tremendously by region. Note also that the time scale is expanded for the most recent 250,000 years.

constitutes what is known as the **Upper Paleolithic** transition. Upper Paleolithic tool kits include increased prominence of "blade" tools: long, thin, precisely shaped pieces of stone demonstrating the considerable skill of their creators. The Upper Paleolithic, lasting until about 10,000 years ago, is best known from archaeological evidence found in Europe where numerous distinctive tool complexes from successive time periods have been documented. In addition, the European archaeological record from this period is rich with cave wall paintings, engravings, and bas-relief sculptures as well as many portable nonutilitarian artifacts.

In Upper Paleolithic times, humans began to manufacture tools for more effective hunting, fishing, and gathering. Cultural adaptation also became more highly specific and regional, thus enhancing human chances for survival under a wide variety of environmental conditions. Instead of manufacturing all-purpose tools,

Upper Paleolithic The last part (40,000 to 10,000 years ago) of the Old Stone Age, featuring tool industries characterized by long slim blades and an explosion of creative symbolic forms.

Upper Paleolithic populations inhabiting a wide range of environments—mountains, marshlands, tundra, forests, lake regions, river valleys, and seashores—all developed specialized devices suited to the resources of their particular habitat and to the different seasons. In the Upper Paleolithic humans found ways and means to cross icy Arctic regions and open water to reach places never previously inhabited by humans. Humans reached Australia between 60,000 and 40,000 years ago and the Americas between about 30,000 and 15,000 years ago.

This degree of regional specialization required improved manufacturing techniques. The blade method of manufacture, invented by archaic *H. sapiens* and later used widely in Europe and western Asia, required less raw material than before and resulted in smaller and lighter tools with a better ratio between weight of flint and length of cutting edge. The pressure-flaking technique—in which a bone, antler, or a wooden tool is used to press off small flakes from a larger flake or blade—gave the Upper Paleolithic toolmaker greater control over the shape of the tool than was possible with percussion flaking.

Invented by Mousterian toolmakers, the *burin* (a stone tool with chisel-like edges) came into common use in the Upper Paleolithic. The burin provided an

The techniques of the Upper Paleolithic allowed for an explosion of artistic expression. Venus figurines, such as this stone figure, were widespread and highly stylized. Art historian LeRoy McDermott has suggested that the distortions and exaggerations of the female form visible in the Venus figurines are a result of perspective taken by female artists as they looked at their own bodies.

excellent means of working bone and antler into tools such as fishhooks and harpoons. The spear-thrower or *atlatl* (a Nahuatl word used by Aztec Indians in Mexico, referring to a wooden device, 1 to 2 feet long, with a hook on the end for throwing a spear) also appeared at this time. By effectively elongating the arm, the atlatl gave hunters increased force behind the throw.

In addition to the creativity evident in their tools and weapons, Upper Paleolithic people produced representational artwork. In some regions, tools and weapons were engraved with beautiful animal figures; pendants were made of bone and ivory, as were female figurines; and small sculptures were modeled out of clay. Spectacular paintings and engravings depicting humans and animals of this period have been found on the walls of caves and rock shelters in southwestern Europe, Australia, and Africa.

The southern African rock art tradition spanned 27,000 years and lasted into historic times; from this continuity, we know that much of it depicts artists' visions when in altered states of consciousness related to spiritual practices. Along with the animals, the art also includes a variety of geometric motifs reminiscent of visual hallucinations spontaneously generated by the human nervous system when in a trancelike state.

Australian cave art, some of it older than European cave art and also associated with trancing, includes similar motifs. The occurrence of the same geometric designs in the cave art of Europe suggests trancing was a part of these prehistoric foraging cultures as well. Some suggest that geometric motifs in Paleolithic art were interpreted as stylized human figures and patterns of descent. Although speculative, the great importance of kinship in all historically known communities of hunters, fishers, and gatherers at least makes such a suggestion plausible.

Whether or not a new kind of human, anatomically modern with correspondingly superior intellectual and creative abilities, is responsible for this cultural explosion is hotly debated within paleoanthropology. The biological and cultural evidence preserved in fossil and archaeological records does not tell a simple story.

THE MODERN HUMAN ORIGINS DEBATE

On a biological level, the great debate can be distilled to a question of whether one, some, or all populations of the archaic groups played a role in the evolution of modern *H. sapiens*. Those supporting the **multiregional hypothesis** argue that the fossil evidence suggests a simultaneous local transition from *H. erectus* to modern *H. sapiens* throughout the parts of the world inhabited by early members of the genus *Homo*. By contrast, those supporting the **recent African origins hypothesis** (also known as the *Eve* or *out of Africa hypothesis*) argue that all anatomically modern humans living today descend directly from one single population of archaic *H. sapiens* in Africa. This theory asserts that improved cultural capabilities allowed members of this group to replace other archaic human forms as they began to spread out of Africa some time after 100,000 years ago. So while both models place human origins firmly in Africa, the first argues that our human ancestors began moving into Asia and Europe as early as 1.8 million years ago, whereas the second maintains that anatomically modern *H. sapiens* evolved only in Africa, completely replacing other members of the genus *Homo* as they spread throughout the world.

multiregional hypothesis The hypothesis that modern humans originated through a process of simultaneous local transition from *Homo erectus* to *Homo sapiens* throughout the inhabited world.

recent African origins hypothesis The hypothesis that all modern people are derived from one single population of archaic *H. sapiens* from Africa who migrated out of Africa after 100,000 years ago, replacing all other archaic forms due to their superior cultural capabilities. Also called the Eve or out of Africa hypothesis.

For many years, the recent African origins hypothesis relied upon genetic evidence. In particular, genetic evidence is said to point to a single mother or "Eve" for all anatomically modern humans by tracing human origins through DNA that is found in the mitochondria—a cellular structure that is maternally inherited. The absence of good fossil evidence from Africa to support the second hypothesis has been a major problem for this theory. In 2003, however, skulls of two adults and one child (discovered in 1997 in the Afar region of Ethiopia) and described as anatomically modern were reconstructed and dated to 160,000 years ago.[15] The discoverers of these fossils called them *Homo sapiens idaltu* (meaning "elder" in the local Afar language). Convinced that they have conclusively proved the recent African origins hypothesis, they argue that their latest evidence verifies that Neandertals represent a dead-end side branch of human evolution.

Though the recent African origins hypothesis has achieved considerable popularity, not every scholar supports it. Among those with opposing views are Chinese paleoanthropologists, who generally favor the multiregional hypothesis in part because it fits better with the fossil discoveries from Australia and Asia but also because it directs attention to China as central for human origins.

By contrast, the recent African origins hypothesis depends more upon the interpretation of genetic evidence, fossils, and cultural remains from Europe, Africa, and southwestern Asia. Proponents of multiregionalism critique this model on several grounds. For example, the molecular evidence upon which it is based has been strongly criticized as more recent genetic studies indicate that Africa was not the sole source of DNA in modern humans.[16]

Recent African origins proponents argue that anatomically modern people co-existed for a time with archaic populations until the superior cultural capacities of the moderns resulted in extinction of the archaic peoples. This may help explain its popularity with Western scholars, as it resonates with European experience of colonial expansion; the difference is that Africa rather than Europe is the origin of the supposedly superior people. It also harmonizes with the historical discomfort with considering Neandertals as humans.

It has been argued that evidence from Europe, where Neandertals and "anatomically moderns" co-existed between 40,000 and 30,000 years ago, supports a model of co-existence and replacement. However, defining some fossils as either Neandertal or anatomically modern is difficult. The latest Neandertals show features (such as chins) more commonly seen in anatomically modern humans, while "early moderns" show features (such as brow ridges and bony masses at the back of the skull) reminiscent of Neandertals.

This mix of modern and Neandertal features is so evident in a child's skeleton recently found in Portugal as to lead several specialists to regard it as clear evidence of hybridization, or successful sexual mating between both human populations.[17] Other specialists argue that some of the modern-appearing features are simply due to the fact that this specimen is a child. But if this child is a hybrid, it would mean that the two human forms belonged to one single species rather than to separate ones. Multiregionalists argue that the simplest way to account for all this evidence is to consider these fossils as belonging to a single varied population, with some individuals showing features more typical of Neandertals than others. They cite archaeological evidence that the cultural achievements of late Neandertals were not fundamentally different from those of "early moderns."[18] as well as evidence that the culture of these European "early moderns" developed in Europe[19] and was not introduced from outside, as out of Africanists assert.

Nevertheless, by 30,000 years ago, many of the distinctive anatomical features seen in archaic groups like Neandertals seem to disappear from the fossil record in Europe. Instead, individuals with higher foreheads, smoother brow ridges, and more distinct chins seemed to have Europe to themselves. However, if one looks at the full range of contemporary human variation across the globe, one can find living people who do not meet the anatomical definition of modernity proposed in the recent African origins model.[20]

RACE AND HUMAN EVOLUTION

The Neandertal debate raises fundamental questions about the complex relationship between biological and cultural human variation. As we reviewed the human

[15]White, T., et al. (2003). Pleistocene *Homo sapiens* from the Middle Awash, Ethiopia. *Nature, 423,* 742–747.

[16]Templeton, A. R. (1995). The "Eve" hypothesis: A genetic critique and reanalysis. *American Anthropologist, 95*(1), 51–72; Gibbons, A. (1997). Ideas on human origins evolve at anthropology gathering. *Science, 276,* 535–536; Pennisi, E. (1999). Genetic study shakes up out of Africa theory. *Science, 283,* 1,828.

[17]Holden, C. (1999). Ancient child burial uncovered in Portugal. *Science, 283,* 169.

[18]D'Errico, F., et al. (1998). Neandertal acculturation in Western Europe? *Current Anthropology, 39,* 521. See also Henry, D. O., et al. (2004). Human behavioral organization in the Middle Paleolithic: Were Neandertals different? *American Anthropologist, 107*(1), 17–31.

[19]Clark, G. A. (2002). Neandertal archaeology: Implications for our origins. *American Anthropologist, 104*(1), 50–67.

[20]Wolpoff, M., & Caspari, R. (1997). *Race and human evolution* (pp. 344–345, 393). New York: Simon & Schuster.

fossil record throughout this chapter, inferences were made about the cultural capabilities of our ancestors partially based on biological features. For instance, the argument of a significantly increased brain size of *Homo habilis* 2.5 million years ago compared to earlier australopithecines was used to support the claim that these ancestors were capable of more complex cultural activities, including the manufacture of stone tools. Can we make the same kinds of assumptions about other more recent biological developments? Can we say that only anatomically modern humans with higher foreheads and reduced brow ridges were capable of making sophisticated tools and beautiful art due to fundamental biological difference?

Supporters of the multiregional hypothesis argue we cannot. They argue instead that the human evolutionary history consists of a long period of a single evolving human species without geographically distinct biological types. Paleoanthropologists looking at the fossil evidence can recognize distinctive suites of features possessed by fossil groups but whether these groups constitute distinct species or variation within a single species is far more difficult to determine.

Without isolation, gene flow tends to keep populations from differentiating into distinct species. As we shall see in the following chapters, since the end of the Ice Age into today's era of globalization, most populations did not live in extreme isolation. The integrating effects of gene flow have become so powerful that dramatic regional variations for suites of traits no longer exist.

Over the course of our long evolutionary history, we have become an amazingly diverse and yet still unified single species inhabiting the entire earth. Some ethnically diverse societies such as the United States, South Africa, and Brazil emphasize differences between types of people, but the vast majority of these differences are social rather than biological. While biological processes account for some aspects of human variation, it is human cultures that shape both the expression and the interpretation of biological variation at every step. Human bipeds do indeed stand with one foot in nature and another in culture.

Chapter Summary

■ Macroevolution focuses upon the formation of new species (speciation) and on the evolutionary relationships between groups of species. Speciation can occur in a branching fashion known as cladogenesis or without branching (anagenesis), as a single population accumulates sufficient new mutations over time to be considered a separate species. Microevolutionary forces of mutation, gene flow, genetic drift, and natural selection can lead to macroevolutionary change but the tempo of evolutionary change varies. A mutation in a regulatory gene can bring about rapid change. Punctuated equilibrium model proposes that macroevolution is characterized by long periods of relative stability with periods of rapid change interspersed.

■ Climate changes led to the appearance of primates about 65 million years ago, following a mass extinction of dinosaurs. These were small, arboreal, nocturnal, insect eaters. Old World and New World species separated by about 40 million years ago. Many of the Old World anthropoid species became ground dwellers. About 23 million years ago, hominoids, the broad-shouldered tailless primates that include all living and extinct apes and humans began to appear in Asia, Africa, and Europe. Genetic studies have confirmed that the African apes—chimpanzees, bonobos, and gorillas—are our closest living relatives. Larger brains and bipedal locomotion constitute the most striking differences between humans and our closest primate relatives. Bipedalism preceded brain expansion, and played a pivotal role in setting us apart from the apes.

■ The earliest members of the bipedal human line diverged from the African apes (chimpanzees, bonobos, and gorillas) sometime between 8 and 5 million years ago. Best known are the australopithecines, well equipped for generalized foraging in a relatively open savannah environment. Although many theories propose that bipedalism reinforced brain expansion by freeing the hands for activities other than locomotion, the increase in brain size did not appear in human evolutionary history until much later with the appearance of the genus *Homo*.

■ With the first members of genus *Homo—Homo habilis—* about 2.5 million years ago, stone tools begin to appear in the archaeological record. Possible earlier tools made of perishable materials such as plant fibers are not preserved. Throughout the course of the evolution of the genus *Homo,* the critical importance of culture as the human mechanism for adaptation imposed selective pressures favoring a larger brain, which in turn made possible improved cultural adaptation.

■ *Homo erectus,* appearing shortly after 2 million years ago, had a brain close in size to that of modern humans and sophisticated behaviors including controlled use of fire for warmth, cooking, and protection. *H. erectus* remains are found throughout Africa, Asia, and Europe, reaching the colder northern areas about 780,000 years ago. The technological efficiency of *H. erectus* is evidenced in improved tool making— first the hand axe and later specialized tools for hunting, butchering, food processing, hide scraping, and defense. Hunting techniques developed by *H. erectus* reflected a considerable advance in organizational ability.

■ Between 400,000 and 200,000 years ago, evolving humans achieved the brain capacity of contemporary *Homo sapiens.* Apparently several local variations of the genus *Homo* existed around this time period, including the Neandertals. Their capacity for cultural adaptation was considerable, doubtless because large brains made sophisticated technology and conceptual thought possible. Those who lived in Europe used fire extensively in their Arctic climate, lived in small bands, and communicated through language. Remains testify to ritual behavior and caretaking for the aged and infirm. Determining the place of Neandertals in the human evolutionary line is one of the major debates of paleoanthropology.

■ Evidence indicates that at least one population of archaic *H. sapiens* evolved into modern humans. Whether this involved the biological evolution of a new species with improved cultural capabilities or a simultaneous worldwide process involving all archaic forms remains one of the most contentious issues in paleoanthropology. The recent African origins hypothesis proposes that modern humans evolved in Africa about 200,000 years ago, replacing other populations as they spread throughout the globe. The multiregional hypothesis proposes that humans originated in Africa some 2 million years ago and that ancient populations throughout the globe are all ancestors of modern humans with unity of a single species maintained through gene flow.

■ The stone tool industries and artwork of Upper Paleolithic cultures surpassed any previously undertaken by humans. Cave paintings and rock art found in Spain, France, Australia, and Africa served a religious purpose and attest to a highly sophisticated aesthetic sensibility. Humans came to inhabit the entire globe during this period, developing watercraft and other technologies suitable for adaptation to a variety of environments.

■ Paleoanthropologists link changes in cultural capacity to changes in brain size and skull shape over most of the course of human evolutionary history. As we get closer to the present, and fossil specimens possess brains the size of contemporary humans, paleoanthropologists debate whether a particular skull shape can be linked to cultural abilities and a behavioral repertoire. With the gene flow that has existed since at least the end of the Ice Age, it is not possible to divide humans into a series of distinct types.

Questions for Reflection

1. Over the course of their evolutionary history, humans came to rely on culture to meet the challenges of survival. They left behind spectacular evidence of their creativity and knowledge in ancient cave paintings from the Upper Paleolithic. These cultural expressions reflect a fundamental need to record and share observations. How do you meet these challenges in your life? What biological adaptations allow you to record and share observations?

2. Do you think evidence from a single bone is enough to determine whether an organism from the past was bipedal?

3. Paleoanthropologists can be characterized as either "lumpers" or "splitters" depending upon their approach to recognizing species in the fossil record. Which of these approaches do you prefer and why?

4. How do you feel about the possibility of having Neandertals as part of your ancestry? How might you relate the Neandertal debate to stereotyping or racism in contemporary society?

5. Do you think that gender has played a role in anthropological interpretations of the behavior of our ancestors and the way that paleoanthropologists and archaeologists conduct their research? Do you believe that feminism has a role to play in the interpretation of the past?

Key Terms

macroevolution	Oldowan
speciation	Lower Paleolithic
cladogenesis	*Homo habilis*
anagenesis.	*Homo erectus*
punctuated equilibria	Neandertals
continental drift	Mousterian
bipedalism	Upper Paleolithic
Australopithecus	multiregional hypothesis
robust autralopithecines	recent African origins
gracile australopithecines	hypothesis

Multimedia Review Tools

Make the Grade in Anthropology with ThomsonNOW

Thomson NOW! This powerful online study tool provides you with a *personalized study plan* based on your responses to a diagnostic pretest. Once you have mastered the material with the help of interactive learning tools, an integrated e-book, and more, you can take a post-test to confirm you are ready to move on to the next chapter. To get started with ThomsonNOW, check the card packaged with your book for the access code. Then go to http://www.thomsonedu.com to create an account through 1pass™. If there is no card in your book, go to http://www.thomsonedu.com to purchase an access code.

Companion Website and Anthropology Resource Center

Go to http://anthropology.wadsworth.com to reach the companion website for your text. This offers many study aids, including self quizzes for each chapter and a practice final exam, as well as links to anthropology websites and information on the latest theories and discoveries in the field.

Also, check out the Anthropology Resource Center for a wealth of learning materials that include interactive maps, video exercises, simulations, and breaking news in anthropology. Be sure to explore InfoTrac College Edition®, your online library that offers full-length articles from thousands of scholarly and popular publications. To reach the Anthropology Resource Center and InfoTrac College Edition, check the card packaged with your book for the access code. Then go to http://www.thomsonedu.com to create an account through 1pass(tm). If there is no card in your book, go to http://www.thomsonedu.com to purchase an access code.

© Erich Lessing/Art Resource, NY

CHALLENGE ISSUE

Beginning some time around 10,000 years ago, some of the world's people embarked on a new way of life, solving the challenges of survival through the gradual domestication of animals and plants and the formation of permanent settlements. The shift from food foraging to food production so drastically transformed human existence that this cultural period, the Neolithic, has been described as revolutionary. While farming and village life solved some of the challenges of existence, these cultural innovations have also posed risks to human health, both in the past and in the present. Crowded living conditions and close contact with animals in Neolithic villages promoted the spread of infectious disease. Diets limited by reliance on single crops sometimes led to malnutrition and even famine when these crops failed. The development of village life, and the domestication of animals and plants, introduced a number of health issues that continue to challenge humans globally.

The Neolithic Revolution: The Domestication of Plants and Animals

6

Throughout the Paleolithic, people depended exclusively on wild sources of food for their survival. They followed wild herds and gathered wild plant foods, relying on their wits and muscles to acquire what nature provided. Whenever favored sources of food became scarce, people adjusted by increasing the variety of foods eaten and incorporating less desirable foods into their diets.

Over time, the subsistence practices of some people began to change in ways that radically transformed their way of life as they became food producers rather than food foragers.[1] Food production had important implications for humans, for it meant that people could lead a more sedentary existence. Moreover, by reorganizing the workload, some individuals could be freed from the food quest to devote their energies to other tasks. Over the course of thousands of years, these changes brought about an unforeseen way of life. With good reason, the **Neolithic,** when this change took place, has been called a revolutionary one in human history.

THE MESOLITHIC ROOTS OF FARMING AND PASTORALISM

By 12,000 years ago, the glaciers that had covered much of the northern hemisphere receded, causing changes in human habitats globally. Throughout the world,

Neolithic The New Stone Age; prehistoric period beginning about 10,000 years ago in which peoples possessed stone-based technologies and depended on domesticated crops and/or animals.

[1]Rindos, D. (1984). *The origins of agriculture: An evolutionary perspective* (p. 99). Orlando: Academic Press.

climates warmed and sea levels were on the rise, ultimately flooding many areas that had been above sea level during periods of glaciation, such as the Bering Strait, parts of the North Sea, and an extensive land area that had joined the eastern islands of Indonesia to mainland Asia. In some northern regions, warmer climates brought about particularly marked changes, allowing the replacement of tundra with forests. In the process, the herd animals—upon which northern Paleolithic peoples had depended for much of their food, clothing, and shelter—disappeared from many areas. Some, like the reindeer and musk ox, moved to colder climates; others, like the mammoths, died out completely. In the new forests, animals were often more solitary in their habits. As a result, large cooperative hunts were less productive than before. Diets shifted to abundant plant foods as well as fish and other foods around lakeshores, bays, and rivers. In Europe, Asia, and Africa this transitional period between the Paleolithic and the Neolithic is called the **Mesolithic,** or Middle Stone Age. In the Americas, comparable cultures are referred to as **Archaic cultures.**

New technologies accompanied the changed postglacial environment. Manufacture began of ground stone tools, shaped and sharpened by grinding the tool against sandstone, often using sand as an additional abrasive. These shaped, sharpened stones were set into wooden or sometimes antler handles to make effective axes and adzes, a cutting tool with a sharp blade set at right angles to a handle. Though such implements take longer to make, they are less prone to breakage under heavy-duty usage than those made of chipped stone. Thus, they were helpful in clearing forest areas and in the woodwork needed for the creation of dugout canoes and skin-covered boats. Evidence for the presence of seaworthy watercraft at Mesolithic sites indicates that human foraging for food likely took place on the water as well as the land. Thus, it was possible to make use of deep-water resources as well as those of coastal areas, rivers, and lakes.

The **microlith,** a small but hard, sharp, blade, was the characteristic tool of the Mesolithic. Although a microlithic tradition existed in Central Africa by about 40,000 years ago,[2] such tools did not become common elsewhere until the Mesolithic. Microliths could be mass produced because they were small, easy to make, and could be fashioned from sections of blades. These small tools could be attached to arrow or other tool shafts by using melted resin (from pine trees) as a binder. Microliths provided Mesolithic people with an important advantage over their Upper Paleolithic forebears: The small size of the microlith enabled them to devise a wider array of composite tools made out of stone and wood or bone. Thus, they could make sickles, harpoons, arrows, knives, and daggers by fitting microliths into slots in wood, bone, or antler handles. Later experimentation with these forms led to more sophisticated tools and weapons such as bows to propel arrows.

Dwellings from the Mesolithic provide some evidence of a more sedentary lifestyle during this period. By contrast, most hunting peoples, and especially those depending on herd animals, are highly mobile. To be successful, hunters must follow migratory game. People subsisting on diets of seafood and plants in the now milder forested environments of the north, did not need to move regularly over large geographical areas.

In the warmer parts of the world, the collection of wild plant foods complemented hunting in the Upper Paleolithic more than had been the case in the colder northern regions. Hence, in areas like Southwest Asia, the Mesolithic represents less of a changed way of life than was true in Europe. Here, the important **Natufian culture** flourished.

The Natufians lived between 12,500 and 10,200 years ago at the eastern end of the Mediterranean Sea in caves, rock shelters, and small villages with stone- and mud-walled houses. They are named after the Wadi en-Natuf, a ravine near Jerusalem, Israel, where the remains of this culture were first found. They buried their dead in communal cemeteries, usually in shallow pits without any other objects or decorations. A small shrine is known from one of their villages, a 10,500-year-old settlement at Jericho in the Jordan River Valley. Basin-shaped depressions in the rocks found outside homes and plastered storage pits beneath the floors of the houses indicate that the Natufians were the earliest Mesolithic people known to have stored plant foods. Certain tools found among Natufian remains bear evidence of their use to cut grain. These Mesolithic sickles consisted of small stone blades set in straight handles of wood or bone.

The new way of life of the various Mesolithic and Archaic cultures generally provided supplies of food sufficiently abundant to permit people in some parts of the world to live in larger and more sedentary groups.

Mesolithic The Middle Stone Age of Europe, Asia, and Africa beginning about 12,000 years ago.

Archaic cultures Term used to refer to Mesolithic cultures in the Americas.

microlith A small blade of flint or similar stone, several of which were hafted together in wooden handles to make tools; widespread in the Mesolithic.

---

[2]Bednarik, R. G. (1995). Concept-mediated marking in the Lower Paleolithic. *Current Anthropology, 36,* 606.

Natufian culture A Mesolithic culture living in the lands that are now Israel, Lebanon, and western Syria, between about 12,500 and 10,200 years ago.

They became village dwellers, and some of these settlements went on to expand into the first farming villages, towns, and ultimately cities.

THE NEOLITHIC REVOLUTION

The Neolithic, or New Stone Age derives its name from the polished stone tools that are characteristic of this period. But more important than the presence of these tools is the transition from a foraging economy based on hunting, gathering, and fishing to one based on food production, representing a major change in the subsistence practices of early peoples. It was by no means a smooth or instantaneous transition; in fact, the switch to food production spread over many centuries—even millennia—and was a direct outgrowth of the preceding Mesolithic. Where to draw the line between the two periods is not always clear.

One of the first regions to undergo this transition, and certainly the most intensively studied, was Southwest Asia. The remains of domesticated plants and animals are known from parts of Israel, Jordan, Syria, Turkey, Egypt, Iraq, and Iran, from well before 10,000 years ago.

The transition to relatively complete reliance on domesticates took several thousand years. Archaeological evidence for food production also exists from other parts of the world such as China and the Americas at similar or somewhat younger dates. The critical point is not which region invented farming first, but rather the independent but more or less simultaneous invention of food production throughout the globe.

Domestication: What Is It?

Domestication is an evolutionary process whereby humans modify, either intentionally or unintentionally, the genetic makeup of a population of plants or animals, sometimes to the extent that members of the population are unable to survive and/or reproduce without human assistance. Domestication is essentially a special case of interdependence between different species frequently seen in the natural world, where one species depends on another (that feeds upon it) for its protection and reproductive success. For example, certain ants native to the American tropics grow fungi in their nests, and these fungi provide the ants with most of their nutrition. Like

human farmers, the ants add manure to stimulate fungal growth and eliminate competing weeds both mechanically and through use of antibiotic herbicides.[3] The fungi are protected and ensured reproductive success while providing the ants with a steady food supply.

Numerous other examples of such cooperation between species exist, all characterized by mutual benefit. In plant–human interactions, for example, domestication ensures the plants' reproductive success while providing humans with food. From a human point of view, domestication involves selectively reproducing to eliminate thorns, toxins, and bad-tasting chemical compounds that in the wild had served to ensure a plant species' survival and selecting for larger, tastier edible parts attractive to humans. U.S. journalist Michael Pollan has turned this idea around by looking at domestication from a plant's perspective. He suggests that domesticated plant species successfully exploit human desires and considers "agriculture as something grasses did to people to conquer trees."[4]

Evidence of Early Plant Domestication

Domesticated plants generally differ from their wild ancestors in ways favored by humans, including increased size, at least of edible parts; reduction or loss of natural means of seed dispersal; reduction or loss of protective devices such as husks or distasteful chemical compounds; loss of delayed seed germination (important to wild plants for survival in times of drought or other adverse conditions of temporary duration); and development of simultaneous ripening of the seed or fruit. Many of these characteristics can be seen in plant remains from archaeological sites. Paleobotanists can often tell the fossil of a wild plant species from a domesticated one, for example, by studying the shape and size of various plant structures.

Wild cereals have a very fragile stem, whereas domesticated ones have a tough stem. Under natural conditions, plants with fragile stems scatter their seed for themselves, whereas those with tough stems do not. When the grain stalks were harvested, their soft stems would shatter at the touch of sickle or flail, and many of their seeds would be lost. Inevitably, though unintentionally, most of the seeds that people harvested would have been taken from the tough plants. Early domesticators probably also tended to select seed from plants having few husks or none at all—eventually breeding them

---

domestication An evolutionary process whereby humans modify, either intentionally or unintentionally, the genetic makeup of a population of plants or animals, sometimes to the extent that members of the population are unable to survive and/or reproduce without human assistance.

---

[3]Diamond, J. (1998). Ants, crops, and history. *Science, 281,* 1,974–1,975.
[4]Pollan, M. (2001). *The botany of desire: A plant's-eye view of the world.* New York: Random House.

out—because husking prior to pounding the grains into meal or flour required extra labor.

Size of plants is another good indicator of the presence of domestication. For example, the large ear of corn (maize) we know today is a far cry from the tiny ears (about an inch long) characteristic of early maize. In fact, the ear of maize may have arisen when a simple gene mutation transformed male tassel spikes of the wild grass called teosinte into small earliest versions of the female maize ear.[5] Small though these were (an entire ear contained less nourishment than a single kernel of modern maize), they were radically different in structure from the ears of teosinte.

Evidence of Early Animal Domestication

Domestication also produced changes in the skeletal structure of some animals. For example, the horns of wild goats and sheep differ from those of their domesticated counterparts. Most domesticated female sheep have no horns altogether. Similarly, the size of an animal or its parts can vary with domestication as seen in the smaller size of certain teeth of domesticated pigs compared to those of wild ones.

A study of age and sex ratios of butchered animals at an archaeological site may indicate whether animal domestication was practiced. Investigators have determined that if the age and/or sex ratios at the site differ from those in wild herds, the imbalances are due to domestication. Archaeologists documented a sharp rise in the number of young male goats killed at 10,000-year-old sites in the Zagros Mountains of Iran. Evidently people were slaughtering the young males for food and saving the females for breeding. Although such herd management does not prove that the goats were fully domesticated, it does indicate a step in that direction.[6]

In the Andean highlands, the high frequency of bones of newborn llamas at archaeological sites (up to 72 percent at some), dating to around 6,300 years ago, is probably indicative of the beginning of domestication. Such high mortality rates for newborn animals are uncommon in wild herds but are common where animals are penned up. Under confined conditions, the inevitable buildup of mud and filth harbors bacteria and viruses that can be deadly to newborn animals.

Beginnings of Domestication

Over the past 30 years, a good deal of information has accumulated about the beginnings of domestication, primarily in Southwest Asia, Central America, and the Andes. We still do not have all the answers about how and why it took place. Nonetheless, some observations

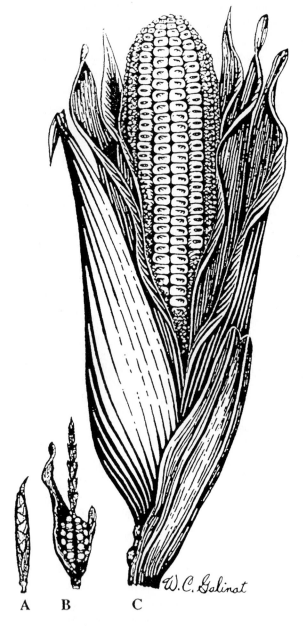

A   B   C

W. C. Galinat

Increased size of edible parts is a common feature of domestication. Teosinte (A), compared to 5,500-year-old maize (B) and modern maize (C). The wild grass from highland Mexico, teosinte, from which maize originated, is far less productive and does not taste very good. Like most plants that were domesticated, it was not a favored food for foraging people. Domestication transformed it into something highly desirable.

[5]Gould, S. J. (1991). *The flamingo's smile: Reflections in natural history* (p. 368). New York: Norton.

[6]Zeder, M. A., & Hesse, B. (2000). The initial domestication of goats (*Capra hircus*) in the Zagros Mountains 10,000 years ago. *Science, 287,* 2,254–2,257.

of general validity can be made that help us to understand how the switch to food production may have taken place.

The first of these observations is that the switch to food production was not the result of people making certain discoveries, such as that seeds, if planted, grow into plants. Contemporary food foragers are far from ignorant about the forces of nature and are perfectly aware of the role of seeds in plant growth, that plants grow better under certain conditions than others, and so forth. Physiologist Jared Diamond aptly describes contemporary food foragers as "walking encyclopedias of natural history with individual names for as many as a thousand or more plant and animal species, and with detailed knowledge of those species' biological characteristics, distribution, and potential uses."[7] What's more, they frequently apply their knowledge so as to manage actively the resources on which they depend. For example, indigenous people living in northern Australia deliberately alter the runoff channels of creeks so as to flood extensive tracts of land, converting them into fields of wild grain. Indigenous Australians choose to continue to forage while also managing the land.

A second observation is that a switch from food foraging to food production does not free people from hard work. In fact, available ethnographic data indicate just the opposite—that farmers, by and large, work far longer hours compared to most food foragers.

A final observation is that food production is not necessarily a more secure means of subsistence than food foraging. Seed crops in particular—of the sort originally domesticated in Southwest Asia, Central America, and the Andean highlands—are highly productive but not stable from an ecological perspective because of low species diversity. Without constant human attention, their productivity suffers.

For these reasons, it is little wonder that food foragers do not necessarily regard farming and animal husbandry as superior to hunting, gathering, or fishing. Thus, there are some people in the world who have remained food foragers into the present. However, it has become increasingly difficult for them, because food-producing peoples (including postindustrial societies) have deprived them of more and more of the land base necessary for their way of life. For food foragers, as long as existing practices work well, there is no need to abandon them especially if they provide an eminently satisfactory way of life. Noting that hunter–gatherers have more leisure time than farmers, U.S. anthropologist Marshall Sahlins has called them "the original affluent

society."[8] Farming brings with it a whole new system of relationships that disturbs an age-old balance between humans and nature.

WHY HUMANS BECAME FOOD PRODUCERS

In view of what has been said so far, we may well ask: Why did any human group abandon food foraging in favor of food production?

Several theories have been proposed to account for this change in human subsistence practices. One older theory, championed by Australian archaeologist V. Gordon Childe, is the desiccation, or oasis, theory, which is based on climatic determinism. Its proponents advanced the idea that the glacial cover over Europe and Asia caused a shift in rain patterns from Europe to northern Africa and Southwest Asia. When the glaciers retreated northward, so did the rain patterns. As a result, northern Africa and Southwest Asia became dryer, and people were forced to congregate at oases for water. Because of the relative food scarcity in such an environment, necessity drove people to collect the wild grasses and seeds growing around the oases, congregating in a part of Southwest Asia known as the Fertile Crescent (Figure 6.1). Eventually they had to cultivate the grasses to provide enough food for the community. According to this theory, animal domestication began because the oases attracted hungry animals, such as wild goats, sheep, and also cattle, which came to graze on the stubble of the grain fields and to drink. Finding that these animals were often too thin to kill for food, people began to fatten them up.

Although Childe's oasis theory can be critiqued on a number of grounds and many other theories have been proposed to account for the shift to domestication, it remains historically significant as the first scientifically testable explanation for the origins of food production. Childe's theory set the stage for the development of archaeology as a science. Later theories build on Childe's ideas and take into account the role of chance environmental circumstances.

The Fertile Crescent

Present evidence indicates that the earliest plant domestication took place gradually in the Fertile Crescent, the lands just east of the Mediterranean Sea. Archaeological data suggest the domestication of rye as early as 13,000 years ago by people living at a site (Abu Hureyra) east of

---

[7]Diamond, J. (1997). *Guns, germs, and steel* (p. 143). New York: Norton.

[8]Sahlins, M. (1972). *Stone age economics*. Chicago: Aldine.

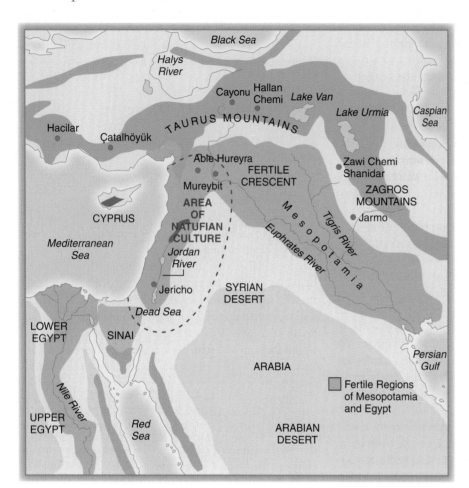

Figure 6.1 **The Fertile Crescent of Southwest Asia and the Area of Natufian Culture**

Aleppo, Syria, although wild plants and animals continued to be their major food sources. Over the next several millennia they became full-fledged farmers, cultivating rye and wheat.[9] By 10,300 years ago, others in the region were also growing crops.

The domestication process was a consequence of a chance convergence of independent natural events and other cultural developments.[10] The Natufians, whose culture we looked at earlier in this chapter, illustrate this process. These people lived at a time of dramatically changing climates in Southwest Asia. With the end of the last glaciation, temperatures not only became significantly warmer but markedly seasonal as well. Between 12,000 and 6,000 years ago, the region experienced the most extreme seasonality in its history, with dry summers significantly longer and hotter than today. As a consequence of increased evaporation, many shallow lakes dried up, leaving just three in the Jordan River Valley. At the same time, the region's plant cover changed dramatically. Those plants best adapted to environmental instability and sea-

sonal dryness were annuals, including wild cereal grains and legumes (such as peas, lentils, and chickpeas). Because they complete their life cycle in a single year, annuals can evolve very quickly under unstable conditions. Moreover, they store their reproductive abilities for the next wet season in abundant seeds, which can remain dormant for prolonged periods.

The Natufians, who lived where these conditions were especially severe, adapted by modifying their subsistence practices in two ways: First, they probably burned the landscape regularly to promote browsing by red deer and grazing by gazelles, the main focus of their hunting activities. Second, they placed greater emphasis on the collection of wild seeds from the annual plants that could be effectively stored to see people through the dry season. The importance of stored foods, coupled with the scarcity of reliable water sources, promoted more sedentary living patterns, reflected in the substantial villages of late Natufian times. The reliance upon seeds in Natufian subsistence was made possible by the fact that they already possessed sickles (originally used to cut reeds and sedges for baskets) for harvesting grain and grinding stones for processing a variety of wild foods.[11]

[9]Pringle, H. (1998). The slow birth of agriculture. *Science, 282,* 1,449.
[10]McCorriston, J., & Hole, F. (1991). The ecology of seasonal stress and the origins of agriculture in the Near East. *American Anthropologist, 93,* 46–69.

[11]Olszewski, D. I. (1991). Comment. *Current Anthropology, 32,* 43.

The use of sickles to harvest grain turned out to have important consequences, again unexpected, for the Natufians. In the course of harvesting, it was inevitable that many easily dispersed seeds would be lost at the harvest site, whereas those from plants that did not readily scatter their seeds would mostly be carried back to where people processed and stored them.[12] The periodic burning of vegetation carried out to promote the deer and gazelle herds may have also affected the development of new genetic variation. Heat is known to affect mutation rates. Also, fire removes individuals from a population, which change the genetic structure of a population drastically and quickly. With seeds for nondispersing variants being carried back to settlements, it was inevitable that some lost seeds would germinate and grow there on dump heaps and other disturbed sites (latrines, areas cleared of trees, or burned-over terrain).

As it turns out, many of the plants that became domesticated were "colonizers," variants that do particularly well in disturbed habitats. Moreover, with people becoming increasingly sedentary, disturbed habitats became more extensive as resources closer to settlements were depleted over time. Thus, variants of plants particularly susceptible to human manipulation had more opportunities to flourish where people were living. Under such circumstances, it was inevitable that eventually people would begin to actively promote their growth, even by deliberately sowing them. Ultimately, people realized that they could play a more active role in the process by deliberately trying to breed the strains they preferred. With this, domestication may be said to have shifted from a process that was unintentional to one that was intentional.

The development of animal domestication in Southwest Asia seems to have proceeded along somewhat similar lines in the hilly country of southeastern Turkey, northern Iraq, and the Zagros Mountains of Iran. Large herds of wild sheep and goats, as well as much environmental diversity, characterized these regions. From the flood plains of the valley of the Tigris and Euphrates rivers, for example, travel to the north or east takes one into high country through three other zones: first steppe; then oak and pistachio woodlands; and, finally, high plateau country with grass, scrub, or desert vegetation. Valleys that run at right angles to the mountain ranges afford relatively easy access across these zones. Today, a number of peoples in the region still graze their herds of sheep and goats on the low steppe in the winter and move to high pastures on the plateaus in the summer.

Moving back in time prior to the domestication of plants and animals, we find the region inhabited by peoples whose subsistence pattern, like that of the Natufians, was one of food foraging. Different plants were found in different ecological zones, and because of the difference in altitude, plant foods matured at different times in different zones. Many animal species were hunted for meat and hides by these people, most notably, the hoofed animals: deer, gazelles, wild goats, and wild sheep. Their bones are far more common in human refuse piles than those of other animals. This is significant, for most of these animals naturally move back and forth from low winter pastures to high summer pastures. People followed these animals in their seasonal migrations, making use along the way of other wild foods in the zones through which they passed: palm dates in the lowlands; acorns, almonds, and pistachios higher up; apples and pears higher still; wild grains maturing at different times in different zones; woodland animals in the forested zone between summer and winter grazing lands. All in all, it was a rich, varied fare.

The archaeological record indicates that, at first, animals of all ages and sexes were hunted by the people of the Southwest Asian highlands. But, beginning about 11,000 years ago, the percentage of immature sheep eaten increased to about 50 percent of the total. At the same time, the percentage of females among animals eaten decreased. Apparently, people were learning that they could increase yields by sparing the females for breeding, while feasting on male lambs. This marks the beginning of human management of sheep. As this management of flocks became more efficient, sheep were increasingly shielded from the effects of natural selection, allowing variants preferred by humans to have increased reproductive success. Variants attractive to humans did not arise out of need but at random, as mutations do. But then humans selectively bred the varieties they favored. In such a way, those features characteristic of domestic sheep—such as greater fat and meat production, excess wool, and so on—began to develop. By 9,000 years ago, the shape and size of the bones of domestic sheep had become distinguishable from those of wild sheep. At about the same time, similar developments were taking place in southeastern Turkey and the lower Jordan River Valley, where pigs were the focus of attention.[13]

Some researchers have recently linked animal domestication to the development of fixed territories and settlements. Without a notion of resource ownership, they suggest that hunters would not be likely to postpone the short-term gain of killing prey for the long-term gain of continued access to animals in the future.[14]

[12]Blumer, M. A., & Byrne, R. (1991). The ecological genetics and domestication and the origins of agriculture. *Current Anthropology, 32,* 30.

[13]Pringle, p. 1,448.

[14]Alvard, M. S., & Kuznar, L. (2001). Deferred harvest: The transition from hunting to animal husbandry. *American Anthropologist, 103*(2), 295–311.

Eventually, animal species domesticated in one area were introduced into areas outside their natural habitat.

To sum up, the domesticators of plants and animals sought only to maximize the food sources available to them. They were not aware of the long-term and revolutionary cultural consequences of their actions. But as the process continued, the productivity of the domestic species increased relative to wild species. Thus they became increasingly more important to subsistence, resulting in further intensification of, interest in, and management of, the domesticates. Inevitably, the result would be further increases in productivity.

OTHER CENTERS OF DOMESTICATION

In addition to Southwest Asia, the domestication of plants and, in some cases, animals took place independently in Southeast Asia, parts of the Americas (Central America, the Andean highlands, the tropical forests of South America, and eastern North America), northern China, and Africa (Figure 6.2). In China, domestication of rice was underway along the middle Yangtze River by about 11,000 years ago.[15] It was not until 4,000 years later, however, that domestic rice dominated wild rice to become the dietary staple.

---

[15]Pringle, p. 1,449.

In Southeast Asia, decorations on pottery dated to some time between 8,800 and 5,000 years ago document rice as the earliest species to be domesticated. This region, however, is primarily known for the domestication of root crops, most notably yams and taro. Root crop farming, or **vegeculture**, typically involves the growing of many different species together in a single field. Because this approximates the complexity of the natural vegetation, vegeculture tends to be more stable than seed crop cultivation. Propagation or breeding of new plants typically occurs through vegetative means—the planting of cuttings—rather than the planting of seeds.

In the Americas, the domestication of plants began about as early as it did in these other regions. One species of domestic squash may have been grown as early as 10,000 years ago in the coastal forests of Ecuador; at the same time another species was being grown in an arid region of highland Mexico.[16] Evidently, these developments were independent of each other. The ecological diversity of the highland valleys of Mexico, like the hill country of Southwest Asia, provided an excellent environment for domestication. Movement of people through a variety of ecological zones as they changed

vegeculture   The cultivation of domesticated root crops, such as yams and taro.

---

[16]Pringle, p. 1,447.

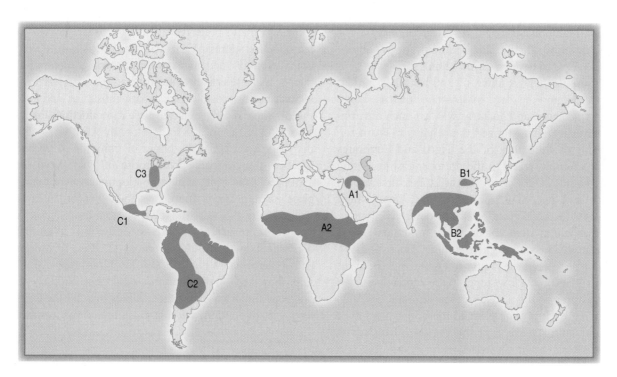

Figure 6.2
Early plant and animal domestication took place in such widely scattered areas as Southwest Asia (A1), Central Africa (A2), China (B1), Southeast Asia (B2), Central America (C1), South America (C2), and North America (C3).

altitude brought plant and animal species into new habitats, providing opportunities for "colonizing" species and humans alike.

Domestication in the Andean highlands of Peru, another environmentally diverse region, emphasized root crops, the best known being potatoes (of which about 3,000 varieties were grown, versus the mere 250 grown today in North America). South Americans also domesticated guinea pigs, llamas, alpacas, and ducks, whereas people in the Mexican highlands never did much with domestic livestock. They limited themselves to dogs, turkeys, and bees. American Indians living north of Mexico developed some of their own indigenous domesticates. These included local varieties of squash and sunflower.

Ultimately, American Indians domesticated over 300 food crops, including two of the four most important ones in the world today: potatoes and maize (the other two are wheat and rice). In fact, 60 percent of the crops grown in the world today were first cultivated by America's indigenous peoples, who not only remain the developers of the world's largest array of nutritious foods but are also the primary contributors to the world's varied cuisines.[17] After all, where would Italian cuisine be without tomatoes? Thai cooking without peanuts? Northern European cooking without potatoes? Small wonder American Indians have been called the world's greatest farmers.[18]

An international team of archaeologists and other scientists is beginning to decipher the farming methods used by Indians in the Amazon rainforest. These ancient methods, which left behind rich dark soils, may have important applications for humans today, as explained in this chapter's Original Study. Reviving these ancient soil-enrichment techniques could contribute to better global management of rainforests and climate today.

_____

[17]Weatherford, J. (1988). *Indian givers: How the Indians of the Americas transformed the world* (pp. 71, 115). New York: Fawcett Columbine.
[18]Weatherford, p. 95.

Original Study

The Real Dirt on Rainforest Fertility

IRANDUBA, AMAZÔNAS STATE, BRAZIL— Above a pit dug by a team of archaeologists here is a papaya orchard filled with unusually vigorous trees bearing great clusters of plump green fruit. Below the surface lies a different sort of bounty: hundreds, perhaps thousands, of burial urns and millions of pieces of broken ceramics, all from an almost unknown people who flourished here before the conquistadors. But surprisingly, what might be most important about this central Amazonian site is not the vibrant orchard or the extraordinary outpouring of ceramics but the dirt under the trees and around the ceramics. A rich, black soil known locally as *terra preta do Indio* (Indian dark earth), it sustained large settlements on these lands for 2 millennia, according to the Brazilian-American archaeological team working here.

Throughout Amazonia, farmers prize terra preta for its great productivity— some farmers have worked it for years with minimal fertilization. Such long-lasting fertility is an anomaly in the tropics. Despite the exuberant growth of rainforests, their red and yellow soils are notoriously poor: weathered, highly acidic, and low in organic matter and essential nutrients. In these oxisols, as they are known, most carbon and nutrients are stored not in the soil, as in temperate regions, but in the vegetation that covers it. When loggers, ranchers, or farmers clear the vegetation, the intense sun and rain quickly decompose the remaining organic matter in the soil, making the land almost incapable of sustaining life—one reason ecologists frequently refer to the tropical forest as a "wet desert."

Because terra preta is subject to the same punishing conditions as the surrounding oxisols, "its existence is very surprising," says Bruno Glaser, a chemist at the Institute of Soil Science and Soil Geography at the University of Bayreuth, Germany. "If you read the textbooks, it shouldn't be there." Yet according to William I. Woods, a geographer at Southern Illinois University, Edwardsville, terra preta might cover as much as 10% of Amazonia, an area the size of France. More remarkable still, terra preta appears to be the product of intensive habitation by precontact Amerindian populations. "They practiced agriculture

here for centuries," Glaser says. "But instead of destroying the soil, they improved it—and that is something we don't know how to do today."

In the past few years, a small but growing group of researchers— geographers, archaeologists, soil scientists, ecologists, and anthropologists—has been investigating this "gift from the past," as terra preta is called by one member of the Iranduba team, James B. Petersen of the University of Vermont, Burlington. By understanding how indigenous groups created Amazonian dark earths, these researchers hope, today's scientists might be able to transform some of the

[continued]

[continued]

region's oxisols into new terra preta. Indeed, experimental programs to produce "terra preta nova" have already begun. Population pressure and government policies are causing rapid deforestation in the tropics, and poor tropical soils make much of the clearing as economically nonviable in the long run as it is ecologically damaging.

The Good Earth

Terra preta is scattered throughout Amazonia, but it is most frequently found on low hills overlooking rivers—the kind of terrain on which indigenous groups preferred to live. According to Eduardo Neves, an archaeologist at the University of São Paulo who is part of the Iranduba team, the oldest deposits date back more than 2,000 years and occur in the lower and central Amazon; terra preta then appeared to spread to cultures upriver. By AD 500 to 1000, he says, "it appeared in almost every part of the Amazon Basin."

Typically, black-soil regions cover 1 to 5 hectares, but some encompass 300 hectares or more. The black soils are generally 40 to 60 centimeters deep but can reach more than 2 meters. Almost always they are full of broken ceramics. Although they were created centuries ago—probably for agriculture, researchers such as Woods believe—patches of terra preta are still among the most desirable land in the Amazon. Indeed, terra preta is valuable enough

that locals sell it as potting soil. To the consternation of archaeologists, long planters full of terra preta, complete with pieces of pre-Columbian pottery, greet visitors to the airport in the lower Amazon town of Santarém.

As a rule, terra preta has more "plant-available" phosphorus, calcium, sulfur, and nitrogen than surrounding oxisols; it also has much more organic matter, retains moisture and nutrients better, and is not rapidly exhausted by agricultural use when managed well.

The key to terra preta's long-term fertility, Glaser says, is charcoal: Terra preta contains up to 70 times as much as adjacent oxisols. "The charcoal prevents organic matter from being rapidly mineralized," Glaser says. "Over time, it partly oxidizes, which keeps providing sites for nutrients to bind to." But simply mixing charcoal into the ground is not enough to create terra preta. Because charcoal contains few nutrients, Glaser says, "high nutrient inputs via excrement and waste such as turtle, fish, and animal bones were necessary." Special soil microorganisms are also likely to play a role in its persistent fertility, in the view of Janice Thies, a soil ecologist who is part of a Cornell University team studying terra preta. "There are indications that microbial biomass is higher in terra preta," she says, which raises the possibility that scientists might be able to create a "package" of charcoal, nutrients, and microfauna that could

be used to transform oxisols into terra preta.

Slash-and-Char

Surprisingly, terra preta seems not to have been created by the "slash-and-burn" agriculture famously practiced in the tropics. In slash-and-burn, farmers clear and then burn their fields, using the ash to flush enough nutrients into the soil to support crops for a few years; when productivity declines, they move on to the next patch of forest. Glaser, Woods, and other researchers believe that the long-ago Amazonians created terra preta by a process that Christoph Steiner, a University of Bayreuth soil scientist, has dubbed "slash-and-char." Instead of completely burning organic matter to ash, in this view, ancient farmers burned it only incompletely, creating charcoal, then stirred the charcoal directly into the soil. Later they added nutrients and, in a process analogous to adding sourdough starter to bread, possibly soil previously enriched with microorganisms. In addition to its potential benefits to the soil, slash-and-char releases much less carbon into the air than slash-and-burn, which has potential implications for climate change. (Charles C. Mann, *Science*, 297, 920–923. Copyright © by the American Association for the Advancement of Science. Reprinted by permission.) ▪ ▪ ▪

Considering the separate innovations of plant domestication, it is interesting to note that in all cases people developed the same categories of foods. Everywhere, starchy grains (or root crops) are accompanied by one or more legumes: wheat and barley with peas, chickpeas, and lentils in Southwest Asia; maize with various kinds of beans in Mexico, for example. Together the amino acids (building blocks of proteins) in these starch and legume combinations provide humans with sufficient protein. The starchy grains are the core of the diet and are eaten at every meal in the form of bread, some sort of food wrapper (like a tortilla) or a gruel or thickening agent in a stew along with one or more legumes. Being rather bland, these sources of carbohydrates and proteins are invariably combined with flavor-giving substances that help the food go down.

In Mexico, for example, the flavor enhancer par excellence is the chili pepper; in other cuisines it may

be a bit of meat, a dairy product, or mushrooms. Anthropologist Sidney Mintz refers to this as the core-fringe-legume pattern (CFLP), noting that only recently has it been upset by the worldwide spread of processed sugars and high-fat foods.[19]

FOOD PRODUCTION AND POPULATION SIZE

Human population has been growing steadily since the Neolithic. The exact relationship between population growth and food production is similar to the old chicken

---

[19]Mintz, S. (1996). A taste of history. In W. A. Haviland & R. J. Gordon (Eds.), *Talking about people* (2nd ed., pp. 81–82). Mountain View, CA: Mayfield.

and egg question. Some assert that population growth creates pressures that result in innovations such as food production while others suggest that population growth is a consequence of food production. As already noted, domestication inevitably leads to higher yields, and higher yields make it possible to feed more people, albeit at the cost of more work.

While increased dependence on farming is associated with increased fertility across human populations,[20] the reasons behind this illustrate the complex interplay between human biology and culture in all human activity. Some researchers have suggested that the availability of soft foods for infants brought about by farming promoted population growth. In humans, frequent breastfeeding has a dampening effect on mothers' ovulation, inhibiting pregnancy in nursing mothers who breastfeed exclusively. Because breastfeeding frequency declines when soft foods are introduced, fertility tends to increase.

However, it would be overly simplistic to limit the explanation for changes in fertility to the introduction

---

[20]Sellen, D. W., & Mace, R. (1997). Fertility and mode of subsistence: A phylogenetic analysis. *Current Anthropology, 38,* 886.

of soft foods. Many other pathways can also lead to fertility changes. For example, among farmers, numerous children are frequently seen as assets to help out with the many household chores. Further, it is now known that sedentary lifestyles and diets emphasizing a narrow range of resources characteristic of the Neolithic led to growing rates of infectious disease and higher mortality. High infant mortality may well have led to a cultural value placed on increased fertility. In other words, the relationship between farming and fertility is far from simple, as explored in this chapter's Biocultural Connection.

THE SPREAD OF FOOD PRODUCTION

Paradoxically, although domestication increases productivity, it also increases instability. This is so because those varieties with the highest yields become the focus of human attention, while other varieties are less valued and ultimately ignored. As a result, farmers become dependent on a rather narrow range of

---

Biocultural Connection

Breastfeeding, Fertility, and Beliefs

Cross-cultural studies indicate that farming populations tend to have higher rates of fertility than hunter–gatherers. These differences in fertility were calculated in terms of the average number of children born per woman and through the average number of years between pregnancies or birth spacing. Hunter–gatherer mothers have their children about 4 to 5 years apart while some contemporary farming populations not practicing any form of birth control have another baby every year and a half.

For many years this difference was interpreted as a consequence of nutritional stress among the hunter–gatherers. This theory was based in part on the observation that humans and many other mammals require a certain percentage of body fat in order to reproduce successfully. The theory was also grounded in the mistaken cultural belief that the hunter–gatherer lifestyle,

supposedly inferior to that of "civilized" people, could not provide adequate nutrition for closer birth spacing. Detailed studies by anthropologists Melvin Konner and Marjorie Shostak, among the !Kung or Ju/'hoansi (pronounced "zhutwasi") people of the Kalahari Desert in southern Africa, disproved this theory, revealing instead a remarkable interplay between cultural and biological processes in human infant feeding.[a, b]

The detailed observations of Ju/'hoansi infant-feeding practices were combined with studies of hormonal levels in nursing Ju/'hoansi mothers conducted by Carol Worthman. Ju/'hoansi mothers do not believe that babies should be fed on schedules, as recommended by some North American child-care experts, nor do they believe that crying is "good" for babies. Instead, they respond rapidly to their infants and breastfeed them whenever the infant

shows any signs of fussing both during the day and night. The resulting pattern is breastfeeding in short very frequent bouts. Together the ethnographic and laboratory studies document that this pattern of breastfeeding stimulates the body to suppress ovulation, or the release of a new egg into the womb for fertilization. The hormonal signals from nipple stimulation through breastfeeding controls the process of ovulation. Thus, the average number of years between children among the Ju/'hoansi is not a consequence of nutritional stress. Instead, Ju/'hoansi infant-feeding practices and beliefs directly affect the biology of fertility. ■ ■ ■

[a]Konner, M., & Worthman, C. (1980). Nursing frequency, gonadal function, and birth spacing among !Kung hunter-gatherers. *Science, 207,* 788–791.

[b]Shostak, M. (1983). *Nisa: The life and words of a !Kung woman.* New York: Random House.

resources, compared to the wide range utilized by food foragers. Today, this range has narrowed further. Modern agriculturists rely on a mere dozen species for about 80 percent of the world's annual tonnage of all crops.[21]

This dependence upon fewer varieties means that when a crop fails, for whatever reason, farmers have less to fall back on than do food foragers. Furthermore, the likelihood of failure is increased by the common farming practice of planting crops together in one locality, so that a disease contracted by one plant can easily spread to others. Moreover, by relying on seeds from the most productive plants of a species to establish next year's crop, farmers favor genetic uniformity over diversity. The result is that if some virus, bacterium, or fungus is able to destroy one plant, it will likely destroy them all. To draw an example for a more recent time period, this is what happened in the terrible Irish potato famine of 1845–1850, which caused the deaths of about 1 million people due to hunger and disease and forced another 2 million to abandon their homes and emigrate. The population of Ireland dropped from 8 million people before the famine to only 5 million after the famine was over.

The Irish potato famine illustrates how the combination of increased productivity and vulnerability may contribute to the geographic spread of farming. Time and time again in the past, population growth, followed by crop failure, has triggered movements of people from one place to another, where they have re-established their familiar subsistence practices. Thus, once farming came into existence, it was more or less guaranteed that it would spread to neighboring regions through such migrations. From Southwest Asia, for instance, farming spread northeastward eventually to all of Europe, westward to North Africa, and eastward to India. Domesticated variants also spread from China and Southeast Asia westward. Those who brought crops to new locations brought other things as well, including languages, beliefs, and new alleles for human gene pools.

A similar spread occurred from West Africa, to the southeast, creating the modern far-reaching distribution of speakers of Bantu languages. Crops including sorghum (so valuable today it is grown in hot, dry areas on all continents), pearl millet, watermelon, black-eyed peas, African yams, oil palms, and kola nuts (source of modern cola drinks) were first domesticated in West Africa but began spreading eastward by 5,000 years ago. Between 3,000 and 2,000 years ago, Bantu speakers with their crops reached the continent's east coast and a few

centuries later reached deep into what is now the country of South Africa. Being well adapted to summer rains, West African crops spread no further, for the Cape of South Africa has a Mediterranean climate with winter rains.

CULTURE OF NEOLITHIC SETTLEMENTS

A number of Neolithic settlements have been excavated, particularly in Southwest Asia. The structures, artifacts, and food debris found at these sites have revealed much about the daily activities of their former inhabitants as they pursued the business of making a living. Perhaps the best known of these sites is Jericho, an early farming community in the Jordan River Valley of Palestine.

Jericho: An Early Farming Community

Excavations at the Neolithic settlement that later grew to become the biblical city of Jericho, revealed the remains of a sizable farming community inhabited as early as 10,350 years ago. Here, in the Jordan River Valley, crops could be grown almost continuously, due to the presence of a bounteous spring and the rich soils of an Ice Age lake that had dried up some 3,000 years earlier. In addition, flood-borne deposits originating in the Judean highlands to the west regularly renewed the fertility of the soil.

To protect their settlement against these floods and associated mudflows, as well as invaders, the people of Jericho built massive walls of stone around it.[22] Within these walls (6½ feet wide and 12 feet high), as well as a large rock-cut ditch (27 feet wide and 9 feet deep), an estimated 400 to 900 people lived in houses of mud brick with plastered floors arranged around courtyards. In addition to these houses, a stone tower that would have taken 100 people 104 days to build was located inside one corner of the wall, near the spring. A staircase inside it probably led to a mud-brick building on top. Nearby were mud-brick storage facilities as well as peculiar structures of possible ceremonial significance. A village cemetery also reflects the sedentary life of these early people; nomadic groups, with few exceptions, rarely buried their dead in a single central location.

Close contact between the farmers of Jericho and other villages is indicated by common features in art,

---

[21]Diamond, p. 132.

[22] Bar-Yosef, O. (1986). The walls of Jericho: An alternative interpretation. *Current Anthropology, 27,* 160.

ritual, use of prestige goods, and burial practices. Other evidence of trade consists of obsidian and turquoise from Sinai as well as marine shells from the coast, all discovered inside the walls of Jericho.

Neolithic Material Culture

Various innovations in the realms of tool making, pottery, housing, and clothing characterized life in Neolithic villages. All of these are examples of material culture.

Tool Making

Early harvesting tools were made of wood or bone into which razor sharp flint blades were inserted. Later tools continued to be made by chipping and flaking stone, but during the Neolithic period, stone that was too hard to be chipped was ground and polished for tools. People developed scythes, forks, hoes, and simple plows to replace their simple digging sticks. Mortars and pestles were used to grind and crush grain. Later, when domesticated animals became available for use as draft animals, plows were redesigned. Along with the development of diverse technologies, individuals acquired specialized skills for creating a variety of implements including leatherworks, weavings, and pottery.

Pottery

Hard work on the part of those producing the food would also support other members of the society who could then apply their skills and energy to various craft specialties such as pottery. In the Neolithic, different

Ancient pottery provides evidence of animal domestication as well as the craft specializations that developed as a consequence of the Neolithic revolution. This pottery vessel from Turkey was made around 7,600 years ago. Pigs were under domestication as early as 11,000 to 10,500 years ago in southeastern Turkey.

©Ankara Archaeological Museum/Ara Guler, Istanbul

forms of pottery were created for transporting and storing food, water, and various material possessions. Because pottery vessels are impervious to damage by insects, rodents, and dampness, they could be used for storing small grain, seeds, and other materials. Moreover, food can be boiled in pottery vessels directly over the fire rather than by such ancient techniques as dropping stones heated directly in the fire into the food being cooked. Pottery was also used for pipes, ladles, lamps, and other objects, and some cultures used large vessels for disposal of the dead. Significantly, pottery containers remain important for much of humanity today.

Widespread use of pottery, which is made of clay and fired in very hot ovens, is a good, though not foolproof, indication of a sedentary community. It is found in abundance in all but a few of the earliest Neolithic settlements. Its fragility and weight make it less practical for use by nomads and hunters, who more typically use woven bags, baskets, and animal hide containers. Nevertheless, there are some modern nomads who make and use pottery, just as there are farmers who lack it. In fact, food foragers in Japan were making pottery by 13,000 years ago, long before it was being made in Southwest Asia.

The manufacture of pottery requires artful skill and some technological sophistication. To make a useful vessel requires knowledge of clay: how to remove impurities from it, how to shape it into desired forms, and how to dry it in a way that does not cause cracking. Proper firing is tricky as well; it must be heated sufficiently so that the clay will harden and resist future disintegration from moisture, but care must be taken to prevent the object from cracking or even exploding as it heats and later cools down.

Pottery is decorated in various ways. For example, designs can be engraved on the vessel before firing, or special rims, legs, bases, and other details may be made separately and fastened to the finished pot. Painting is the most common form of pottery decoration, and there are literally thousands of painted designs found among the pottery remains of ancient cultures.

Housing

Food production and the new sedentary lifestyle brought about another technological development— house building. Permanent housing is of limited interest to most food foragers who frequently are on the move. Cave shelters, pits dug in the earth, and simple lean-tos made of hides and tree limbs serve the purpose of keeping the weather out. In the Neolithic, however, dwellings became more complex in design and more diverse in type. Some were constructed of wood, while others included more elaborate shelters made of stone, sun-dried brick, or branches plastered together with mud or clay.

Although permanent housing frequently goes along with food production, there is evidence that substantial housing could exist without food production. For example, on the northwestern coast of North America, people lived in substantial houses made of heavy planks hewn from cedar logs, yet their food consisted entirely of wild plants and animals, especially salmon and sea mammals.

Clothing

During the Neolithic, for the first time in human history, clothing was made of woven textiles. The raw materials and technology necessary for the production of clothing came from several sources: flax and cotton from farming; wool from domesticated sheep, llamas, or goats; silk from silk worms. Human invention contributed the spindle for spinning and the loom for weaving.

Social Structure

Evidence of all the economic and technological developments listed thus far have enabled archaeologists to draw certain inferences concerning the organization of Neolithic societies. Although indication of ceremonial activity exists, little evidence of a centrally organized and directed religious life has been found. Burials, for example, show a marked absence of social differentiation. Early Neolithic graves were rarely constructed of or covered by stone slabs and rarely included elaborate objects. Evidently, no person had attained the kind of exalted status that would have required an elaborate funeral. The smallness of most villages and the absence of elaborate buildings suggest that the inhabitants knew one another very well and were even related, so that most of their relationships were probably highly personal ones, with equal emotional significance.

The general picture that emerges is one of a relatively egalitarian society with minimal division of labor but some development of new and more specialized social roles. Villages seem to have been made up of several households, each providing for most of its own needs. The organizational needs of society beyond the household level were probably met by kinship groups.

Neolithic Cultures in the Americas

In the Americas the shape and timing of the Neolithic revolution differed compared to other parts of the world. For example, Neolithic agricultural villages were common in Southwest Asia between 9,000 and 8,000 years

ago, but similar villages did not appear in the Americas until about 4,500 years ago, in **Mesoamerica** (southern Mexico and northern Central America) and the Andean highlands. Moreover, pottery, which developed in Southwest Asia shortly after plant and animal domestication, did not emerge in the Americas until about 4,500 years ago. The potter's wheel was not used by early Neolithic people in the Americas. Instead, elaborate pottery was manufactured by hand. Looms and the hand spindle appeared in the Americas about 3,000 years ago.

None of these absences indicate any backwardness on the part of Native American peoples, many of whom, as we have already seen, were highly sophisticated farmers and plant breeders. Rather, the effectiveness of existing practices was such that they continued to be satisfactory. When food production developed in Mesoamerica and the Andean highlands, it did so wholly independently of Europe and Asia, with different crops, animals, and technologies.

Outside Mesoamerica and the Andean highlands, hunting, fishing, and the gathering of wild plant foods remained important elements in the economy of Neolithic peoples in the Americas. Apparently, most American Indians chose not to make as complete a change from a food-foraging to a food-producing mode of life, even though maize and other domestic crops came to be cultivated just about everywhere that climate permitted.

THE NEOLITHIC AND HUMAN BIOLOGY

Although we tend to think of the invention of food production in terms of its cultural consequences, it obviously had a biological impact as well. From studies of human skeletons from Neolithic burials, physical anthropologists have found evidence for a somewhat lessened mechanical stress on peoples' bodies and teeth. Although there are exceptions, the teeth of Neolithic peoples generally show less wear, their bones are less robust, and osteoarthritis (the result of stressed joint surfaces) is not as marked as in the skeletons of Paleolithic and Mesolithic peoples.

On the other hand, there is clear evidence for a marked deterioration in health and mortality. Skeletons from Neolithic villages show evidence of severe and chronic nutritional stress as well as pathologies related to infectious and deficiency diseases. High starch diets led to increased dental decay during the Neolithic as well.

Mesoamerica   The region encompassing southern Mexico and northern Central America.

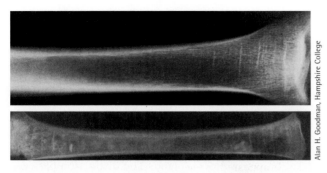

Harris lines near the ends of these youthful thigh bones, found in a prehistoric farming community in Arizona, are indicative of recovery after growth arrest, caused by famine or disease.

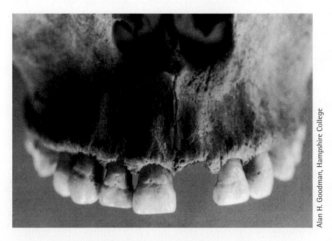

Enamel hypoplasias, such as those shown on these teeth, are indicative of arrested growth caused by famine or disease. These teeth are from an adult who lived in an ancient farming community in Arizona.

For the most part, the crops on which Neolithic peoples came to depend were selected for their higher productivity and storability rather than nutritional balance. Moreover, as already noted, their nutritional shortcomings would have been exacerbated by their susceptibility to periodic failure, particularly as populations grew in size. Thus, the worsened health and higher mortality of Neolithic peoples is not surprising. Some have gone so far as to assert that the switch from food foraging to food production was the worst mistake that humans ever made!

Another key contributor to the increased incidence of disease and mortality was probably the new mode of life in Neolithic communities. Sedentary life in fixed villages brings with it sanitation problems as garbage and human waste accumulate. These are not a problem for small groups of people who move about from one campsite to another. Moreover, airborne diseases are more easily transmitted where people are gathered into villages. Farming practices also created the ideal environment for the species of mosquito that spreads malaria.

Another factor, too, was the close association between humans and their domestic animals, a situation conducive to the transmission of some animal diseases to humans. A host of life-threatening diseases—including smallpox, chicken pox, and in fact all of the infectious diseases of childhood that were not overcome by medical science until the latter half of the 20th century—were transmitted to humans through their close association with domestic animals (Table 6.1).

Scientists have recently documented dental drilling of teeth in a 9,000-year-old Neolithic site in Pakistan.[23]

Domestication encourages a sedentary lifestyle with the great potential for overpopulation relative to the resource base. Under these conditions, even minor environmental fluctuations can lead to widespread hunger and malnutrition. Evidence of stress and disease increased proportionally with population density and the reliance on intensive agriculture.[24] Further, the crowded conditions in settlements and competition among settlements for resources also led to increased mortality due to warfare.

---

[23]Coppa, A., et al. (2006). Early Neolithic tradition of dentistry. *Nature, 440*, 755–756.

[24]Cohen, M. N., & Armelagos, G. J. (1984). *Paleopathology at the origins of agriculture.* Orlando: Academic Press; Goodman, A., & Armelagos, G. J. (1985). Death and disease at Dr. Dickson's mounds. *Natural History Magazine, 94*(9), 12–18.

TABLE 6.1	DISEASES ACQUIRED FROM DOMESTICATED ANIMALS
Disease	**Animal with Most Closely Related Pathogen**
Measles	Cattle (rinderpest)
Tuberculosis	Cattle
Smallpox	Cattle (cowpox) or other livestock with related pox viruses
Influenza	Pigs, ducks
Pertussis ("whooping cough")	Pigs, dogs

Some of the diseases that humans have acquired from domestic animals. For example, humans have developed symptoms from infection with avian influenza (bird flu) following contact with domesticated birds. Close contact with animals provides a situation in which variants of animal pathogens may establish themselves in humans.

Source: Diamond, J. (1997). *Guns, germs, and steel* (p. 207). New York: Norton.

THE NEOLITHIC
AND THE IDEA OF PROGRESS

Despite the fact that the overall health of Neolithic peoples often worsened as a consequence of this cultural shift, many view the transition from food foraging to food production as a great step upward on a ladder of progress. In part this interpretation is due to one of the more widely held beliefs of Western culture, that human history is basically a record of steady progress over time. To be sure, farming allowed people to increase the size of their populations, to live together in substantial sedentary communities, and to reorganize the workload in ways that permitted craft specialization. This is not progress in a universal sense but, rather, a set of cultural beliefs about the nature of progress. Each culture, after all, defines progress (if it does so at all) in its own terms.

Whatever the benefits of food production, however, a substantial price was paid. As anthropologists Mark Cohen and George Armelagos put it, "Taken as a whole, indicators fairly clearly suggest an overall decline in the quality—and probably in the length—of human life associated with the adoption of agriculture."[25]

Rather than imposing ethnocentric notions of progress on the archaeological record, it is best to view the advent of food production as but one more factor contributing to the diversification of cultures, something that had begun in the Paleolithic. Although some societies continued to practice various forms of hunting, gathering, and fishing, others became **horticultural**—small communities of gardeners working with simple hand tools and using neither irrigation

---

[25] Cohen, M. N., & Armelagos, G. J. (1984). Paleopathology at the origins of agriculture: Editors' summation. In *Paleopathology at the origins of agriculture* (p. 594). Orlando: Academic Press.

nor the plow. Horticulturists typically cultivate a variety of crops in small gardens they have cleared by hand. Some horticultural societies, however, developed **agriculture.** Technologically more complex than horticultural societies, agriculturalists practice intensive crop cultivation, employing plows, fertilizers, and possibly irrigation. They may use a wooden or metal plow pulled by one or more harnessed draft animals, such as the horse, oxen, or water buffalo, to produce food on larger plots of land. The distinction between horticulturalist and intensive agriculturalist is not always an easy one to make. For example, the Hopi Indians of the North American Southwest traditionally employed irrigation in their farming while at the same time using basic hand tools.

Pastoralism arose in environments that were too dry, too grassy, too steep, too cold, or too hot for effective horticulture or intensive agriculture. Pastoralists breed and manage migratory herds of domesticated grazing animals, such as goats, sheep, cattle, llamas, or camels. For example, the Russian steppes, with their heavy grass cover, were not suitable to farming without a plow, but they were ideal for herding. Thus, a number of peoples living in the arid grasslands and deserts that stretch from northwestern Africa into Central Asia kept large herds of domestic animals, relying on their neighbors for plant foods. Finally, some societies went on to develop civilizations—the subject of the next chapter.

> **horticulture** Cultivation of crops carried out with simple hand tools such as digging sticks or hoes.
> **agriculture** Intensive crop cultivation, employing plows, fertilizers, and/or irrigation.
> **pastoralism** Breeding and managing migratory herds of domesticated grazing animals, such as goats, sheep, cattle, llamas, or camels.

Chapter Summary

■ The end of the glacial period saw great physical changes in human habitats. Sea levels rose, vegetation changed, and herd animals disappeared from many areas. The Mesolithic period marked a shift from big game hunting to the hunting of smaller game and gathering a broad spectrum of plants and aquatic resources. Increased reliance on seafood and plants made the Mesolithic a more sedentary period for many peoples. Ground stone tools, including axes and adzes, met the needs for new technologies in the postglacial world. Many Mesolithic tools in the Old World were made with microliths—small, hard, sharp blades of flint or similar stone that could be mass produced and hafted with others to produce implements like sickles. In

the Americas, Archaic cultures are comparable to the Old World Mesolithic.

■ The change to food production took place independently and more or less simultaneously in various regions of the world. Along with food production, people became more sedentary, allowing for a reorganization of the workload, so that some people could pursue other tasks. From the end of the Mesolithic, some human groups became larger and more permanent as people domesticated plants and animals.

■ A domesticated plant or animal is one that has become genetically modified as an intended or unintended consequence of human manipulation. Analysis of plant and animal remains at a site usually indicate whether its occupants were food producers. Wild cereal grasses, for example, typically have fragile stems, whereas cultivated ones have tough stems. Domesticated plants can also be identified because their edible parts are generally larger than those of their wild counterparts. Domestication produces skeletal changes in some animals. The horns of wild goats and sheep, for example, differ from those of domesticated ones. Age and sex imbalances in herd animals may also indicate manipulation by human domesticators.

■ The most probable theory to account for the Neolithic revolution is that domestication came about as a consequence of a chance convergence of separate natural events and cultural developments. This happened independently at basically the same time in Southwest and Southeast Asia, highland Mexico and Peru, South America's Amazon forest, eastern North America, China, and Africa. In all cases, however, people developed food complexes based on starchy grains and/or roots that were consumed with protein-containing legumes plus flavor enhancers.

■ Human population sizes have increased steadily since the Neolithic. Some scholars believe that pressure from increasing population size led to innovations such as intensive agriculture. Others suggest that these innovations allowed population size to grow.

■ Two major consequences of domestication are that crops become more productive but also more vulnerable. This combination periodically causes population size to outstrip food supplies, whereupon people are apt to move into new regions. In this way, farming has often spread from one region to another, as into Europe from Southwest Asia. Sometimes, food foragers will adopt the cultivation of crops from neighboring peoples in response to a shortage of wild foods.

■ Among the earliest known sites containing domesticated plants and animals, about 10,300 to 9,000 years old, are those of Southwest Asia. These sites were mostly small villages of mud huts with individual storage pits and clay ovens. There is evidence not only of cultivation and domestication but also of trade. At ancient Jericho, remains of tools, houses, and clothing indicate the oasis was occupied by Neolithic people as early as 10,350 years ago. At its height, Neolithic Jericho had a population of 400 to 900 people. Comparable villages developed independently in Mexico and Peru by about 4,500 years ago.

■ During the Neolithic, stone that was too hard to be chipped was ground and polished for tools. People developed scythes, forks, hoes, and plows to replace simple digging sticks. The Neolithic was also characterized by the extensive manufacture and use of pottery. The widespread use of pottery is a good indicator of a sedentary community. It is found in all but a few of the earliest Neolithic settlements. The manufacture of pottery requires knowledge of clay and the techniques of firing or baking. Other technological developments that accompanied food production and the sedentary life were the building of permanent houses and the weaving of textiles.

■ Archaeologists have been able to draw some inferences concerning the social structure of Neolithic societies. No evidence has been found indicating that religion or government was yet a centrally organized institution. Social organization was probably relatively egalitarian, with minimal division of labor and little development of specialized social roles.

■ The development of food production had biological, as well as cultural, consequences. New diets, living arrangements, and farming practices led to increased incidence of disease and higher mortality rates. Increased fertility, however, more than offset mortality, and globally human population has grown since the Neolithic.

Questions for Reflection

1. The changed lifeways of the Neolithic included the domestication of plants and animals as well as settlement into villages. How did these cultural transformations both solve the challenges of existence while creating new challenges for humans of the past and today?

2. Why do you think some people of the past chose not to make the change from food foragers to food producers? What problems existing in today's world have their origins in the lifeways of the Neolithic?

3. Though human biology and culture are always interacting, the rates of biological change and culture change uncoupled at some point in the history of our development. Think of examples of how the differences in these rates had consequences for humans in the Neolithic and in the present.

4. Why are the changes of the Neolithic sometimes mistakenly associated with progress? Why have the social forms that originated in the Neolithic come to dominate the earth?

5. Although the archaeological record indicates some differences in the timing of domestication of plants and animals in different parts of the world, why is it incorrect to say that one region was more advanced than another?

Key Terms

Neolithic	vegeculture
Mesolithic	Mesoamerica
Archaic cultures	horticulture
microlith	agriculture
Natufian culture	pastoralism
domestication	

Multimedia Review Tools

Make the Grade in Anthropology with ThomsonNOW

Thomson NOW! This powerful online study tool provides you with a *personalized study plan* based on your responses to a diagnostic pretest. Once you have mastered the material with the help of interactive learning tools, an integrated e-book, and more, you can take a post-test to confirm you are ready to move on to the next chapter. To get started with ThomsonNOW, check the card packaged with your book for the access code. Then go to http://www.thomsonedu.com to create an account through 1pass™. If there is no card in your book, go to http://www.thomsonedu.com to purchase an access code.

Companion Website and Anthropology Resource Center

Go to http://anthropology.wadsworth.com to reach the companion website for your text. This offers many study aids, including self quizzes for each chapter and a practice final exam, as well as links to anthropology websites and information on the latest theories and discoveries in the field.

Also, check out the Anthropology Resource Center for a wealth of learning materials that include interactive maps, video exercises, simulations, and breaking news in anthropology. Be sure to explore InfoTrac College Edition®, your online library that offers full-length articles from thousands of scholarly and popular publications. To reach the Anthropology Resource Center and InfoTrac College Edition, check the card packaged with your book for the access code. Then go to http://www.thomsonedu.com to create an account through 1pass™. If there is no card in your book, go to http://www.thomsonedu.com to purchase an access code.

© Susan Zheng/UNEP/Peter Arnold, Ir

CHALLENGE ISSUE

With the emergence of cities and states, people began to face the challenge of social stratification in which a ruling elite controls the means of subsistence and many other aspects of daily life, often resulting in the oppression of others. While the people of such societies are interdependent, the elite classes have disproportionate access to and control of all resources including human labor. The centralized governments that emerged with cities and states have commonly used their power to mobilize and supervise labor for the construction of large-scale dwellings, monuments, and military works, all of which served to strengthen or extend their rule. One such monumental undertaking was the Great Wall of China, a 4,163-mile wall built over 2,000 years ago, for protection from plundering nomadic peoples to the north.

The Emergence
of Cities and States

7

A walk down a busy street of a city such as New York or San Francisco brings us in contact with numerous activities essential to life in North American society. Sidewalks are crowded with people going to and from offices and stores. Heavy traffic of cars, taxis, and trucks periodically comes to a standstill. A brief two-block stretch may contain a grocery store; shops selling clothing, appliances, or books; a restaurant; a newsstand; a gasoline station; and a movie theater. Other features such as a museum, a police station, a school, a hospital, or a church distinguish some neighborhoods.

Each of these services or places of business is dependent on others from outside this two-block radius. A butcher shop, for instance, depends on slaughterhouses and beef ranches. A clothing store could not exist without designers, farmers who produce cotton and wool, and workers who manufacture synthetic fibers. Restaurants rely on refrigerated trucking and vegetable and dairy farmers. Hospitals need insurance companies, pharmaceutical companies, and medical equipment industries to function. All institutions, finally, depend on the public utilities—the telephone, gas, water, and electric companies. Although interdependence is not immediately apparent to the passerby, it is an important aspect of modern cities.

The interdependence of goods and services in a big city makes a variety of products readily available to people. But interdependence also creates vulnerability. If strikes, bad weather, or acts of violence cause one service to stop functioning, other services can deteriorate. At the same time, cities are resilient in their response to stresses. When one service breaks down, others take over its functions. During a long newspaper strike in New York City in the 1960s, for example, several new magazines were launched, and television networks expanded their coverage of news and events. In many parts of the world the violence of war has caused extensive damage to basic infrastructure, leading to the development of alternative systems to cope with everything from the most basic tasks such as procuring food to communication within global political systems.

On the surface, city life seems so orderly that we take it for granted; but a moment's reflection reminds us that the intricate fabric of city life did not always exist, and the concentrated availability of diverse goods is a very recent development in human history.

DEFINING CIVILIZATION

The word *civilization* comes from the Latin *civis*, which refers to one who is an inhabitant of a city, and *civitas*, which refers to the urban community in which one dwells. The concept of civilization therefore contains the idea of "citification" or "the coming-to-be of cities."

In everyday North American and European usage, the word *civilization* carries the notion of refinement and progress, and the term may imply judgments about cultures according to an ethnocentric standard. In anthropology, by contrast, the term has a more precise meaning that avoids culture-bound notions. As used by anthropologists, **civilization** refers to societies in which large numbers of people live in cities, are socially stratified, and are governed by a ruling elite working through centrally organized political systems called states. We shall elaborate on all of these points in the course of this chapter.

As Neolithic villages grew into towns, the world's first cities developed. This happened between 6,000 and 4,500 years ago, first in Mesopotamia (modern-day Iraq), then in Egypt's Nile Valley and the Indus Valley (today's India and Pakistan). In China, civilization was underway by 5,000 years ago. Independent of these developments in Eurasia and Africa, the first American Indian cities appeared in Peru around 4,000 years ago and in Mesoamerica about 2,000 years ago (Figure 7.1).

What characterized these first cities? Why are they called the birthplaces of civilization? The first feature of cities—and of civilization—is their large size and population.

> **civilization** In anthropology a type of society marked by the presence of cities, social classes, and the state.

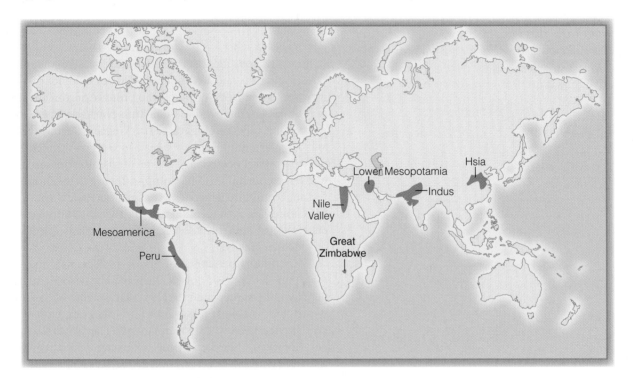

Figure 7.1
The major early civilizations sprang from Neolithic villages in various parts of the world. Those of the Americas developed wholly independently of those in Africa and Eurasia; Chinese civilization seems to have developed independently of Southwest Asia (including the Nile and Indus) civilizations.

But cities are more than overgrown towns. Consider the case of Çatalhöyük, a compact 9,500-year-old village settlement in south-central Turkey.[1] The tightly packed houses for its more than 5,000 inhabitants left no room for streets. People traversed the roofs of neighboring houses and dropped through a hole in the roof to get into their own homes. While house walls were covered with all sorts of paintings and bas-reliefs, the houses were structurally similar to one another, and no known public architecture existed. People grew some crops and tended livestock but also collected significant amounts of food from wild plants and animals, never intensifying their agricultural practices. Evidence of a division of labor or of a centralized authority is minimal or nonexistent. It was as if several Neolithic villages were crammed together in one place at Çatalhöyük.

Archaeological evidence from early urban centers, by contrast, demonstrates organized planning by a central authority, technological intensification, and social stratification. For example, flood control and protection were vital components of the great ancient cities of the Indus River Valley, located in today's India and Pakistan. Mohenjo-Daro an urban center at its peak some 4,500 years ago with a population of at least 20,000, was built on an artificial mound, safe from flood waters. Further, the streets of this densely populated city were laid out in a grid pattern and included individual homes with sophisticated drainage systems.

Ancient peoples incorporated their spiritual beliefs and social order into the cities they built. For example, the layout of the great Mesoamerican city Teotihuacan, founded 2,200 years ago, translated the solar calendar into a unified spatial pattern. The Street of the Dead—a grand north-south axis bordered by the Pyramid of the Sun and the Pyramid of the Moon and a royal palace compound—was deliberately oriented to an astronomical marker, east of true north. Ancient city planners even channeled the San Juan River to conform to the grid where it runs through the city. Surrounding this core were thousands of apartment compounds, separated from one another by a grid of narrow streets, maintaining the east-of-north orientation throughout the city. It is estimated that over 100,000 people inhabited this great city until its sudden collapse possibly in the 7th century.

Finally, clear evidence for both social and economic diversity exists in Teotihuacan. Some six levels of society can be recognized by variation in size and quality of apartment rooms. Those at and near the top of the social scale lived on or near the Street of the Dead. The Pyramid of the Sun along this avenue was built above a cave, which was seen as a portal to the underworld and as the home of deities associated with death. Teotihuacan artisans worked on exotic goods and raw materials imported from afar, and at least two neighborhoods housed people with foreign affiliations—one with Oaxaca, the other (the "merchant's barrio") with the Gulf and Maya lowlands. Farmers, whose labor in fields (some of them irrigated) supplied the food to fellow city dwellers, also resided in the city.[2]

Mohenjo-Daro and Teotihuacan, like other early cities throughout the globe, were far more than expanded Neolithic villages. Such great changes took place in the transition from village to city that the emergence of urban living is considered by some to be one of the great developments in human culture. The following case study gives us a glimpse of another of the world's ancient cities, how archaeologists studied it, and how it may have grown from a smaller farming community.

TIKAL: A CASE STUDY

The ancient city of Tikal, one of the largest lowland Maya centers in existence, is situated in Central America about 300 kilometers north of Guatemala City. Tikal was built on a broad limestone terrace in a rainforest. Here the Maya settled 3,000 years ago. Because the Maya calendar can be precisely correlated with our own, it is known that their civilization flourished until 1,100 years ago.

At its height, Tikal covered about 120 square kilometers (km^2), and its center or nucleus was the Great Plaza, a large, paved area surrounded by about 300 major structures and thousands of houses. Starting from a small, dispersed population, Tikal swelled to at least 45,000 people. By 1,550 years ago, its population density had reached 600 to 700 persons per square kilometer, which was three times that of the surrounding region.

Tikal and the surrounding region were intensively explored under the joint auspices of the University of

---

[1]Material on Çatalhöyük is drawn from Balter, M. (1998). Why settle down? The mystery of communities. *Science, 282,* 1,442–1,444; Balter, M. (1999). A long season puts Çatalhöyük in context. *Science, 286,* 890–891; Balter, M. (2001). Did plaster hold Neolithic society together? *Science, 294,* 2,278–2,281; Kunzig, R. (1999). A tale of two obsessed archaeologists, one ancient city and nagging doubts about whether science can ever hope to reveal the past. *Discover, 20*(5), 84–92.

[2]Cowgill, G. L. (1997). State and society at Teotihuacan, Mexico. *Annual Review of Anthropology, 26,* 129–161.

At Tikal only the tallest temples are visible above the forest canopy. The two farthest temples are at either end of the Great Plaza, the civic and ceremonial heart of the city. (Those familiar with the original *Star Wars* movie will recognize this view.)

Pennsylvania Museum and the Guatemalan government from 1956 through the 1960s. At the time, it was the most ambitious archaeological project undertaken in the western hemisphere.

In the first few years of the Tikal Project, archaeologists investigated only major temple and palace structures found in the vicinity of the Great Plaza, at the site's epicenter. But in 1959, aiming to gain a balanced view of Tikal's development and composition, they turned their attention to hundreds of small mounds that surrounded larger buildings and were thought to be the remains of dwellings. In some senses, this represented a shift in the practice of archaeology toward studying the complexities of everyday life. Imagine how difficult it would be to get a realistic view of life in a major city such as Washington, D.C., or Beijing by looking only at their monumental public buildings. Similarly, a realistic view of Tikal cannot be reconstructed without examining the full range of ruins in the area.

The excavation of small structures, most of which were probably houses, permitted the estimation of Tikal's population size and density. This information was critical for testing hypotheses regarding the city's Maya inhabitants. These data allowed archaeologists to test the conventional assumption that the Maya's subsistence practices were inadequate to sustain large population concentrations.

Extensive excavation also provided a sound basis for a reconstruction of the everyday life and social organization of the Maya, a people who had been known almost entirely through the study of ceremonial remains. For example, differences in architecture, house construction, and associated artifacts and burials suggest social class differences. Features of house distribution might reflect the existence of extended families or other types of kin groups. The excavation of both large and small structures revealed the social structure of the total population of Tikal.[3]

Surveying and Excavating the Site

Mapping crews extensively surveyed 6 km² of forested land surrounding the Great Plaza, providing a preliminary map to guide the small structure excavation process.[4] Aerial photography could not be used for this mapping, because the tree canopy in this area is often 30 meters (about 100 feet) above the ground, obscuring all but the tallest temples. Many of the small ruins are practically invisible even to observers on the ground. Four years of mapping revealed that ancient Tikal was far larger than the originally 6 km² surveyed. More time and money were required to continue surveying the area in order to fully define the city's boundaries and calculate its overall size.[5]

The initial excavation of six structures, two plazas, and a platform revealed new structures not visible before excavation, the architectural complexity of the structures, and an enormous quantity of artifacts that had to be washed and catalogued. Consequently, not every structure was completely excavated, and some remained uninvestigated. Following this initial work, the

[3]Haviland, W. A. (2002). Settlement, society and demography at Tikal. In J. Sabloff (Ed.), *Tikal*. Santa Fe: School of American Research.
[4]Haviland, W. A., et al. (1985). *Excavations in small residential groups of Tikal: Groups 4F-1 and 4F-2*. Philadelphia: University Museum.
[5]Puleston, D. E. (1983). *The settlement survey of Tikal*. Philadelphia: University Museum.

archaeological team excavated over 100 additional small structures in different parts of the site in order to ensure investigation of a representative sample. The team also sunk numerous test pits in various other small structure groups to supplement the information gained from more extensive excavations.

Evidence from the Excavation

Excavation at Tikal produced considerable evidence about the social organization, technology, and diversity in this ancient city, as well as the relationship between people in Tikal and other regions. For example, the site provides evidence of trade in nonperishable items. Granite, quartzite, hematite, pyrite, jade, slate, and obsidian all were imported, either as raw materials or finished products. Marine materials came from Caribbean and Pacific coastal areas. Tikal is located on top of an abundant source of chert (a flintlike stone used to manufacture tools), which may have been exported in the form of raw material and finished objects. The site is located between two river systems to the east and west, and so may have been on a major overland trade route between the two. Also, evidence exists for trade in perishable goods such as textiles, feathers, salt, and cacao. We can safely conclude that there were full-time traders among the Tikal Maya.

In the realm of technology, specialized woodworking, pottery, obsidian, and shell workshops have been found. The skillful stone carving displayed on stone monuments suggests that occupational specialists did this work. The same is true of the fine artwork exhibited on ceramic vessels. Ancient artists had to envision what their work would look like after their pale, relatively colorless ceramics had been fired.

To control the large population, some form of bureaucratic organization must have existed in Tikal. From Maya written records (glyphs), we know that the government was headed by a hereditary ruling dynasty with sufficient power to organize massive construction and maintenance. This included a system of defensive ditches and embankments on the northern and southern edges of the city. The longest of these ran for a distance of perhaps 19 to 28 km. Although we do not have direct evidence, there are clues to the existence of textile workers, dental workers, makers of bark cloth "paper," scribes, masons, astronomers, and other occupational specialists.

The religion of the Tikal Maya may have developed initially as a means to cope with the uncertainties of agriculture. Soils at Tikal are thin, and the only available water comes from rain that has been collected in ponds. Rain is abundant in season, but its onset tends to be unreliable. Conversely, the elevation of Tikal, high relative to surrounding terrain, may have caused it to be perceived as a "power place," especially suited for making contact with supernatural forces and beings.

The Maya priests tried not only to win over and please the deities in times of drought but also to honor them in times of plenty. Priests, the experts on the Maya calendar, determined the most favorable time to plant crops and were concerned with other agricultural matters. This tended to keep people in or near the city. The population in and around Tikal depended upon their priesthood to influence supernatural beings and forces on their behalf, so that their crops would not fail.

As the population increased, land for agriculture became scarce, forcing the Maya to find new methods of food production that could sustain the dense population concentrated at Tikal. They added the planting and tending of fruit trees and other crops that could be grown around their houses in soils enriched by human waste (unlike houses at Teotihuacan, those at Tikal were not built close to one another). Along with increased reliance on household gardening, the Maya constructed artificially raised fields in areas that were flooded each rainy season. In these fields, crops could be intensively cultivated year after year, as long as they were carefully maintained. Measures were taken to maximize collection of water for the dry season, by converting low areas into reservoirs and constructing channels to carry runoff from plazas and other architecture into these reservoirs. As these changes were taking place, a class of artisans, craftspeople, and other occupational specialists emerged to serve the needs of an elite consisting of the priesthood and a ruling dynasty. The Maya built numerous temples, public buildings, and various kinds of houses appropriate to the distinct social classes of their society.

For several hundred years, Tikal was able to sustain its ever-growing population. When the pressure for food and land reached a critical point, population growth stopped. At the same time, warfare with other cities was becoming increasingly destructive. All of this is marked archaeologically by abandonment of houses on prime land in rural areas, by the advent of nutritional problems visible in skeletons recovered from burials, and by the construction of the previously mentioned defensive ditches and embankments. In other words, a period of readjustment set in, which must have been directed by an already strong central authority. Activities then continued as before, but without further population growth for another 250 years or so.

As this case study shows, excavations at Tikal demonstrated the splendor, the social organization, the belief systems, the agricultural practices of the ancient Maya civilization among other things. This chapter's Anthropology Applied feature illustrates a very different approach to another Maya site, just a day's walk from Tikal.

Anthropology Applied

Action Archaeology and the Community at El Pilar

Resource management and conservation are palpable themes of the day. Nowhere is this more keenly felt than the Maya forest, one of the world's most biodiverse areas and among the last terrestrial frontiers. Over the next two decades this area's population will double, threatening the integrity of the tropical ecosystems with contemporary development strategies. Curiously, in the past the Maya forest was home to a major civilization with at least three to nine times the current population of the region.

I began my work as an archaeologist in the Maya forest in 1972. I was interested in the everyday life of the Maya through the study of their cultural ecology—the multifaceted relationships of humans and their environment— rather than monumental buildings. Despite my interest in daily life in the forest, monumental buildings became a part of my work. While conducting a settlement survey in the forest, I discovered El Pilar, a Maya urban center with temples and plazas covering more than 50 hectares. The observation that the ancient Maya evolved a sustainable economy in the tropics of Mesoamerica led my approach to developing El Pilar.

Astride the contemporary border separating Belize from Guatemala, El Pilar has been the focus of a bold conservation design for an international friendship park on a troubled border. My vision for El Pilar is founded on the preservation of cultural heritage in the context of the natural environment. With a collaborative and interdisciplinary team of local villagers, government administrators, and scientists, we have established the El Pilar Archaeological Reserve for Maya Flora and Fauna. Since 1993, the innovations of the El Pilar program have forged new ground in testing novel strategies for community participation in the

conservation development of the El Pilar Reserve. This program touches major administrative themes of global importance: tourism, natural resources, foreign affairs, and rural development and education. Yet the program's impacts go further. Working with traditional forest gardeners impacts agriculture, rural enterprise, and capacity building. There are few areas untouched by the program's inclusive sweep, and more arenas can contribute to its evolution.

At El Pilar, I practice what I call "action archaeology," a pioneering conservation model that draws on lessons learned from the recent and distant past to benefit contemporary populations. For example, the co-evolution of Maya society and the environment provide clues about sustainability in this region today. At El Pilar we have advanced programs that will simulate "Maya forest gardens" as an alternative to resource-diminishing, plow and pasture farming methods. The forest survives and demonstrates resilience to impacts brought on by human expansion. The ancient Maya lived with this forest for

millennia, and the El Pilar program argues there are lessons to be learned from that past.

The El Pilar Program recognizes the privilege it has enjoyed in forging an innovative community participatory process, in creating a unique management planning design, and in developing a new tourism destination. The success of local outreach at El Pilar can best be seen in the growth of the community organization Amigos de El Pilar (Friends of El Pilar). With groups based in both Belize and Guatemala, the Amigos de El Pilar have worked together with the El Pilar program to build an inclusive relationship between the community and the reserve that is mutually beneficial. The development of this dynamic relationship lies at the heart of the El Pilar philosophy—resilient and with the potential to educate communities, reform local-level resource management, and inform conservation designs for the Maya Forest. *(By Anabel Ford, Director of Mesoamerican Research Center, University of California, Santa Barbara.)* ■■■

© Rolox Awards for Enterprise, Susan Gray

CITIES AND CULTURE CHANGE

If someone who grew up in a rural North American village today moved to Chicago, Montreal, or Los Angeles, that person would experience a number of marked changes in his or her way of life. Similarly, changes in daily life would have been felt 5,500 years ago by a Neolithic village dweller upon moving into one of the world's first cities in Mesopotamia. Four basic changes mark the transition from Neolithic village life to life in the first urban centers: agricultural innovation, diversification of labor, central government, and social stratification.

Agricultural Innovation

The first culture change characteristic of early civilizations occurred in farming methods. The ancient Sumerians, for example, built an extensive system of dikes, canals, and reservoirs to irrigate their farmlands. With such a system, they could control water resources at will; water could be held and then run off into the fields as necessary. Irrigation was an important factor affecting an increase of crop yields. Free-

The University Museum, University of Pennsylvania

This clay tablet map of farmland outside the Mesopotamian city of Nippur dates to 3,000 years ago. Shown are irrigation canals separating the various fields, each of which is identified with the name of the owner.

dom from seasonal rain cycles allowed farmers to harvest more crops in one year. Increased crop yields, resulting from agricultural innovations, were undoubtedly a factor contributing to the high population densities of ancient civilizations.

Diversification of Labor

The second culture change characteristic of early civilizations was the diversification of labor. In a Neolithic village without irrigation or plow farming, every family member participated in the raising of crops. The high crop yields made possible by new farming methods and the increased population permitted a sizable number of people to pursue nonagricultural activities on a full-time basis.

Ancient public records document a variety of specialized workers. For example, an early Mesopotamian document from the old Babylonian city of Lagash lists the artisans, craftspeople, and others paid from crop surpluses stored in the temple granaries. These lists included coppersmiths, silversmiths, sculptors, merchants, potters, tanners, engravers, butchers, carpenters, spinners, barbers, cabinetmakers, bakers, clerks, and brewers.

With specialization came the expertise that led to the invention of new ways of making and doing things. In Eurasia and Africa, civilization ushered in what archaeologists often refer to as the **Bronze Age**, a period marked by the production of tools and ornaments made of this metal. Metals were in great demand for the manufacture of farmers' and artisans' tools, as well as for weapons. Copper and tin (the raw materials from which bronze is made) were smelted, or separated from their ores, then purified, and cast to make plows, swords, axes, and shields. Later, such tools were made from smelted iron. In wars over border disputes or to extend a state's territory, stone knives, spears, and slings could not stand up against metal spears, arrowheads, swords, helmets, or armor.

The indigenous civilizations of the Americas also used metals. In South America, copper, silver, and gold were used for tools as well as ceremonial and ornamental objects. The Aztecs and Maya used the same soft metals for ceremonial and ornamental objects while continuing to rely on stone for their everyday tools. To those who assume that metal is inherently superior, this

Bronze Age In the Old World, the period marked by the production of tools and ornaments of bronze; began about 5,000 years ago in China and Southwest Asia and about 500 years earlier in Southeast Asia.

The construction of elliptical granite walls held together without any mortar at Great Zimbabwe in southern Zimbabwe, Africa, attest to the skill of the people who built these structures. When European explorers, unwilling to accept the notion of civilization in sub-Saharan Africa, discovered these magnificent ruins, they wrongly attributed them to white non-Africans. This false notion persisted until archaeologists demonstrated that these structures were part of a city with 12,000 to 20,000 inhabitants that served as the center of a medieval Bantu state.

© Robert Holmes/Corbis

seems puzzling. However, the ready availability of obsidian (a glass formed by volcanic activity), its extreme sharpness (many times sharper than the finest steel), and the ease with which it could be worked made it perfectly suited to their needs. Moreover, unlike bronze and especially iron, copper, silver, and gold are soft metals and have limited practical use. Obsidian tools provide some of the sharpest cutting edges ever made.

Early civilizations developed extensive trade systems to procure the raw materials needed for their technologies. In many parts of the world, boats gave greater access to trade centers for transporting large loads of imports and exports between cities at less cost than if they had been carried overland. A one-way trip from the ancient Egyptian cities along the Nile River to the Mediterranean port city of Byblos in Phoenicia (not far from the present city of Beirut, Lebanon) took far less time by rowboat compared to the overland route. With a sailboat, it took even less time.

Egyptian kings, or pharaohs, sent expeditions south to Nubia (northern Sudan) for gold; east to the Sinai Peninsula for copper; to Arabia for spices and perfumes; to Asia for lapis lazuli (a blue semiprecious stone) and other jewels; north to Lebanon for cedar, wine, and funerary oils; and southwest to central Africa for ivory, ebony, ostrich feathers, leopard skins, cattle, and the captives they enslaved. Evidence of trading from Great Zimbabwe in southern Africa indicates that these trading networks extended throughout the "Old World." Increased contact with foreign peoples through trade brought new knowledge into trading economies, furthering the spread of innovations and even bodies of knowledge such as geometry and astronomy.

Central Government

The third culture change characteristic of early civilizations was the emergence of a governing elite, a strong central authority required to deal with the challenges new cities faced because of their size and complexity. The governing elite saw to it that different interest groups, such as farmers or craft specialists, provided their respective services and did not infringe on one another's rights (to the extent that they had rights).

The government ensured that the city was safe from its enemies by constructing fortifications and raising an army. It levied taxes and appointed tax collectors so that construction workers, the army, and other public expenses could be paid. It saw to it that merchants, carpenters, or farmers who made legal claims received justice according to standards of the legal system. It guaranteed safety for the lives and property of ordinary people and assured them that any harm done to one person by another would be justly handled. In addition, surplus food had to be stored for times of scarcity, and public works such as extensive irrigation systems or fortifications had to be supervised by competent, fair individuals. The mechanisms of government served all these functions.

Evidence of Centralized Authority

Evidence of centralized authority in ancient civilizations comes from such sources as law codes, temple records, and royal chronicles. Excavation of the city structures themselves provides further evidence because they can show definite signs of city planning. The precise astronomical layout of the Mesoamerican city Teotihuacan, described earlier, attests to strong, centralized control.

Monumental buildings and temples, palaces, and large sculptures are usually found in ancient civilizations. For example, the Great Pyramid, which is the tomb of Khufu, the Egyptian pharaoh, is 755 feet long and 481 feet high. It contains about 2,300,000 stone blocks, each with an average weight of 2.5 tons. The Greek historian Herodotus reports that it took 100,000 men 20 years to build this tomb. Such gigantic structures could be built only because a powerful central authority could harness the considerable labor force, engineering skills, and raw materials necessary for their construction.

Another indicator of the existence of centralized authority is writing, or some form of recorded information. With writing, central authorities could disseminate information and store, systematize, and deploy memory for political, religious, and economic purposes.

Scholars attribute the initial motive for the development of writing in Mesopotamia to record keeping of state affairs. Writing allowed early governments to track accounts of their food surplus, tribute records, and other business receipts. Some of the earliest documents appear to be just such records—lists of vegetables and animals bought and sold, tax lists, and storehouse inventories.

Before 5,500 years ago, records consisted initially of "tokens," ceramic pieces with different shapes indicative of different commercial objects. Thus, a cone shape could represent a measure of grain, or a cylinder could be an animal. As the system developed, tokens represented different animals; processed foods such as oil, trussed ducks, or bread; and manufactured or imported goods such as textiles and metal.[6] Ultimately, clay tablets with impressed marks representing objects replaced these tokens.

In the Mesopotamian city of Uruk, by 5,100 years ago, a new writing technique emerged, in which writers used a reed stylus to make wedge-shaped markings on a tablet of damp clay. Originally, each marking stood for a word. Because most words in this language were monosyllabic, the markings came, in time, to stand for syllables.

Controversy surrounds the question of the earliest evidence of writing. Traditionally, the earliest writing was linked to Mesopotamia. However, in 2003 archaeologists working in the Henan Province of western China discovered signs carved into 8,600-year-old tortoise shells; these markings resemble later-written characters and predate the Mesopotamian evidence by about 2,000 years.[7]

In the Americas, writing systems came into use among various Mesoamerican peoples, but the Maya system was particularly sophisticated. The Maya writing system, like other aspects of Maya culture, appears to have roots in the earlier writing system of the Olmec civilization.[8] The Maya hieroglyphic system had less to do with keeping track of state properties than with extravagant celebrations of the accomplishments of their rulers. Maya lords glorified themselves by recording their dynastic genealogies, important conquests, and royal marriages; by using grandiose titles to refer to themselves; and by associating their actions with important astronomical events. Different though this may be from the record keeping of ancient Mesopotamia, all writing systems share a concern with political power and its maintenance.

Carved monuments like this were commissioned by Tikal's rulers to commemorate important events in their reigns. Portrayed on this one is a king who ruled about 1,220 years ago. Such skilled stone carving could only have been accomplished by a specialist. The translation of the text shows that this monument recorded the dynastic genealogy of some Maya rulers.

© Anita de Laguna Haviland

---

[6]Lawler, A. (2001). Writing gets a rewrite. *Science, 292,* 2,419.

[7]Li, X., et al. (2003). The earliest writing? Sign use in the seventh millennium BC at Jiahu, Henan Province, China. *Antiquity, 77,* 31–44.

[8]Pohl, M. E. D., Pope, K. O., & von Nagy, C. (2002). Olmec origins of Mesoamerican writing, *Science, 298,* 1,984–1,987.

The Earliest Governments

A king and his advisors typically headed the earliest city governments. Of the many ancient kings known, one stands out as truly remarkable for the efficient government organization and highly developed legal system characterizing his reign. This is Hammurabi, the Babylonian king who lived in Mesopotamia sometime between 3,950 and 3,700 years ago. He issued a set of laws for his kingdom, now known as the Code of Hammurabi, notable for its thorough detail and standardization. It prescribed the correct form for legal procedures and determined penalties for perjury and false accusation. It contained laws applying to property rights, loans and debts, family rights, and even damages paid for malpractice by a physician. It defined fixed rates to be charged in various trades and branches of commerce and mechanisms to protect the poor, women, children, and slaves against injustice.

Officials had the code publicly displayed on huge stone slabs so that no one accused could plead ignorance. Even the poorest citizen was supposed to know his or her rights and responsibilities. Distinct social classes were clearly reflected in the law ("rule of law" does not necessarily mean "equality before the law"). For example, if an aristocrat put out the eye of a fellow aristocrat, the law required that his own eye be put out in turn; hence, the saying "an eye for an eye." However, if the aristocrat put out the eye of a commoner, the punishment was simply a payment of silver.[9]

While some civilizations flourished under a single ruler with extraordinary governing abilities, other civilizations possessed a widespread governing bureaucracy that was very efficient at every level. The government of the Inca empire is one such example.

The Inca civilization of Peru and its surrounding territories reached its peak 500 years ago, just before the arrival of the Spanish invaders. By 1525, it stretched 2,500 miles from north to south and 500 miles from east to west, making it at the time one of the largest empires on the face of the earth. Its population, which numbered in the millions, was composed of people of many different ethnic groups. In the achievements of its governmental and political system, Inca civilization surpassed every other civilization of the Americas and most of those of Eurasia. An emperor, regarded as the divine son of the Sun God, headed the government. Under him came the royal family, the aristocracy, imperial administrators, and lower nobility, and below them the masses of artisans, craftspeople, and farmers.

The empire was divided into four administrative regions, further subdivided into provinces, and so on down to villages and families. Government agricultural and tax officials closely supervised farming activities such as planting, irrigation, and harvesting. Teams of professional relay runners could carry messages up to 250 miles in a single day over a network of roads and bridges that remains impressive even today.

Considering the complexity of the Inca civilization, it is surprising that they had no known form of conventional writing. Instead, public records and historical chronicles were kept in the form of an ingenious coding system of colored strings with knots.

Social Stratification

The rise of large, economically diversified populations presided over by centralized governing authorities brought with it the fourth culture change characteristic of civilization: social stratification, or the emergence of social classes. For example, symbols of special status and privilege appeared in the ancient cities of Mesopotamia, and people were ranked according to the kind of work they did or the family into which they were born.

People who stood at or near the head of government were the earliest holders of high status. Although specialists of one sort or another—metal workers, tanners, traders, or the like—generally outranked farmers, such specialization did not necessarily bring with it high status. Rather, people engaged in these kinds of economic activities were either members of the lower classes or outcasts.[10] Merchants of the past could sometimes buy their way into a higher class. With time, the possession of wealth and the influence it could buy became in itself a requisite for high status, as it is in some cultures today.

Evidence of Social Stratification

How do archaeologists know that different social classes existed in ancient civilizations? As described earlier, laws and other written documents as well as archaeological features including dwelling size and location can reflect social stratification.

It is also revealed by burial customs. Graves excavated at early Neolithic sites are mostly simple pits dug in the ground, containing few, if any, **grave goods**. Grave goods consist of things such as utensils, figurines,

grave goods Items such as utensils, figurines, and personal possessions, symbolically placed in the grave for the deceased person's use in the afterlife.

---

[9]Moscati, S. (1962). *The face of the ancient orient* (p. 90). New York: Doubleday.

[10]Sjoberg, G. (1960). *The preindustrial city* (p. 325). New York: Free Press.

© Courtesy of Tavid Hingham

Grave goods frequently indicate the status of deceased individuals in stratified societies. For example, China's first emperor was buried with 7,000 life-size terra cotta figures of warriors.

and personal possessions, symbolically placed in the grave for the deceased person's use in the afterlife. Early Neolithic grave sites reveal little variation, indicating essentially classless societies. Graves excavated in civilizations, by contrast, vary widely in size, mode of burial, and the number and variety of grave goods. This reflects a stratified society, divided into social classes. The graves of important persons contain not only various artifacts made from precious materials, but sometimes, as in some early Egyptian burials, the remains of servants evidently killed to serve their master in the afterlife.

Skeletons from the burials may also provide evidence of stratification. Age at death as well as presence of certain diseases can be determined from skeletal remains. In stratified societies of the past, the dominant groups usually lived longer, ate better, and enjoyed an easier life than lower-ranking members of society, just as they do today.

THE MAKING OF STATES

From northeastern Africa to China to the South American Andes, ancient civilizations are almost always associated with magnificent palaces built high above ground; sculptures so perfect as to be unrivaled by those of today's artists; and engineering projects so vast and daring as to awaken in us a sense of wonder. These impressive accomplishments could indicate that civilization is better than other cultural forms, particularly when civilizations have come to dominate peoples with other social systems. It is important to bear in mind that

domination relates more to an aggressive attitude, size and power than to cultural superiority. In other words, the emergence of centralized governments, characteristic of civilizations, has allowed some cultures to dominate others and for civilizations to flourish. Anthropologists have proposed several theories to account for the transition from small, egalitarian farming villages to large urban centers in which population density, social inequality, and diversity of labor required a centralized government.

Ecological Approaches

Ecological approaches emphasize the role of the environment in the development of states. Among these, the irrigation or **hydraulic theory** holds that civilizations developed when Neolithic peoples realized that the best farming occurred in the fertile soils of river valleys, provided periodic flooding was controlled.[11] The centralized effort to control the irrigation process blossomed into the first governing body, elite social class, and civilization.

> **hydraulic theory** The theory that explains civilization's emergence as the result of the construction of elaborate irrigation systems, the functioning of which required full-time managers whose control blossomed into the first governing body and elite social class.

[11]Wittfogel, K. A. (1957). *Oriental despotism, a comparative study of total power.* New Haven, CT: Yale University Press.

Another theory suggests that in regions of ecological diversity, trade is necessary to procure scarce resources. In Mexico, for example, trade networks distributed chilies grown in the highlands, cotton and beans from intermediate elevations, and salt from the coasts to people throughout the region. Some form of centralized authority developed to organize trade for the procurement of these commodities and to redistribute them.

A third theory suggests that states develop where populations are hemmed in by such environmental barriers as mountains, deserts, seas, or other human populations.[12] As these populations grow, they have no space in which to expand, and so they begin to compete for increasingly scarce resources. Internally, this may result in the development of social stratification, in which an elite controls important resources to which lower classes have limited access. Externally, this leads to warfare and even conquest, which, to be successful, require elaborate organization under a centralized authority.

Problems exist with each of these ecological theories. Across the globe and through time, cultures can be found that do not fit these models. For example, some of the earliest large-scale irrigation systems developed in highland New Guinea, where strong centralized governments never emerged. North American Indians possessed trade networks that extended from Labrador in northeastern Canada to the Gulf of Mexico and the Yellowstone region of the Rocky Mountains and even to the Pacific without centralized control.[13] In many of the cultures that do not fit the theories of environmental determinism, neighboring cultures learned to co-exist rather than pursuing warfare to the point of complete conquest.

Although few anthropologists would deny the importance of the human–environment relationship, many are dissatisfied with theories that do not take into account the beliefs and values that regulate the interaction between people and their environment.[14] For example, as described in the case study of Tikal, while religion was tied to the earth in that the priests determined the most favorable time for planting crops, the beliefs and power relations that developed within Maya culture were not environmentally determined. Human societies past and present bring their beliefs and values into their interactions with the environment.

Action Theory

One criticism of the above theories is that they fail to recognize the capacity of aggressive, charismatic leaders to shape the course of human history. Accordingly, anthropologists Joyce Marcus and Kent Flannery have developed what they call **action theory**.[15] This theory acknowledges the relationship of society to the environment in shaping social and cultural behavior, but it also recognizes that forceful leaders strive to advance their positions through self-serving actions. In so doing, they may create change.

In the case of Maya history, for example, local leaders, who once relied on personal charisma for the economic and political support needed to sustain them in their positions, may have seized upon religion to solidify their power. Through religion they developed an ideology that endowed them and their descendants with supernatural ancestry and privileged access to the gods on which their followers depended. In this case, certain individuals could monopolize power and emerge as divine kings, using their power to subjugate any rivals.

As the above example makes clear, the context in which a forceful leader operates is critical. In the case of the Maya, the combination of existing cultural and ecological factors combined to open the way to the emergence of political dynasties. Thus, explanations of civilization's emergence are likely to involve multiple causes, rather than just one. Furthermore, we may also have the cultural equivalent of what biologists call *convergence,* where similar societies come about in different ways. Consequently, a theory that accounts for the rise of civilization in one place may not account for its rise in another.

CIVILIZATION AND ITS DISCONTENTS

Living in the context of civilization ourselves, we are inclined to view its development as a great step upward on a so-called ladder of progress. Whatever benefits civilization has brought, the cultural changes it represents has produced new problems. Among them is the problem of waste disposal. In fact, waste disposal

---

[12]Carneiro, R. L. (1970). A theory of the origin of the state. *Science, 169,* 733–738.

[13]Haviland, W. A., & Power, M. W. (1994). *The original Vermonters* (2nd ed., chs. 3 & 4). Hanover, NH: University Press of New England.

[14]Adams, R. M. (2001). Scale and complexity in archaic states. *Latin American Antiquity, 11,* 188.

action theory The theory that self-serving actions by forceful leaders play a role in civilization's emergence.

---

[15]Marcus, J., & Flannery, K. V. (1996). *Zapotec civilization: How urban society evolved in Mexico's Oaxaca Valley.* New York: Thames & Hudson.

probably began to be a problem in settled, farming communities even before civilizations emerged. But as villages grew into towns and towns grew into cities, the problem became far more serious, as crowded conditions and the buildup of garbage and sewage created optimum environments for infectious diseases such as bubonic plague, typhoid, and cholera. Early cities therefore tended to be disease-ridden places, with relatively high death rates.

Genetically based adaptation to diseases may also have influenced the course of civilization. In northern Europeans, for example, the mutation of a gene on chromosome 7 makes carriers resistant to cholera, typhoid, and other bacterial diarrheas.[16] Because of the mortality caused by these diseases, selection favored spread of this allele among northern Europeans. But, as with sickle-cell anemia, protection comes at a price. That price is cystic fibrosis, a usually fatal disease present in people who are homozygous for the altered gene.

The rise of towns and cities brought with it other acute, infectious diseases. In a small population, diseases such as chicken pox, influenza, measles, mumps, pertussis, polio, rubella, and smallpox will kill or immunize so high a proportion of the population that the virus cannot continue to propagate.

Measles, for example, is likely to die out in any human population with fewer than half a million people.[17] Hence, such diseases, when introduced into small communities, spread immediately to the whole population and then die out. Their continued existence depends upon the presence of large population aggregates as found in cities. Survivors possessed immunity to these deadly diseases.

Infectious disease played a major role in European colonization of the Americas. When Europeans with immunity to "Old World" diseases came to the Americas for the first time, they brought these devastating diseases with them. Millions of Native Americans who had never been in contact with the microbes that cause diseases such as small pox, typhus, measles, and bubonic plague died as a result.

Not until relatively recent times did public health measures reduce the risk of living in cities, and had it not been for a constant influx of rural peoples, areas of high population density might not have persisted. Europe's urban population, for example, did not become self-sustaining until early in the 20th century.[18]

What led people to live in such unhealthy places? Most likely, people were attracted by the same things that lure people to cities today: They are vibrant, exciting places that provide people with new opportunities and protection in times of warfare. Of course, people's experience in the cities did not always live up to advance expectations, particularly for the poor, as described in this chapter's Biocultural Connection.

In addition to health problems, many early cities faced social problems strikingly similar to those found in many cities all over the world today. Dense population and the inequalities of class systems and oppressive centralized governments created internal stress. The poor saw that the wealthy had all the things that they themselves lacked. It was not just a question of luxury items; the poor did not have enough food or space in which to live with comfort, dignity, and health.

Evidence of warfare in early civilizations is common. Cities were fortified. Ancient documents list battles, raids, and wars between groups. Cylinder seals, paintings, and sculptures depict battle scenes, victorious kings, and captured prisoners of war. Increasing population and the accompanying scarcity of good farming land often led to boundary disputes and quarrels over land between civilized states or between so-called tribal peoples and a state. When war broke out, people crowded into walled cities for protection and to be near irrigation systems.

What we would call "development" today also posed problems in the past. At the Maya city of Copan, in the present-day country of Honduras, much of the fertile bottom lands along the Copan River were paved over as the city grew, making the people more and more dependent on food grown in the fragile soils of the valley slopes. This ultimately led to catastrophic soil loss through erosion and a breakdown of food production. Similarly, in ancient Mesopotamia, evaporation of water from extensive irrigation works resulted in a buildup of salt in the soil, ruining it for agricultural use.

It is discouraging to note that many of the problems associated with the first civilizations are still with us. Waste disposal, pollution-related health problems, crowding, social inequities, and warfare continue to be serious problems. Through the study of past civilizations, and through comparison of contemporary societies, we now stand a chance of understanding such problems. Such understanding represents a central part of the anthropologist's mission. In this sense, then, anthropology represents an effort to adapt, so that the next cultural revolution may see our species transcend these problems.

---

[16]Ridley, M. (1999). *Genome, the autobiography of a species in 23 chapters* (p. 142). New York: HarperCollins.

[17]Diamond, J. (1997). *Guns, germs, and steel* (p. 203). New York: Norton.

[18]Diamond, p. 205.

Biocultural

Connection

Social Stratification and Diseases of Civilization: Tuberculosis

Before the discovery of antibiotics in the early 20th century, individuals infected with the bacteria causing the disease tuberculosis (TB) would invariably waste away and die. But before the development of cities, the disease TB in humans was rare. The bacteria that cause TB cannot survive in the presence of sunlight and fresh air. Therefore, TB, like many other sicknesses, can be called a disease of civilization.

Before humans lived in dark, crowded urban centers, if an infected individual coughed and released the TB bacteria into the air, sunlight would prevent the spread of infection. But civilization affects disease in another powerful way. The social distribution of TB indicates that social stratification is as much a determinant of disease as any bacterium, past and present.

For example, Ashkenazi Jews of eastern Europe were forced into urban ghettos over several centuries, becoming especially vulnerable to the TB

thriving in crowded, dark, confined neighborhoods. As we have seen with the genetic response to malaria (sickle cell and other abnormal hemoglobins) and bacterial diarrheas (the cystic fibrosis gene), TB triggered a genetic response in the form of the Tay-Sachs allele. Individuals heterozygous for the Tay-Sachs allele were protected from this disease.[a]

Unfortunately, homozygotes for the Tay-Sachs allele develop a lethal, degenerative condition that remains common in Ashkenazi Jews. Without the selective pressure of TB, the frequency of the Tay-Sachs allele would never have increased. Similarly, without the strict social rules confining poor Jews to the ghettos (compounded by rules about marriage), the frequency of the Tay-Sachs allele would never have increased. In recent times, cultural mechanisms such as prenatal and premarital genetic testing have resulted in a decrease in the frequency of the Tay-Sachs allele.

While antibiotics have reduced deaths from TB, resistant forms of the bacteria require an expensive regime of multiple drugs. Not only are poor individuals more likely to become infected with TB, they are also less likely to be able to afford expensive medicines required to treat this disease. For people in poor countries and for disadvantaged people in wealthier countries TB—like AIDS—can be an incurable, fatal, infectious disease. As Holger Sawert from the World Health Organization has said, "Both TB and HIV thrive on poverty." The difficult living conditions in urban slums promote the spread of infectious disease. Poverty also makes medical treatment inaccessible.

Before the social stratification accompanying the emergence of cities and states, as far as infectious microbes were concerned, all humans were the same.

[a]Ridley, M. (1999). *Genome, the autobiography of a species in 23 chapters* (p. 191). New York: HarperCollins. ■ ■ ■

Chapter Summary

■ The world's first cities grew out of Neolithic villages between 6,000 and 4,500 years ago—first in Mesopotamia, then in Egypt and the Indus Valley. In China, the process was underway by 5,000 years ago. Somewhat later, and completely independently, similar changes took place in Mesoamerica and the central Andes. Four basic culture changes mark the transition from Neolithic village life to life in civilized urban centers: agricultural innovation, diversification of labor, emergence of centralized government, and social stratification.

■ Agricultural innovation involved the development of new farming methods, such as irrigation, that increased crop yields. Agricultural innovations, in turn, brought about other changes such as increased population size.

■ Diversification of labor occurred as a result of population growth in cities. Some people could provide sufficient food for others who devoted themselves fully to specialization as artisans and craftspeople. With specialization came the development of new technologies, leading to the beginnings of extensive trade systems. An outgrowth of technological innovation

and increased contact with foreign people through trade was new knowledge; within the early civilizations sciences such as geometry and astronomy were first developed.

■ The emergence of central government provided an authority to deal with the complex problems associated with cities. Evidence of a central governing authority comes from such sources as law codes, temple records, and royal chronicles. With the invention of writing, governments could keep records of their transactions and/or boast of their own power and glory. Further evidence of centralized government comes from monumental public structures and signs of centralized planning. Typically, the first cities were headed by a king and his special advisors.

■ Social stratification, or the emergence of social classes, is another culture change characteristic of cities and states. Symbols of status and privilege appeared, and individuals were ranked according to the work they did or the position of their families. Archaeologists have been able to verify the existence of social classes in ancient civilizations by studying burial customs, as well as skeletons, through grave excavations; by noting the size of dwellings in excavated cities; and by examining preserved records in writing and art.

■ A number of theories have been proposed to explain why cities and states developed; these ecological theories emphasize the interrelation of the actions of ancient people and their environment. According to these theories, civilizations developed as centralized governments began to control irrigation systems, trade networks, or scarce resources. While these factors coincide with the emergence of states, it is difficult to establish whether the environmental condition caused the culture changes. Further, these theories omit the importance of the beliefs and values of the cultures of the past as well as the actions of forceful, dynamic leaders, whose efforts to promote their own interests may play a role in social change. Probably, several factors acted together, rather than singly, to bring about the emergence of cities and states.

■ Early cities were beset by many problems. Poor sanitation in early cities, coupled with large numbers of people living in close proximity, created environments in which infectious diseases were rampant. Early urban centers also faced social problems strikingly similar to those persisting in the world today. Dense population, class systems, and a strong centralized government created internal stress. Warfare was common; cities were fortified, and armies served to protect the state.

Questions for Reflection

1. In large-scale societies of the past and present, people face the challenge of social stratification. Elite classes have disproportionate access to and control of all resources. Is social stratification an inevitable consequence of the emergence of cities and states? How can the study of social stratification in the past contribute to the resolution of contemporary issues of social justice?

2. In previous chapters it was emphasized that human evolutionary history should not be thought of as progress. Why is it similarly incorrect to think of the shift from village to city to state as progress?

3. What are some of the ways that differences in social stratification are expressed in your community? Does your community have any traditions surrounding death that serve to restate the social differentiation of individuals?

4. With today's global communication and economic networks, will it be possible to shift away from social systems involving centralized governments or will a centralized authority have to control the entire world?

5. With many archaeological discoveries there is a value placed on "firsts," such as the earliest writing, the first city, or the earliest government. Given the history of the independent emergence of cities and states throughout the world, do you think that scientists should place more value on some of these events just because they are older?

Key Terms

civilization	hydraulic theory
Bronze Age	action theory
grave goods	

Multimedia Review Tools

Make the Grade in Anthropology with ThomsonNOW

Thomson NOW! This powerful online study tool provides you with a *personalized study plan* based on your responses to a diagnostic pretest. Once you have mastered the material with the help of interactive learning tools, an integrated e-book, and more, you can take a post-test to confirm you are ready to move on to the next chapter. To get started with ThomsonNOW, check the card packaged with your book for the access code. Then go to http://www.thomsonedu.com to create an account through 1pass™. If there is no card in your book, go to http://www.thomsonedu.com to purchase an access code.

Companion Website and Anthropology Resource Center

Go to http://anthropology.wadsworth.com to reach the companion website for your text. This offers many study aids, including self quizzes for each chapter and a practice final exam, as well as links to anthropology websites and information on the latest theories and discoveries in the field.

Also, check out the Anthropology Resource Center for a wealth of learning materials that include interactive maps, video exercises, simulations, and breaking news in anthropology. Be sure to explore InfoTrac College Edition®, your online library that offers full-length articles from thousands of scholarly and popular publications. To reach the Anthropology Resource Center and InfoTrac College Edition, check the card packaged with your book for the access code. Then go to http://www.thomsonedu.com to create an account through 1pass™. If there is no card in your book, go to http://www.thomsonedu.com to purchase an access code.

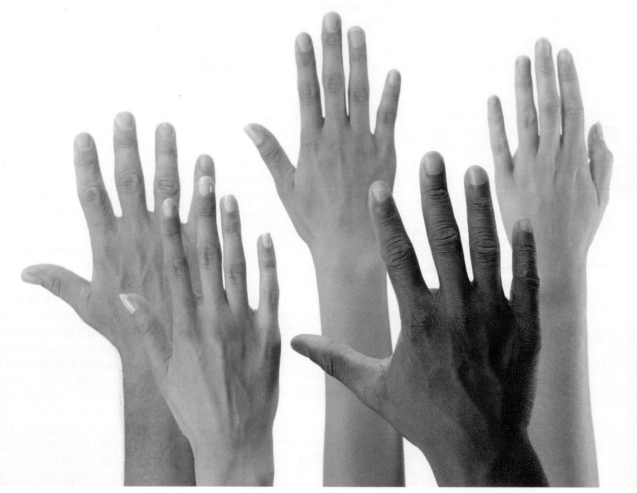

© White Packert / Iconica / Getty Images

CHALLENGE ISSUE

Biological diversity contributes to our ability to adapt to a variety of environments. It is also a challenge, calling upon us to recognize our common origins and to avoid oversimplification, discrimination, bigotry, and even bloodshed. While some people view so-called racial groups as natural and separate divisions within our species based on visible physical differences, biological evidence demonstrates that separate races do not exist. Broadly defined geographic "racial" groupings differ from one another in only 7 percent of their genes. Having exchanged genes throughout history, human populations continue to do so today. Instead of leading to the development of distinctive subspecies (biologically defined races), this genetic exchange has maintained all of humankind as a single species. While race is an important social and political category in some societies, it is a cultural construct without objective scientific merit.

Modern Human Diversity: Race and Racism

8

From male to female, short to tall, light to dark, biological variation can be categorized in a number of ways, but in the end we are all members of the same species. Minute variations of our DNA give each of us a unique genetic fingerprint, yet this variation remains within the bounds of being genetically human. Visible differences among modern humans are expressed within the framework of biological features shared throughout the species, and as a species, humans are highly variable.

Human genetic variation generally is distributed across the globe in a continuous fashion. From a biological perspective, this variation sometimes follows a pattern imposed by interaction with the environment through the evolutionary process of natural selection. At other times, the variation results from random genetic drift. The significance we give our biological variation, however, is always patterned because the way we perceive variation—in fact, whether we perceive it at all—is determined by culture. For example, in many Polynesian cultures, where skin color is not a determinant of social status, people pay little attention to this physical characteristic. By contrast, in countries such as the United States, Brazil, and South Africa, where skin color is a significant social and political category, it is one of the first things people notice.

Biological diversity, therefore, cannot be studied without an awareness of the cultural dimensions that shape the questions asked about diversity as well as the history of how this knowledge has been used. When European scholars first began their systematic study of human variation in the 18th and 19th centuries, they were concerned with documenting differences among human groups in order to divide them hierarchically into progressively better "types" of humans. Today, this hierarchical approach has been appropriately abandoned. Before exploring how contemporary biological variation is studied today, we will examine the effects of social ideas about race and racial hierarchy on the interpretation of biological variation, past and present.

THE HISTORY OF HUMAN CLASSIFICATION

Early European scholars tried to systematically classify *Homo sapiens* into subspecies, or races, based on geographic location and phenotypic features such as skin color, body size, head shape, and hair texture. The 18th-century Swedish naturalist Carolus Linnaeus originally divided humans into subspecies based on geographical location and classified all Europeans as "white," Africans as "black," American Indians as "red," and Asians as "yellow."

The German medical doctor Johann Blumenbach (1752–1840) introduced some significant changes to this four-race scheme in the 1795 edition of his book *On the Natural Variety of Mankind*. Most notably this book formally put forth the notion of a hierarchy of human types. Based on a comparative examination of his human skull collection, Blumenbach judged as most beautiful the skull of a woman from the Caucasus Mountain range (located between the Black Sea and the Caspian Sea of southeastern Europe and southwestern Asia). It was more symmetrical than the others, and he saw it as a reflection of nature's ideal form: the circle. Surely, Blumenbach reasoned, this "perfect" specimen resembled God's original creation. Moreover, he thought that the living inhabitants of the Caucasus region were the most "beautiful" in the world. Based on these criteria, he concluded that this high mountain range, not far from the lands mentioned in the Bible, was the place of human origins.

Blumenbach determined that all light-skinned peoples in Europe and adjacent parts of western Asia and northern Africa belonged to the same race. On this basis, he dropped the "European" race label and replaced it with "Caucasian." Although he continued to distinguish American Indians as a separate race, he regrouped dark-skinned Africans as "Ethiopian" and split those Asians not considered Caucasian into two separate races: "Mongolian" (referring to most inhabitants of Asia, including China and Japan) and "Malay" (indigenous Australians, Pacific Islanders, and others).

Convinced that Caucasians were closest to the original ideal humans supposedly created in God's image, Blumenbach ranked them as superior. The other races, he argued, were the result of "degeneration";

moving away from their place of origin and adapting to different environments and climates, they had degenerated physically and morally into what many Europeans came to think of as inferior races.[1]

Critically reviewing this and other historical efforts at classifying humanity into higher and lower forms, we now clearly recognize their factual errors and ethnocentric prejudices with respect to the concept of race. Especially disastrous is the notion of superior and inferior races, as this has been used to justify brutalities ranging from repression to slavery to mass murder or genocide. It has also been employed to rationalize cruel

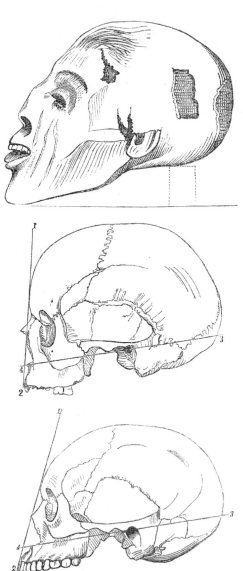

The work of 19th-century Philadelphia physician Samuel Morton is an example of ideologically biased research conducted to justify popular prejudices about so-called racial hierarchies. He measured a series of skulls in an attempt to demonstrate the supposed biological superiority of groups of people through features of skull shape and size.

[1]Gould, S. J. (1994). The geometer of race. *Discover, 15*(11), 65–69.

mockery, as painfully illustrated in the tragic story of Ota Benga, an African pygmy man who in the early 1900s was caged in a New York zoo with an orangutan.

Captured in a raid in Congo, Ota Benga somehow came into the possession of a North American missionary-explorer looking for exotic "savages" for exhibition in the United States. In 1904, Ota and a group of fellow pygmies were shipped across the Atlantic and exhibited at the World's Fair in Saint Louis, Missouri. About 23 years old at the time, Ota was 4 feet 11 inches in height and weighed 103 pounds. Throngs of visitors came to see displays of dozens of indigenous peoples from around the globe, shown in their traditional dress and living in replica villages doing their customary activities. The fair was a success for the organizers, and all the pygmies survived to be shipped back to their homeland. The enterprising missionary also returned to Congo and with Ota's help collected artifacts to be sold to the American Museum of Natural History in New York City.

In the summer of 1906 Ota came back to the United States with the missionary, who soon went bankrupt and lost his entire collection to the bank. Left stranded in the big city, Ota was placed in the care of the museum and then taken to the Bronx Zoo and exhibited in the monkey house, with an orangutan as company. Ota's sharpened teeth (a cultural practice among his own people) were seen as evidence of his supposedly cannibal nature. After intensive protest, zoo officials released Ota from his cage and during the day let him roam free in the park, where he was often harassed by teasing visitors. Ota (usually referred to as a "boy") was then turned over to an orphanage for African American children. In 1916, upon hearing that he would never return to his homeland, he took a revolver and shot himself through the heart.[2]

The racist display at the Bronx Zoo a century ago was by no means unique. Just a tip of the ethnocentric iceberg, it was the manifestation of a powerful ideology in which one small part of humanity sought to demonstrate and justify its claims of biological and cultural superiority. This had particular resonance in North America, where people of European descent were thrown together in a society with Native Americans, African slaves, and (later) Asians imported as a source of cheap labor. Indeed, such claims, based on false notions of race, have resulted in the oppression and genocide of millions of humans because of the color of their skin or the shape of their skulls.

Fortunately, by the early 20th century, some scholars began to challenge the concept of racial hierarchies.

Among the strongest critics was Franz Boas (1858–1942), a Jewish scientist who immigrated to the United States because of rising anti-Semitism in his German homeland and went on to become a founder of North America's academic anthropology. As president of the American Association for the Advancement of Science, Boas criticized false claims of racial superiority in an important speech titled "Race and Progress," published in the prestigious journal *Science* in 1909.

Ashley Montagu (1905–1999), a student of Boas and one of the best-known anthropologists of his time, devoted much of his career to combating scientific racism. Born Israel Ehrenberg to a working-class Jewish family in England, he also felt the sting of anti-Semitism. After changing his name in the 1920s, he immigrated to the United States, where he went on to fight racism in his writing and in academic and public lectures. Of all his works, none is more important than his book *Man's Most Dangerous Myth: The Fallacy of Race*. Published in 1942, it took the lead in debunking the concept of clearly bounded races as a "social myth." The book has since gone through six editions, the last in 1999. Montagu's once controversial ideas have now become mainstream, and his text remains one of the most comprehensive treatments of its subject.

RACE AS A BIOLOGICAL CONCEPT

To understand why the "racial" approach to human variation has been so unproductive and even damaging, we must first understand the race concept in strictly biological terms. In biology, a **race** is defined as a subspecies, or a population of a species differing geographically, morphologically, or genetically from other populations of the same species.

Simple and straightforward though such a definition may seem, there are three very important things to note about it. First, it is arbitrary; there is no agreement on how many differences it takes to make a race. For example, if one researcher emphasizes skin color while another emphasizes blood group differences, they will not classify people in the same way. Ultimately, it proved impossible to reach agreement on the number of genes and precisely which ones are the most important for defining races.

---

[2]Bradford, P. V., & Blume, H. (1992). *Ota Benga: The pygmy in the zoo.* New York: St. Martin's Press.

race In biology, the taxonomic category of subspecies that is not applicable to humans because the division of humans into discrete types does not represent the true nature of human biological variation. In some societies race is an important social category.

Fingerprint patterns of loops, whorls, and arches are genetically determined. Grouping people on this basis would place most Europeans, sub-Saharan Africans, and East Asians together as "loops," Australian aborigines and the people of Mongolia together as "whorls," and central Europeans and the Bushmen of southern Africa together as "arches."

After arbitrariness, the second thing to note about the biological definition of race is that it does not mean that any one race has exclusive possession of any particular variant of any gene or genes. In human terms, the frequency of a trait like the type O blood group, for example, may be high in one population and low in another, but it is present in both. In other words, populations are genetically "open," meaning that genes flow between them. Because populations are genetically open, no fixed racial groups can exist. The only reproductive barriers that exist for humans are cultural.

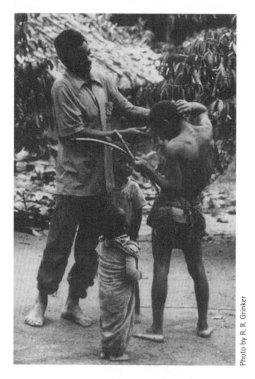

In this photograph, taken in Africa's Democratic Republic of Congo, we see full-grown men of noticeably different heights. The short man is an Efe (pygmy), who traditionally inhabit the Ituri rainforest. The tall man is a member of the Lese ethnic group, who traditionally live and cultivate open land at the edge of the forest. Standing side-by-side, these neighbors illustrate the wide range of variation seen within a single so-called racial category.

Another important consideration about the biological definition of race with respect to humans is that the differences among individuals and *within* a population are generally greater than the differences *among* populations. Evolutionary biologist Richard Lewontin demonstrated this through genetic analyses in the 1970s. He compared the amount of genetic variation within populations and among so-called racial types, finding a mere 7 percent of human variation existing among groups.[3] Instead, the vast majority of genetic variation exists within groups. As the science writer James Shreeve puts it, "most of what separates me genetically from a typical African or Eskimo also separates me from another average American of European ancestry."[4] This follows from the genetic openness of races; no one race has an exclusive claim to any particular form of a gene or trait.

THE CONCEPT OF HUMAN RACES

While the biological race concept is not applicable to human variation, nevertheless, race exists as a significant cultural category. Human groups frequently insert a false notion of biological difference into the cultural category of race to make it appear more factual and objective. In various ways, cultures define religious, linguistic, and ethnic groups as "races," thereby confusing linguistic and cultural traits with physical traits.

For example, in many Central and South American countries, people are commonly classified as Indian, Mestizo (mixed), or Ladino (of Spanish descent). But despite the biological connotations of these terms, the criteria used for assigning individuals to these categories consist of things such as whether they wear shoes, sandals, or go barefoot; speak Spanish or an Indian language; live in a thatched hut or a European-style house; and so forth. Thus, an Indian—by speaking Spanish, wearing Western-style clothes, and living in a house in a non-Indian neighborhood—ceases to be an Indian, no matter how many "Indian genes" he or she may possess.

This sort of confusion of nonbiological characteristics with the biological notion of heredity is by no means limited to Central and South American societies. To various extents, such confusion is found in most societies of Europe and North America. Take, for example, the fact that the racial categories used by the U.S. Census Bureau change with every census. The current large catch-all categories (white, black, American Indian or Alaskan Native, Asian, and Pacific Islander or native Hawaiian)

[3]Lewontin R. C. (1972). The apportionment of human diversity. In T. Dobzhansky, et al. (Eds.), *Evolutionary biology* (pp. 381–398). New York: Plenum Press.
[4]Shreeve, J. (1994). Terms of estrangement. *Discover, 15*(11), 60.

The Concept of Human Races   137

include diverse peoples. Asian, for example, includes such different people as Chinese and East Indians, whereas native Hawaiian and Alaskan are far more restrictive. The Census Bureau also asks people to identify Hispanic ethnicity, a category that includes people who, in their countries of origin, might be classified as Indian, Mestizo, or Ladino. The addition of categories for native Hawaiians, Middle Easterners, and people who consider themselves multiracial does nothing to improve the situation. To compound the confusion, inclusion in one or another of these categories is usually based on self-identification, which means that these are not biological categories at all, but rather cultural constructs.

In the United States, the Census Bureau statistics are applied in a variety of ways that add to the confusion between biological and social categories. For example, health statistics are gathered using the same Census Bureau categories for the purposes of correcting health disparities among social groups. Unfortunately, the false biological concept of race is frequently inferred in these analyses. As a result, the increased risk of dying from a heart attack for African Americans compared to "whites" is attributed to biological difference rather than health-care disparities or other social factors contributing to the development of heart attacks.

Similarly, medical genetics research is regularly oversimplified into the comparisons among the racial types defined in the 18th and 19th centuries. Whether this genetic research will avoid the trap of recreating false genetic types that do not reflect the true nature of human variation remains to be seen. The recent claims made for race-specific drugs and vaccines based on limited scientific data indicate that the social category of race may again be limiting our ability to grasp the true nature of human genetic diversity.

To make matters worse, the confusion of social with biological factors is frequently combined with prejudices that then serve to exclude whole categories of people from certain roles or positions in society. Take for example, the racial hierarchy among European settlers, American Indians, and Africans imported as slaves that characterized colonial North America. A "racial" worldview that had antecedents in the unequal power relations between the English or Saxon "race" and the Irish or Celtic "race" in Europe assigned some groups to perpetual low status on the basis of their supposed biological inferiority, whereas access to privilege, power, and wealth was reserved for favored groups of European descent.[5]

Because of the colonial association of lighter skin with greater power and higher social status, people whose history includes domination by lighter-skinned Europeans have sometimes valued this phenotype. In Haiti, for example, the "color question" has been the dominant force in social and political life. Skin texture, facial features, hair color, and socioeconomic class collectively play a role in the ranking. According to Haitian anthropologist Michel-Rolph Trouillot, "a rich black becomes a mulatto, a poor mulatto becomes black."[6]

The Nazis in Germany elevated a racialized worldview to state policy, with particularly evil consequences. The Nuremberg race laws of 1935 declared the superiority of the Aryan "race" and the inferiority of the Gypsy and Jewish "races." The Nazi doctrine justified, on supposed biological grounds, political repression and extermination. In all, 11 million people (Jews, Gypsies, homosexuals, and other so-called inferior people, as well as political opponents of the Nazi regime) were deliberately put to death.

© Scott Nelson / Getty Images

Persecution and killing based on race or ethnic identity is far from being a thing of the past. Conflict in the Darfur region of western Sudan between the *Janjaweed*, a militia group recruited from local *Arab* tribes, and the non-Arab peoples of the region is a major humanitarian crisis today. A January 2005 United Nations report documented serious violations of human rights, including attacks on villages, killing of civilians, torture, rape, pillaging, and forced displacement. As of this report, the number of internally displaced persons in Darfur was estimated to be 1.65 million people with more than an additional 200,000 refugees from Darfur fleeing to neighboring Chad. In this photo, refugees stop to take water from a muddy well dug in an intermittent stream on the border between Sudan and Chad.

5American Anthropological Association. (1998). Statement on "race." www.ameranthassn.org.

6Trouillot, M. R. (1996). Culture, color, and politics in Haiti. In S. Gregory & R. Sanjek (Eds.), *Race*. New Brunswick, NJ: Rutgers University Press.

Tragically, the Nazi Holocaust (from the Greek word for "wholly burnt" or "sacrificed by fire") is not unique in human history. Such genocides, programs of extermination of one group by another, have a long history that predates World War II and continues today. Recent and ongoing genocide in parts of South America, Africa, Europe, and Asia, like previous genocides, are accompanied by a rhetoric of dehumanization and a depiction of the people being exterminated as a lesser type of human.

Considering the problems, confusion, and horrendous consequences, it is small wonder that most anthropologists have abandoned the race concept as being of no particular utility in understanding human biological variation. Instead, they have found it more productive to study the distribution and significance of single, specific, genetically based characteristics and continuous traits related to adaptation. They examine human variation within small breeding populations, the smallest units in which evolutionary change occurs.

THE SOCIAL SIGNIFICANCE OF RACE: RACISM

Scientific facts, unfortunately, have been slow to change what people think about race. **Racism,** a doctrine of superiority by which one group justifies the dehumanization of others based on their distinctive physical characteristics, is not just about discriminatory ideas, values, or attitudes but is also a political problem. Indeed, politicians have often exploited this concept as a means to mobilizing support, demonizing opponents, and eliminating rivals. Racial conflicts result from social stereotypes, not known scientific facts.

Race and Behavior

The assumption that behavioral differences exist among human "races" remains an issue to which many people today cling tenaciously. Throughout history, certain characteristics have been attributed to groups of people under a variety of names—national character, spirit, temperament—all of them vague and standing for a number of concepts totally unrelated to any biological phenomena. Common myths involve the coldness of Scandinavians or the warlike character of Germans or the lazy nature of Africans. Such unjust characterizations rely upon a false notion of biological difference.

racism A doctrine of superiority by which one group justifies the dehumanization of others based on their distinctive physical characteristics.

To date, no innate behavioral characteristic can be attributed to any group of people (which the nonscientist might term a "race") that cannot be explained in terms of cultural practices. If the Chinese happen to exhibit exceptional visual-spatial skills, it is probably because the business of learning to read Chinese characters requires a visual-spatial kind of learning that is not needed to master Western alphabets.[7] Similarly, the exclusion of "blacks" from honors in the sport of golf (until Tiger Woods) had more to do with the social rules of country clubs and the sport's expense. All such differences or characteristics can be explained in terms of culture.

Similarly, high crime rates, alcoholism, and drug use among certain groups can be explained with reference to culture rather than biology. Individuals alienated and demoralized by poverty, injustice, and unequal opportunity tend to display "antisocial behaviors" more frequently than those who are integrated into the dominant culture. In a racialized society, poverty and all its ill consequences disproportionately affect some groups of people more than others.

Race and Intelligence

A question frequently asked by those unfamiliar with the fallacy of biological race in humans is whether some "races" are inherently more intelligent than others. First we must ask, what do we mean by the term *intelligence*? Unfortunately, there is no general agreement as to what abilities or talents actually make up what we call intelligence, even though some psychologists insist that it is a single quantifiable thing measured by IQ tests. Many more psychologists consider intelligence to be the product of the interaction of different sorts of cognitive abilities: verbal, mathematical-logical, spatial, linguistic, musical, bodily kinesthetic, social, and personal.[8] Each may be thought of as a particular kind of intelligence, unrelated to the others. This being so, they must be independently inherited (to the degree they are inherited), just as height, blood type, skin color, and so forth are independently inherited. Thus, the various abilities that constitute intelligence are independently distributed like other phenotypic traits such as skin color and blood type.

The next question is, Are IQ tests a valid measure of inborn intelligence? Unfortunately, an IQ test measures

[7]Chan, J. W. C., & Vernon, P. E. (1988). Individual differences among the peoples of China. In J. W. Berry (Ed.), *Human abilities in cultural context* (pp. 340–357). Cambridge, England: Cambridge University Press.
[8]Jacoby, R., & Glauberman, N. (Eds.). (1995). *The Bell Curve debate* (pp. 7, 55–56, 59). New York: Random House.

performance (something that one does) rather than genetic disposition (something that the individual was born with). Performance reflects past experiences and present motivational state, as well as innate ability. In sum, it is fair to say that an IQ test is not a reliable measure of inborn intelligence.

Attempts to prove the existence of significant differences in intelligence among human populations have been going on for at least a century. In the United States systematic comparisons of intelligence between "whites" and "blacks" began in the early 20th century and were frequently combined with data gathered by physical anthropologists about skull shape and size. During World War I, for example, a series of IQ tests known as Alpha and Beta were regularly given to draftees. The results showed that the average score attained by European Americans was higher than that obtained by African Americans. Even though African Americans from the urban northern states scored higher than European Americans from the rural South, and some African Americans scored higher than most European Americans, many people took this as proof of the intellectual superiority of "white" people. But all the tests really showed was that, on the average, "whites" outperformed "blacks" in the social situation of IQ testing. The tests did not measure intelligence per se, but the ability, conditioned by culture, of certain individuals to respond appropriately to certain questions conceived by Americans of European descent for comparable middle-class "whites." These tests frequently require knowledge of "white" middle-class values and linguistic behavior.

For such reasons, intelligence tests continue to be the subject of controversy. Many psychologists as well as anthropologists are convinced that they are of limited use, because they are applicable only to particular cultural circumstances. When cultural and environmental factors are held constant, African and European Americans tend to score equally well.[9]

Nevertheless some researchers still insist that significant differences in intelligence among human populations exist. Recent proponents of this view are the psychologist Richard Herrnstein and Charles Murray, a social scientist who at the time was a fellow of the American Enterprise Institute, a conservative think tank in the United States. Their argument, in a lengthy (and highly publicized) book entitled *The Bell Curve,* is that the difference in IQ scores between Americans of African, Asian, and European descent is primarily determined by genetic factors and therefore immutable.

Herrnstein and Murray's book has been justly criticized on many grounds, including violation of basic rules of statistics and their practice of utilizing studies, no matter how flawed, that appear to support their thesis while ignoring or barely mentioning those that contradict it. In addition, they are also wrong on purely theoretical grounds. Because genes are inherited independently of one another, whatever alleles that may be associated with intelligence bear no relationship with the ones for skin pigmentation or with any other aspect of human variation such as blood type.

Further, the expression of genes always occurs in an environment. Among humans, culture shapes all aspects of the environment. In the following Original Study, U.S. physical anthropologist Jonathan Marks extends the discussion of race and intelligence to stereotypes about athletic abilities of different so-called races.

---

[9]Sanday, P. R. (1975). On the causes of IQ differences between groups and implications for social policy. In M. F. A. Montagu (Ed.), *Race and IQ* (pp. 232–238). New York: Oxford.

Original Study

A Feckless Quest for the Basketball Gene

You know what they say about a little knowledge. Here's some: The greatest sprinters and basketball players are predominantly black. Here's some more: Nobel laureates in science are predominantly white.

What do we conclude? That blacks have natural running ability, and whites have natural science ability? Or perhaps that blacks have natural running ability, but whites don't have natural science ability, because that would be politically incorrect?

Or perhaps that we can draw no valid conclusions about the racial distribution of abilities on the basis of data like these.

That is what modern anthropology would say.

But it's not what a new book, *Taboo: Why Black Athletes Dominate Sports and Why We're Afraid to Talk About It,* says. It says that blacks dominate sports because of their genes and that we're afraid to talk about it on account of a cabal of high-ranking politically correct postmodern professors—myself, I am flattered to observe, among them.

The book is a piece of good old-fashioned American anti-intellectualism (those dang perfessers!) that plays to vulgar beliefs about group differences of the sort we recall from *The Bell*

[continued]

[continued]

Curve six years ago. These are not, however, issues that anthropologists are "afraid to talk about"; we talk about them a lot. The author, journalist and former television producer Jon Entine, simply doesn't like what we're saying. But to approach the subject with any degree of rigor, as anthropologists have been trying to do for nearly a century, requires recognizing that it consists of several related questions.

First, how can we infer a genetic basis for differences among people? The answer: Collect genetic data. There's no substitute. We could document consistent differences in physical features, acts, and accomplishments until the Second Coming and be entirely wrong in thinking they're genetically based. A thousand Nigerian Ibos and a thousand Danes will consistently be found to differ in complexion, language, and head shape. The first is genetic, the second isn't, and the third we simply don't understand.

What's clear is that, developmentally, the body is sufficiently plastic that subtle differences in the conditions of growth and life can affect it profoundly. Simple observation of difference is thus not a genetic argument.

Which brings us to the second question: How can we accept a genetic basis for athletic ability and reject it for intelligence? The answer: We can't. Both conclusions are based on the same standard of evidence. If we accept that blacks are genetically endowed jumpers because "they" jump so well, we are obliged to accept that they are genetically unendowed at schoolwork because "they" do so poorly.

In either case, we are faced with the scientifically impossible task of drawing conclusions from a mass of poorly controlled data. Controls are crucial in science: If every black schoolboy in America knows he's supposed to be good at basketball and bad at algebra, and we have no way to measure

schoolboys outside the boundaries of such an expectation, how can we gauge their "natural" endowments? Lots of things go into the observation of excellence or failure, only one of which is genetic endowment.

But obviously humans differ. Thus, the last question: What's the relationship between patterns of human genetic variation and groups of people? The answer: It's complex.

All populations are heterogeneous and are built in some sense in opposition to other groups. Jew or Muslim, Hutu or Tutsi, Serb or Bosnian, Irish or English, Harvard or Yale—one thing we're certain of is that the groups of most significance to us don't correspond to much in nature.

Consider, then, the category "black athlete"—and let's limit ourselves to men here. It's broad enough to encompass Arthur Ashe, Mike Tyson, and Kobe Bryant.

When you read about the body of the black male athlete, whose body do you imagine? Whatever physical gift these men share is not immediately apparent from looking at them.

Black men of highly diverse builds enter athletics and excel.

Far more don't excel. In other words, there is a lot more to being black and to being a prominent athlete than mere biology. If professional excellence or overrepresentation could be regarded as evidence for genetic superiority, there would be strong implications for Jewish comedy genes and Irish policeman genes.

Inferring a group's excellence from the achievements of some members hangs on a crucial asymmetry: To accomplish something means that you had the ability to do it, but the failure to do it doesn't mean you didn't have the ability. And the existing genetic data testify that known DNA variations do not respect the boundaries of human groups.

To be an elite athlete, or elite anybody, presumably does require some kind of genetic gift. But those gifts must be immensely diverse, distributed broadly across the people of the world—at least to judge from the way that the erosion of social barriers consistently permits talent to manifest itself in different groups of people.

In an interview with *The Philadelphia Daily News* in February, Mr. Entine observed that Jews are overrepresented among critics of the views he espouses. But is that a significantly Jewish thing? Or is it simply a consequence of the fact that among any group of American intellectuals you'll find Jews overrepresented because they are a well-educated minority? There's certainly no shortage of non-Jews who find the ideas in "Taboo" to be demagogic quackery.

Of course, Jewish academics may sometimes be speaking as academics, not as Jews. Likewise black athletes may perform as athletes, not just as embodied blackness.

How easy it is to subvert Michael Jordan, the exceptional and extraordinary man, into merely the representative of the black athlete.

The problem with talking about the innate superiority of the black athlete is that it is make-believe genetics applied to naïvely conceptualized groups of people. It places a spotlight on imaginary natural differences that properly belongs on real social differences.

More important, it undermines the achievements of individuals as individuals. Whatever gifts we each have are far more likely, from what we know of genetics, to be unique individual constellations of genes than to be expressions of group endowments. (Jonathan Marks, "A Feckless Quest for the Basketball Gene," *New York Times*, April 8, 2000. Copyright © 2000 by the New York Times Co. Reprinted by permission.) ∎ ∎ ∎

There are enormous problems in attempting to separate genetic components of intelligence from environmental contributors.[10] Most studies of intelligence rely on comparisons between identical twins, genetically identical individuals raised in the same or different environments. As biologists Richard Lewontin and Steven Rose with psychologist Leon Kamin observe, twin studies are plagued by a host of problems: inadequate sample sizes, biased subjective judgments, failure to make sure

---

[10]Andrews, L. B., & Nelkin, D. (1996). The bell curve: A statement. *Science, 271,* 13.

that "separated twins" really were raised separately, unrepresentative samples of adoptees to serve as controls, untested assumptions about similarity of environments. In fact, children reared by the same mother resemble her in IQ to the same degree, whether or not they share her genes.[11] Clearly, the degree to which intelligence is inherited through genes is far from understood.[12]

Undoubtedly, the effects of social environment are important for intelligence. This should not surprise us, as other genetically determined traits are influenced by environmental factors. Height in humans, for example, has a genetic basis while also being dependent both upon nutrition and health status (severe illness in childhood arrests growth, and renewed growth never makes up for this loss). While it is possible to see the effects of the environment on growth, the exact relative contributions of genetic and environmental factors on either the height or the intelligence of an individual is unknown. Nevertheless documentation of the importance of the environment in the expression of intelligence exposes further the problems with generalizations about IQ and "race." For example, IQ scores of all groups in the United States, as in most industrial and postindustrial countries, have risen some 15 points since World War II. In addition, the gap between Americans of African and European descent, for example, is narrower today than in the past. Other studies show impressive IQ scores for African American children from socially deprived and economically disadvantaged backgrounds who have been adopted into highly educated and prosperous homes. It is now known that underprivileged children adopted into such privileged families can boost their IQs by 20 points. It is also well known that IQ scores rise in proportion to the test-takers' amount of schooling. More such cases could be cited, but these suffice to make the point: The assertion that IQ is biologically fixed and immutable is clearly false. Ranking human beings with respect to their intelligence scores in terms of "racial" difference is doubly false.

But despite such efforts, the hypothesis that differences in intelligence exist among "races" remains unproved. Nor is it ever likely to be proved, in view of the major thrust in the evolution of the genus *Homo*. Over the past 2.5 million years, all populations of this genus have adapted primarily through culture—actively inventing solutions to the problems of existence, rather than relying only on biological adaptation. Thus, we would expect a comparable degree of intelligence in all present-day human populations.

The only way to be sure that individual human beings develop their innate abilities and skills to the fullest is to make sure they have access to the necessary resources and the opportunity to do so. This certainly cannot be accomplished if whole populations are assumed at the outset to be inferior.

HUMAN BIOLOGICAL DIVERSITY

Although the biological category of race is not valid when considering groups of humans, this is not to say that differences in various biological traits such as skin color do not exist. In fact, skin color provides an excellent example of the role of natural selection in shaping human variation.

Skin Color: A Case Study in Adaptation

Skin color is subject to great variation and is attributed to several key factors: the transparency or thickness of the skin; a copper-colored pigment called carotene; reflected color from the blood vessels (responsible for the rosy color of lightly pigmented people); and, most significantly, the amount of melanin (from *melas*, a Greek word meaning "black")—a dark pigment in the skin's outer layer. People with dark skin have more melanin-producing cells than those with light skin, but everyone (except albinos) has a measure of melanin. Exposure to sunlight increases melanin production, causing skin color to deepen.

Melanin is known to protect skin against damaging ultraviolet solar radiation;[13] consequently, dark-skinned peoples are less susceptible to skin cancers and sunburn than are those with less melanin. They also seem to be less susceptible to destruction of certain vitamins under intense exposure to sunlight. Because the highest concentrations of dark-skinned people tend to be found in the tropical regions of the world, it appears that natural selection has favored heavily pigmented skin as a protection against exposure where ultraviolet radiation is most constant.[14]

In northern latitudes light skin has an adaptive advantage related to the skin's important biological function as the manufacturer of vitamin D through a chemical reaction dependent upon sunlight. Vitamin D is vital for maintaining the balance of calcium in the body. In northern climates with little sunshine, light skin

[11]Lewontin, R. C., Rose, S., & Kamin, L. J. (1984). *Not in our genes* (pp. 100, 113, 116). New York: Pantheon.
[12]Lewontin, Rose, & Kamin, pp. 9, 121.

[13]Neer, R. M. (1975). The evolutionary significance of vitamin D, skin pigment, and ultraviolet light. *American Journal of Physical Anthropology, 43,* 409–416.
[14] Branda, R. F., & Eatoil, J. W. (1978). Skin color and photolysis: An evolutionary hypothesis. *Science, 201,* 625–626.

allows enough sunlight to penetrate the skin and stimulate the formation of vitamin D, essential for healthy bones. Dark pigmentation interferes with this process. The severe consequences of vitamin D deficiency can be avoided through culture. Until recently, children in northern Europe and northern North America were regularly fed a spoonful of cod liver oil during the dark winter months. Today, pasteurized milk is often fortified with vitamin D.

Given what we know about the adaptive significance of human skin color, and the fact that, until 800,000 years ago, members of the genus *Homo* were exclusively creatures of the tropics, it is likely that lightly pigmented skins are a recent development in human history. Conversely, and consistent with humanity's African origins, darkly pigmented skins likely are quite ancient.

The enzyme tyrosinase, which converts the amino acid tyrosine into the compound that forms melanin, is present in lightly pigmented peoples in sufficient quantity to make them very "black." The reason it does not is that they have genes that inactivate or inhibit it.[15] Human skin, more liberally endowed with sweat glands and lacking heavy body hair compared to other primates, effectively eliminates excess body heat in a hot climate. This would have been especially advantageous to our ancestors on the savannah, who could have avoided confrontations with large carnivorous animals by carrying out most of their activities in the heat of the day. For the most part, tropical predators rest during this period, hunting primarily from dusk until early morning. Without much hair to cover their bodies, selection would have favored dark skin in our human ancestors. In short, based on available scientific evidence, all humans appear to have a "black" ancestry, no matter how "white" some of them may appear to be today.

Obviously, one should not conclude that, because it may be a more recent development, lightly pigmented skin is better, or more highly evolved, than heavily pigmented skin. The latter is clearly better evolved to the conditions of life in the tropics or at high altitudes, although with cultural adaptations like protective clothing, hats, and more recently invented sunscreen lotions, lightly pigmented peoples can survive there. Conversely, the availability of supplementary sources of vitamin D allows more heavily pigmented peoples to do quite well far away from the tropics. In both cases, culture has rendered skin color differences largely irrelevant from a purely biological perspective. With time and with the efforts we see being made in many cultures today, skin color may lose its social significance as well.

Culture and Biological Diversity

While cultural adaptation has reduced the importance of biological adaptation and physical variation, at the same time, cultural forces impose their own selective pressures. For example, take the reproductive fitness of individuals with diabetes—a disease with a known genetic predisposition. In North America and Europe today, where medication is relatively available, people with diabetes are as biologically fit as anyone else. However, if diabetics are denied access to the needed medication, as they are in many parts of the world, their biological fitness is lost and they die out. In fact, one's financial status affects one's access to medication, and so, however unintentional it may be, one's biological fitness may be decided by one's financial status.

Cultural factors can also contribute directly to the development of disease. For example, one type of diabetes is very common among overweight individuals who get little exercise—a combination that describes 61 percent of people from the United States today who are increasingly beset by this condition. As people from traditional cultures throughout the world adopt a Western high sugar diet and activity pattern, the frequency of diabetes and obesity increases.

Another example of culture acting as an agent of biological selection has to do with lactose tolerance: the ability to digest **lactose,** the primary constituent of fresh milk. This ability depends on the capacity to make a particular enzyme, **lactase.**

Most mammals as well as most human populations—especially Asian, Native Australian, Native American, and many (but not all) African populations—do not continue to produce lactase into adulthood. Failure to retain lactase production into adulthood causes gas pains and diarrhea for individuals who consume milk. Only 10 to 30 percent of Americans of African descent and 0 to 30 percent of adult Asians are lactose tolerant.[16] By contrast, lactase retention and lactose tolerance are normal for over 80 percent of adults of northern European descent. Eastern Europeans, Arabs, and some East Africans are closer to northern Europeans in lactase retention than they are to Asians and other Africans. Generally speaking, a high retention of lactase is found in populations with a long tradition of dairying. For them, fresh milk is an important

lactose A sugar that is the primary constituent of fresh milk.
lactase An enzyme in the small intestine that enables humans to assimilate lactose.

[15]Wills, C. (1994). The skin we're in. *Discover, 15*(11), 79.

[16]Harrison, G. G. (1975). Primary adult lactase deficiency: A problem in anthropological genetics. *American Anthropologist, 77,* 815–819.

The "got milk?" ad campaign emphasizes that milk is good for all people's health, yet the vast majority of adults globally are unable to digest milk. Only populations with long traditions of dairying have high frequencies of the alleles for this biological capacity.

dietary item. In such populations, selection in the past favored those individuals with the allele that confers the ability to assimilate lactose, selecting out those without this allele.

Because milk is associated with health in North American and European countries, powdered milk has long been a staple of economic aid to other countries. In fact, such practices work against the members of populations in which lactase is not commonly retained into adulthood. Those individuals who are not lactose tolerant will be unable to utilize the many nutrients in milk. Frequently they will also suffer diarrhea, abdominal cramping, and even bone degeneration, with serious results. In fact, the shipping of powdered milk to victims of South American earthquakes in the 1960s caused many deaths among them.

Among Europeans, lactose tolerance is linked with the evolution of a non-thrifty genotype as opposed to the **thrifty genotype** that characterized humans until about 6,000 years ago.[17] The thrifty genotype permits efficient storage of fat to draw on in times of food shortage. In times of scarcity individuals with the thrifty genotype conserve glucose (a simple sugar) for use in brain and red blood cells (as opposed to other tissues such as muscle), as well as nitrogen (vital for growth and health).

Regular access to glucose through the lactose in milk led to selection for the non-thrifty genotype as protection against adult-onset diabetes, or at least its

thrifty genotype Human genotype that permits efficient storage of fat to draw on in times of food shortage and conservation of glucose and nitrogen.

onset relatively late in life (at a nonreproductive age). Populations that are lactose intolerant retain the thrifty genotype. As a consequence, when they are introduced to Western-style diets (characterized by abundance, particularly of foods high in sugar content), the incidence of obesity and diabetes skyrockets. This chapter's Biocultural Connection describes how a return to a Paleolithic lifestyle can reduce the prevalence of chronic health problems such as obesity, diabetes, and heart disease, regardless of genotype "thriftiness."

In view of the consequences for human biology of such seemingly benign innovations as dairying or farming, we may wonder about many recent practices—for example, the effects of increased exposure to radiation from use of x-rays, nuclear accidents, production of radioactive wastes, ozone depletion (which increases human exposure to solar radiation), and the like. In addition to exposure to radiation, humans also face increased exposure to other known mutagenic agents, including a wide variety of chemicals.

Hormone-disrupting chemicals are of particular concern because they interfere with the reproductive process. For example, in 1938 a synthetic estrogen known as DES (diethylstilbestrol) was developed and subsequently prescribed for a variety of ailments ranging from acne to prostate cancer. Moreover, DES was routinely added to animal feed. It was not until 1971, however, that researchers realized that DES causes vaginal cancer in young women. Subsequent studies have shown that DES causes problems with the male reproductive system and causes deformities of the female reproductive tract of individuals exposed to DES *in utero.* DES mimics the natural hormone, binding with appropriate receptors in and on cells, and thereby turns on biological activity associated with the hormone.[18]

DES is not alone in its effects: At least fifty-one chemicals—many of them in common use—are now known to disrupt hormones, and even this could be the tip of the iceberg. Some of these chemicals mimic hormones in the manner of DES, whereas others interfere with other parts of the endocrine system, such as thyroid and testosterone metabolism. Included are such supposedly benign and inert substances as plastics widely used in laboratories and chemicals added to polystyrene and polyvinyl chloride (PVCs) to make them more stable and less breakable. These plastics are widely used in plumbing, food processing, and food packaging.

Hormone-disrupting chemicals are also found in many detergents and personal care products, contracep-

[17]Allen, J. S., & Cheer, S. M. (1996). The non-thrifty genotype. *Current Anthropology, 37,* 831–842.

[18]Colburn, T., Dumanoski, D., & Myers, J. P. (1996). Hormonal sabotage. *Natural History,* (3), 45–46.

Biocultural Connection

Paleolithic Prescriptions for Today's Diseases

Though increased life expectancy is often hailed as one of modern civilization's greatest accomplishments, in some ways people in the "developed" world are far less healthy than our ancestors. Throughout most of our evolutionary history, humans led more physically active lives and ate a more varied low-fat diet than people do now. They did not drink or smoke. They spent their days scavenging or hunting for animal protein while gathering vegetable foods with some insects thrown in for good measure. They stayed fit through traveling great distances each day over the savannah and beyond.

Today humans may survive longer but survival entails skyrocketing rates of obesity and chronic disease. Heart disease, diabetes, high blood pressure, and cancer plague individuals in wealthy industrialized nations. These diseases become global threats as Western diets and "couch potato" habits replace traditional lifeways.

Anthropologists Melvin Konner and Marjorie Shostak and physician Boyd Eaton have suggested that our Paleolithic ancestors have provided a prescription for a cure. They propose that

as "stone-agers in a fast lane," people's health will improve by returning to the lifestyle to which their bodies are adapted.[a] Such Paleolithic prescriptions are an example of evolutionary medicine—a branch of medical anthropology that uses evolutionary principles to contribute to human health.

Evolutionary medicine bases its prescriptions on the idea that rates of culture change exceed the rates of biological change. Our food forager physiol-

© Gusto/Photo Researchers

ogy was shaped over millions of years, and our bodies are best adapted to this lifestyle. By contrast the culture changes leading to contemporary lifestyles have occurred rapidly, in mere instants in evolutionary terms.

The downward trajectory for human health began with the earliest human village settlements some 10,000 years ago. While nutritional deficiencies and an increase in infectious diseases have troubled humans since the start of the Neolithic, the main health threats to humans have shifted over the past 50 years.

The invention of antibiotics has effectively controlled or eliminated many infectious diseases at the same time that decreased physical activity and increased calorie consumption has led to obesity and chronic disease. Returning to the lifestyle of our Paleolithic forebears, high physical activity along with a diet characterized by moderate consumption of varied but unprocessed foods can contribute substantially to the improvement of human health today. ■ ■ ■

[a]Eaton, S. B, Konner, M., & Shostak, M. (1988). Stone-agers in the fast lane: Chronic degenerative diseases in evolutionary perspective. *American Journal of Medicine, 84*(4), 739–749.

---

tive creams, the giant jugs used to bottle drinking water, and plastic linings in cans. About 85 percent of food cans in the United States are so lined. Similarly, the health effects of the release of compounds from plastic wrap during microwaving are currently being debated. As with the Neolithic revolution and the development of civilization, each invention creates new challenges for humans.

The implications of all these developments are sobering. We know that pathologies result from extremely low levels of exposure to harmful chemicals. Yet, besides those used domestically, the United States exports millions of pounds of these chemicals to the rest of the world.[19] Hormone disruptions may be at least partially responsible for certain trends that have recently become causes for concern among scientists. These range from increasingly early onset of puberty in human females to dramatic declines in human

sperm counts. With respect to the latter, some sixty-one separate studies confirm that sperm counts have dropped almost 50 percent from 1938 to 1990. Most of these studies were carried out in the United States and Europe, but some from Africa, Asia, and South America show that this is essentially a worldwide phenomenon. If this trend continues, it will have profound results.

One of the difficulties with predicting trends is that serious health consequences of new cultural practices are often not apparent until years or even decades later. By then, of course, these practices are fully embedded in the cultural system. Today, cultural practices, probably as never before, are currently having an impact on human gene pools.

It remains to be seen just what the long-term effects on the human species as a whole will be. Unquestionably, this impact is deleterious to those individuals, whose misery and death are the price paid for

[19]Colburn, Dumanoski, & Myers, p. 47.

many of the material benefits of civilization we enjoy today. Can the new cultural practice of genetic engineering alleviate some of the misery that result from our own practices? Possibly, but it also raises the specter

of removing genetic variants that might turn out to be of future adaptive value, or that might turn out to make us immediately susceptible to new problems that we do not even know about today.

Chapter Summary

■ Present-day humans are a single, highly variable species inhabiting the entire globe. Though biological processes are responsible for human variation, the biological concept of race or subspecies cannot be applied to human diversity. Contemporary human variation is not divided into discrete racial types. Instead, individual traits appear in continuous gradations from one population to another without sharp breaks. In addition, because of the independent inheritance of individual traits and the genetic openness of human populations, the vast majority of human variation exists within populations rather than among populations. While anthropologists work actively to show that the biological concept of race is false when applied to human diversity, they recognize the significance of race as a sociopolitical category in many countries such as the United States, Haiti, Brazil, and South Africa.

■ Racism can be viewed solely as a social problem. Racial conflicts result from social stereotypes and not known scientific facts. Racists of the past and present frequently invoke the notion of biological difference to support unjust social practices.

■ Notwithstanding the impossibility of defining biologically valid human "races," many people have assumed that there are behavioral differences among human races. The innate behavioral characteristics attributed to race can be explained in terms of experience as well as a hierarchical social order affecting the opportunities and challenges faced by different groups of people, rather than biology.

■ In the United States, intelligence or IQ testing was used in the 20th century to try to establish racial differences in intelligence. In addition to problems relating to the cultural and environmental specificity of these tests, comparisons among people divided according to the false biological category of race are unwarranted. Furthermore, at present, it is not possible to separate the inherited components of intelligence from those that are culturally acquired. There is still no consensus on what intelligence really is, but it is generally agreed that intelligence is made up of several different talents and abilities.

■ In many parts of the world, "race" is commonly thought of in terms of skin color. Subject to tremendous variation, skin color is a function of several factors: transparency or thickness of the skin, distribution of blood vessels, and amount of carotene and melanin in a given area of skin. Exposure to sunlight increases the amount of melanin, darkening the skin. Natural selection has favored heavily pigmented skin as protection against the strong solar radiation of equatorial latitudes. In northern latitudes, natural selection has favored relatively depigmented skin, which can utilize relatively weak solar radiation in the production of vitamin D. Cultural

factors such as selective mating, as well as geographic location, play a part in skin color distribution globally.

■ Although the human species has come to rely on cultural rather than biological adaptation for survival, human gene pools still change in response to external factors. Many of these changes are brought about by cultural practices; for example, peoples with a dairying tradition possess the ability to digest milk sugars (lactose) into adulthood and a non-thrifty genotype. Populations that are lactose intolerant retain the thrifty genotype. As a consequence, when they are introduced to Western-style diets (characterized by abundance, particularly of foods high in sugar content), the incidence of obesity and diabetes skyrockets.

■ Today hormone-disrupting chemicals, used in plastics and other industries, are of particular importance to human health because they interfere with the reproductive process. One of the difficulties with predicting trends is that serious health consequences of new cultural practices are often not apparent until years or even decades later. By then, of course, these practices are fully embedded in the cultural system.

Questions for Reflection

1. Although biological diversity contributes to our ability to adapt to a variety of environments, it also challenges us to recognize our common origins and to avoid oversimplification, discrimination, bigotry, and even bloodshed. How have cultural beliefs about race affected the interpretation of biological diversity in the past? What are the cultural beliefs about biological diversity in your community today?

2. While we can see and scientifically explain population differences in skin color, why isn't the biological concept of subspecies or race valid for humans? Can you imagine another species of animal, plant, or microorganism for which the subspecies concept makes sense?

3. Globally, health statistics are gathered by country. In addition, some countries such as the United States gather health statistics by race. How are these two endeavors different and similar? Should health statistics be gathered by group?

4. How do you define the concept of intelligence? Do you think scientists will ever be able to discover the genetic basis of intelligence?

5. Cultural practices impact ongoing microevolutionary changes in the human species often seen through dramatic effects on human health. As the world becomes increasingly interconnected, how should humans regulate these kinds of actions globally?

Key Terms

race

racism

lactose

lactase

thrifty genotype

Multimedia Review Tools

Make the Grade in Anthropology with ThomsonNOW

Thomson NOW! This powerful online study tool provides you with a *personalized study plan* based on your responses to a diagnostic pretest. Once you have mastered the material with the help of interactive learning tools, an integrated e-book, and more, you can take a post-test to confirm you are ready to move on to the next chapter. To get started with ThomsonNOW, check the card packaged with your book for the access code. Then go to http://www.thomsonedu.com to create an account through 1pass™. If there is no card in your book, go to http://www.thomsonedu.com to purchase an access code.

Companion Website and Anthropology Resource Center

Go to http://anthropology.wadsworth.com to reach the companion website for your text. This offers many study aids, including self quizzes for each chapter and a practice final exam, as well as links to anthropology websites and information on the latest theories and discoveries in the field.

Also, check out the Anthropology Resource Center for a wealth of learning materials that include interactive maps, video exercises, simulations, and breaking news in anthropology. Be sure to explore InfoTrac College Edition®, your online library that offers full-length articles from thousands of scholarly and popular publications. To reach the Anthropology Resource Center and InfoTrac College Edition, check the card packaged with your book for the access code. Then go to http://www.thomsonedu.com to create an account through 1pass™. If there is no card in your book, go to http://www.thomsonedu.com to purchase an access code.

©David Wells/The Image Bar

CHALLENGE ISSUE

Culture is inscribed almost everywhere we look. One of its most visible expressions is self-adornment—the distinctive ways groups of people dress, style their hair, and otherwise decorate their bodies. Beyond individual style, the function of such shared visual expression is to mark group identities, to signal who is insider and who is outsider. This photograph, taken in front of the western city wall of Jerusalem, includes people from three different religious/cultural groups. For each, that ancient holy city has distinct symbolic meaning, and their clothing reveals what the particular perspective and behavior of each person is likely to be. This is very useful, because part of the challenge of survival is having a sense of who others are.

The Characteristics of Culture

9

Students of anthropology are bound to find themselves studying a seemingly endless variety of human societies, each with its own distinctive environment and system of economics, politics, and religion. Yet for all this variation, these societies have one thing in common: Each is a group of people cooperating to ensure their collective survival and well-being. For this to work, some degree of predictable behavior is required of each person within the society, for group living and cooperation are impossible unless individuals know how others are likely to behave in any given situation. In humans, it is culture that sets the limits of behavior and guides it along predictable paths that are generally acceptable to members of the group.

THE CONCEPT OF CULTURE

Anthropologists conceived the modern concept of culture toward the end of the 19th century. The first really clear and comprehensive definition came from the British anthropologist Sir Edward Tylor. Writing in 1871, he defined culture as "that complex whole which includes knowledge, belief, art, law, morals, custom, and any other capabilities and habits acquired by man as a member of society." Since Tylor's time, definitions of culture have proliferated, so that by the early 1950s, North American anthropologists A. L. Kroeber and Clyde Kluckhohn were able to collect over a hundred of them from the academic literature. Recent definitions tend to distinguish more clearly between actual behavior and the abstract ideas, values, and perceptions of the world that inform that behavior. To put it another way,

culture goes deeper than observable behavior; it is a society's shared and socially transmitted ideas, values, and perceptions, which are used to make sense of experience and generate behavior and are reflected in that behavior.

CHARACTERISTICS OF CULTURE

Through the comparative study of many human cultures, past and present, anthropologists have gained an understanding of the basic characteristics evident in all of them: Every culture is learned, shared, based on symbols, integrated, and dynamic. A careful study of these characteristics helps us to see the importance and the function of culture itself.

Culture Is Learned

All culture is learned rather than biologically inherited, prompting anthropologist Ralph Linton to refer to it as humanity's "social heredity." One learns one's culture by growing up with it, and the process whereby culture is transmitted from one generation to the next is called **enculturation.**

Most animals eat and drink whenever the urge arises. Humans, however, are enculturated to do most of their eating and drinking at certain culturally prescribed times and feel hungry as those times approach. These eating times vary from culture to culture, as does what is eaten, how it is prepared, how it is eaten, and where. To add complexity, food is used to do more than merely satisfy nutritional requirements. When used to celebrate rituals and religious activities, as it often is, food "establishes relationships of give and take, of cooperation, of sharing, of an emotional bond that is universal."[1]

Through enculturation every person learns the socially appropriate way of satisfying the basic biologically determined needs: food, sleep, shelter, companionship, safety, and sexual activity. It is important to distinguish between the needs themselves, which are not learned, and the learned ways in which they are satisfied—for each culture determines in its own way how these needs

> **culture** A society's shared and socially transmitted ideas, values, and perceptions, which are used to make sense of experience and generate behavior and are reflected in that behavior.
>
> **enculturation** The process by which a society's culture is transmitted from one generation to the next and individuals become members of their society.

will be met. For instance, a North American's idea of a comfortable way to sleep may vary greatly from that of a Japanese person.

Learned behavior is exhibited in some degree by most, if not all, mammals. Several species may even be said to have elementary culture, in that local populations share patterns of behavior that, just like humans, each generation learns from the one before and that differ from one population to another. Elizabeth Marshall Thomas, for example, has described a distinctive pattern of behavior among lions of southern Africa's Kalahari Desert—behavior that fostered nonaggressive interaction with the region's indigenous hunters and gatherers and that each generation of lions passed on to the next.[2] She has shown as well how Kalahari lion culture changed over a 30-year period in response to new circumstances. That said, it is important to note that not all learned behavior is cultural. For instance, a pigeon may learn tricks, but this behavior is reflexive, the result of conditioning by repeated training, not the product of enculturation.

Beyond our species, examples of cultural behavior are particularly evident among other primates. A chimpanzee, for example, will take a twig, strip it of all leaves, and smooth it down to fashion a tool for extracting termites from their nest. Such tool making, which juveniles learn from their elders, is unquestionably a form of cultural behavior once thought to be exclusively human. In Japan, macaques that learned the advantages of washing sweet potatoes before eating them passed the practice on to the next generation. And so it goes; what is interesting is that within any given primate species, the culture of one population often differs from that of others, just as it does among humans.

We have discovered both in captivity and in the wild that primates in general and apes in particular "possess a near-human intelligence generally, including the use of sounds in representational ways, a rich awareness of the aims and objectives of others, the ability to engage in tactical deception, and the ability to use symbols in communication with humans and each other."[3] Given the remarkable degree of biological similarity between apes and humans, it should come as no surprise that they are like us in other ways as well. In fact, in many respects the differences between apes and humans are differences of degree rather than kind (although the degree *does* make a major difference). Growing knowledge of ape/human similarities contradicts a belief that is

[1]Caroulis, J. (1996). Food for thought. *Pennsylvania Gazette, 95*(3), 16.

[2]Thomas, E. M. (1994). *The tribe of the tiger: Cats and their culture* (pp. 109–186). New York: Simon & Schuster.

[3]Reynolds, V. (1994). Primates in the field, primates in the lab. *Anthropology Today, 10*(2), 4.

deeply embedded in Western cultures: the idea that there is a vast and unbridgeable gap between people and animals. It has not been easy to overcome this bias, and indeed we still have not come to grips fully with the moral implications with respect to the way humans treat fellow primates in research laboratories.

Culture Is Shared

As a shared set of ideas, values, perceptions, and standards of behavior, culture is the common denominator that makes the actions of individuals intelligible to other members of their society. It enables them to predict how others are most likely to behave in a given circumstance, and it tells them how to react accordingly. A group of people from different cultures, stranded for a time on a desert island, may become a society of sorts. They would have a common interest—survival—and would develop techniques for living and working together. However, each person would retain his or her own cultural identity, and the group would disintegrate without further ado once rescued from the island. It would have been merely an aggregate in time and not a cultural entity. **Society** may be defined as an organized group or groups of interdependent people who generally share a common territory, language, and culture and who act together for collective survival and well-being. The way in which these people depend upon one another can be seen in such features as their economic, communication, and defense systems. They are also bound together by a general sense of common identity.

Because culture and society are such closely related concepts, anthropologists study both. Obviously, there can be no culture without a society. Conversely, there are no known human societies that do not exhibit culture. This cannot be said for all other animal species. Ants and bees, for example, instinctively cooperate in a manner that clearly indicates a remarkable degree of social organization, yet this instinctual behavior is not a culture.

Although a culture is shared by members of a society, it is important to realize that all is not uniform. For one thing, no two people share the exact same version of their culture. And there are bound to be other variations. At the very least, there is some difference between the roles of men and women. This stems from the fact that women give birth but men do not and that there

are obvious differences between male and female reproductive anatomy and physiology. Every culture gives meaning to sexual differences by explaining them and specifying what is to be done about them. Moreover, every culture stipulates how the kinds of people resulting from the differences should relate to others. Because each culture does this in its own way, there can be tremendous variation from one society to another. Anthropologists use the term **gender** to refer to the cultural elaborations and meanings assigned to the biological differentiation between the sexes. So, although one's sex is biologically determined, one's sexual identity or gender is socially constructed within the context of one's particular culture.

The distinction between sex, which is biological, and gender, which is cultural, is an important one. Presumably, gender differences are as old as human culture—about 2.5 million years—and arose from the biological differences between early human males and females, which appear to have been greater than those of modern humans. As in gorillas today, one of the species most closely related to humans, early human

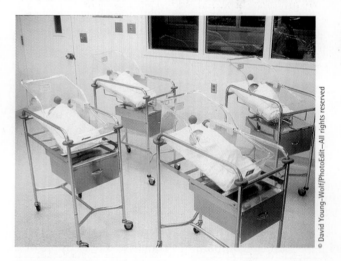

© David Young-Wolff/PhotoEdit—All rights reserved

In the United States, culture requires that newborn infants be assigned a sexual identity of either male or female. Yet, significant numbers of infants are born each year whose genitalia do not conform to cultural expectations. Because only two genders are recognized, the usual reaction is surgery to make the young bodies conform to cultural requirements. In most cases, male genitals are constructed, merely because they are easier. This is in contrast to many Native American cultures in which more than two genders are recognized and socially acceptable.[4]

---

society An organized group or groups of interdependent people who generally share a common territory, language, and culture and who act together for collective survival and well-being.

gender The cultural elaborations and meanings assigned to the biological differentiation between the sexes.

---

[4]For statistics on this, see Blackless, M., et al. (2000). How sexually dimorphic are we? Review & synthesis. *American Journal of Human Biology, 12,*151–166.

males were on average substantially larger than females. Moreover, technological advancements in the home and workplace over the last century or two have greatly diminished the cultural significance of most remaining male–female biological differences in many societies all across the world. Thus, apart from sexual differences directly related to reproduction, any biological basis for contrasting gender roles has largely disappeared in modern industrialized and postindustrial societies. (For example, using a hydraulic lift to move heavy automobile engines in an assembly line eliminates the need for muscular strength in that task.) Nevertheless, all cultures exhibit at least some role differentiation related to biology—some far more than others.

In addition to cultural variation associated with gender, there is also variation related to age. In any society, children are not expected to behave as adults, and the reverse is equally true. But then, who is a child and who is an adult? Again, although age differences are "natural," cultures give their own meaning and timetable to the human life cycle. In North America, for example, individuals are generally not regarded as adults until the age of 18; in many others, adulthood begins earlier—often around age 12. That said, the status of adulthood often has less to do with age than with passage through certain prescribed rituals.

Besides age and gender variation, there may be cultural variation between subgroups in societies. These may be occupational groups in societies where there is a complex division of labor, or social classes in a stratified society, or ethnic groups in some other societies. When such groups exist within a society, each functioning by its own distinctive standards of behavior while still sharing some common standards, we speak of **subcultures.** The word *subculture* carries no suggestion of lesser status relative to the word *culture.*

Amish communities comprise one example of a subculture in North America. Specifically, they are an **ethnic group**—people who collectively and publicly identify themselves as a distinct group based on various cultural features such as shared ancestry and common origin, language, customs, and traditional beliefs. The Amish originated in Central Europe during the Christian Protestant revolutions that swept through Europe in the 16th century. Today members of this group number about 100,000 and live mainly in Pennsylvania, Ohio, Illinois, and Indiana in the United States, and in Ontario, Canada. These pacifistic, rural people base their lives on their traditional Anabaptist religion, which holds that only adult baptism is valid and that "true Christians" should not hold government office, bear arms, or use force. They prohibit marriage outside their faith, which calls for obedience to radical Christian teachings, including social separation from the wider "evil world" and rejection of material wealth. Among themselves they usually speak a German dialect known as Pennsylvania Dutch (from *Deutsch,* meaning "German"). They use High German for religious purposes, and children learn English in school. Valuing simplicity, hard work, and a high degree of neighborly cooperation, they dress in a distinctive plain garb, and even today rely on the horse for transportation as well as agricultural work.[5] In short, they share the same **ethnicity.** This term, rooted in the Greek word *ethnikos* ("nation") and related to *ethnos* ("custom") is the expression of the set of cultural ideas held by an ethnic group.

The goal of Amish education is to teach youngsters reading, writing, and arithmetic, as well as Amish values. Adults in the community reject what they regard as "worldly" knowledge and the idea of schools producing good citizens for the state. Resisting all attempts to force their children to attend regular public schools, they insist that education take place near home and that teachers be committed to Amish ideals. Their nonconformity to many standards of mainstream culture has caused frequent conflict with state authorities, as well as legal and personal harassment. Pressed to compromise, they have introduced "vocational training" beyond junior high to fulfill state requirements, but they have managed to retain control of their schools and maintain their way of life. Confronted with economic challenges that make it impossible for most Amish communities to subsist solely on farming, some work outside their communities. Many more have established cottage industries and actively market homemade goods to tourists and other outsiders. Yet, while their economic separation from mainstream society has declined over the past four decades, their cultural separation has not.[6] They remain

---

subculture A distinctive set of standards and behavior patterns by which a group within a larger society operates.

ethnic group People who collectively and publicly identify themselves as a distinct group based on various cultural features such as shared ancestry and common origin, language, customs, and traditional beliefs.

---

ethnicity This term, rooted in the Greek word *ethnikos* ("nation") and related to *ethnos* ("custom") is the expression of the set of cultural ideas held by an ethnic group.

---

[5]Hostetler, J., & Huntington, G. (1971). *Children in Amish society.* New York: Holt, Rinehart and Winston.
[6]Kraybill, D. B. (2001). *The riddle of Amish culture* (pp. 1–6, 244, 268–69). Baltimore: Johns Hopkins University Press.

© Dennis MacDonald/PhotoEdit—All rights reserved

The Amish people have held on to their traditional agrarian way of life in the midst of industrialized North American society. By maintaining their own schools to instill Amish values in their children, prohibiting mechanized vehicles and equipment, and dressing in their distinctive plain clothing, the Amish proclaim their own special identity.

a defensive community, more distrustful than ever of the dominant North American culture surrounding them and mingling as little as possible with non-Amish people.

The Amish are but one example of the way a subculture may develop and be dealt with by the larger culture within which it functions. In contrast to these European immigrants, North American Indian

Anthropology Applied

New Houses for Apache Indians

The United States, in common with other industrialized countries of the world, contains a number of more or less separate subcultures. Those who live by the standards of one particular subculture have their closest relationships with one another, receiving constant reassurance that their perceptions of the world are the only correct ones, and coming to take it for granted that the whole culture is as they see it. As a consequence, members of one subcultural group frequently have trouble understanding the needs and aspirations of other such groups. For this reason anthropologists, with their special understanding of cultural differences, are frequently employed as go-betweens in situations requiring interaction between peoples of differing cultural traditions.

As an example, George S. Esber, Jr., while still a graduate student in anthropology, was hired to work with architects and a band of Apache Indians in designing a new community for the Apaches.[a] Although architects knew of cross-cultural differences in the use of space,

they had no idea of how to get relevant information from the Indians. For their part, the Apaches had no explicit awareness of their needs, for these were based on unconscious patterns of behavior. Moreover, the idea that patterns of behavior could be acted out unconsciously was an alien one to them.

Esber's task was to persuade the architects to hold back on their planning long enough for him to gather, through fieldwork and review of written records, the kind of data from which Apache housing needs could be abstracted. At the same time, he had to overcome Apache anxieties over an outsider coming into their midst to learn about matters as personal as their daily lives. With these hurdles overcome, Esber was able to identify and successfully communicate to the architects features of Apache life with important implications for community design. At the same time, discussions of findings with the Apaches themselves enhanced awareness of their own unique needs.

As a result of Esber's work, Apaches moved into houses that had been

designed with *their* participation, for *their* specific needs. Among other things, account was taken of their need to ease into a social situation rather than to jump right in. Apache etiquette requires that all people be in full view of one another so each can assess from a distance the behavior of others in order to act appropriately with them. This requires a large, open living space. At the same time, hosts must be able to offer food to guests as a prelude to further social interaction. Thus, cooking and dining areas cannot be separated from living space. Nor can standard middle-class Anglo kitchen equipment be installed; the need for handling large quantities of food requires large pots and pans, for which extra-large sinks and cupboards are necessary. Built with such ideas in mind, the new houses accommodated long-standing native traditions. ■ ■ ■

[a]See Esber, G. (1987). Designing Apache houses with Apaches. In R. M. Wulff & S. J. Fiske (Eds.), *Anthropological praxis: Translating knowledge into action.* Boulder, CO: Westview.

subcultures are formerly independent cultural groups that underwent colonization by European settlers and were forcibly brought under the control of the federal government in the United States and Canada. Although all American Indian groups have experienced enormous changes due to colonization, many have held on to traditions significantly different from those of the dominant Euramerican culture surrounding them, so that it is sometimes difficult to decide whether they remain as distinct cultures as opposed to subcultures. In this sense, *culture* and *subculture* represent opposite ends of a continuum, with no clear dividing line in the gray area between. The Anthropology Applied feature examines the intersection of culture and subculture with an example concerning Apache Indian housing.

This raises the issue of the multi-ethnic or **pluralistic society** in which two or more ethnic groups or nationalities are politically organized into one territorial state but maintain their cultural differences. Pluralistic soci-

> **pluralistic society** A society in which two or more ethnic groups or nationalities are politically organized into one territorial state but maintain their cultural differences.

eties could not have existed before the first politically centralized states arose a mere 5,000 years ago. With the rise of the state, it became possible to bring about the political unification of two or more formerly independent societies, each with its own culture, thereby creating what amounts to a more complex order that transcends the theoretical one culture–one society linkage. Pluralistic societies, which are common in the world today (Figure 9.1), all face the same challenge: They are comprised of groups that, by virtue of their high degree of cultural variation, are all essentially operating by different sets of rules. Since social living requires predictable behavior, it may be difficult for the members of any one subgroup to accurately interpret and follow the different standards by which the others operate. This can lead to significant misunderstandings, such as the following case reported in the *Wall Street Journal* of May 13, 1983:

> Salt Lake City—Police called it a cross-cultural misunderstanding. When the man showed up to buy the Shetland pony advertised for sale, the owner asked what he intended to do with the animal. "For my son's birthday," he replied, and the deal was closed.

Figure 9.1
Shown here are some of the ethnic groups of the Russian Federation, which is by far the largest and most important part of the former Union of Soviet Socialist Republics.

The buyer thereupon clubbed the pony to death with a two-by-four, dumped the carcass in his pickup truck and drove away. The horrified seller called the police, who tracked down the buyer. At his house they found a birthday party in progress. The pony was trussed and roasting in a *luau pit*. "We don't ride horses, we eat them," explained the buyer, a recent immigrant from Tonga [an island in the Pacific Ocean].

Unfortunately, the difficulty members of one subgroup within a pluralistic society may have making sense of the standards by which members of other groups operate can go far beyond mere misunderstanding. It can intensify to the point of anger and violence.

Every culture includes individuals who behave in abnormal ways that earn them such labels as "oddball," "eccentric," or "crazy." Typically, because they differ too much from the acceptable standard, they are looked upon with disapproval by their society. And if their behavior becomes too peculiar, they are sooner or later excluded from participating in the activities of the group. Such exclusion acts to keep what is defined as deviant behavior outside the group. Interestingly, behavior viewed as deviant in one society may not be in another. In many American Indian societies, for example, a few exceptional individuals were permitted to assume for life the role normally associated with people of the opposite sex. Thus, a man could dress as a woman and engage in what were conventionally defined as female activities; conversely, women could achieve renown in activities normally in the masculine domain. In effect, four different gender identities were available: masculine men, feminine men, feminine women, and masculine women. Furthermore, masculine women and feminine men were not merely accepted but were highly respected.

Culture Is Based on Symbols

Human thought and behavior involve **symbols**—signs, sounds, gestures, and other things that are arbitrarily linked to something else and represent it in a meaningful way. Because there is no inherent or necessary relationship between a thing and its representation, symbols are arbitrary, acquiring specific meanings when people agree on usage in their communications. In fact, symbols—ranging from spoken and written words to national flags to wedding rings to money—enter into every aspect of culture, from social life and religion to politics and economics. We're all familiar with the fervor and devotion that a religious symbol can elicit from a believer. An Islamic crescent, Christian cross, or a Jewish Star of David, as well as the sun among the Inca, a cow among the Hindu, a white buffalo calf among Plains Indians, or any other object of worship may bring to mind years of struggle and persecution or may stand for a whole philosophy or creed.

The most important symbolic aspect of culture is language—using words to represent objects and ideas. Through language humans are able to transmit culture from one generation to another. In particular, language makes it possible to learn from cumulative, shared experience. Without it, one could not inform others about events, emotions, and other experiences to which they were not a party.

Culture Is Integrated

For purposes of comparison and analysis, anthropologists customarily imagine a culture as a well-structured system made up of distinctive parts that function together as an organized whole. While they may sharply distinguish each part as a clearly defined unit with its own characteristic features and special place within the larger system, anthropologists recognize that reality is more convoluted, and divisions between cultural units are often blurry. However, because all aspects of a culture must be reasonably well integrated in order to function properly, anthropologists seldom focus on an individual feature in isolation. Instead, they view each in terms of its larger context and carefully examine its connections to related cultural features.

Broadly speaking, a society's cultural features fall within three categories: social structure, infrastructure, and superstructure. **Social structure** concerns the rule-governed relationships that hold members of a society together, with all their rights and obligations. Households, families, associations, and power relations, including politics, are all part of social structure. It establishes group cohesion and enables people to consistently satisfy their basic needs, including food and

symbols Signs, sounds, gestures, and other things that are arbitrarily linked to something else and represent it in a meaningful way.

social structure The rule-governed relationships—with all their rights and obligations—that hold members of a society together. This includes households, families, associations, and power relations, including politics.

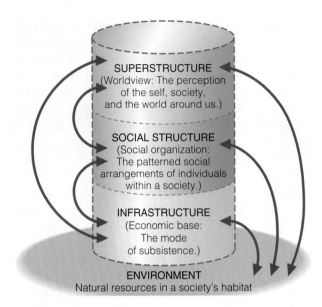

Figure 9.2
Every culture is an integrated and dynamic system of adaptation that responds to a combination of internal factors (economic, social, ideological) and external factors (environmental, climatic). Within a cultural system, there are functional relationships among the economic base (infrastructure), the social organization (social structure), and the ideology (superstructure). A change in one leads to a change in the others.

shelter for themselves and their dependents, by means of work. So, there is a direct relationship between a group's social structure and its economic foundation, which includes subsistence practices and the tools and other material equipment used to make a living. Because subsistence practices involve tapping into available resources to satisfy a society's basic needs, this aspect of culture is known as **infrastructure.** Supported by this economic foundation, a society is also held together by a shared sense of identity and worldview. This collective body of ideas, beliefs, and values by which a group of people makes sense of the world— its shape, challenges, and opportunities—and their place in it is known as ideology or **superstructure.** Including religion and national ideology, it structures the overarching ideas that people in a society have about themselves and everything else that exists around them—and it gives meaning and direction to their lives. Influencing and reinforcing one another, these three in-

infrastructure The economic foundation of a society, including its subsistence practices, and the tools and other material equipment used to make a living.

superstructure A society's shared sense of identity and worldview. The collective body of ideas, beliefs, and values by which a group of people makes sense of the world—its shape, challenges, and opportunities—and their place in it. This includes religion and national ideology.

terdependent structures together form part of a cultural system (Figure 9.2).

The integration of economic, social, and ideological aspects of a culture can be illustrated by the Kapauku Papuans, a mountain people of western New Guinea (Figure 9.3), studied in 1955 by the North American anthropologist Leopold Pospisil.[7] The Kapauku economy relies on plant cultivation, along with pig breeding, hunting, and fishing. Although plant cultivation provides most of the people's food, it is through pig breeding that men achieve political power and positions of legal authority.

Figure 9.3

Among the Kapauku, pig breeding is a complex business. Raising lots of pigs requires lots of food to feed them. The primary fodder is sweet potatoes, grown in garden plots. Kapauku culture defines the caring of pigs, plus certain essential gardening activities, as women's work alone. So, to raise a lot of pigs, a man has to have many women in the household. Thus, in Kapauku society, multiple wives (polygyny) are not only permitted, they are highly desired. For each wife, however, a man must pay a bride price, and this can be expensive. Furthermore, wives have to be compensated for their care of pigs. Put simply, it takes pigs, by which wealth is measured, to get wives, without whom pigs cannot be raised in the first place. Needless to say, this requires considerable entrepreneurship. It is this ability that produces leaders in Kapauku society.

The interrelatedness of the various parts of Kapauku culture is even more complicated. For example, one condition that encourages polygyny is a surplus of adult females, sometimes caused by loss of males through warfare. Among the Kapauku, recurring warfare has long been viewed as a necessary evil. By the rules of Kapauku warfare, men may be killed but women may not. This system works to promote the sort of imbalanced sex ratio that fosters polygyny. Polygyny tends to work best if a man's wives all come to live in his village, and so it is among the Kapauku. With this arrangement, the men of a village are typically "blood" relatives of one another, which enhances their

---

[7]Pospisil, L. (1963). *The Kapauku Papuans of west New Guinea.* New York: Holt, Rinehart and Winston.

ability to cooperate in warfare. Considering all of this, it makes sense that Kapauku typically reckon descent (ancestry) through men.

Descent reckoning through men, coupled with near-constant warfare, tends to promote male dominance. So it is not surprising to find that positions of leadership in Kapauku society are held exclusively by men, who appropriate the products of women's labor in order to play their political "games." Such male dominance is by no means characteristic of all human societies. Rather, as in the Kapauku case, it arises only under particular sets of circumstances that, if changed, will alter the way in which men and women relate to each other.

In sum, for a culture to function properly, its various parts must be consistent with one another. But consistency is not the same as harmony. In fact, there is often friction and potential for conflict within every culture—among individuals, factions, and competing institutions. Even on the most basic level of a society, individuals rarely experience the enculturation process in precisely the same way, nor do they perceive their reality in precisely identical fashion. Moreover, conditions may change, brought on by inside or outside forces. A society will function reasonably well as long as its culture is capable of handling the daily strains and tensions. However, when a culture no longer provides adequate solutions or when its component parts are no longer consistent, a situation of cultural crisis ensues.

Culture Is Dynamic

Cultures are dynamic systems that respond to motions and actions within and around them. When one element within the system shifts or changes, the entire system strives to adjust, just as it does when an outside force applies pressure. To function adequately, a culture must be flexible enough to allow such adjustments in the face of unstable or changing circumstances. All cultures are, of necessity, dynamic, but some are far less so than others. When a culture is too rigid or static and fails to provide its members with the means required for long-term survival under changing conditions, it is not likely to endure. On the other hand, some cultures are so fluid and open to change that they may lose their distinctive character. The Amish mentioned earlier in this chapter typically resist change as much as possible but are constantly making balanced decisions to adjust when absolutely necessary. North Americans in general, however, have created a culture in which change has become a positive ideal. This dynamic aspect of culture is discussed in more detail later in this chapter under the heading "Culture and Adaptation."

Describing another culture is like trying to describe a new game. Like American baseball, the British game of cricket (pictured here) involves a ball, a bat, and bases. However, to describe cricket in the language of baseball would be at best a caricature of the game as the British know it. The challenge in anthropology is to describe another culture for an audience unfamiliar with it, so that the description captures its distinct nuances.

STUDYING CULTURE IN THE FIELD

Equipped now with some basic knowledge about culture, we can raise the question, How does an anthropologist study culture in the field? Since every culture is comprised of rules or standards that are rarely obvious, an anthropologist faces the challenge of gleaning those rules through an analysis of observed behavior. In fieldwork, an anthropologist's most important research tools are his or her social skills as well as skills of observation, documentation, and analysis. By carefully watching, questioning, listening, and analyzing over a period of time, one can usually identify, explain, and often predict a group's social behavior. The task is similar to that of a linguist who tries to develop a set of rules to account for the ways a group of people combine sounds into meaningful phrases.

To further explore the anthropologist's task of identifying the rules that underlie each culture, consider the difference between cultural ideals and the way people actually behave—as noted in our Chapter 1 discussion of William Rathje's Garbage Project. Given such discrepancies, common in any social group, an anthropologist must be extremely careful to come up with an accurate description of a culture. To play it safe, he or she needs to seek out and consider three kinds of data:

1. The people's own understanding of their culture and the general rules they share—that is, their ideal sense of the way their own society ought to be.

2. The extent to which people believe they are observing those rules—that is, how they think they really behave.

3. The behavior that can be directly observed—that is, what the anthropologist actually sees happening.

Clearly, the way people think they *should* behave, the way in which they think they *do* behave, and the way in which they *actually* behave may be distinctly different. By carefully and objectively examining and comparing these elements, the anthropologist can draw up a set of rules that may explain the acceptable range of behavior within a culture. Of course, the anthropologist is only human, and it is difficult to completely cast aside one's personal feelings and biases, which have been shaped by one's own culture, as well as gender and age. Yet it is important to recognize this challenge and make every effort to overcome it, for otherwise one may seriously misinterpret what one sees.

CROSS-CULTURAL COMPARISONS

Ideally, as noted in Chapter 1, theories in cultural anthropology are generated from worldwide comparisons, facilitated by various collections of cross-indexed ethnographic and archaeological data put together by anthropologists over the years. For example, Peggy Reeves Sanday examined a sample of 156 societies in an attempt to answer such questions as: Why do women play a more dominant role in some societies than others? Why, and under what circumstances, do men dominate women? Her 1981 study, *Female Power and Male Dominance*, disproves the common perception that women are universally subordinate to men, sheds light on the way men and women relate to each other, and ranks as a major landmark in the study of gender.[8]

Cultural comparisons are not restricted to contemporary ethnographic data. Indeed, anthropologists frequently turn to archaeological or historical data to test hypotheses about culture change. Cultural characteristics thought to be caused by certain specified conditions can be tested archaeologically by investigating similar situations where such conditions actually occurred. Also useful are written and oral historical data stored in archives and libraries or obtained by interviewing elders and other persons of knowledge in the community. The historical analysis of cultures, like archaeology, is a valuable approach to understanding change. This chapter's Biocultural Connection provides an example of the type of understanding one can gain about a culture from bioarchaeological analysis.

---

[8]Sanday, P. R. (1981). *Female power and male dominance*. New York: Cambridge University Press. See also Sanday, P. R. (2002). *Women at the center: Life in a modern matriarchy*. Ithaca: Cornell University Press.

Biocultural Connection

Adult Human Stature and the Effects of Culture: An Archaeological Example

Each human being is genetically programmed at conception to achieve a certain stature as an adult. Whether we actually wind up as tall as our genes would allow, however, is influenced by experiences during our growth and development. For example, if an individual becomes severely ill, this may arrest growth temporarily, a setback that will not be made up when growth resumes. Critically important as well is the quality of diet. Without adequate nutrition, a person will not grow to be as tall as would otherwise be possible. Thus, in class-structured societies, individuals of higher class standing have tended to be the tallest individuals, as they generally have access to the best diets and are shielded from many of life's harsher realities. Conversely, individuals of lower class standing have tended to be shorter, owing to poor diets and generally harsher lives.

At the ancient Maya city of Tikal, in the Central American country of Guatemala, analysis of human skeletons from burials reveal stature differences characteristic of stratified societies. On average, males interred in rich "tombs" were taller than those in simple graves associated with relatively small houses. Those buried near intermediate-sized houses were generally taller than those from simple graves, but not as tall as those from "tombs." Thus, the analysis provides strong support for a reconstruction of Tikal society into three tiers: lower class commoners, higher class commoners, and (at the top) the ruling elite. ■ ■ ■

CULTURE AND ADAPTATION

In the course of their evolution, humans, like all living creatures, have continually faced the challenge of adapting to their environment. The term *adaptation* refers to a gradual process by which organisms adjust to the conditions of the locality in which they live. Species have generally adapted biologically, relying on advantageous anatomical and physiological mechanisms through a process known as natural selection (detailed in Chapter 2). For example, body hair coupled with certain other physiological traits protects mammals from extremes of temperature; specialized teeth help them to procure the kinds of food they need; and so on. Humans, however, have increasingly come to depend on cultural adaptation, using a unique combination of brain power and physical skills to alter their circumstances. Biology has not provided them with built-in fur coats to protect them in cold climates, but it has given them the ability to make their own coats, build fires, and construct shelters to shield themselves against the cold. They may not be able to run as fast as a cheetah, but they are able to invent and build vehicles that can carry them faster and further than any other creature. Through culture and its many constructions, the human species has secured not just its survival but its expansion as well. By manipulating environments through cultural means, people have been able to move into a vast range of environments, from the icy Arctic to the Sahara Desert. They have even set foot on the moon.

This is not to say that everything that humans do they do *because* it is adaptive to a particular environment. For one thing, people do not just react to an environment as given; rather, they react to it as they perceive it, and different groups of people may perceive the same environment in radically different ways. They also react to things other than the environment: their own biological natures; their beliefs and attitudes; and the short- and long-term consequences of their behavior for themselves and other life forms that share their habitats. Although people maintain cultures to deal with problems, it is clear that some cultural practices prove to be maladaptive and actually create new problems—such as toxic water and air caused by certain industrial practices or North America's obesity epidemic brought on by the culture of cars, fast food, television, and personal computers.

A further complication is the relativity of any given adaptation: What is adaptive in one context may be seriously maladaptive in another. For example, the sanitation practices of food-foraging peoples—their toilet habits and methods of garbage disposal—are appropriate to contexts of low population levels and

What is adaptive at one time may not be at another. In the United States, the principal source of fruits, vegetables, and fiber is the Central Valley of California, where irrigation works have made the desert bloom. As happened in ancient Mesopotamia, evaporation concentrates salts in the water, but here pollution is made even worse by chemical fertilizers. These poisons are now accumulating in the soil and threaten to make the valley a desert again.

some degree of residential mobility. But these same practices become serious health hazards in the context of large, fully sedentary populations. Similarly, behavior that is adaptive in the short run may be maladaptive over the long run. Thus, the development of irrigation in ancient Mesopotamia (modern-day Iraq) made it possible over the short run to increase food production, but over time it favored the gradual accumulation of salts in the soils. This, in turn, contributed to the collapse of civilization there about 4,000 years ago.

Similarly, the development of prime farmland today in places like the eastern United States for purposes other than food production makes us increasingly dependent on food raised in marginal environments. High yields are presently possible through the application of expensive technology, but continuing loss of topsoil, increasing salinity of soils through evaporation of irrigation waters, and silting of irrigation works, not to mention impending shortages of water and fossil fuel, make continuing high yields over the long term unlikely. All of this said, it should be clear that for a culture to survive, it must produce behavior that is generally adaptive to the natural environment.

Functions of Culture

A culture cannot survive if it fails to provide its people with the necessary guidance and know-how to deal effectively with basic problems. Through it, people must provide for the production and distribution of goods and services considered necessary for life. As a design for living, it must meet the biological and psychological needs of its members and provide some structure for reproduction in order to ensure biological continuity. It must offer ways to enculturate new members so they can become functioning adults. It must facilitate conflict resolution and the maintenance of order among its members, as well as between them and outsiders. It must motivate its members to survive and engage in those activities necessary for survival. On top of all of this, a culture must be able to change if it is to remain adaptive under shifting conditions.

Culture and Change

Cultures have always changed over time, although rarely as rapidly or as massively as many are doing today. Changes take place in response to such events as population growth, technological innovation, environmental crisis, the intrusion of outsiders, or modification of behavior and values within the culture. In our current age of globalization, we are witnessing a much accelerated pace of widespread and radical cultural change, discussed in detail in the last two chapters of this book.

Although cultures must have some flexibility to remain adaptive, culture change can also bring unexpected and often disastrous results. For example, consider the relationship between culture and the droughts that periodically afflict so many people living in African countries just south of the Sahara Desert. The lives of some 14 million pastoral nomadic people native to this region are centered on cattle and other livestock, herded from place to place as required for pasturage and water. For thousands of years these people have been able to go about their business, efficiently utilizing vast areas of arid lands in ways that allowed them to survive severe droughts many times in the past. Unfortunately for them, their nomadism annoys the central governments of modern states in the region, for it takes them across relatively new international boundaries and makes them difficult to track for purposes of taxation and other governmental controls.

Seeing nomads as a challenge to their authority, these governments have gone all out to stop them from ranging through their traditional grazing territories and to convert them into sedentary villagers. Imposed loss of mobility has resulted in overgrazing; moreover, the problem has been compounded by government efforts to press pastoralists into a market economy by giving them incentives to raise many more animals than required for their own needs in order to have a surplus to sell and thus add to the tax base. The resulting devastation, where there had previously been no significant overgrazing or erosion, now makes droughts far more disastrous than they would otherwise

be. In fact, it places the very existence of the nomads' traditional way of life in jeopardy.

CULTURE, SOCIETY, AND THE INDIVIDUAL

Ultimately, a society is no more than a union of individuals, all of whom have their own special needs and interests. To survive, it must succeed in balancing the self-interest of its members against the demands of the society as a whole. To accomplish this, a society offers rewards for adherence to its cultural standards. In most cases, these rewards assume the form of social acceptance. For example, in contemporary North American society a man who holds a good job, is faithful to his wife, and does volunteer work in the community may be described as a "model citizen" by his neighbors. To ensure the survival of the group, each person must learn to postpone certain immediate personal satisfactions. Yet the needs of the individual cannot be suppressed too far, lest levels of stress become too much to bear.

Consider, for example, the matter of sexual expression, which, like anything that people do, is shaped by culture. Sexuality is important in any society, for it helps to strengthen cooperative bonds between members of society, ensuring the perpetuation of society itself. Yet sex can be disruptive to social living. If the issue of who has sexual access to whom is not clearly spelled out, competition for sexual privileges can destroy the cooperative bonds on which human survival depends. Uncontrolled sexual activity, too, can result in reproductive rates that cause a society's population to outstrip its resources. Hence, as it shapes sexual behavior, every culture must balance the needs of society against the individual's sexual needs and desires so that frustration does not build up to the point of being disruptive in itself.

Cultures vary widely in the way they go about this. On one end of the spectrum, societies such as the Amish in North America or groups in Saudi Arabia have taken an extremely restrictive approach, specifying no sex outside of marriage. On the other end are such societies as the Norwegians in northern Europe who generally accept premarital sex and often choose to have children outside marriage, or even more extreme, the Canela Indians in Brazil, whose social codes guarantee that, sooner or later, everyone in a given village has had sex with just about everyone of the opposite sex. Yet, even as permissive as the latter situation may sound, there are nonetheless strict rules as to how the system operates.[9]

---

[9]Crocker, W. A., & Crocker, J. (1994). *The Canela, bonding through kinship, ritual and sex* (pp. 143–171). Fort Worth, TX: Harcourt Brace.

Not just in sexual matters, but in all life issues, cultures must strike a balance between the needs and desires of individuals and those of society as a whole. When those of society take precedence, people experience excessive stress. Symptomatic of this are increased levels of mental illness and behavior regarded as antisocial: violence, crime, abuse of alcohol and other drugs, depression, suicide, or simply alienation. If not corrected, the situation can result in cultural breakdown. But just as problems develop if the needs of society take precedence over those of the individual, so too do they develop if the balance is upset in the other direction.

EVALUATION OF CULTURE

We have knowledge of numerous highly diverse cultural solutions to the challenges of human existence. The question often arises, Which is best? Anthropologists have been intrigued to find that all cultures tend to see themselves as the best of all possible worlds. This is reflected in the way individual societies refer to themselves: Typically, a society's traditional name for itself translates roughly into "true human beings." In contrast, their names for outsiders commonly translate into various versions of "subhumans," including "monkeys," "dogs," "weird-looking people," "funny talkers," and so forth. We now know that any adequately functioning culture regards its own ways as the only proper ones, a view known as **ethnocentrism.**

Anthropologists have been actively engaged in the fight against ethnocentrism ever since they started to study and actually live among traditional peoples with radically different cultures and thus learned by personal experience that they were no less human than anyone else. Resisting the common urge to rank cultures, anthropologists have instead aimed to understand individual cultures and the general concept of culture. To do so, they have examined each culture on its own terms, aiming to discern whether or not the culture satisfies the needs and expectations of the people themselves. If a people practiced human sacrifice or capital punishment, for example, they asked about the circumstances that made the taking of human life acceptable according to their values. The idea that one must suspend judgment on other peoples' practices in order to understand them in their own cultural terms is called **cultural relativism.** Only through such an approach can one gain a meaningful view of the values and beliefs that underlie the behaviors and institutions of other peoples and societies as well as clearer insights into the underlying beliefs and practices of one's own society.

Take, for example, the 16th-century Aztec practice of sacrificing humans for religious purposes. Few (if any) North Americans today would condone such a practice, but by suspending judgment one can get beneath the surface and discern how it functioned to reassure the populace that the Aztec state was healthy and that the sun would remain in the heavens. Moreover, an impartial and open-minded exploration of Aztec sacrifices may offer fresh insight on how the death penalty functions in the United States today. Numerous studies by a variety of social scientists have clearly shown that the death penalty does not deter violent crime, any more than Aztec sacrifice really provided sustenance for the sun. In fact, cross-cultural studies show that homicide rates mostly decline after its abolition.[10] Similar to Aztec human sacrifice, capital punishment may be seen as an institutionalized magical response to perceived disorder, reassuring people that there is security when state authorities guarantee supreme law and order and are willing to demonstrate their commitment into the extreme.

Clearly, cultural relativism is essential as a research tool. However, employing it as a tool does not mean suspending judgment forever, nor does it require the anthropologist to defend a people's right to engage in any cultural practice, no matter how destructive. All that is necessary is that we avoid *premature* judgments until we have a full understanding of the culture in which we are interested. Then, and only then, may the anthropologist adopt a critical stance and in an informed way consider the advantages and disadvantages particular beliefs and behaviors have for a society and its members.

A culture is essentially a maintenance system to ensure the continued well-being of a group of people. Therefore, it may be deemed successful as long as it secures the survival of a society in a way that its members find to be reasonably fulfilling. What complicates matters is that any society is made up of groups with different interests, raising the possibility that some people's interests may be better served than others. For this reason, the anthropologist must always ask, Whose needs and whose survival are best served by

cultural relativism The idea that one must suspend judgment of other people's practices in order to understand them in their own cultural terms

ethnocentrism The belief that the ways of one's own culture are the only proper ones.

[10]Ember, C. J., & Ember, M. (1996). What have we learned from cross-cultural research? *General Anthropology, 2*(2), 5.

the culture in question? Only by looking at the overall situation can a reasonably objective judgment be made as to how well a culture is working. Indicators that help us measure a culture's effectiveness include the nutritional status and general physical and mental health of the population, the incidence of violence, the stability of domestic life, and the group's relationship to its resource base.

Chapter Summary

■ Culture, to the anthropologist, is a society's shared and socially transmitted ideas, values, and perceptions, which are used to make sense of experience and to generate behavior and are reflected in that behavior. All cultures share certain basic characteristics; study of these sheds light on the nature and function of culture itself. Culture cannot exist without society: an organized group or groups of interdependent people who generally share a common territory, language, and culture and who act together for collective survival and well-being. Culture, which is learned, is distinct from shared instinctive behavior.

■ Although culture involves a group's shared values, ideas, and, behavior; everything within a culture is not uniform. For instance, in all cultures there is some difference between men and women's roles. Anthropologists use the term gender to refer to the cultural elaborations and meanings assigned to the biological differences between sexes. Age variation is also universal, and in some cultures there are other subcultural variations as well. A subculture (for example, the Amish) shares certain overarching assumptions of the larger culture, while observing its own set of distinct rules. Pluralistic societies are those in which two or more ethnic groups or nationalities are politically organized into one territorial state but maintain their cultural differences.

■ All cultures have the following characteristics: In addition to being shared, they are learned, with individual members learning the accepted norms of social behavior through the process of enculturation; culture is based on symbols—transmitted through the communication of ideas, emotions, and desires expressed in symbols, especially language; culture is integrated, so that all aspects function as an integrated whole (albeit not without tension, friction, and even conflict); finally, all cultures are dynamic and changeable.

■ As illustrated in the barrel model, all aspects of a culture fall into one of three broad, interrelated categories: infrastructure (the subsistence practices or economic system), social structure (the rule-governed relationships), and superstructure (the ideology or worldview).

■ The job of the anthropologist is to abstract a set of rules from what he or she observes in order to explain social behavior. To arrive at a realistic description of a culture free from personal and cultural biases, the anthropologist must examine a people's notion of how their society ought to function, determine how a people think they behave, and compare these with how a people actually do behave. It is also the anthropologist's job to free him- or herself as much as possible from the biases of his or her own culture. As well, anthropologists must acknowledge that gender can slant research findings. Through worldwide comparison of cultures, anthropologists develop general theories of culture.

■ Cultural adaptation has enabled humans to survive and expand into a wide variety of environments. Sometimes what is adaptive in one set of circumstances or over the short run is maladaptive over time. To survive, a culture must satisfy the basic biological and psychological needs of its members, provide some structure for reproduction to ensure their continuity, and maintain order among its members as well as between its members and outsiders.

■ Culture change takes place in response to such events as population growth, technological innovation, environmental crisis, intrusion of outsiders, or modification of values and behavior within the culture. Although cultures must change to adapt to new circumstances, sometimes the unforeseen consequences of change are disastrous for a society. As well, a society must strike a balance between the self-interest of individuals and the needs of the group.

■ Ethnocentrism is the belief that one's own culture is superior to all others. To avoid making ethnocentric judgments, anthropologists adopt the approach of cultural relativism, which requires suspending judgment in order to understand each culture in its own terms.

■ The least biased measure of a culture's success may be based on answering this question: How well does a particular culture satisfy the physical and psychological needs of those whose behavior it guides? These indicators provide answers: the nutritional status and general physical and mental health of the population, the incidence of violence, the stability of domestic life, and the group's relationship to its resource base.

Questions for Reflection

1. What are some of the cultural symbols that would help you identify emergency workers in your town should a natural disaster strike and wounded survivors need to be evacuated? Would you be able to recognize such vitally important individuals in a completely foreign country? If so, how?

2. Anthropological fieldwork is based on participant observation. Imagine a foreign anthropologist choosing your town or neighborhood for such research. Would you, your family, or your friends react differently to a female researcher than to a male? If so, how and why? And what if this male or female anthropologist came from Congo or Ireland? Which would play a more significant role in terms of acceptance and research findings—the researcher's gender or national origin?

3. Many large modern societies are pluralistic. Are you familiar with any subcultures in your own society? How different are these subcultures from one another? Could you make friends or even marry someone from another subculture? What kind of problems would you be likely to encounter?

4. Although all cultures across the world display some degree of ethnocentrism, some are more ethnocentric than others. In what ways is your own society ethnocentric? Considering the modern fact of globalization (as described in Chapter 1), do you think ethnocentrism poses more of a problem in today's world than in the past?

5. The barrel model offers a simple framework to imagine what a culture looks like from an analytical point of view. How would you apply that model to your own community?

Key Terms

culture	pluralistic society
enculturation	symbols
society	social structure
gender	infrastructure
subculture	superstructure
ethnic group	ethnocentrism
ethnicity	cultural relativism

Multimedia Review Tools

Make the Grade in Anthropology with ThomsonNOW

Thomson NOW! This powerful online study tool provides you with a *personalized study plan* based on your responses to a diagnostic pretest. Once you have mastered the material with the help of interactive learning tools, an integrated e-book, and more, you can take a post-test to confirm you are ready to move on to the next chapter. To get started with ThomsonNOW, check the card packaged with your book for the access code. Then go to http://www.thomsonedu.com to create an account through 1pass™. If there is no card in your book, go to http://www.thomsonedu.com to purchase an access code.

Companion Website and Anthropology Resource Center

Go to http://anthropology.wadsworth.com to reach the companion website for your text. This offers many study aids, including self quizzes for each chapter and a practice final exam, as well as links to anthropology websites and information on the latest theories and discoveries in the field.

Also, check out the Anthropology Resource Center for a wealth of learning materials that include interactive maps, video exercises, simulations, and breaking news in anthropology. Be sure to explore InfoTrac College Edition®, your online library that offers full-length articles from thousands of scholarly and popular publications. To reach the Anthropology Resource Center and InfoTrac College Edition, check the card packaged with your book for the access code. Then go to http://www.thomsonedu.com to create an account through 1pass™. If there is no card in your book, go to http://www.thomsonedu.com to purchase an access code.

© Yavuz Arslan/Peter Arnol

© Yavuz Arslan/Peter Arnol

CHALLENGE ISSUE

As social creatures dependent upon one another for survival, humans face the challenge of finding effective ways to communicate clearly in a multiplicity of situations about countless things connected to our well-being. We do this in many ways, including touch, gesture, and posture. Our most distinctive and complex form of communication, however, is language—a foundation stone of culture.

Language and Communication 10

All normal humans are born with the ability to communicate through language and may spend a considerable part of each day doing so. Indeed, language is so much a part of our lives that it involves everything we do, and everything we do involves language. There is no doubt that our ability to communicate, whether through sounds or gestures (sign languages, such as the American Sign Language used by the hearing impaired, are fully developed languages in their own right), rests squarely upon our biological makeup. We are "programmed" for language, although only in a general sort of way. Beyond the cries of babies, which are not learned but which do communicate, humans must learn their language. So it is that any normal child from anywhere in the world readily learns the language of his or her culture.

We define **language** as a system of communication using sounds and/or gestures that are put together according to certain rules, resulting in meanings that are intelligible to all who share that language. These sounds and gestures fall into the category of *symbols* (defined in Chapter 9 as signs, sounds, gestures, and other things that are arbitrarily linked to something else and represent it in a meaningful way). For example, the word *crying* is a symbol, a combination of sounds to which we assign the meaning of a particular action and which we can use to communicate that meaning, whether or not anyone around us is actually crying. **Signals,** unlike culturally learned

language A system of communication using sounds and/or gestures that are put together in meaningful ways according to a set of rules.

signals Instinctive sounds or gestures that have a natural or self-evident meaning.

165

symbols, are sounds and gestures that have a natural or self-evident meaning. A scream, a cough, and the sound of crying itself are signals that convey some kind of emotional or physical state.

Today's language experts are not certain how much credit to give to animals, such as dolphins or chimpanzees, for the ability to use symbols as well as signals, even though these animals and many others have been found to communicate in remarkable ways. Several chimpanzees, gorillas, and orangutans have been taught American Sign Language, and researchers have discovered that even vervet monkeys utilize distinct calls for communication.

These calls go beyond merely signaling levels of fear or arousal. These small African monkeys have specific calls to signify the type of predator threatening the group. According to primatologist Allison Jolly,

> [The calls] include which direction to look in or where to run. There is an audience effect: calls are given when there is someone appropriate to listen . . . monkey calls are far more than involuntary expressions of emotion.[1]

What are the implications for our understanding of the nature and evolution of language? No final answer will be evident until we gain more knowledge about the various systems of animal communication. In the mean time, even as debate continues over how human and animal communication relate to each other, we cannot simply dismiss communication among nonhuman species as a set of simple instinctive reflexes or fixed action patterns.[2] A remarkable example of the many scientific efforts underway on this subject is the story of an orangutan named Chantek, featured in the following Original Study. Among other things, it illustrates the creative process of language development and the capacity of a nonhuman primate to cognize symbols.

---

[1] Jolly, A. (1991). Thinking like a vervet. *Science, 251,* 574. See also Seyfarth, R.M., et al. (1980). Monkey responses to three different alarm calls: Evidence for predator classification and semantic communication. *Science, 210,* 801–803.

[2] Armstrong, D. F., Stokoe, W. C., & Wilcox, S. E. (1993). Signs of the origin of syntax. *Current Anthropology, 34,* 349–368; Burling, R. (1993). Primate calls, human language, and nonverbal communication. *Current Anthropology, 34,* 25–53.

Original Study

Language and the Intellectual Abilities of Orangutans

In 1978, after researchers began to use American Sign Language for the deaf to communicate with chimpanzees and gorillas, I began the first long-term study of the language ability of an orangutan named Chantek. There was criticism that symbol-using apes might just be imitating their human caregivers, but there is now growing agreement that orangutans, gorillas, and both chimpanzee species can develop language skills at the level of a 2- to 3-year-old human child. The goal of Project Chantek was to investigate the mind of an orangutan through a developmental study of his cognitive and linguistic skills. It was a great ethical and emotional responsibility to engage an orangutan in what anthropologists call "enculturation," since I would not only be teaching a form of communication, I would be teaching aspects of the culture upon which that language was based. If my project succeeded, I would create a symbol-using creature that would be somewhere between an ape living under natural conditions and an

adult human. This threatened to raise as many questions as I sought to answer.

A small group of caregivers at the University of Tennessee, Chattanooga, began raising Chantek when he was 9 months old. They communicated with him by using gestural signs based on the American Sign Language for the deaf. After a month, Chantek produced his own first sign and eventually learned to use approximately 150 different signs, forming a vocabulary similar to that of a very young child. Chantek learned names for people (LYN, JOHN), places (YARD, BROCK-HALL), things to eat (YOGURT, CHOCOLATE), actions (WORK, HUG), objects (SCREW-DRIVER, MONEY), animals (DOG, APE), colors (RED, BLACK), pronouns (YOU, ME), location (UP, POINT), attributes (GOOD, HURT), and emphasis (MORE, TIME-TO-DO). We found that Chantek's signing was spontaneous and nonrepetitious. He did not merely imitate his caregivers, but rather he actively used signs to initiate communications and meet his needs. Almost immediately, he

began using signs in combinations and modulated their meanings with slight changes in how he articulated and arranged his signs. He commented "COKE DRINK" after drinking his coke, "PULL BEARD" while pulling a caregiver's hair through a fence, and "TIME HUG" while locked in his cage as his caregiver looked at her watch. But, beyond using signs in this way, could he use them as symbols, that is, more abstractly to represent a person, thing, action, or idea, even apart from its context or when it was not present?

One indication of the capacity of both deaf and hearing children to use symbolic language is the ability to point, which some researchers argued that apes could not do spontaneously. Chantek began to point to objects when he was 2 years old, somewhat later than human children. First, he showed and gave us objects, and then he began pointing where he wanted to be tickled and to where he wanted to be carried. Finally, he could answer questions like WHERE HAT? WHICH

Though the orangutans diverged from humans, chimps, and gorillas about 12 million years ago, all of these ape species share a number of qualities. Orangutans have an insightful, humanlike thinking style characterized by longer attention spans and quiet deliberate action. Orangutans make shelters, tie knots, recognize themselves in mirrors, use one tool to make another, and are very skilled at manipulating objects. In this photo, an orangutan named Chantek, now an adult, begins the sign for tomato.

DIFFERENT? and WHAT WANT? by pointing to the correct object.

As Chantek's vocabulary increased, the ideas that he was expressing became more complex, such as when he signed BAD BIRD at noisy birds giving alarm calls, and WHITE CHEESE FOOD-EAT for cottage cheese. He understood that things had characteristics or attributes that could be described. He also created combinations of signs that we had never used before. In the way that a child learns language, Chantek began to over- or under-extend the meaning of his signs, which gave us insight into his emotions and how he was beginning to classify his world. For example, he used the sign DOG for actual dogs, as well as for a picture of a dog in his Viewmaster, orangutans on television, barking noises on the radio, birds, horses, a tiger at the circus, a herd of cows, a picture of a cheetah, and a noisy helicopter that presumably sounded like it was barking. For Chantek, the sign BUG included crickets, cockroaches, a picture of a cockroach, beetles, slugs, small moths, spiders, worms, flies, a picture of a graph shaped like a butterfly, tiny brown pieces of cat food, and small bits of feces. He signed BREAK before he broke and shared pieces of crackers, and after he broke his toilet. He signed BAD to himself before he grabbed a cat, when he bit into a radish, and for a dead bird.

We also discovered that Chantek could comprehend our spoken English (after the first couple of years we used speech as well as signing). When he was 2 years old, Chantek began to sign for things that were not present. He frequently asked to go to places in his yard to look for animals, such as his pet squirrel and cat, who served as playmates. He also made requests for ICE CREAM, signing CAR RIDE and pulling us toward the parking lot for a trip to a local ice-cream shop. We learned that an orangutan can tell lies. Deception is an important indicator of language abilities since it requires a deliberate and intentional misrepresentation of reality. In order to deceive, you must be able to see events from the other person's perspective and negate his or her perception. Chantek began to deceive from a relatively early age, and we caught him in lies about three times a week. He learned that he could sign DIRTY to get into the bathroom to play with the washing machine, dryer, soap, and so on, instead of using the toilet. He also used his signs deceptively to gain social advantage in games, to divert attention in social interactions, and to avoid testing situations and coming home after walks on campus. On one occasion, Chantek stole food from my pocket while he simultaneously pulled my hand away in the opposite direc-

tion. On another occasion, he stole a pencil eraser, pretended to swallow it, and "supported" his case by opening his mouth and signing FOOD-EAT, as if to say that he had swallowed it. However, he really held the eraser in his cheek, and later it was found in his bedroom where he commonly hid objects.

We carried out tests of Chantek's mental ability using measures developed for human children. Chantek reached a mental age equivalent to that of a 2- to 3-year-old child, with some skills of even older children. On some tasks done readily by children, such as using one object to represent another and pretend play, Chantek performed as well as children, but less frequently. He engaged in chase games in which he would look over his shoulder as he darted about, although no one was chasing him. He also signed to his toys and offered them food and drink.

By 4$^1/_2$ years of age, Chantek showed evidence of planning, creative simulation, and the use of objects in novel relations to one another to invent new meanings. For example, he simulated the context for food preparation by giving his caregiver two objects needed to prepare his milk formula and staring at the location of the remaining ingredient. A further indication that Chantek had mental images is found in his ability to respond to his caregiver's request that he improve the articulation of a sign. When his articulation became careless, we would ask him to SIGN BETTER. Looking closely at us, he would sign slowly and emphatically, taking one hand to put the other into the proper shape.

Chantek was extremely curious and inventive. When he wanted to know the name of something, he offered his hands to be molded into the shape of the proper sign. But language is a creative process, so we were pleased to see that Chantek began to invent his own signs. He invented: NO-TEETH (to show us that he would not use his teeth during rough play); EYE-DRINK (for contact lens solution used by his caregivers); and DAVE-MISSING-FINGER (a name for a favorite university employee who had a hand injury). Like our ancestors, Chantek had become a creator of language. *(Adapted from H. L. W. Miles (1993). Language and the orangutan: The old "person" of the forest. In*

[continued]

[continued]

P. Cavalieri & P. Singer (Eds.), The great ape project (pp. 45–50). New York: St. Martin's Press.)

2004 update: My relationship and research with Chantek continues, through the Chantek Foundation in Atlanta, Georgia. Chantek now uses several hundred signs and has invented new signs for CAR WATER (bottled water that I bring in my car), KATSUP, and ANNOYED. He makes stone tools, arts and crafts, necklaces, and other jewelry, and small percussion instruments used in my rock band Animal Nation. He even co-composes songs with the band. Plans are in the making for Chantek and other enculturated apes to live in culture-based preserves where they have more range of choices and learning opportunities than zoos or research centers. An exciting new project under the auspices of ApeNet will give Chantek an opportunity to communicate with other apes via the Internet. It is of special note that based on great ape language skills, efforts will be underway in the next decade to obtain greater legal rights for these primates, as well as greater recognition of them as another type of "person." For more information, see www.chantek.org. ■■■

While language studies such as the one involving Chantek are fascinating and reveal much about primate cognition, the fact remains that human culture is ultimately dependent on an elaborate system of communication far more complex than that of any other species—including our fellow primates. The reason for this is the sheer amount of what must be learned by each person from other individuals in order to control the knowledge and rules for behavior necessary for full participation in society. Of course, a significant amount of learning can and does take place in the absence of language by way of observation and imitation, guided by a limited number of meaningful signs or symbols. However, all known human cultures are so rich in content that they require communication systems that not only can give precise labels to various classes of phenomena but also permit people to think and talk about their own and others' experiences and expectations—past, present, and future. The central and most highly developed human system of communication is language. Knowledge of the workings of language, then, is essential to a full understanding of what culture is about and how it operates.

THE NATURE OF LANGUAGE

Any human language—Chinese, English, Swahili, or whatever—is obviously a means of transmitting information and sharing with others both collective and individual experiences. Because we tend to take language for granted, it is perhaps not so obvious that language is also a system that enables us to translate our concerns, beliefs, and perceptions into symbols that can be understood and interpreted by others. In spoken language, this is done by taking a few sounds—no language uses more than about fifty—and developing rules for putting them together in meaningful ways. Sign languages, such as American Sign Language, do the same thing but with gestures rather than sounds. The many languages presently in existence all over the world—some 6,000 or so different ones—may well astound and mystify us by their great variety and complexity, but this should not blind us to the fact that all languages, as far back as we can trace them, are organized in the same basic way.

The roots of **linguistics**—the systematic study of all aspects of language—go back a long way, to the works of ancient language specialists in India more than 2,000 years ago. The European age of exploration from the 16th through the 18th centuries set the stage for a great leap forward in the scientific study of language. Explorers, invaders, and missionaries accumulated information about a huge diversity of languages from all around the world. An estimated 10,000 languages still existed when they began their inquiries. Nineteenth-century linguists, including anthropologists, made a significant contribution in discovering system, regularity, and relationships in the data and tentatively formulating laws and regular principles concerning language. In the 20th century, while still collecting data, they made considerable progress in unraveling the reasoning process behind language construction, testing and working from new and improved theories. Insofar as theories and facts of language are verifiable by independent researchers looking at the same materials, there may now be said to be a science of linguistics. This science has three main branches: descriptive linguistics, historical linguistics, and a third branch that focuses on the close relationship between language and culture.

DESCRIPTIVE LINGUISTICS

How can an anthropologist, a trader, a missionary, a diplomat, or anyone else approach and make sense of a language that has not yet been described and analyzed,

linguistics The systematic study of all aspects of language.

or for which there are no readily available written materials? There are hundreds of such undocumented languages in the world; fortunately, effective methods have been developed to help with the task. Descriptive linguistics involves unraveling a language by recording, describing, and analyzing all of its features. It is a painstaking process, but it is ultimately rewarding in that it provides deeper understanding of a language—its structure, its unique linguistic repertoire (figures of speech, word plays, and so on), and its relationship to other languages.

The process of unlocking the underlying rules of a spoken language requires a trained ear and a thorough understanding of the way multiple different speech sounds are produced. Without such know-how, it is extremely difficult to write out or make intelligent use of any data concerning a particular language. To satisfy this preliminary requirement, most people need special training in phonetics. As for the biology that makes human speech possible, that is explained in this chapter's Biocultural Connection.

Phonology

Rooted in the Greek word *phone* (meaning "sound"), **phonetics** is defined as the systematic identification and description of the distinctive sounds of a language. Phonetics is basic to **phonology,** the study of language sounds. In order to analyze and describe any language, one needs first an inventory of all its distinctive sounds. While some of the sounds used in other languages may seem very much like those of the researcher's own speech pattern, others may be unfamiliar. For example, the "th" sound common in English does not exist in the Dutch language and is difficult for most Dutch speakers to pronounce, just as the "r" sound used in numerous languages is tough for Japanese speakers. And the unique "click" sounds used in Bushman languages in southern Africa are difficult for speakers of just about every other language.

While collecting speech sounds or utterances, the linguist works to isolate the **phonemes**—the smallest units of sound that make a difference in meaning. This isolation and analysis may be done by a process called the minimal-pair test. The researcher tries to find two short words that appear to be exactly alike except for one sound, such as *bit* and *pit* in English. If the substitution of *b* for *p* in this minimal pair makes a difference in meaning, as it does in English, then those two sounds have been identified as distinct phonemes of the language and will require two different symbols to record. If, however, the linguist finds two different pronunciations (as when "butter" is pronounced "budder") and then finds that there is no difference in their meaning for a native speaker, the sounds represented will be considered variants of the same phoneme. In such cases, for economy of representation only one of the two symbols will be used to record that sound wherever it is found.

Morphology

While making and studying an inventory of distinctive sounds, linguists also look into **morphology:** the study of the patterns or rules of word formation in a language (including such things as rules concerning verb tense, pluralization, and compound words). They do this by marking out specific sounds and sound combinations that seem to have meaning. These are called **morphemes**—the smallest units of sound that carry a meaning in a language.

Morphemes are distinct from phonemes, which can alter meaning but have no meaning by themselves. Such units may consist of words or parts of words. For example, a linguist studying English in a North American farming community would soon learn that *cow* is a morpheme—a meaningful combination of the phonemes *c, o,* and *w*. Pointing to two of these animals, the linguist would elicit the word *cows* from local speakers. This would reveal yet another morpheme—the *s*—which can be added to the original morpheme to indicate "plural." In time, discovering that the *s* does not occur in the language on its own or unattached, the linguist identifies it as a "bound morpheme." *Cow,* however, is noted as a "free morpheme" because it can occur unattached.

Grammar and Syntax

The next step in unraveling a language is to see how morphemes are put together to form phrases or sentences.

---

phonetics The systematic identification and description of distinctive speech sounds in a language.

phonology The study of language sounds.

phonemes The smallest units of sound that make a difference in meaning in a language.

---

morphology The study of the patterns or rules of word formation in a language (including such things as rules concerning verb tense, pluralization, and compound words).

morphemes The smallest units of sound that carry a meaning in language. They are distinct from phonemes, which can alter meaning, but have no meaning by themselves.

Biocultural Connection

The Biology of Human Speech

While other primates have shown some capacity for language (a socially agreed upon code of communication), actual speech is unique to humans. It comes at a price, for the anatomical organization of the human throat and mouth that make speech possible also increase the risk of choking.

Of particular importance are the positions of the human larynx (voice box) and the epiglottis. The larynx, situated in the respiratory tract between the pharynx (throat) and trachea (wind pipe), contains the vocal chords. The epiglottis is the structure that separates the esophagus or food pipe from the wind pipe as food passes from the mouth to the stomach. (See Figure 10.1 for comparative diagrams of the anatomy of this region in chimps and humans.)

The overlapping routes of passage for food and air can be seen as a legacy of our evolutionary history. Fish, the earliest vertebrates (animals with backbones), obtained both food and oxygen from water entering through their mouths. As

land vertebrates evolved, separate means for obtaining food and air developed out of the preexisting combined system. As a result, the pathways for air and food overlap. In most mammals, including human infants and apes of all ages, choking on food is not a problem because the larynx is relatively high in the throat so that the epiglottis seals the windpipe from food with every swallow. The position of the larynx and trachea make it easy for babies to coordinate breathing with eating.

However, as humans mature and develop the neurological and muscular coordination for speech, the larynx and epiglottis shift to a downward position. The human tongue bends at the back of the throat and is attached to the pharynx, the region of the throat where the food and airways share a common path. Sound occurs as air exhaled from the lungs passes over the vocal cords and causes them to vibrate.

Through continuous interactive movements of the tongue, pharynx,

lips, and teeth, as well as nasal passages, the sounds are alternately modified to produce speech—the uniquely patterned sounds of a particular language. Based on long-standing socially learned patterns of speech, different languages stress certain distinctive types of sounds as significant and ignore others. For instance, languages belonging to the Iroquoian family, such as Mohawk, Seneca, and Cherokee, are among the few in the world that have no bilabial stops (*b* and *p* sounds). They also lack the labio-dental spirants (*f* and *v* sounds), leaving the bilabial nasal *m* sound as the only consonant requiring lip articulation.

It takes many years of practice for people to master the muscular movements needed to produce the precise sounds of any particular language. But no human could produce the finely controlled speech sounds without a lowered position of the larynx and epiglottis. ■ ■ ■

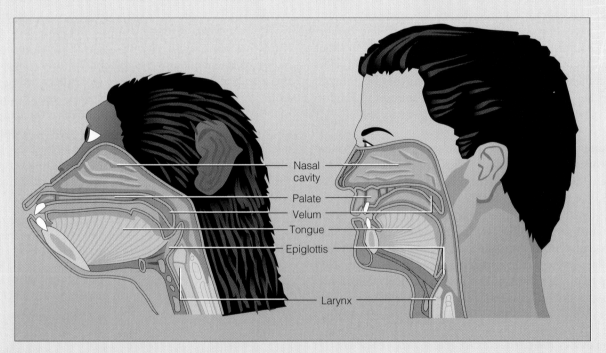

Figure 10.1

This process is known as identifying the syntactic units of the language, or the way morphemes are put together into larger chains or strings that have meaning. This begins to establish the rules or principles of phrase and sentence making, the **syntax** of the language. The **grammar** of the language will ultimately consist of all observations about its morphemes and syntax.

One of the strengths of modern descriptive linguistics is the objectivity of its methods. For example, an English-speaking anthropologist who specializes in this will not approach a language with the idea that it must have nouns, verbs, prepositions, or any other of the form classes identifiable in English. She or he instead sees what turns up in the language and makes an attempt to describe it in terms of its own inner workings. This allows for unanticipated discoveries. For instance, unlike many other languages, English does not distinguish between feminine and masculine nouns. So it is that English speakers use the definite article *the* in front of any noun, while the French require two types of such definite articles: *la* for feminine nouns and *le* for masculine—as in *la lune* (the moon) and *le soleil* (the sun). German speakers go one step further, utilizing three types of articles: *der* in front of masculine nouns, *die* for feminine, and *das* for neutral. It is also interesting to note that in contrast to their French neighbors, Germans consider the moon as masculine, so they say *der Mon,* and the sun as feminine, which makes it *die Sonne.* In another corner of the world, the highlands of Peru and Bolivia in South America, indigenous peoples who speak Quechua are not concerned about such gendered nouns, for there are no definite articles in their language.

HISTORICAL LINGUISTICS

In contrast to descriptive linguistics, which focuses on all features of a particular language as it is at any one moment in time, historical linguistics deals with the fact that languages change. In addition to deciphering "dead" languages that are no longer spoken, specialists in this field investigate relationships between earlier and later forms of the same language, study older languages for developments in modern ones, and examine interrelationships among older languages. For example, they attempt to sort out the development of Latin (spoken almost 1,500 years ago in southern Europe) into Italian, Spanish, Portuguese, French, and Romanian by identifying

natural shifts in the original language, as well as modifications brought on by direct contact during the next few centuries with Germanic-speaking invaders from northern Europe. That said, historical linguists are not limited to the faraway past, for even modern languages are constantly transforming—adding new words, dropping others, or changing meaning. Over the last decade or so, Internet use has widened the meaning of a host of already existing English words—from *hacking* to *surfing* to *spam.*

Especially when focusing on long-term processes of change, historical linguists depend on written records of languages. They have achieved considerable success in working out the relationships among different languages, and these are reflected in schemes of classification. For example, English is one of approximately 140 languages classified in the larger Indo-European **language family.** This family is subdivided into some eleven subgroups, which reflects the fact that there has been a long period (6,000 years or so) of **linguistic divergence** from an ancient unified language (reconstructed as Proto-Indo-European) into separate "daughter" languages. English is one of several languages in the Germanic subgroup (Figure 10.2), all of which are more closely related to one another than they are to the languages of any other subgroup of the Indo-European family.

So it is that, despite the differences between them, the languages of one subgroup share certain features when compared to those of another. As an illustration, the word for "father" in the Germanic languages always starts with an *f* or closely related *v* sound (Dutch *vader,* German *Vater,* Gothic *Fadar*). Among the Romance languages, by contrast, the comparable word always starts with a *p*: French *père,* Spanish and Italian *padre*—all derived from the Latin *pater.* The original Indo-European word for "father" was *p'te¯r,* so in this case, the Romance languages have retained the earlier pronunciation, whereas the Germanic languages have diverged. Thus, many words that begin with *p* in the Romance languages, like Latin *piscis* and *pes,* become words like English *fish* and *foot* in the Germanic languages.

In addition to describing the changes that have taken place as languages have diverged from ancient parent languages, historical linguists have also developed methods to estimate when such divergences occurred. One such technique is known as **glottochronology,** a

syntax The patterns or rules for the formation of phrases and sentences in a language.
grammar The entire formal structure of a language, including morphology and syntax.

language family A group of languages descended from a single ancestral language.
linguistic divergence The development of different languages from a single ancestral language.
glottochronology In linguistics, a method for identifying the approximate time that languages branched off from a common ancestor. It is based on analyzing core vocabularies.

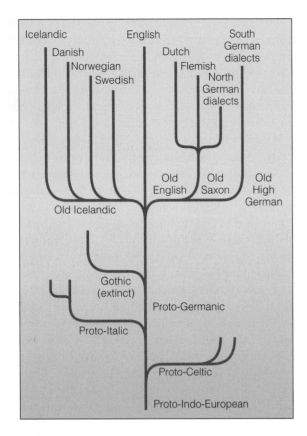

Figure 10.2
English is one of a group of languages in the Germanic subgroup of the Indo-European family. This diagram shows its relationship to other languages in the same subgroup. The root was Proto-Indo-European, an ancestral language originally spoken by early farmers and herders who spread north and west over Europe, bringing with them both their customs and their language.

term derived from the Greek word *glottis,* which means "tongue" or "language." This method compares the **core vocabularies** of languages—pronouns, lower numerals, and names for body parts and natural objects. It is based on the assumption that these elemental vocabularies change more slowly than other words and at a more or less constant rate of 14 to 19 percent per 1,000 years. (Linguists determined this rate by calculating changes documented in thirteen historic written languages.) By applying a mathematical formula to two related core vocabularies, one can determine the approximate number of years since the languages separated. Although not as precise as we might like, glottochronology, in conjunction with other chronological dating methods such as those based on archaeological and genetic data, can help determine the time of linguistic divergence.

core vocabularies The most basic and long-lasting words in any language—pronouns, lower numerals, and names for body parts and natural objects.

Processes of Linguistic Divergence

Studying modern languages in their particular cultural contexts can help us understand the processes of change that may have led to linguistic divergence. Clearly, one force for change is *selective borrowing* by one language from another. This is evident in the many French words present in the English language—and in the growing number of English words cropping up in languages all around the world due to globalization. Technological breakthroughs resulting in new equipment and products also prompt linguistic shifts. For instance, the electronic revolution that brought us radio, television, and computers has created entirely new vocabularies. Increasing professional specialization is another driving force. We see one of many examples in the field of biomedicine where today's students must learn the specialized vocabulary and idioms of the profession—over 6,000 new words in the first year of medical school. There is also a tendency for any group within a larger society to create its own unique vocabulary, whether it is a street gang, sorority, religious group, prison inmates, or platoon of soldiers. By changing the meaning of existing words or inventing new ones, members of the "in-group" can communicate with fellow members while effectively excluding outsiders who may be within hearing range. Finally, there seems to be a human tendency to admire the person who comes up with a new and clever idiom, a useful word, or a particularly stylish pronunciation, as long as these do not seriously interfere with communication. All of this means that no language stands still.

Phonological differences among groups may be regarded in the same light as vocabulary differences. In a class-structured society, for example, members of the upper class may try to keep their pronunciation distinct from that of lower classes, or vice versa, as a means of reinforcing social boundaries.

Language Loss and Revival

Perhaps the most powerful force for linguistic change is the domination of one society over another, as demonstrated during 500 years of European colonialism. Such dominations persist in many parts of the world to the present time. In many cases, foreign political control has resulted in linguistic erosion or even complete disappearance, sometimes only leaving a faint trace in old, indigenous names for geographic features such as hills and rivers. In fact, over the last 500 years 4,000 of the world's 10,000 or so languages have become extinct as a direct result of warfare, epidemics, and forced assimilation brought on by colonial powers and other aggressive outsiders. Most of the remaining 6,000 languages are spoken by very few people, and many of them are losing speakers rapidly due to globalization. In fact, half have fewer than 10,000 speakers each, and a quarter have fewer than 1,000. In North America, for instance, only 150 of the original 300 indigenous languages still exist, and many of these surviving tongues are seriously threatened.

Some anthropologists predict that the number of languages still spoken in the world today will be cut in half by the year 2100, in large part due to printed and electronic media. The printing press, radio, satellite television, Internet, and instant messaging on cellular phones are driving the need for sharing languages that many understand, and increasingly that is English. In the past 500 years, this language originally spoken by about 2.5 million people living only in part of the British Isles in northwestern Europe has spread around the world. Today more than 375 million people claim English as their native tongue. Another 375 million people speak it as a second language and 700 million as a foreign language. While a common language allows people to communicate easily, many contend that a global tongue should not come at the cost of language diversity—for with the disappearance of each language, a measure of humankind's richly varied cultural heritage, including countless insights on life, is lost.

Sometimes, in reaction to a real or perceived threat of cultural dominance by powerful foreign societies, ethnic groups and even entire countries may seek to maintain or reclaim their unique identity by purging their vocabularies of "foreign" terms. Emerging as a significant force for linguistic change, such **linguistic nationalism** is particularly characteristic of the former colonial countries of Africa and Asia today. It is by no means limited to those countries, however, as one can see by periodic French attempts to purge their language of such Americanisms as *le hamburger*. A recent example of this is France's decision to substitute the word *e-mail* with the newly minted government-approved term *couriel*.

Also in the category of linguistic nationalism are revivals of languages long out of daily use by ethnic minorities and sometimes even whole nations. Among the few successful examples is the recent revival of ancient Hebrew (after it had not been spoken as a daily language for almost 2,000 years) as the basis for the national language of Jews in the modern state of Israel.

For many ethnic minorities, efforts to counter the threat of linguistic extinction form part of their struggle to maintain a sense of cultural identity and dignity. A prime means by which powerful groups try to assert their dominance over minorities living within their borders is to actively suppress their languages. A dramatic illustration of this is the government-sanctioned effort to repress Native American cultures in Canada and the United States and fully absorb these cultures into the main body of North American society. Government polices included taking Indian children away from their parents and putting them in boarding schools where only English was allowed, and students were often punished for speaking their traditional languages. Upon returning to their homes, many could no longer communicate with their own close relatives and neighbors. While now abolished, these institutions and the historical policies that shaped them did lasting damage to American Indian groups striving to maintain their cultural heritage. Especially over the past three decades many of these besieged indigenous communities have been actively involved in language reclamation efforts, often with the aid of anthropologists specializing in linguistics.

LANGUAGE IN ITS SOCIAL AND CULTURAL SETTINGS

As discussed in the section on descriptive linguistics, language is not simply a matter of combining sounds according to certain rules to come up with meaningful utterances. It is important to remember that languages are spoken by people who are members of distinct societies. In addition to the fact that most societies have their own unique cultures, individuals within a society tend to vary in the ways they use language based on social variables such as gender, class, and ethnicity. We choose words and sentences to communicate meaning, and what is meaningful in one community or culture may not be in another. The fact is that our use of language reflects, and is reflected by, the rest of our culture. Thus, linguistic anthropologists also examine language in relation to its social and cultural contexts. This area of study falls into two categories: sociolinguistics and ethnolinguistics.

Sociolinguistics

Sociolinguistics, the study of the relationship between language and society, examines how social categories

linguistic nationalism The attempt by ethnic minorities and even countries to proclaim independence by purging their language of foreign terms.

sociolinguistics The study of the relationship between language and society through examining how social categories influence the use and interpretation of distinctive styles of speech.

(such as age, sex, ethnicity occupation, religion and class) influence the use and interpretation of distinctive styles of speech.

Language and Gender

As a powerful feature of personal and social identity, gender is often reflected in language use, so it is not surprising that numerous intriguing and thought-provoking sociolinguistic topics fall under the category of language and gender. These include research on **gendered speech**—distinct male and female speech patterns, which vary across social and cultural settings. One of the first in-depth studies in this vein, done in the early 1970s, asserted that neither language nor gender can be studied independently of the socially constructed communities in which we live. Written by linguist Robin Lakoff, it explored the relationship of gender and power, addressing specific issues including social factors thought to contribute to North American women exhibiting less decisive speech styles than men. This study and a subsequent wave of related works by other scholars have produced new insights (and often heated discussions) about languages as socially produced speech performances in both private and public settings.[3]

Gendered speech research also includes the study of distinct male and female syntax exhibited in various languages around the world, such as the Lakota language, still spoken at the Pine Ridge and Rosebud Indian reservations in South Dakota. When a Lakota woman asks someone, "How are you?" she says, "*Tonikthkahe?*" But when her brother poses the same question, he says, "*Toniktukahwo?*" As explained by Michael Two Horses, "Our language is gender-specific in the area of commands, queries, and a couple of other things."[4]

Learning these nuances of language is not difficult for a child growing up surrounded by Lakota speakers, but it can be hard for newcomers. So it was for Kevin Costner and other actors in the 1990 film *Dances with Wolves*, which tells the fictional story of a white soldier's relationship with a Lakota Indian community in the 1800s. Since Costner (who plays the soldier) and several of the Native American actors did not speak Lakota, the producers hired a Lakota woman to coach them, aiming

> **gendered speech** Distinct male and female speech patterns, which vary across social and cultural settings.

---

[3]See Lakoff, R. T. (2004). *Language and woman's place*, Mary Bucholtz (Ed.), New York: Oxford University Press. This re-release of Lakoff's 1975 seminal book on gender and language features annotations by Lakoff plus twenty-five short essays by scholars whose own language and gender research grew out of positive and negative reactions to her original work.

[4]Personal communication, April 2003.

to make the feature film as culturally authentic as possible. Upon release, the film won critical acclaim and drew crowds to cinemas all across the country. When it showed in a theater in Rapid City, South Dakota, Lakota people from the nearby reservations arrived on the scene eager to see this movie about their ancestors. But when they heard Costner and his on-screen warrior friends talk, they began to snicker. As the dramatic scenes unfolded, their laughter grew. What was so hilarious? While it was true that Lakota in the audience were generally pleased to hear their own language in a major Hollywood film, they thought it very funny to hear the white hero, along with some non-Lakota Indian actors dressed as warriors, speak Lakota like women. Because the language coach had had to teach both male and female actors, and because they found the language difficult to learn, she had decided not to bother them with the complexities of gendered speech.

Social Dialects

Sociolinguists are also interested in **dialects**—varying forms of a language that reflect particular regions, occupations, or social classes and that are similar enough to be mutually intelligible. Distinguishing dialects from "languages" and revealing the relationship between power and language, the noted linguist/political activist Noam Chomsky stated that a language is a dialect with an army. Technically, all dialects are languages—there is nothing partial or sublinguistic about them—and the point at which two different dialects become distinctly different languages is roughly the point at which speakers of one are almost totally unable to communicate with speakers of the other. Boundaries may be psychological, geographical, social, or economic, and they are not always very clear. In the case of regional dialects, there is frequently a transitional territory, or perhaps a buffer zone, where features of both are found and understood, as between central and southern China. The fact is that if you learn the Chinese of Beijing, you cannot communicate with someone who comes from Canton or Hong Kong, although both languages—or dialects—are usually lumped together as Chinese.

A classic example of the kind of dialect that may set one group apart from others within a single society is one spoken by many inner-city African Americans. Technically known as African American Vernacular English (AAVE), it has often been referred to as "black English" and "Ebonics." Unfortunately, there is a widespread misperception among non-AAVE speakers that this

> **dialects** Varying forms of a language that reflect particular regions, occupations, or social classes and that are similar enough to be mutually intelligible.

dialect is somehow substandard or defective. A basic principle of linguistics is that the selection of a so-called prestige dialect—in this case, what we may call "Standard English" as opposed to Ebonics—is determined by social historical forces such as wealth and power and is not dependent on virtues or shortcomings of the dialects themselves. In fact, African American Vernacular English is a highly structured mode of speech with patterned rules of sounds and sequences like any other language or dialect. Many of its distinctive features stem from a retention of sound patterns, grammatical rules concerning verbs, and even words of the West African languages spoken by the ancestors of present-day African Americans.[5]

Humans have been talking in this world for an extremely long time, and every language or dialect now known has a long history and has developed its own particular subtleties and complexities that reflect its speakers' way of life and what they want or need to communicate with others. Thus, anthropologists recognize that all languages are more or less equally effective as systems of communication within their own particular cultural contexts.

Ethnolinguistics

The study of the relationships between language and culture, and how they mutually influence and inform each other, is the domain of **ethnolinguistics.** In this type of research, anthropologists may investigate how a language reflects the culturally significant aspects of a certain people's natural habitat. Among the Inuit in the Canadian Arctic, for instance, we'll find numerous words for different types of snow, whereas Americans in a city like Detroit most likely possess a rich vocabulary allowing them to precisely distinguish between different types of cars, categorized by model, year, and manufacturer. This is an example of **linguistic relativity**—the idea that distinctions encoded in one language are unique to that language alone. Another example of linguistic relativity concerns cultural categories of color. Languages have different ways of dividing and naming elements of the color spectrum, which is actually a continuum of multi-

ple hues with no clear-cut boundaries between them. In English we speak of violet, red, orange, yellow, green, and blue, but other languages mark out different groupings. For instance, Indians in Mexico's northwestern mountains speaking Tarahumara have only one word for both green and blue—*siyoname.*

Related to linguistic relativity is the principle of **linguistic determinism,** the idea that language to some extent shapes the way in which we view and think about the world around us. An extreme version of this principle holds that language actually determines thought and thereby shapes behavior and culture itself. A more widely accepted view holds that thought is merely influenced by language. Linguistic determinism is associated with the pioneering ethnolinguistic research of anthropologist Edward Sapir and his student Benjamin Lee Whorf during the 1930s and '40s. Their research resulted in what is now known as the *Sapir-Whorf hypothesis:* that each language provides particular grooves of linguistic expression that predispose speakers of that language to perceive the world in a certain way. In Whorf's own words, "The structure of the language one habitually uses influences the manner in which one understands his environment. The picture of the universe shifts from tongue to tongue."[6]

Whorf gained many of these insights while translating English into Hopi, a North American Indian language still spoken in Arizona. Doing this work, he discovered that Hopi differs from English not only in vocabulary but also in terms of its grammatical categories such as nouns and verbs. For instance, Hopi use numbers for counting and measuring things that have physical existence, but they do not apply numbers to abstractions like time. They would have no problem translating an English sentence such as, "I see fifteen sheep grazing on three acres of grassland," but an equally simple sentence such as, "Three weeks ago, I enjoyed my fifteen minutes of fame" would require a much more complex translation into Hopi. It is also of note that Hopi verbs do not express tenses in the same way that English verbs do. Rather than marking past, present, and future, with *-ed, -ing,* or *will,* Hopi requires additional words to indicate if an event is completed, still ongoing, or is expected to take place. So instead of saying, "Three strangers stayed for fifteen days in our village," a Hopi would say something like, "We

ethnolinguistics A branch of linguistics that studies the relationships between language and culture and how they mutually influence and inform each other.

linguistic relativity The idea that distinctions encoded in one language are unique to that language alone.

linguistic determinism The idea that language to some extent shapes the way in which we view and think about the world around us; sometimes called the Sapir-Whorf hypothesis after its originators Edward Sapir and his student Benjamin Lee Whorf.

[5]Monaghan, L., Hinton, L., & Kephart, R. (1997). Can't teach a dog to be a cat? The dialogue on ebonics. *Anthropology Newsletter, 38*(3), 1, 8, 9.

[6]Quoted in Hoebel, E. A. (1958). *Man in the primitive world: An introduction to anthropology* (p. 571). New York: McGraw-Hill.

remember three strangers stay in our village until the sixteenth day." In addition, the Hopi language can express the fact that the event talked about is a regular thing that generally occurs.

Considering such linguistic distinctions in connection with observed Hopi behavior, Whorf concluded that the Hopi language structures thinking and behavior with a focus on the present—on getting ready and carrying out what needs to be done right. He summed it up like this: "A characteristic of Hopi behavior is the emphasis on preparation. This includes announcing and getting ready for events well beforehand, elaborate precautions to insure persistence of desired conditions, and stress on good will as the preparer of good results."[7]

In the 1990s linguistic anthropologists devised new research strategies to actually test Sapir and Whorf's original hypothesis.[8] One study found that speakers of Swedish and Finnish (neighboring peoples who speak radically different languages) working at similar jobs in similar regions under similar laws and regulations show significantly different rates of on-the-job accidents. The rates are substantially lower among the Swedish speakers. What emerges from comparison of the two languages is that Swedish (one of the Indo-European languages) emphasizes information about movement in three-dimensional space. Finnish (a Ural-Altaic language, like Estonian and Hungarian, unrelated to Indo-European languages) emphasizes more static relations among coherent temporal entities. As a consequence, it seems that Finns organize the workplace in a way that favors the individual person over the temporal organization in the overall production process. This in turn leads to frequent production disruptions, haste, and (ultimately) accidents. Intriguing as such studies may be, they are not sufficient by themselves for a full understanding of the relation between language and thought. Supplementary approaches are necessary and are being developed.

A more obvious ethnolinguistic observation is that language mirrors or reflects, rather than determines, cultural reality. Aymara Indians living in the Bolivian highlands, for example, depend on the potato (or *luki*) as their major source of food. Their language has over 200 words for potatoes, reflecting the many varieties they traditionally grow and the many different ways that they preserve and prepare this food.

If language does mirror cultural reality, it would follow that changes in a culture will sooner or later be reflected in changes in the language. We see this is happening all around the world today, including in the English language. Consider, for example, the cultural practice of marriage. Historically, English-speaking North Americans have defined marriage as a legally binding union between one man and one woman. However, a growing tolerance toward homosexuals over the past two decades or so, coupled with legislation prohibiting sexual discrimination, resulted in a ruling by Canada's Supreme Court in summer 2003 that it is illegal to exclude same-sex unions from the definition of marriage. Consequently, the meaning of the word *marriage* is now being stretched. It is no longer possible to automatically assume that the term refers to the union of a man and a woman—or that a woman who mentions her "spouse" is speaking of a man. Such changes in the English language reflect the wider process of change in North America's cultural reality.

Linguists have found that although language is generally flexible and adaptable, established terminologies do tend to perpetuate themselves, reflecting and revealing the social structure and worldview of groups and people. For example, American English has a wide array of words having to do with conflict and warfare. It also features an abundance of militaristic metaphors, such as "conquering" space, "fighting" the "battle" of the budget or the bulge, carrying out a "war" against drugs, making a "killing" on the stock market, "shooting down" an argument, "torpedoing" a plan, "spearheading" a movement, "decapitating" a foreign government, or "bombing" on an exam, to mention just a few. An observer from an entirely different and perhaps less aggressive culture, such as the Hopi in Arizona or the Jain in India, could gain considerable insight into the importance of open competition, winning, and military might in American society simply by tuning into such commonly used phrases.

LANGUAGE VERSATILITY

In many societies throughout the world, it is not unusual for individuals to be fluent in two, three, or more different languages. They succeed in this in large part because they experience training in multiple languages as children—not as high school or college students, which is the educational norm in the United States. In some regions where groups speaking different languages co-exist and interact, people often understand one another but may choose not to speak the other's language. Such is the case in the borderlands of northern Bolivia and southern Peru where Quechua-speaking and Aymara-speaking Indians are neighbors. When an Aymara farmer speaks to a Quechua herder in Aymara, the Quechua will reply in Quechua, and vice versa, each

---

[7]Carroll, J. B. (Ed.). (1956). *Language, thought and reality: Selected writings of Benjamin Lee Whorf* (p. 148). Cambridge, MA: MIT Press.
[8]Lucy, J. A. (1997). Linguistic relativity. *Annual Review of Anthropology, 26,* 291–312.

© John Chellmann/Animals Animals Earth Scenes—All rights reserved

© Jutta Klee/Corbis

Humans talk, using the highly nuanced vocabularies of speech, while other primates communicate through nonlanguage vocal systems. But all primates, including humans, communicate with gestures or body language, including facial expression, as shown here.

knowing that the other understands both languages even if speaking just one. The ability to comprehend two languages but express oneself in only one is known as "receptive" or "passive" bilingualism.

In the United States, perhaps reflecting the country's enormous size and power, many citizens are not interested in learning a second or foreign language. This is especially significant—and troubling—since the United States is not only one of the world's most ethnically diverse countries but is also the world's largest economy and heavily dependent on international trade relations. Moreover, in our globalized world, being bilingual or multilingual opens doors of communication not only for trade but for diplomacy, art, and friendship.

BEYOND WORDS: THE GESTURE-CALL SYSTEM

Efficient though languages are at naming and talking about ideas, actions, and things, all are insufficient to some degree in communicating certain kinds of information that people need to know in order to fully understand what is being said. For this reason, human language is always embedded within a gesture-call system of a type that we share with nonhuman primates. The various sounds and gestures of this system serve to "key" speech, providing listeners with the appropriate frame for interpreting what a speaker is saying. Messages about human emotions and intentions are effectively communicated by this gesture-call system: Is the speaker happy, sad, mad, enthusiastic, tired, or in some other emotional state? Is he or she requesting information, denying something, reporting factually, or lying?

Very little of this information is conveyed by spoken language alone. In English, for example, at least 90 percent of emotional information is transmitted not by the words spoken but by "body language" and tone of voice.

Body Language

The **gesture** component of the gesture-call system consists of facial expressions and bodily postures and motions that convey intended as well as subconscious messages. The method for notating and analyzing this "body language" is known as **kinesics.** Humankind's repertoire of body language is enormous. This is evident if you consider just one aspect of it: the fact that a human being has 80 facial muscles and is thereby capable of making more than 7,000 facial expressions! This given, it should not be surprising to hear that at least 60 percent of our total communication takes place nonverbally. Often, gestural messages complement spoken messages—for instance, nodding the head while affirming something verbally, raising eyebrows when asking a question, or using hands to illustrate or emphasize what is being talked about. However, nonverbal signals are sometimes at odds with verbal ones, and they have the power to override or undercut them. For example, a person may say the words "I love you" a thousand times to someone, but if it's not true, the nonverbal signals will

gesture Facial expressions and bodily postures and motions that convey intended as well as subconscious messages.

kinesics A system of notating and analyzing postures, facial expressions, and body motions that convey messages.

likely communicate that falseness and will probably be perceived as what really matters.

Communication took a radical turn in the 1990s with the widespread use of e-mail and Internet chat rooms. These new forms resemble the spontaneity and speed of face-to-face communication but lack the body signals and voice intonations that nuance what is being said (and hint at how it is being received). According to a recent study, the intended tone of e-mail messages is perceived correctly only 56 percent of the time.[9] A misunderstood message can quickly turn into "flame bait," inviting hostile and insulting messages, which can escalate into "flame wars." Because the risk of miscommunication on the Internet abounds, even with the use of interpretation signals such as LOL (laugh out loud) or the smiley face ☺, certain sensitive exchanges are better made in person.

Little scientific notice was taken of body language prior to the 1950s, but since then a great deal of research has been devoted to this intriguing subject. Cross-cultural studies in this field have shown that there are many similarities around the world in such basic facial expressions as smiling, laughing, crying, and displaying shock or anger. The smirks, frowns, and gasps that we have inherited from our primate ancestry require little learning and are harder to "fake" than conventional or socially obtained gestures that are shared by members of a group, albeit not always consciously so. Routine greetings are also similar around the world. Europeans, Balinese, Papuans, Samoans, Bushmen, and at least some South American Indians all smile and nod, and if the individuals are especially friendly, they will raise their eyebrows with a rapid movement, keeping them raised for a fraction of a second. By doing so, they signal a readiness for contact. The Japanese, however, suppress the eyebrow flash, regarding it as indecent, which goes to show that there are important differences, as well as similarities, cross-culturally. This can be seen in gestural expressions for yes and no. In North America, one nods the head down then up for yes or shakes it left and right for no. The people of Sri Lanka also nod to answer yes to a factual question, but if asked to do something, a slow sideways movement of the head means yes. In Greece, the nodded head means yes, but no is indicated by jerking the head back so as to lift the face, usually with the eyes closed and the eyebrows raised.

Another aspect of body language has to do with social space: how people position themselves physically in relation to others. **Proxemics,** the cross-cultural study of humankind's perception and use of space, came to the fore through the work of anthropologist Edward Hall, who coined the term. Growing up in the culturally diverse southwestern United States, Hall glimpsed the complexities of intercultural relations early on in life. As a young man in the 1930s, he worked with construction crews of Hopi and Navajo Indians, building roads and dams. In 1942 he earned his doctorate in anthropology under the famous Franz Boas, who stressed the point that "communication constitutes the core of culture."

This idea was driven home for Hall during World War II when he commanded an African American regiment in Europe and the Philippines and again when he worked with the U.S. State Department to develop the new field of intercultural communication at the Foreign Service Institute (FSI). It was during his years at FSI (1950–1955), while training some 2,000 Foreign Service workers, that Hall's ideas about proxemics began to crystallize. He articulated them and other aspects of nonverbal communication in his 1959 book, *The Silent Language,* now recognized as the founding document for the field of intercultural communication.

His work showed that people from different cultures have different frameworks for defining and organizing space—the personal space they establish around their bodies, as well as the macrolevel sensibilities that shape cultural expectations about how streets, neighborhoods, and cities should be arranged. Among other things, his investigation of personal space revealed that every culture has distinctive norms for closeness. (You can see this for yourself if you are watching a foreign film, visiting a foreign country, or find yourself in a multicultural group. How close to one another do the people you are observing stand when talking in the street or riding in a subway or elevator? Does the pattern match the one you are accustomed to in your own cultural corner?) Hall identified four categories of proxemically relevant spaces or body distances: intimate (0–18 inches), personal-casual (1½–4 feet), social-consultive (4–12 feet), and public distance (12 feet and beyond). Hall warned that different cultural definitions of socially accepted use of space within these categories can lead to serious failures of communication and understanding in cross-cultural settings. His research has been a foundation stone for the present-day training of international businesspeople, diplomats, and others involved in intercultural work.

---

[9]Kruger, J., et al. (2005). *Journal of Personality and Social Psychology,* 89(6), 925–936.

proxemics The cross-cultural study of humankind's perception and use of space.

Paralanguage

The second component of the gesture-call system is **paralanguage**—specific voice effects that accompany speech and contribute to communication. These include vocalizations such as giggling, groaning, or sighing, as well as voice qualities such as pitch and tempo. The importance of paralanguage is suggested by the comment, "It's not so much *what* was said as *how* it was said." Recent studies have shown, for example, that subliminal messages communicated below the threshold of conscious perception by seemingly minor differences in phrasing, tempo, length of answers, and the like are far more important in courtroom proceedings than even the most perceptive trial lawyer may have realized. Among other things, how a witness gives testimony alters the reception it gets from jurors and influences the witness' credibility.[10]

TONAL LANGUAGES

There is an enormous diversity in the ways languages are spoken. In addition to hundreds of vowels and consonants, sounds can be divided into tones—rises and falls in pitch that play a key role in distinguishing one word from another. About 70 percent of the world's languages are **tonal languages** in which the various distinctive sound pitches of spoken words are not only an essential part of their pronunciation but also key to their meaning, and at least one-third of the people in the world speak a tonal language.

Many languages in Africa, Central America, and East Asia are tonal. For instance, the tone or pitch level of a spoken word is an essential part of its pronunciation in Mandarin Chinese, the most common language in China. Mandarin has four contrasting tones: flat, rising, falling, and falling then rising. These tones are used to distinguish among normally stressed syllables that are otherwise identical. Thus, depending on intonation, *ba* can mean "to uproot," "eight," "to

> **paralanguage** Voice effects that accompany language and convey meaning. These include vocalizations such as giggling, groaning, or sighing, as well as voice qualities such as pitch and tempo.
>
> **tonal language** A language in which the sound pitch of a spoken word is an essential part of its pronunciation and meaning.

hold," or "a harrow" (farm tool).[11] Cantonese, the primary language in southern China and Hong Kong, uses six contrasting tones, and some Chinese dialects have as many as nine. In nontonal languages such as English, tone can be used to convey an attitude or to change a statement into a question, but tone alone does not change the meaning of individual words as it does in Mandarin, where careless use of tones with the syllable *ma* could cause one to call someone's mother a horse!

FROM SPEECH TO WRITING

When anthropology developed as an academic discipline over a century ago, it concentrated its attention on small traditional communities that relied primarily on personal interaction and oral communication for survival. Cultures that depend on talking and listening often have rich traditions of storytelling and speechmaking. For them, oration (from the Latin *orare*, "to speak") plays a central role in education, conflict resolution, political decision making, spiritual or supernatural practices, and many other aspects of life. Consequently, people capable of making expressive and informed speeches usually enjoy great prestige in such societies.

Today as in the past, traditional orators are typically trained from childhood in memorizing genealogies, ritual prayers, customary laws, and diplomatic agreements. In ceremonies that can last many hours, even days, they eloquently recite the oral traditions by heart. Their extraordinary memories are often enhanced by oral devices such as rhyme, rhythm, and melody. Orators may also employ special objects to help them remember proper sequences and points to be made—memory devices such as notched sticks, knotted strings, bands embroidered with shells, and so forth. Traditional Iroquois Indian orators, for example, performed their formal speeches often with wampum belts made of hemp string and purple-blue and white shell beads (quahog and whelk shells) woven into distinctive patterns. More than artful motifs, wampum designs were used to represent any of a variety of important messages, including treaties with other nations.

Such symbolic designs are found all over the world, some dating back more than 30,000 years. When ancient artifacts of bone, antler, stone, or some other material have been etched or painted, anthropologists try to determine if these markings were created to symbolize

---

[10]O'Barr, W. M., & Conley, J. M. (1993). When a juror watches a lawyer. In W. A. Haviland & R. J. Gordon (Eds.), *Talking about people* (2nd. ed., pp. 42–45). Mountain View, CA: Mayfield.

[11]Catford, J. C. (1988). *A practical introduction to phonetics* (p. 183). Oxford, England: Clarendon Press.

specific ideas such as seasonal calendars, kinship relations, trade records, and so forth. From basic visual signs such as these emerged a few writing systems, including the alphabet.

Thousands of languages, past and present, have existed only in spoken form, but many others have been documented in graphic symbols of some sort. Over time, visual representations in the form of simplified pictures of things (pictographs) evolved into more stylized symbolic forms. Although different peoples invented a variety of graphic styles, anthropologists distinguish an actual **writing system** as a set of visible or tactile signs used to represent units of language in a systematic way. Recently discovered symbols carved into 8,600-year-old tortoise shells found in western China may represent the earliest evidence of elementary writing found anywhere.[12] A fully developed early writing system is Egyptian hieroglyphics, developed some 5,000 years ago and in use for about 3,500 years. One of the other oldest systems in the world is cuneiform, an arrangement of wedge-shaped imprints developed in

> **writing system** A set of visible or tactile signs used to represent units of language in a systematic way.

---

[12] Li, X., et al. (2003). The earliest writing? Sign use in the seventh millennium BC at Jiahu, Henan Province, China. *Antiquity, 77*, 31–44.

Mesopotamia mostly (present-day Iraq), which lasted nearly as long. Cuneiform writing stands out among other early forms in that it led to the first and only phonetic writing system (that is, an alphabet), ultimately spawning a wide array of alphabetic writing systems. About 2,500 years or so after these systems were established, others began to appear, developing independently in distant locations around the world, such as the hieroglyphics invented in the Mexican state of Oaxaca and subsequently elaborated by the Maya.

Although thousands of years have passed since literacy first emerged, today more than 860 million adults worldwide cannot read and write. Illiteracy condemns already disadvantaged people to ongoing poverty—migrant rural workers, refugees, ethnic minorities, and those living in rural backlands and urban slums throughout the world. For example, a third of India's 1 billion inhabitants cannot read and write, and some 113 million children around the world are not enrolled in school. Declaring literacy a human right, the United Nations established International Literacy Day (September 8) and proclaimed the period 2003 to 2012 as the Literacy Decade with the objective of extending literacy to all humanity. Every September 8 during this decade, the UN Education, Scientific, and Cultural Organization (UNESCO) awards prizes to individuals or groups who devote themselves year after year to advancing the cause of literacy for all.

Chapter Summary

■ Anthropologists need to understand the workings of language, because it is through language that people in every society are able to share their experiences, concerns, and beliefs, over the past and in the present, and to communicate these to the next generation. Language makes communication of infinite meanings possible by employing a few sounds or gestures that, when put together according to certain rules, result in meanings that are intelligible to fellow speakers.

■ Linguistics is the systematic study of all aspects of language by anthropologists, psychologists, and other specialists. Phonetics focuses on the production, transmission, and reception of speech sounds, or phonemes. Phonology studies the sound patterns of language in order to extract the rules that govern the way sounds are combined. Morphology is concerned with the smallest units of meaningful combinations of sounds—morphemes—in a language. Syntax refers to the principles according to which phrases and sentences are built. The entire formal structure of a language, consisting of all observations about its morphemes and syntax, constitutes the grammar of a language.

■ There are three main branches of linguistics. Descriptive linguists mark out and explain the features of a language at a particular time in its history. Historical linguists investigate relationships between earlier and later forms of the same language—including identifying the forces behind the changes that have taken place in languages in the course of linguistic divergence. Their work provides a means of roughly dating certain migrations, invasions, and contacts of people. A third group of linguists study language as it relates to society and culture—research areas known as sociolinguistics and ethnolinguistics.

■ All languages change—borrowing terms from other languages or inventing new words for new technologies or social realities. A major cause of language change is the domination of one society over another, which over the last 500 years led to the disappearance of about 4,000 of the world's 10,000 languages. A reaction to this loss and to the current far-reaching spread and domination of the English language is linguistic nationalism—purging foreign terms from a language's vocabulary and pressing for the revitalization of lost or threatened languages. Dialects are varying forms of a language that are similar enough to be mutually intelligible.

■ Some linguistic anthropologists, following Edward Sapir and Benjamin Lee Whorf, have proposed that language shapes the way people think and behave. Others have argued that language reflects reality. Although language is flexible and adaptable, a terminology once established tends to perpetuate itself and to reflect much about the speakers' beliefs and social relationships.

■ Human language is embedded in a gesture-call system inherited from our primate ancestors that serves to "key" speech, providing the appropriate frame for interpreting linguistic form. The gestural component of this system consists of body motions (including facial expressions) used to convey messages. The system of notating and recording these motions is known as kinesics. Another aspect of body language is proxemics, the study of how people perceive and use space. The call component of the gesture-call system is represented by paralanguage, consisting of extralinguistic sounds involving various voice qualities and vocalizations.

■ About 70 percent of the world's languages are tonal, in which the musical pitch of a spoken word is an essential part of its pronunciation and meaning.

■ The first actual writing systems—Egyptian hieroglyphics and cuneiform—developed about 5,000 years ago, Chinese perhaps earlier.

Questions for Reflection

1. In what ways do you feel prepared or unprepared to meet the challenge of communicating effectively in our increasingly globalized world?

2. Up to 4,000 languages have disappeared over the last 500 years, most of them vanishing without a trace. Only 6,000 languages remain. If the same rate of extinction continues, and just one or two languages exist in the year 2500, would that be a loss or a gain? How so?

3. Applying the principle of linguistic determinism to your own language, consider how your perceptions of objective reality might have been shaped by your language and how your sense of reality might have been different if you grew up speaking Hopi.

4. Think about the gestures commonly used in your own family. Are they more or less powerful than the words expressed?

5. From its earliest days writing was linked to political power. How does that apply to modern media and globalization?

Key Terms

language	linguistic nationalism
signals	sociolinguistics
linguistics	gendered speech
phonetics	dialects
phonology	ethnolinguistics
phonemes	linguistic relativity
morphology	linguistic determinism
morphemes	gesture
syntax	kinesics
grammar	proxemics
language family	paralanguage
linguistic divergence	tonal language
glottochronology	writing system
core vocabularies	

Multimedia Review Tools

Make the Grade in Anthropology with ThomsonNOW

Thomson NOW! This powerful online study tool provides you with a personalized study plan based on your responses to a diagnostic pretest. Once you have mastered the material with the help of interactive learning tools, an integrated e-book, and more, you can take a post-test to confirm you are ready to move on to the next chapter. To get started with ThomsonNOW, check the card packaged with your book for the access code. Then go to http://www.thomsonedu.com to create an account through 1pass™. If there is no card in your book, go to http://www.thomsonedu.com to purchase an access code.

Companion Website and Anthropology Resource Center

Go to http://anthropology.wadsworth.com to reach the companion website for your text. This offers many study aids, including self quizzes for each chapter and a practice final exam, as well as links to anthropology websites and information on the latest theories and discoveries in the field.

Also, check out the Anthropology Resource Center for a wealth of learning materials that include interactive maps, video exercises, simulations, and breaking news in anthropology. Be sure to explore InfoTrac College Edition®, your online library that offers full-length articles from thousands of scholarly and popular publications. To reach the Anthropology Resource Center and InfoTrac College Edition, check the card packaged with your book for the access code. Then go to http://www.thomsonedu.com to create an account through 1pass™. If there is no card in your book, go to http://www.thomsonedu.com to purchase an access code.

© Danny Lehman/Corbis

CHALLENGE
ISSUE Every society faces the challenge of humanizing its children, teaching them the values and social codes that will enable them to be functioning and contributing members in the community. This is essential, for it helps ensure that the society will perpetuate itself culturally as well as biologically. Ethnographic research has revealed a wide range of approaches to raising children in order to meet this goal. These different child-rearing methods and their possible effects on adult personalities have long been of interest to anthropologists.

Social Identity, Personality, and Gender

11

In 1690 English philosopher John Locke presented his *tabula rasa* theory in *An Essay Concerning Human Understanding*. This notion held that a newborn human was like a blank slate, and what the individual became in life was written on the slate by his or her life experiences. The implication is that all individuals are biologically identical at birth in their potential for personality development and that their adult personalities are exclusively the products of their postnatal experiences, which differ from culture to culture.

Locke's idea offered high hopes for the all-embracing impact of education on a child's character formation, but it missed the mark, for it did not take into consideration what we now know: Based on recent breakthroughs in human genetic research, some scientists suggest that a substantial portion of our behavior may be due to genetic factors.[1] That means that each person is born with unique inherited tendencies that help determine his or her adult personality. While this genetic inheritance sets certain broad potentials and limitations, an individual's cultural identity and unique personal life experiences, particularly in the early years, also play a significant role in this formation. Since different cultures handle the raising and education of children in different ways, these practices and their effects on personalities are important subjects of anthropological inquiry. Such studies gave rise to the specialization of psychological anthropology and are the subjects of this chapter.

---

[1]http://www.healthanddna.com/behavioralgenetics.html.

THE SELF AND THE BEHAVIORAL ENVIRONMENT

From the moment of birth, a person faces multiple challenges to survive as an individual human being. Obviously, newborns cannot take care of their own biological needs. Only in myths and romantic fantasies do we encounter stories about children successfully coming of age alone in the wilderness or accomplishing this feat having been raised by animals in the wild. For example, Italians in Rome still celebrate the mythological founders of their city, the twin brothers Romulus and Remus, who according to legend were suckled as infants by a she-wolf. Also, millions of children around the world have been fascinated by stories about Tarzan and the apes or the jungle boy Mowgli and the wolves. Moreover, young and old alike have been captivated by newspaper hoaxes about "wild" children, such as a 10-year-old boy reported to have been found running among gazelles in the Syrian desert in 1946.

Fanciful imaginations aside, human children are biologically ill-equipped to survive without culture. This point has been driven home by several documented cases about feral children (feral comes from *fera*, which is Latin for "wild animal") who grew up deprived of human contact. None of them had a happy ending. For instance, there was nothing romantic about the girl Kamala, supposedly rescued from a wolf den in India in 1920: She moved about on all fours and could not feed herself. And everyone in Paris considered the naked "wild boy" captured in the woods outside Aveyron village in 1800 an incurable idiot. Clearly, the biological capacity for what we think of as human, which entails culture, must be nurtured to be realized.

Because culture is socially constructed and learned rather than biologically inherited, all societies must somehow ensure that culture is adequately transmitted from one generation to the next—a process we have already defined as *enculturation*. Since each group lives by a particular set of cultural rules, a child will have to learn the rules of his or her society in order to survive. Most of that learning takes place in the first few years when a child learns how to feel, think, speak, and, ultimately, act like an adult who embodies being Japanese, Kikuyu, Lakota, Norwegian, or whatever ethnic or national group it was born into.

The first agents of enculturation in all societies are the members of the household into which a person is born. Initially, the most important member of this household is the newborn's mother. (In fact, cultural factors are at work even before a child is born, through what a pregnant mother eats, drinks, and inhales.) Soon thereafter, other household members come to play roles in the enculturation process. Just who these others are depends on how households are structured in the particular society. As the young person matures, individuals outside the household are brought into the enculturation process. These usually include other relatives and certainly the individual's peers. The latter may be included informally in the form of playgroups or formally in age associations, where children actually teach other children. In some societies, and the United States is a good example, professionals are brought into the process to provide formal instruction. In many societies, however, children are pretty much allowed to learn through observation and participation, at their own speed.

The Self

Enculturation begins with the development of **self-awareness**—the ability to identify oneself as an individual creature, to reflect on oneself, and to evaluate oneself. Humans do not have this ability at birth, even though it is essential for their successful social functioning. It is self-awareness that permits one to assume responsibility for one's conduct, to learn how to react to others, and to assume a variety of roles in society. An important aspect of self-awareness is the attachment of positive value to one's self. Without this, individuals cannot be motivated to act to their advantage rather than disadvantage.

Self-awareness does not come all at once. In modern industrial and postindustrial societies, for example, self and non-self are not clearly distinguished until a child is about 2 years of age. This development of self-awareness in children growing up in such large-scale societies, however, may lag somewhat behind other cultures. Self-awareness develops in concert with neuromotor development, which is known to proceed at a slower rate in infants from industrial societies than in infants in many, perhaps even most, small-scale farming or foraging communities. The reasons for this slower rate are not yet clear, although the amount of human contact and stimulation that infants receive seems to play an important role. In the United States, for example, infants generally do not sleep with their parents, most often being put in rooms of their own. This is seen as an important step in making them into individuals, "owners" of themselves and their capacities, rather than part of some social whole. As a consequence, they do not experience the steady stream of personal stimuli, including touch, smell, movement, and warmth, that they would if co-sleeping. Private sleeping also takes away the opportunity for frequent nursing through the night.

self-awareness The ability to identify oneself as an individual, to reflect on oneself, and to evaluate oneself.

In traditional societies, infants routinely sleep with their parents, or at least their mothers. Also, they are carried or held most other times, usually in an upright position. The mother typically responds to a cry or "fuss" literally within seconds, usually offering the infant her breast. So it is among traditional Ju/'hoansi (pronounced "zhutwasi") people of southern Africa's Kalahari Desert, whose infants are nursed about four times an hour, for 1 or 2 minutes at a time. Overall, a 15-week-old Ju/'hoansi infant is in close contact with its mother about 70 percent of the time, as compared with 20 percent for home-reared infants in the United States. Moreover, they usually have contact with numerous other adults and children of virtually all ages.

Overall, infants in traditional societies are usually exposed to a steady stream of various stimuli far more than most babies in contemporary North America and most other industrial and postindustrial societies. This is significant, for recent studies show that stimulation plays a key role in the "hard wiring" of the brain—it is necessary for development of the neural circuitry. Looking at breastfeeding in particular, studies show that the longer a child is breastfed, the higher it will score on cognitive tests and the lower its risk of attention deficit hyperactivity disorder. Furthermore, breastfed children have fewer allergies, fewer ear infections, less diarrhea, and are at less risk of sudden infant death syndrome. Nonetheless breastfeeding tends to be relatively short-lived at best in the industrialized world, in part due to workplace conditions that rarely facilitate it.[2]

---

[2]Dettwyler, K. A. (1997, October). When to wean. *Natural History,* 49; Stuart-MacAdam, P., & Dettwyler, K. A. (Eds.). (1995). *Breastfeeding: Biocultural perspectives.* New York: Aldine de Gruyter.

Social Identity Through Personal Naming

Personal names are important devices for self-definition in all cultures. It is through naming that a social group acknowledges a child's birthright and establishes its social identity. Without a name, an individual has no identity, no self. For this reason, many cultures consider name selection to be an important issue and mark the naming of a child with a special event or ritual known as a **naming ceremony.** For instance, Aymara Indians in the Bolivian highland village of Laymi do not consider an infant truly "human" until they have given it a name. And naming does not happen until the child begins to speak the Aymara language, typically around the age of 2. Once the child shows the ability to speak like a human, he or she is considered fit to be recognized as such with a proper name. The naming ceremony marks their social transition from a state of "nature" to "culture" and consequently to full acceptance into the Laymi community.

There are countless contrasting approaches to naming. Icelanders still follow an ancient naming custom in which children use their father's personal given name as their last name. A son adds the suffix *sen* to the name and a daughter adds *dottir.* Thus, a brother and sister whose father is named Sven Olafsen would have the last names Svensen and Svendottir. In some Nigerian ethnic groups, parents and other relatives often give a child three or more names at birth. The first is a personal name that may relate to the family's circumstances; the second expresses what the family hopes the child will become;

naming ceremony A special event or ritual to mark the naming of a child.

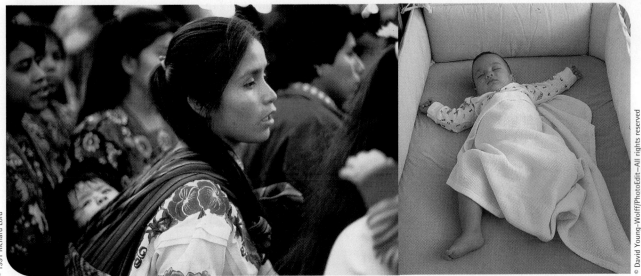

© 1991 Richard Lord

© David Young-Wolff/PhotoEdit—All rights reserved

In traditional societies around the world, infants are never left by themselves and so receive constant stimulation, an important element in their development. In the United States, by contrast, many infants spend considerable time isolated from human interaction.

the third relates to the child's lineage or clan and may refer to a founding ancestor such as a legendary hero or a god, or even a thing considered sacred by the family. When the child has matured, she or he may take two of these given names and use them in combination with the name of her or his father or some other forefather's name.

In many cultures, a person receives a name soon after birth but may acquire new names during subsequent phases in their life. A Hopi child, for instance, is born into its mother's clan. Cared for by the elder women, the newborn spends the first 19 days of its life wrapped in a blanket and secluded indoors. Placed next to the infant are two perfectly shaped ears of corn, referred to as "Mother Corn." On the 20th day, the father's sister gives the baby its name in a sunrise ceremony. At age 6, the child receives another name in a religious ceremony. Reaching adulthood, the person gets yet another name and keeps that one till the end of her or his life. Yet one more name is bestowed upon a Hopi at death, a name that is not to be mentioned after it is given.

Finally, among the Netsilik Inuit in Arctic Canada, women experiencing a difficult delivery would call out the names of deceased people of admirable character. The name being called at the moment of birth was thought to enter the infant's body and help the delivery, and the child would bear that name thereafter. Inuit parents may also name their children for deceased relatives in the belief that the spiritual identification will help shape their character.[3]

Among the many cultural rules that exist in each society, those having to do with naming are unique because they individualize a person while at the same time identify one as part of a group and even connect the person to the spirit world. In short, name-giving customs play an important role in a person's life journey as a socially accepted member of a culture.

The Behavioral Environment

The development of self-awareness requires basic orientations that structure the psychological field in which the self acts. These include object orientation, spatial orientation, temporal orientation, and normative orientation.

First, each individual must learn about a world of objects other than the self. Each culture singles out for attention certain environmental attributes, while ignoring other features or lumping them together into broad categories. A culture also *explains* the perceived environment.

This is important, for a cultural explanation of one's surroundings imposes a measure of order and provides the individual with a sense of direction needed to act meaningfully and effectively. Behind this lies a powerful psychological drive to reduce uncertainty—part of the common human need for a balanced and integrated perspective on the relevant universe. When confronted with ambiguity and uncertainty, people invariably strive to clarify and give structure to the situation; they do this, of course, in ways that their particular culture deems appropriate. Thus, we should not be surprised to find that observations and explanations of the universe are largely culturally constructed and mediated symbolically through language. In fact, everything in the physical environment varies in the way it is *perceived and experienced* by humans. In short, we might say that the world around us is perceived through cultural lenses.

The behavioral environment in which the self acts also involves *spatial orientation,* or the ability to get from one object or place to another. In all societies, the names and significant features of places are important references for spatial orientation. Traditionally, geographic place names often contain references to significant features in the landscape. For instance, the name of the Mississippi in North America means literally "big river"; the English coastal city of Plymouth is located at the mouth of the river Plym; and the riverside city of Bamako, Mali, in West Africa translates as "crocodile river." Finding your way to class, remembering where you left your car keys, and directing someone to the nearest bus stop are examples of highly complex cognitive tasks based on spatial orientation and memory. So is a desert nomad's ability to travel from one oasis to another, gauging his location by the position of the sun in daytime or by the stars at night. Without these functions, navigating through daily life would be impossible.

Temporal orientation, which gives people a sense of their place in time, is also part of the behavioral environment. Connecting past actions with those of the present and future provides a sense of self-continuity. This is the function of calendars, for example. Derived from the Latin word *kalendae,* which originally referred to a public announcement at the first day of a new month, or moon, such a chart gives people a sense of where they are in the annual cycle. Just as the perceived environment of objects is organized in cultural terms, so too are time and space.

A final aspect of the behavioral environment is the *normative orientation.* Moral values, ideals, and principles, which are purely cultural in origin, are as much a part of the individual's behavioral environment as are trees, rivers, and mountains. Without them people would have nothing by which to gauge their own actions or those of others. In short, the self-evaluation aspect of self-awareness could

---

[3]Balikci, A. (1970). *The Netsilik Eskimo.* Garden City, NY: Natural History Press.

not be made functional. Normative orientation includes standards that indicate what ranges of behavior are acceptable for males and females in a particular society. Such behavior is embedded in biology but modified by culture, so it should not be surprising that they vary cross-culturally. (A compelling example of this appears in the Original Study later in this chapter.)

PERSONALITY

In the process of enculturation, we have seen that each individual is introduced to the ideas of self and the behavioral environment characteristic of his or her culture. The result is the creation of a kind of mental map of how the world looks and operates in which the individual will think and act. It is his or her particular map of how to run the maze of life. It is an integrated, dynamic system of perceptual assemblages, including the self and its behavioral environment. When we speak of someone's personality, we are generalizing about that person's cognitive map over time. Hence, personalities are products of enculturation, as experienced by individuals, each with his or her distinctive genetic makeup.

Personality does not lend itself to a formal definition, but for our purposes we may take it as the distinctive way a person thinks, feels, and behaves. Derived from the Latin word *persona,* meaning "mask," the term relates to the idea of learning to play one's role on the stage of daily life. Gradually, the mask, as it is placed on the face of a child, begins to shape the latter until there is little sense of the mask as a superimposed alien force. Instead it feels natural, as if one were born with it. The individual has successfully internalized the culture.

The Development of Personality

Although *what* one learns is important to personality development, most anthropologists assume that *how* one learns is no less important. Along with psychological theorists, anthropologists view childhood experiences as strongly influencing adult personality.

Psychological literature tends to be long on speculative concepts, clinical data, and studies that are culture-bound. Anthropologists, for their part, are most interested in studies that seek to prove, modify, or at least shed light on the cultural differences in shaping personality. For example, the traditional ideal in Western societies has been for men to be tough, aggres-

personality The distinctive way a person thinks, feels, and behaves.

sive, assertive, dominant, and self-reliant, whereas women have been expected to be gentle, passive, obedient, and caring. To many, these personality contrasts between the sexes seem so natural that they are thought to be biologically grounded and therefore fundamental, unchangeable, and universal. But are they? Have anthropologists identified any psychological or personality characteristics that universally differentiate men and women?

North American anthropologist Margaret Mead is well known as a pioneer in the cross-cultural study of both personality and gender. In the early 1930s she studied three ethnic groups in Papua New Guinea—the Arapesh, Mundugamor, and Tchambuli. This comparative research suggested that whatever biological differences exist between men and women, they are extremely malleable. In short, she concluded, biology is not destiny. Mead found that among the Arapesh, relations between men and women were expected to be equal, with both genders exhibiting what most North Americans traditionally consider feminine traits (cooperative, nurturing, and gentle).[4] She also discovered gender equality among the Mundugamor (now generally called Biwat), however, in that both genders in that community displayed supposedly masculine traits (individualistic, assertive, volatile, aggressive). Among the Tchambuli (now called Chambri), however, Mead found that women dominated men.

Recent anthropological research suggests that some of Mead's interpretations of gender roles were incorrect—for instance, Chambri women neither dominate Chambri men, nor vice versa. Yet, overall her research generated new insights into the human condition, showing that male dominance is a cultural construct and, consequently, that alternative gender arrangements can be created. Although biological influence in male–female behavior cannot be ruled out (in fact, debate continues about the genetic and hormonal factors at play), it has nonetheless become clear that each culture provides different opportunities and has different expectations for ideal or acceptable male–female behavior.[5]

To understand the importance of child-rearing practices for the development of gender-related personality characteristics, we may take another brief look at the already mentioned Ju/'hoansi people native to the Kalahari Desert of Namibia and Botswana in south-

[4]Mead, M. (1950) (orig. 1935). *Sex and temperament in three primitive societies.* New York: New American Library.
[5]Errington, F. K., & Gewertz, D. B. (2001). *Cultural alternatives and a feminist anthropology: An analysis of culturally constructed gender interests in Papua New Guinea.* Cambridge, England, and New York: Cambridge University Press.

ern Africa (Figure 11.1). The Ju/'hoansi are one of a number of groups traditionally referred to as Bushmen, who were once widespread through much of southern Africa. Traditionally subsisting as nomadic hunter–gatherers ("foragers"), in the past three decades many Ju/'hoansi have been forced to settle down—tending small herds of goats, planting gardens for their livelihood, and engaging in occasional wage labor.[6] Among those who traditionally forage for a living, equality is stressed, and dominance and aggressiveness are not tolerated in either gender. Ju/'hoansi men are as mild mannered as the women, and women are as energetic and self-reliant as the men. By contrast, among the Ju/'hoansi who have recently settled in permanent villages, men and women exhibit personality characteristics resembling those traditionally thought of as typically masculine and feminine in North America and other industrial societies.

Among the food foragers, each newborn child receives lengthy, intensive care from its mother during the first few years of life, for the space between births is typically 4 to 5 years. This is not to say that mothers are constantly with their children. For instance, when women go to collect wild plant foods in the bush, they do not always take their offspring with them. At such times, the children are supervised by their fathers or

other community adults, one-third to one-half of whom are always found in camp on any given day. Because these include men as well as women, children are as much habituated to the male as to the female presence.

Within village households, gender typecasting begins early. As soon as girls are old enough, they are expected to attend to many of the needs of their younger siblings, thereby allowing their mothers more time to deal with other domestic tasks. This not only shapes but also limits the behavior of girls, who cannot range as widely or explore as freely and independently as they could without little brothers and sisters in tow. Indeed, they must stay close to home and be more careful, more obedient, and more sensitive to the wishes of others than they otherwise might be. Boys, by contrast, have little to do with the handling of infants, and when they are assigned work, it generally takes them away from the household. Thus, the space that girls occupy becomes restricted, and they are trained in behaviors that promote passivity and nurturance, whereas boys begin to learn the distant, controlling roles they will later play as adult men.

From this comparison, we may begin to understand how a society's economy helps structure the way a child is brought up, and how this, in turn, influences the adult personality. It also shows that alternatives exist to the way that children are raised—which means that changing the societal conditions in which one's children grow up can alter significantly the way men and women act and interact.

Dependence Training

Some years after Margaret Mead's pioneering comparative research on gender in three Papua communities, psychological anthropologists carried out a significant and more wide-ranging series of cross-cultural studies on the effects of child rearing on personality. Among other things, their work showed that it is possible to distinguish between two general patterns of child rearing. These patterns stem from a number of practices that, regardless of the reason for their existence, have the effect of emphasizing independence on the one hand and dependence on the other. Thus, for convenience, we may speak of "dependence training" and "independence training."[7]

Dependence training socializes people to think of themselves in terms of the larger whole. Its effect is to create community members whose idea of selfhood transcends individualism, promoting compliance in the

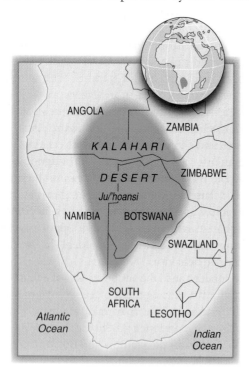

Figure 11.1

> **dependence training** Child-rearing practices that foster compliance in the performance of assigned tasks and dependence on the domestic group, rather than reliance on oneself.

---

[6]Draper, P. (1975). !Kung women: Contrasts in sexual egalitarianism in foraging and sedentary contexts. In R. Reiter (Ed.), *Toward an anthropology of women* (pp. 77–109). New York: Monthly Review Press.

[7]Whiting, J. W. M., & Child, I. L. (1953). *Child training and personality: A cross-cultural study*. New Haven, CT: Yale University Press.

performance of assigned tasks and keeping individuals within the group. This pattern is typically associated with extended families, which consist of several husband-wife-children units within the same household. It is most likely to be found in societies with an economy based on subsistence farming but also in foraging groups where several family groups may live together for at least part of the year. Big extended families are important, for they provide the labor force necessary to till the soil, tend whatever flocks are kept, and carry out other part-time economic pursuits considered necessary for existence. These large families, however, have built into them certain potentially disruptive tensions. For example, important family decisions must be collectively accepted and followed. In addition, the in-marrying spouses—husbands and/or wives who come from other groups—must conform themselves to the group's will, something that may not be easy for them.

Dependence training helps to keep these potential problems under control and involves both supportive and corrective aspects. On the supportive side, indulgence is shown to young children, particularly in the form of prolonged breastfeeding. Nursing continues for several years and is virtually provided on demand. This may be interpreted as rewarding the child for seeking support within the family, the main agent in meeting the child's needs. Also on the supportive side, children at a relatively early age are assigned a number of child-care and domestic tasks, all of which make significant and obvious contributions to the family's welfare. Thus, family members all actively work to help and support one another.

On the corrective side, behavior the adults interpret as aggressive or selfish is likely to be actively discouraged. Moreover, the adults tend to be insistent on overall obedience, which commonly inclines the individual toward being subordinate to the group. This combination of encouragement and discouragement in the socialization process teaches individuals to put the group's needs above their own—to be obedient, supportive, noncompetitive, and generally responsible, to stay within the fold and not do anything potentially disruptive. Indeed, a person's very definition of self comes from the individual being a part of a larger social whole rather than from his or her mere individual existence.

Independence Training

By contrast, **independence training** fosters individual independence, self-reliance, and personal achievement. It is typically associated with societies in which a basic

> **independence training** Child-rearing practices that promote independence, self-reliance, and personal achievement on the part of the child.

social unit consisting of parent(s) and offspring fends for itself. Independence training is particularly characteristic of mercantile (trading), industrial, and postindustrial societies where self-sufficiency and personal achievement are important traits for success, if not survival—especially for men, increasingly for women.

Again, this pattern of training involves both encouragement and discouragement. On the negative side, infant feeding is prompted more by schedule than demand. In North America, as noted above, babies are rarely nursed for more than a year, if that. Many parents resort to an artificial nipple or teething ring (pacifier) to satisfy the baby's sucking instincts—typically doing so to calm the child rather than out of an awareness that infants need sucking to strengthen and train coordination in the muscles used for feeding and speech.

In addition, North American parents are comparatively quick to start feeding infants baby food and even try to get them to feed themselves. Many are delighted if they can prop their infants up in the crib or playpen so that they can hold their own bottles. Moreover, as soon after birth as possible, children are commonly given their own private space, away from their parents. As already noted, infants do not receive the amount of attention they so often do in nonindustrial societies. In the United States a mother may be very affectionate with her 15-week-old infant during the 20 percent of the time she is in contact with it, but typically for the other 80 percent of the time the baby is more or less on its own, usually within hearing range of the mother or caretaker(s). Collective responsibility is not pushed in children; they are not usually given responsible tasks to perform until later in childhood, and these are often carried out for personal benefit (such as to earn an allowance to spend as they wish) rather than as contributions to the family's welfare.

Displays of individual will, assertiveness, and even aggression are encouraged, or at least tolerated to a greater degree than where dependence training is the rule. In schools, and even in the family, competition and winning are emphasized. Schools in the United States, for example, devote considerable resources to competitive sports. Competition is fostered within the classroom as well: overtly through such devices as spelling bees and awards, covertly through such devices as grading on a curve. In addition, there are various popularity contests, such as crowning a prom queen and king or holding an election to choose the classmate who is "best looking" or "most likely to succeed."

Thus, by the time individuals have grown up in U.S. society, they have received a clear message: Life is about winning or losing, and losing is equal to failure. Often, success is viewed as something that comes at someone else's expense. As anthropologist Colin Turnbull observed, "Even the team spirit, so loudly touted" in U.S.

school athletics (or out of school in Little League baseball and the like), "is merely a more efficient way, through limited cooperation, to 'beat' a greater number of people more efficiently."[8]

In sum, independence training generally encourages individuals to seek help and attention rather than to give it, and to try to exert individual dominance. Such qualities are useful in societies with hierarchical social structures that emphasize personal achievement and where individuals are expected to look out for their own interests.

Combined Dependence/Independence Training

In actuality, dependence and independence training represent extremes along a continuum, and particular situations may include elements of both. This is the case in child-rearing practices in food-foraging societies, for example. "Share and share alike" is the order of the day, so competitive behavior, which can interfere with the cooperation on which all else depends, is discouraged. Thus, infants receive much in the way of positive, affectionate attention from adults, including extended breast-feeding from the mother. This, as well as low pressure for compliance and a lack of emphasis on competition, encourages individuals to be more supportive of one another than is often the case in modern industrial and postindustrial societies. At the same time, personal achievement and independence are encouraged, for those individuals most capable of self-reliance are apt to be the most successful in the food quest.

In the United States the argument is sometimes made that "permissive" child rearing produces irresponsible adults. Yet the practices of food foragers seem to be about as "permissive" as they can get, and socially responsible adults are produced. The fact is that none of these child-rearing systems is inherently better or worse than any other; what matters is whether the system is functional or dysfunctional in the context of a particular society. If compliant adults who are accepting of authority are required, then independence training will not work well in that society. Nor will dependence training serve very well a society whose adults are expected to be self-reliant, questioning of authority, and ready to explore and embrace new ways of doing things.

Group Personality

From studies such as those reviewed here, it is clear that personality, child-rearing practices, and other aspects of culture are systematically interrelated. The existence of a close, if not causal, relationship between child-rearing practices and personality development, coupled with variation in child-rearing practices from one society to

another, have led to a number of attempts to characterize whole societies in terms of particular kinds of personalities. Indeed, common sense suggests that personalities appropriate for one culture may be less appropriate for others. For example, an egocentric, aggressive personality would be out of place where cooperation and sharing are the keys to success.

Unfortunately, common sense, like conventional wisdom in general, is not always the truth. A question worth asking is: Can we describe a group personality without falling into stereotyping? The answer appears to be a qualified yes; in an abstract way, we may speak of a generalized "cultural personality" for a society, so long as we do not expect to find a uniformity of personalities within that society. Put another way, each individual develops certain personality characteristics that, from common experience, resemble those of other people. Yet, each human being also acquires distinct personality traits because every individual is exposed to unique sets of experiences and may react to shared experiences in novel ways. Moreover, each person brings to these experiences a one-of-a-kind genetic potential (except in the case of identical twins) that plays a role in determining personality.

This is evident, if not obvious, in every society—including even the most traditional ones. Consider for example the Yanomami people, who subsist on foraging and horticulture in the tropical forests of northern Brazil and southern Venezuela. Commonly, Yanomami men strive to achieve a reputation for fierceness and aggressiveness, and they defend that reputation at the risk of serious personal injury and death. Yet, among the Yanomami there are men who have quiet and somewhat retiring personalities. It is all too easy for an outsider to overlook these individuals when other, more typical Yanomami are in the front row, pushing and demanding attention.

Modal Personality

Obviously, any fruitful approach to the problem of group personality must recognize that each individual is unique to a degree in both genetic inheritance and life experiences and it must leave room for a range of personality types in any society. In addition, personality traits that may be regarded as appropriate in men may not be so regarded in women, and vice versa. Given all this, we may focus our attention on the **modal personality** of a group, defined as the body of character traits that occur with the highest frequency in a culturally bounded population. Modal personality is a statistical concept rather than the particular personality of a par-

---

[8]Turnbull, C. M. (1983). *The human cycle* (p. 74). New York: Simon & Schuster.

modal personality The body of character traits that occur with the highest frequency in a culturally bounded population.

© N. Chagnon/Anthro-Photo

Yanomami men living in the Amazon rainforest of South America display their fierceness. While flamboyant, belligerent personalities are especially compatible with the Yanomami ideal of male fierceness, some men are quiet and retiring.

ticular person. As such, it opens up for investigation the questions of how societies organize diversity and how diversity relates to culture change. Such questions are easily missed if one associates a certain type of personality with one particular culture, as did some earlier anthropologists. At the same time, modal personalities of different groups can be compared.

Data on modal personality are best gathered by means of psychological tests (such as the Rorschach or "ink blot" test) administered to a sample of the population in question. In addition, observing and recording the frequency of certain behaviors, the collection and analysis of life histories and dreams, and the analysis of popular tales, jokes, legends, and traditional myths are helpful in eliciting data on modal personality.

While having much to recommend it, the concept of modal personality as a means of dealing with group personality nevertheless presents certain difficulties. One is the complexity of the measurement techniques, which may be difficult to do in the field. For instance, an adequate representative sample of subjects is necessary. The problem here is twofold: making sure the sample is really representative and having the time and personnel necessary to administer the tests, conduct interviews, and so on, all of which can be lengthy proceedings. Also, the tests themselves constitute a problem, for those devised in one cultural setting may not be appropriate in another. Still, to minimize any cultural bias, it is best not to rely on projective tests alone. In addition to all this, language differences or conflicting cultural values

between the researcher and the individuals being studied may inhibit communication and/or lead to misinterpretation. Finally, what is being measured must be questioned. Just what, for example, is aggression? Does everyone define it the same way? Is it a legitimate entity, or does it involve other variables?

National Character

In summer 2003, Italy's tourism minister publicly commented on "typical characteristics" of Germans, referring to them as "hyper-nationalistic blondes" and "beer drinking slobs" holding "noisy burping contests" on his country's beaches.[9] Outraged (and proud of his country's excellent beer), Germany's prime minister canceled his planned vacation to Italy and demanded an official apology. Of course, many Germans think of Italians as dark-eyed, hot-blooded spaghetti eaters. To say so in public, however, might cause an uproar.

Unflattering stereotypes about foreigners are deeply rooted in cultural traditions everywhere. Many Japanese believe Koreans are stingy, crude, and aggressive, while many Koreans see the Japanese as cold and arrogant. Similarly, we all have in mind some image, perhaps not well defined, of the typical citizen of Russia or Japan or England. Essentially, these are simply stereotypes. We might well ask, however, if these stereotypes have any basis in fact. In reality, does such a thing as national character exist?

Some anthropologists once thought that the answer might be yes. Accordingly, they embarked upon national character studies in the 1930s and 1940s, aiming to discover basic personality traits shared by the majority of the people of modern state societies. In what came to be known as the culture and personality movement, their research emphasized child-rearing practices and education as the factors theoretically responsible for such characteristics. During and immediately after World War II, techniques were developed for studying "culture at a distance" through the analysis of newspapers, books, photographs, popular films, and interviews with refugees and emigrants from the enemy countries in question. By investigating memories of childhood and cultural attitudes, and by examining graphic material for the appearance of recurrent themes and values, researchers attempted to portray national character.

Objections to National Character Studies

Critics of national character theories have emphasized the tendency for such work to be based on relatively

---

[9]Italy-Germany verbal war hots up (2003, July 9). *Deccan Herald.* (Bangalore India).

small samples of informants and on unscientific and overgeneralized data. The concept of modal personality has a certain statistical validity, they argue, but to generalize the qualities of a complex country on the basis of such limited data is to lend insufficient recognition to the countless individuals who vary from the generalization. Further, such studies tend to be highly subjective; for example, the tendency during the late 1930s and 1940s for anthropologists to characterize the German people as aggressive paranoids was obviously a reflection of wartime hostility rather than scientific objectivity. Finally, it has been pointed out that occupation and social status tend to cut across national boundaries. A French farmer may have less in common with a French lawyer than he does with a German farmer.

An alternative approach to national character—one that allows for the fact that not all personalities will conform to cultural ideals—is that of anthropologist Francis Hsu. His approach was to study **core values** (values especially promoted by a particular culture) and related personality traits. The Chinese, he suggested, value kin ties and cooperation above all else. To them, mutual dependence is the very essence of personal relationships and has been for thousands of years. Compliance and subordination of one's will to that of family and kin transcend all else, while self-reliance is neither promoted nor a source of pride.

Perhaps the core value held in highest esteem by North Americans of European descent is "rugged individualism," traditionally for men but in recent decades for women as well. Each individual is supposed to be able to achieve anything he or she likes, given a willingness to work hard enough. From their earliest years, individuals are subjected to relentless pressures to excel, and as we have already noted, competition and winning are seen as crucial to this. Undoubtedly, this contributes to the restlessness and drive seen as characteristic for much of North American society today, and to the

degree that it motivates individuals to work hard and to go where the jobs are, it fits well with the demands of a modern market. Thus, while individuals in Chinese traditional society are firmly bound into a larger group to which they have lifelong obligations, most urban North Americans are isolated from relatives other than their young children and spouse, and even the commitment to marriage has lessened.[10]

ALTERNATIVE GENDER MODELS FROM A CROSS-CULTURAL PERSPECTIVE

As we have already discussed, the gender roles assigned to each sex vary from culture to culture and have an impact on personality formation. But what if the sex of an individual is not self-evident, as revealed in the following Original Study? Written when the author was an undergraduate student of philosophy at Bryn Mawr College in Pennsylvania, this narrative offers a compelling personal account of the emotional difficulties associated with gender ambiguity, while making the important point that attitudes toward gender vary cross-culturally. However, some of the cultural information is overgeneralized and therefore not quite accurate, including the idea that all or most Native American spiritual-religious worldviews were and are nonhierarchical.[11]

intersexuals People born with reproductive organs, genitalia, and/or sex chromosomes that are not exclusively male or female.

[10]Observations on North American culture in this paragraph are drawn primarily from Natadecha-Sponsal, P. (1993). The young, the rich and the famous: Individualism as an American cultural value. In P. R. DeVita & J. D. Armstrong (Eds.), *Distant mirrors: America as a foreign culture* (pp. 46–53). Belmont, CA: Wadsworth.

[11]For scholarly accounts of the issues presented here, readers may turn to several excellent books, including the one mentioned in the Original Study: Roscoe, W. (1991). *Zuni man-woman*. Albuquerque: University of New Mexico Press.

core values Those values especially promoted by a particular culture.

Original Study

The Blessed Curse

One morning not so long ago, a child was born. This birth, however, was no occasion for the customary celebration. Something was wrong: something very grave, very serious, very sinister. This child was born between sexes, an "intersexed" child. From the day of its birth, this child would be caught in a series of struggles involving virtually every aspect of its life. Things that required little thought under "ordinary" circumstances were, in this instance, extraordinarily difficult. Simple questions now had an air of complexity: "What is it, a girl or a boy?" "What do we name it?" "How shall we raise it?" "Who (or what) is to blame for this?"

A Foot in Both Worlds

The child referred to in the introductory paragraph is myself. As the great-granddaughter of a Cherokee woman, I was exposed to the Native American view of people who were born intersexed, and those who exhibited transgendered characteristics. This view, unlike the Euro-American one, sees such individuals in a very positive and affirming light. Yet my immediate family (mother, father, and brothers) were firmly fixed in a negative Christian Euro-American point of view. As a result, from a very early age I was presented with two different and conflicting views of myself. This resulted in a lot of confusion within me about what I was, how I came to be born the way I was, and what my intersexuality meant in terms of my spirituality as well as my place in society.

I remember, even as a small child, getting mixed messages about my worth as a human being. My grandmother, in keeping with Native American ways, would tell me stories about my birth. She would tell me how she knew when I was born that I had a special place in life, given to me by God, the Great Spirit, and that I had been given "a great strength that girls never have, yet a gentle tenderness that boys never know" and that I was "too pretty and beautiful to be a boy only and too strong to be a girl only." She rejoiced at this "special gift" and taught me that it meant that the Great Spirit had "something important for me to do in this life." I remember how good I felt inside when she told me these things and how I soberly contemplated, even at the young age of five, that I must be diligent and try to learn and carry out the purpose designed just for me by the Great Spirit.

My parents, however, were so repulsed by my intersexuality that they would never speak of it directly. They would just refer to it as "the work of Satan." To them, I was not at all blessed with a "special gift" from some "Great Spirit," but was "cursed and given over to the Devil" by God. My father treated me with contempt, and my mother wavered between contempt and distant indifference. I was taken from one charismatic church to another in order to have the "demon of mixed sex" cast out of me. At some of these "deliverance" services I was even given a napkin to cough out the demon into!

In the end, no demon ever popped out of me. Still I grew up believing that there was something inherent within me that caused God to hate me, that my intersexuality was a punishment for this something, a mark of condemnation.

Whenever I stayed at my grandmother's house, my fears would be allayed, for she would once again remind me that I was fortunate to have been given this special gift. She was distraught that my parents were treating me cruelly and pleaded with them to let me live with her, but they would not let me stay at her home permanently. Nevertheless, they did let me spend a significant portion of my childhood with her. Had it not been for that, I might not have been able to survive the tremendous trials that awaited me in my walk through life.

Blessed Gift: The Native American View

It is now known that most, if not all, Native American societies had certain individuals that fell between the categories of "man" and "woman." The various nations had different names for such people, but a term broadly used and recognized is *berdache*, a word of French origin that designated a male, passive homosexual. [The preferred term today is *two-spirit*.] Some of these individuals were born physically intersexed. Others appeared to be anatomically normal males, but exhibited the character and the manners of women—or vice versa. The way native people treated such individuals reveals some interesting insights into Native American belief systems.

The Spirit

The extent to which Native Americans see spirituality is reflected in their belief that all things have a spirit: "Every object—plants, rocks, water, air, the moon, animals, humans, the earth itself—has a spirit. The spirit of one thing (including a human) is not superior to the spirit of any other. . . . The function of religion is not to try to condemn or to change what exists, but to accept the realities of the world and to appreciate their contributions to life. Everything that exists has a purpose."

This paradigm is the core of Native American thought and action. Because everything has a spirit, and no spirit is superior to that of another, there is no "above" or "below," no "superior" or "inferior," no "dominant" and "subordinate." These are only illusions that arise from unclear thinking. Thus, an intersexed child is not derided or viewed as a "freak of nature" in many traditional Native American cultures. Intersexuality (as well as masculinity in a female or effeminacy in a male) is seen as the manifestation of the spirit of the child, so an intersexed child is respected as much as a girl child or a boy child. It is the spirit of the child that determines what the gender of the child will ultimately be. According to a Lakota, Lame Deer, "the Great Spirit made them *winktes* [two-spirit], and we accepted them as such." In this sense, the child has no control over what her or his gender will be. It follows that where there is no choice, there can be no accountability on the part of the child. Indeed, the child who is given the spirit of a *winkte* is unable to resist becoming one.

"When an Omaha boy sees the Moon Being [a feminine Spirit] on his vision quest, the spirit holds in one hand a man's bow and arrow and in the other a woman's pack strap. . . . 'When the youth tried to grasp the bow and arrows, the Moon Being crossed hands very quickly, and if the youth was not very careful he seized the pack strap instead of the bow and arrows, thereby fixing his lot in later life. In such a case he could not help acting [like a] woman, speaking, dressing, and working just as . . . women . . . do.'"

[continued]

[continued]

The Curse: The Euro-American View

In contrast to the view of respect and admiration of physical intersexuality and transgendered behavior traditionally held by Native Americans, the Europeans who came to "Turtle Island" (the Cherokee name for North America) brought with them their worldview, shaped by their Judaeo-Christian beliefs. According to this religious perspective, there had to be, by mandate of God, a complete dichotomy of the sexes. . . .

Will Roscoe, in his book *The Zuni Man-Woman*, reports (pp. 172–73): "Spanish oppression of 'homosexual' practices in the New World took brutal forms. In 1513, the explorer Balboa had some forty berdaches thrown to his dogs [to be eaten alive]—'a fine action by an honorable and Catholic Spaniard,' as one Spanish historian commented. In Peru, the Spaniards burned 'sodomites, . . . and in this way they frightened them in

such a manner that they left this great sin.'" It is abundantly clear that Christian Euro-Americans exerted every effort to destroy Native American culture: "In 1883, the U.S. Office of Indian Affairs issued a set of regulations that came to be known as the Code of Religious offenses, or Religious Crimes Code. . . . Indians who refused to adopt the habits of industry, or to engage in 'civilized pursuits or employments' were subject to arrest and punishment. . . . By interfering with native sexuality [and culture], the agents of assimilation effectively undermined the social fabric of entire tribes" (Roscoe, p. 176).

A Personal Resolution

For me, the resolution to the dual message I was receiving was slow in coming, largely due to the fear and self-hatred instilled in me by Christianity. Eventually, though, the Spirit wins out. I came to adopt my grandmother's teaching about my intersexuality. Through

therapy, and a new, loving home environment, I was able to shed the constant fear of eternal punishment I felt for something I had no control over. After all, I did not create myself.

Because of my own experience, and drawing on the teaching of my grandmother, I am now able to see myself as a wondrous creation of the Great Spirit—but not only me. All creation is wondrous. There is a purpose for everyone in the gender spectrum. Each person's spirit is unique in her or his or her-his own way. It is only by living true to the nature that was bestowed upon us by the Great Spirit, in my view, that we are able to be at peace with ourselves and be in harmony with our neighbor. This, to me, is the Great Meaning and the Great Purpose . . . (*Adapted from R. K. Williamson (1995). The blessed curse: Spirituality and sexual difference as viewed by Euro-American and Native American cultures. The College News, 18(4).*)

The biological facts of human nature are not always as clear-cut as most people assume. At the level of chromosomes, biological sex is determined according to whether a person's 23rd chromosomal set is XX (female) or XY (male). Some of the genes on these chromosomes control sexual development. This standard biological package does not apply to all humans, for a considerable number are born as **intersexuals**—people having reproductive organs, genitalia, and/or sex chromosomes that are not exclusively male or female. These individuals do not fit neatly into a binary gender standard.[12]

For example, some people are born with a genetic disorder that gives biological females only one X chromosome instead of the usual two. A person with this chromosomal complex, known as Turner's syndrome, develops female external genitalia but has nonfunctional ovaries and is therefore infertile. Other individuals are born with the XY sex chromosomes of a male but have

an abnormality on the X chromosome that affects the body's sensitivity to androgens (male hormones). This is known as androgen insensitivity syndrome (AIS). An adult XY person with complete AIS appears fully female with a normal clitoris, labia, and breasts. Internally, these individuals possess testes (up in the abdomen, rather than in their usual descended position in the scrotal sac), but they are otherwise born without a complete set of either male or female internal genital organs. They generally possess a short, blind-ended vagina.

"Hermaphrodites" comprise a distinct category of intersexuality—although the terms *male pseudohermaphrodite* and *female pseudohermaphrodite* are often used to refer to a range of intersex conditions. The name, objected to by many, comes from a figure in Greek mythology: Hermaphroditus (son of Hermes, messenger of the gods, and Aphrodite, goddess of beauty and love) who became half-male and half-female when he fell in love with a nymph and his body fused with hers. True hermaphrodites have both testicular and ovarian tissue. They may have a separate ovary and testis, but more commonly they have an ovotestis containing both sorts of tissue. About 60 percent of hermaphrodites possess XX (female) sex chromosomes, and the remainder may have XY or a mosaic (a mixture). Their external genitalia may be ambiguous or female, and they may have a uterus or (more commonly) a hemi-uterus (half uterus).

---

[12]This paragraph and the two following are based on several sources: Chase, C. (1998). Hermaphrodites with attitude. *Gay and Lesbian Quarterly, 4*(2), 189–211; Dumurat-Dreger, A. (1998, May/June). "Ambiguous sex" or ambivalent medicine? *The Hastings Center Report, 28*(3), 2,435 (posted on the Intersex Society of North America website: www.isna.org); Fausto-Sterling, A. (1993). The five sexes: Why male and female are not enough. *The Sciences, 33*(2), 20–24; the Mayo Clinic website.

Biologist Anne Fausto-Sterling, a specialist in this area, notes that the concept of intersexuality is "rooted in the very ideas of male and female," in an idealized biological world in which:

> human beings are divided into two kinds: a perfectly dimorphic species. Males have an X and a Y chromosome, testes, a penis and all of the appropriate internal plumbing for delivering urine and semen to the outside world. They also have well-known secondary sexual characteristics, including a muscular build and facial hair. Women have two X chromosomes, ovaries, all of the internal plumbing to transport urine and ova to the outside world, a system to support pregnancy and fetal development, as well as a variety of recognizable secondary sexual characteristics.
>
> That idealized story papers over many obvious caveats: some women have facial hair, some men have none; some women speak with deep voices, some men veritably squeak. Less well known is the fact that on close inspection, absolute dimorphism disintegrates even at the level of basic biology. Chromosomes, hormones, the internal sex structures, the gonads and external genitalia all vary more than most people realize. Those born outside of the . . . dimorphic mold are called intersexuals.[13]

Intersexuality may be unusual but is not uncommon. In fact, about 1 percent of all humans are intersexed in some (not necessarily visible) way—in other words, about 60 million people worldwide.[14] Until recently, it was rarely discussed publicly in many societies. Since the mid-20th century, individuals with financial means in postindustrial parts of the world have had the option of reconstructive surgery and hormonal treatments to alter such conditions, and many parents faced with raising a visibly intersexed child in a culture intolerant of such minorities have chosen this option for their baby. However, there is a growing movement to put off such irreversible procedures indefinitely or until the child becomes old enough to be the one to make the choice.

Obviously, a society's attitude toward these individuals can impact their personality—their fundamental sense of self and how they express it.

In addition to people who are genetically intersexed, throughout history some individuals have been subjected to a surgical removal of some of their sexual organs. In many cultures, male prisoners or war captives have undergone forced castration, crushing or cutting the testicles. While castration of adult males did not eliminate the sex drive or the possibility of having an erection, it did take away the ability of procreating. Archaeological evidence from Egypt, Mesopotamia, Persia, and China suggests that the cultural practice of castrating war captives may have begun several thousand years ago. Young boys captured during war or slave-raiding expeditions were often castrated before being sold and shipped off to serve in foreign households, including royal courts. In the Ottoman Empire, where they could occupy a variety of important functions in the sultan's household from the mid-15th century onward, they became known as *eunuchs*. As suggested by the original meaning of the word, which is Greek for "guardian of the bed," castrated men were often put in charge of a ruler's harem, the women's quarters in a household. Eunuchs could also rise to high status as priests and administrators and were even appointed to serve as army commanders. Some powerful lords, kings, and emperors kept hundreds of eunuchs in their castles and palaces.

In addition to forced castration, there were also men who engaged in self-castration or underwent voluntary castration. For example, early Christian monks in Egypt and neighboring regions voluntarily abstained from sexual relationships and sometimes castrated themselves for the sake of the kingdom of heaven. Such genital mutilation was also practiced among Coptic monks, until the early 20th century.[15] In the late 15th century, Europe saw the emergence of a category of musical eunuchs known as *castrati*. These eunuchs sang female parts in church choirs after Roman Catholic authorities banned women singers on the basis of Saint Paul's instruction, "Let your women keep silence in the churches." Simultaneously, castrati began performing female roles in operas. Castrated before they reached puberty so as to retain their high voices, these selected boys were often orphaned or came from poor families. Without a functioning testis to produce male sex hormones, physical development into manhood is aborted, so deeper voices, as well as body hair, semen production, and other usual male attributes, were not part of a castrati's biology.

[13]Fausto-Sterling, A. (2000, July). The five sexes revisited. *The Sciences*, 20–24.

[14]Fausto-Sterling, A. (2003, August 2). Personal e-mail communication from this recognized expert on the subject. For published statistics, see her article co-authored with Blackless, M., et al. (2000). How sexually dimorphic are we? Review and synthesis. *American Journal of Human Biology, 12,* 151–166.

[15]Abbot, E. (2001). *A history of celibacy.* Cambridge, MA: Da Capo Press.

During the 1700s, at the height of castrati popularity, an estimated 4,000 boys a year were castrated in Italy alone. Some became celebrated performers, drawing huge fees, adopting fantastic stage names, and gaining notoriety for their eccentricity on and off stage. Not necessarily homosexual, castrati were "gender benders" who could engage in sexual relations with men or women, or both. The phenomenon of castrati continued until about 1900, when Roman Catholic authorities in the Vatican banned their role in church music. By then, the eunuch systems in the Chinese and Ottoman Empires were also about to be abolished.[16]

Although human castration was not practiced among North American Indians, many indigenous communities in the Great Plains and Southwest created alternative social space for intersexed or transgendered individuals. (**Transgenders** are people who cross over or occupy a culturally accepted intermediate position in the binary male–female gender construction.) For example, the Lakota of the northern Plains had an intermediate category of culturally accepted transgendered males who dressed as women and were thought to possess both male and female spirits. They called (and still call) these third-gender individuals *winkte,* applying the term to a male "who wants to be a woman." Thought to have special curing powers, *winktes* traditionally enjoyed considerable prestige in their communities. Among the neighboring Cheyenne, such a person was called *hemanah,* literally meaning "half-man, half-woman."[17]

French traders who came to the Great Plains in the 1600s eventually encountered cross-dressing Native American men, whom they called *berdache* (also spelled *burdash*). The name derived from the Persian word *bardah,* which referred to eunuchs or slaves. The French term *berdache* had acquired obvious contemptuous applications for effeminacy and celibacy, as well as cowardice, and it was broadly used for eunuchs, castrati, crossdressers, and homosexuals alike. Although early anthropological literature adopted the word, the preferred term among North American Indians today is "two-spirits," which avoids the negative connotations associated with the term *berdache.*[18]

transgenders People who cross over or occupy a culturally accepted intermediate position in the binary male–female gender construction.

[16]Taylor, G. (2000). *Castration: Abbreviated history of western manhood.* (pp. 38–44, 252–259). New York: Routledge.

[17]Medicine, B. (1994). Gender. In M. B. Davis (Ed.), *Native America in the twentieth century.* New York: Garland.

[18]Jacobs, S. E. (1994). Native American two-spirits. *Anthropology Newsletter, 35*(8), 7.

© Photography Hugh Heartshorne. Copyright © Re Angle Pictures

Transgendering occurs in many cultures but is not always publicly tolerated. Among Polynesians inhabiting Pacific Ocean islands such as Tonga and Samoa, however, such male transvestites are culturally accepted. Samoans refer to these third genders as *fa'afafines* ("the female way").

Mapping the sexual landscape, anthropologists have come to realize that gender bending exists in many cultures all around the world, playing a significant role in shaping behaviors and personalities. For instance, third-gender individuals are well known in Samoa, where males who take on the identity of females are referred to as *fa'afafines* ("the female way"). Becoming a *fa'afafine* is an accepted option for boys who prefer to dance, cook, clean house, and care for children and the elderly. In large families, it is not unusual to find two or three boys being raised as girls to take on domestic roles in their households. As North American anthropologist Lowell Holmes recently reported,

In fact, they tend to be highly valued because they can do the heavy kinds of labor that most women find difficult. A Samoan nun once told me how fortunate it is to have a fa'afafine in the family to help with the household chores. [There] is also the claim made that fa'afafines never have sexual relations with each other but, rather, consider themselves to be "sisters." [They] are religious and go to church regularly dressed as women and . . . some are even Sunday school teachers. Fa'afafines often belong to women's athletic teams, and some even serve as coaches.[19]

Among many other third genders, the best known may be the *hijra* (or *hijadas*) in India. *Hijra* is an Urdu term that covers transgendered men, castrated males, and hermaphrodites who dress and behave like women in an exaggerated way. As Hindu devotees of the Mother Goddess Bahuchara Mata, their cultural role is to perform blessings for young married couples and male babies. Beyond small earnings for those rituals, they survive by begging, chanting, running bathhouses, and sometimes prostitution.[20]

None of these transgendered cultural types can be simply lumped together as homosexuals. For example, the Tagalog-speaking people in the Philippines use the word *bakla* to refer to a man who views himself "as a male with a female heart." These individuals cross-dress on a daily basis, often becoming more female than females in their use of heavy makeup, in the clothing they wear, and in the way they walk. Like the Samoan *fa'afafines,* they are generally not sexually attracted to other *bakla* but are drawn to heterosexual men instead.

Since some people are gender variants, permanent or incidental transvestites, without being homosexuals, it is obvious that the cross-cultural sex and gender scheme is complex. Indeed, the late 19th-century "homosexuality" label is quite inadequate to cover the full range of sex and gender diversity.

In sum, human cultures in the course of thousands of years have creatively dealt with a wide range of inherited and artificially imposed sexual features. The importance of studying complex categories involving intersexuality and transgendering is that doing so enables us to recognize the existing range of gender alternatives and to debunk false stereotypes. It is one more piece of the human puzzle—an important one that prods us to rethink social codes and the range of forces that shape personality as well as each society's definition of normal.

NORMAL AND ABNORMAL PERSONALITY

The standards that define normal behavior for any culture are determined by that culture itself. So it is that in

mainstream North American culture, in contrast to those just noted, transgender behavior has traditionally been regarded as abnormal, emotionally disturbed, or even mentally ill. If a North American man dresses as a woman, it is still widely viewed as a mental health problem and is likely to lead to psychiatric intervention. There are countless examples of the fact that what seems normal or socially acceptable (if not always popular) in one culture is often considered abnormal or ridiculous and shameful (if not even criminal) in another.

It is also true that the abnormal may become normal. In this vein, anthropologist Emily Martin cites changing attitudes toward "manic depression" (more properly called "bipolar disorder") and attention deficit hyperactivity disorder (ADHD).[21] Commonly regarded as dreaded liabilities, she suggests that, in North America, the manic and hyperactivity aspects are gradually becoming viewed as assets in the quest for success. More and more, they are interpreted as indicative of "finely wired, exquisitely alert nervous systems" that make one highly sensitive to signs of change, able to fly from one thing to another while pushing the limits of everything, and doing it all with an intense level of energy focused totally in the future. These are extolled as high virtues in the corporate world, and to be called "hyper" or "manic" is increasingly an expression of approval.

Not only do attitudes concerning a wide range of mental and physical disorders change over time within a society, they also vary across cultures—as evident in this chapter's Biocultural Connection.

Is all of this to suggest that "normalcy" is a meaningless concept when applied to personality? Within the context of a particular culture, the concept of normal personality is quite meaningful. Irving Hallowell, a major figure in the development of psychological anthropology, somewhat ironically observed that it is normal to share the delusions traditionally accepted by one's society. Abnormality involves the development of a delusional system of which the culture does not approve. The individual who is disturbed because he or she cannot adequately measure up to the norms of society and be happy may be termed *neurotic.* When a person's delusional system is so different that it in no way reflects his or her society's norms, the individual may be termed *psychotic.*

If severe enough, culturally induced conflicts can produce psychosis and also determine the form of the psychosis. In a culture that encourages aggressiveness and suspicion, the insane person may be one who is

[19]Holmes, L. D. (2000). Paradise bent (film review). *American Anthropologist, 102*(3), 604–605.
[20]Nanda, S. (1990). *Neither man nor woman: The hijras of India.* Belmont, CA: Wadsworth.

[21]Martin, E. (1999). Flexible survivors. *Anthropology News, 40*(6), 5–7.

Biocultural Connection

Down's Syndrome Across Cultures

Biological anthropologist Katherine Dettwyler compares the cultural experience of Down's syndrome, the biological state of having an extra 21st chromosome, in Peter, her son, and in Abi, a child she meets while conducting fieldwork in Mali. She writes:

Down's syndrome children are often (though not always!) sweet, happy, and affectionate kids, and many families of children with Down's syndrome consider them to be special gifts from God and refer to them as angels. . . .

A little girl had just entered the hut, part of a large family with many children. She had a small round head, and all the facial characteristics of a child with Down's syndrome—Oriental-shaped eyes with epicanthic folds, a small flat nose, and small ears. There was no mistaking the diagnosis. Her name was Abi, and she was about 4 years old, the same age as Peter.

I knelt in front of the little girl. "Hi there, sweetie," I said in English. "Can I have a hug?" I held out my arms, and she willingly stepped forward and gave me a big hug.

I looked up at her mother. "Do you know that there's something 'different' about this child?" I asked, choosing my words carefully.

"Well, she doesn't talk," said her mother, hesitantly, looking at her husband for confirmation. "That's right," he said. "She's never said a word."

"But she's been healthy?" I asked.

"Yes," the father replied. "She's like the other kids, except she doesn't talk. She's always happy. She never cries. We know she can hear, because she does what we tell her to. Why are you so interested in her?"

"Because I know what's the matter with her. I have a son like this." Excitedly, I pulled a picture of Peter out of my bag and showed it to them. They couldn't see any resemblance, though. The difference in skin color swamped the similarities in facial features. But then, Malians think all white people look alike. And it's not true that all kids with

Down's syndrome look the same. They're "different in the same way," but they look most like their parents and siblings.

"Have you ever met any other children like this?" I inquired, bursting with curiosity about how rural Malian culture dealt with a condition as infrequent as Down's syndrome. Children with Down's syndrome are rare to begin with, occurring about once in every 700 births. In a community where 30 or 40 children are born each year at the most, a child with Down's syndrome might be born only once in 20 years. And many of them would not survive long enough for anyone to be able to tell that they were different. Physical defects along the midline of the body (heart, trachea, intestines) are common among kids with Down's syndrome; without immediate surgery and neonatal intensive care, many would not survive. Such surgery is routine in American children's hospitals but nonexistent in rural Mali. For the child without any major physical defects, there are still the perils of rural Malian life to survive: malaria, measles, diarrhea, diphtheria, and polio. Some, like Peter, have poor immune systems, making them even more susceptible to childhood diseases. The odds against finding a child with Down's syndrome, surviving and healthy in a rural Malian village, are overwhelming.

Not surprisingly, the parents knew of no other children like Abi. They asked if I knew of any medicine that could cure her. "No," I explained, "this condition can't be cured. But she will learn to talk, just give her time. Talk to her a lot. Try to get her to repeat things you say. And give her lots of love and attention. It may take her longer to learn some things, but keep trying. In my country, some people say these children are special gifts from God." There was no way I could explain cells and chromosomes and nondisjunction to them, even with a translator's help. And how, I thought to myself, would that have helped them anyway? They just accepted her as she was.

We chatted for a few more minutes, and I measured the whole family, including Abi, who was, of course, short for her age. I gave her one last hug and a balloon and sent her out the door after her siblings. . . .

I walked out of the hut, . . . trying to get my emotions under control. Finally I gave in, hugged my knees close to my chest, and sobbed. I cried for Abi—what a courageous heart she must have; just think what she might have achieved given all the modern infant stimulation programs available in the West. I cried for Peter—another courageous heart; just think of what he might achieve given the chance to live in a culture that simply accepted him, rather than stereotyping and pigeonholing him, constraining him because people didn't think he was capable of more. I cried for myself—not very courageous at all; my heart felt as though it would burst with longing for Peter, my own sweet angel.

There was clearly some truth to the old adage that ignorance is bliss. Maybe pregnant women in Mali had to worry about evil spirits lurking in the latrine at night, but they didn't spend their pregnancies worrying about chromosomal abnormalities, the moral implications of amniocentesis, or the heart-wrenching exercise of trying to evaluate handicaps, deciding which ones made life not worth living. Women in the United States might have the freedom to choose not to give birth to children with handicaps, but women in Mali had freedom from worrying about it. Children in the United States had the freedom to attend special programs to help them overcome their handicaps, but children in Mali had freedom from the biggest handicap of all—other people's prejudice.

I had cried myself dry. I splashed my face with cool water from the bucket inside the kitchen and returned to the task at hand. *(Adapted from Katherine A. Dettwyler. (1994).* Dancing Skeletons: Life and Death in West Africa *(CH. 8). Reprinted by permission of Waveland Press, Inc., Long Grove, IL.* ▪ ▪ ▪

passive and trusting. In a culture that encourages passivity and trust, the insane person may be the one who is aggressive and suspicious. Just as each society establishes its own norms, each individual is unique in his or her perceptions.

Many anthropologists see the only meaningful criterion for personality evaluation as the correlation between personality and social conformity. From their point of view, insanity is a culturally constructed mental illness, and people are considered insane when they fail to conform to a culturally defined range of normal behavior. This is not to say that psychosis is simply a matter of a particularly bad fit between an individual and his or her particular culture.

Although it is true that each particular culture defines what is and is not normal behavior, the situation is complicated by findings suggesting that major categories of mental disorders may be universal types of human affliction. Take, for example, schizophrenia, probably the most common of all psychoses, and one that may be found in any culture, no matter how it may manifest itself. Individuals afflicted by schizophrenia experience distortions of reality that impair their ability to function adequately, so they withdraw from the social world into their own psychological shell. Although environmental factors play a role, evidence suggests that schizophrenia is caused by a biochemical disorder for which there is an inheritable tendency. One of its more severe forms is paranoid schizophrenia. Those suffering from it fear and mistrust nearly everyone. They hear voices that whisper dreadful things to them, and they are convinced that someone is "out to get them." Acting on this conviction, they engage in bizarre behaviors, which lead to their removal from society.

Ethnic psychoses are mental disorders specific to particular ethnic groups. Among these is Windigo psychosis, limited to northern Algonquian Indian groups such as the Cree and Ojibwa. In their traditional belief systems, these Indians recognized the existence of

cannibalistic monsters called Windigos. Individuals afflicted by the psychosis developed the delusion that, under the control of these monsters, they were themselves transformed into Windigos, with a craving for human flesh. As this happened, the psychotic individuals saw people around them turning into various edible animals—fat, juicy beavers, for instance. Although there are no known instances where sufferers of Windigo psychosis actually ate another human being, they were acutely afraid of doing so, and people around them were genuinely fearful that they might.

Windigo psychosis may seem different from clinical cases of paranoid schizophrenia found in Euramerican cultures, but a closer look suggests otherwise; the disorder was merely being expressed in ways compatible with traditional northern Algonquian culture. Ideas of persecution, instead of being directed toward other humans, were directed toward supernatural beings (the Windigo monsters); cannibalistic panic replaced panic expressed in other forms. Northern Algonquian Indians, like Euramericans, expressed their problems in terms compatible with the appropriate view of the self and its behavioral environment. However, the Algonquians dealt with Windigo victims by killing them, rather than committing them to mental institutions.

Windigo behavior has seemed exotic and dramatic to Euramericans, but psychotic individuals draw upon whatever imagery and symbolism their culture has to offer, and in northern Algonquian culture, these include myths featuring cannibal giants. By contrast, the delusions of Irish schizophrenics draw upon the images and symbols of Irish Catholicism and feature virgin and savior motifs. Euramericans, on the other hand, tend toward secular or electromagnetic persecution delusions.

The underlying structure of the mental disorder is the same in all cases, but its expression is culturally specific. Anthropologists view mental health issues in their cultural context, in recognition of the fact that each individual's social identity, unique personality, and overall sense of mental health is molded by the particular culture within which the person is born and raised to function as a valued member of the community.

ethnic psychoses Mental disorders specific to particular ethnic groups.

Chapter Summary

■ Enculturation, the process by which individuals become members of their society, begins soon after birth. Its first agents are the members of an individual's household, but later, other members of society become involved. For enculturation to proceed, individuals must possess self-awareness, the ability to perceive and reflect upon themselves as individuals. For self-awareness to emerge and function, four basic orientations are necessary to structure the behavioral environment in which the self acts. First among these is object orientation, learning about a world of objects other than the self. Also required is a sense of both spatial and temporal orientation. Finally, the growing individual needs a normative orientation, or an understanding of the values, ideals, and standards that constitute the behavioral environment.

■ A child's birthright and social identity are established through personal naming, a universal practice with numerous cross-cultural variations. A name is an important device for self-definition—without one, an individual has no identity, no self. Many cultures mark the naming of a child with a special ceremony.

■ Personality refers to the distinctive ways a person thinks, feels, and behaves. Along with psychoanalysts, most anthropologists believe early childhood experiences play a key role in shaping adult personality. A prime goal of anthropologists has been to produce objective studies that test this theory. Cross-cultural studies of gender-related personality characteristics, for example, show that whatever biologically based personality differences exist between men and women, they are extremely malleable. A society's economy helps structure the way children are brought up, which in turn influences their adult personalities.

■ Psychological anthropologists, on the basis of cross-cultural studies, have established the interrelation of personality, child-rearing practices, and other aspects of culture. For example, dependence training, usually associated with traditional farming societies, tries to ensure that members of society will willingly and routinely work for the benefit of the group, performing the jobs assigned to them. At the opposite extreme, independence training, typical of societies characterized by small, independent families, puts a premium on self-reliance and independent behavior. Although a society may emphasize one sort of behavior over the other, it may not emphasize it to the same degree in both sexes. Some psychological anthropologists contend that child-rearing practices have their roots in a society's customs for meeting the basic physical needs of its members and that these practices produce particular kinds of adult personalities.

■ Gender behaviors and relations are extremely malleable and vary cross-culturally. Each culture presents different opportunities and expectations concerning ideal or acceptable male–female behavior. In some cultures, male–female relations are based on equal status, with both genders expected to behave similarly. In others, however, male–female relations are based on inequality and are marked by different standards of expected behavior. Anthropological research demonstrates that gender dominance is a cultural construct and, consequently, that alternative male–female social arrangements can be created if so desired.

■ Early on, anthropologists began to work on the problem of whether it is possible to delineate a group personality without falling into stereotyping. Each culture chooses, from the vast array of possibilities, those traits that it sees as normative or ideal. Individuals who conform to these traits are rewarded; the rest are not. The modal personality of a group is the personality typical of a culturally bounded population, as indicated by the central tendency of a defined frequency distribution. As a statistical concept, it opens up for investigation how societies organize the diverse personalities of their members, some of which conform more than others to the modal "type."

■ National character studies have focused on the modal characteristics of modern countries. They have attempted to determine the child-rearing practices and education that shape such a group personality. Many anthropologists believe national character theories are based on unscientific and overgeneralized data; others have chosen to focus on the core values promoted in particular societies while recognizing that success in instilling these values in individuals may vary considerably.

■ Intersexuals are individuals who do not fit neatly into either a male or female biological standard or into a binary gender standard. Many cultures have created social space for transgendered individuals who are culturally accepted as a third gender category.

■ What defines normal behavior in any culture is determined by the culture itself, and what may be acceptable, or even admirable, in one may not be in another. Abnormality involves developing personality traits not accepted by a culture. Culturally induced conflicts not only can produce psychological disturbance but can determine the form of the disturbance as well. Similarly, mental disorders that have a biological cause, like schizophrenia, will be expressed by symptoms specific to the culture of the afflicted individual.

Questions for Reflection

1. Every society faces the challenge of humanizing its children, teaching them the values and social codes that will enable them to be functioning and contributing members in the community. What child-rearing practices did you experience that embody the values and social codes of your society?

2. Considering the cultural significance of naming ceremonies in so many societies, what do you think motivated your parents when they named you? Does that have any influence on your sense of self?

3. Do you fit within the acceptable range of your society's modal personality? How so?

4. Given that about 60 million people currently are intersexed, and in light of the fact that a very small fraction of these people have access to reconstructive sexual surgery, what do you think of societies that have created cultural space for a third gender option?

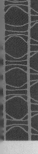

Key Terms

self-awareness
naming ceremony
personality
dependence training
independence training

modal personality
core values
intersexuals
transgenders
ethnic psychoses

Multimedia Review Tools

Make the Grade in Anthropology with ThomsonNOW

Thomson NOW! This powerful online study tool provides you with a *personalized study plan* based on your responses to a diagnostic pretest. Once you have mastered the material with the help of interactive learning tools, an integrated e-book, and more, you can take a post-test to confirm you are ready to move on to the next chapter. To get started with ThomsonNOW, check the card packaged with your book for the access code. Then go to http://www.thomsonedu.com to create an account through 1pass™. If there is no card in your book, go to http://www.thomsonedu.com to purchase an access code.

Companion Website and Anthropology Resource Center

Go to http://anthropology.wadsworth.com to reach the companion website for your text. This offers many study aids, including self quizzes for each chapter and a practice final exam, as well as links to anthropology websites and information on the latest theories and discoveries in the field.

Also, check out the Anthropology Resource Center for a wealth of learning materials that include interactive maps, video exercises, simulations, and breaking news in anthropology. Be sure to explore InfoTrac College Edition®, your online library that offers full-length articles from thousands of scholarly and popular publications. To reach the Anthropology Resource Center and InfoTrac College Edition, check the card packaged with your book for the access code. Then go to http://www.thomsonedu.com to create an account through 1pass™. If there is no card in your book, go to http://www.thomsonedu.com to purchase an access code.

© 1991 Richard Lord

CHALLENGE ISSUE

All humans face the challenge of gaining and maintaining access to resources needed for survival. This is true for Nigerian farmers, Icelandic fishers, and Mongolian herders. Whatever they lack, they may seek through exchange or trade. In such economic transactions, humans forge and affirm their social networks. These friendships, partnerships, and alliances, in turn, are essential in their search for safety and well-being. A basic feature of the concept of "market" in nonindustrial societies is that it refers to a specific place where people meet face to face to exchange goods at certain designated times. At this market in the highlands of Guatemala, people from the region exchange items they have produced for things they need but can only get from others.

Subsistence and Exchange

All living beings must satisfy certain basic needs to survive—including food, water, and shelter. Moreover, because these needs must be met on a regular basis, no creature could long survive if its relations with its environment were random and chaotic. People have a huge advantage over other animals in this challenge: We have culture. With the passing of time, culture has become our primary means of adapting to the limitations and possibilities within any given environment.

ADAPTATION

As discussed earlier in this book, adaptation is the process organisms undergo to achieve a beneficial adjustment to a particular environment. What makes human adaptation unique among all other species is our capacity to produce and reproduce culture, enabling us to creatively adapt to an extraordinary range of radically different environments. How humans adjust to the burdens and opportunities presented in daily life is the basic concern of all cultures. A people's **cultural adaptation** consists of a complex of ideas, activities, and technologies that enable them to survive and even thrive. The process of adaptation establishes an ever-shifting balance between the needs of a population and its environment.

Indeed, organisms and environments form dynamic interacting systems. (See this chapter's Biocultural

cultural adaptation A complex of ideas, activities, and technologies that enable people to survive and even thrive.

203

Biocultural Connection

The Cultural and Political Ecology of Disease

An ecological perspective considers organisms in the context of their environment. Because local human environments are shaped not only by local culture but by global political and economic systems, these features must all be included in a comprehensive examination of human health. Simply describing disease in terms of biological processes leaves out the deeper, ultimate reasons that some individuals are more likely than others to become sick. A strictly biological approach also fails to account for differences in the resources available to individuals, communities, and states to regain health.

Kuru, a fatal disease that afflicted the Fore (pronounced "foray") people of Papua New Guinea at high rates during the 20th century, provides an excellent example of the political ecology of disease. Kuru does not fit neatly into biomedical categories. For instance, its slow progress contradicts typical infectious disease models. Because the disease seemed to be limited to genetically related individuals, particularly women and their children, an international health care team, including cultural anthropologists Shirley Lindenbaum from Australia and Robert Glasse from the United States, investigated possible familial mechanisms of transmission.[a]

When their investigation of Fore kinship relationships did not reveal a pattern of genetic transmission, the team returned to the notion of a slow infectious disease. Later, it was determined that a prion—a completely new kind of infectious particle lacking any genetic material—was responsible for kuru.

Local cultural practices, along with global influences, help to clarify why Fore women and children were more likely to get kuru compared to men. As Lindenbaum explained in her book *Kuru Sorcery,* Fore women are responsible for preparing the bodies of their loved ones for the afterlife, putting them at greater risk for exposure to kuru through touching their dead relatives. In the middle of the 20th century this risk was compounded. Colonial rule by Australia had changed the fabric of Fore society, threatening traditional subsistence patterns and resulting in a shortage of pigs, their main protein source. Because Fore men are responsible for raising, slaughtering, and distributing pig meat, the limited amount of meat available was distributed by men preferentially to other men. As a practical solution to their hunger, Fore women turned to eating the bodies of their loved ones who had died in a relatively "meaty" state from kuru. The temporary practice of cannibalism was abandoned as Fore subsistence practices recovered, and the

biological mechanisms of transmission were communicated to the Fore.

Today, postindustrial societies are beset by prion diseases far more than the Fore. Prion diseases are nearly always transmitted through infected foods, although they may also be transmitted in transplant surgery. The beef supply of several countries in Europe and North America has been tainted by prions in the form of Mad Cow disease. As with the Fore, cultural practices spread the disease, but this time on a much larger scale.

As the biology of kuru was being unraveled, a similar neurodegenerative disease, scrapie, was identified in sheep. Prion disease then jumped from sheep to cows through the cultural practice of grinding up sheep carcasses and adding them to the commercial feed of beef cattle. Thus, through the wide distribution of tainted feed, prion disease was spread.

Today countries without confirmed Mad Cow disease ban the importation of beef from neighboring countries with documented prion disease. Such bans have tremendous effects on the local economies. Prion disease illustrates that political and economic forces play as big a role as biological factors in the distribution of disease in societies. ■ ■ ■

[a]Lindenbaum, S. (1978). *Kuru sorcery: Disease and danger in the New Guinea highlands.* New York: McGraw-Hill.

Connection for an example.) And although environments do not determine culture, they do present certain possibilities and limitations: People might just as easily farm as fish, but we do not expect to find farmers in Siberia's frozen tundra or fishermen in the middle of North Africa's Sahara Desert.

Some anthropologists have adopted the ecologists' concept of **ecosystem,** defined as a system composed of both the natural environment and all the organisms living within it. The system is bound by the activities of the organisms, as well as by such physical processes as

erosion and evaporation. **Cultural ecology** is a term that refers to the dynamic interaction of specific cultures with their natural environments.

Adaptation in Cultural Evolution

Human groups adapt to their environments by means of their cultures. However, cultures may change over the course of time; they evolve. This is called **cultural evolution.** The process is sometimes confused with the

ecosystem A system, or a functioning whole, composed of both the natural environment and all the organisms living within it.

cultural ecology The dynamic interaction of specific cultures with their natural environments.

cultural evolution Culture change over time (not to be confused with progress).

idea of **progress**—the notion that humans are moving forward to a better, more advanced stage in their development toward perfection. Yet, not all changes turn out to be positive in the long run, nor do they improve conditions for every member of a society even in the short run. Complex, urban societies are not more "highly evolved" than those of food foragers. Rather, both are "highly evolved," but in quite different ways.

To fit into an ecosystem, humans (like all organisms) must have the potential to adjust to or become a part of it. A good example of this is the Comanche, whose history begins in the highlands of southern Idaho.[1] Living in that harsh, arid region, these North American Indians traditionally subsisted on wild plants, small animals, and occasionally larger game. Their material equipment was simple and limited to what they (and their dogs) could carry or pull. The size of their groups was restricted, and what little social power could develop was in the hands of the shaman, who was a combination of healer and spiritual guide.

At some point in their nomadic history, the Comanche moved east onto the Great Plains, where bison were abundant, and they could hunt. As larger groups could be supported by the new and plentiful food supply, the Comanche needed a more complex political organization.

Eventually the Comanche acquired horses and guns from European settlers, which enhanced their hunting capabilities significantly and led to the emergence of powerful hunting chiefs. The Comanche became raiders in order to get horses (which they did not breed for themselves), and their hunting chiefs evolved into war chiefs. The once materially "poor" and peaceful hunter–gatherers of the dry highlands became wealthy, and raiding became a way of life.

In the late 18th and early 19th centuries, they dominated the southern Plains (now primarily Texas and Oklahoma). In moving from one regional environment to another, and in adopting a new technology, the Comanche were able to take advantage of existing cultural capabilities to thrive in their new situation.

Sometimes societies that developed independently of each other find similar solutions to similar problems. For example, the Cheyenne Indians moved from the woodlands of the Great Lakes region to the Great Plains and took up a form of Plains Indian culture resembling that of the Comanche even though the cultural historical

backgrounds of the two groups differed significantly. (Before they transformed into horse-riding bison hunters, the Cheyenne had cultivated crops and gathered wild rice, which fostered a distinct set of social, political, and religious practices.) This is an example of **convergent evolution**—the development of similar cultural adaptations to similar environmental conditions by different peoples with different ancestral cultures.

Especially interesting is that the Cheyenne gave up crop cultivation completely and focused exclusively on hunting and gathering after their move into the vast grasslands of the northern High Plains. Contrary to the popular notion of evolution as a progressive movement toward increased manipulation of the environment, this ethnographic example shows that cultural historical changes in subsistence practices do not always go from dependence on wild food to farming; they may go the other way as well.

Analogous to the phenomenon of convergent evolution is **parallel evolution,** in which similar cultural adaptations to similar environmental conditions are achieved by peoples whose ancestral cultures were already somewhat alike. For example, the development of farming in Southwest Asia and Mesoamerica took place independently, as people in both regions, whose life ways were already comparable, became dependent on a narrow range of plant foods that required human intervention for their protection and reproductive success. Both developed intensive forms of agriculture, built large cities, and created complex social and political organizations.

It is important to recognize that stability as well as change is involved in cultural adaptation and evolution; episodes of major adaptive change may be followed by long periods of relative stability in a cultural system. For example, about 5,500 years ago a way of life had evolved in northwestern New England and southern Quebec that was well attuned to the natural environmental conditions of the times. Since those conditions remained fairly stable over the next 5,000 years or so, it is understandable that people's lifeways remained so as well. This is not to say that culture change was entirely absent, for it was not. Periodically, people refined and enhanced their way of life: They replaced spears and spear-throwers with far-reaching bows and arrows; they enhanced cooking methods by using pottery vessels

---

progress The ethnocentric notion that humans are moving forward to a higher, more advanced stage in their development toward perfection.

convergent evolution In cultural evolution, the development of similar cultural adaptations to similar environmental conditions by different peoples with different ancestral cultures.

parallel evolution In cultural evolution, the development of similar cultural adaptations to similar environmental conditions by peoples whose ancestral cultures were already somewhat alike.

---

[1]Wallace, E., & Hoebel, E. A. (1952). *The Comanches*. Norman: University of Oklahoma Press.

Saying that a society is stable is not to say it is changeless. Maintaining a stable way of life for 5,000 years, Western Abenakis nevertheless incorporated new elements into their culture during that time, including longhouses such as the one here. Today, 400 years after first contact with Europeans, Abenaki houses are like those of European Americans, but many traditional values and practices endure, and ceremonial longhouses still exist.

instead of containers made from bark, wood, or animal hide; they substituted heavy and cumbersome dugout boats with lightweight birch-bark canoes; and they supplemented foods gained in hunting, gathering, and fishing with cultivated corn, beans, and squash.

Despite these changes, however, the native peoples of the region retained the basic structure of their culture and maintained a balance with their resource base well into the 17th century, when the culture had to adjust to pressures associated with European invasions of North America. Such enduring stability suggests success. Had this culture not effectively satisfied people's physical and psychological needs, it would not have endured as it did for thousands of years.

That said, not every group has implemented the changes needed for long-term survival—and some have made changes that failed to bring expected benefits. Moreover, not everybody benefits from changes, especially if change is forced upon them. As history painfully demonstrates, all too often humans have made changes that have had disastrous results, leading to the deaths of thousands, even millions of people—not to mention other creatures—and to the destruction of the natural environment. In short, we must avoid falling into the ethnocentric trap of equating change with progress or seeing everything as adaptive.

MODES OF SUBSISTENCE

Human societies all across the world have developed a cultural infrastructure that is compatible with the natural resources they have available to them and within the limitations of their various habitats. Each mode of

subsistence involves not only resources but also the technology required to effectively capture and utilize them, as well as the kinds of work arrangements that are developed to best suit a society's needs. In the next few pages, we will discuss the major types of cultural infrastructure, beginning with the oldest and most universal mode of subsistence: food foraging.

Food-Foraging Societies

Before the domestication of plants and animals, all people supported themselves through **food foraging,** a mode of subsistence involving some combination of hunting, fishing, and gathering wild plant foods. When food foragers had the earth to themselves, they had their pick of the best environments. But gradually areas with rich soils and ample supplies of water were appropriated by farming societies and, more recently, by industrial and postindustrial societies. As a result, small foraging communities were edged out of their traditional habitats by these expanding groups.

Today at most a quarter of a million people—less then 0.005 percent of the world population of about 6 billion—still support themselves mainly as foragers. They are found only in the world's most marginal areas—frozen Arctic tundra, deserts, and inaccessible forests—and typically lead a migratory existence that makes it impractical to accumulate too many material possessions. Because foraging cultures have nearly

food foraging   Hunting, fishing, and gathering wild plant foods.

disappeared in areas having a natural abundance of food and fuel resources, anthropologists are necessarily cautious when it comes to making generalizations about the ancient human past based on in-depth studies of still-existing foraging groups that have adapted to more marginal habitats.

Anthropological research shows that forager diets are typically ample and balanced and that foragers are less likely to experience severe famine than farmers. The material possessions of foragers may be limited, but so is their desire to amass things. Notably, they have plenty of leisure time for concentrating on family ties, social life, and spiritual development—apparently far more than people living in farming and industrial societies. Such findings clearly challenge the once widely held view that food foragers live a miserable existence.

It is important to note that present-day people who subsist by hunting, fishing, and wild plant collection are not following an ancient way of life because they do not know any better. Rather, they have been forced by circumstances into situations where foraging is the best means of survival or they simply prefer to live this way. In fact, foraging constitutes a rational response to particular ecological, economic, and sociopolitical realities. Moreover, for at least 2,000 years, hunters, fishers, and gatherers have met the demands for commodities such as furs, hides, feathers, ivory, pearls, fish, nuts, and honey within larger trading networks. Like everyone else, most food foragers are now part of a larger system with social, economic and political relations extending far beyond regional, national, or even continental boundaries.

Characteristics of the Food-Foraging Life

The hallmarks of food-foraging societies, particularly those still (or until recently) surviving in marginal areas that are not naturally as rich in food and fuel, include mobility, small group size, egalitarianism, communal property, and flexible division of labor by gender. We will discuss the last three points in the economics section of this chapter. In this section we zero in on mobility and population.

Food foragers move as needed within a circumscribed region that is their home range to tap into naturally available food sources. Some groups, such as the Ju/'hoansi in the Kalahari Desert of southern Africa, who depend on the reliable and highly drought-resistant mongongo nut, may keep to fairly fixed annual routes and cover only a restricted territory. Others, such as the traditional Shoshone in the western highlands of North America, had to cover a wider territory, their course determined by the local availability of the erratically productive pine nut. A crucial factor in this mobility is availability of water. The distance between the food

supply and water must not be so great that more energy is required to fetch water than can be obtained from the food.

Another characteristic of the food-foraging adaptation is the small size of local groups, typically fewer than a hundred people. No completely satisfactory explanation for this has been offered, but both ecological and social factors are involved. Among the ecological factors is the **carrying capacity** of the land—the number of people that the available resources can support at a given level of food-getting techniques. This requires adjusting to seasonal and long-term changes in resource availability.

Most food-foraging populations stabilize at numbers well below the carrying capacity of their land. In fact, the home ranges of most food foragers can support from three to five times as many people as they typically do. In the long run, it may be more adaptive for a group to keep its numbers low rather than to expand indefinitely and risk destruction by a sudden and unexpected natural reduction in food resources. The population density of foraging groups surviving in marginal environments today rarely exceeds one person per square mile, a very low density.

Food-Producing Societies

The domestication of plants and animals began about 10,000 years ago with the **Neolithic revolution;** it led to radical transformations in cultural systems with foragers developing new social and economic patterns based either on plant cultivation or pastoralism. Although food production gave people alternative sources for nutrition and some control over vital resources, the new ways of life were not always more reliable than foraging.

Pastoralism

One of the more striking examples of human adaptation to the environment is *pastoralism*: breeding and managing migratory herds of domesticated grazing animals, such as goats, sheep, cattle, llamas, or camels. Pastoralism is an effective way of living—far more so than sheep or cattle ranching—in places that are too dry, cold, steep, or rocky for farming, such as the vast, arid grasslands that stretch eastward from northern Africa through the

carrying capacity The number of people that the available resources can support at a given level of food-getting techniques.
Neolithic revolution Domestication of plants and animals by peoples with stone-based technologies, beginning about 10,000 years ago and leading to radical transformations in cultural systems.

© Reinhold Loeffler

Pastoral nomadism is a cultural ecological adaptation that is effective in many parts of the world that are too hot, cold, dry, rocky, or rugged for farming. In the unforgiving Zagros Mountains of Iran, Bakhtiari herders follow seasonal pastures, migrating with their flocks over perilously steep, snowy passes and fast ice-cold rivers.

Arabian Desert, across the plateau of Iran and into Turkistan and Mongolia.

Today, in Africa and Asia alone, more than 21 million people are pastoralists, still migrating with their herds. These nomadic groups regard movement as a natural part of life. Although some herding groups depend on nearby farmers for certain supplies, and may even earn more from other sources than from their own herds, the nomadic herding lifestyle remains central to their identities.

Counted among the world's pastoral groups are the Bakhtiari, a fiercely independent people who live in the Zagros Mountains of western Iran. The Bakhtiari way of life, uniquely adapted to the seasonal fluctuations in their rugged mountainous environment, involves **transhumance**—a subsistence strategy in which people move their grazing animals from winter pastures in low steppe lands to summer pastures on high plateaus. For many thousands of years the Bakhtiari have tended herds of goats and fat-tailed sheep this way. Their lives revolve around two seasonal migrations needed to provide good grazing lands for their flocks—long hazardous journeys that take them over mountains as high as 12,000 feet and through deep chasms and churning water courses.

Central to Bakhtiari subsistence, sheep and goats provide milk, cheese, butter, meat, hides, and wool.

Women and girls spend considerable time spinning wool into yarn—sometimes doing so while riding atop donkeys on the less rugged parts of their migration. They use the yarn not only to make rugs and tents, but also clothing, storage bags, and other essentials.

Bakhtiari people also engage in very limited horticulture: They own lands that contain orchards, producing fruit for themselves and to sell to townspeople. The division of labor is according to gender. The chief task of the men is tending the flocks. The women cook, sew, weave, care for the children, and carry fuel and water.

Crop Cultivation: Horticulture

With the advent of plant domestication, some societies took up *horticulture*, in which small communities of gardeners work with simple hand tools, using neither irrigation nor the plow.

Typically, horticulturists cultivate several varieties of crops together in small, hand-cleared plots. Because they do not usually fertilize the soil, they use a given garden plot for only a few years before abandoning it in favor of a new one. A horticultural way of life involves producing enough food for the group's subsistence. And although they often can (and sometimes do) produce more than they need for purposes such as inter-village feasts and exchange, horticulturists do not produce a surplus to sell on the market.

One of the most widespread forms of horticulture, especially in the tropics, is **swidden farming** (also known as slash-and-burn). This is an ecologically sophisticated and sustainable way of raising food when carried out under the right conditions: low population densities and adequate amounts of land. It mimics the diversity of the natural ecosystem, growing several different crops in the same field. Mixed together, the crops are less vulnerable to pests and plant diseases than a single crop. Not only is the system ecologically sound, but it is far more energy efficient than modern farming methods used in developed countries such as the United States where natural resources such as land and fuel are still relatively cheap and abundant, and many farms operate with financial support in the form of government subsidies or tax breaks. While high-tech farming requires more energy input than it yields, swidden farming produces between 10 and 20 units of energy for every unit expended. A good example of how such a system works is provided by the Mekranoti Kayapo Indians of Brazil's Amazon forest, profiled in the following Original Study.

transhumance A subsistence strategy in which people move their grazing animals from winter pastures in low steppe lands to summer pastures on high plateaus.

swidden farming Also known as slash-and-burn. An extensive form of horticulture in which the natural vegetation is cut, the slash is subsequently burned, and crops are then planted among the ashes.

Original Study

Gardens of the Mekranoti Kayapo

The planting of a Mekranoti garden always follows the same sequence. First, men clear the forest and then burn the debris. In the ashes, both men and women plant sweet potatoes, manioc, bananas, corn, pumpkins, papaya, sugar cane, pineapple, cotton, tobacco, and annatto, whose seeds yield achiote, the red dye used for painting ornaments and people's bodies. Since the Mekranoti don't bother with weeding, the forest gradually invades the garden. After the second year, only manioc, sweet potatoes, and bananas remain. And after three years or so there is usually nothing left but bananas. Except for a few tree species that require hundreds of years to grow, the area will look like the original forest 25 or 30 years later.

This gardening technique, known as slash-and-burn, is one of the most common in the world. At one time critics condemned the technique as wasteful and ecologically destructive, but today we know that, especially in the humid tropics, slash-and-burn may be one of the best gardening techniques possible.

Continuous high temperatures encourage the growth of the microorganisms that cause rot, so organic matter quickly breaks down into simple minerals. The heavy rains dissolve these valuable nutrients and carry them deep into the soils, out of the reach of plants. The tropical forest maintains its richness because the heavy foliage shades the earth, cooling it and inhibiting the growth of the decomposers. A good deal of the rain is captured by leaves before ever reaching the ground.

When a tree falls in the forest and begins to rot, other plants quickly absorb the nutrients that are released. In contrast, with open-field agriculture, the sun heats the earth, the decomposers multiply, and the rains quickly leach the soils of their nutrients. In a few years a lush forest, if cleared for open one-crop agriculture, can be transformed into a barren wasteland.

A few months after the Mekranoti plant banana and papaya, these trees shade the soil, just as the larger forest trees do. The mixing of different kinds of plants in the same area means that minerals can be absorbed as soon as they are released; corn picks up nutrients very fast, while manioc is slow. Also, the small and temporary clearings mean that the forest can quickly reinvade its lost territory.

Because decomposers need moisture as well as warmth, the long Mekranoti dry season could alter this whole picture of soil ecology. But soil samples from recently burned Mekranoti fields and the adjacent forest floor showed that, as in most of the humid tropics, the high fertility of the Indians' garden plots comes from the trees that are burned there, not from the soil, as in temperate climes.

Getting a good burn is a tricky operation. Perhaps for this reason its timing was left to the more experienced and knowledgeable members of the community. If the burn is too early, the rains will leach out the minerals in the ash before planting time. If too late, the debris will be too wet to burn properly. Then, insects and weeds that could plague the plants will not die and few minerals will be released into the soil. If the winds are too weak, the burn will not cover the entire plot. If they are too strong, the fire can get out of hand.

Shortly after burning the plots and clearing away of some of the charred debris, people began the long job of planting, which took up all of September and lasted into October. In the center of the circular garden plot the women dug holes and threw in a few pieces of sweet potatoes. After covering the tubers with dirt they usually asked a male—one of their husbands or anyone else who happened to be nearby—to stomp on the mound and make a ritual noise resembling a Bronx cheer. This magic would ensure a large crop, I was told. Forming a large ring around the sweet potatoes, the Indians rapidly thrust pieces of manioc stems into the ground, one after the other.

When grown, the manioc stems form a dense barrier to the sweet potato patch, and some of the plants must be cut down to gain entrance. Outside of the ring of manioc, the women plant yams, cotton, sugar cane, and annatto. Banana stalks and papaya trees, planted by simply throwing the seeds on the ground, form the outermost circle. The Indians also plant corn, pumpkins, watermelons, and pineapple throughout the garden. These grow rapidly and are harvested long before the manioc matures. The garden appears to change magically from corn and pumpkins to sweet potatoes and manioc without replanting.

Mekranoti gardens grew well. A few Indians complained now and then about a peccary that had eaten a watermelon they were looking forward to eating, or that had reduced their corn harvest. Capybara, large rodents usually found near the river banks, were known for their love of sugar cane, but in general the animals seemed to leave the crops alone. Even the leaf-cutting ants that are problems in other areas did not bother the Mekranoti. Occasionally a neighbor who had not planted a new garden would make off with a prized first-year crop, such as pumpkin, watermelon, or pineapple. But even these thefts were rare. In general, the Mekranoti could depend on harvesting whatever they planted.

Eventually, I wanted to calculate the productivity of Mekranoti gardens. Western agronomists knew very little about slash-and-burn crop cultivation.

[continued]

[continued]

They were accustomed to experiments in which a field was given over to one crop only, and in which the harvest happened all at once. Here, the plants were all mixed together, and people harvested piecemeal whenever they needed something. The manioc could stay in the ground, growing for several years before it was dug up.

I began measuring off areas of gardens to count how many manioc plants, ears of corn, or pumpkins were found there. The women thought it strange to see me struggling through the tangle of plants to measure off areas, 10 meters by 10 meters, placing string along the borders, and then counting what was inside. Sometimes I asked a woman to dig up all of the sweet potatoes within the marked-off area. The requests were bizarre, but the women cooperated just the same, holding on to the ends of the measuring tapes, or sending their

children to help. For some plants, like bananas, I simply counted the number of clumps of stalks in the garden, and the number of banana bunches I could see growing in various clumps. By watching how long it took the bananas to grow, from the time I could see them until they were harvested, I could calculate a garden's total banana yield per year.

After returning from the field, I was able to combine the time allocation data with the garden productivities to get an idea of how hard the Mekranoti need to work to survive. The data showed that for every hour of gardening one Mekranoti adult produces almost 18,000 kilocalories of food. (As a basis for comparison, people in the United States consume approximately 3,000 kilocalories of food per day.) As insurance against bad years, and in case they receive visitors from other villages, they grow far more produce than they

need. But even so, they don't need to work very hard to survive. A look at the average amount of time adults spend on different tasks every week shows just how easy-going life in horticultural societies can be:

8.5 hours	Gardening
6.0 hours	Hunting
1.5 hours	Fishing
1.0 hour	Gathering wild foods
33.5 hours	All other jobs

Altogether, the Mekranoti need to work less than 51 hours a week, and this includes getting to and from work, cooking, repairing broken tools, and all of the other things we normally don't count as part of our work week. *(Adapted from D. Werner. (1990). Amazon Journey (pp. 105–112). Englewood Cliffs, NJ: Prentice Hall. Reprinted by permission of Pearson Education.)* ▪ ▪ ▪

Crop Cultivation: Agriculture

In contrast to horticulture, *agriculture* is crop cultivation that involves using technologies other than hand tools, such as irrigation, fertilizers, and the wooden or metal plow pulled by harnessed draft animals. In the so-called developed countries of the world, it relies on fuel-powered tractors to produce food on larger plots of land.

In contrast to horticulturists, agriculturists are able to grow surplus food—providing not only for their own needs but for those of various full-time specialists and nonproducing consumers as well. This surplus may be sold for cash, or it may be coerced out of the farmers through tribute, taxes, or rent paid to landowners. These landowners and specialists—such as traders, carpenters, blacksmiths, sculptors, basket makers, and stonecutters—typically reside in substantial towns or cities, where political power is centralized in the hands of a socially elite class. Dominated by an urban elite, much of what the farmers do is governed by political and economic forces over which they have little control.

Industrialization: Replacing Human Labor and Hand Tools with Machines

Until about 200 years ago, human societies all across the world had developed a cultural infrastructure based on

foraging, horticulture, agriculture, pastoralism, crafts, trade, or some combination of these. This changed with the invention of the steam engine in England, which brought about an industrial revolution that quickly spread to other parts of the globe. Machines and tools powered by water, wind, and steam (followed by oil, gas, and diesel) replaced human labor and hand tools, increasing factory production and facilitating mass transportation.

Throughout the 1800s and 1900s, this resulted in large-scale industrialization of many societies. Technological inventions utilizing oil, electricity, and nuclear energy (since the 1940s) brought about more dramatic changes in social and economic organization on a worldwide scale. In the late 20th century, the electronic-digital revolution made the production and distribution of information the center of economic activity in some wealthy societies.

SUBSISTENCE AND ECONOMICS

An **economic system** is an organizational arrangement for producing, distributing, and consuming goods. Since a people, in pursuing a particular means of subsistence,

economic system An organizational arrangement for producing, distributing, and consuming goods.

necessarily produces, distributes, and consumes things, it is obvious that our discussion of subsistence patterns involved economic matters. Yet economic systems encompass much more than we have covered so far.

Although anthropologists have adopted theories and concepts from economists, most recognize that theoretical principles derived from the study of capitalist market economies have limited applicability to economic systems in societies that are not industrialized and where people do not produce and exchange goods for private profit. This is because, in these nonstate societies, the economic sphere of behavior is not separate from the social, religious, and political spheres.

In every society, particular customs and rules govern the kinds of work done, who does the work, attitudes toward the work, how it is accomplished, and who controls the resources necessary to produce desired goods, knowledge, and services. The primary resources in any culture are raw materials, technology, and labor. The rules directing the use of these are embedded in a people's culture and determine the way the economy operates within any given natural environment.

Control of Land and Water Resources

All societies regulate the allocation of valuable natural resources—especially land and water. Food foragers must determine who will hunt game and gather plants in their home range and where these activities take place. Groups that rely on fishing or growing crops need to make similar decisions concerning who carries out which task on which stretch of water or land. Farmers must have some means of determining title to land and access to water supplies for irrigation. Pastoralists require a system that determines rights to watering places and grazing land, as well as the right of access to land where they move their herds.

In industrialized Western societies, a system of private ownership of land and rights to natural resources generally prevails. Although elaborate laws have been enacted to regulate the buying, owning, and selling of land and water resources, if individuals wish to reallocate valuable farmland to some other purpose, for instance, they generally can.

In traditional nonindustrialized societies, land is often controlled by kinship groups such as the band or lineage rather than by individuals. For example, among the Ju/'hoansi of the Kalahari Desert, each band, a local group of anywhere from ten to thirty people, lives on roughly 250 square miles of land, which they consider to be their territory—their own country. These territories are defined not in terms of boundaries but in terms of water holes that are located within them. The land is said to be "owned" by those who have lived the longest in the band, usually a group of brothers and sisters or cousins. Their concept of ownership, however, is not something easily translated in modern Western terms. Suffice it to say that within their traditional worldview, no part of their homeland can be sold for money or traded away for goods. Outsiders must ask permission to enter the territory—but denying the request would be unthinkable.

A Ju/'hoansi water hole. The practice of defining territories on the basis of core features such as water holes is typical of food foragers, such as these people of the Kalahari Desert in southern Africa.

Technology Resources

All societies have some means of creating and allocating tools that are used to produce goods, as well as traditions concerning passing them on to succeeding generations. The number and kinds of tools a society uses—which, together with knowledge about how to make and use them constitute its **technology**—are related to the lifestyles of its members. Food foragers and pastoral nomads who are frequently on the move are apt to have fewer and simpler tools than more settled peoples such as sedentary farmers. A great number of complex tools would impair mobility. Thus, the average weight of an individual's personal belongings among the Ju'hoansi is just under 25 pounds, limited to the barest essentials such as implements for hunting, gathering, fishing, building, and cooking.

Food foragers make and use a variety of tools, many of which are ingenious in their effectiveness. Some of these they make for their individual use, but codes of generosity are such that a person may not refuse to give or loan what is requested. Tools may be given or loaned to others in exchange for the products resulting from their use. For example, a Ju/'hoansi who gives his arrow to another hunter has a right to a share in any animals the hunter kills. Game is considered to "belong" to the man whose arrow killed it, even when he is not present on the hunt. In this context, it makes little sense for them to accumulate luxuries or surplus goods, and the fact that no one owns significantly more than another helps to limit status differences.

Among horticulturists, the axe, digging stick, and hoe are the primary tools. Since these are relatively easy to produce, every person can make them. Whoever makes a tool has first rights to it, but when he or she is not using it, any family member may ask to use it and the request is rarely denied. Refusal would cause people to treat the tool owner with scorn for this singular lack of concern for others. If a relative helps raise the crop traded for a particular tool, that relative becomes part owner of the implement, and it may not be traded or given away without his or her permission.

In permanently settled agricultural communities, tools and other productive goods are more complex, and more difficult and costly to make. In such settings, individual ownership tends to be more absolute, as are the conditions under which people may borrow and use such equipment. It is easy to replace a knife lost by a relative during palm cultivation but much more difficult to replace an iron plow or a diesel-fueled harvesting machine. Rights to the ownership of complex tools are more rigidly applied; generally the person who has funded the purchase of a complex piece of machinery is considered the sole owner and may decide how and by whom it will be used.

Labor Resources and Patterns

In addition to raw materials and technology, labor is a key resource in any economic system. A look around the world reveals many different labor patterns, but two features are almost always present in human cultures: a basic division of labor by gender and by age.

Division of Labor by Gender

Anthropologists have studied extensively the social division of labor by gender in cultures of all sorts. Whether men or women do a particular job varies from group to group, but typically work is divided into the tasks of either one or the other. For example, the practices most commonly regarded as "women's work" tend to be those that can be carried out near home and that are easily resumed after interruption. The tasks historically often regarded as "men's work" tend to be those requiring physical strength, rapid mobilization of high bursts of energy, frequent travel at some distance from home, and assumption of high levels of risk and danger.

Many exceptions occur, however, as in those societies where women regularly carry burdensome loads or put in long hours of hard work cultivating crops in the fields. In some societies, women perform almost three-quarters of all work, and in several societies they have served as warriors. For example, in the 19th-century West African kingdom of Dahomey, in what is now called Benin, thousands of women served in the armed forces of the Dahomean king, and some considered the women to be better fighters than their male counterparts.

Instead of looking for key biological factors to explain the social division of labor, a more useful strategy is to examine the kinds of work that men and women do in the context of specific societies to see how it relates to other cultural and historical factors. Researchers find a continuum of patterns, ranging from flexible integration of men and women to rigid segregation by gender.[2]

The *flexible/integrated pattern* is exemplified by the Ju/'hoansi discussed above and is seen most often among food foragers and subsistence farmers. In such

---

technology Tools and other material equipment, together with the knowledge of how to make and use them.

---

[2]Sanday, P. R. (1981). *Female power and male dominance: On the origins of sexual inequality* (pp. 79–80). Cambridge, England: Cambridge University Press.

Food foragers such as the Ju/'hoansi have a division of labor in which men usually do the hunting, and women gather and prepare "bush food" (here an ostrich egg omelet). However, this labor division is not rigid.

societies, men and women perform up to 35 percent of activities with approximately equal participation, and tasks deemed especially appropriate for one gender may be performed by the other, without loss of face, as the situation warrants. Where these practices prevail, boys and girls grow up in much the same way, learn to value cooperation over competition, and become equally habituated to adult men and women, who interact with each other on a relatively equal basis.

Societies following a *segregated pattern* define almost all work as either masculine or feminine, so men and women rarely engage in joint efforts of any kind. In such societies, it is inconceivable that someone would even think of doing something considered the work of the opposite sex! This pattern is frequently seen in pastoral nomadic, intensive agricultural, and industrial societies, where men's work keeps them outside the home for much of the time. Typically, men in such societies are expected to be tough, aggressive, and competitive—and this often involves assertions of male superiority, and hence authority, over women. Historically, societies segregated by gender often have imposed their control on those featuring integration, upsetting the egalitarian nature of the latter.

In the third pattern of labor division by gender, sometimes called the *dual sex configuration,* men and women carry out their work separately, as in societies segregated by gender, but the relationship between them is one of balanced complementarity rather than inequality. Although competition is a prevailing ethic, each gender manages its own affairs, and the interests of both men and women are represented at all levels. Thus, as in integrated societies, neither gender exerts dominance over the other. The dual sex orientation may be seen among certain American Indian peoples whose economies were based upon subsistence farming, as well as among several West African kingdoms, including that of the aforementioned Dahomeans.

Division of Labor by Age

Division of labor according to age is also typical of human societies. Among the Ju/'hoansi, for example, children are not expected to contribute significantly to subsistence until they reach their late teens. Indeed, until they possess adult levels of strength and endurance, many "bush foods" that are tough to gather—edible tubers, for example—are not readily accessible to them.

The Ju/'hoansi equivalent of "retirement" comes somewhere around the age of 60, which is many years beyond their average life expectancy. Elderly people, while they will usually do some foraging for themselves, are not expected to contribute much food. However, older men and women alike play an essential role in spiritual matters. Freed from food taboos and other restrictions that apply to younger adults, they may handle ritual substances considered dangerous to those still involved with hunting or having children. By virtue of their old age, they have recollections of things that happened far in the past. Thus, they are repositories of accumulated wisdom—the "libraries" of a nonliterate people—and are able to suggest solutions to problems younger adults have never before had to face.

Considered useful for their knowledge, they are far from being unproductive members of society.

In many traditional farming societies, children as well as older people may make a greater contribution to the economy in terms of work and responsibility than is common in industrial or postindustrial societies. For instance, in Maya peasant communities in southern Mexico and Guatemala, children not only look after their younger brothers and sisters but also help with housework. Girls begin to make a substantial contribution to the work of the household by age 7 or 8. By age 11 they are constantly busy with an array of chores—grinding corn, making tortillas, fetching wood and water, sweeping, and so forth. Young boys have less to do but are given small tasks, such as bringing in the chickens or playing with a baby. However, by age 12 they are carrying toasted tortillas to the men out working in the fields and returning with loads of corn.[3]

Children also work in industrial societies, where poor families depend on every possible contribution to the household. There, however, economic desperation may easily lead to the cold exploitation of children in factory settings.[4] The use of child labor has become a matter of increasing concern as large capitalist corporations rely more and more on the low-cost manufacture of goods in the world's poorer countries. Although reliable figures are hard to come by, it is estimated that there are some 15 million bonded child laborers in South Asia alone, including some as young as 4 years old. Although the United States long ago passed laws prohibiting institutionalized child labor, the country imports at least $100 million worth of products manufactured by poorly paid children, ranging from rugs and carpets to clothing and soccer balls.[5]

Cooperative Labor

Cooperative work groups can be found everywhere—in foraging as well as food- producing, and in nonindustrial as well as industrial societies. Often, if the effort involves the whole community, a festive spirit permeates the work. In some parts of East Africa, work parties begin with the display of a pot of millet beer to be consumed after the tasks have been finished. Yet, the beer is not payment for the work; indeed, the labor involved is worth far more than the beer consumed. Rather, the beverage is more of a symbol, whereas recompense comes as individuals sooner or later participate in work parties for others.

Craft Specialization

In contemporary industrial and postindustrial societies, there is a great diversity of specialized tasks to be performed. By contrast, in small-scale foraging and traditional crop-cultivating societies, where division of labor typically occurs along lines of age and gender, each person has knowledge and competence in all aspects of work appropriate to his or her age and gender. Yet, even in these nonindustrial societies there is a measure of specialization. For instance, in food-foraging groups the arrow points of one man may be in particular demand because of his distinct skill at making them. Among larger groups, especially people who produce their own food, specialization is more apt to occur. In the Trobriand Islands, for example, if a man wanted stone to make axe blades, he had to travel some distance to a particular island where the appropriate kind of stone was quarried; clay pots, on the other hand, were made by people living on yet another island.

DISTRIBUTION AND EXCHANGE

In societies without a money economy, the rewards for labor are usually direct. The workers in a family group consume what they harvest, eat what the hunter or gatherer brings home, and use the tools they themselves make. But even where no formal medium of exchange such as money exists, some distribution of goods takes place. Anthropologists often classify the cultural systems of distributing material goods into three modes: reciprocity, redistribution, and market exchange.[6]

Reciprocity

Reciprocity refers to a transaction between two parties whereby goods and services of roughly equivalent value are exchanged. This may involve gift giving. Notably, individuals or groups in most cultures like to think that the main point of the transaction is the gift itself, yet what actually matters are the social ties that are created or rein-

reciprocity The exchange of goods and services, of approximately equal value, between two parties.

---

[3]Vogt, E. Z. (1990). *The Zinacantecos of Mexico, a modern Maya way of life* (2nd ed., pp. 83–87). Fort Worth: Holt, Rinehart and Winston.

[4]Goddard, V. (1993). Child labor in Naples. In W. A. Haviland & R. J. Gordon (Eds.), *Talking about people* (pp. 105–109). Mountain View, CA: Mayfield.

[5]It's the law: Child labor protection. (1997, November/December). *Peace and Justice News*, 11.

[6]Polanyi, K. (1968). The economy as instituted process. In E. E. LeClair, Jr., & H. K. Schneider (Eds.), *Economic anthropology: Readings in theory and analysis* (pp. 127–138). New York: Holt, Rinehart and Winston.

These Ju/'hoansi are cutting up meat that will be shared by others in the camp. The food distribution practices of such food foragers are an example of generalized reciprocity.

forced between givers and receivers. Because reciprocity is about a relationship between the self and others, gift giving is seldom really "selfless." The overriding (if unconscious) motive is to fulfill social obligations and perhaps to gain a bit of prestige in the process.

For example, when an animal is killed by a group of indigenous hunters in Australia, the meat is divided among the hunters' families and other relatives. Each person in the camp gets a share, the size depending on the nature of the person's kinship tie to the hunters. The least desirable parts may be kept by the hunters themselves. The giving and receiving is obligatory, as is the particularity of the distribution. Such sharing of food reinforces community bonds and ensures that everyone eats. By giving away part of a kill, the hunters get social credit for a similar amount of food in the future. It is a bit like buying a collective insurance policy.

Reciprocity falls into several categories. The Australian food-distribution example just noted constitutes an example of **generalized reciprocity**—exchange in which the value of what is given is not calculated, nor is the time of repayment specified. Gift giving, in the unselfish sense, also falls in this category. So, too, does the act of a kindhearted soul who stops to help a stranded motorist or someone else in distress and refuses payment with the admonition: "Pass it on to the next person in need."

Most generalized reciprocity, however, occurs among close kin or people who otherwise have very close ties with one another. Within such circles of intimacy, people give to others when they have the means and can count on receiving from others in time of need. This sort of giving, receiving, and sharing constitutes a form of social security or insurance. Typically, participants will deny that the exchanges are economic and will couch them explicitly in terms of kinship and friendship obligations.

Balanced reciprocity differs in that it is not part of a long-term process. The giving and receiving, as well as the time involved, are more specific. One has a direct obligation to reciprocate promptly in equal value in order for the social relationship to continue. Examples of balanced reciprocity in North American society include such practices as trading baseball cards or buying drinks when one's turn comes at a gathering of friends or associates. A classic anthropological example from the other side of the world is the Kula ring, described ahead.

Negative reciprocity is a third form of exchange, in which the aim is to get something for as little as possible. The parties involved have opposing interests and are not usually closely related; they may be strangers or even enemies. They are people with whom exchanges are often neither fair nor balanced and are usually not expected to be such. It may involve hard bargaining, ma-

---

generalized reciprocity A mode of exchange in which the value of the gift is not calculated, nor is the time of repayment specified.

balanced reciprocity A mode of exchange in which the giving and the receiving are specific as to the value of the goods and the time of their delivery.

negative reciprocity A form of exchange in which the aim is to get something for as little as possible. Neither fair nor balanced, it may involve hard bargaining, manipulation, outright cheating, and even theft.

nipulation, or outright cheating. An extreme form of negative reciprocity is to take something by force, while realizing that one's victim may seek compensation or retribution for losses.

Barter and Trade

Exchanges that occur within a group of people generally take the form of generalized or balanced reciprocity. When they occur between two groups, there is the potential for hostility and competition. Therefore, such exchanges may well be in the form of negative reciprocity, unless some sort of arrangement has been made to ensure at least an approach to balance. *Barter* is one form of reciprocity by which surplus items from one group are exchanged for desirable goods from another group. Although each party seeks to get the best possible deal, both may negotiate until a relative balance has been found and each feels satisfied at having achieved the better of the deal. Relative value is calculated, and despite an outward show of indifference, sharp trading is more the rule, when compared to the more balanced nature of exchanges within a group.

The Kula Ring

Because trade can be essential in the quest for survival and is often undertaken for the sake of luxury, people may go to great lengths to establish and maintain good trade relations. A classic example of this is the **Kula ring**, a form of balanced reciprocity that reinforces trade relations among a group of seafaring Melanesians inhabiting a large ring of islands in the southern Pacific off the eastern coast of Papua New Guinea. First described by Polish anthropologist Bronislaw Malinowski who observed it during ethnographic research among Trobriand Islanders, this centuries-old ceremonial exchange system involves thousands of men and continues to this day.[7]

Kula participants are men of influence who travel to islands within the Trobriand ring to exchange prestige items—red shell necklaces (*soulava*), which are circulated around the ring of islands in a clockwise direction, and white shell armbands (*mwali*), which are carried in the opposite direction (Figure 12.1). Each man in the Kula is linked to partners on the islands that neighbor his own. To a partner residing on an island in the clockwise direc-

Kula ring A form of balanced reciprocity that reinforces social relations among the seafaring Trobriand people and other Melanesians.

---

[7]Malinowski, B. (1922). *Argonauts of the western Pacific.* London: Routledge & Kegan Paul; Weiner, A. B. (1988). *The Trobrianders of Papua New Guinea.* New York: Holt, Rinehart and Winston.

Figure 12.1 The Kula Ring
The ceremonial trading of shell necklaces and armbands in the Kula ring encourages trade throughout Melanesia.

tion, he offers a *soulava* and receives in return a *mwali.* He makes the reverse exchange of a *mwali* for a *soulava* to a partner living in the counterclockwise direction. Each of these trade partners eventually passes the object on to a Kula partner further along the chain of islands.

Soulava and *mwali* are ranked according to their size, their color, how finely they are polished, and their particular histories. Such is the fame of some that, when they appear in a village, they create a sensation.

Traditionally, men make their Kula journeys in elaborately carved dugout canoes, sailing and paddling these 20- to 25-feet long boats across open waters to shores some 60 miles or more away. The adventure is often dangerous and may take men away from their homes for several weeks, sometimes even months. Although men on Kula voyages may use the opportunity to trade for practical goods, acquiring such goods is not always the reason for these voyages—nor is Kula exchange a necessary part of regular trade expeditions.

Perhaps the best way to view the Kula is as an indigenous insurance policy in an economic order fraught with danger and uncertainty. It establishes and reinforces social partnerships for traders doing business on distant shores, ensuring a welcome reception from people who have similar vested interests. That said, this ceremonial exchange network does more than simply smooth or enhance the trade of foods and other goods essential for survival. Melanesians participating in the Kula ring have no doubt that their social position has to do with the company they keep, the circles in which they move. They derive their social prestige from the reputations of their partners and the valuables that they circulate. By giving and receiving armbands and necklaces that accumulate the histories of their travels and names of those who have possessed them, men proclaim their individual fame and talent, gaining considerable influence for themselves in the process.

Like other forms of currency, *soulava* and *mwali* must flow from hand to hand; once they stop flowing, they may lose their value. A man who takes these valuables out of their inter-island circuit invites criticism. He may lose not only prestige or "social capital" as a man of influence, but may become a target of sorcery for unraveling the cultural fabric that holds the islands together as a functioning social and economic order.

As an elaborate complex of ceremony, political relationships, economic exchange, travel, magic, and social integration, the Kula illustrates how inseparable economic matters are from the rest of culture. This is just as true in modern industrial societies as it is in traditional Trobriand society.

Redistribution

Redistribution is a form of exchange in which goods flow into a central place where they are sorted, counted, and reallocated. Commonly, it involves an element of power. In societies with a sufficient surplus to support some sort of government, goods in the form of gifts, tribute, taxes, and the spoils of war are gathered into storehouses controlled by a chief or some other type of leader. From there they are handed out again. The leadership has three motives in redistributing this income: The first is to gain or maintain a position of power through a display of wealth and generosity; the second is to assure those who support the leadership an adequate standard of living by providing them with desired goods; and the third is to establish alliances with leaders of other groups by hosting them at lavish parties and giving them valuable goods.

Taxes imposed by central governments of countries all around the world today are one form of redistribution—required payments typically based on a percentage of one's income and property value. Typically, a portion of the taxes goes toward supporting the government itself while the rest are redistributed either in cash (such as welfare payments and government loans or subsidies to businesses) or in the form of services (such as military defense, law enforcement, food and drug inspection, schools, highway construction, and the like). Tax codes vary greatly among countries. In many

European countries, wealthy citizens pay considerably higher percentages of their incomes than those in the United States.

Spending Wealth to Gain Prestige

In societies where people devote most of their time to subsistence activities, gradations of wealth are small, kept that way through various cultural mechanisms and systems of reciprocity that serve to spread quite fairly what little wealth exists. It is a different situation in ranked societies where substantial surpluses are produced, and the gap between the have-nots and the have-lots can be considerable. In these societies, showy display for social prestige—known as **conspicuous consumption**—is a strong motivator for the distribution of wealth.

Obviously, excessive efforts to impress others with one's wealth or status also play a prominent role in industrial and postindustrial societies, as individuals compete for prestige. Indeed, many North Americans and Europeans spend much of their lives trying to impress others. This requires the display of symbolic prestige items—designer clothes, substantial jewelry, mansions, big cars, private planes—and fits neatly into an economy based on consumer wants.

A form of conspicuous consumption also occurs in some crop-cultivating and foraging societies—as illustrated by potlatches given by the chiefs among the Kwakwaka'wakw, including the Kwakiutl and neighboring indigenous groups living along North America's northwest coast. A **potlatch** is a ceremonial event in which a village chief publicly gives away stockpiled food and other goods that signify wealth. (The term comes from the Chinook Indian word *patshatl*, which means "gift.")

In extreme displays of wealth, chiefs even destroyed some of their precious possessions. This occurred with some frequency in the second half of the 19th century, after European contact triggered a process of culture change that included new trade wealth. Outsiders might view such grandiose displays as wasteful in the extreme. However, these extravagant giveaway ceremonies have played an ecologically adaptive role in a coastal region where villages alternately faced periods of scarcity and abundance and relied upon alliances and trade relations with one another for long-term survival. The potlatch provided a ceremonial opportunity to

redistribution A form of exchange in which goods flow into a central place, where they are sorted, counted, and reallocated.

conspicuous consumption The display of wealth for social prestige.
potlatch On the northwest coast of North America, a ceremonial event in which a village chief publicly gives away stockpiled food and other goods that signify wealth.

strategically redistribute surplus food and goods among allied villages in response to periodic fluctuations in fortune.

A strategy that features this sort of accumulation of surplus goods for the express purpose of displaying wealth and giving it away to raise one's status is known as a **prestige economy.** In contrast to conspicuous consumption in industrial and postindustrial societies, the emphasis is not on amassing goods that then become unavailable to others. Instead, it is on gaining wealth in order to give it away for the sake of prestige and status.

Leveling Mechanisms

The potlatch is an example of a **leveling mechanism**—a cultural obligation compelling prosperous members of a community to give away goods, host public feasts, provide free service, or otherwise demonstrate generosity so that no one permanently accumulates significantly more wealth than anyone else. With leveling mechanisms at work, greater wealth brings greater social pressure to spend and give generously. In exchange for such demonstrated altruism, a person not only increases his or her social standing in the community but may also keep disruptive envy at bay.

Underscoring the value of collective well-being over individual self-interest, leveling mechanisms are important in the long-term survival of traditional communities. The potlatch is just one of many cultural variations of leveling mechanisms. Another example can be found in Maya Indian towns in the highlands of Guatemala and southern Mexico. In these traditional communities, the higher public offices are those of councilmen, judges, and mayors, in addition to various ceremonial leadership positions. Because the people who are called upon to fill these roles are not paid, the positions are known as *cargos* (Spanish for "burdens"). In fact, Maya Indian officeholders are expected to personally pay for the food, liquor, music, fireworks, or whatever is required for community festivals or for feast meals associated with their particular post. For some cargos, the cost can be as much as a man can earn in four years!

After holding a cargo position, a man usually returns to his normal life for a period, during which he may accumulate sufficient resources to campaign for a higher office. Each successful male citizen of the community is socially obliged to serve in the community's cargo system at least once, and the social pressure to do so drives individuals who have once again accumulated surplus wealth to apply for higher offices in order to raise their social status. Ideally, while some individuals gain appreciably more prestige than others in their community, no one has appreciably more wealth in the long run than anyone else.

By pressuring members into sharing their wealth in their own community rather than keeping it to themselves or privately investing it elsewhere, such a system does more than keep resources in circulation. It also reduces social tensions among relatives, neighbors, and fellow town folk, promoting a collective sense of togetherness. An added practical benefit is that they ensure that necessary services within the community are performed.

Market Exchange

To an economist, **market exchange** has to do with the buying and selling of goods and services, with prices set by rules of supply and demand. Personal loyalties and moral values are not supposed to play a role, but they often do. Since the actual location of the transaction is not always relevant in today's world, we must distinguish between the "marketplace" and "market exchange."

Typically, until well into the 20th century, market exchange was carried out in specific localities or *marketplaces*. This is still the case in much of the nonindustrial world and even in numerous centuries-old European and Asian towns and cities. In agrarian societies, marketplaces overseen by a centralized political authority provide the opportunity for farmers in the surrounding rural territories to exchange some of their livestock and produce for needed items manufactured in factories or in the workshops of craft specialists living (usually) in towns and cities. Thus, some sort of complex division of labor as well as centralized political organization is necessary for the appearance of markets.

The traditional market is local, specific, and contained. Prices are typically set on the basis of face-to-face bargaining rather than by "market forces" wholly removed from the transaction itself. Notably, sales do not necessarily involve money; instead, goods may be directly exchanged through some form of barter among the specific individuals involved.

In industrial and postindustrial societies, some market transactions still take place in a specific identifiable

---

prestige economy Creation of a surplus for the express purpose of gaining prestige through a public display of wealth that is given away as gifts.

leveling mechanism A cultural obligation compelling prosperous members of a community to give away goods, host public feasts, provide free service, or otherwise demonstrate generosity so that no one permanently accumulates significantly more wealth than anyone else.

---

market exchange The buying and selling of goods and services, with prices set by rules of supply and demand.

location—including international trade fairs such as the semi-annual Canton Trade Fair in Guangzhou, China, which in spring 2005 featured some 10,000 Chinese enterprises and drew buyers from over 200 countries. However, it is possible and increasingly common for people living in technologically wired parts of the world to buy and sell everything from cattle to cars without ever being in the same city, let alone the same space, as those with whom they are doing business. For example, think of Internet companies such as eBay where all buying and selling occurs electronically. Thus, when people talk about a market in today's industrial or postindustrial world, the particular geographical location where something is bought or sold is often not important at all.

The faceless market exchanges that take place in industrial and postindustrial societies stand in stark contrast to experiences in the marketplaces of nonindustrial societies, which have much of the excitement of a fair. Traditional exchange centers are colorful places where a host of sights, sounds, and smells awaken the senses. Typically, vendors and/or their family members pro-

In many societies, particularly in developing countries, the market is an important focus of social as well as economic activity, as typified by this market in Toubokru, Ivory Coast.

© 1998 Richard Lord

duced the goods they are selling, thereby personalizing the transactions. Dancers and musicians may perform, and feasting and fighting may mark the end of the day. In these markets social relationships and personal interactions are key elements, and noneconomic activities may even overshadow the economic. In short, such markets are gathering places where people renew friendships, see relatives, gossip, and keep up with the world, while procuring needed goods they cannot produce for themselves.

Although there have been marketplaces without money of any sort, money does facilitate trade. **Money** may be defined as something used to make payments for other goods and services as well as to measure their value. Its critical attributes are durability, portability, divisibility, recognizability, and fungibility (exchangeable or replaceable for any other monetary item of the same value, as when four quarters are substituted for a dollar bill). Items that have been used as money in various societies include salt, shells, stones, beads, feathers, fur, bones, teeth, and of course metals, from iron to gold and silver.

Among the Tiv of West Africa, brass rods might be exchanged for cattle, with the seller then using the rods to purchase slaves (the economic value of the cattle being converted into the rods and then reconverted into slaves). In their culture the money in question is (or was) used only for special purposes. To a Tiv, the idea of exchanging a brass rod for subsistence foods is repugnant, and most market exchanges involve direct barter. Special-purpose monies usually have some moral restrictions on their use, as contrasted with general-purpose monies, which can be used to purchase just about anything. Even the latter category, however, has limits. For example, in the United States it is considered immoral, as well as illegal, to exchange money for sexual or political favors.

This also raises the issue of the distinction between the informal and formal sectors of the market economy. The **informal economy** may be defined as a network of producing and circulating marketable commodities, labor, and services that for various reasons escape government control (enumeration, regulation, or other type of public monitoring or auditing). Such enterprises may encompass a range of activities: gardening, house cleaning, child care, making and selling beer or other

money Anything used to make payments for other things (goods or labor) as well as to measure their value; may be special purpose or multipurpose.

informal economy Network of producing and circulating marketable commodities, labor, and services that for various reasons escape government control.

alcoholic beverages, doing repair or construction work, begging, selling things on the street, performing ritual services, lending money, dealing drugs, picking pockets, and gambling, to mention just a few.

These "off-the-books" or black market activities have been known for a long time but generally have long been dismissed by economists as of marginal importance. Yet, in many countries of the world, the informal economy is, in fact, more important than the formal economy. In many places, large numbers of under- and unemployed people, who have only limited access to the formal economic sector, in effect improvise, "getting by" on scant resources. Meanwhile, more affluent members of society may dodge various regulations in order to maximize returns and/or to vent their frustrations at their perceived loss of self-determination in the face of increasing government regulation.

ECONOMICS, CULTURE, AND THE WORLD OF BUSINESS

Failing to overcome cultural biases can have serious economic consequences, especially in this era of globalization. For example, it has led prosperous countries to impose inappropriate development schemes in parts of the world that they regard as economically "underdeveloped." Typically, these schemes focus on increasing the target country's gross national product through large-scale production that all too often boosts the well-being of a few but results in poverty, poor health, discontent, and a host of other ills for many.

In northeastern Brazil, for example, development of large-scale plantations to grow sisal for export to the United States took over numerous small farms where peasants grew food to feed themselves. With this change, peasants were forced into the ranks of the unemployed or poorly paid wage laborers. Because they no longer had land for growing their own crops and did not earn enough to buy basic foodstuffs, they faced a dramatic increase in the incidence of malnutrition.[8]

Such failures are tied to the fact that every culture is an integrated system (as illustrated by the barrel model) and that a shift in the infrastructure, or economic base, impacts interlinked elements of the society's social structure and superstructure. As the ethnographic examples of the potlatch and the Kula ring show, economic activities in traditional cultures such as the Kwakiutl and the Trobrianders are intricately intertwined with social and political relations and even involve spiritual elements. Development programs that do not take such complexities into consideration may have unintended negative consequences on a society. Fortunately, there is now a growing awareness on the part of development officials that future projects are unlikely to succeed without the expertise that anthropologically trained people can bring to bear.

---

[8]Bodley, J. H. (1990). *Victims of progress* (3rd ed., p. 141). Mountain View, CA: Mayfield.

Chapter Summary

■ Adaptation, essential for survival, is the ongoing process organisms undergo to achieve beneficial adjustments to a particular environment. It results in biological changes in the organisms, which in turn impact the environment. Humans are unique in the degree to which they adapt through culture, which has made it possible for them to inhabit an extraordinary range of environments. Cultural adaptation is the complex of ideas, activities, and technologies that enable people to survive in a certain environment and in turn impact the environment.

■ The food-foraging way of life, the oldest and most universal type of human adaptation, requires that people move their residence according to changing food sources. Local group size is kept small, possibly because small numbers fit the land's capacity to sustain the groups. Obviously, a habitat rich in natural resources can sustain more people than marginal lands that are home to the world's few surviving foragers.

■ The transition from food foraging to food production, known as the Neolithic revolution, began about 10,000 years ago. With it came the development of permanent settlements as people practiced horticulture using simple hand tools. One common form of horticulture is swidden or slash-and-burn farming. Agriculture, a more complex activity, involves plows, irrigation, and/or fertilizers. Pastoralism is a means of subsistence that relies on raising and managing herds of domesticated migratory grazing animals, such as cattle, sheep, and goats. Pastoralists are usually nomadic, moving as needed to provide animals with pasture and water. Transhumance is a subsistence strategy in which people move their grazing animals from winter pastures in low steppe lands to summer pastures on high plateaus.

■ The industrial revolution began 200 years ago with the invention of the steam engine. It replaced human labor and hand tools with machines and resulted in massive culture change in many societies.

■ An economic system is an organizational arrangement for producing, distributing and consuming goods. Studying the economics of nonliterate, nonindustrialized societies can be undertaken only in the context of the total culture of each society. Each society solves the problem of subsisting by allocating raw materials, land, labor, and technology and by distributing goods according to its own priorities.

■ Labor is a major productive resource, and the allotment of work is commonly governed by rules according to gender and age. Only a few broad generalizations can be made covering the kinds of work performed by men and women cross-culturally. A more productive strategy is to examine the kinds of work that men and women do in the context of specific societies to see how it relates to other cultural and historical factors. The cooperation of many people working together is a typical feature of both nonindustrial and industrial societies. Specialization of craft is important even in societies with very simple technologies.

■ All societies regulate the allocation of land and other valuable resources. In nonindustrial societies, individual ownership of land is rare; generally land is controlled by kinship groups, such as the lineage or band. The band provides flexibility of land use, since the size of a band and its territories can be adjusted according to availability of resources in any particular place. The technology of a people, in the form of the tools they use and associated knowledge, is related to their mode of subsistence.

■ A characteristic of food-foraging societies is their egalitarianism. Since this way of life requires mobility, people accumulate only the material goods necessary for survival, so that status differences are limited to those based on age and gender. Status differences associated with gender, however, do not imply subordination of women to men. Food resources are distributed equally throughout the groups; thus no individual can achieve the wealth or status that hoarding might bring. In food-foraging societies, codes of generosity promote free access to tools, even though individuals may have made these for their own use. Settled farming communities offer greater opportunities to accumulate material belongings, and inequalities of wealth may develop. In many such communities, though, a relatively egalitarian social order may be maintained through leveling mechanisms, such as the potlatch and the cargo system.

■ Nonindustrial peoples consume most of what they produce themselves, but they do exchange goods. The processes of distribution may be distinguished as reciprocity, redistribution, and market exchange. Reciprocity is a transaction between individuals or groups, involving the exchange of goods and services of roughly equivalent value. Usually it is prescribed by ritual and ceremony. Barter and trade take place between groups. Trading exchanges have elements of reciprocity but involve a greater calculation of the relative value of goods exchanged. Barter is one form of negative reciprocity, whereby surplus goods from one group are exchanged for desirable goods from another group. A classic example of exchange that partakes of both reciprocity and sharp trading is the Kula ring of the Trobriand Islanders.

■ Display for social prestige is a motivating force in societies that produce some surplus of goods. In the United States, goods accumulated for display generally remain in the hands of those who accumulated them, whereas in other societies they are generally given away; the prestige comes from publicly divesting oneself of valuables, as in the potlatch ceremony.

■ Strong, centralized political organization is necessary for redistribution to occur. The government assesses each citizen a tax or tribute, uses the proceeds to support the governmental and religious elite, and redistributes the rest, usually in the form of public services. The collection of taxes and delivery of government services and subsidies in the United States is a form of redistribution.

■ Exchange in the marketplace serves to distribute goods in a region. In nonindustrial societies, the marketplace is usually a specific site where produce, livestock, and material items the people make are exchanged. It also functions as a social gathering place and a news medium. Although market exchanges may take place without money through bartering and other forms of reciprocity, some form of money at least for special transactions makes market exchange more efficient. In market economies, the informal sector may become more important than the formal sector as large numbers of under- and unemployed people with marginal access to the formal economy seek to survive. The informal economy consists of those economic activities that escape official scrutiny and regulation.

■ The anthropological approach to economics has taken on new importance in today's world of international development and commerce. Without it, development schemes for so-called underdeveloped countries are prone to failure, and international trade is handicapped as a result of cross-cultural misunderstandings.

Questions for Reflection

1. Since the beginning of human existence, humans have been challenged to adapt to the resources available. Having read this chapter, you know that not all adaptations are successful. Can you think of any failures? From an ecological point of view, what may have caused those failures?

2. What was so radical about the Neolithic revolution? Can you think of any equally radical changes going on in the world today?

3. Consider the differences between reciprocity and market exchange. What role does each play in your own society?

4. As the potlatch ceremony shows, prestige may be gained by giving away wealth. Does such a prestige-building mechanism exist in your own society? If so, how does it work?

5. As discussed in this chapter, economic relations in traditional cultures are usually wrapped up in social, political, and even spiritual issues. Can you think of any examples in your own society in which the economic sphere is inextricably intertwined with other structures in the cultural system? Would tinkering with the economic sphere affect these other aspects of your culture?

Key Terms

cultural adaptation

ecosystem

cultural ecology

cultural evolution

progress

convergent evolution

parallel evolution

food foraging

carrying capacity

Neolithic revolution

transhumance

swidden farming

economic system

technology

reciprocity

generalized reciprocity

balanced reciprocity

negative reciprocity

Kula ring

redistribution

conspicuous
   consumption

potlatch

prestige economy

leveling mechanism

market exchange

money

informal economy

Multimedia Review Tools

Make the Grade in Anthropology with ThomsonNOW

Thomson NOW! This powerful online study tool provides you with a *personalized study plan* based on your responses to a diagnostic pretest. Once you have mastered the material with the help of interactive learning tools, an integrated e-book, and more, you can take a post-test to confirm you are ready to move on to the next chapter. To get started with ThomsonNOW, check the card packaged with your book for the access code. Then go to http://www.thomsonedu.com to create an account through 1pass™. If there is no card in your book, go to http://www.thomsonedu.com to purchase an access code.

Companion Website and Anthropology Resource Center

Go to http://anthropology.wadsworth.com to reach the companion website for your text. This offers many study aids, including self quizzes for each chapter and a practice final exam, as well as links to anthropology websites and information on the latest theories and discoveries in the field.

Also, check out the Anthropology Resource Center for a wealth of learning materials that include interactive maps, video exercises, simulations, and breaking news in anthropology. Be sure to explore InfoTrac College Edition®, your online library that offers full-length articles from thousands of scholarly and popular publications. To reach the Anthropology Resource Center and InfoTrac College Edition, check the card packaged with your book for the access code. Then go to http://www.thomsonedu.com to create an account through 1pass™. If there is no card in your book, go to http://www.thomsonedu.com to purchase an access code.

© Richard T. Nowitz/Corbis

CHALLENGE ISSUE

All around the world humans face the challenge of managing sexual relations and establishing social alliances essential to the survival of individuals and their offspring. Marriage and family, in various forms, provide cultural structures for meeting this challenge. Because each generation becomes responsible for maintaining a group's overall well-being and advancing its collective interests, children are an essential investment for a group's long-term survival. Each group has to pass on the necessary cultural know-how and thus ensure enduring success. Adjusting to distinct environments and facing specific challenges, each group establishes its own arrangements in terms of child-rearing tasks, gender relations, household and family structures, and residence patterns. Changes in these conditions may cause social tensions and thus require adjustments.

Sex, Marriage, and Family

13

Among Trobriand Islanders, whose Kula voyages we examined in the previous chapter, children who have reached the age of 7 or 8 years begin playing erotic games and imitating adult seductive attitudes. Within another 4 or 5 years they begin to pursue sexual partners in earnest—experimenting sexually with a variety of individuals. By the time they are in their mid-teens, meetings between lovers may take up most of the night, and affairs are apt to last for several months. Ultimately, lovers begin to meet the same partner again and again, rejecting the advances of others. When the couple is

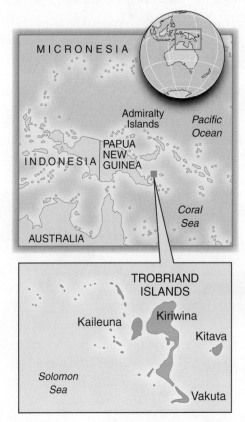

ready, they appear together one morning outside the young man's house as a way of announcing their intention to be married.

For young Trobrianders, attracting sexual partners is an important matter, and they spend a great deal of time making themselves look attractive and seductive. Youthful conversations during the day are loaded with sexual innuendo, and magical spells as well as small gifts are employed to entice a prospective sex partner to the beach at night or to the house in which boys sleep apart from their parents. Because girls, too, sleep apart from their parents, youths and adolescents have considerable freedom in arranging their love affairs. Boys and girls play this game as equals, with neither having an advantage over the other.

Until the latter part of the 20th century, the Trobriand attitude toward adolescent sexuality was in marked contrast to that of most Western cultures in Europe and North America where individuals were not supposed to have sexual relations before or outside of marriage. Since then, practices in much of Europe and North America have converged toward those of the Trobrianders, even though the traditional ideal of premarital abstinence has not been abandoned entirely.

CONTROL OF SEXUAL RELATIONS

Culture plays a significant role in sexual behavior, helping to determine when, how, and between whom sex takes place. For instance, in some human societies, intercourse during pregnancy is thought to promote the growth of the fetus. Also, same-sex relations are sharply condemned in some societies but accepted in others. Many languages do not even have a special term to distinguish homosexuality as significant in its own right. In fact, in some cultures certain prescribed male-to-male

sexual acts are part of male initiation rituals required of all boys to become respected adult men.[1] Certain New Guinea cultures, for example, consider the transmission of semen from older to younger boys, through oral sex, as vital for building up the strength needed to protect against the supposedly debilitating effects of adult heterosexual intercourse.[2] Clearly, the social rules and cultural meanings of all sexual behavior are subject to great variability from one society to another.

Regulating Sexual Relations and Marriage

In the absence of effective birth control devices, the usual outcome of sexual activity between fertile individuals of opposite sex is that, sooner or later, the woman becomes pregnant. Given the intricate array of social responsibilities involved in rearing the children that are born of sexual relations, it is not surprising that all societies have cultural rules that seek to regulate those relations.

In much of North America and Europe, the traditional ideal was that all sexual activity outside of marriage was taboo. Individuals were expected to establish a family through marriage, by which one gained an exclusive right of sexual access to another person. According to strict Judeo-Christian law, as prescribed in the Book of Leviticus (20:10), adultery was punishable by death: "And the man that committeth adultery with another man's wife . . . , the adulterer and the adulteress shall surely be put to death." Deuteronomy (22:24) adds:

---

[1]Kirkpatrick, R. C. (2000). The evolution of human homosexual behavior. *Current Anthropology, 41*, 385.

[2]Herdt, G. H. (1993). Semen transactions in Sambia culture. In D. N. Suggs & A. W. Mirade (Eds.), *Culture and human sexuality* (pp. 298–327). Pacific Grove, CA: Brooks/Cole.

Although homosexuality is a widespread human phenomenon, in some societies it faces repression or ridicule. In parts of the United States, for example, public displays of same-sex affection between men in particular are often looked upon as distasteful or even disgusting. One nationwide exception is the football field, where an extreme measure of rough-and-tumble masculine behavior makes it possible for players to pat each other on the behind, exchange celebratory hugs, and even leap into each other's arms without bringing their sexual orientation into question.

© Lisa Krantz/The Image Works

© Catherine Karnow/CORBIS

"Then ye shall bring them both out unto the gate of that city, and ye shall stone them with stones that they die."

Many centuries later, among Christian colonists in 17th- and 18th-century New England, adultery by women remained a serious crime. While it did not lead to stoning, women so accused were shunned by the community and could even be imprisoned. As recounted in *The Scarlet Letter* by Nathaniel Hawthorne, the adulteress was forced to have the letter "A" stitched on her dress, publicly signifying her crime.

Such restrictions exist today in many traditional Muslim societies in northern Africa and western Asia, where age-old "Shariah" law continues or has been reinstated to regulate social behavior in strict accordance with religious standards of morality. Under this law, women found guilty of having sexual relations outside marriage can be sentenced to death by stoning. In northern Nigeria, for example, a Muslim woman who committed adultery and had a child outside marriage was sentenced to death in 2002. Her sentence was ultimately overturned by an Islamic appeals court, but it nonetheless drove home the rule of Shariah law. Turning legal transgressions into a public spectacle, authorities reinforce public awareness of the rules of social conduct.

One positive side effect of such restrictive rules of sexual behavior is that they limit the spread of sexually transmitted diseases. For instance, the global epidemic of HIV/AIDS has had relatively little impact in sexually restrictive societies. Such societies, however, are a minority. In fact, most cultures in the world are much more relaxed about sexuality and do not sharply regulate personal practices. Indeed, a majority of all cultures are considered sexually permissive or semi-permissive (the former having few or no restrictions on sexual experimentation before marriage, the latter allowing some experimentation but less openly). A minority of known societies—about 15 percent—have rules requiring that sexual involvement take place only within marriage.

This brings us to an anthropological definition of **marriage**—a culturally sanctioned union between two or more people that establishes certain rights and obligations between the people, between them and their children, and between them and their in-laws. Such marriage rights and obligations most often include, but are not limited to, sex, labor, property, child rearing, exchange, and status. Thus defined, marriage is universal.

marriage A culturally sanctioned union between two or more people that establishes certain rights and obligations between the people, between them and their children, and between them and their in-laws. Such marriage rights and obligations most often include, but are not limited to, sex, labor, property, child rearing, exchange, and status.

Notably, our definition of marriage refers to "people" rather than "a man and a woman" because in some countries same-sex marriages are considered socially acceptable and allowed by law, even though opposite-sex marriages are far more common. We will return to this point later in the chapter.

Incest Taboo

Just as marriage in its various forms is found in all cultures, so is the **incest taboo**—the absolute forbiddance of sexual contact between certain close relatives. But, what is defined as "close" is not the same in all cultures. Moreover, such definitions may be subject to change over time. The scope and details of the taboo vary across cultures and time, but almost all societies past and present strongly forbid sexual relations at least between parents and children and nearly always between siblings. In some societies the taboo extends to other close relatives, such as cousins, and even some relatives linked through marriage.

Anthropologists have long been fascinated by the incest taboo and have proposed many explanations for its cross-cultural existence and variation. The simplest explanation, based on the idea of "human nature," is that our species has an "instinctive" repulsion for incest. It has been documented that human beings raised together have less sexual attraction for one another. However, by itself this "familiarity breeds contempt" argument may simply substitute the result for the cause. The incest taboo ensures that children and their parents, who are constantly in close contact, avoid regarding one another as sexual objects. Besides this, if an instinctive horror of incest exists, how do we account for the far from rare violations of the incest taboo? (In the United States, for instance, an estimated 10 to 14 percent of children under 18 years of age have been involved in incestuous relations.[3])

Moreover, so-called instinctive repulsion doesn't explain institutionalized incest, such as that requiring the divine ruler of the Inca empire in ancient Peru be married to his own (half) sister. Sharing the same father, both siblings belonged to the political dynasty that derived its sacred right to rule the empire from Inti, its

incest taboo The prohibition of sexual relations between specified individuals, usually parent and child and sibling relations at a minimum.

[3]Whelehan, P. (1985). Review of incest, a biosocial view. *American Anthropologist, 87,* 678. See also Langan, P., & Harlow, C. (1994). *Child rape victims, 1992.* Washington, DC: Bureau of Justice Statistics, U.S. Department of Justice.

ancestral Sun God. And by virtue of this royal lineage's godly origin, their children could claim the same sacred political status as their human god-father and mother. Ancient emperors in Egypt also practiced such religiously prescribed incest based on a similar claim to godly status.

Early students of genetics argued that the incest taboo prevents the harmful effects of inbreeding. While this is so, it is also true that, as with domestic animals, inbreeding can increase desired characteristics as well as detrimental ones. Furthermore, undesirable effects will show up sooner than without inbreeding, so whatever genes are responsible for them are quickly eliminated from the population. That said, a preference for a genetically different mate does tend to maintain a higher level of genetic diversity within a population, and in evolution this generally works to a species' advantage. Without genetic diversity a species cannot adapt biologically to a changed environment if necessary.

Nonetheless, the inbreeding- or biological-avoidance theory can be challenged on several fronts. Detailed census records made in Roman Egypt about 2,000 years ago show that brother–sister marriages were not uncommon among ordinary members of the farming class.[4] Moreover, in a sample of 129 societies, anthropologist Nancy Thornhill found that only 57 had specific rules against parent–child or sibling incest. Twice that number (114) had explicit rules to control activity with cousins, in-laws, or both.[5] Some anthropologists have argued that the incest taboo exists as a cultural means to preserve the stability and integrity of the family, which is essential to maintaining social order. Sexual relations between members other than the husband and wife would introduce competition, destroying the harmony of a social unit fundamental to social order. A truly convincing explanation of the incest taboo has yet to be advanced.

Endogamy and Exogamy

Closely related to prohibitions against incest are cultural rules against **endogamy,** or marriage within a particular group of individuals (cousins and in-laws, for example).

> **endogamy** Marriage within a particular group or category of individuals.

[4]Leavitt, G. C. (1990). Sociobiological explanations of incest avoidance: A critical review of evidential claims. *American Anthropologist, 92,* 982.

[5]Thornhill, N. (1993). Quoted in W. A. Haviland & R. J. Gordon (Eds.), *Talking about people* (p. 127). Mountain View, CA: Mayfield.

If the group is defined as one's immediate family alone, then societies generally prohibit or at least discourage endogamy, thereby promoting **exogamy,** or marriage outside the group. Yet, a society that practices exogamy at one level may practice endogamy at another. Among the Trobriand Islanders, for example, each individual has to marry outside of his or her own clan and lineage (exogamy). However, since eligible sex partners are to be found within one's own community, village endogamy is commonly practiced.

Interestingly, societies vary widely concerning which relatives are or are not covered by rules of exogamy. For example, first cousins are prohibited from marrying each other in many countries where the Roman Catholic Church has long been a dominant institution. Such marriages are also illegal in thirty-one of the United States. Yet, in numerous other societies, first cousins are preferred spouses. (See a discussion of marriage prohibitions in the Biocultural Connection.)

Some anthropologists have suggested that our ancestors discovered the advantage of intermarriage as a means of creating bonds of friendship. French anthropologist Claude Lévi-Strauss elaborated on this idea. He saw exogamy as a form of exchange in which wife-giving and wife-taking created social alliances between distinct groups. By widening the human network, a larger number of people could pool natural resources and cultural information, including technology and other useful knowledge. Building on Lévi-Strauss's theory, other anthropologists have proposed that exogamy is an important means of promoting trade between groups, thereby ensuring access to needed goods and resources not otherwise available. Forging wider kinship networks, exogamy also functions to integrate distinctive groups and thus potentially reduces violent conflict.

Distinction Between Marriage and Mating

Having defined marriage, in part, in terms of sexual access, we must make clear the distinction between marriage and mating. All animals, including humans, mate—some for life and some not, some with a single individual and some with several. Mates are secured and held solely through individual effort, as opposed to marriage, which is a culturally recognized right. Only marriage is backed by social, political, and ideological factors that regulate sexual relations as well as reproductive rights and obligations. Thus, while mating is bi-

> **exogamy** Marriage outside the group.

Biocultural Connection

Marriage Prohibitions in the United States

In the United States, every state has laws prohibiting some type of relatives from marrying each other. There is complete agreement when it comes to prohibiting parent–child marriage and preventing full siblings from marrying, but the laws vary when it comes to more distant relatives. Thirty-one states prohibit first cousins from marrying while nineteen do not. Furthermore, the prohibitions are not limited to people related by birth. A dozen states also forbid certain step-relatives and in-laws from intermarrying.

Although the marriage prohibitions apply to people not related by birth, North Americans commonly believe that these prohibitions are based on biological factors. It is assumed that the prohibitions protect families from potential genetic defects in children of parents who are biologically "too close." The

first-cousin prohibitions, in particular, are often defended for this reason.

There are two major problems with this idea. First, the cousin prohibitions began to be enacted in the United States around the middle of the 19th century, long before the emergence of modern genetics. Second, modern genetic research has shown that first-cousin marriage does not present any significantly greater risk to offspring than that from parents who are not related. Why, then, do some North Americans maintain this myth?

In the 19th century United States, an evolutionary model of humans that included a notion about human progress depending upon outbreeding became widely accepted. Cousin marriage was thought to be characteristic of savagery, considered a form of degeneration based on inbreeding, believed to inhibit the

intellectual development of humans, and feared as a threat to civilized life. With the development of modern genetics, it was wrongly assumed that genetic data supported this now-discredited evolutionary dogma.

Human reproduction is a biological process situated in a cultural context. Each culture develops a particular understanding about the nature of reproduction. This can change over time. At present, the Western model of reproduction is undergoing a transformation stimulated by the recent discovery of mitochondrial DNA and the introduction of new reproductive technologies. The process well illustrates that biological processes and culture are intimately intertwined, each affecting and being affected by the other. *(By M. Ottenheimer, Kansas State University.)* ■ ■ ■

ological, marriage is cultural. This is evident when we consider the various forms that marriage takes cross-culturally.

FORMS OF MARRIAGE

Within societies, and all the more so across cultures, we see contrasts in the constructs and contracts of marriage. Indeed, as evident in the definition of marriage given above, this institution comes in various forms—and these forms are distinct in terms of the number and gender of spouses involved.

Monogamy

Monogamy—marriage in which both partners have just one spouse—is the most common form of marriage worldwide. In North America and most of Europe, it is the only legally recognized form of marriage. Not only are other forms prohibited there, but also systems of in-

heritance, whereby property and wealth are transferred from one generation to the next, are based on the institution of monogamous marriage. In some parts of the world, such as North America and Europe where divorce rates are high and divorcees typically remarry, an increasingly common form of marriage is **serial monogamy,** whereby an individual marries a series of partners in succession.

Polygamy

While monogamy is the most common marriage form worldwide, it is not the most preferred. That distinction goes to **polygamy** (one individual having multiple spouses)—specifically to **polygyny,** in which a man is married to more than one woman. Favored in about 80

monogamy Marriage in which both partners have just one spouse.

serial monogamy A marriage form in which an individual marries or lives with a series of partners in succession.

polygamy One individual having multiple spouses at the same time; from the Greek words *poly* ("many") and *gamous* ("marriage").

polygyny Marriage of a man to two or more women at the same time; a form of polygamy.

to 85 percent of the world's cultures, polygyny is commonly practiced in parts of Asia and much of sub-Saharan Africa.[6]

Nonetheless, monogamy exceeds polygyny in these places, and the reason for this is economic rather than moral. In many polygynous societies, where a groom is usually expected to compensate a bride's family in cash or kind, a man must be fairly wealthy to be able to afford more than one wife. Recent multiple surveys of twenty-five sub-Saharan African countries where polygyny is common show that it has declined by about half between the 1970s and 2001 but nonetheless remains highly significant with an overall average of 25 percent of married women in polygynous unions.[7]

Polygyny is particularly common in societies that support themselves by growing crops and where women do the bulk of cultivation. Under these conditions, women are valued both as workers and as child bearers. Because the labor of wives in polygynous households generates wealth, and little support is required from husbands, the wives have a strong bargaining position within the household. Often, they have considerable freedom of movement and some economic independence from the sale of crops. Wealth-increasing polygyny is found in its fullest elaboration in parts of sub-Saharan Africa, though it is known elsewhere as well.[8]

In societies practicing wealth-generating polygyny, most men and women do enter into polygynous marriages, although some are able to do so earlier in life than others. This is made possible by a female-biased sex ratio and/or a mean age at marriage for females significantly below that for males. In fact, this marriage pattern is frequently found in societies where violence, including war, is common and where many young males lose their lives in fighting. Their high combat mortality results in a population where women outnumber men.

By contrast, in societies where men are more heavily involved in productive work, generally only a small minority of marriages are polygynous. Under these circumstances, women are more dependent on men for support, so they are valued as child bearers more than for the work they do. This is commonly the case in pastoral nomadic societies where men are the primary owners and tenders of livestock. This makes women especially vulnerable if they prove incapable of bearing children, which is one reason a man may seek another wife.

Another reason for a man to take on secondary wives is to demonstrate his high position in society. But where men do most of the productive work, they must work extremely hard to support more than one wife, and few actually do so. Usually, it is the exceptional hunter or male shaman ("medicine man") in a food-foraging society or a particularly wealthy man in a horticultural, agricultural, or pastoral society who is most apt to practice polygyny. When he does, it is usually of the *sororal* type, with the co-wives being sisters. Having lived their lives together before marriage, the sisters continue to do so with their husband, instead of occupying separate dwellings of their own.

Polygyny also occurs in a few places in Europe. In 1972, for example, English laws concerning marriage changed to accommodate immigrants who traditionally practiced polygyny. Since that time polygamous marriages have been legal in England for some specific religious minorities, including Muslims and Sephardic Jews. According to one family law specialist, the real impetus behind this law change was a growing concern that "destitute immigrant wives, abandoned by their husbands, [were] overburdening the welfare state."[9]

Even in the United States where it is illegal, somewhere between 20,000 and 60,000 people in the Rocky Mountain states live in households made up of a man with two or more wives.[10] Most consider themselves Mormons, even though the official Mormon Church does not approve of the practice. A growing minority, however, call themselves "Christian polygamists," citing the Bible as justification. Despite its illegality, regional law enforcement officials have adopted a "live and let live" attitude toward polygyny in their region. One woman—a lawyer and one of nine co-wives—expresses her attitude toward polygyny as follows:

> I see it as the ideal way for a woman to have a career and children. In our family, the women can help each other care for the children. Women in monogamous relationships don't have that luxury. As I see it, if this lifestyle didn't already exist, it would have to be invented to accommodate career women.[11]

[6]Lloyd, Cynthia B., Ed. (2005). *Growing up global: The changing transitions to adulthood in developing countries* (pp. 450–453). Washington, DC: National Academies Press, Committee on Population, National Research Council and Institute of Medicine of the National Academies.
[7]Lloyd.
[8]White, D. R. (1988). Rethinking polygyny: Co-wives, codes, and cultural systems. *Current Anthropology, 29,* 529–572.

[9]Cretney, S. (2003). *Family law in the twentieth century: A history* (pp. 72–73). New York: Oxford University Press.
[10]Egan, T. (1999, February 28). The persistence of polygamy. *New York Times Magazine,* 52.
[11]Johnson, D. (1996). Polygamists emerge from secrecy, seeking not just peace but respect. In W. A. Haviland & R. J. Gordon, (Eds.), *Talking about people* (2nd ed., pp. 129–131). Mountain View, CA: Mayfield.

A Christian polygamist poses with his three wives and children in front to their dormitory-style home in Utah, and a Baranarna man of Upper Guinea poses with his two wives and children.

Although monogamy and polygyny are the most common forms of marriage in the world today, other forms do occur. **Polyandry,** the marriage of one woman to two or more men simultaneously, is known in only a few societies, perhaps in part because a woman's life expectancy is usually longer than a man's, and female infant mortality is somewhat lower, so a surplus of women in a society is likely.

Fewer than a dozen societies are known to have favored this form of marriage, but they involve people as widely separated from one another as the eastern Inuit (Eskimos), Marquesan Islanders of Polynesia, and Tibetans. In Tibet, where inheritance is in the male line and arable land is limited, the marriage of brothers to a single woman (*fraternal polyandry*) keeps the land together by preventing it from being repeatedly subdivided among sons from one generation to the next. Unlike monogamy, it also holds down population growth, thereby avoiding increased pressures on resources. Finally, among Tibetans who practice a mixed economy of farming, herding, and trading, fraternal polyandry provides the household with an adequate pool of male labor for all three subsistence activities.[12]

Group Marriage

Group marriage (also known as *co-marriage*), in which several men and women have sexual access to one another, occurs rarely. Among Eskimos in northern Alaska, for instance, sexual relations between unrelated individuals implied ties of mutual aid and support. In order to create or strengthen such ties, a man could lend his wife to another man for temporary sexual relationships: Thus in attracting and holding members of a hunting crew, an *umialik* (whaleboat headman) could lend his wife to a crew member and take his in turn. These men thereafter entered into a partnership relationship, one virtually as strong as kinship. The children of such men, in fact, retained a recognized relationship to each other by virtue of the wife exchange of their parents.[13]

CHOICE OF SPOUSE

The Western egalitarian ideal that an individual should be free to marry whomever he or she chooses is an unusual arrangement, certainly not universally embraced. In many societies, marriage and the establishment of a

polyandry Marriage of a woman to two or more men at one time; a form of polygamy.

group marriage Marriage in which several men and women have sexual access to one another. Also called co-marriage.

[12]Levine, N. E., & Silk, J. B. (1997). Why polyandry fails. *Current Anthropology, 38*, 375–398.

[13]Spencer, R. F. (1984). North Alaska Coast Eskimo. In D. Damas (Ed.), *Arctic*, Vol. 5, *Handbook of North American Indians* (pp. 320–337). Washington, DC: Smithsonian Institution.

family are considered far too important to be left to the whims of young people. The marriage of two individuals who are expected to spend their lives together and raise their children together is viewed as incidental to the more serious matter of making allies of two families through the marriage bond. Marriage involves a transfer of rights between families, including rights to property and rights over children, as well as sexual rights. Thus, marriages tend to be arranged for the economic and political advantage of the family unit.

Although arranged marriages are rare in North American society, they do occur. Among ethnic minorities, they may serve to preserve traditional values that people fear might otherwise be lost. Among families of wealth and power, marriages may be arranged by segregating their children in private schools and carefully steering them toward "proper" marriages. The following Original Study illustrates how marriages may be arranged in societies where such practices are commonplace.

Original Study

Arranging Marriage in India

Six years [after my first field trip to India] I returned to do fieldwork among the middle class in Bombay, a modern, sophisticated city. From the experience of my earlier visit, I decided to include a study of arranged marriages in my project. By this time I had met many Indian couples whose marriages had been arranged and who seemed very happy. Particularly in contrast to the fate of many of my married friends in the United States who were already in the process of divorce, the positive aspects of arranged marriages appeared to me to outweigh the negatives. In fact, I thought I might even participate in arranging a marriage myself. I had been fairly successful in the United States in "fixing up" many of my friends, and I was confident that my matchmaking skills could be easily applied to this new situation, once I learned the basic rules. "After all," I thought, "how complicated can it be?"

An opportunity presented itself almost immediately. A friend from my previous India trip was in the process of arranging for the marriage of her eldest son. Since my friend's family was eminently respectable and the boy himself personable, well educated, and nice looking, I was sure that by the end of my year's fieldwork, we would have found a match.

The basic rule seems to be that a family's reputation is most important. It is understood that matches would be arranged only within the same caste and general social class, although some crossing of subcastes is permissible if the class positions of the bride's and groom's families are similar. Although

dowry is now prohibited by law in India, extensive gift exchanges took place with every marriage. Even when the boy's family does not "make demands," every girl's family nevertheless feels the obligation to give the traditional gifts, to the girl, to the boy, and to the boy's family. Particularly when the couple would be living in the joint family—that is, with the boy's parents and his married brothers and their families, as well as with unmarried siblings, which is still very common even among the urban, upper-middle class in India—the girl's parents are anxious to establish smooth relations between their family and that of the boy. Offering the proper gifts, even when not called "dowry," is often an important factor in influencing the relationship between the bride's and groom's families and perhaps, also, the treatment of the bride in her new home.

In a society where divorce is still a scandal and where, in fact, the divorce rate is exceedingly low, an arranged marriage is the beginning of a lifetime relationship not just between the bride and groom but between their families as well. Thus, while a girl's looks are important, her character is even more so, for she is being judged as a prospective daughter-in-law as much as a prospective bride. . . .

My friend is a highly esteemed wife, mother, and daughter-in-law. She is religious, soft-spoken, modest, and deferential. She rarely gossips and never quarrels, two qualities highly desirable in a woman. A family that has the reputation for gossip and conflict among its womenfolk will not find it easy to get good wives for their sons. Parents

will not want to send their daughter to a house in which there is conflict.

Originally from North India, my friend's family had lived for forty years in Bombay, where her husband owned a business. The family had delayed in seeking a match for their eldest son because he had been an Air Force pilot for several years, stationed in such remote places that it had seemed fruitless to try to find a girl who would be willing to accompany him. In their social class, a military career, despite its economic security, has little prestige and is considered a drawback in finding a suitable bride. Many families would not allow their daughters to marry a man in an occupation so potentially dangerous and that requires so much moving around.

The son had recently left the military and joined his father's business. Since he was a college graduate, modern, and well traveled, from such a good family, and, I thought, quite handsome, it seemed to me that he, or rather his family, was in a position to pick and choose. I said as much to my friend. While she agreed that there were many advantages on their side, she also said, "We must keep in mind that my son is both short and dark; these are drawbacks in finding the right match." While the boy's height had not escaped my notice, "dark" seemed to me inaccurate; I would have called him "wheat" colored perhaps, and in any case, I did not realize that color would be a consideration. I discovered, however, that while a boy's skin color is a less important consideration than a girl's, it is still a factor.

An important source of contacts in trying to arrange her son's marriage was my friend's social club in Bombay. Many of the women had daughters of the right age, and some had already expressed an interest in my friend's son. I was most enthusiastic about the possibilities of one particular family who had five daughters, all of whom were pretty, demure, and well educated. Their mother had told my friend, "You can have your pick for your son, whichever one of my daughters appeals to you most." I saw a match in sight. "Surely," I said to my friend, "we will find one there. Let's go visit and make our choice." But my friend held back; she did not seem to share my enthusiasm, for reasons I could not then fathom.

When I kept pressing for an explanation of her reluctance, she admitted, "See, Serena, here is the problem. The family has so many daughters, how will they be able to provide nicely for any of them? We are not making any demands, but still, with so many daughters to marry off, one wonders whether she will even be able to make a proper wedding. Since this is our eldest son, it's best if we marry him to a girl who is the only daughter, then the wedding will truly be a gala affair." I argued that surely the quality of the girls themselves made up for any deficiency in the elaborateness of the wedding. My friend admitted this point but still seemed reluctant to proceed.

"Is there something else," I asked her, "some factor I have missed?" "Well," she finally said, "there is one other thing. They have one daughter already married and living in Bombay. The mother is always complaining to me that the girl's in-laws don't let her visit her own family often enough. So it makes me wonder, will she be that kind of mother who always wants her

daughter at her own home? This will prevent the girl from adjusting to our house. It is not a good thing." And so, this family of five daughters was dropped as a possibility.

Somewhat disappointed, I nevertheless respected my friend's reasoning and geared up for the next prospect. This was also the daughter of a woman in my friend's social club. There was clear interest in this family and I could see why. The family's reputation was excellent; in fact, they came from a subcaste slightly higher than my friend's own. The girl, who was an only daughter, was pretty and well educated and had a brother studying in the United States. Yet, after expressing an interest to me in this family, all talk of them suddenly died down and the search began elsewhere.

"What happened to that girl as a prospect?" I asked one day. "You never mention her anymore. She is so pretty and so educated, what did you find wrong?"

"She is too educated. We've decided against it. My husband's father saw the girl on the bus the other day and thought her forward. A girl who 'roams about' the city by herself is not the girl for our family." My disappointment this time was even greater, as I thought the son would have liked the girl very much. . . . I learned that if the family of the girl has even a slightly higher social status than the family of the boy, the bride may think herself too good for them, and this too will cause problems. Later my friend admitted to me that this had been an important factor in her decision not to pursue the match. . . .

[After one more candidate, who my friend decided was not attractive enough for her son,] almost six months had passed [and I had become anxious]. My friend laughed at my impatience: "Don't be so much in a hurry," she said. "You Americans want everything done so quickly. You get married quickly and then just as quickly get divorced. Here we take marriage more seriously. We must take all the factors into account. It is not enough for us to learn by our mistakes. This is too serious a business. If a mistake is made we have not only ruined the life of our son or daughter, but we have spoiled the reputation of our family as well. And that will make it

much harder for their brothers and sisters to get married. So we must be very careful."

What she said was true and I promised myself to be more patient. I had really hoped and expected that the match would be made before my year in India was up. But it was not to be. When I left India my friend seemed no further along in finding a suitable match for her son than when I had arrived.

Two years later, I returned to India and still my friend had not found a girl for her son. By this time, he was close to 30, and I think she was a little worried. Since she knew I had friends all over India, and I was going to be there for a year, she asked me to "help her in this work" and keep an eye out for someone suitable. I was flattered that my judgment was respected, but I had lost my earlier confidence as a matchmaker. Nevertheless, I promised that I would try.

It was almost at the end of my year's stay in India that I met a family with a marriageable daughter whom I felt might be a good possibility for my friend's son. . . . This new family had a successful business in a medium-sized city in central India and were from the same subcaste as my friend. The daughter was pretty and chic; in fact, she had studied fashion design in college. Her parents would not allow her to go off by herself to any of the major cities in India where she could make a career, but they had compromised with her wish to work by allowing her to run a small dress-making boutique from their home. In spite of her desire to have a career, the daughter was both modest and home-loving and had had a traditional, sheltered upbringing.

I mentioned the possibility of a match with my friend's son. The girl's parents were most interested. Although their daughter was not eager to marry just yet, the idea of living in Bombay—a sophisticated, extremely fashion-conscious city where she could continue her education in clothing design—was a great inducement. I gave the girl's father my friend's address and suggested that when they went to Bombay on some business or whatever, they look up the boy's family.

Returning to Bombay on my way to New York, I told my friend of this newly

[continued]

[continued]

discovered possibility. She seemed to feel there was potential but, in spite of my urging, would not make any moves herself. She rather preferred to wait for the girl's family to call upon them.

A year later I received a letter from my friend. The family had indeed come to visit Bombay, and their daughter and my friend's daughter, who were near in age, had become very good friends. During that year, the two girls had frequently visited each other. I thought things looked promising.

Last week I received an invitation to a wedding: My friend's son and the girl were getting married. Since I had found the match, my presence was particularly requested at the wedding.

I was thrilled. Success at last! As I prepared to leave for India, I began thinking, "Now, my friend's younger son, who do I know who has a nice girl for him . . . ?" *(By S. Nanda, (1992). Arranging a marriage in India. In P. R. De Vita (Ed.). The naked anthropologist (pp. 139–143). Belmont, CA: Wadsworth.)* ▪ ▪ ▪

Cousin Marriage

While cousin marriage is prohibited in some societies, certain cousins are the preferred marriage partners in others. A **parallel cousin** is the child of a father's brother or a mother's sister (Figure 13.1). In some societies, the preferred spouse for a man is his father's brother's daughter (or, from the woman's point of view, her father's brother's son). This is known as *patrilateral parallel-cousin marriage*. Although not obligatory, such marriages have been favored historically among Arabs, the ancient Israelites, and the ancient Greeks. All of these societies are (or were) hierarchical in nature—that is, some people are ranked higher than others because they have more power and property—and although male dominance and descent are emphasized, property of value to men is inherited by daughters as well as sons. Thus, when a man marries his father's brother's daughter (or a woman marries her father's brother's son), property is retained within the single male line of descent. In these societies, generally speaking, the greater the property, the more this form of parallel-cousin marriage is apt to occur.

A **cross cousin** is the child of a mother's brother or a father's sister (Figure 13.1). Some societies favor *matrilateral cross-cousin marriage*—marriage of a man to his mother's brother's daughter, or a woman to her father's sister's son. This preference exists among food foragers (such as the Australian aborigines) and some farming cultures (including various peoples of South India). Among food foragers, who inherit relatively little in the way of property, such marriages help establish and maintain ties of solidarity between social groups. In agricultural societies, however, the transmission of property is an important determinant. In societies that trace descent exclusively in the female line, for instance, property and other important rights usually pass from a man to his sister's son; under cross-cousin marriage, the sister's son is also the man's daughter's husband.

Same-Sex Marriage

As noted earlier in this chapter, our definition of marriage refers to a union between "people" rather than

parallel cousin   Child of a father's brother or a mother's sister.

cross cousin   Child of a mother's brother or a father's sister.

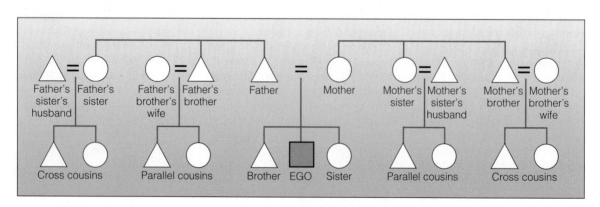

Figure 13.1
Anthropologists use diagrams of this sort to illustrate kinship relationships. Shown in this one is the distinction between cross and parallel cousins. In such diagrams, males are always shown as triangles, females as circles, marital ties by an =, sibling relationships as a horizontal line, and parent–child relationships as a vertical line. Terms are given from the perspective of the individual labeled EGO, who can be female or male.

"a man and a woman" because in some societies same-sex marriages are socially acceptable and officially allowed by law. Marriages between individuals of the same sex may provide a way of dealing with problems for which opposite-sex marriage offers no satisfactory solution. This is the case with woman–woman marriage, a practice permitted in many societies of sub-Saharan Africa, although in none does it involve more than a small minority of all women.

Details differ from one society to another, but woman–woman marriages among the Nandi of western Kenya may be taken as representative of such practices in Africa.[14] The Nandi are a pastoral people who also do considerable farming. Control of most significant property and the primary means of production—livestock and land—is exclusively in the hands of men and may only be transmitted to their male heirs, usually their sons. Since polygyny is the preferred form of marriage, a man's property is normally divided equally among his wives for their sons to inherit. Within the household, each wife has her own home in which she lives with her children, but all are under the authority of the woman's husband, who is a remote and aloof figure within the household. In such situations, the position of a woman who bears no sons is difficult; not only does she not help perpetuate her husband's male line—a major concern among the Nandi—but also she has no one to inherit the proper share of her husband's property.

To get around these problems, a woman of advanced age who bore no sons may become a female husband by marrying a young woman. The purpose of this arrangement is for the young wife to provide the male heirs her female husband could not. To accomplish this, the woman's wife enters into a sexual relationship with a man

other than her female husband's male husband; usually it is one of his male relatives. No other obligations exist between this woman and her male sex partner, and her female husband is recognized as the social and legal father of any children born under these conditions.

In keeping with her role as female husband, this woman is expected to abandon her female gender identity and, ideally, dress and behave as a man. In practice, the ideal is not completely achieved, for the habits of a lifetime are difficult to reverse. Generally, it is in the context of domestic activities, which are most highly symbolic of female identity, that female husbands most completely assume a male identity.

The individuals who are parties to woman–woman marriages enjoy several advantages. By assuming male identity, a barren or sonless woman raises her status considerably and even achieves near equality with men, who otherwise occupy a far more favored position in Nandi society than women. A woman who marries a female husband is usually one who is unable to make a good marriage, often because she (the female husband's wife) has lost face as a consequence of premarital pregnancy. By marrying a female husband, she too raises her status and also secures legitimacy for her children. Moreover, a female husband is usually less harsh and demanding, spends more time with her, and allows her a greater say in decision making than a male husband does. The one thing she may not do is engage in sexual activity with her marriage partner. In fact, female husbands are expected to abandon sexual activity altogether, even with their male husbands to whom they remain married even though the women now have their own wives.

In contrast to woman–woman marriages among the Nandi are same-sex marriages that include sexual activity between partners. Over the past decade, the legal recognition of such unions has become a matter of vigorous debate in some parts of the world. Several countries, including Spain, Belgium, Canada, and the Netherlands, have passed laws legalizing gay marriages, as has the state of Massachusetts. Meanwhile numerous U.S. states have adopted constitutional amendments barring same-sex marriage.

The arguments most commonly marshaled by opponents of same-sex unions are, first, that marriage has always been between males and females, but as we have just seen, this is not true. Same-sex marriages have been documented not only for a number of societies in Africa but in other parts of the world as well. As among the Nandi, they provide acceptable positions in society for individuals who might otherwise be marginalized.

A second argument against same-sex unions is that they legitimize gays and lesbians, whose sexual orientations have been widely regarded as unnatural. But again, as discussed in earlier chapters, neither cross-cultural studies nor studies of other animal species suggest that homosexual behavior is unnatural.

A third argument, that the function of marriage is to produce children, is at best a partial truth, as marriage involves economic, political, and legal considerations as

---

[14]The following is based on Obler, R. S. (1982). Is the female husband a man? Woman/woman marriage among the Nandi of Kenya. *Ethnology, 19,* 69–88.

well. Moreover, it is increasingly common for same-sex partners to have children through adoption or by turning to modern reproductive technologies. There is also the fact that in many societies, such as the Nandi, there is a separation between the sexual and reproductive attributes of women.

MARRIAGE AND ECONOMIC EXCHANGE

Marriages in many human societies are formalized by some sort of economic exchange. This may take the form of a gift exchange or something known as **bride-price** or *bride wealth*, which involves payments of money or valuable goods to a bride's parents or other close kin. This usually happens in patrilineal societies where the bride will become a member of the household where her husband grew up; this household will benefit from her labor as well as from the offspring she produces. Thus, her family must be compensated for their loss.

Not only is bride-price *not* a simple "buying and selling" of women, but the bride's parents may use the money to purchase jewelry or household furnishings for her or to finance an elaborate and costly wedding celebration. It also contributes to the stability of the marriage, because it usually must be refunded if the couple separates. Other forms of compensation are an exchange of women between families—"My son will marry your daughter if your son will marry my daugh-

ter." Yet another is **bride service,** a period of time during which the groom works for the bride's family.

In a number of societies more or less restricted to the western, southern, and eastern margins of Eurasia, where the economy is based on agriculture, women often bring a dowry with them at marriage. A form of dowry in the United States is the custom of the bride's family paying the wedding expenses. In effect, a **dowry** is a woman's share of parental property that, instead of passing to her upon her parents' death, is distributed to her at the time of her marriage. This does not mean that she retains control of this property after marriage. In some European countries, for example, a woman's property traditionally falls exclusively under her husband's control. Having benefited by what she has brought to the marriage, however, he is obligated to look out for her future well-being, including her security after his death.

Thus, one of the functions of dowry is to ensure a woman's support in widowhood (or after divorce), an important consideration in a society where men carry out the bulk of productive work and women are valued for their reproductive potential rather than for the work they do. In such societies, women incapable of bearing children are especially vulnerable, but the dowry they bring with them at marriage helps protect them against desertion. Another function of dowry is to reflect the economic status of the woman in societies where differences in wealth are important. It also permits women, with the

bride-price Compensation the groom or his family pays to the bride's family upon marriage. Also called bride wealth.

bride service A designated period of time after marriage when the groom works for the bride's family.

dowry Payment of a woman's inheritance at the time of her marriage, either to her or to her husband.

In some societies when a woman marries, she receives her share of the family inheritance (her dowry), which she brings to her new family (unlike bride-price, which passes from the groom's family to the bride's family). Shown here are Slovakian women carrying the objects of a woman's dowry.

© John Eastcott/Yva Momatiuk/Woodfin Camp & Associates

aid of their parents and kin, to compete through dowry for desirable (that is, wealthy) husbands.

DIVORCE

Like marriage, divorce in most societies is a matter of great concern to the couple's families. Since marriage is less often a religious matter than it is an economic one, divorce arrangements can be made for a variety of reasons and with varying degrees of difficulty. Among the Gusii farmers of western Kenya, sterility or impotence are grounds for a divorce. Among the Chenchu foragers inhabiting the thickly forested hills in central India and certain aboriginal peoples in northern Canada, divorce was discouraged after children were born; couples usually were urged by their families to adjust their differences. By contrast, in the southwestern United States, a Hopi Indian woman in Arizona could divorce her husband at any time merely by placing his belongings outside the door to indicate he was no longer welcome.

An adult unmarried woman is very rare in most non-Western societies where a divorced woman usually soon remarries. In many societies, economic considerations are often the strongest motivation to wed. On the island of New Guinea, a man does not marry because of sexual needs, which he can readily satisfy out of wedlock, but because he needs a woman to make pots and cook his meals, to fabricate nets and weed his plantings. Likewise, women in communities that depend for security upon males capable of fighting need husbands who are raised to be able warriors as well as good hunters.

Although divorce rates may be high in various corners of the world, they have become so high in Western industrial and postindustrial societies that many worry about the future of what they view as traditional and familiar forms of marriage and the family. It is interesting to note that although divorce was next to impossible in Western societies between 1000 and 1800, few marriages lasted more than about 10 or 20 years, owing to high mortality rates, due in part to inadequate health care and medical expertise with often deadly consequences for young and old alike.[15] With increased longevity, separation by death has diminished, and separation by legal action has grown. In the United States, some 50 percent of first marriages end in divorce—twice the 1960 divorce rate but slightly less than the high point in the early 1980s.[16]

---

[15]Stone, L. (1998). *Kinship and gender: An introduction* (p. 235). Boulder, CO: Westview Press.

[16]Whitehead, B. D. & Popenoe, D. (2004). *The state of our unions: The social health of marriage in America 2004*. Rutgers, NJ: Rutgers University National Marriage Project.

FAMILY AND HOUSEHOLD

Dependence on group living for survival is a basic human characteristic. We have inherited this from primate ancestors, although we have developed it in our own distinctly human way. However each culture may define what constitutes a family, this social unit forms the basic cooperative structure that ensures an individual's primary needs and provides the necessary care for children to develop as healthy and productive members of the group and thereby help ensure its future.

In most human societies, new families are **conjugal,** that is, established through marriage. That said, historical and cross-cultural studies of the family reveal a wide variety of family patterns, and these patterns may change over time. Thus, the definition of **family** is necessarily broad: Two or more people related by blood, marriage, or adoption. The family may take many forms, ranging from a single parent with one or more children, to a married couple or polygamous spouses with offspring, to several generations of parents and their children.

In all known cultures, past and present, gender plays at least some role in determining the household division of labor. An effective way to facilitate economic cooperation between men and women and simultaneously provide for a close bond between mother and child is through the establishment of residential groups that include adults of both sexes. The differing nature of male and female roles, as defined by different cultures, makes it advantageous for a child to have an adult of the same sex available to serve as a proper model for the appropriate adult role. The presence of adult men and women in the same residential group provides for this. The men, however, need not be the women's husbands. In some societies they are the women's brothers.

Well suited though the family may be for these tasks, other arrangements exist. In many food-foraging societies (such as the Ju/'hoansi discussed in earlier chapters), all adult members of a community share in the responsibilities of child care. Thus, when parents go off to hunt or to collect plants and herbs, they may leave their children behind, secure in the knowledge they will be looked after by whatever adults remain in the camp.

---

conjugal family A family established through marriage.
family Two or more people related by blood, marriage, or adoption. The family may take many forms, ranging from a single parent with one or more children, to a married couple or polygamous spouses with offspring, to several generations of parents and their children.

Yet another domestic arrangement may be seen among the Mundurucu, a horticultural people living in the center of Brazil's Amazon rainforest. In Mundurucu Indian villages, boys live in houses with their mothers and sisters, separate from all men until the age of 13. At that point the boys move into the men's house. Their sisters, on the other hand, continue to live with their mothers and the younger boys in two or three houses grouped around the men's house. Married men and women are members of separate households, meeting periodically for sexual activity. This illustrates that *family* and *household* are not always synonymous.

For purposes of cross-cultural comparison, anthropologists define the **household** as the basic residential unit where economic production, consumption, inheritance, child rearing, and shelter are organized and carried out. Given this broad definition, the household is considered universally present and comes in many forms. In the vast majority of human societies, most households are made up of families. Although some households consist of a single individual, typically they include more than one person. Often, a household may consist of one nuclear family along with some other relatives. But there are many other arrangements. For instance, among the Mundurucu, just noted, the men's house constitutes one household inhabited by adult males and their sexually mature sons, and the women's houses, inhabited by adult women and prepubescent boys and girls, constitute others. In other situations, coresidents of a household may be unrelated, such as the service personnel in an elaborate royal household, apprentices in the household of craft specialists, or low-status clients in the household of rich and powerful patrons.

Forms of the Family

According to a cross-cultural survey of family types in 192 cultures around the world, the extended family is most common, present in about 48 percent of those cultures, compared to the nuclear family at 25 percent, and polygamous at 22 percent.[17] Each of these is discussed below.

---

household   The basic residential unit where economic production, consumption, inheritance, child rearing, and shelter are organized and carried out.

---

[17]Winick, C. (Ed.). (1970). *Dictionary of anthropology* (p. 202). Totowa, NJ: Littlefield, Adams, & Co.

The Nuclear Family

The smallest family unit is known as the **nuclear family,** a group consisting of one or two parents and dependent offspring, which may include a stepparent, stepsiblings, and adopted children. Until recently, the term *nuclear family* referred solely to the mother, father, and child(ren) unit—the family form that Europeans and North Americans generally regarded as the "normal" or "natural" nucleus of larger family units. In the United States father/mother/child(ren) nuclear family households reached their highest frequency around 1950, when 60 percent of all households conformed to this model.[18] Today such families comprise only 24 percent of U.S. households.[19]

Industrialization has played a role in shaping the nuclear family. One reason for this is that industrial economies require a mobile labor force; people must be prepared to move to where the jobs are, something that is most easily done without excess kin in tow. Also, in the United States and many European countries it is not generally considered desirable for young people to live with their parents beyond a certain age, nor is it considered a moral responsibility for a couple to take their aged parents into their home when the old people can no longer care for themselves. Retirement communities and nursing homes provide these services, and younger members of the industrialized world's mobile workforce increasingly rely on them to care for their parents.

The nuclear family is also likely to be prominent in foraging societies such as that of the Inuit people who live in the harsh Arctic environments of Canada and Greenland. In the winter the traditional Inuit husband and wife, with their children, roam the vast snowscape in their quest for food. The husband hunts and makes shelters. The wife cooks, is responsible for the children, and makes the clothing and keeps it in good repair. One of her chores is to chew her husband's boots to soften the leather for the next day so that he can resume his quest for game. The wife and her children could not survive without the husband, and life for a man is unimaginable without a wife.

---

nuclear family   A group consisting of one or more parents and dependent offspring, which may include a stepparent, stepsiblings, and adopted children. (Until recently this term referred only to the father/mother/children unit.)

---

[18]Stacey, J. (1990). *Brave New families* (pp. 5, 10). New York: Basic Books.
[19]Irvine, M. (1999, November 24). Mom-and-pop houses grow rare. *Burlington Free Press*; *Current population survey*. (2002). U.S. Census Bureau.

Among Inuit people who still hunt for much of their food, nuclear families such as the one shown here are typical. However, in contrast to nuclear families in Europe and the United States, their isolation from other relatives is usually temporary. Much of the time they are found in groups of at least a few related families.

Similar to nuclear families in industrial societies, those living under especially harsh environmental conditions must be prepared to fend for themselves. Such isolation comes with its own set of challenges, including the difficulties of rearing children without multigenerational support and a lack of familial care for the elderly. Nonetheless, this form of family is well adapted to a mode of subsistence that requires a high degree of geographical mobility. For the Inuit, this mobility permits the hunt for food; for other North Americans, the hunt for jobs and improved social status requires a mobile form of family unit.

The Extended Family

When two or more closely related nuclear families cluster together into a large domestic group, they form a unit known as the **extended family.** This larger family unit, common in traditional farming and herding cultures around the world, typically consists of siblings with their spouses and offspring, and often their parents. All of these kin, some related "by blood" and some by marriage, live and work together for the common good and deal with outsiders as a single unit. Because members of the younger generation bring their husbands or wives to live in the family, extended families have continuity through time. As older members die off, new members are born into the family. Extended families have built into them particular challenges. Among these

are difficulties that the in-marrying spouse is likely to have in adjusting to his or her spouse's family.

Nontraditional Families and Nonfamily Households

In North America and parts of Europe, increasing numbers of people live in nonfamily households, either alone or with nonrelatives (Figure 13.2). In fact, some 32 percent of households in the United States fall into this category.[20] Many others live as members of what are often called nontraditional families. These include single-parent households. Such households are often the result of divorce or a marriage partner's death. They also stem from increased sexual activity outside of wedlock, combined with declining marriage rates among women of childbearing age, as well as a rise in the number of women actively choosing single motherhood. About a third of all births in the United States occur outside of marriage, and in several northwestern European countries, the nonmarital birthrate is close to 50 percent.[21]

The percentage of single-parent households in the United States has grown to 9 percent, while the number comprised of married couples with children has dropped to 24 percent. Although single-parent households account for just 9 percent of all households in the United States, they are home to 28 percent of all

extended family Several closely related nuclear families clustered together into a large domestic group.

[20]*Current population survey.*
[21]*Recent demographic developments in Europe—2000.* Council of Europe.

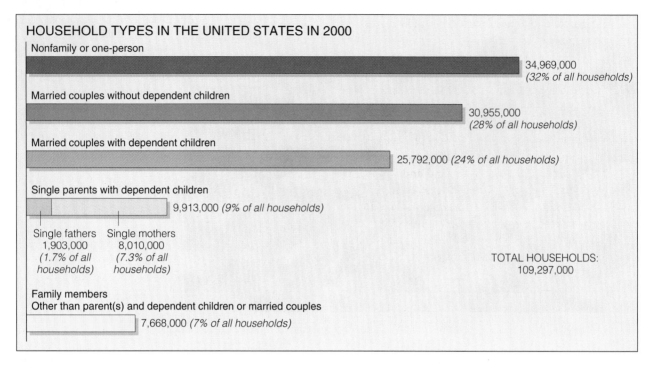

Figure 13.2
Household types in the United States, based on U.S. Census Bureau figures for 2000.
Current population survey. (2002). U.S. Census Bureau.

children (under 18 years of age) in the country.[22] In the vast majority of cases, a child living in a single-parent household is with his or her mother. Fathers are usually required to pay child support but are not always able or willing to do so. And when they do pay, the amount is often insufficient for essential food, clothing and medical care, let alone the cost of child care so that the woman can seek or continue income-producing work to support herself. Notably, single fathers in the United States are three times more likely to have a cohabiting partner in the home than are single mothers.

RESIDENCE PATTERNS

Where some form of conjugal or extended family is the norm, family exogamy requires that either the husband or wife, if not both, must move to a new household upon marriage. There are five common patterns of residence that a newly married couple may adopt—the prime determinant being ecological circumstances,

although other factors enter in as well. Thus, postmarital residence arrangements, far from being arbitrary, are adaptive in character. Here we will mention only the three most common arrangements.

Patrilocal residence is when a woman goes to live with her husband in his father's place of residence. This arrangement is favorable in situations where men play a predominant role in subsistence, particularly if they own property that can be accumulated, if polygyny is customary, if warfare is prominent enough to make cooperation among men especially important, and if an elaborate political organization exists in which men wield authority. These conditions are most often found together in societies that rely on animal husbandry and/or intensive agriculture for their subsistence. Where patrilocal residence is customary, the bride often must move to a different band or community. In such cases, her parents' family is not only losing the services of a useful family member, but they are losing her potential offspring as well. Hence, some kind of compensation to her family, most commonly bride-price, is usual.

patrilocal residence   A residence pattern in which a married couple lives in the locality associated with the husband's father's relatives.

---

[22]*Current population survey.*

Matrilocal residence, where the man leaves the family he grew up in to go live with his wife in her mother's place of residence, household, is a likely result if ecological circumstances make the role of the woman predominate for subsistence. It is found most often in horticultural societies, where political organization is relatively uncentralized and where cooperation among women is important. The Hopi Indians provide one example. Although it is the Hopi men who do the farming, the women control access to land and "own" the harvest. Indeed, men are not even allowed in the granaries. Under matrilocal residence, men usually do not move very far from the family in which they were raised so they are available to help out there from time to time. Therefore, marriage usually does not involve compensation to the groom's family.

Under **neolocal residence,** a married couple forms a household in a separate location. This occurs where the independence of the nuclear family is emphasized. In industrial societies such as the United States, where most economic activity occurs outside rather than inside the family and where it is important

> **matrilocal residence** A residence pattern in which a married couple lives in the locality associated with the wife's parents.
> **neolocal residence** A pattern in which a married couple establish their household in a location apart from either the husband's or the wife's parents.

for individuals to be able to move where jobs can be found, neolocal residence is better suited than any of the other patterns.

FAMILY IN OUR GLOBALIZED AND TECHNOLOGIZED WORLD

In many countries the mosaic of family forms has become more varied in recent decades. Many factors contribute to this, including global capitalism and large-scale emigration of peoples moving across cultural boundaries. Also significant are high rates of divorce and remarriage, resulting in *blended families* comprised of a married couple raising children together from previous unions. Other contributing factors include *new reproductive technologies* (NRTs), such as in vitro fertilization, as well as open adoption, which makes it possible for a child to have a relationship with both the biological and adoptive parents.

As the ethnographic examples in this chapter illustrate, our species has invented a wide variety of marriage, household, and family forms, each in correspondence with related features in the social structure and conforming to the larger cultural system. In the face of new challenges, we explore and tinker in search of solutions, sometimes resulting in finding completely new forms, and other times returning to time-tested formulas of more traditional varieties.

Chapter Summary

■ Managing sexual relations and establishing social alliances are essential to the survival of individuals and their offspring. Every society has incest and marriage rules that help accomplish this. Marriage can be broadly defined as a culturally sanctioned union between two or more people that establishes certain rights and obligations between the people, between them and their children, and between them and their in-laws.

■ Incest taboos forbid sexual relations between certain close relatives—usually between parent–child and siblings at a minimum. A truly convincing explanation of the incest taboo has yet to be advanced, but it is related to the practices of endogamy (marrying within a group of individuals) and exogamy (marrying outside a group). If the group is limited to the immediate family, almost all societies can be said to prohibit endogamy and practice exogamy. Likewise, societies that practice exogamy at one level may practice endogamy at another.

■ A majority of cultures are sexually permissive and do not sharply regulate personal sexual practices. Others are restrictive and explicitly prohibit all sexual activity outside of marriage. Of these, a few punish adultery by imprisonment, social exclusion, or even death, as traditionally prescribed by some religious laws.

■ Marriage, in contrast to mating, is backed by social, legal, and economic forces. It falls into several broad categories. Monogamy, or the taking of a single spouse, is the most common form of marriage, primarily for economic reasons. Serial monogamy, in which a man or woman marries a series of partners, has become common among Europeans and North Americans. Polygamy, in which one individual has multiple spouses, comes in two forms: polygyny and polyandry. A man must have a certain amount of wealth to be able to afford polygyny, or marriage to more than one wife at the same time. Yet in societies where women do most of the productive work, polygyny may serve as a means of generating wealth for a household. Although few marriages in a given society may be polygynous, it is regarded as an appropriate, and even preferred, form of marriage in the majority of the world's societies. Since few communities have a surplus of men, polyandry, or the custom of a woman having several husbands, is uncommon. Also rare is group marriage, in which several men and several women have sexual access to one another.

■ In industrial and postindustrial countries of the West, marriages are generally based on ideals of romantic love. Other parts of the world do not risk marriages based on such youthful whims. In non-Western societies, economic considerations are of major concern in arranging marriages, and marriage serves to bind two families as allies.

■ Preferred marriage partners in many societies are particular cross cousins (mother's brother's daughter if a man; father's sister's son if a woman) or, less commonly, parallel cousins on the paternal side (father's brother's son or daughter). Cross-cousin marriage is a means of establishing and maintaining solidarity between groups.

■ In many human societies, marriages are formalized by some sort of economic exchange—such as a reciprocal gift exchange between the bride's and groom's relatives. More common is bride-price, the payment of money or other valuables from the groom's to the bride's kin. Bride service occurs when the groom is expected to work for a period for the bride's family. A dowry is the payment of a woman's inheritance at the time of marriage to her or her husband. Its purpose is to ensure support for women in societies where men do most of the productive work, and women are valued primarily for their reproductive potential.

■ Same-sex marriages exist in some societies. For example, woman–woman marriages as practiced in some African cultures provide a socially approved way to deal with problems for which heterosexual marriages offer no satisfactory solution. In recent years Belgium, Canada, Spain, and the Netherlands legalized same-sex marriage.

■ Divorce is possible in all societies, although reasons and frequency vary cross-culturally.

■ Dependence on group living for survival is a basic human characteristic, and gender plays at least some role in the division of labor. The presence of adults of both sexes in a residential group is advantageous, providing children with adult models from whom they can learn the gender-appropriate roles as defined in that society.

■ The family may take many forms, ranging from a single parent with one or more children, to a married couple or polygamous spouses with offspring, to several generations of parents and their children. A family is distinct from a household, which is the basic residential unit where economic production, consumption, inheritance, child rearing, and shelter are organized and carried out. In the vast majority of human societies, most households are made up of families or parts of families, but there are many other household arrangements.

■ The smallest domestic unit is the nuclear family—a group consisting of one or two parents and dependent offspring, which may include a stepparent, stepsiblings, and adopted children. Until recently, the term referred solely to the mother, father, and child(ren) unit. This family form is common in the industrial and postindustrial countries of North America and Europe and also in societies that live in harsh environments, as do the Inuit. It is well suited to the mobility required both in food-foraging groups and in industrial societies where job changes are frequent. The extended family consists of several closely related nuclear families living and often working together in a single household.

■ Three common residence patterns are patrilocal (in which a married couple lives in the locality of the husband's father's place of residence), matrilocal (living in the locality of the wife's mother's place of residence), and neolocal (living in a locality apart from the husband's or wife's parents).

■ In North America and parts of Europe, increasing numbers of people live in nonfamily households, either alone or with nonrelatives. Many others live as members of what are often called nontraditional families, including single-parent households and blended families. New reproductive technologies are adding a new dimension to familial relationships.

Questions for Reflection

1. Raising children is a challenge not only for parents but also for the larger community. Why do you think your own culture has developed the kind of family and household organization most familiar to you? Why do you think those particular organizational forms came into being? Can you imagine under which circumstances these arrangements may become inadequate?

2. Members of traditional communities in countries where the state is either weak or absent depend on relatives to help meet the basic challenges of survival. In such traditional societies, why would it be risky to have romantic love as the exclusive basis for marriage? Can you imagine other factors playing a role if the long-term survival of your community is at stake?

3. Many people in North America and Europe choose to have children outside marriage. Considering some of the major functions of marriage, do you think there is a relationship between the type of society an individual belongs to and the choice to forgo the traditional benefits of marriage? Under what cultural conditions might the choice to remain unmarried present serious challenges?

4. Although most women in Europe and North America view polygyny as a marriage practice exclusively benefiting men, women in cultures where such marriages are traditional sometimes stress more positive sides of sharing a husband with several co-wives. Under which conditions do you think polygyny could be considered as relatively beneficial for women?

5. Single motherhood in North America has typically been seen as something tied to low income, yet it is becoming increasingly common among women across the economic spectrum. What do you consider to be the reasons for this, based on the barrel model of culture with its three tiers of infrastructure, social structure, and superstructure?

Key Terms

marriage
incest taboo
endogamy
exogamy
monogamy
serial monogamy
polygamy
polygyny
polyandry
group marriage
parallel cousin
cross cousin

bride-price
bride service
dowry
conjugal family
family
household
nuclear family
extended family
patrilocal residence
matrilocal residence
neolocal residence

Multimedia Review Tools

Make the Grade in Anthropology with ThomsonNOW

Thomson NOW! This powerful online study tool provides you with a *personalized study plan* based on your responses to a diagnostic pretest. Once you have mastered the material with the help of interactive learning tools, an integrated e-book, and more, you can take a post-test to confirm you are ready to move on to the next chapter. To get started with ThomsonNOW, check the card packaged with your book for the access code. Then go to http://www.thomsonedu.com to create an account through 1pass™. If there is no card in your book, go to http://www.thomsonedu.com to purchase an access code.

Companion Website and Anthropology Resource Center

Go to http://anthropology.wadsworth.com to reach the companion website for your text. This offers many study aids, including self quizzes for each chapter and a practice final exam, as well as links to anthropology websites and information on the latest theories and discoveries in the field.

Also, check out the Anthropology Resource Center for a wealth of learning materials that include interactive maps, video exercises, simulations, and breaking news in anthropology. Be sure to explore InfoTrac College Edition®, your online library that offers full-length articles from thousands of scholarly and popular publications. To reach the Anthropology Resource Center and InfoTrac College Edition, check the card packaged with your book for the access code. Then go to http://www.thomsonedu.com to create an account through 1pass™. If there is no card in your book, go to http://www.thomsonedu.com to purchase an access code.

©Wally Turnbull

All humans face the challenge of creating and maintaining social networks that reach beyond the capabilities of immediate family or household to provide support and security. On a very basic level such networks are arranged by kinship. In the highlands of Scotland, as among many traditional peoples around the world, large kinship groups known as clans have been important units of social organization. Now dispersed all over the world, Scottish clan members gather and express their kinship with one another by wearing a tartan skirt, or kilt, with a distinct plaid pattern and color identifying clan membership. Shown here is a Turnbull clan gathering in Stone Mountain, Georgia.

Kinship and Other Methods of Grouping

14

All societies rely on some form of family and/or household organization to effectively deal with basic human challenges: regulating sexual activities, coordinating work, and organizing child rearing. As efficient and flexible as family and household organization may be for meeting such challenges, many societies confront problems that are beyond the coping ability of family and household organization. For example, members of one independent local group often need some means of interacting with neighboring groups, of claiming support and protection from individuals in another group. This can be important for defense against natural or human-made disasters. Also, a group frequently needs to share rights to a natural resource that is difficult to divide or exclusively control, such as a large tract of land, stretch of water, or a wild herd of migratory animals. Finally, people often need some means of providing cooperative work forces for tasks that require more participants than households alone can provide.

Many ways to deal with such challenges exist. One is through a formal political system, with personnel to make and enforce laws, keep the peace, allocate resources, and perform other regulatory and societal functions. A more common way in nonindustrial societies—especially foraging, crop-cultivating, and pastoral societies—is by means of **kinship**, a network of relatives within which individuals possess certain mutual rights and obligations.

kinship A network of relatives within which individuals possess certain mutual rights and obligations.

DESCENT GROUPS

A common way of organizing a society along kinship lines is by creating what anthropologists call descent groups. Found in many societies, a **descent group** is any kinship group with a membership lineally descending from a real (historical) or fictional common ancestor. The addition of a few culturally meaningful obligations and taboos acts as a kind of glue to help hold the structured social group together.

Besides acting as economic units providing mutual aid to their members, descent groups may act to support the aged and infirm and help with marriages and deaths. Often, they play a role in determining who an individual may or may not marry. Also, the descent group may act as a repository of religious traditions. Ancestor worship, for example, is often a powerful force acting to reinforce group solidarity.

Descent group membership must be sharply defined in order to operate effectively. If membership is allowed to overlap, it is unclear where someone's primary loyalty belongs. Membership can be restricted in a number of ways. The most common way is by tracing membership exclusively through one gender in what anthropologists refer to as *unilineal descent*.

Unilineal Descent

Unilineal descent (sometimes called *unilateral descent*) establishes descent group membership exclusively through the male or the female line. In non-Western societies, unilineal descent groups are quite common. The individual is assigned at birth to membership in a specific descent group, which may be traced either by **matrilineal descent**, through the female line, or by **patrilineal descent**, through the male line, depending on the culture. In patrilineal societies the males are far more important than the females, for they are considered responsible for the group's continued existence. In matrilineal societies, this responsibility falls on the female members of the group, whose importance is thereby enhanced.

The two major forms of a unilineal descent group, be it patrilineal or matrilineal, are the lineage and the clan. A **lineage** is a unilineal kinship group descended from a known ancestor or founder, who commonly lived about five generations ago, and in which relationships between each member can be exactly stated in genealogical terms. A **clan** is an extended unilineal kinship group, often consisting of several lineages, whose members claim common descent from a remote ancestor, usually legendary or mythological.[1]

Patrilineal Descent and Organization

Patrilineal descent is the more widespread of the two unilineal descent systems. The male members of a patrilineal descent group trace through forefathers their descent from a common ancestor (Figure 14.1). Brothers and sisters belong to the descent group of their father's father, their father, their father's siblings, and their father's brother's children. A man's son and daughter also trace their descent back through the male line to their common ancestor. In the typical patrilineal group, authority over the children rests with the father or his elder brother. A woman belongs to the same descent group as her father and his brothers, but her children cannot trace their descent through them.

Matrilineal Descent and Organization

As the term implies, matrilineal descent is traced exclusively through the female line (Figure 14.2), just as patrilineal descent is through the male line. However, the matrilineal pattern differs from the patrilineal in that it does not automatically confer gender authority. Although descent passes through the female line and women may have considerable power, they do not hold exclusive authority in the descent group. They share it with men. Usually, these are the brothers, rather than the husbands, of the women through whom descent is traced. Apparently, the adaptive purpose of matrilineal systems is to provide continuous female solidarity within the female work group. Matrilineal systems are usually found in horticultural societies in which women perform much of the work in the house and nearby gardens. In part because women's labor as crop cultivators is regarded as so important to the society, matrilineal descent prevails.

---

descent group Any kinship group with a membership lineally descending from a real (historical) or fictional common ancestor.

unilineal descent Descent that establishes group membership exclusively through either the male or female line.

matrilineal descent Descent traced exclusively through the female line to establish group membership.

patrilineal descent Descent traced exclusively through the male line to establish group membership.

---

lineage A unilineal kinship group descended from a known ancestor or founder, who commonly lived about five generations ago, and in which relationships between each member can be exactly stated in genealogical terms.

clan An extended unilineal kinship group, often consisting of several lineages, whose members claim common descent from a remote ancestor, usually legendary or mythological.

---

[1] See Hoebel, E.A. (1949) *Man in the primitive world: An introduction to anthropology* (pp. 646, 652). New York: McGraw-Hill.

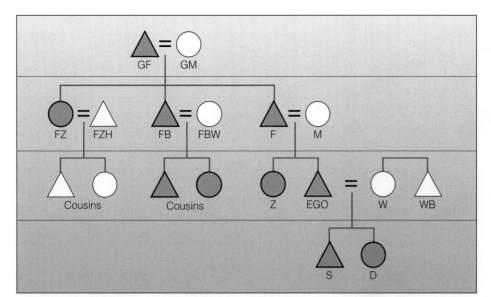

Figure 14.1
How patrilineal descent is traced. Only the individuals symbolized by a filled-in circle or triangle are in the same descent group as EGO. The abbreviation F stands for father, B for brother, H for husband, S for son, M for mother, Z for sister, D for daughter, and W for wife.

In a matrilineal system, brothers and sisters belong to the descent group of the mother, the mother's mother, the mother's siblings, and the mother's sisters' children. Thus, every male belongs to the same descent group as his mother, and a man's own children belong to his wife's descent group, not his.

Although not true of all matrilineal systems, a common feature is the relative weakness of the social tie between wife and husband. A woman's husband lacks authority in the household they share. Her brother, and not the husband-father, distributes goods, organizes work, settles disputes, administers inheritance and succession rules, and supervises rituals. Meanwhile, her husband fulfills the same role in his own sister's household. Furthermore, his property and status are inherited by his sister's son rather than his son. Thus, brothers and sisters maintain lifelong ties with one another, whereas

marital ties are easily severed. In matrilineal societies, unsatisfactory marriages are more easily ended than in patrilineal societies.

Other Forms of Descent

Among Samoan Islanders (and many other cultures in the Pacific as well as in Southeast Asia) a person has the option of affiliating with either the mother's or the father's descent group. Known as *ambilineal descent*, such a kin-ordered system provides a measure of flexibility. However, this flexibility also introduces a possibility of dispute and conflict as unilineal groups compete for members.

This problem does not arise under *double descent*, or double unilineal descent, a very rare system whereby descent is reckoned both patrilineally and matrilineally

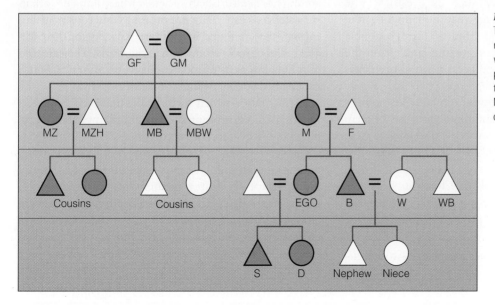

Figure 14.2
This diagram, which traces descent matrilineally, can be compared with that in Figure 14.1, showing patrilineal descent. The two patterns are virtually mirror images. Note that a man cannot transmit descent to his own children.

Arizona State Museum, University of Arizona, Helga Teiwes, Photographer

Hopi Indians in Arizona are a matrilineal farming people. At birth, every Hopi is assigned to his or her mother's clan. Hopi villages feature several lineages, each headed by a senior woman, and Hopi households consist of the women of a lineage with their husbands and unmarried sons. The lineages function as landholding corporations, allocating land for the support of member households.

at the same time. Here descent is matrilineal for some purposes and patrilineal for others. Generally, where double descent is traced, the matrilineal and patrilineal groups take action in different spheres of society. For example, among the Yakö of eastern Nigeria, property is divided into both patrilineal possessions and matrilineal possessions.[2] The patrilineage owns perpetual productive resources, such as land, whereas the matrilineage owns consumable property, such as livestock. The legally weaker matriline is somewhat more important in religious matters than the patriline. Through double descent, a Yakö might inherit grazing lands from the father's patrilineal group and certain ritual privileges from the mother's matrilineal group.

Finally, when descent derives from both the mother's and father's families equally, anthropologists use the term *bilateral descent*. In such a system people trace their descent from all ancestors, regardless of their gender or side of the family. We may recognize bilateral descent when individuals apply the same genealogical terms to identify similarly related individuals on both sides of the family—when they speak of a "grandmother" or "grandfather," for instance,

[2]Forde, C. D. (1968). Double descent among the Yakö. In P. Bohannan & J. Middleton (Eds.), *Kinship and social organization.* (pp. 179–191). Garden City, NY: Natural History Press.

no indication is given whether these relatives are on the paternal or maternal side of the family. Bilateral descent exists in various foraging cultures and is also quite common in many contemporary state societies with agricultural, industrial, or postindustrial economies. For example, although most people in Europe, Australia, and North America typically inherit their father's family name (indicative of a culture's history in which patrilineal descent was the norm), they usually consider themselves as much a member of their mother's as their father's family.

DESCENT AS A FEATURE INTEGRATED IN THE CULTURAL SYSTEM

Descent groups are ancestor oriented; membership in a lineage is recognized only if relationship to a common real historical ancestor can be genealogically traced. In many societies an individual has no legal or political status except as a lineage member. Since "citizenship" is derived from lineage membership and legal status depends on it, political and religious powers are derived from it as well. Because a lineage endures after the deaths of members with new members continually born into it, it has a continuing existence that enables it to act like a corporation, as in owning property, organizing productive activities, distributing goods and labor power, assigning status, and regulating relations with other groups. Thus it is a strong, effective base of social organization.

There is a close relationship between the descent system and a cultural system's infrastructure. Generally, patrilineal descent predominates where male labor is considered of prime importance, as among pastoralists and agriculturalists. Matrilineal descent predominates mainly among horticulturists in societies where female work in subsistence is especially important. Numerous matrilineal societies are found in southern Asia, one of the earliest cradles of food production in the world. They are also prominent in parts of indigenous North America, South America's tropical lowlands, and parts of Africa.

No matter which form of descent predominates, the kin of both mother and father are important components of the social structure in all societies. Just because descent may be traced patrilineally, for example, does not mean that matrilineal relatives are necessarily unimportant. It simply means that, for purposes of group membership, the mother's relatives are excluded. Similarly, under matrilineal descent, the father's relatives are excluded for purposes of group membership.

By way of example, we have seen in preceding chapters how important paternal relatives are among the matrilineal Trobriand Islanders of the southern

Pacific. Although children belong to their mother's descent groups, fathers play an important role in nurturing and educating them. Upon marriage, the bride's and groom's paternal relatives contribute to the exchange of gifts, and, throughout life, a man may expect his paternal kin to help him improve his economic and political position in society. Eventually, sons may expect to inherit personal property from their fathers.

Lineage Exogamy

A common characteristic of lineages is *exogamy*. As defined in the previous chapter, this means that lineage members must find their marriage partners in other lineages. One advantage of exogamy is that potential sexual competition within the group is curbed, promoting the group's solidarity. Lineage exogamy also means that each marriage is more than a union between two individuals; it is as well a new alliance between lineages. This helps to maintain them as components of larger social systems. Finally, lineage exogamy maintains open communication within a society, promoting the diffusion of knowledge from one lineage to another.

In contemporary North American Indian communities, kinship and descent play an essential role in tribal membership—as illustrated in this chapter's Anthropology Applied.

Anthropology Applied

Resolving a Native American Tribal Membership Dispute

In autumn 1998, I received a call from the tribal chief of the Aroostook Band of Micmacs in Northern Maine asking for help in resolving a bitter tribal membership dispute. The conflict centered on the fact that several hundred individuals had become tribal members without proper certification of their Micmac kinship status. Traditionalists in the community argued that their tribe's organization was being taken over by "non-Indians." With the formal status of so many members in question, the tribal administration could not properly determine who was entitled to benefit from the available health, housing, and education programs. After some hostile confrontations between the factions, tribal elders requested a formal inquiry into the membership controversy, and I was called in as a neutral party with a long history of working with the band.

My involvement as an advocacy anthropologist began in 1981, when these Micmacs (also spelled Mi'kmaq) first employed me (with Bunny McBride) as co-Director of Research and Development. At the time, they formed a poor and landless community not yet officially recognized as a tribe. During that decade, we helped the band define its political strategies, which focused on

petitioning for federal recognition of their Indian status, claiming traditional rights to hunt, trap, and fish, and even demanding return of lost ancestral lands. To generate popular support for the effort, I co-produced a film about the community (*Our Lives in Our Hands*, 1986). Most important, we gathered oral histories and detailed archival documentation to address kinship issues and other government criteria for tribal recognition. The latter included important genealogi-

The Sanipass-Lafford family cluster in Chapman, Maine, represents a traditional Micmac residential kin group. Such extended families typically include grandchildren and bilaterally related family members such as in-laws, uncles, and aunts. Taken from the Sanipass family album, this picture shows a handful of members in the mid-1980s: Marline Sanipass Morey with two of her nephews and uncles.

cal records showing that most Micmac adults in the region were at least "half-blood" (having two of their grandparents officially recorded as Indians).

Based on this evidence, we effectively argued that Aroostook Micmacs could claim aboriginal title to lands in the region and convinced politicians in Washington, D.C., to introduce a special bill to acknowledge their tribal status and settle their land claims. When formal hearings were held in 1990, I testified in the U.S. Senate as expert witness for the Micmacs. The following year, the Aroostook Band of Micmacs Settlement Act became federal law. This made the band eligible for the financial assistance (health, housing, education and child welfare) and economic development loans available to all federally recognized tribes in the United States. Moreover, it provided the band with funding to buy a 5,000-acre territorial base in Maine.

Flush with federal funding and rapidly expanding its activities, the 500-member band became overwhelmed by complex bureaucratic regulations now governing their existence. Without formally established ground rules determining who could apply for tribal membership, and

Continued

Continued

overlooking federally imposed regulations, hundreds of new names were
rather casually added to its tribal rolls.

By 1997, the Aroostook band population had ballooned to almost 1,200
members, and Micmac traditionalists
were questioning the legitimacy of many
whose names had been added to the
band roll. With mounting tension threatening to destroy the band, the tribal
chief invited me to evaluate critically the
membership claims of more than half
the tribe. In early 1999, I reviewed kinship records submitted by hundreds of
individuals whose membership on the
tribal rolls was in question. Several
months later, I offered my final report to
the Micmac community. After traditional
prayers, sweetgrass burning, drumming,
and a traditional meal of salmon and
moose, I formally presented my findings:
Based on the official criteria, about 100
lineal descendants of the original members and just over 150 newcomers met
the minimum required qualifications for
membership; several hundred would
have to be stripped from the tribal rolls.
After singing, drumming, and closing
prayers, the Micmac gathering dispersed.

Today, the band numbers about 850
members and is doing well. It has purchased several tracts of land (collectively
over 600 acres), including a small residential reservation near Presque Isle,
now home to about 200 Micmacs. Also
located here are new tribal administration offices, a health clinic, and a cultural center. *(By Harald Prins, co-author
of this textbook.)* ■ ■ ■

From Lineage to Clan

In the course of time, as generation succeeds generation and new members are born into the lineage, the kinship group's membership may become too large to be manageable or too much for the lineage's resources to support. When this happens, **fission** occurs; that is, the original lineage splits into new, smaller lineages. Usually the members of the new lineages continue to recognize their original relationship to one another. The result of this process is the appearance of a larger kind of descent group: the clan.

As already noted, a clan—typically consisting of several lineages—is an extended unilineal descent group whose members claim common descent from a remote ancestor (usually legendary or mythological) but are unable to trace the precise genealogical links back to that ancestor. This stems from the great genealogical depth of the clan, whose founding ancestor lived so far in the past that the links must be assumed rather than known in detail. A clan differs from a lineage in another respect: It lacks the residential unity generally—although not invariably—characteristic of a lineage's core members. As with the lineage, descent may be patrilineal, matrilineal, or ambilineal.

Because clan membership is dispersed rather than localized, it usually does not hold tangible property corporately. Instead, it tends to be more a unit for ceremonial and political matters. Only on special occasions will the membership gather together for specific purposes.

Clans, however, may handle important integrative functions. Like lineages, they may regulate marriage through exogamy. Because of their dispersed membership, they give individuals the right of entry into local groups other than their own. Members usually are expected to give protection and hospitality to others in the clan. Hence, these can be expected in any local group that includes people who belong to a single clan.

Clans, lacking the residential unity of lineages, frequently depend on symbols—of animals, plants, natural forces, colors, and special objects—to provide members with solidarity and a ready means of identification. These symbols, called totems, often are associated with the clan's mythical origin and reinforce for clan members an awareness of their common descent. The word *totem* comes from the Ojibwa American Indian word *ototeman*, meaning "he is a relative of mine." **Totemism** was defined by the British anthropologist A. R. Radcliffe-Brown as a set of "customs and beliefs by which there is set up a special system of relations between the society and the plants, animals, and other natural objects that are important in the social life."[3] For example, Hopi Indian matriclans (matrilineal clans) bear such totemic names as Bear, Bluebird, Butterfly, Lizard, Spider, and Snake.

In addition to the above mentioned matriclans, there are also patriclans tracing descent exclusively through men from a founding ancestor. Historically, a few dozen such clans existed in the Scottish highlands, often identified with the prefix "Mac" or "Mc" (from an old Celtic word meaning "son of"). During the past few

totemism The belief that people are related to particular animals, plants, or natural objects by virtue of descent from common ancestral spirits.

fission The splitting of a descent group into two or more new descent groups.

[3]Radcliffe-Brown, A. R. (1931) Social organization of Australian tribes. *Oceana Monographs, 1,* 29.

hundred years, large Scottish clans such as McGregor and Mackenzie broke apart as many members moved away in search of economic opportunity. Today, their descendents are dispersed all across the globe, especially in countries such as Australia, Canada, England, New Zealand, and the United States. During the past few decades, widely scattered descendants have sought to re-establish their kinship ties to ancestral clans, and many travel from afar to attend the annual gathering of their clan, preferably in their traditional ancient homeland in the highlands of Scotland. As this chapter's opening photograph illustrates, these clan members express their kinship with one another by wearing woolen shawls, kilts, or other pieces of clothing made of their clan tartan—a distinct plaid pattern and color identifying their particular clan membership.

Phratries and Moieties

Larger kinds of descent groups are phratries and moieties (Figure 14.3). A **phratry** (after the Greek word for "brother") is a unilineal descent group composed of at least two clans that supposedly share a common ancestry, whether or not they really do. Like individuals in the clan, phratry members cannot trace precisely their descent links to a common ancestor, although they firmly believe such an ancestor existed.

If the entire society is divided into only two major descent groups, whether they are equivalent to clans or phratries, each group is called a **moiety** (after the French word for "half"). Members of the moiety believe themselves to share a common ancestor but cannot prove it through definite genealogical links. As

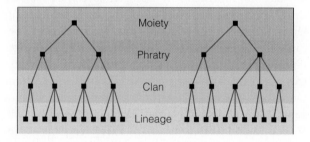

Figure 14.3
This diagram shows how lineages, clans, phratries, and moieties form an organizational hierarchy. Each moiety is subdivided into phratries, each phratry is subdivided into clans, and each clan is subdivided into lineages.

> **phratry** A unilineal descent group composed of at least two clans that supposedly share a common ancestry, whether or not they really do.
>
> **moiety** Each group that results from a division of a society into two halves on the basis of descent.

a rule, the feelings of kinship among members of lineages and clans are stronger than those of members of phratries and moieties. This may be due to the much larger size and more diffuse nature of the latter groups.

Like lineages and clans, phratries and moieties are often exogamous and so are bound together by marriages between their members. And like clans, they provide members rights of access to other communities. In a community that does not include one's clan members, one's phratry members are still there to turn to for hospitality. Finally, moieties may perform reciprocal services for one another. Among them, individuals turn to members of the opposite "half" in their community for the necessary mourning rituals when a member of their own moiety dies. Such interdependence between moieties, again, serves to maintain the cohesion of the entire society.

The kin-ordered social structure of the Winnebago (since 1993, known as the Ho-Chunk Nation—"People of the Sacred Language") offers an interesting ethnographic example of the moiety system. Organized in twelve patrilineal clans, these North American Indians, traditionally ranging the woodlands and prairies of southern Wisconsin, were divided between "those who are above" (Sky) and "those who are below" (Earth). The Sky moiety included the Eagle, Hawk, Pigeon, and Thunder clans, whereas those belonging to the Earth "half " consisted of the Bear, Buffalo, Deer, Elk, Fish, Snake, Water Spirit, and Wolf clans. These exogamous moieties not only regulated marriage and leadership positions among the Ho-Chunk, but even structured their traditional settlement patterns, with Sky clans inhabiting the southwest half of each village and those of the Earth moiety the northeast.[4] For archaeologists excavating ancient Ho-Chunk village sites, of course, the physical reflection in a traditional village layout of such clearly demarcated kinship patterns has considerable interpretive potential.

BILATERAL KINSHIP AND THE KINDRED

Important though descent groups are in many societies, they are not found in all societies, nor are they the only kinds of extended kinship groups to be found. *Bilateral kinship*, a characteristic of most contemporary European and American societies as well as a number of food-foraging cultures, affiliates a person with genetically

---

[4]Radin, P. (1923). The Winnebago tribe. In *37th annual report of the Bureau of American Ethnology, 1915–1916* (pp. 33–550). Washington, DC: Government Printing Office.

close relatives (but not in-laws) through both sexes. In other words, the individual traces descent through both parents, all four grandparents, and so forth, recognizing multiple ancestors. Theoretically, one is associated equally with all "blood" relatives on both the mother's and father's sides of the family. Thus, this principle relates an individual lineally to all eight great-grandparents and laterally to all third and fourth cousins.

Since such a huge group is too big to be socially practical, it is usually reduced to a smaller circle of paternal and maternal relatives, called the kindred. The **kindred** may be defined as an individual's close "blood" relatives on the maternal and paternal side of his or her family. Since the kindred is laterally rather than lineally organized—that is, ego, or the focal person from whom the degree of each relationship is reckoned, is the center of the group—it is not a true descent group.

Most North Americans are familiar with the kindred; those who belong are simply referred to as relatives. It includes those "blood" relatives on both sides of the family who are seen on important occasions, such as family weddings, reunions, and funerals. They can identify the members of their kindred up to grandparents and first, if not always second, cousins. The limits of the kindred, however, are variable and indefinite. No one ever can be absolutely certain which relatives to invite to every important function and which to exclude. Inevitably, situations arise that require some debate about whether or not to invite particular, usually distant, relatives. Kindreds are thus not clearly bounded and lack the distinctiveness of the lineage. (They are also temporary, lasting only as long as the functions for which they are assembled.)

Because of its bilateral structure, a kindred is never the same for any two people except siblings (brothers and sisters). Thus, no two people other than siblings belong to the same kindred. The kindred of ego's first cousin on the father's side, for example, includes not only the father's sister (or brother), as does ego's, but the father's sister's (or brother's) spouse, as well as blood relatives of the latter. As for the kindreds of ego's parents, these will range lineally to grandparents and laterally to cousins too distant for ego to know, and the same is true of ego's aunts and uncles. Thus, the kindred is not composed of people with an ancestor in common but with a living relative in common—ego. Furthermore, as ego goes through life, the kindreds he or she is affiliated with will change. When young, individuals belong to the kindreds of their parents. Ultimately, they belong to the kindreds of their offspring as well as their nieces and nephews.

Kindreds are frequently found in industrial and postindustrial state societies where capitalist wage labor conditions bring on mobility and promote individualism, thereby weakening the importance of a strong kinship organization.

CULTURAL EVOLUTION OF THE DESCENT GROUP

Just as different types of families occur in different societies, so do different kinds of nonfamily kin groups. Descent groups, for example, are not a common feature of food-foraging societies, which are usually small. In many crop-cultivating or herding societies, however, the descent group usually provides the basic structural framework of the social system.

It is generally agreed that lineages arise from extended family organization, so long as organizational challenges exist that such structures help solve. All that is required, really, is that as members of existing extended families find it necessary to split off and establish new households elsewhere, they not move too far away; that the core members of such related families explicitly acknowledge their descent from a common ancestor; and that they continue to participate in common activities in an organized way. As this process proceeds, lineages will develop, and these may with time give rise to clans and ultimately moieties.

Another way that clans may arise is as fictive kin groups to politically integrate otherwise autonomous ethnic groups. The six Iroquois Indian nations of what now is New York State, for example, developed clans by simply behaving as if lineages of the same name in different villages were related. Thus, their members became fictitious "brothers" and "sisters." By this device, members of, say, a Bear clan in a Mohawk village could travel to a nearby Oneida village, or more distant Onondaga, Cayuga, Tuscarora, or even Seneca villages some 200 miles west of their homeland, and be welcomed in and hosted in any of these Iroquois settlements by members of local Bear clans. In this way, the six neighboring Iroquois nations achieved a wider cultural unity than had previously existed.

As larger, dispersed descent groups develop, the conditions that gave rise to extended families and lineages may change. For example, lineages may lose their economic bases if developing political institutions take control of resources. In such circumstances, lineages would be expected to disappear as important organizational units. Clans, however, might survive, if they continue to provide an important integrative function. Such

kindred An individual's genetically close relatives on the maternal and paternal sides of his or her family.

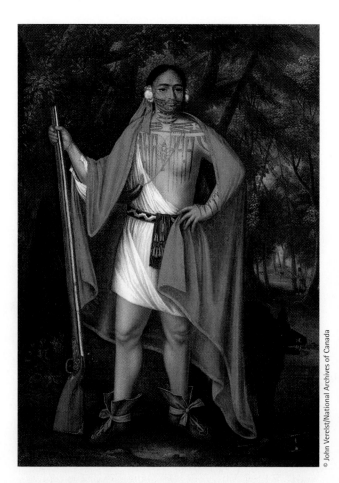

© John Verelst/National Archives of Canada

Clans among the "Six Nations" of the Iroquois confederacy in New York State are a kinship construct that allowed people to freely travel among multiple member villages. This portrait, done in 1710, shows Sa Ga Yeath Qua Pieth Tow, a chief of the Mohawk Nation. Behind him stands a bear, which represents his clan.

is the case with the Scottish clans discussed earlier. This helps explain their continued strength and vitality even far outside Scotland today. They perform an integrative function among kin who are geographically dispersed as well as socially diverse—and they do this in a way that does not conflict with the mobility characteristic of industrial or postindustrial societies.

In societies where small domestic units—nuclear families or single-parent households—are of primary importance, bilateral kinship and kindred organization are likely to result. This can be seen in modern industrial and postindustrial societies, in newly emerging societies in the "underdeveloped" world, and in still-existing food-foraging societies throughout the world.

KINSHIP TERMINOLOGY AND KINSHIP GROUPS

Any system of organizing people who are relatives into different kinds of groups—whether kindreds, lineages,

or clans—influences how relatives are labeled in a given society. Kinship terminology systems vary considerably across cultures, reflecting the positions individuals occupy within their respective societies and helping to differentiate one relative from another. Distinguishing factors include gender, generational differences, or genealogical differences. In the various systems of kinship terminology, any one of these factors may be emphasized at the expense of others.

By looking at the terms people in a particular society use for their relatives, an anthropologist can tell how kinship groups are structured, what relationships are considered especially important, and sometimes what the prevailing attitudes are concerning various relationships. For instance, a number of languages use the same term to identify a brother and a cousin, and others have a single word for cousin, niece, and nephew. Some cultures find it useful to distinguish an oldest brother from his younger brothers and have different words for these brothers. And unlike English, many languages distinguish between an aunt who is mother's sister and one who is father's sister.

Regardless of the factors emphasized, all kinship terminologies accomplish two important tasks. First, they classify similar kinds of individuals into single specific categories; second, they separate different kinds of individuals into distinct categories. Generally, two or more kin are merged under the same term when the individuals have more or less the same rights and obligations with respect to the person referring to them as such. Such is the case among most English-speaking North Americans, for instance, when someone refers to a mother's sister and father's sister both as an "aunt." As far as the speaker is concerned, both relatives possess a similar status.

Several different systems of kinship terminology result from the application of the above principles just mentioned, including the Eskimo, Hawaiian, Iroquois, Crow, Omaha, Sudanese, Kariera, and Aranda systems, each named after the ethnographic example best described by anthropologists. The last five of these systems are fascinating in their complexity and are found among only a few of the world's societies. However, to illustrate some of the basic principles involved, we will focus our attention on the first three systems.

Eskimo System

The Eskimo system, comparatively rare among all the world's systems, is the one used by Euramericans, as well as by a number of food-foraging peoples (including the Inuit and other Eskimos; hence the name).

Sometimes referred to as the *lineal system*, the **Eskimo system** emphasizes the nuclear family by specifically identifying mother, father, brother, and sister while lumping together all other relatives into a few large categories (Figure 14.4). For example, the father is distinguished from the father's brother (uncle); but the father's brother is not distinguished from the mother's brother (both are called "uncle"). The mother's sister and father's sister are treated similarly, both called "aunt." In addition, all the sons and daughters of aunts and uncles are called "cousin," thereby making a generational distinction but without indicating the side of the family to which they belong or even their gender.

Unlike other terminologies, the Eskimo system provides separate and distinct terms for the nuclear family members. This is probably because the Eskimo system is generally found in bilateral societies where the dominant kin group is the kindred, in which only

> **Eskimo system** Kinship reckoning in which the nuclear family is emphasized by specifically identifying the mother, father, brother, and sister, while lumping together all other relatives into broad categories such as uncle, aunt, and cousin. Also referred to as lineal system.

immediate family members are important in day-to-day affairs. This is especially true of modern North American societies, where many families are independent, living apart from, and not directly involved with, other relatives except on special occasions. Thus, most North Americans (and others) generally distinguish between their closest kin (parents and siblings) but lump together (as aunts, uncles, cousins) other kin on both sides of the family.

Hawaiian System

The **Hawaiian system** of kinship terminology, common (as its name implies) in Hawaii and other areas in the Pacific but found elsewhere as well, is the least complex system, in that it uses the fewest terms. The Hawaiian system is also called the generational system, since all relatives of the same generation and sex are referred to by the same term (Figure 14.5). For example, in one's parents' generation, the term used to refer to one's

> **Hawaiian system** Kinship reckoning in which all relatives of the same sex and generation are referred to by the same term.

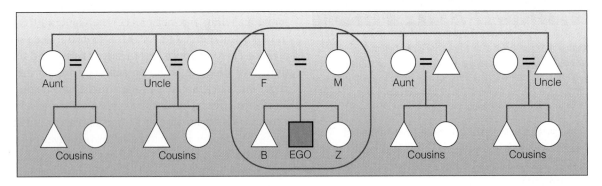

Figure 14.4
The Eskimo system of kinship terminology emphasizes the nuclear family (circled). EGO's father and mother are distinguished from EGO's aunts and uncles, and siblings from cousins.

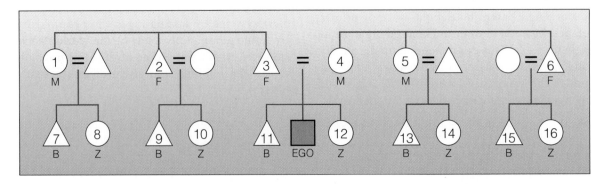

Figure 14.5
In the Hawaiian kinship system the men numbered 2 and 6 are called by the same term as father (3) by EGO; the women numbered 1 and 5 are called by the same term as mother (4). All cousins of EGO's own generation (7–16) are considered brothers (B) and sisters (Z).

father is used as well for the father's brother and mother's brother. Similarly, one's mother, mother's sister, and father's sister are all lumped together under a single term. In ego's generation, male and female cousins are distinguished by gender and are equated with brothers and sisters.

The Hawaiian system reflects the absence of strong unilineal descent, and members on both the father's and the mother's side are viewed as more or less equal. Thus, ego's father's and mother's siblings are all recognized as being similar relations and are merged under a single term appropriate for their gender. In like manner, the children of the mother's and father's siblings are related to ego in the same way brother and sister are. Falling under the incest taboo, they are ruled out as potential marriage partners.

Iroquois System

In the **Iroquois system** of kinship terminology, the father and father's brother are referred to by a single term, as are the mother and mother's sister; however, the father's sister and mother's brother are given separate terms (Figure 14.6). In one's own generation, brothers, sisters, and parallel cousins (offspring of parental siblings of the same sex, that is, the children of the mother's sister or father's brother) of the same sex are referred to by the same terms, which is logical enough considering that they are the offspring of people who are classified in the same category as ego's actual mother and father. Cross

Iroquois system Kinship reckoning in which a father and father's brother are referred to by a single term, as are a mother and mother's sister, but a father's sister and mother's brother are given separate terms. Parallel cousins are classified with brothers and sisters, while cross cousins are classified separately but not equated with relatives of some other generation.

cousins (offspring of parental siblings of opposite sex, that is, the children of the mother's brother or father's sister) are distinguished by terms that set them apart from all other kin. In fact, cross cousins are often preferred as spouses, for marriage to them reaffirms alliances between related lineages or clans.

Iroquois terminology, named for the Iroquoian Indians of northeastern North America's woodlands, is in fact very widespread and is usually found with unilineal descent groups. It was, for example, the terminology in use until recently in rural Chinese society.

Kinship Terms and New Reproductive Technologies

If systems of kinship reckoning other than one's own seem strange and complex, consider the implications of an event that took place in 1978: the production of the world's first test-tube baby, outside the womb, without sexual intercourse. Since then, thousands of babies have been created in this way, and all sorts of new technologies have become part of the reproductive repertoire. Known as NRTs, **New reproductive technologies (NRTs)** Alternative means of reproduction such as surrogate motherhood and in vitro fertilization. These technologies have opened up a large—and sometimes mind-boggling—array of reproductive possibilities. For example, it is now possible for a woman to give birth to her genetic uncle; does that make her his niece or his mother? If a child is conceived from a donor egg, implanted in another woman's womb to be raised by yet another woman, who is its mother? To complicate matters even further, the egg

New reproductive technologies (NRTs) Alternative means of reproduction such as surrogate motherhood and in vitro fertilization.

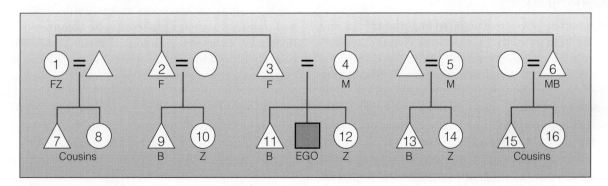

Figure 14.6
According to the Iroquois system of kinship terminology, the father's brother (2) is called by the same term as the father (3); the mother's sister (5) is called by the same term as the mother (4); but the people numbered 1 and 6 have separate terms for themselves. Those people numbered 9 to 14 are all considered siblings, but 7, 8, 15, and 16 are considered cousins.

may have been fertilized by sperm from a donor not married to, or in a sexual relationship with, any of these women. Indeed, it has been suggested that we need nearly a dozen different terms to cover the concepts of "mother" and "father" in today's changing societies.[5]

Clearly, the new reproductive technologies are impacting traditional notions of kinship. Beyond transforming our sense of being human, they force us to redefine established ideas about the status of relatives— challenging us to rethink what being "related" to others is about and, specifically, what our rights and obligations are toward such unfamiliar categories of kin.

GROUPING BEYOND KINSHIP

Because ties of kinship and household are not always sufficient to handle all the challenges of human survival, people also form groups based on gender, age, common interest, and social rank (including class).

Grouping by Gender

As shown in preceding chapters, division of labor along gender lines occurs in all human societies. In some cultures—the previously discussed Ju/'hoansi in southern Africa for example— many tasks that men and women undertake may be shared. People may perform work normally assigned to the opposite sex without loss of face. In others, however, men and women are rigidly segregated in what they do. For instance, among the Mundurucu Indians of Brazil's Amazon rainforest. men and women work, eat, and sleep separately. From age 13 onward males live together in one large house, while women, girls, and preteen boys occupy two or three houses grouped around the men's house. For all intents and purposes, men associate with men, and women with women.

Grouping by Age

Age grouping is so familiar and so important that it and sex have been called the only universal factors that determine a person's positions in society. In North America today, for instance, a child's first friends are usually children of his or her own age. They begin preschool or kindergarten with age mates and typically move through a dozen or more years in the educational system together. At specified ages they are allowed to see certain movies, drive a car, and do things reserved for adults, such as voting, drinking alcoholic beverages, and serving in the military. Ultimately, North Americans

retire from their jobs at a specified age and, more and more, spend the final years of their lives in retirement communities, segregated from the rest of society. As North Americans age, they are labeled "teenagers," "middle-aged," and "senior citizens," whether they like it or not and for no other reason than the number of years they have lived.

Age classification also plays a significant role in non-Western societies, which, at a minimum, make a distinction between immature, mature, and older people whose physical powers are waning. In these societies old age often has profound significance, bringing with it the period of greatest respect (for women it may mean the first social equality with men). Rarely are the elderly shunted aside or abandoned. Even the Inuit of the Canadian Arctic, who are often cited as a people who literally abandon their aged relatives, do so only in truly desperate circumstances, when the group's physical survival is at stake. In all oral tradition societies, elders are the repositories of accumulated wisdom for their people. Recognized as such and no longer expected to carry out many subsistence activities, they play a major role in passing on cultural knowledge to their grandchildren.

All human societies recognize a number of life stages. The demarcation and duration of these stages vary across cultures. Each successive life stage provides distinctive social roles and comes with certain cultural features such as specific patterns of activity, attitudes, prohibitions, and obligations. In many cultures, the social position of an individual in a specific life stage is also marked by a distinctive outward appearance in terms of dress, hairstyle, body paint, tattoos, insignia, or some other symbolic distinction. Typically, these stages are designed to help the transition from one age to another, to teach needed skills, or to lend economic assistance. Often they are taken as the basis for the formation of organized groups.

Institutions of Age Grouping

An organized category of people with membership on the basis of age is known as an **age grade.** Entry into and transfer out of age grades may be accomplished individually, either by a biological distinction, such as puberty, or by a socially recognized status, such as marriage or childbirth. Whereas age-grade members may have much in common, may engage in similar activities, may cooperate with one another, and may share the same orientation and aspirations, their membership may not be entirely parallel with physiological age. A specific time is often ritually established for moving from a

---

[5]Stone, L. (1998). *Kinship and gender* (p. 272). Boulder, CO: Westview Press.

age grade An organized category of people based on age; every individual passes through a series of such categories over his or her lifetime.

In many societies it is common for children of the same age to play, eat, and learn together, such as these East African Maasai boys, who are gathering for the first time to receive instruction for their initiation into an age grade. As members of the same age set, they will move together through a series of age grades in the course of their lives.

younger to an older grade. An example of this is the traditional Jewish ceremony of the bar mitzvah (a Hebrew term meaning "son of the commandment"), marking that a 13-year-old boy has reached the age of religious duty and responsibility. Although members of senior groups commonly expect deference from and acknowledge certain responsibilities to their juniors, this does not necessarily mean that one grade is seen as better, or worse, or even more important than another.

In addition to age grades, some societies feature age sets (sometimes referred to as age classes). An **age set** is a formally established group of people born during a certain time span who move through the series of age-grade categories together. Age sets, unlike age grades, do not cease to exist after a specified number of years; the members of an age set usually remain closely associated throughout their lives.

The age-set notion implies strong feelings of loyalty and mutual support. Because such groups may possess property, songs, shield designs, and rituals and are internally organized for collective decision making and leadership, age sets are distinct from simple age grades. One also may distinguish between transitory age grades—which initially concern younger men (sometimes women too) but become less important and disintegrate as the members grow older—and the comprehensive systems that affect people through the whole of their lives.

Age Grouping in African Societies

Although age is a criterion for group membership in many parts of the world, its most varied and elaborate use is found in Africa, south of the Sahara. An example may be seen among the Tiriki, one of several pastoral nomadic groups living in Kenya.[6] In this culture of herders, each boy born within a 15-year period becomes a member of a particular age set then open for membership. Seven such named age sets exist, only one of which is open for membership at a time; when membership in one is closed, the next one is open for a 15-year period, and so on until the passage of 105 years (7 times 15), when the first set once again takes in new "recruits."

Members of Tiriki age sets remain together for life as they move through four successive age grades: Advancement occurs at 15-year intervals at the same time one age set closes and another opens for membership. Each age grade has its particular duties and responsibilities. Traditionally, the first, or "Warrior" age grade, served as guardians of the country, and members gained renown through fighting. Under British colonial rule, however, this traditional function fell by the wayside with the cessation of warfare, and members of this age grade now find excitement and adventure by leaving their community for extended employment or study elsewhere.

age set A formally established group of people born during a certain time span who move through the series of age grade categories together.

[6]Sangree, W. H. (1965). The Bantu Tiriki of western Kenya. In J. L. Gibbs, Jr. (Ed.), *Peoples of Africa* (pp. 69–72). New York: Holt, Rinehart and Winston.

The next age grade, the "Elder Warriors," had few specialized tasks in earlier days beyond learning skills they would need later on by assuming an increasing share of administrative activities. For example, they would chair the postfuneral gatherings held to settle property claims after someone's death. Traditionally, Elder Warriors also served as envoys between elders of different communities. Nowadays, they hold nearly all of the administrative and executive roles opened up by the creation and growth of a centralized Tiriki administrative bureaucracy.

"Judicial Elders," the third age grade, traditionally handled most tasks connected with the administration and settlement of local disputes. Today, they still serve as the local judiciary body. Members of the "Ritual Elders," the senior age grade, used to preside over the priestly functions of ancestral shrine observances on the household level, at subclan meetings, at semiannual community appeals, and at rites of initiation into the various age grades. They also were credited with access to special magical powers. With the decline of ancestor worship over the past several decades, many of these traditional functions have been lost, and no new ones have arisen to take their places. Nonetheless, Ritual Elders continue to hold the most important positions in the initiation ceremonies, and their power as sorcerers and expungers of witchcraft are still recognized.

Grouping by Common Interest

The rise of urban, industrialized societies in which individuals are often separated from their kin has led to a proliferation of **common-interest associations**—associations that result from an act of joining and are based on sharing particular activities, objectives, values, or beliefs. Moreover, common-interest associations help people meet a range of needs from companionship to safe work conditions to learning a new language and customs upon moving from one country to another.

Because common-interest associations are by nature flexible, they have often been turned to, both in cities and in traditional villages, as a way of meeting these needs. Common-interest associations are not, however, restricted to modernizing societies alone. They also are found in many traditional societies, and there is reason to believe they arose with the emergence of the first horticultural villages. Furthermore, associations in traditional societies may be just as complex and

highly organized as those of countries such as the United States and Canada.

Kinds of Common-Interest Associations

The variety of common-interest associations is astonishing. In the United States, they include such diverse entities as women's clubs of all sorts, street gangs, private militias, sport and service clubs, churches and other religious organizations, political parties, labor unions, environmental organizations—the list could go on and on. Their goals may include the pursuit of friendship, recreation, and promotion of certain values, as well as governing and the pursuit or defense of economic interests.

Associations also have served to preserve traditional songs, history, language, and moral beliefs among various ethnic minorities. In nonindustrial societies, such organizations are frequently exclusive, but a prevailing characteristic is their concern for the general well-being of an entire village or group of villages. The rain that falls as a result of the work of Hopi rainmakers nourishes the crops of members and nonmembers alike. Such organizations, often operating secretly, have kept traditions alive among North American Indians, who are undergoing a resurgence of ethnic pride despite generations of schooling designed to stamp out their cultural identity.

Over the last decade or so, common-interest associations have had a boost in societies that have access to the Internet. The cyber world has seen an explosion of what are, in effect, virtual common-interest associations, all of which have their own particular rules on matters such as what members may or may not post and how they should behave online.

Grouping by Social Rank in Stratified Societies

Social stratification is a common and powerful structuring force in many of the world's societies. Basically, **stratified societies** are those in which people are hierarchically divided and ranked into social strata, or layers, and do not share equally in basic resources that support survival, influence, and prestige. Members of low-ranked strata typically have fewer privileges and less power than those in higher ranked strata. In addition, the restrictions and obligations they face are usually more oppressive, and they must work harder for less re-

---

common-interest associations Associations that result from an act of joining based on sharing particular activities, objectives, values, or beliefs.

---

stratified societies Societies in which people are hierarchically divided and ranked into social strata, or layers, and do not share equally in basic resources that support survival, influence, and prestige.

Increasingly common among women around the world are common-interest groups centered on sports, as seen in this photo of the Swedish national women's soccer team.

© Chris Trotman/New Sport/Corbis

ward. In short, social stratification amounts to institutionalized inequality. Without ranking—high versus low—no stratification exists; social differences without this do not constitute stratification.

Stratified societies stand in sharp contrast to **egalitarian societies,** in which everyone has about equal rank, access to, and power over basic resources. As we saw in earlier chapters, foraging societies are characteristically egalitarian, although there are some exceptions.

Social Class and Caste

A **social class** may be defined as a category of individuals of equal or nearly equal prestige according to the system of evaluation. The qualification "nearly equal" is important, for a certain amount of inequality may occur even within a given class. Class distinctions are not always clear-cut and obvious in societies that have a wide and continuous range of differential privileges.

A **caste** is a closed social class in which membership is not based on personal achievement or wealth but determined by birth and fixed for life. The opposite of the principle that all humans are born equal, the caste system is based on the principle that humans neither are nor can be equal. Castes are strongly endogamous, and offspring are automatically members of their parents' caste.

> **egalitarian societies** Societies in which everyone has about equal rank, access to, and power over basic resources.
>
> **social class** A category of individuals who enjoy equal or nearly equal prestige according to the system of evaluation.
>
> **caste** A closed social class in which membership is determined by birth and fixed for life.

The classic ethnographic example is the traditional Hindu caste system of India. Perhaps the world's longest surviving social hierarchy, it encompasses a complex ranking of social groups on the basis of "ritual purity." Each of some 2,000 different castes considers itself as a distinct community higher or lower than other castes, although their particular ranking varies among geographic regions and over time. The different castes are associated with specific occupations and customs, such as food habits and styles of dress, along with rituals involving notions of purity and pollution. Differences in status are traditionally justified by the religious doctrine of karma, a belief that one's place in life is determined by one's deeds in previous lifetimes.

All of these castes, or jatis, are organized into four basic orders or varnas (literally meaning "colors"), distinguished partly by occupation and ranked in order of descending religious status of purity. The religious foundation for this social hierarchy is found in a sacred text known as the Laws of Manu, an ancient work about 2,000 years old and considered by traditional Hindus as the highest authority on their cultural institutions. It defines the Brahmans as

the purest and therefore highest varna. As priests and law-givers, Brahmans represent the world of religion and learning. Next comes the order of fighters and rulers, known as the Kshatriyas. Below them are the Vaisyas (merchants and traders), who are engaged in commercial, agricultural, and pastoral pursuits. At the bottom are the Shudras (artisans and laborers), an order required to serve the other three varnas and who also make a living by handicrafts. Falling outside the varna system is a fifth category of degraded individuals known as "untouchables" or Dalits. Considered the most impure of all people, these outcasts can own neither land nor the tools of their trade. Untouchables constitute a large pool of cheap labor at the beck and call of those controlling economic and political affairs. In an effort to bestow some dignity on these poverty-stricken victims of the caste system, Hindu nationalist leader Mahatma Gandhi renamed them harijan or "children of God."

Although India's national constitution of 1950 sought to abolish caste discrimination and the practice of untouchability, the caste system remains deeply entrenched in Hindu culture and is still widespread throughout southern Asia, especially in rural India. In what has been called India's "hidden apartheid," entire villages in many Indian states remain completely segregated by caste. Representing about 15 percent of India's population—or some 160 million people—the widely scattered Dalits endure near complete social isolation, humiliation, and discrimination based exclusively on their birth status. Even a Dalit's shadow is believed to pollute the upper castes. They may not cross the line dividing their part of the village from that occupied by higher castes, drink water from public wells, or visit the same temples as the higher castes. Dalit children are still often made to sit at the back of classrooms.

Castelike situations are known elsewhere in the world. In Bolivia, Ecuador, and several other South and Central American countries, for example, the wealthy upper class is almost exclusively white and rarely intermarries with people of non-European descent. In contrast, the lower class of working poor in those countries is primarily made up of American Indian laborers and peasants. Racial segregation also existed in the United States, where the nation's upper class was made up exclusively of individuals of white European descent.

After the American Revolution, several states in New England joined Virginia and other southern states and made it illegal for whites to marry blacks or American Indians. In 1924, Virginia's General Assembly passed the Racial Integrity Act to prevent light-skinned individuals with some African ancestry from "passing" as whites. Known as the "one-drop" rule, it codified the idea of white racial purity by classifying individuals as black if just one of their multiple ancestors was of African origin ("one drop of Negro blood"). However light-skinned, they were subject to a wide range of discriminatory practices not applicable to whites. Such institutionalized racial discrimination continued for a century after slavery was abolished, and today self-segregation exists in many parts of the United States. The Biocultural Connection painfully illustrates the effects of this institutionalized racism.

Social classes are manifest through various ways, including *symbolic indicators*. For example, in the United States certain activities and possessions are indicative of class: occupation (a garbage collector has different class status than a medical specialist); wealth (rich people are generally in a higher social class than poor people); dress ("white collar" versus "blue collar"); form of recreation (upper-class people are expected to play golf rather than shoot pool down at the pool hall—but they can shoot pool at home or in a club); residential location (upper-class people do not ordinarily live in slums); kind of car; and so on. All sorts of status symbols are indicative of class position, including measures such as the number of

Although the caste system has been outlawed for some 50 years in India, huge, caste-based gaps in wealth, prestige, and power continue, as evidenced in these photos contrasting the palace of the Maharajas in Jaipur and the street shanties inhabited by low caste families in Bombay.

Biocultural Connection

African Burial Ground Project

In 1991, construction workers in lower Manhattan unearthed what turned out to be New York City's African Burial Ground, the final resting place of some 10,000 enslaved African captives brought to New York in the 17th and 18th centuries to build the city and provide the labor for its thriving economy. The discovery sparked controversy as the African American public held protests and prayer vigils to stop the part of a federal building project that nearly destroyed the site. A research team led by biological anthropologist Michael Blakey, then at Howard University, worked together with the descendant African American community to develop a plan that included both extensive biocultural research and the humane retention of the sacred nature of the site ultimately through reburial and the creation of a fitting memorial. The research also involved archaeological and historical studies that used a broad African diaspora context for understanding the lifetime experiences of these people who were enslaved and buried in New York.

Studying a sample population of 419 individuals from the burial ground,

Blakey and his team used an exhaustive range of skeletal biological methods, producing a database containing more than 200,000 observations of genetics, morphology, age, sex, growth and development, muscle development, trauma, nutrition, and disease. The bones revealed an unmistakable biocultural connection: physical wear and tear of an entire community brought on by the social institution of slavery. We now know, based on this study, that life for Africans in colonial New York was characterized by poor nutrition, grueling physical labor that enlarged and often tore muscles, and death rates that were unusually high for 15- to 25-year-olds. Many of these young adults died soon after arriving on slaving ships. Few Africans lived past 40 years of age, and less than 2 percent lived beyond 55. Church records show strikingly different mortality trends for the Europeans of New York: About eight times as many English as Africans lived past 55 years of age, and mortality in adolescence and the early 20s was relatively low.

Skeletal research also showed that those Africans who died as children and

were most likely to have been born in New York exhibited stunted and disrupted growth and exposure to high levels of lead pollution—unlike those with evidence of having been born in Africa (filed teeth). Fertility was very low among enslaved women in New York, and infant mortality was high. In these respects, this northern colonial city was very similar to South Carolina and the Caribbean to which its economy was tied—regions where conditions for African captives were among the harshest.

Individuals in this deeply troubling burial ground came from warring African states including Calibar, Asante, Benin, Dahomey, Congo, Madagascar, and many others—states that wrestled with the European demand for human chattel. They resisted their enslavement through rebellion, and they resisted their dehumanization by carefully burying their dead and preserving what they could of their cultures. *(By Michael Blakey (2003). African Burial Ground Project. Manuscript © by author, Department of Anthropology, College of William & Mary.)* ■ ■ ■

---

bathrooms in a person's house. That said, class rankings do not fully correlate with economic status or pay scales. The local garbage collector or unionized car-factory laborer typically makes more money than an average college professor with a doctorate.

Social Mobility

All stratified societies offer at least some *social mobility*, the ability to change one's class position. This helps to ease the strains inherent in any system of inequality. Even the Indian caste system, with its guiding ideology that all hierarchical social arrangements within it are fixed, has a degree of flexibility and mobility, not all of it associated with the recent changes modernization has brought to India. Although individuals cannot move up or down the caste hierarchy, whole groups can do so depending on claims they make for higher status and on how well they can manipulate others into acknowledging their claims.

With their limited mobility, caste-structured societies exemplify *closed-class societies*. Those that permit a great deal of mobility are referred to as *open-class societies*. Yet even in these, mobility is apt to be more limited than one might suppose. In the United States, despite its rags-to-riches ideology, most mobility involves a move up or down only a notch, although if this continues in a family over several generations, it may add up to a major change. Nonetheless, U.S. society makes much of relatively rare examples of great upward mobility consistent with its cultural values and does its best to overlook the numerous cases of little or no upward, not to mention downward, mobility.

The degree of mobility in a stratified society is related to the prevailing kind of family organization. In societies where the extended family is the usual form, mobility tends to be more difficult, because each individual is strongly tied to many relatives. Hence, for a person to move up to a higher social class, his or her family must move up as well. Mobility is easier for independent nuclear families where the individual is closely tied to fewer people. Moreover, under neolocal residence, individuals normally leave their family of birth. So it is, then, that through careful marriage, occupational success, and disassociation from the lower-class family in which they grew up, individuals can more easily "move up" in society.

Maintaining Stratification

Because social stratification of any kind generally makes life difficult for large segments of a population, the lower classes are usually kept quiet through the cultural system's superstructure, including religions promising them a better existence in the hereafter. In India, for example, belief in reincarnation and the existence of an incorruptible supernatural power that assigns people to a particular caste position as a reward or punishment for the deeds and misdeeds of past lives justifies one's position in this life. If, however, individuals faithfully perform the duties appropriate to their caste in this lifetime, then they can expect to be reborn into a higher caste in a future existence. In the minds of orthodox Hindus, then, one's caste position is something earned rather than the accident of birth as it appears to outside observers. Thus, although the caste system explicitly recognizes (and accepts as legitimate) inequality among people, an implicit assumption of ultimate equality underlies it. This contrasts with the situation in the United States, where the equality of all people is proclaimed even while various groups are discriminated against.

Although the cost is great—social classes do, after all, make life oppressive for large numbers of people—classes may nevertheless perform an integrative function in society.

By cutting across some or all lines of kinship, residence, occupation, and age group, depending on the particular society, they counteract potential tendencies for society to fragment into separate entities.

Chapter Summary

■ In nonindustrial societies, kinship groups commonly deal with challenges that families and households cannot handle alone—challenges involving defense, allocation of property, and the pooling of other resources. As societies become larger and more complex, formal political systems take over many of these matters. A common form of kinship group is the descent group, which has as its criterion of membership descent from a common ancestor through a series of parent–child links. Unilineal descent establishes kin group membership exclusively through the male or female line. Matrilineal descent is traced through the female line; patrilineal, through the male.

■ The descent system is closely tied to a society's economic base. Generally, patrilineal descent predominates where males do the majority of the primary productive work and matrilineal where females do it. Anthropologists recognize that in all societies the kin of both mother and father are important elements in the social structure, regardless of how descent group membership is defined.

■ The male members of a patrilineage trace their descent from a common male ancestor. In a patrilineage a female belongs to the same descent group as her father and his brother, but her children cannot trace their descent through them. Typically, authority over the children lies with the father or his elder brother. The requirements for younger men to defer to older men and for women to defer to men, as well as to the women of a household they marry into, are common sources of tension in a patrilineal society.

■ Matrilineal descent is traced exclusively through the female line, just as patrilineal descent is through the male line. However, the matrilineal pattern differs from the patrilineal in that it does not automatically confer gender authority.

■ The matrilineal system is common in societies where women perform much of the productive work. This system may be a source of family tension, since the husband's authority lies not in his own household but in that of his sister. This, and the ease with which unsatisfactory marriages may be ended, often result in higher divorce rates in matrilineal than in patrilineal societies. Double descent is matrilineal for some purposes and patrilineal for others. Ambilineal descent provides a measure of flexibility in that an individual has the option of affiliating with either the mother's *or* father's descent group. When descent derives from *both* the mother's and father's families equally, anthropologists use the term *bilateral descent*.

■ Descent groups are often highly structured economic units that function to provide aid and security to their members. They also may be repositories of religious tradition, with group solidarity enhanced by worship of a common ancestor.

■ A lineage is a unilineal descent group descended from a known ancestor, or founder, and in which relationships between each member can be exactly stated in genealogical terms. Since lineages are commonly exogamous, sexual competition within the group is largely avoided. In addition, marriage of a group member represents an alliance of two lineages. Lineage exogamy also serves to maintain open communication within a society and fosters the exchange of information among lineages.

■ Fission is the splitting of a large lineage group into new, smaller ones, with the original lineage becoming a clan. Clan members claim common descent from a remote ancestor, usually legendary or mythological. Unlike lineages, clan residence is usually dispersed rather than localized. In the absence of residential unity, clan identification is often reinforced by totems, usually symbols from nature that remind members of their common ancestry. A phratry is a unilineal descent group of two or more clans that supposedly share a common ancestry. When a society is divided into two halves, each half consisting of one or more clans, these two major descent groups are called moieties.

■ In bilateral societies, such as industrial, postindustrial, and many food-foraging societies, individuals are affiliated equally with all relatives on both the mother's and father's sides. Such a large group is socially impractical and is usually reduced to a small circle of paternal and maternal relatives called the kindred. A kindred is never the same for any two people except siblings. Different types of descent systems appear in different societies. In those where the nuclear family predominates, bilateral kinship and kindred organization are likely to prevail.

■ In any society cultural rules dictate the way kinship relationships are defined. Factors such as gender and generational or genealogical differences help distinguish one kin from another. The Hawaiian system is the simplest system of kinship terminology, with all relatives of the same generation and gender referred to by the same term. The Eskimo system, also used by English-speaking North Americans and many others, emphasizes the nuclear family and merges all other relatives in a given generation into a few large, generally undifferentiated categories. In the Iroquois system, a single term is used for father and his brother and another for a mother and her sister. Parallel cousins are equated with brothers and sisters but distinguished from cross cousins.

■ With new reproductive technologies that separate conception from birth and eggs from wombs, traditional notions of kinship and gender are being challenged, and new social categories are emerging.

■ Grouping by gender separates men and women to varying degrees in different societies; in some, they may be together much of the time, while in others they may spend much of their time apart, even to the extreme of eating and sleeping separately.

■ Age grouping is another form of association that may augment or replace kinship grouping. An age grade is a category of people organized by age. Some societies have not only age grades, but also age sets, comprised of individuals who are initiated into an age grade at the same time and move together through a series of life stages. The most varied use of age grouping is found in African societies south of the Sahara. Among the Tiriki of East Africa, for example, seven named age sets pass through four successive age grades.

■ Common-interest associations are linked with rapid social change and urbanization. They have increasingly assumed the roles formerly played by kinship or age groups. In urban areas they help new arrivals cope with the changes demanded by the move. Common-interest associations also are seen in traditional societies, and their roots may be found in the first horticultural villages.

■ A stratified society is divided into two or more categories of people who do not share equally in wealth, influence, or prestige. Societies may be stratified by gender, age, social class, or caste. Class differences are not always clear-cut and obvious. Caste is a closed form of social class in which membership is determined by birth and fixed for life. Endogamy is particularly marked within castes, and children automatically belong to their parents' caste.

■ Social class is based on role differentiation, although this by itself is not sufficient for stratification. Also necessary are formalized positive and negative attitudes toward roles and restricted access to the more valued ones. Social classes are given expression in several ways. One is through symbolic indicators: activities and possessions indicative of class position.

■ Social mobility is present to a greater or lesser extent in all stratified societies. Open-class societies are those with the easiest mobility. In most cases, however, the move is limited to one rung up or down the social ladder. The degree of mobility is related to factors such as access to higher education or the type of family organization that prevails in a society. Where the extended family is the norm, mobility tends to be severely limited. The independent nuclear family makes mobility easier.

Questions for Reflection

1. Suppose that for reasons of support and security, you were forced to create and maintain a social network of relatives beyond your immediate family or household. How would you meet that challenge?

2. People growing up in modern industrial and postindustrial societies generally treasure ideas of personal freedom, individuality, and privacy as essential in their pursuit of happiness. Considering the social functions of kinship relations in traditional non-state societies, why do you think that such ideas may be considered unsociable and even dangerously selfish?

3. Why do you think that one of the most simple kinship terminology systems imaginable, namely the Eskimo system, is functionally adequate for most Europeans, North Americans, and others living in complex modern societies?

4. When teenagers leave their parental home to go to college or find employment in a distant part of the country, they face the challenge of establishing social relationships that are not based on kinship but on common interest. To which common-interest associations do you belong and why?

5. Why do you think that members of an upper class or caste in a socially stratified system have a greater vested interest in the idea of "law and order" than those forced to exist on the bottom of such societies?

Key Terms

kinship
descent group
unilineal descent
matrilineal descent
patrilineal descent
lineage
clan
fission
totemism
phratry
moiety
kindred

Eskimo system
Hawaiian system
Iroquois system
new reproductive
    technologies
age grade
age set
common-interest
    associations
stratified societies
egalitarian societies
social class
caste

Multimedia Review Tools

Make the Grade in Anthropology with ThomsonNOW

Thomson NOW! This powerful online study tool provides you with a *personalized study plan* based on your responses to a diagnostic pretest. Once you have mastered the material with the help of interactive learning tools, an integrated e-book, and more, you can take a post-test to confirm you are ready to move on to the next chapter. To get started with ThomsonNOW, check the card packaged with your book for the access code. Then go to http://www.thomsonedu.com to create an account through 1pass™. If there is no card in your book, go to http://www.thomsonedu.com to purchase an access code.

Companion Website and Anthropology Resource Center

Go to http://anthropology.wadsworth.com to reach the companion website for your text. This offers many study aids, including self quizzes for each chapter and a practice final exam, as well as links to anthropology websites and information on the latest theories and discoveries in the field.

Also, check out the Anthropology Resource Center for a wealth of learning materials that include interactive maps, video exercises, simulations, and breaking news in anthropology. Be sure to explore InfoTrac College Edition®, your online library that offers full-length articles from thousands of scholarly and popular publications. To reach the Anthropology Resource Center and InfoTrac College Edition, check the card packaged with your book for the access code. Then go to http://www.thomsonedu.com to create an account through 1pass™. If there is no card in your book, go to http://www.thomsonedu.com to purchase an access code.

© AP Photo/Santiago Andrade/World Wide Photo

CHALLENGE ISSUE

In all societies, from the largest to the smallest, people must decide who gets what, when, where, and how. This is the basic challenge of politics. Political organization takes many forms, of which the state is just one. Often, states are controlled by members of one nationality who use power to repress (or even exterminate) other nationalities within the state. Here, Ecuador's Quechua Indians burn an effigy of the president of that South American country in protest against government policies that they feel enrich the wealthy at the expense of poor indigenous communities.

Politics, Power, and Violence

15

Complex political structures known as states first began to emerge over 5,000 years ago. Commonly unstable, many have disappeared in the course of history, some temporarily and others forever. Some were annexed by other states, and others collapsed or fragmented into small political units. Although some present-day states are very old—such as Japan, which has endured as a state for almost 1,500 years—few are older than the United States, an independent country since 1783.

Despite the predominance of state societies today, there are still groups where political organization consists of flexible and informal kinship systems whose leaders lack real **power**—the ability of individuals or groups to impose their will upon others and make them do things even against their own wants or wishes. Between these two polarities of kin-ordered and state-organized political systems lies a world of variety.

KINDS OF POLITICAL SYSTEMS

The term **political organization** refers to the way power is distributed and embedded in society, whether in organizing a giraffe hunt, managing irrigated farmlands, or raising an army. In short, it is the means through which a society creates and maintains social

power The ability of individuals or groups to impose their will upon others and make them do things even against their own wants or wishes.

political organization The way power is distributed and embedded in society; the means through which a society creates and maintains social order and reduces social disorder.

267

order. It assumes a variety of forms among the peoples of the world, but anthropologists have simplified this complex subject by identifying four basic kinds of political systems: bands, tribes, chiefdoms, and states (Figure 15.1). The first two are uncentralized systems; the latter two are centralized.

Uncentralized Political Systems

Until recently, many non-Western peoples have had neither chiefs with established rights and duties nor any fixed form of government, as those who live in modern states understand the term. Instead, marriage and kinship have formed their principal means of social organization. The economies of these societies are primarily of a subsistence type, and populations are typically small.

Leaders do not have real power to force compliance with the society's customs or rules, but if individuals do not conform, they may become targets of scorn and gossip or even be banished. Important decisions are usually made in a collective manner by agreement among adults. Dissenting members may decide to act with the majority, or they may choose to adopt some other course of action, including leaving the group. This egalitarian form of political organization provides great flexibility, which in many situations offers an adaptive advantage. Since power in these kin-ordered communities is shared, with nobody exercising exclusive control over collective resources or public affairs, individuals typically enjoy much more freedom

TYPES OF POLITICAL ORGANIZATION
The symbol ➛ indicates that the attribute varies between less and more complex societies of that type.

	BAND	TRIBE	CHIEFDOM	STATE
MEMBERSHIP				
Number of people	Dozens and up	Hundreds and up	Thousands and up	Tens of thousands and up
Settlement pattern	Mobile	Mobile or fixed: 1 or more villages	Fixed: 2 or more villages	Fixed: Many villages and cities
Basis of relationships	Kin	Kin, descent groups	Kin, rank, and residence	Class and residence
Ethnicities and languages	1	1	1	1 or more
GOVERNMENT				
Decision making, leadership	"Egalitarian"	"Egalitarian" or Big-Man	Centralized, hereditary	Centralized
Bureaucracy	None	None	None, or 1 or 2 levels	Many levels
Monopoly of force and information	No	No	No ➛ Yes	Yes
Conflict resolution	Informal	Informal	Centralized	Laws, judges
Hierarchy of settlement	No	No	No ➛ Paramount village or head town	Capital
ECONOMY				
Food production	No	No ➛ Yes	Yes ➛ Intensive	Intensive
Labor specialization	No	No	No ➛ Yes	Yes
Exchanges	Reciprocal	Reciprocal	Redistributive ("tribute")	Redistributive ("taxes")
Control of land	Band	Descent group	Chief	Various
SOCIETY				
Stratified	No	No	Yes, ranked by kin	Yes, by class or caste
Slavery	No	No	Some, small-scale	Some, large-scale
Luxury goods for elite	No	No	Yes	Yes
Public architecture	No	No	No ➛ Yes	Yes
Indigenous literacy	No	No	No ➛ Some	Often

Figure 15.1 Four Kinds of Political Systems

than those who form part of larger and more complex political systems.

Band Organization

The **band** is a relatively small and loosely organized kin-ordered group that inhabits a specific territory and that may split periodically into smaller extended family groups that are politically independent. Typically, bands are found among food foragers and other nomadic societies where people organize into politically autonomous extended-family groups that usually camp together, although the members of such families may periodically break up into smaller groups to forage for food or visit other relatives. The band is probably the oldest form of political organization, since all humans were once food foragers and remained so until the development of farming and pastoralism over the past 10,000 years.

Since bands are egalitarian and small, numbering at most a few hundred people, no real need exists for formal, centralized political systems. Because everyone is related to—and knows on a personal basis—everyone else with whom dealings are required, there is high value placed on "getting along." Conflicts that do arise are usually settled informally through gossip, ridicule, direct negotiation, or mediation. When negotiation or mediation are used, the focus is on reaching a solution considered fair by all concerned parties, rather than on conforming to some abstract law or rule. Where all else fails, disgruntled individuals have the option of leaving the band to go live in another where they may have relatives or trying to establish a new community of their own.

Decisions affecting a band are made with the participation of all its adult members, with an emphasis on achieving consensus—a collective agreement—rather than a simple majority. Individuals become leaders by virtue of their abilities and serve in that capacity only as long as they retain the confidence of the community. They have no real power to force people to abide by their decisions. A leader who exceeds what people are willing to accept quickly loses followers.

An example of the informal nature of band leadership is found among the Ju/'hoansi Bushmen of the Kalahari Desert mentioned in earlier chapters. Each Ju/'hoansi band is composed of a group of families that live together, linked through kinship to one another and to the headman (or, less often, headwoman). Although each band has rights to the territory it occupies and the resources within it, two or more bands may range over the same land. The head, called the *kxau,* or "owner," is the focal point for the band's claims on the territory. He or she does not personally own the land or resources but symbolically represents the rights of band members to them. If the head leaves the area to live elsewhere, people turn to someone else to lead them.

The head coordinates band migration when resources are no longer adequate for subsistence in a particular habitat. This leader's major duty is to plan when and where the group will move, and when the move begins his or her position is at the head of the line. The leader selects the site for the new settlement and has the first choice of a spot for his or her own fire. There are few other material rewards or duties. For example, a Ju/'hoansi head is not a judge and does not punish other band members. Wrongdoers are judged and held accountable by public opinion, usually expressed by gossip—which can play an important role in curbing socially unacceptable behavior. A prime technique for resolving disputes, or even avoiding them in the first place, is mobility. Those unable to get along with others of their group simply move to another group where kinship ties may give them rights of entry.

Tribal Organization

The second type of uncentralized authority system is the tribe. This term is problematic because it has many meanings, and over time it has come to be widely used as a label for any people not organized into states. In anthropology, **tribe** refers to a wide range of kin-ordered groups that are politically integrated by some unifying factor and whose members share a common ancestry, identity, culture, language, and territory. In these larger political entities, people sacrifice a degree of household autonomy in return for greater security against such perils as enemy attacks or starvation.

Typically, though not invariably, a tribe has an economy based on some form of crop cultivation or herding. Since these subsistence methods usually yield more food than those of the food-foraging band, tribal membership is typically larger than band membership. While band population densities are usually less than one person per square mile, tribal population densities generally exceed that and may be as high as 250 per square mile. Greater population density brings a new set of problems to be solved as opportunities for bickering,

---

band A relatively small and loosely organized kin-ordered group that inhabits a specific territory and that may split periodically into smaller extended family groups that are politically independent.

tribe In anthropology, refers to a range of kin-ordered groups that are politically integrated by some unifying factor and whose members share a common ancestry, identity, culture, language, and territory.

begging, adultery, and theft increase markedly, especially among people living in permanent villages.

Each tribe consists of one or more self-supporting and self-governing local communities that may then form alliances with others for various purposes. As in the band, political organization in the tribe is informal and temporary. Whenever a situation requiring political integration of all or several groups within the tribe arises—perhaps for defense, to carry out a raid, to pool resources in times of scarcity, or to capitalize on a windfall that must be distributed quickly lest it spoil—groups join to deal with the situation in a cooperative manner. When the problem is satisfactorily solved, each group then resumes autonomy.

In many tribal societies the organizing unit and seat of political authority is the clan, comprised of people who consider themselves descended from a common ancestor. Within the clan, elders or headmen and/or headwomen regulate members' affairs and represent their clan in interactions with other clans. As a group, the elders of all the clans may form a council that acts within the community or for the community in dealings with outsiders. Because clan members usually do not all live together in a single community, clan organization facilitates joint action with members of related communities when necessary.

Leadership among tribes is also relatively informal, as evident in a wide array of past and present examples. The Navajo Indians in the southwestern United States, for example, traditionally did not think of government as something fixed and all-powerful, and leadership was not vested in a central authority. A local leader was a man respected for his age, integrity, and wisdom. Therefore, people sought his advice frequently, but he had no formal means of control and could not force any decision on those who asked for his help. Group decisions were made by public consensus, although the most influential man usually played a key role in reaching a decision. Social mechanisms that induced members to abide by group decisions included gossip, criticism, withdrawal of cooperation, and the belief that antisocial actions caused sickness and other misfortune.

Another example of tribal leadership is the Big Man. Common in the southern Pacific, such men are leaders of localized descent groups or of a territorial group. The Big Man combines a small amount of interest in his tribe's welfare with a great deal of cunning and calculation for his own personal gain. His authority is personal; he does not come to office in any formal sense, nor is he elected. His status is the result of acts that raise him above most other tribe members and attract to him a number of loyal followers.

The Kapauku of western New Guinea typify this form of political organization. Among them, the Big Man is called the *tonowi,* or "rich one." To achieve this status, one must be male, wealthy, generous, and eloquent. Physical bravery and an ability to deal with the supernatural are also common *tonowi* characteristics, but they are not essential. The *tonowi* functions as the headman of the village unit in a wide variety of situations within and beyond the community. He represents his group in dealing with outsiders and other villages and acts as negotiator and/or judge when disputes break out among his followers.

Because Kapauku culture places a high value on wealth, a well-to-do man is considered successful and admirable—provided he is also generous when it comes to making loans. Those who refuse to lend money to other villagers may be ostracized, ridiculed, and, in extreme cases, actually executed by a group of warriors. Such responses to tightfistedness ensure that economic wealth is distributed throughout the group.

The *tonowi's* wealth comes from his success at breeding pigs—the focus of the entire Kapauku economy. It is not uncommon for a *tonowi* to lose his fortune rapidly due to bad management or bad luck with his pigs. Thus the Kapauku political structure shifts

This Big Man from New Guinea is wearing his "official" regalia.

© George Holton/Photo Researchers, Inc.

frequently; as one man loses wealth and consequently power, another gains it and becomes a *tonowi*. These changes confer a degree of flexibility on the political organization and prevent any one *tonowi* from holding political power for too long. Although it is far more common for tribal chiefs to be men, in some cultures women serve in such leadership positions, as discussed later in this chapter.

Political Integration Beyond the Kin Group

Age sets, age grades, and common-interest groups discussed in the previous chapter are among the mechanisms used by tribal societies as means of political integration. Cutting across territorial and kin groupings, these organizations link members from different lineages and clans. For example, among many Indian nations inhabiting North America's Great Plains in the 19th century, the band comprised the basic territorial and political unit. In addition, however, there existed a number of military societies or warrior clubs.

Among the Cheyenne, for instance, there were seven of these groups. A boy might be invited to join one of these societies when he achieved warrior status, whereupon he became familiar with the society's particular insignia, songs, and rituals. Beyond military functions, the warrior societies also had ceremonial and social functions. The Cheyenne warriors' daily tasks consisted of overseeing activities in the village, protecting families on the move to the next camping site, and enforcing rules against individual hunting when the whole tribe was on a buffalo hunt. In addition, each warrior society had its own repertoire of dances, performed on special ceremonial occasions. Since each Cheyenne band had identical military societies bearing identical names, the societies served to integrate the entire tribe for military and political purposes.[1]

Centralized Political Systems

In bands and tribes, political authority is not centralized, and each group is economically and politically autonomous. Political organization is vested in kinship, age, and common-interest groups. Populations are small and relatively homogeneous, with people engaged for the most part in the same sorts of activities throughout their lives. However, as a society's social life becomes more complex—as population rises, technology becomes more intricate, and specialization of labor and trade networks produce surplus goods—the opportunity increases for some individuals or groups to exercise control at the expense of others. In such societies, political authority and power are concentrated in a single individual (the chief) or in a body of individuals (the state).

Chiefdoms

A **chiefdom** is a regional polity in which two or more local groups are organized under a single ruling individual—the chief—who is at the head of a ranked hierarchy of people. An individual's status in such a polity is determined by the closeness of his or her relationship to the chief. Those closest are officially superior and receive deferential treatment from those in lower ranks.

The office of the chief is usually for life and often hereditary. Typically, it passes from a man to his son or his sister's son, depending on whether descent is reckoned patrilineally or matrilineally. Unlike the headmen or headwomen in bands and tribes, the leader of a chiefdom is generally a true authority figure, whose authority serves to unite members in all affairs and at all times. For example, a chief can distribute land among community members and recruit people into military service. Chiefdoms have a recognized hierarchy consisting of major and minor authorities who control major and minor subdivisions. Such an arrangement is, in effect, a chain of command, linking leaders at every level. It serves to bind groups in the heartland to the chief's headquarters, be it a mud and dung hut or a marble palace. Although leaders of chiefdoms are almost always men, in some cultures a politically astute wife, sister, or single daughter of a deceased male chief could inherit such a powerful position as well.

Chiefs usually control the economic activities of those who fall under their political rule. Typically, chiefdoms involve redistributive systems, and the chief has control over surplus goods and perhaps even over the community's labor force. Thus, he (and sometimes she) may demand a quota of rice from farmers, which will then be redistributed to the entire community. Similarly, laborers may be recruited to build irrigation works, a palace, or a temple.

The chief may also amass a great amount of personal wealth and pass it on to offspring. Land, cattle, and luxury goods produced by specialists can be collected by the chief and become part of the power base. Moreover, high-ranking families of the chiefdom may engage in the same practice and use their possessions as evidence of noble status.

---

[1]Hoebel, E. A. (1960). *The Cheyennes: Indians of the Great Plains*. New York: Holt, Rinehart and Winston.

chiefdom A regional polity in which two or more local groups are organized under a single chief, who is at the head of a ranked hierarchy of people.

An example of this form of political organization may be seen among the Kpelle of Liberia in West Africa.[2] Among them is a class of paramount chiefs, each of whom presides over one of the Kpelle chiefdoms (each of which is now a district of the Liberian state). The paramount chiefs' traditional tasks are hearing disputes, preserving order, seeing to the upkeep of trails, and various other supervising functions. In addition, they are now salaried officials of the Liberian government, mediating between it and their own people. Also, a paramount chief receives government commissions on taxes and court fees collected within his chiefdom, plus a commission for furnishing the rubber plantations with laborers. Moreover, he gets a stipulated amount of rice from each household and gifts from people who come to request favors and intercessions. In keeping with his exalted station in life, a paramount chief has at his disposal uniformed messengers, a literate clerk, and the symbols of wealth: many wives, embroidered gowns, and freedom from manual labor.

In a ranked hierarchy beneath each Kpelle paramount chief are several lesser chiefs: one for each district within the chiefdom, one for each town with-in a district, and one for each quarter of all but the smallest towns. Each acts as a kind of lieutenant for his chief of the next higher rank and also serves as a liaison between him and those of lower rank. Unlike paramount or district chiefs, who are comparatively remote, town and quarter chiefs are readily accessible to people at the local level.

Traditionally, chiefdoms in all parts of the world have been highly unstable, with lesser chiefs trying to take power from higher ranking chiefs or paramount chiefs vying with one another for supreme power. In precolonial Hawaii, for example, war was the way to gain territory and maintain power; great chiefs set out to conquer one another in an effort to become paramount chief of all the islands. When one chief conquered another, the loser and all his nobles were dispossessed of all property and were lucky if they escaped alive. The new chief then appointed his own supporters to positions of political power. As a consequence, there was very little continuity of governmental or religious administration.

State Systems

The **state,** the most formal of political organizations, is one of the hallmarks of what is commonly referred to as civilization. It is a centralized political system involving large numbers of people within a defined territory who are organized and directed by a formal government that has the capacity and authority to make laws and use force to defend the social order. From the perspective of the political elite in control of the state, its formation and endurance are typically represented as something positive—as progress. This view is not necessarily shared by those who exist on the political underside and do not possess much personal freedom to say and do as they please.

A large population in a state-organized society requires increased food production and wider distribution networks. Together, these result in a transformation of the landscape by way of irrigation and terracing, carefully managed crop rotation cycles, and intensive competition for clearly demarcated lands and roads, plus enough farmers and other rural workers to support market systems and a specialized urban sector. Under such conditions, corporate groups that stress exclusive membership proliferate, ethnic differentiation, and ethnocentrism become more pronounced, and the potential for social conflict increases dramatically. Given these circumstances, state institutions, which minimally involve a bureaucracy, a military, and (usually) an official religion, provide a means for numerous and diverse groups to function together as an integrated whole.

Although their guiding ideology is that they are permanent and stable, the truth is, since their first appearance some 5,000 years ago, states have been anything but permanent. Whatever stability they have achieved has been short term at best; over the long term, they show a clear tendency toward instability and transience. Nowhere have states even begun to show the staying power exhibited by less centralized political systems, the longest lasting social forms invented by humans.

An important distinction to make at this point is between state and nation. As noted in Chapter 1, a **nation** is a people who share a collective identity based on a common culture, language, territorial base, and history. Today, there are roughly 200 internationally recognized states in the world, most of which did not exist

---

[2]Gibbs, J. L., Jr. (1965). The Kpelle of Liberia. In J. L. Gibbs, Jr. (Ed.), *Peoples of Africa* (pp. 216–218). New York: Holt, Rinehart and Winston.

state In anthropology, a centralized political system that has the capacity and authority to make laws and use force to maintain social order.

nation A people who share a collective identity based on a common culture, language, territorial base, and history.

before the end of World War II (1945). By contrast, there are about 5,000 nations (including tribes), many of which have existed since "time immemorial." Rarely do state and nation coincide, as they do, for example, in Iceland, Japan, and Swaziland.

About 73 percent of the world's states are pluralistic societies, having within their boundaries peoples of more than one nation. Often, smaller nations (including tribes) and other groups find themselves at the mercy of one or more dominant nations or ethnic groups controlling the state. Frequently facing discrimination, even repression, some minority nations seek to improve their political position by founding an independent state. In the process, they usually encounter stiff opposition, even violent confrontations. So it is with the Kurdish people inhabiting the borderlands of Iran, Iraq, and Turkey (Figure 15.2), the Palestinians whose lands have been occupied by Israel for several decades, and the Chechens in the Russian federation, to cite but a few examples. While the outcome of armed struggle may be the formation of a new state (such as Bosnia's recent split from Serb-dominated Yugoslavia), some nations have forged their own states without open violence. Papua New Guinea in the southern Pacific, which became an independent state in 1975, is one example of this.

An important aspect of the state is its delegation of authority to maintain order within and outside its borders. Police, foreign ministries, war ministries, and other bureaucracies function to control and punish disruptive acts of crime, terror, and rebellion. By such agencies the state asserts authority impersonally and in a consistent, predictable manner. Western forms of government, like that of the United States (in reality, a superstate), of course, are state governments, and their organization and workings are undoubtedly familiar to most everyone.

POLITICAL SYSTEMS AND THE QUESTION OF LEGITIMACY

Whatever form a society's political system may take, it must find some way to obtain and retain the people's allegiance. In uncentralized systems, where every adult participates in all decision making, loyalty and cooperation are freely given, since each person is considered a part of the political system. As the group grows larger, however, and the organization becomes more formal, the problem of obtaining and keeping public support becomes greater.

Centralized political systems may rely upon coercion as a means of social control. This, however, carries a measure of risk since the personnel needed to apply force must be numerous and may grow to be a political power. Also, the emphasis on force may create resentment and lessen cooperation. Thus, police states are generally short-lived, and most societies choose less extreme forms of social coercion. In the United States, this is reflected in the increasing emphasis placed on cultural, as opposed to social, control.

Also basic to the political process is the concept of **legitimacy,** or the right of political leaders to govern. Like force, legitimacy is a form of support for a political system; unlike force, legitimacy is based on the values a particular society holds. For example, among the Kapauku the legitimacy of the *tonowi's* power comes from his wealth; the kings of Hawaii, and of England and France before their revolutions, were thought to have a divine right to rule; and the head of the traditional Dahomey state in what is now Benin, West Africa, acquired legitimacy through his age, as he was always the oldest living male.

Legitimacy grants the right to hold, use, and allocate power. Power based on legitimacy results in authority. It is distinct from power based solely on force: Obedience to authority results from the belief that obedience is "right"; compliance to power based on force results from fear of being deprived of liberty, physical well-being, life, or material property. Thus, power based on legitimacy is symbolic and depends upon the positive expectations of those who recognize and accept it. If the expectations are not met regularly (if the head of state fails to deliver economic prosperity or the leader is continuously unsuccessful in preventing or dealing

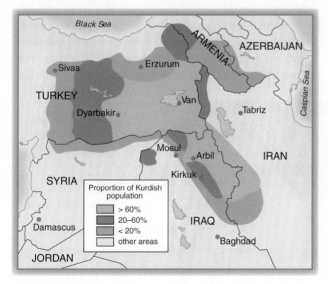

Figure 15.2
The Kurds, most of whom live in Iran, Iraq, and Turkey, are an example of a nation without a state.

legitimacy The right of political leaders to govern—to hold, use, and allocate power—based on the values a particular society holds.

with calamities), the legitimacy of the recognized power figure erodes or may collapse altogether.

POLITICS AND RELIGION

Religion is often intricately connected with politics. Frequently it is religion that legitimizes the political order. Religious beliefs may influence laws: Acts that people believe to be sinful, such as incest, are often illegal as well.

In both industrial and nonindustrial societies, belief in the supernatural is important and is reflected in people's governments. One place where the effect of religion on politics was well exemplified was in medieval Europe: Holy wars were fought over the smallest matter; labor was mobilized to build immense cathedrals in honor of the Virgin Mary and other saints; kings and queens ruled by "divine right" and (in the West) pledged allegiance to the pope and asked his blessing in all important ventures, were they marital or martial.

In Peru, the divine ruler of the Inca empire proclaimed absolute authority based on the proposition that he was descended from the Sun God. Mexico's ancient Aztec state was also a politico-religious one, having a divine ruler and engaging in nearly constant warfare to procure captives for human sacrifices thought necessary to assuage or please the gods. Modern Iran was proclaimed an "Islamic republic," and its first head of state was the most holy of all Shiite Muslim holy men. The fact that the president of the United States takes the oath of office by swearing on the Bible is another instance of the use of religion to legitimize political power, as is the phrase "one nation, under God" in the Pledge of Allegiance. In the U.S., coins feature the saying "In God We Trust," many meetings of government bodies begin with a prayer or invocation, and the phrase "so help me God" is routinely used in legal proceedings. In spite of an official separation of church and state, religious legitimization of government lingers.

POLITICAL LEADERSHIP AND GENDER

Irrespective of cultural configuration or type of political organization, women hold important positions of political leadership far less often than men. Furthermore, when they do occupy publicly recognized offices, their power and authority rarely exceed those of men. But significant exceptions occur. Historically, one might cite the female chiefs, or *sachems,* of Algonquian Indian communities in southern New England, as well as powerful queens in several Asian, African, and European monarchies. One historical example is Aimata, who succeeded her deceased half-brother Pomare III as leader of the Polynesian chiefdom of Tahiti in 1827, ruling as Queen Pomare IV until her death 50 years later. Perhaps most notable is Queen Victoria, the long-reigning queen of England, Scotland, Wales, and Ireland. Also recognized as monarch in a host of colonies all over the world, Victoria even acquired the title Empress of India. Ruling the British empire from 1837 until 1901, she was perhaps the world's most powerful leader.

In addition to inheriting high positions of political leadership, growing numbers of women have also been elected as presidents or prime ministers. Countries with female heads of state now or in recent years include Indonesia, Pakistan, Ireland, Sri Lanka, Norway, India, Turkey, Liberia, Chile, Germany, and the Philippines, to mention just a few. While such high profile female leadership is still relatively rare, women regularly enjoy as much political power as men in a number of societies. In band societies, for example, it is common for females to have as much of a say in public affairs as males, even though more often than not the latter are the nominal leaders of their groups.

Among the Iroquois nations of New York State, all leadership positions above the household and clan level were, without exception, filled by men. Thus men held all positions on the village and tribal councils, as well as

In contrast to countries such as the United States, where religion and state are constitutionally separated, countries such as Iran and Great Britain permit a much closer relationship between political and religious affairs. For instance, Shiite Muslim religious leader Ayatollah Khamenei is not only Iran's supreme spiritual leader but also his country's highest political authority. In England, Queen Elizabeth is not only her country's nominal head of state but also head of the Anglican Church.

© Reuters/Corbis

© K. Prouse/Pressnet/Topham/The Image Works

on the great council of the Iroquois Confederacy. However, they were completely beholden to women, for only women could nominate men to high office. Moreover, women actively lobbied the men on the councils and could have someone removed from office whenever it suited them.

Lower visibility in politics does not necessarily indicate that women lack power in political affairs. And just as there are various ways in which women play a role behind the scenes, so it is when they have more visible roles, as in the dual-sex system of the Igbo in Nigeria, West Africa. Among the Igbo, each political unit has separate political institutions for men and women, so that both have an autonomous sphere of authority, as well as an area of shared responsibility.[3] At the head of each political unit was a male *obi*, considered the head of government although in fact he presided over the male community, and a female *omu*, the acknowledged mother of the whole community but in practice concerned with the female section of the community. Unlike a queen (though both she and the *obi* were crowned), the *omu* was neither the *obi's* wife nor the previous *obi's* daughter.

Just as the *obi* had a council of dignitaries to advise him and act as a check against any arbitrary exercise of power, the *omu* was served by a council of women in equal number to the *obi's* male councilors. The duties of the *omu* and her councilors involved such tasks as establishing rules and regulations for the community market (marketing was a woman's activity) and hearing cases involving women brought to her from throughout the town or village. If such cases also involved men, then she and her council would cooperate with the *obi* and his council. Widows also went to the *omu* for the final rites required to end their period of mourning for dead husbands. Since the *omu* represented all women, she had to be responsive to her constituency and would seek their approval and cooperation in all major decisions.

In addition to the *omu* and her council, the Igbo women's government included a representative body of women chosen from each quarter or section of the village or town. Moreover, political pressure groups of women acted at the village or lineage level to stop quarrels and prevent wars. These pressure groups included women born into a community (most of whom lived elsewhere since villages were exogamous and residence was patrilocal) and women who had married into the community. Their duties included helping companion wives in times of illness and stress and meting out discipline to lazy or recalcitrant husbands.

In the Igbo system, then, women managed their own affairs, and their interests were represented at all levels of government. Moreover, they had the right to enforce their decisions and rules with sanctions similar to those employed by men, including strikes, boycotts, and "sitting on a man" or woman. Political scientist Judith Van Allen, senior fellow at Cornell University's Institute for African Development, describes the latter:

> To "sit on" or "make war on" a man involved gathering at his compound, sometimes late at night, dancing, singing scurrilous songs which detailed the women's grievances against him and often called his manhood into question, banging on his hut with the pestles women used for pounding yams, and perhaps demolishing his hut or plastering it with mud and roughing him up a bit. A man might be sanctioned in this way for mistreating his wife, for violating the women's market rules, or for letting his cows eat the women's crops. The women would stay at his hut throughout the day, and late into the night if necessary, until he repented and promised to mend his ways.[4]

Given the high visibility of women in the Igbo political system, it may come as a surprise to learn that when the British imposed colonial rule on the Igbo in the late 1800s, they failed to recognize the autonomy and power of the women. One reason is that the British were blinded by their own cultural values, reflecting a male-dominated society in which the domestic sphere was seen as the ideal place for women. This is ironic because the long-reigning and powerful head of the British empire at the time was, as mentioned earlier, Queen Victoria. Nevertheless, unable to imagine that Igbo women might play important roles in politics, the British introduced "reforms" that destroyed traditional forms of female autonomy and power without providing alternative forms in exchange. As a result, Igbo women lost much of their traditional equality and became subordinate to men.

---

[3]Okonjo, K. (1976). The dual-sex political system in operation: Igbo women and community politics in midwestern Nigeria. In N. Hafkin & E. Bay (Eds.), *Women in Africa*. Stanford, CA: Stanford University Press.

[4]Van Allen, J. (1997). Sitting on a man: Colonialism and the lost political institutions of Igbo women. In R. Grinker & C. Steiner (Eds.), *Perspectives on Africa* (p. 450). Boston: Blackwell Press.

POLITICAL ORGANIZATION AND THE MAINTENANCE OF ORDER

Political organization always includes means of maintaining order that ensure people behave in acceptable ways and define what action will be taken when they do not. In chiefdoms and states, some sort of authority has the power to regulate the affairs of society. In bands and tribes, however, people behave generally as they are expected to, without the direct intervention of any centralized political authority. To a large degree, gossip, criticism, fear of supernatural forces, and the like serve as effective deterrents to antisocial behavior.

As an example of how such seemingly informal considerations serve to keep people in line, we may look at the Wape people of Papua New Guinea, who believe the spirits of deceased ancestors roam lineage lands, protecting them from trespassers and helping their hunting descendants by driving game their way.[5] These ancestral spirits also punish those who have wronged them or their descendants by preventing hunters from finding game or causing them to miss their shots, thereby depriving people of much needed meat.

Nowadays, the Wape hunt with shotguns, which the community purchases for the use of one man, whose job it is to hunt for all the others. The cartridges used in the hunt, however, are invariably supplied by individual community members. Thus, if the gunman shoots and misses, it is not viewed as his failing. Rather, it is because the owner of the fired shell, or some close relative, has quarreled or wronged another person whose deceased relative is securing revenge by causing the hunter to miss. Or, if the gunman cannot even find game, it is because vengeful ancestors have chased the animals away. As a proxy hunter for the villagers, the gunman is potentially subject to sanctions by ancestral spirits in response to collective wrongs by those for whom he hunts.

For the Wape, then, successful hunting depends upon avoiding quarrels and maintaining tranquility within the community so as not to antagonize anybody's deceased ancestor. Unfortunately, complete harmony is impossible to achieve in any human community, and the Wape are no exception. Thus, when hunting is poor, the gunman must discover what quarrels and wrongs have occurred within his village to identify the proper ancestral spirits to appeal to for renewed success. Usually, this is done in a special meeting where confessions of wrongdoing may be forthcoming. If not, questioning accusations are bandied about until resolution occurs, but even with no resolution, the meeting must end amicably to prevent new antagonisms. Thus,

everyone's behavior comes under public scrutiny, reminding all of what is expected of them and encouraging all to avoid acts that will cast them in an unfavorable light.

Internalized Controls

The Wape concern about ancestral spirits is a good example of internalized, or cultural, controls—beliefs that are so thoroughly ingrained that each person becomes personally responsible for his or her own conduct. **Cultural control** may be thought of as control through beliefs and values deeply internalized in the minds of individuals, as opposed to **social control,** which involves external enforcement through open coercion.

Cultural controls are embedded in our consciousness and may rely on deterrents such as fear of supernatural punishment—ancestral spirits sabotaging the hunting, for example—and magical retaliation. Like the devout Christian who avoids sinning for fear of hell, the individual expects some sort of punishment, even though no one in the community may be aware of the wrongdoing.

Cultural controls can also be framed in positive terms, with customary ways and means that encourage individual sacrifice for the common good. For example, many cultures honor traditions of giving to, or volunteering for, charitable or humanitarian institutions. Performed out of a desire to help those in need, such personal sacrifices (Latin: *sacer,* "holy"; *facere,* "making") may be motivated by a spiritual or religious worldview. Often deeply rooted in basic ideas of a wider community and reciprocity, they are also cultural controls against self-seeking, self-serving, greedy opportunism that threaten the well-being of a larger community.

Externalized Controls

Because internalized controls are not wholly sufficient even in bands and tribes, every society develops externalized social controls known as **sanctions** designed to encourage conformity to social norms. Operating within social groups of all sizes and involving a mix of cultural and social controls, sanctions may vary significantly within a given society, but they fall into one of two categories: positive or negative.

---

cultural control Control through beliefs and values deeply internalized in the minds of individuals.

social control External control through open coercion.

sanctions Externalized social controls designed to encourage conformity to social norms.

---

[5]Mitchell, W. E. (1973, December). A new weapon stirs up old ghosts. *Natural History Magazine,* 77–84.

Positive sanctions consist of incentives to conformity such as awards, titles, and recognition by one's neighbors. Negative sanctions consist of threats such as imprisonment, fines, corporal punishment, or ostracism from the community for violation of social norms.

For sanctions to be effective, they cannot be arbitrary. They must be applied consistently, and they must be generally known among members of the society. If some individuals are not convinced of the advantages of social conformity, they are still more likely to obey society's rules than to accept the consequences of not doing so.

Sanctions may also be categorized as either formal or informal, depending on whether or not a legal statute is involved. In the United States, the man who goes shirtless in shorts to a church service may be subject to a variety of informal sanctions, ranging from disapproving glances from the clergy to the chuckling of other parishioners. If, however, he were to show up without any clothing at all, he would be subject to the formal negative sanction of arrest for indecent exposure. Only in the second instance would he have been guilty of breaking the law.

Formal sanctions, such as laws, are always organized, because they attempt to precisely and explicitly regulate people's behavior. Other examples of organized sanctions include, on the positive side, military decorations and monetary rewards. On the negative side are loss of face, exclusion from social life and its privileges, seizure of property, imprisonment, and even bodily mutilation or death. Informal sanctions emphasize cultural control and are diffuse in nature, involving spontaneous expressions of approval or disapproval by members of the group or community. They are, nonetheless, very effective in enforcing a large number of seemingly unimportant customs. Because most people want to be accepted, they are willing to acquiesce to the rules that govern dress, eating, and conversation, even in the absence of actual laws.

Social Control Through Witchcraft

In societies with or without centralized political systems, witchcraft sometimes functions as an agent of social control and involves both internal and external controls. An individual will think twice before offending a neighbor if convinced that the neighbor could retaliate by resorting to black magic. Similarly, individuals may not wish to be accused of practicing witchcraft, and so they behave with greater circumspection. Among the Azande of the Sudan, people who think they have been bewitched may consult an oracle, who, after performing the appropriate mystical rites, then may establish or confirm the identity of the offending witch.[6] Confronted with this evidence, the "witch" will usually agree to cooperate in order to avoid any additional trouble. Should the victim die, the relatives of the deceased may choose to make magic against the witch, ultimately accepting the death of some villager both as evidence of guilt and of the efficacy of their magic.

For the Azande, witchcraft provides not only a sanction against antisocial behavior but also a means of dealing with natural hostilities and death. No one wishes to be thought of as a witch, and surely no one wishes to be victimized by one. By institutionalizing their emotional responses, the Azande successfully maintain social order.

SOCIAL CONTROL THROUGH LAW

Among the Inuit of northern Canada, all offenses are considered to involve disputes between individuals; thus, they must be settled between the disputants themselves. A traditional way of doing this is through a song duel, in which the individuals involved heap insults upon one another in songs specially composed for the occasion. Although society does not intervene, its interests are represented by spectators, whose applause determines the outcome. If, however, social harmony cannot be restored—and that is the goal, rather than assigning and punishing guilt—one or the other disputant may move to another band. Ultimately, there is no binding legal authority.

In Western society, by contrast, someone who commits an offense against another person may become subject to a series of complex legal proceedings. In criminal cases the primary concern is to assign and punish guilt

Having a song duel is the traditional approach to dispute resolution among the Inuit of northern Canada.

---

[6]Evans-Pritchard, E. E. (1937). *Witchcraft, oracles and magic among the Azande.* London: Oxford University Press.

rather than to help out the victim. The offender will be arrested by the police; tried before a judge and, perhaps, a jury; and, depending on the severity of the crime, may be fined, imprisoned, or even executed. Rarely does the victim receive restitution or compensation. Throughout this chain of events, the accused party is dealt with by police, judges, jurors, and jailers, who may have no personal acquaintance whatsoever with the plaintiff or the defendant. How strange this all seems from the standpoint of traditional Inuit culture! Clearly, the two systems operate under distinctly different assumptions.

Definition of Law

Once two Inuit settle a dispute by engaging in a song contest, the affair is considered closed; no further action is expected. Would we choose to describe the outcome of such a contest as a legal decision? If every law is a sanction but not every sanction is a law, how are we to distinguish between social sanctions in general and those to which we apply the label "law"?

The definition of law has been a lively point of contention among anthropologists. In 1926, Bronislaw Malinowski argued that the rules of law are distinguished from the rules of custom in that "they are regarded as the obligation of one person and the rightful claim of another, sanctioned not by mere psychological motive, but by a definite social machinery of binding force based . . . upon mutual dependence."[7] In other words, laws exemplify social control because they employ overt coercion.

An example of one rule of custom in contemporary North American society might be the dictate that guests at a dinner party should repay the person who gave the party with entertainment in the future. A host or hostess who does not receive a return invitation may feel cheated out of something thought to be owed but has no legal claim against the ungrateful guest for the $30 spent on food and drinks. If, however, an individual was cheated out of the same sum by the grocer when shopping, the law could be invoked. Although Malinowski's definition introduced several important elements of law, his failure to distinguish adequately between legal and nonlegal sanctions left the problem of formulating a workable definition of law in the hands of later anthropologists.

According to E. Adamson Hoebel, an important pioneer in the anthropological study of law, "A social norm is legal if its neglect or infraction is regularly met, in threat or in fact, by the application of physical force by an individual or group possessing the socially recognized privilege of so acting."[8] In stressing the legitimate use of physical coercion, Hoebel de-emphasized the traditional association of law with a centralized court system. Although rules enacted by an authorized legislative body and enforced by the judicial mechanisms of the state are fundamental features of Western jurisprudence, they are not the universal backbone of human law. Can any concept of law be applied to societies for whom the notion of a centralized judiciary is virtually meaningless? How shall we categorize duels, song contests, and other socially condoned forms of self-help that seem to meet some but not all of the criteria of law?

Ultimately, it is always of greatest value to consider each case within its cultural context. After all, law reflects a society's basic postulates, so to understand any society's laws, one must understand the underlying values and assumptions. Nonetheless, a working definition of law is useful for purposes of discussion and cross-cultural comparison, and for this, **law** is adequately characterized as formal rules of conduct that, when violated, lead to negative sanctions.

Functions of Law

In Hoebel's 1954 book, *The Law of Primitive Man,* he described the generous sharing of private property as a fundamental principle in traditional Cheyenne Indian culture. However, he wrote, this principle shifted after some men assumed the privilege of borrowing other men's horses without bothering to obtain permission. When Wolf Lies Down complained of such unauthorized borrowing to the members of the Elk Soldier Society, the Elk Soldiers not only had his horse returned to him but also secured an award for damages from the offender. The Elk Soldiers then announced that, to avoid such difficulties in the future, horses no longer could be borrowed without permission. Furthermore, they declared their intention to retrieve any such property and whip anyone who resisted the return of improperly borrowed goods.

This case illustrates three basic functions of law. First, it defines relationships among society's members and marks out proper behavior under specified circumstances. Knowledge of the law permits each person to

law Formal rules of conduct that, when violated, lead to negative sanctions.

---

[7]Malinowski, B. (1951). *Crime and custom in savage society* (p. 55). London: Routledge.

[8]Hoebel, E. A. (1954). *The law of primitive man: A study in comparative legal dynamics* (p. 28). Cambridge, MA: Harvard University Press.

know his or her rights and duties with respect to every other member of society. Second, law allocates the authority to employ coercion in the enforcement of sanctions. In societies with centralized political systems, such authority is generally vested in the government and its judiciary system. In societies that lack centralized political control, the authority to employ force may be allocated directly to the injured party. Third, law functions to redefine social relations and to ensure social flexibility. As new situations arise, law must determine whether old rules and assumptions retain their validity and to what extent they must be altered. Law, if it is to operate efficiently, must allow room for change.

In practice, law is never as neat as a written description about it. In any given society, the power to employ sanctions may vary from level to level within the larger group. For example, the head of a Kapauku household in Papua New Guinea may punish a household member by slapping or beating, but the authority to confiscate property is vested exclusively in the headman of the lineage. Analogous distinctions exist in the United States among municipal, state, and federal jurisdictions. The complexity of legal jurisdiction within each society makes it difficult to generalize about law.

Crime

As we have observed, an important function of negative sanctions, legal or otherwise, is to discourage the breach of social norms. A person contemplating theft is aware of the possibility of being caught and punished. Yet, even in the face of severe sanctions, individuals in every society sometimes violate the norms and subject themselves to the consequences of their behavior.

In Western societies a clear distinction is made between offenses against the state and offenses against an individual. However, in non-state societies such as bands and tribes, all offenses are viewed as transgressions against individuals or kin-groups (families, lineages, clans, and so on).

Disputes between individuals or kin-groups may seriously disrupt the social order, especially in small groups where the number of disputants, though small in absolute numbers, may be a large percentage of the total population. For example, although the Inuit traditionally have no effective domestic or economic unit beyond the family, a dispute between two people will interfere with the ability of members of separate families to come to one another's aid when necessary and is consequently a matter of wider social concern. The goal of judicial proceedings in such instances is restoring social harmony rather than punishing an offender. When distinguishing between offenses of concern to the community as a whole and those of concern only to a few individuals, we may refer to them as collective or personal.

Basically, disputes are settled in one of two ways. First, disputing parties may, through argument and compromise, voluntarily arrive at a mutually satisfactory agreement. This form of settlement is referred to as **negotiation** or, if it involves the assistance of an unbiased third party, **mediation.** In bands and tribes a third party mediator has no coercive power and thus cannot force disputants to abide by such a decision, but as a person who commands great personal respect, the mediator frequently may help bring about a settlement.

Second, in chiefdoms and states, an authorized third party may issue a binding decision that the disputing parties will be compelled to respect. This process is referred to as **adjudication.** The difference between mediation and adjudication is basically a difference in authorization. In a dispute settled by adjudication, the disputing parties present their positions as compellingly as they can, but they do not participate in the ultimate decision making.

Although the adjudication process is not universally characteristic, every society employs some form of negotiation to settle disputes. Often negotiation acts as a prerequisite or an alternative to adjudication. For example, in the resolution of U.S. labor disputes, striking workers may first negotiate with management, often with the mediation of a third party. If the state decides the strike constitutes a threat to the public welfare, the disputing parties may be forced to submit to adjudication. In this case, the responsibility for resolving the dispute is transferred to a presumably impartial judge.

The judge's work is difficult and complex. In addition to sifting through evidence presented, he or she must consider a wide range of norms, values, and earlier rulings to arrive at a decision intended to be considered fair not only by the disputing parties but by the public and other judges as well.

Punitive justice, such as imprisonment, may be the most common approach to justice in North America, but it has not proven to be an effective way of changing criminal behavior. There are cultural alternatives. For a number of years, Native American communities in Canada urged their federal government to reform justice services to make them more consistent with indigenous values and traditions. Native communities

---

negotiation The use of direct argument and compromise by the parties to a dispute to arrive voluntarily at a mutually satisfactory agreement.

mediation Settlement of a dispute through negotiation assisted by an unbiased third party.

adjudication Mediation with an unbiased third party making the ultimate decision.

have pressed especially for restorative justice techniques such as the Talking Circle, traditionally used by Native American groups. For this, parties involved in a conflict come together in a circle with equal opportunity to express their views—one at a time, free of interruption. Usually, a "talking stick" (or eagle feather or some other symbolic tool) is held by whoever is speaking to signal that she or he has the right to talk at that moment and others have the responsibility to listen.

In tribal and band societies, agreement is less likely to be coercive because all concerned individuals can negotiate and mediate on relatively equal terms. The United States, by contrast, has great disparities in power, and evidence indicates that it is the stronger parties that prefer mediation and negotiation. That said, leaders in the field of dispute resolution in the United States and other parts of the industrial and postindustrial world are drawing upon anthropological expertise to find effective ways to bring about balanced solutions to conflict. An example of this appears in this chapter's Anthropology Applied feature.

Anthropology Applied

Dispute Resolution and the Anthropologist

In an era when the consequences of violent approaches to dispute resolution are more far-reaching than ever, conflict management is of growing importance. A world leader in this profession is William L. Ury, an independent negotiations specialist who earned his Ph.D. in anthropology at Harvard University.

In his first year at graduate school, Ury began looking for a way to apply anthropology to practical problems, including conflicts of all dimensions. He wrote a paper about the role of anthropology in peacemaking and on a whim sent it to Roger Fisher, a law professor noted for his work in negotiation and world affairs. Fisher, in turn, invited the young graduate student to co-author a kind of how-to book for international mediators. The book they researched and wrote together turned out to have a far wider audience, for it presented basic principles of negotiation that could be applied to household spats, management–employee conflicts, or international crises. Titled *Getting to Yes: Negotiating Agreement Without Giving In* (1981), it sold millions of copies, was translated into twenty-one languages, and earned the nickname "negotiator's bible."

While working on *Getting to Yes*, Ury and Fisher co-founded the Program on Negotiation (PON) at Harvard Law School, pulling together an interdisciplinary group of academics interested in new approaches to and applications of the negotiation process. Today this applied research center is a multiuniversity consortium that trains mediators, businesspeople, and government officials in negotiation skills. It has four key goals: (1) design, implement, and evaluate better dispute resolution practices; (2) promote collaboration among practitioners and scholars; (3) develop education programs and materials for instruction in negotiation and dispute resolution; (4) increase public awareness and understanding of successful conflict resolution efforts.

In 1982, Ury earned his Ph.D. with a dissertation titled *Talk Out or Walk Out: The Role and Control of Conflict in a Kentucky Coal Mine*. Afterward, he taught for several years while maintaining a leadership role at PON. In particular, he devoted himself to PON's Global Negotiation Project (initially known as the Project on Avoiding War). Today, having left his teaching post at Harvard, Ury continues to serve as director of the Global Negotiation Project, writing, consulting, and running regular workshops on dealing with difficult people and situations.

Utilizing a cross-cultural perspective sharpened through years of anthropological research, he specializes in ethnic and secessionist disputes, including those between white and black South Africans, Serbs and Croats, Turks and Kurds, Catholics and Protestants in Northern Ireland, and Russians and Chechens in the former Soviet Union.

Among the most effective tools in Ury's applied anthropology work are his books on dispute resolution. In 1993 he wrote *Getting Past No: Negotiating Your Way from Confrontation*, which explores ways to reach out to hostile parties who are not interested in negotiation. His 1999 book, *Getting to Peace: Transforming Conflict at Home, at Work, and in the World*, examines what he calls the "third side," which is the role that the surrounding community can play in preventing, resolving, and containing destructive conflict between two parties.[a] His 2002 edited volume *Must We Fight?* challenges entrenched ideas that violence and war are inevitable and presents convincing evidence that human beings have as much inherent potential for cooperation and co-existence as they do for violent conflict. The key point in this book is that violence is a choice. In

© Jay Dickman

Ury's words, "Conflict is not going to end, but violence can."[b]

What Ury and others in this field are doing is helping create a culture of negotiation in a world where adversarial, win–lose attitudes are out of step with the increasingly interdependent relations between people. ■ ■ ■

[a]Pease, T. (2000). Taking the third side. *Andover Bulletin*, spring.

[b]Ury, W. (2002). A global immune system. *Andover Bulletin*, winter; see also www.PON.harvard.edu and www.thirdside.org.

VIOLENT CONFLICT AND WARFARE

Although the regulation of internal affairs is an important function of any political system, it is by no means the sole function. Another is the management of external affairs—relations not just among different states but among different bands, lineages, clans, or whatever the largest autonomous political unit may be. And just as the threatened or actual use of force may be used to maintain order within a society, it also may be used in the conduct of external affairs.

Our species has a horrific track record when it comes to violence. Far more lethal than spontaneous and individual outbursts of aggression, organized violence in the form of war is responsible for enormous suffering and deliberate destruction of life and property. In the past 5,000 years or so, some 14,000 wars have been fought, resulting in many hundreds of millions of casualties.

Generally, we may distinguish among different motives, objectives, methods, and scales of warfare as organized violence. For instance, some societies engage in defensive wars only and avoid armed confrontations with others unless seriously threatened or actually attacked. Others initiate aggressive wars to pursue particular strategic objectives, including material benefits in the form of precious resources such as slaves, gold, or oil, as well as territorial expansion or control over trade routes. In some cultures, aggressive wars are waged for ideological reasons, such as spreading one's own worldview or religion and defeating "evil" ideas or heresies elsewhere.

The scope of violent conflict is wide, ranging from individual fights, local feuds and raids to formally declared international wars fought by professional armed forces. In addition, we may distinguish among various civil wars (in which armies from different geographical sections, ethnic or religious groups, or political parties within the same state are pitted against each other) and low-intensity guerilla warfare involving small-scale hit-and-run tactical operations instead of pitched battles.

Why do wars occur? Some argue that males of the human species are naturally aggressive (see this chapter's Biocultural Connection). As evidence, they point to aggressive group behavior exhibited by chimpanzees in Tanzania where researchers observed one group systematically destroy another and take over their territory. Also, they cite the behavior of people such as the Yanomami Indians who range on either side of the border between Brazil and Venezuela. These tropical horticulturists and foragers have been described as living in a chronic state of war, and some scientists suggest this exemplifies the way all humans once behaved. However, as discussed in earlier chapters, warfare among humans, as well as aggressive group behavior among apes, may be situation specific rather than an unavoidable expression of biological predisposition.

This is not to say that violence was unknown among ancient humans. The occasional discovery of stone spear points embedded in human skeletons, such as that of a more than 9,000-year-old man found in Kennewick in the northwestern United States or even older ones from the Grimaldi caves in Italy, prove otherwise. Nevertheless, it is clear that war is not a universal phenomenon, for in various parts of the world there are societies that do not practice warfare as we know it. Examples include people as diverse as the Ju/'hoansi Bushmen and pygmy peoples of southern Africa, the Arapesh of New Guinea, and the Jain of India, as well as the Amish of North America. Among societies that do practice warfare, levels of violence may differ dramatically.

We have ample reason to suppose that war has become a problem only in the last 10,000 years, since the invention of food-production techniques and especially since the formation of centralized states 5,000 years ago. It has reached crisis proportions in the past 200 years, with the invention of modern weaponry and increased direction of violence against civilian populations. In contemporary warfare, casualties not just of civilians but also of *children* far outnumber those of soldiers. Thus, war is not so much an age-old problem as it is a relatively recent one.

Among food foragers, with their uncentralized political systems, violence may erupt sporadically, but warfare was all but unknown until recent times. There are several reasons for this. First of all, since territorial boundaries and membership among food-foraging

Biocultural Connection

Gender, Sex, and Human Violence

At the start of the 21st century, war and violence are no longer the strictly male domains that they were in many societies in the past. War has become embedded in civilian life in many parts of the world and impacts the daily lives of women and children. Moreover, women now serve in the military forces of several states, although their participation in combat is often limited. Some female soldiers in the United States argue that gender should not limit their participation in combat as they consider themselves as strong, capable, and well trained as their male counterparts. Others believe that biologically based sex differences make war a particularly male domain.

Scientists have long argued that males are more suited to combat because natural selection has made them on average larger and stronger than females. This idea, known as sexual selection, was first put forth by Darwin in the 19th century. At that time he proposed that the physical specializations of males in animal species—such as horns, vibrant plumage, and, in the case of humans, intelligence and tool use—demonstrate selection acting upon males to aid in the competition for mates. In these scenarios, male reproductive success is thought to be optimized through a strategy of "spreading seed"—in other words, by being sexually active with as many females as possible. Females, on the other hand, are considered gatekeepers who optimize

their reproductive success through caring for individual offspring. According to this theory of sexual selection, in species where male–male competition is high, males will be considerably larger than females, and aggression will serve males well. In monogamous species, males and females will be of similar sizes.

Primatologist Richard Wrangham has taken the idea of sexual selection even further. In his book *Demonic Males*, he explores the idea that both male aggression and patriarchy have an evolutionary basis. He states that humans, like our close cousins the chimpanzees, are "party gang" species characterized by strong bonds among groups of males who have dominion over an expandable territory. These features "suffice to account for natural selection's ugly legacy, the tendency to look for killing opportunities when hostile neighbors meet."[a] Violence in turn generates a male-dominated social order: "Patriarchy comes from biology in the sense that it emerges from men's temperaments out of their evolutionarily derived efforts to control women and at the same time have solidarity with fellow males in competition against outsiders."[b] While Wrangham allows that evolutionary forces have shaped women as well, he suggests that females' evolutionary interests cannot be met without cooperation with males.

Feminist scholars have pointed out that these scientific models are

"gendered" in that they incorporate the gender norms derived from the scientists' culture. Darwin's original model of sexual selection incorporated the Victorian gender norms of the passive female and active male. U.S. primatologist Laura Fedigan suggests that in Darwinian models women evolved in positive directions only by a "coat tails" process whereby females were "pulled along" toward improved biological states by virtue of the progress of the genes they shared with males.[c] Wrangham's more recent *Demonic Males* theory is similarly shaped by culture. It incorporates the dominant world order (military states) and the gender norms (aggressive males) it values. In both cases, the putatively scientific theory has created a natural basis for a series of social conventions.

This does not mean that biological differences between the sexes cannot be studied in the natural world. Instead, scientists studying sex differences must be especially aware of how they may project cultural beliefs onto nature. Meanwhile, the attitudes of some women soldiers continue to challenge generalizations regarding "military specialization" by gender. ■ ■ ■

[a]Wrangham, R., & Peterson, D. (1996). *Demonic males* (p. 168), Boston: Houghton Mifflin.
[b]Wrangham & Peterson, p. 125.
[c]Fedigan, L. M. (1986). The changing role of women in models of human evolution. *Annual Review of Anthropology, 15,* 25–66.

bands are usually fluid and loosely defined, a man who hunts with one band today may hunt with a neighboring band next month. This renders warfare impractical. So, too, does the systematic exchange of marriage partners among food-foraging groups, which makes it likely that someone in each band will have a sister, a brother, or a cousin in a neighboring band. Moreover, the absence of a food surplus among foragers makes prolonged combat difficult. Finally, a worldview in which people perceive themselves as part of the natural world rather than superior to it tends to work against exploitation of other people. In sum, where populations are small and see themselves as part of the natural world, where food surpluses are absent, property ownership minimal, and no

state organization exists, the likelihood of organized violence by one group against another is small.[9]

Despite the traditional view of the gardener or farmer as a gentle tiller of the soil, it is among such people, along with pastoralists, that warfare becomes prominent. One reason may be that food-producing peoples have a more exploitative worldview than do food foragers. Another is that they are far more prone to population growth than are food foragers, whose numbers are generally maintained well below carrying capacity. This population growth, if unchecked, can lead

[9]Knauft, B. (1991). Violence and sociality in human evolution. *Current Anthropology, 32,* 391–409.

Often depicted as warlike by nature, the Yanomami may be no such thing; rather, Yanomami warfare is likely a recent phenomenon related to outside pressures originating in the Brazilian and Venezuelan states.

© Napoleon Chagnon/Anthro-Photo

to resource depletion, one solution to which may be seizure of some other people's resources. In addition, the commitment to a fixed piece of land inherent in farming makes such societies somewhat less fluid in their membership than those of food foragers. Instead of marrying distantly, farmers marry locally, depriving them of long-distance kin networks. In rigidly matrilocal or patrilocal societies, each new generation is bound to the same territory, no matter how small it may be or how large the group trying to live within it.

The availability of unoccupied lands may not serve as a sufficient detriment to the outbreak of war. Among swidden farmers, for example, competition for land cleared of old growth forest frequently leads to hostility and armed conflict. The centralization of political control and the possession of valuable property among farming people provide many more stimuli for warfare.

It is among such peoples, especially those organized into states, where the violence of warfare is most apt to result in indiscriminate killing. This development has reached its peak in modern states. Indeed, much (but not all) of the warfare that has been observed in recent stateless societies (so-called tribal warfare) has been induced by states as a reaction to colonial expansion.[10]

Although competition for scarce resources may turn violent and lead to war, ideological motivations and justifications for war are typically embedded in a society's superstructure or worldview—the collective

body of ideas that members of a culture generally share concerning the ultimate shape and substance of their reality. There are many examples of this, ranging from the Crusades (a series of "Wars of the Cross" by European Christian armies between 700 and 900 years ago to push the Muslims out of Palestine, a territory they viewed as "Holy Land") to Aztec Indian warfare in Mexico (conducted some 500 years ago in part to capture people for sacrifice to Aztec gods).

Currently, there are several dozen wars going on in the world, often resulting in massive killing fields (Figure 15.3). And many contemporary wars are not between states but often occur within countries where the government is either corrupt, ineffective, or without popular support. The following examples offer some specific data. Between 1975 and 1979, Khmer Rouge soldiers in Cambodia murdered 1.7 million fellow citizens, or 20 percent of that country's population. In the 1990s, between 2 and 3 million died due to warfare in the southern Sudan. Another 5 million died in the recent war in Congo (1998–2003), which involved armies from a handful of neighboring states as well. Moreover, there are hundreds of violent flashpoints or hot spots. Moreover, many armies around the world recruit not only women but also children. Today, there are more than 300,000 child soldiers, many as young as 12 years old.

As the above examples show, the causes of warfare are complex, involving economic, political, and ideological factors. The challenge of eliminating human warfare has never been greater than it is in today's world—nor has the cost of *not* finding a way to do so.

---

[10]Whitehead, N. L., & Ferguson, R. B. (1993, November). Deceptive stereotypes about tribal warfare. *Chronicle of Higher Education,* A48.

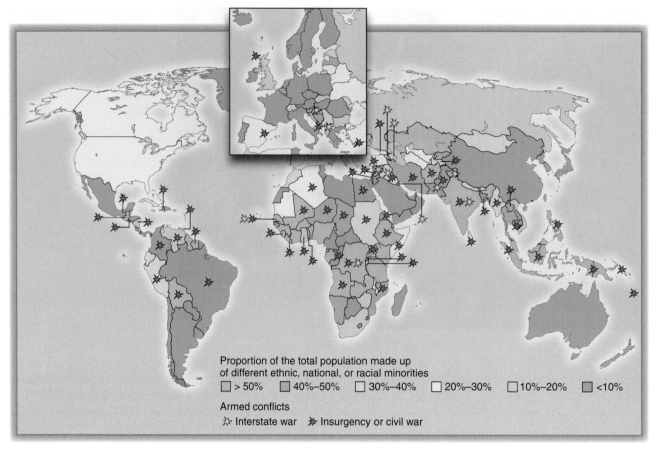

Figure 15.3
In multinational states, warfare is common as one nationality suppresses others within the country.

Chapter Summary

■ Through political organization, societies impose and maintain social order, manage public affairs, and reduce social disorder. No group can function without persuading or coercing its members to conform to agreed-upon rules of conduct.

■ Four basic types of political systems may be identified, ranging from uncentralized bands and tribes to centralized chiefdoms and states. The band is a relatively small and loosely organized kin-ordered group that inhabits a specific territory and that may split into smaller extended family groups that are politically independent. Political organization in bands is democratic, and informal control is exerted by public opinion in the form of gossip and ridicule. Band leaders are usually older men whose personal authority lasts only as long as members believe they are leading well.

■ In anthropology, *tribe* refers to a range of kin-ordered groups that are politically integrated by some unifying factor and whose members share a common ancestry, identity, culture, language, and territory. With an economy usually based on crop cultivation or herding, the tribe's population is larger than that of the band, although family units within the tribe

are still relatively autonomous and egalitarian. As in the band, political organization is transitory, and leaders have no coercive means of maintaining authority.

■ One type of authority in tribes is the Big Man, who builds up his wealth and political power until he must be reckoned with as a leader. In many tribal societies the organizing political unit is the clan, comprised of people who consider themselves descended from a common ancestor. A group of elders or headmen or headwomen regulate the affairs of members and represent their group in relations with other clans.

■ As societies include larger numbers of people and become more heterogeneous socially, politically, and economically, leadership becomes more centralized. A chiefdom is a regional polity in which two or more local kin-ordered groups are organized under a chief who heads a ranked hierarchy of people. An individual's status is determined by his or her position in a descent group and distance of relationship to the chief, whose role is to unite his community in all matters. The chief may accumulate great personal wealth, which enhances his power base and which he may pass on to his heirs.

■ The most centralized of political organizations is the state—a complex political institution involving large numbers of people within a defined territory. Its members are organized and directed by a formal government that has the capacity and authority to make laws and use force to maintain the social order. The state is found in diverse, stratified societies, with unequal distribution of wealth and power. States are inherently unstable and transitory and differ from nations, which are communities of people who share a collective identity based on a common culture, language, territorial base, and history.

■ Legitimacy, or the right of political leaders to exercise power, is required to govern with authority. Legitimate government may be distinguished from rule based on intimidation or force. To a greater or lesser extent, most governments use ideology, including religion, to legitimize political power.

■ Research shows that far fewer women than men have held important positions of political leadership. Nonetheless, in a number of societies, women have enjoyed political equality with men, as among the Iroquoian peoples in northeastern North America. Under centralized political systems, women are traditionally most likely to be subordinate to men.

■ Two kinds of control exist: internalized and externalized. Internalized controls are cultural in nature, self-imposed by enculturated individuals. They rely on personal shame, fear of divine punishment, and magical retaliation. Externalized controls, called sanctions, mix cultural and social control (involving actions taken by others). Positive sanctions are rewards or recognition by others, whereas negative sanctions include threat of imprisonment, fines, corporal punishment, or loss of face. Sanctions are either formal, including actual laws, or informal, involving norms. Other important agents of social control are witchcraft beliefs and religious sanctions. Sanctions serve to assure conformity to group norms, including actual law, and to maintain the place of each social faction in a community.

■ Law, formal negative sanctions, defines relationships, prescribes and prohibits behavior among a society's members, and allocates authority to enforce sanctions. In centralized political systems, this authority rests with the government and court system, whereas uncentralized societies give this authority directly to the injured party.

■ In contrast to bands, tribes, and chiefdoms, state societies distinguish between crimes (offenses against the state) and offenses against an individual. A dispute may be settled in two ways: negotiation or adjudication. All societies use negotiation to settle individual disputes. In negotiation the parties to the dispute reach an agreement themselves, with or without the help of a third party. In adjudication, an authorized third party issues a binding decision.

■ Political systems also attempt to regulate external affairs, or relations between politically autonomous units. In doing so they may resort to the threat or use of force. The scope of violent conflict is wide, ranging from individual fights, local feuds and raids to formally declared international wars fought by professional armed forces. Some societies engage in defensive wars only and avoid armed confrontations with others unless seriously threatened or actually attacked. Others initiate aggressive wars to pursue material or ideological objectives. War is not a universal phenomenon.

Questions for Reflection

1. The basic challenge for people in all societies is to decide who gets what, when, where, and how. In many states, political power is concentrated in the hands of an elite few belonging to a dominant nationality or ethnic group. Imagine you belong to a repressed group such as the Quechua of Ecuador, depicted in the chapter's opening photograph. What would you do if you were systematically frustrated in the exercise of your human rights in a political system that discriminates against your ethnic group?

2. Given the basic definition of politics presented in the beginning of this chapter, why do you think that power in egalitarian societies plays a relatively insignificant role?

3. If political organization functions to impose or maintain order and to resolve conflicts, why do you think that a government in a country such as your own is so interested in legitimizing its power? What happens when a government loses such legitimacy?

4. Which nationalities or ethnic groups do you know that are dominant, and which can you identify that are in a minority position or are repressed? What is the basis for this inequality?

5. When your own government declares war against another country, on which basis does it seek to justify its decision to send soldiers into battle? Do you know the death ratio of noncombatants to soldiers in your country's most recent war?

Key Terms

power	legitimacy
political organization	cultural control
band	social control
tribe	sanctions
chiefdom	law
state	negotiation
nation	mediation
	adjudication

Multimedia Review Tools

Make the Grade in Anthropology with ThomsonNOW

Thomson NOW! This powerful online study tool provides you with a *personalized study plan* based on your responses to a diagnostic pretest. Once you have mastered the material with the help of interactive learning tools, an integrated e-book, and more, you can take a post-test to confirm you are ready to move on to the next chapter. To get started with ThomsonNOW, check the card packaged with your book for the access code. Then go to http://www.thomsonedu.com to create an account through 1pass™. If there is no card in your book, go to http://www.thomsonedu.com to purchase an access code.

Companion Website and Anthropology Resource Center

Go to http://anthropology.wadsworth.com to reach the companion website for your text. This offers many study aids, including self quizzes for each chapter and a practice final exam, as well as links to anthropology websites and information on the latest theories and discoveries in the field.

Also, check out the Anthropology Resource Center for a wealth of learning materials that include interactive maps, video exercises, simulations, and breaking news in anthropology. Be sure to explore InfoTrac College Edition®, your online library that offers full-length articles from thousands of scholarly and popular publications. To reach the Anthropology Resource Center and InfoTrac College Edition, check the card packaged with your book for the access code. Then go to http://www.thomsonedu.com to create an account through 1pass™. If there is no card in your book, go to http://www.thomsonedu.com to purchase an access code.

© Photographer: Hester & Hardaway Photographers. The Menil Collection, Housto[n]

CHALLENGE ISSUE

As self-conscious and self-reflecting beings, humans face challenges beyond biological survival; they face mental ones born of the need to make sense of their existence. Among other concerns, they wrestle with questions about human origin and destiny. Thus, cultures have origin-of-life stories that are passed on from one generation to the next, helping to define the individual and the group's place in the world. For example, the Jains, a Hindu sect in India, believe that all life springs from a cosmic being that has existed since the beginning of time, such as the one pictured here.

Spirituality, Religion, and the Supernatural

16

From an anthropological point of view, spirituality and religion are part of a cultural system's superstructure, earlier defined as a society's shared sense of identity and the ideas, beliefs, and values by which its people makes sense of the world and their place in it. In their studies of different religious and spiritual beliefs and practices, anthropologists seek to remain unbiased regarding any particular cultural tradition. Instead, they examine spirituality and religion in terms of a society's **worldview**— the collective body of ideas that members of a culture generally share concerning the ultimate shape and substance of their reality.

Among people in all cultures, particular spiritual or religious beliefs and practices fulfill numerous social and psychological needs, such as the need to confront and explain suffering and death. Religion gives meaning to individual and group life, drawing power from spiritual forces or beings and offering continuity of existence beyond death. It can provide the path by which people transcend a burdensome and mortal existence and attain, if only momentarily, spiritual hope and relief.

Religion and spirituality also serve an array of social needs. A traditional religion reinforces group norms, provides moral sanctions for individual conduct, and furnishes the ideology of common purpose and values that support the well-being of the community. Also of note, people often turn to religion or spirituality in the hope of reaching a specific goal, such as the healing of physical, emotional, or social ills. Perhaps it is because they fulfill these and numerous other social and

worldview The collective body of ideas that members of a culture generally share concerning the ultimate shape and substance of their reality.

289

psychological needs shared by humans across cultures that belief in the supernatural is universal. While recognizing that not all *individuals* believe in a supernatural force or entity, anthropologists know of no *group* of people anywhere on the face of the earth who, at any time over the past 100,000 years, has been without some manifestation of spirituality or religion.

In the 19th century, the European intellectual tradition gave rise to the idea that modern science would ultimately replace religion by showing people the irrationality of their spiritual beliefs and practices. The expectation was that as valid scientific explanations became available, people would abandon their religious beliefs and rituals as superstitious myths and false worship. But to date, despite tremendous scientific advancements, that has not occurred. In fact, in many places, the opposite trend seems to prevail.

Although traditional mainline Christian religions have shown some decline, nondenominational spirituality is on the rise. Also on the rise are fundamentalist religions, which often take a strong antiscience position. Examples include Islamic fundamentalism in countries such as Afghanistan, Algeria, and Iran; Jewish fundamentalism in Israel and the United States; and Hindu fundamentalism in India. Christian fundamentalism is represented in the dramatic growth of evangelical denominations in the United States, Central America, and sub-Saharan Africa.

Within the United States, non-Christian religions are also growing: Islam (5 to 7 million followers—up from 527,000 in 1990), Buddhism (1.1 million—up from 401,000 in 1990), Hinduism (800,000—up from 227,000 in 1990), not to mention various New Age options such as Wicca (a modern, nature-oriented religion that draws upon ancient western European and pre-Christian beliefs and now counting about 310,000 adherents).[1] Notably, a mere 14 percent of the adult population throughout the world claims to be nonreligious (Figure 16.1).

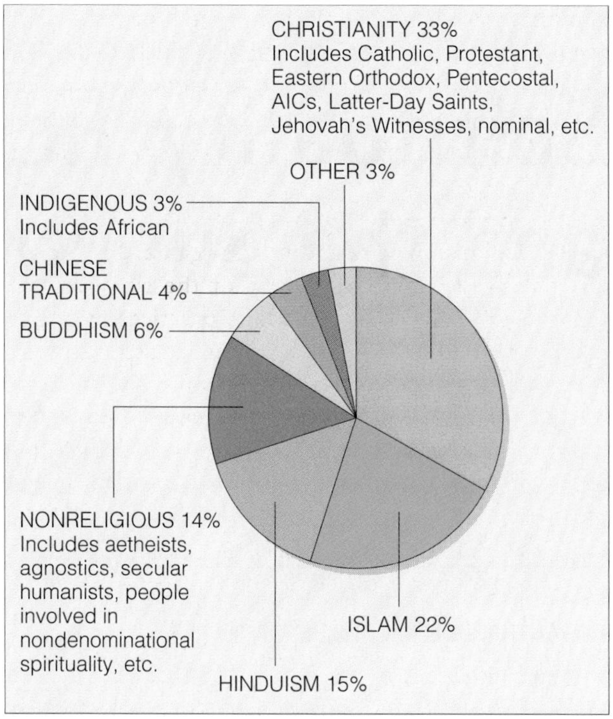

Beyond noting that science has not destroyed spiritual beliefs or religion, one could even say that it has actually created, in its technological applications, a host of new anxieties. These include nuclear catastrophe, threats of chemical or biological terrorism, health hazards from pollution, and unease about the consequences of new developments in biotechnology such as cloning, production of new strains of genetically engineered organisms, ability to store human sperm and eggs for future fertilization, and manipulation of human DNA. On top of these, many people face emotional turmoil and psychological upheaval brought on by the breakup of traditional communities due to globalization, plus invasions

CHRISTIANITY 33%
Includes Catholic, Protestant, Eastern Orthodox, Pentecostal, AICs, Latter-Day Saints, Jehovah's Witnesses, nominal, etc.

OTHER 3%

INDIGENOUS 3%
Includes African

CHINESE TRADITIONAL 4%

BUDDHISM 6%

NONRELIGIOUS 14%
Includes aetheists, agnostics, secular humanists, people involved in nondenominational spirituality, etc.

HINDUISM 15%

ISLAM 22%

Figure 16.1 **Major Religions of the World and Their Percentage of All Believers, 2002**

of foreign ideas and values through mass media controlled by unfamiliar powers. In the face of these and other modern anxieties confronting the human species, religion offers social and psychological support.

The continuing strength of religion in the face of Western scientific rationalism clearly reveals that it remains a dominant and dynamic force in society. Although anthropologists are not qualified to pass judgment on the metaphysical truth of any particular religion or spiritual belief, they can show how each embodies a number of revealing facts about humans and society.

THE ANTHROPOLOGICAL APPROACH TO RELIGION

Anthropologist Anthony F. C. Wallace defined religion as "a set of rituals, rationalized by myth, which mobilizes supernatural powers for the purpose of achieving or preventing transformations of state in man and nature."[2] Behind his definition lies a recognition that when people are unable to "fix" serious, anxiety-causing problems through technological or organizational means, they try to do so through manipulation of

---

[1] U.S. Census 2000; www.adherents.com.

[2] Wallace, A. F. C. (1966). *Religion: An anthropological view.* New York: Random House.

supernatural or spiritual beings and powers. This requires ritual, or "religion in action," which can be seen as a basic expression of religion. Its major functions are to reduce anxiety and boost confidence, thereby helping people cope with reality. It is this that gives religion survival value.

With these aspects in mind, we offer a somewhat simpler definition of **religion:** an organized system of ideas about the spiritual sphere or the supernatural, along with associated ceremonial practices by which people try to interpret and/or influence aspects of the universe otherwise beyond their control. Similar to religion, **spirituality** is also concerned with the sacred, as distinguished from material matters, but it is often individual rather than collective and does not require a distinctive format or traditional organization. Both are indicators that many aspects of the human experience are thought to be beyond scientific explanation.

Since no known culture, including those of modern industrial societies, has achieved complete certainty in controlling existing or future conditions and circumstances, spirituality and/or religion play a role in all known cultures. However, considerable variability exists here. At one end of the spectrum are food-foraging peoples, whose technological ability to manipulate their environment is limited and who tend to see themselves as part of, rather than masters of nature. This may be referred to as a *naturalistic worldview*. Among food foragers religion is likely to be inseparable from the rest of daily life. It also mirrors and confirms the egalitarian nature of social relations in their societies, in that individuals do not plead with high-ranking deities for aid the way members of stratified societies do. At the other end of the spectrum is Western civilization, with its ideological commitment to overcoming problems through technological and organizational skills. Here religion is less a part of daily activities and is restricted to more specific occasions. Moreover, with its hierarchy of supernatural beings—for instance, God, and (in some religions) the angels, saints or holy people—it reflects and confirms the stratified nature of the society in which it is embedded.

Religious activity may be less prominent in the lives of social elites, who may see themselves as more in control of their own destinies, than it is in the lives of peasants or members of lower classes. Among the latter, religion may afford some compensation for a dependent position in society. Yet religion is still important to elite members of society, in that it rationalizes the system in such a way that less advantaged people are not as likely to question the existing social order as they might otherwise be. With hope for a better existence after death, one may be more willing to put up with a disadvantaged position in life. Thus, religious beliefs serve to influence and perpetuate certain ideas about the relationships, if not the actual relations, between different classes of people.

religion An organized system of ideas about the spiritual sphere or the supernatural, along with associated ceremonial practices by which people try to interpret and/or influence aspects of the universe otherwise beyond their control.

spirituality Concern with the sacred, as distinguished from material matters. In contrast to religion, spirituality is often individual rather than collective and does not require a distinctive format or traditional organization.

During the funeral of Pope John Paul II, onlookers held signs pronouncing "Santo Subito" ("Saint Now"), calling for his immediate sainthood. Roman Catholicism, with its hierarchy of supernatural beings—God, Christ, angels, and saints or holy people—reflects and confirms the stratified nature of the society in which it is embedded.

© Francesco Caampani Photography/photographersdirect

THE PRACTICE OF RELIGION

Much of religion's value comes from the activities called for by its prescriptions and rules. Participation in religious ceremonies may bring a sense of personal lift—a wave of reassurance, an emotion of being overpowered by joy, and even a sense of being raised into a trancelike state—or a feeling of closeness to fellow participants. The beliefs and ceremonial practices of religions vary considerably. Yet, rituals that seem bizarre to an outsider can be shown to serve the same basic social and psychological functions as do his or her own distinct rituals.

Supernatural Beings and Powers

A hallmark of religion is belief in spiritual beings and forces. In attempting to control by religious means what cannot be controlled in other ways, humans turn to prayer, sacrifice, and other religious or spiritual rituals. These presuppose the existence of spiritual forces that can be tapped into, or spiritual beings interested in human affairs and available for aid. For convenience we may divide these beings into three categories: major deities (gods and goddesses), ancestral spirits, and other sorts of spirit beings. Although the variety of deities and spirits recognized by the world's cultures is tremendous, it is possible to make certain generalizations about them.

Gods and Goddesses

Gods and goddesses are the great and more remote beings. They are usually seen as controlling the universe. If more than one is recognized (known as **polytheism**), each has charge of a particular part of the universe. Such was the case with the gods and goddesses of ancient Greece: Zeus was lord of the sky, Poseidon was ruler of the sea, and Hades was lord of the underworld and ruler of the dead.

In addition to these three brothers, Greek mythology features a host of other deities, female as well as male, each similarly concerned with specific aspects of life and the universe. A **pantheon,** or the collection of gods and goddesses such as those of the Greeks, is common in non-Western states as well. Since states commonly have grown through conquest, often their pantheons have expanded as local deities of conquered peoples were incorporated into the official state pantheon. Another frequent though not invariable feature of pantheons is the presence of a supreme deity, who

> **polytheism** Belief in several gods and/or goddesses (as contrasted with monotheism—belief in one god or goddess).
>
> **pantheon** The several gods and goddesses of a people.

may be all but totally ignored by humans. The Aztecs of the Mexican highlands, for instance, recognized a supreme pair to whom they paid little attention. After all, being so remote, this divine duo was unlikely to be interested in human affairs. The sensible practice, then, was to focus attention on less remote deities who were more directly concerned with human affairs.

Whether or not a people recognize gods, goddesses, or both has to do with how men and women relate to each other in everyday life. Generally speaking, societies that subordinate women to men define the supreme deity in masculine terms. For instance, in traditional Christian religions believers speak of God as a "father" who had a divine "son" but do not entertain thoughts of God as a "mother" nor of a divine "daughter." Such male-privileging religions developed in traditional societies with economies based upon the herding of animals or intensive agriculture carried out or controlled by men, who are dominating figures to their children.

Goddesses, by contrast, are likely to be most prominent in societies where women play a significant role in the economy, where women enjoy relative equality with men, and where men are less controlling figures to their wives and children. Such societies are most often those that depend upon crop cultivation carried out solely or mostly by women.

Ancestral Spirits

A belief in ancestral spirits is consistent with the widespread notion that human beings are made up of two closely intertwined parts: a physical body and some mental component or spiritual self. For example, traditional belief of the Penobscot Indians in Maine holds that each person has a vital spirit capable of traveling apart from the body. Given such a concept, the idea of the spirit being freed from the body in trance and dreams or by death, and having an existence thereafter, seems quite reasonable. Frequently, where a belief in ancestral spirits exists, these beings are seen as retaining an active interest and even membership in society.

In the previous chapter, for instance, we discussed how the Wape Papuans in New Guinea believe that ancestral spirits act to provide or withhold meat from their living descendants. Like living persons, such spirit beings are viewed as benevolent or malevolent, but no one is ever quite sure what their behavior will be. The same feeling of uncertainty—How will they react to what I have done?—may be displayed toward ancestral spirits as it often is toward people of an older generation who hold authority over individuals. Beyond this, ancestral spirits closely resemble living humans in their appetites, feelings, emotions, and behavior. Thus, they reflect and reinforce social reality.

Belief in ancestral spirits of one sort or another is found in many parts of the world, especially among people having unilineal descent systems with their associated ancestor orientation. In several such African societies, the concept is highly elaborate. Here one frequently finds ancestral spirits behaving just like humans. They are able to feel hot, cold, and pain, and they may be capable of dying a second death by drowning or burning. They even may participate in family and lineage affairs, and seats will be provided for them, even though the spirits are invisible. If they are annoyed, they may send sickness or death. Eventually, they are reborn as new members of their lineage, and, in societies that hold such beliefs, adults need to observe infants closely to determine just who has been reborn. Such beliefs provide a strong sense of continuity that links the past, present, and future.

Animism

One of the most widespread concepts concerning supernatural beings is **animism,** a belief that nature is animated (enlivened or energized) by distinct personalized spirit beings separable from bodies. Spirits such as souls and ghosts are thought to dwell in humans and animals, but also in human-made artifacts, plants, stones, mountains, wells, and other natural features. So too the woods may be full of a variety of unattached or free-ranging spirits. The various spirits involved are a highly diverse lot. Generally speaking, though, they are less remote from people than gods and goddesses and are more involved in daily affairs. They may be benevolent, malevolent, or just plain neutral. They also may be awesome, terrifying, lovable, or even mischievous. Since they may be pleased or irritated by human actions, people are obliged to be concerned about them.

Animism is typical of those who see themselves as being a part of nature rather than superior to it. This includes most food foragers, as well as those food-producing peoples who acknowledge little qualitative difference between a human life and any living entity from turtles to trees, or even rivers and mountains. In such societies, gods and goddesses are relatively unimportant, but the woods are full of spirits. Gods and goddesses, if they exist at all, may be seen as having created the world and perhaps making it fit to live in; but in animism, spirits are the ones to beseech when ill, the ones to help or hinder the shaman, and the ones who the ordinary hunter may meet when off in the woods.

animism A belief that nature is enlivened or energized by distinct personalized spirit beings separable from bodies.

Animatism

Although supernatural power is often thought of as being vested in supernatural beings, it does not have to be. Such is the case with **animatism**—the belief that nature is enlivened or energized by an impersonal spiritual power or supernatural potency. The Melanesians, for example, think of *mana* as a force inherent in all objects—not unlike the idea of a cosmic energy passing into and through everything, affecting living and nonliving matter alike (similar to "The Force" in the *Star Wars* films). It is not in itself physical, but it can reveal itself physically. A warrior's success in fighting is not attributed to his own strength but to the *mana* contained in an amulet that hangs around his neck. Similarly, a farmer may know a great deal about horticulture, soil conditioning, and the correct time for sowing and harvesting, but nevertheless may depend upon *mana* for a successful crop, often building a simple altar to this power at one end of the field. If the crop is good, it is a sign that the farmer has in some way appropriated the necessary *mana*. Far from being a personalized force, *mana* is abstract in the extreme, a power or potency lying always just beyond reach of the senses.

This concept of impersonal potency or energy was also widespread among North American Indians. The Mohawk called it *orenda;* to the Lakota it was *wakonda;* to the Algonquins, *manitou*. Nevertheless, though found on every continent, the concept is not necessarily universal. In some cultures this impersonal spirit power is turned to for healing purposes. For example, Ju/'hoansi Bushmen healers rely on a supernatural force called *n/um,* which generally remains dormant within them until activated, usually through a "trance dance."[3] Notably, animism (as a belief in distinct spirit beings) and animatism (which lacks particular substance or individual form) are not mutually exclusive. They are often found in the same culture, as in Melanesian societies and also in the North American Indian societies just mentioned.

People trying to comprehend beliefs in the supernatural beings and powers that others recognize frequently ask how such beliefs are maintained. In part, the answer is through manifestations of power. Given a belief in animatism and/or the powers of supernatural beings, one is predisposed to see what appear to be results of the application of such powers. For example, if a Melanesian warrior is convinced of his power because

animatism A belief that nature is enlivened or energized by an impersonal spiritual power or supernatural potency.

[3]Shostak, M. (1983). *Nisa: The life and words of a !Kung woman* (pp. 291–293). New York: Vintage.

he possesses the necessary *mana* and he is successful, he is likely to interpret this success as proof of the power of *mana*. "After all, I would have lost had I not possessed it, wouldn't I?" Beyond this, because of his confidence in his *mana*, he may be willing to take more chances in his fighting, and this indeed could mean the difference between success or failure.

Failures, of course, do occur, but they can be explained. Perhaps one's prayer was not answered because a deity or spirit was still angry about some past insult. Or perhaps the Melanesian warrior lost his battle because he was not as successful in bringing *mana* to bear as he thought, or because his opponent had more mana than he did. In any case, humans generally emphasize successes over failures, and long after many of the latter have been forgotten, tales probably still will be told of striking cases of the workings of supernatural powers.

Beliefs are also maintained through myths—explanatory narratives that rationalize and reinforce religious beliefs and practices. We will discuss myths in more detail later in the chapter.

Religious Specialists

All human societies include individuals who guide and supplement the religious practices of others. Such individuals are seen to be highly skilled at contacting and influencing supernatural beings and utilizing supernatural forces. Often their qualification for this is that they have undergone special training. In addition, they may display certain distinctive personality traits that make them particularly well suited to perform these tasks.

Priests and Priestesses

Societies with the resources to support full-time occupational specialists give the role of guiding religious practices and influencing the supernatural to the **priest** or **priestess**. He or she is the socially initiated, ceremonially inducted member of a recognized religious organization, with a rank and function that belong to him or her as the holder of a position others have held before. The sources of power are the society and the institution within which the priest or priestess functions.

The priest, if not the priestess, is a familiar figure in Western societies; he is the priest, minister, imam, lama, rabbi, or whatever the official title may be in an

priest or priestess A full-time religious specialist formally recognized for his or her role in guiding the religious practices of others and for contacting and influencing supernatural powers.

© Irven DeVore/Anthro-Photo

Interceding with the spirits is the task of Ju/'hoansi Bushmen healers, men and women who possess the powerful healing force called *n/um*. *N/um* generally remains dormant in a healer until an effort is made to activate it. The usual way of doing this is through the "trance dance." To the sound of undulating melodies sung by women, healers dance around a fire, sometimes for hours. The music, strenuous dancing, smoke, heat of the fire, and healers' intense concentration cause their *n/um* to heat up. When it comes to a boil, trance is achieved. Here, a Ju/'hoansi healer entering trance is assisted by a trance dancer.

organized religion. With their god defined historically in masculine, authoritarian terms, it is not surprising that, in the Judaic, Christian, and Islamic religions, the most important positions traditionally have been filled by men. Female religious specialists are likely to be found only in societies where women make a major publicly recognized contribution to the economy and where gods and goddesses are both recognized. In Western Europe and North America, for instance, where women are now wage-earners in almost every profession and occupy leadership positions in the workforce, they are now also increasingly admitted into the leadership of many Judeo-Christian religious groups.[4]

Shamans

Societies that lack full-time occupational specialization have existed far longer than those with such specialization,

[4]Lehman, E. C., Jr. (2002). Women's path into the ministry. *Pulpit & Pew Research Reports*, 1(Fall), 4.

and have always included individuals with special powers and skills that enable them to connect with and manipulate supernatural beings and forces. These powers and skills have come to them through some personal experience, usually in solitude. In an altered state of consciousness, they receive a vision that empowers them to heal the sick, change the weather, control the movements of animals, and foretell the future. As they perfect these and related skills, they assume the role of shaman.

The word *shaman* originally referred to medical-religious specialists, or spiritual guides, among the Tungus and other Siberian pastoral nomads with animist beliefs. By means of various techniques such as fasting, drumming, chanting, or dancing, as well as hallucinogenic mushrooms, these Siberian shamans enter into a trance, or altered state of consciousness. While in this waking dream state, they experience visions of an alternate reality inhabited by spirit beings such as guardian animal spirits who may assist in the healing.

Cross-cultural research of shamanism shows that similar medical-religious healing practices also exist in traditional cultures outside Siberia. For that reason, the term *shaman* has also been applied to a variety of part-time spiritual leaders and traditional healers ("medicine men") active in North and South American indigenous communities and beyond.

As defined by US anthropologist Michael Harner, famous for his participant observation among Shuar (or Jivaro) Indian shamans in the Amazon rainforest, a **shaman** is

> a man or woman who enters an altered state of consciousness—at will—to contact and utilize an ordinarily hidden reality in order to acquire knowledge, power, and to help other persons. The shaman has at least one, and usually more, "spirits" in his or her personal service.[5]

The term *shaman* has become so popular in recent decades that any non-Western local priest, healer, or diviner is often loosely referred to as one. In addition to so-called New Age enthusiasts, among whom shamanism is particularly popular, the faith healers and many other evangelists among fundamentalist Christians share many of the characteristics of shamanism.

Typically, one becomes a shaman by passing through stages of learning and practical experience, often

---

shaman A person who enters an altered state of consciousness—at will—to contact and utilize an ordinarily hidden reality in order to acquire knowledge, power, and to help others.

---

[5]Harner, M. (1980). *The way of the shaman: A guide to power and healing* (p. 20). San Francisco: Harper & Row.

---

involving psychological and emotional ordeals brought about by isolation, fasting, physical torture, sensory deprivation, and/or hallucinations. These hallucinations (derived from the Latin word for "mental wandering") occur when the shaman is in a trance, which may occur spontaneously but can also be induced by drumming or consuming mind-altering drugs such as psychoactive vines or mushrooms.

Among the Penobscot Indians in northern New England, for example, any person could become a shaman, since no formal institution provided rules and regulations to guide religious consciousness. The search for shamanic visions was pursued by most adult Penobscot males, who would go off alone and, through meditation, sensory deprivation, and hyperventilation, induce an altered state of consciousness in which they hoped to receive a vision. Not all were successful, but failure did not result in social disgrace. Those who did achieve success experienced a sense of being freed from their bodily existence in which they established a special relationship with a particular animal spirit that appeared in their trance state. This became the shaman's animal helper—a common element in shamanism—who thereafter would assist the shaman in performing his tasks.

Because shamanism is rooted in altered states of consciousness and the human nervous system that produces these trance states is universal, individuals involved in shamanism experience similarly structured visual, auditory, somatic (touch), olfactory (smell), and gustatory (taste) hallucinations. The widespread occurrence of shamanism and the remarkable similarities among shamanic traditions everywhere are consequences of this universal neurological inheritance. At the same time, the meanings ascribed to sensations experienced in altered states and made of their content are culturally determined; hence, despite their overall similarities, local traditions always vary in their details. The Biocultural Connection examines such experiences with a special focus on Ju/'hoansi Bushman culture where about half of all men and a third of the older women are shamans.

This chapter's shaman is essentially a religious go-between who acts on behalf of some human client, often to bring about healing or to foretell some future event. To do so, the shaman intervenes to influence or impose his or her will on supernatural powers. The shaman can be contrasted with the priest or priestess, whose "clients" are the deities. Priests and priestesses frequently tell people what to do; the shaman tells supernaturals what to do. In return for services rendered, the shaman may collect a fee—fresh meat, yams, or a favorite possession. In some cases, the added prestige, authority, and social power attached to the shaman's status are reward enough.

Biocultural Connection

Altered States, Art, and Archaeology

Many human societies not only accept the practice of inducing altered states of consciousness but actively encourage it as an accepted means of contacting and interacting with supernatural beings and powers.

Because all human beings have essentially the same nervous system—be they urban dwellers in the United States, food foragers in southern Africa, or horticulturists in the Amazon forest— they all progress through the same three stages when entering trance. In the first stage, the nervous system generates a variety of luminous, pulsating, revolving, and constantly shifting geometric patterns known as *entoptic phenomena* (anyone who has suffered from migraine headaches is familiar with these). Typical imagery includes grids, parallel lines, zigzags, dots, nested curves, and filigrees, often in a spiral pattern.

As one goes into deeper trance, the brain tries to "make sense" of these abstract forms, just as it does of sensations received when in an unaltered state of consciousness. This process is known as *construal*, and here differences in culture and experience come into play. Commonly, a South African Bushman in trance will construe a grid pattern as markings on the skin on a giraffe, nested curves as a honeycomb (honey is a local delicacy, and the auditory sensation of buzzing that often accompanies trance promotes the illusion), and dots as *n/um*, the potency seen only by shamans in trance. Obviously, we would not expect an Inuit or someone from Los Angeles to construe these patterns in the same way.

In the third and deepest trance stage, people cease to be observers of their visions and seem to become part of them. As this happens, they feel them- selves passing into a rotating tunnel or vortex with latticelike sides on which appear images of animals, humans, and monsters of various sorts. In the process, the entoptic forms of the earlier stages become integrated into these *iconic images*. These are also culture specific: Individuals see what their culture disposes them to see, and often the images are things having high emotional content. Bushmen often see the eland, an animal thought to be imbued with especially strong potency, particularly for rainmaking. Given this, one of the things shamans try to do in trance is to "capture" elands—"rain animals"—for purposes of making rain.

In many societies, individuals recorded the visions they saw when in trance. The Bushmen are a prime example; as early as 27,000 years ago, they began to paint or engrave their visions on rock faces. Such depictions inevitably include the geometric elements and various distortions that are universal components of the trance experience. For archaeologists, this is of enormous importance, for it has allowed them to identify such diverse prehistoric art as the famous cave paintings of Europe or graffiti etched into the plaster walls of ancient Maya palaces as related to the trance experience. ▪ ▪ ▪

When a shaman acts on behalf of a client, he or she may put on something of a show—one that heightens the basic drama with a sense of danger. Typically, the shaman enters a trance state, in which he or she experi- ences the sensation of traveling to the alternate world and seeing and interacting with spirit beings. The shaman tries to impose his or her will upon these spirits, an inherently dangerous contest, considering the super- human powers that spirits are usually thought to possess.

In many human societies, sleight-of-hand tricks and ventriloquism occur at the same time as trancing. Among Arctic peoples, for example, a shaman may sum- mon spirits in the dark and produce all sorts of flapping noises and strange voices to impress the audience. Some Western observers regard this kind of trickery as evidence that shamanism is fraudulent. However, those who have studied shamanic practices all agree that even though shamans know perfectly well that they are ma- nipulating people with their tricks, they really believe in their power to deal with supernatural forces and spirit beings. Their power, verified by the trance experience, gives them the right as well as the ability to manipulate people in minor technical matters. In short, the shaman

regards his or her ability to perform extraordinary tricks as further proof of superior powers.

The importance of shamanism in a society should not be underestimated. It promotes, through the drama of performance, a trancelike feeling of and release of tension. And it provides psychological assurance that prevailing upon supernatural powers and spirits otherwise beyond human control can bring about invulnerability from attack, success at love, or the return of health. In fact, a frequent reason for a shamanic performance is poor health—a concept that is difficult to define effec- tively in cross-cultural terms. Not only do people in diverse cultures recognize and experience different types of illnesses, they may also view and explain them in different terms. The culturally defined diagnosis of an illness, in turn, determines how the patient will be treated according to the beliefs of the culture, in order to achieve healing.

Although the shamanic treatment may not be physiologically effective, the psychological state of mind induced in the patient is often critical to his or her recovery. From an anthropological perspective, shamanic healings can be understood by means of a three-cornered model we call the *shamanic complex* (Figure 16.2). This triangle is created by the relationships among the shaman and the patient and the community to which both belong.

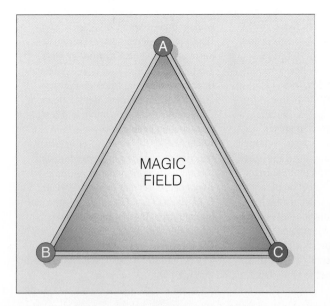

Figure 16.2 **The Shamanic Complex**
Shamanic healing takes place within a "magic field" created when the shaman (A) and patient (B), as well as their community (C), are all convinced that the shaman is a genuine healing master using appropriate techniques that are effective and beneficial. Similar psychological processes are involved in Western medical treatments.

For healing to take place, the shaman needs to be convinced of the effectiveness of his or her spiritual powers and techniques. Likewise, the patient must see the shaman as a genuine healing master using appropriate techniques. Finally, to close the triangle's "magic field," the community within which the shaman operates on the patient must view the healing ceremony and its practitioner as potentially effective and beneficial.

Such dynamics are not unique to shamanic healing ceremonies, for similar social psychological processes are involved in Western medical treatments as well. Some people involved in modern medicine work collaboratively with practitioners of traditional belief systems toward the healing of various illnesses—as illustrated in this chapter's Anthropology Applied feature.

RITUALS AND CEREMONIES

Rituals, or ceremonial acts, are not all religious in nature (consider, for example, college graduation ceremonies in North America), but those that are play a crucial role in religious activity. Religious ritual is the means through which people relate to the supernatural; it is religion in action. Ritual serves to relieve social tensions and reinforce a group's collective bonds. More than this, it provides a means of marking many important events and lessening the social disruption and individual suffering of crises, such as death.

Reconciling Modern Medicine with Traditional Beliefs in Swaziland

Although the biomedical germ theory is generally known and accepted in Western societies today, this is not the case in many other societies around the world. In southern Africa's Swaziland, for example, many illnesses are generally thought to be caused by sorcery or by loss of ancestral protection. (Sexually transmitted diseases—STDs—and other contagious diseases are exceptions to these beliefs.)

Even where the effectiveness of Western medicine is recognized, the ultimate question remains: Why did a disease come to a particular person in the first place? Thus, for the treatment of disease, the Swazi have traditionally relied upon herbalists, diviner mediums

through whom ancestor spirits are thought to work, and (more recently) Christian faith healers. Unfortunately, such individuals have usually been regarded as quacks and charlatans by the medical establishment. Yet, the herbal medicines used by traditional healers are effective in several ways, and the reassurance provided patient and family alike through rituals that reduce stress and anxiety plays an important role in the patient's recovery. In a country where there is 1 traditional healer for every 110 people, but only 1 physician for every 10,000, the potential benefit of cooperation between physicians and healers seems self-evident. Nevertheless, it was largely unrecognized until

proposed by anthropologist Edward C. Green.

Green, a senior researcher at the Harvard School of Public Health, went to Swaziland in 1981 as a researcher for the Rural Water-Borne Disease Control Project, funded by the United States Agency for International Development. Assigned the task of finding out about knowledge, attitudes, and practices related to water and sanitation, and aware of the serious deficiencies of conventional surveys that rely on precoded questionnaires, Green used instead the traditional anthropological techniques of open-ended interviews with key informants, along with participant observation. The key

[continued]

[continued]

informants were traditional healers, their patients, and rural health motivators (individuals chosen by communities to receive 8 weeks of training in preventive health care in regional clinics). Without such anthropological research, Green would have found it impossible to design and interpret a reliable survey instrument, but the added payoff was that Green learned a great deal about Swazi theories of illness and its treatment.

Disposed at the outset to recognize the positive value of many traditional practices, Green could also see how cooperation with physicians might be achieved. For example, traditional healers already recognized the utility of Western medicines for treatment of diseases considered not indigenous to Africa, and traditional medicines were routinely given to children through inhalation and a kind of vaccination. Thus, nontraditional medicines and

vaccinations might be accepted, if presented in traditional terms.

Realizing the suspicion existing on both sides, Green and his Swazi associate Lydia Makhubu (a chemist who had studied the properties of native medicines) recommended to the minister of health a cooperative project focused on a problem of concern to health professionals and native healers alike: infant diarrheal diseases. These had recently become a health problem of high concern to the general public; healers wanted a means to prevent such diseases, and a means of treatment existed—oral rehydration therapy—that was compatible with traditional treatments for diarrhea (herbal preparations taken orally over a period of time). Packets of oral rehydration salts, along with instructions, were provided to healers in a pilot project, with positive results. This helped convince health professionals of the benefits of cooperation,

while the healers saw the distribution of packets to them as a gesture of trust and cooperation on the part of their government.

Since then, further steps toward cooperation have been taken, such as work in prevention of AIDS, STDs, and TB. All of this demonstrates the importance of finding how to work in ways compatible with existing belief systems. Directly challenging traditional beliefs, as all too often happens, does little more than create stress, confusion, and resentment among people. *(Adapted from E. C. Green (1987). The planning of health education strategies in Swaziland, and the integration of modern and traditional health sectors in Swaziland. In R. M. Wulff & S. J. Fiske (Eds.), Anthropological praxis: Translating knowledge into action (pp. 15–25, 87–97). Boulder, CO: Westview Press. 2003 update by authors based on personal communication with Green.)* ■ ■ ■

One important type of ritual is the rite of passage. **Rites of passage** mark important stages in an individual's life cycle. In one of anthropology's classic works, French folklorist Arnold van Gennep analyzed the rites of passage that help individuals through the crucial crises or major social transitions in their lives, such as birth, puberty, marriage, parenthood, advancement to a higher class, occupational specialization, and death.[6] He found it useful to divide ceremonies for all of these life crises into three stages: **separation, transition,** and **incorporation**—first ritual removal of the individual from everyday society, followed by a period of isolation, and, finally, formal return and readmission back into society in his or her new status.

This sequence of stages is something that takes place in many forms in all cultures around the world, from military boot camps to fraternity and sorority initiation ceremonies in the United States to a global array of puberty ceremonies that mark the transition from childhood to adulthood. For example, take the male initiation rites of the Australian aborigines. When the elders decide the time for initiation, the boys are taken from the village (separation), while the women cry and make a ritual show of resistance. At a place distant from the camp, groups of men from many villages gather. The elders sing and dance, while the initiates act as though they are dead. The climax of this part of the ritual is a bodily operation, such as circumcision or the knocking out of a tooth. Anthropologist A. P. Elkin comments:

> This is partly a continuation of the drama of death. The tooth-knocking, circumcision or other symbolical act "killed" the novice; after this he does not return to the general camp and normally may not be seen by any woman. He is dead to the ordinary life of the tribe.[7]

---

rites of passage Rituals that mark important stages in an individual's life cycle, such as birth, marriage, and death.

separation In rites of passage, the ritual removal of the individual from society.

transition In rites of passage, isolation of the individual following separation and prior to incorporation into society.

incorporation In rites of passage, incorporation of the individual into society in his or her new status.

---

[6]Van Gennep, A. (1960). *The rites of passage.* Chicago: University of Chicago Press.

[7]Elkin, A. P. (1964). *The Australian aborigines.* Garden City, NY: Doubleday/Anchor Books.

In this transitional stage, the novice may be shown secret ceremonies and receive some instruction, but the most significant element is his complete removal from society. In the course of these Australian puberty rites, the initiate must learn the lore that all adult men are expected to know; he is given, in effect, a "cram course." The trauma of the occasion is a pedagogical technique that ensures he will learn and remember everything; in a nonliterate society the perpetuation of cultural traditions requires no less, and so effective teaching methods are necessary.

On his return to society (incorporation) the novice is welcomed with ceremonies, as though he had returned from the dead. This alerts the society at large to the individual's new status—that people can expect him to act in certain ways, and in return they must act in the appropriate ways toward him. The individual's new rights and duties are thus clearly defined. He is spared, for example, the problems faced by North Americans in their teeenage years, a time of ill-defined status when an individual is neither adult nor child.

In the Australian case just cited, boys are prepared not just for adulthood but also for *manhood*. In their society, for example, courage and endurance are considered important masculine virtues, and the pain of tooth-knocking and circumcision help instill these in initiates. In a similar way, female initiation rites help prepare Mende girls in West Africa for womanhood. After they have begun to menstruate, the girls are removed from society to spend weeks, or even months, in seclusion. There they discard the clothes of childhood, smear their bodies with white clay, and dress in short skirts and many strands of beads.

Shortly after entering this transitional stage, the girls undergo clitoridectomy, a form of female circumcision that they and Mende in general believe enhances their reproductive potential. Until their incorporation back into society, they are trained in the moral and practical responsibilities of potential child bearers by experienced women in the Sande association, an organization to which the initiates will belong once their training has ended. This training is not all harsh, however, for it is accompanied by a good deal of singing, dancing, and story-telling and the initiates are very well fed. Thus, they acquire both a positive image of womanhood and a strong sense of sisterhood. Once their training is complete, a medicine made by brewing leaves in water is used for a ritual washing, removing the magical protection that has shielded them during the period of their confinement. Having gone through this ritual, a traditional Mende woman knows she is "all woman."

Anthropological commitment to cultural relativism permits an understanding of the practice of clitoridectomy in the Mende female initiation rites.

Waris Dirie, a Somali woman who underwent female genital mutilation at age 6, holds the book in which she recounts her experience.

However, as discussed early on in this book, cultural relativism does not preclude the anthropologist from criticizing a given practice. Apart from the pain and the effect of the operation on a woman's future sexual satisfaction, significant numbers of young women die from excessive bleeding, shock, various infections, or damage to the urethra or anus brought on by the procedure. Others face later risks when giving birth as scar tissue tears.

Not surprisingly, female circumcision—commonly referred to as female genital mutilation (FGM) and practiced in various forms in Asia and Africa especially—has been much condemned as a human rights violation in recent years. Committees to end the practice have been set up in twenty-two African countries. (It is of note that some compare breast implant surgery to FGM—the Western version of what it takes to be "all woman." The Original Study in the final chapter of this book addresses this issue in detail.)

RELIGION, MAGIC, AND WITCHCRAFT

Among the most fascinating of ritual practices is application of the belief that supernatural powers can be compelled to act in certain ways for good or evil purposes by recourse to certain specified formulas. This is a classical anthropological notion of magic. Many societies have magical rituals to ensure good crops, the replenishment of game, the fertility of domestic animals, and the avoidance or healing of illness in humans.

Although many Western peoples today, seeking to objectify and demythologize their world, have often tried to suppress the existence of magic mysteries in their own consciousness, they continue to be fascinated by them. Not only are books and films about demonic possession and witchcraft avidly devoured and discussed, but horoscope columns are a regular feature of daily newspapers in the United States. And magical rituals are still commonly practiced by many Westerners—from lighting a votive candle for someone going through a hard time, to wearing your "lucky boxers" on a hot date, to the weird things baseball pitchers do before each throw.

In the 19th century Scottish anthropologist Sir James George Frazer made a useful distinction between two fundamental principles of magic. The first principle, that "like produces like," he named **imitative magic** (sometimes called *sympathetic magic*). In Burma (Myanmar) in Southeast Asia, for example, a rejected lover might engage a sorcerer to make an image of his would-be love. If this image were tossed into water, to the accompaniment of certain charms, it was expected that the hapless girl would go mad. Thus, the girl would suffer a fate similar to that of her image.

Frazer's second principle is **contagious magic**—the idea that things or persons once in contact can influence each other after the contact is broken. The most common example of contagious magic is the permanent relationship between an individual and any part of his or her body, such as hair, fingernails, or teeth. Frazer cited the Basutos of Lesotho in southern Africa, who were careful to conceal their extracted teeth, because these might fall into the hands of certain mythical beings who could harm the owners of the teeth by working magic on them. Related to this is the custom, in Western societies, of treasuring things that have been touched by special people. Such things range from a saint's relics to possessions of other admired or idolized individuals, such as the singer Elvis Presley or England's Princess Diana.

Witchcraft

In Salem, Massachusetts, 200 innocent citizens suspected of being witches were arrested in 1692; of these, 13 women and 6 men were hanged and one 80-year-old farmer was tortured to death. Despite awarding damages to descendants of some of the victims 19 years later, it was not until 1957 that the last of the Salem witches were exonerated by the Massachusetts legislature. **Witchcraft** is an explanation of events based on the belief that certain individuals possess an innate psychic power capable of causing harm, including sickness and death.

Although many North Americans suppose it to be something that belongs to a less enlightened past, witchcraft is alive and well in the United States today. Indeed, starting in the 1960s, a "witch cult" known as Wicca began to undergo something of a boom in this country, including among highly educated segments of society. And, contrary to popular belief, the self-styled witches belonging to this neo-pagan religion are *not* concerned with "working evil."

Ibibio Witchcraft

Witchcraft exists in a variety of societies today. For example, as the Ibibio of Nigeria have become increasingly exposed to modern education and scientific training, their reliance on witchcraft as an explanation for misfortune has increased.[8] Furthermore, it is often the younger, more educated members of Ibibio society who accuse others of bewitching them. Frequently, the accused are older, more traditional members of society; thus, we have an expression of the intergenerational hostility that often exists in fast-changing traditional societies.

Among the Ibibio of Nigeria, as among most traditional peoples of sub-Saharan Africa, witchcraft beliefs are highly developed and long-standing. A rat that eats a person's crops is not really a rat but a witch that changed into one; if a young and enterprising man cannot get a job or fails an exam, he has been bewitched; if someone's money is wasted or if the person becomes sick, is bitten by a snake, or is struck by lightning, the reason is always the same—witchcraft.

---

imitative magic Magic based on the principle that like produces like; sometimes called sympathetic magic.

contagious magic Magic based on the principle that things once in contact can influence each other after the contact is broken.

witchcraft An explanation of events based on the belief that certain individuals possess an innate psychic power capable of causing harm, including sickness and death.

---

[8]Offiong, D. (1985). Witchcraft among the Ibibio of Nigeria. In A. C. Lehmann & J. E. Myers (Eds.), *Magic, witchcraft, and religion* (pp. 152–165). Palo Alto, CA: Mayfield.

Indeed, among traditional Ibibio virtually all misfortune, illness, or death is attributed to the malevolent activity of witches. The modern Ibibio's knowledge of such facts as the role microorganisms play in disease has little impact; after all, it says nothing about why these were sent to the afflicted individual. Although Ibibio religious beliefs provide alternative explanations for misfortune, they carry negative connotations and do not elicit nearly as much sympathy from others. Thus, if evil befalls a person, witchcraft is a far more satisfying explanation than something such as offspring disobedience or violation of a taboo.

Ibibio witches are thought to be men or women who have within them a special substance acquired from another established witch. From swallowing this substance—made up of needles, colored threads, and other ingredients—one is believed to become endowed with a special power that causes injury, even death, to others regardless of whether its possessor intends harm or not. Witches do not perform rites or make use of "bad medicine." Their power is purely psychic and it is believed to give them the ability to transform into animals and travel any distance at incredible speed to get at their unsuspecting victims, whom they may torture or kill by transferring the victim's soul or vital spirit into an animal, which is then eaten.

To identify a witch, an Ibibio looks for any person living in the region whose behavior is considered odd, out of the ordinary, immoral, or unsocial. Witches are apt to look and act mean and to be socially disruptive people in the sense that their behavior exceeds the range of variance considered acceptable.

The Ibibio make a distinction between sorcerers, whose acts are especially diabolical and destructive, and benign witches, whose witchcraft is relatively harmless, even though their powers are thought to be greater than those of their malevolent counterparts. Sorcerers are the very embodiment of a society's conception of evil—beings that flout the rules of sexual behavior and disregard every other standard of decency. Benign witches are often the community's nonconformists. Typically, they are morose, arrogant, and unfriendly people who keep to themselves but otherwise cause little disturbance. Such witches are thought to be dangerous when offended—likely to retaliate by causing sickness, death, crop failure, cattle disease, or any number of lesser ills. Not surprisingly, people viewed as witches are usually treated with considerable caution, respect, and even fear.

The Functions of Witchcraft

Why witchcraft? We might better ask, why not? In a world where there are few proven techniques for dealing with everyday crises, especially sickness, a belief in witches is not foolish; it is indispensable.[9] No one wants to resign oneself to illness, and if the malady is caused by a witch's curse, then magical countermeasures should cure it.

Not only does the idea of personalized evil answer the problem of unmerited suffering, but it also provides an explanation for many happenings for which no cause can be discovered. Witchcraft, then, cannot be refuted. Even if we could convince a person that his or her illness was due to natural causes, the victim would still ask, as the Ibibio do, Why me? Why now? Such a view leaves no room for pure chance; everything must be assigned a cause or meaning. Witchcraft offers an explanation and, in so doing, also provides both the basis and the means for taking counteraction.

A witch-hunt is, in fact, a systematic investigation, through a public hearing, into all social relationships involving the victim of the sickness or death. Was a husband or wife unfaithful or a son lacking in the performance of his duties? Were an individual's friends uncooperative, or was the victim guilty of any of these wrongs? Accusations are reciprocal, and before long just about every unsocial or hostile act that has occurred in that society since the last outbreak of witchcraft (as manifested in sickness, death, or some other misfortune) is brought into the open.[10]

Through such periodic public scrutiny of everyone's behavior, people are reminded of what their society regards as both strengths and weaknesses of character. This encourages individuals to suppress as best they can those personality traits that are looked upon with disapproval, for if they do not, they at some time may be accused of being a witch. A belief in witchcraft thus serves a function of social control.

Anthropological research suggests that witchcraft, in spite of its often negative image, frequently functions in a very positive way to manage tensions within a society. Nonetheless, events may get out of hand, particularly in crisis situations, when widespread accusations may cause great suffering. This certainly was the case in the Salem witch trials, but even those pale in comparison to the half a million individuals executed as witches in Europe from the 15th through the 17th centuries. This was a time of profound change in European society, marked by a good deal of political and religious conflict. At such times, it is all too easy to search out scapegoats to blame for what people believe are undesirable changes.

---

[9]Mair, L. (1969). *Witchcraft* (p.37). New York: McGraw-Hill.
[10]Turnbull, C. M. (1983). *The human cycle* (p. 181). New York: Simon & Schuster.

In North America, interest in and practice of witchcraft have grown significantly over the past 30 years, often among highly educated segments of society. Contrary to popular belief, witchcraft is *not* concentrated exclusively or even primarily, with working evil.

RELIGION AND CULTURE CHANGE: REVITALIZATION MOVEMENTS

No anthropological consideration of religion is complete without some mention of **revitalization movements**—movements for radical cultural reform in response to widespread social disruption and collective feelings of great stress and despair. Many such movements developed in indigenous societies where European colonial exploitation caused enormous upheaval.

Among the various types of revitalization movements is the **cargo cult**—a spiritual movement (especially

> **revitalization movements** Movements for radical cultural reform in response to widespread social disruption and collective feelings of anxiety and despair.
>
> **cargo cults** Spiritual movements (especially noted in Melanesia) in reaction to disruptive contact with Western capitalism, promising resurrection of deceased relatives, destruction or enslavement of European foreigners, and the magical arrival of utopian riches.

noted in Melanesia in the Southwest Pacific) in reaction to disruptive contact with Western capitalism, promising resurrection of deceased relatives, destruction or enslavement of foreigners, and the magical arrival of utopian riches. Indigenous Melanesians referred to the European's wealth as "cargo" (pidgin English for European trade goods). In times of great social stress, native prophets emerged, predicting that the time of suffering would come to an end and a new paradise on earth would soon arrive. Their deceased ancestors would return to life, and the rich "white man" would magically disappear—swallowed by an earthquake or swept away by a huge wave. However, their cargo would be left for the prophets and their cult followers who performed rituals to hasten this supernatural redistribution of wealth.[11]

One of many cargo cults took place in 1931 at Buka, in the Solomon Islands (in the Pacific Ocean). A native religious movement suddenly emerged there when prophets predicted that a deluge would soon engulf all european foreigners, and a ship would then arrive filled with Western industrial commodities. The prophets told their followers to construct a storehouse for the goods and to prepare themselves to repulse the colonial police. They also spread word that the ship would come only after the natives had used up all their own supplies, and for this reason believers ceased working in the fields. Although the leaders of the movement were arrested, the cult continued for some years.

As deliberate efforts to construct a more satisfying culture, revitalization movements aim to reform not just the religious sphere of activity but an entire cultural system. Such drastic measures are taken when a group's anxiety and frustration have become so intense that the only way to reduce the stress is to overturn the entire social system and replace it with a new one. From the cargo cults of Melanesia to the 1890 Ghost Dance of many North American Indians to the Mau Mau of the Kikuyu in Kenya in the 1950s, extreme and sometimes violent religious reactions to European domination are so common that anthropologists have sought to formulate their underlying causes and general characteristics.

Revitalization movements are by no means restricted to the colonial world, and in the United States alone hundreds of them have sprung up. Among the more widely known in that part of the world are Mormonism, which began in the 19th century, and the more recent Unification Church of the Reverend Sun Myung Moon. As all of these examples suggest, revitalization movements show a great deal of diversity, and some have been more successful than others. Indeed, revitalization

---

[11]See Worsley, P. (1959). Cargo cults. *Scientific American, 200* (May), 117–128.

movements lie at the root of all known religions—Judaism, Christianity, and Islam included.

From the ongoing need to make sense of their existence, humans continue to explore metaphysically or spiritually as well as scientifically. All around the globe we see indications of the effort, not only in buildings and other structures created for religious purposes but in natural places that people have designated as sacred sites. The search for meaning is also evident in many works of art, which along with religion forms part of the superstructure in the barrel model of culture.

RELIGION AND ART

Humans in all cultures throughout time have creatively articulated their feelings and ideas about themselves and the world around them in aesthetic forms— visual, verbal, musical, dance, and so on. Although difficult to define, **art** may be understood as the creative use of the human imagination to symbolically interpret, express, and enjoy life. While many contemporary Western peoples consider art as purely aesthetic, serving no other purpose, most societies past and present have used art to symbolically express almost every part of their culture, including ideas about religion, kinship, and ethnic identity.

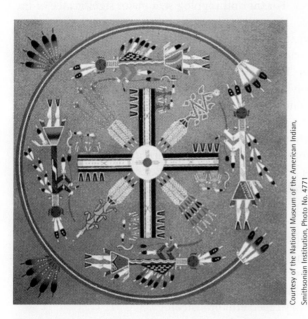

Courtesy of the National Museum of the American Indian, Smithsonian Institution, Photo No. 4771

A traditional Navajo Indian healer creates an intricate sand painting—symbolic designs made with natural colored powders on a surface of smooth clean sand—as part of a ritual healing act. The ill person is positioned in the center of the painting, and when the ceremony is over, the painting is destroyed. Sand paintings such as this are one of countless examples of the interconnections between religion and art.

art The creative use of the human imagination to symbolically interpret, express, and enjoy life.

Art and religion are often intricately intertwined. In an elaborate ceremony involving ornamentation, masks, costumes, songs, dances, and effigies, it is not easy to say precisely where art stops and religion begins. Furthermore music, dance, and other arts may be used, like magic, to "enchant"—to take advantage of the emotional or psychological predispositions of another person or group so as to cause them to perceive reality in a way favorable to the interests of the "enchanter." Indeed, the arts may be used to manipulate a seemingly inexhaustible list of human passions, including desire, terror, wonder, love, fantasy, and vanity.

The Anthropological Study of Art

Anthropologists have found that art often reflects a society's collective ideas, values, and concerns. This is especially true of the verbal, musical, and visual arts—myths, songs, paintings, carvings, and so on. From these, anthropologists may learn how a people imagine their reality and understand themselves and other beings around them. Through the cross-cultural study of art and creativity, we discover much about different worldviews and religious beliefs, as well as political ideas, social values, kinship structures, economic relations, and historical memory.

In approaching art as a cultural phenomenon, anthropologists have the pleasant task of cataloguing, photographing, recording, describing, and analyzing all possible forms of imaginative activity in any particular culture. An enormous variety of forms and modes of artistic expression exists in the world. Because people everywhere continue to create and develop in ever-new ways, there is no end in sight to the interesting process of collecting and describing the world's ornaments, ceremonial masks, body decorations, clothing variations, blanket and rug designs, pottery and basket styles, monuments, architectural embellishments, legends, work songs, dances, and other art forms—many of them rich with religious symbolism.

Visual Art

For many people, the first thing that springs to mind in connection with the word *art* is some sort of visual image, be it a painting, drawing, sketch, or whatever. And indeed, in many parts of the world, people have been making pictures in one way or another for a very long time—etching in bone, engraving in rock, painting on cave walls and rock surfaces, carving and painting on wood, gourds, and clay pots, or painting on textiles, bark cloth, animal hide, or even their own bodies. Some form of visual art is a part of every historically known human culture.

As a type of symbolic expression, visual art may be representational (imitating closely the forms of nature) or abstract (drawing from natural forms but represent-

Courtesy of the Burke Museum of Natural History and Culture, catalogue #1163

The art of the Indians in southern Alaska and British Columbia often portrays animals such as the bear painted on this ceremonial shirt. While not depicted in a representational or naturalistic style, such stylized animals are recognizable to those who share the culture of the artist.

ing only their basic patterns or arrangements). In some of the Indian art of North America's northwest coast, for example, animal figures may be so highly stylized as to be difficult for an outsider to identify. Although the art appears abstract, the artist has created it based on nature, even though he or she has exaggerated and deliberately transformed various shapes to express a particular feeling toward the animals. Because artists do these exaggerations and transformations according to the aesthetic principles of their Indian culture, their meanings are understood not just by the artist but by other members of the community as well.

Verbal Art

The verbal arts include narratives, dramas, poetry, incantations, proverbs, riddles, word games, and even naming procedures, compliments, and insults, when these take structured and special forms. Narratives seem to be among the easiest kinds of the verbal arts to record or collect. Perhaps because they also are the most publishable, with popular appeal in North American culture, they have received the most study and attention.

Generally, narratives have been divided into several basic and recurring categories, including myth and legend.

Derived from the Greek word *mythos*, meaning "speech" or "story," a **myth** is a sacred narrative that explains the fundamentals of human existence (where we and everything in our world came from, why we are here, and where we are going). Beyond this explanatory function, a myth provides a rationale for religious beliefs and practices and sets cultural standards for "right" behavior. Insofar as it is believed, accepted, and perpetuated in a culture, a myth may be said to express part of the traditional worldview of a people. It is a product of creative imagination, and is a work of art, as well as a potentially religious statement.

A **legend** is a story about a memorable event or figure handed down by tradition and told as true but without historical evidence. Commonly, legends consist of pseudo-historical narratives that account for the deeds of heroes, the movements of peoples, and the establishment of local customs, typically with a mixture of realism and the supernatural or extraordinary. As stories, they are not necessarily believed or disbelieved, but they usually serve to entertain as well as to instruct and to inspire or bolster pride in family, community, or nation. Legends all around the world tell us something about the cultures in which they are found.

For the anthropologist, a major significance of the secular and apparently realistic portions of legends, whether long or short, is the clues they provide to what constitutes a culture's approved or ideal ethical behavior. The subject matter of legends is essentially problem solving and mentoring, and the content is likely to include physical and psychological trials of many kinds. Questions may be answered explicitly or implicitly. In what circumstances, if any, does the culture permit homicide? What kinds of behavior are considered brave or cowardly? What is the etiquette of combat or warfare? Does the culture honor or recognize a concept of altruism or self-sacrifice?

Musical Art

The study of music in specific cultural settings, beginning in the 19th century with the collection of folksongs, has developed into a specialized field of anthropological study called **ethnomusicology.**

myth A sacred narrative that explains the fundamentals of human existence—where we and everything in our world came from, why we are here, and where we are going.

legend A story about a memorable event or figure handed down by tradition and told as true but without historical evidence.

ethnomusicology The study of a society's music in terms of its cultural setting.

Music is a form of communication that includes a nonverbal auditory component. The information it transmits is often abstract emotion rather than concrete ideas and is experienced in a variety of ways by different listeners. Such factors make music tough to define. In fact, not even a single definition of music can be agreed upon, because different peoples may include or exclude different ideas within that category. Ethnomusicologists must often rely upon a working definition as the basis for their investigations and often distinguish between "music" and that which is "musical." The way to approach an unfamiliar kind of musical expression is to define it either in indigenous terms or in orthodox musicological terms such as melody, rhythm, and form.

In general, human music is said to differ from natural music—the songs of birds, wolves, and whales, for example—by being almost everywhere perceived in terms of a repertoire of tones at fixed or regular intervals: in other words, a scale. Scale systems and their modifications comprise what is known as **tonality** in music. These vary cross-culturally, so it is not surprising that something that sounds musical to one group of people may come across as noise to another.

> **tonality** In music, scale systems and their modifications.

As another organizing factor in music, rhythm—whether regular or irregular—may be more important than tonality. One reason for this may be our constant exposure to natural rhythms, such as our own heartbeat. The rhythms of traditional European music is most often measured into recurrent patterns of two, three, and four beats, with combinations of weak and strong beats to mark the division and form patterns. Non-European music is likely to move in patterns of five, seven, or eleven beats, with complex arrangements of internal beats and sometimes polyrhythms: one instrument or singer using a pattern of three beats, for example, while another uses a pattern of five or seven. Polyrhythms are frequent in the drum music of West Africa, which shows remarkable precision in the overlapping of rhythmic lines.

Like other art forms, music is often created for religious purposes. Shamans drum to help create a trance state, Buddhist monks chant to focus their meditation, Christians sing hymns to praise their God, and so on. Indeed, the division between art and religion is by no means sharply defined. However uniquely imagined or creatively expressed, art and religion are about feelings, values, and ideas people have about themselves and the world around them and as such form part of a culture's superstructure.

Chapter Summary

■ Religion, an organized system of ideas about spiritual reality, or the supernatural, is a key part of every culture's worldview. It consists of beliefs and practices by which people try to interpret and control aspects of the universe otherwise beyond their control. Among food-foraging peoples, religion is intertwined in everyday life. As societies become more complex, religion may be restricted to particular occasions.

■ Religion is characterized by a belief in supernatural beings and forces, which can be appealed to for aid through prayer, sacrifice, and other rituals. Supernatural beings may be grouped into three categories: major deities (gods and goddesses), ancestral spirits, and other sorts of spirit beings. Gods and goddesses are great but remote beings that control the universe or a specific part of it. Whether people recognize gods, goddesses, or both has to do with how men and women relate to each other in everyday life. Belief in ancestral spirits is based on the idea that human beings are made up of a body and a soul or vital spirit. Freed from the body at death, the spirit continues to participate in human affairs. It is characteristic of descent-based groups with their associated ancestor orientation.

■ Animism, common among peoples who see themselves as part of nature, is a belief that nature is animated or energized by distinct personalized spirit beings separable from bodies. Closer to humans than gods and goddesses, these spirit beings are intimately concerned with human activities. Animatism, sometimes found alongside animism, is a belief that nature is animated or energized by an impersonal spiritual power, which may make itself manifest in any object.

■ Belief in supernatural beings and powers is maintained through what people perceive as manifestations of power. Belief is also fueled by the fact that supernatural beings seem real because they possess certain attributes that are familiar to people. Finally, they are explained and reinforced by myths.

■ All human societies have specialists—priests and priestesses and/or shamans—to guide religious practices and to intervene with the supernatural world. Shamans are individuals skilled at contacting and manipulating supernatural beings and powers through altered states of consciousness. Their performances promote a release of tension among individuals in a society, and the shaman can help to maintain social control. The benefits of shamanism for the shaman are prestige, sometimes wealth, and an outlet for artistic self-expression.

■ Religious rituals are religion in action. Through ritual acts, social bonds are reinforced. Rituals carried out to mark important stages in an individual's life cycle are rites of passage and include three stages: separation, transition, and incorporation. Magic, which can be viewed as a ritual practice that makes supernatural powers act in certain ways, can be differentiated into imitative magic and contagious magic.

■ Witchcraft functions as an effective way for people to explain away personal misfortune without having to shoulder any personal blame. Even malevolent witchcraft may function positively in the realm of social control. It may also provide an outlet for feelings of hostility and frustration without disturbing the norms of the larger group.

■ Religion (including magic and witchcraft) serves several important social functions. These include sanctioning conduct by providing notions of right and wrong; setting standards for acceptable behavior and helping perpetuate an existing social order; lifting the burden of decision making from individuals and placing responsibility with the gods; maintaining social solidarity; enhancing the learning of traditional lore and thereby ensuring continuity in a nonliterate culture; and building hope for reaching a specific goal, such as the healing of physical, emotional, or social ills.

■ Revitalization movements, which can happen in any culture, arise when people seek radical cultural reform in response to widespread social disruption and collective feelings of anxiety and despair. Among Melanesian islanders radically disturbed by Western colonization and capitalism, these movements have often taken the form of cargo cults, which have appeared spontaneously at different times since the beginning of the 20th century. No matter where they occur, revitalization movements follow a common sequence, and all religions stem from such movements.

■ Religion is often intricately intertwined with art—the creative use of the human imagination to symbolically interpret, express, and enjoy life. It stems from the uniquely human ability to use symbols to give shape and significance to the physical world for more than just a utilitarian purpose. Anthropologists are interested in art as a reflection of the cultural values and concerns of people.

■ Three major art categories are visual, verbal, and musical. Visual art may be regarded as either representational or abstract. Verbal arts include myths (sacred narratives that explain how the world came to be as it is) and legends (stories told as if true that often recount the exploits of heroes, the movements of people, and the establishment of local customs). Both provide clues about what constitutes model ethical behavior in a culture. The study of music in specific cultural settings has developed into the specialized field of ethnomusicology. Almost everywhere human music is perceived in terms of tonality (scale systems and their modifications) and rhythm, both of which vary across cultures.

■ Aside from adding beauty and pleasure to everyday life, art serves a wide and varied number of functions, many of them relating to religion—such as setting values and standards for behavior; identifying and reinforcing beliefs; and honoring or beseeching the aid of a deity, an ancestral spirit, or an animal spirit.

Questions for Reflection

1. Beyond biological survival, humans face mental challenges born of the need to make meaningful sense of their existence. Do you ever ponder questions such as the meaning of your life and big issues such as the origin or destiny of the human species? How does your culture, including your religious or spiritual beliefs, offer you guidance in finding meaningful answers to such big questions?

2. Do the basic dynamics of the shamanic complex also apply to preachers or priests in modern churches and medical doctors working in modern hospitals? Can you think of some similarities among the shaman, preacher, and medical doctor in terms of their respective fields of operation?

3. Revitalization movements occur in reaction to the upheavals caused by rapid colonization and modernization. Do you think that the rise of Christian fundamentalism in the North American Bible Belt today is a response to such upheavals as well?

4. In postindustrial societies such as western Europe, the United States, and Canada, there is growing interest in shamanism and alternative healing techniques. Is there any relationship between globalization and this phenomenon?

5. Many museums and private collectors in Europe and North America are interested in so-called tribal art such as African statues or American Indian masks originally used in or made for sacred rituals. Do you know of any sacred objects such as paintings or carvings that have a place in your own religion that might also be collected, bought, or sold as art?

Key Terms

worldview	incorporation
religion	imitative magic
spirituality	contagious magic
polytheism	witchcraft
pantheon	revitalization movements
animism	cargo cults
animatism	art
priest or priestess	myth
shaman	legend
rites of passage	ethnomusicology
separation	tonality
transition	

Multimedia Review Tools

Make the Grade in Anthropology with ThomsonNOW

Thomson NOW! This powerful online study tool provides you with a *personalized study plan* based on your responses to a diagnostic pretest. Once you have mastered the material with the help of interactive learning tools, an integrated e-book, and more, you can take a post-test to confirm you are ready to move on to the next chapter. To get started with ThomsonNOW,

check the card packaged with your book for the access code. Then go to http://www.thomsonedu.com to create an account through 1pass™. If there is no card in your book, go to http://www.thomsonedu.com to purchase an access code.

Companion Website and Anthropology Resource Center

Go to http://anthropology.wadsworth.com to reach the companion website for your text. This offers many study aids, including self quizzes for each chapter and a practice final exam, as well as links to anthropology websites and information on the latest theories and discoveries in the field.

Also, check out the Anthropology Resource Center for a wealth of learning materials that include interactive maps, video exercises, simulations, and breaking news in anthropology. Be sure to explore InfoTrac College Edition®, your online library that offers full-length articles from thousands of scholarly and popular publications. To reach the Anthropology Resource Center and InfoTrac College Edition, check the card packaged with your book for the access code. Then go to http://www.thomsonedu.com to create an account through 1pass™. If there is no card in your book, go to http://www.thomsonedu.com to purchase an access code.

© Staffan Widstrand/C

CHALLENGE ISSUE

For long-term survival, human cultures have been required to adapt to different environments and shifting circumstances. Today's technological and other major changes challenge us to adjust at an ever-faster pace. These challenges are all the more unsettling for traditional peoples around the world, for whom changes are often imposed by powerful outside forces undermining their customary ways of life. However, there are also many examples of traditional peoples accepting change on their own terms, welcoming certain new ideas, products, or practices into their lives as improvements. So it was with Saami reindeer herders in Scandinavia's arctic tundra, who adopted newly invented snowmobiles in the 1960s, convinced that these modern machines would make traditional herding physically easier and economically more advantageous. Here, a young Saami man stands besides his tent and snowmobile, searching for his reindeer with binoculars.

Processes of Change 17

Culture has become the primary medium through which the human species adapts to changes and solves the problems of existence. Various cultural institutions—such as religion, kinship and marriage, and political and economic organization—mesh to form an integrated cultural system. Because systems generally work to maintain stability, cultures are often fairly stable and remain so unless there is a critical change in one or more significant factors such as natural environment, technology, population density—or in human perceptions of the various conditions to which they are adapted.

Archaeological studies reveal how elements of a culture may persist for long periods. In northeastern North America, for example, the cultures of indigenous inhabitants remained relatively consistent over thousands of years because they successfully adapted to relatively minor fluctuations in their social conditions and natural environments, making changes from time to time in tools, utensils, and other material support.

Although stability may be a striking feature of many traditional cultures, all cultures are capable of adapting to changing conditions—climatic, economic, political, or ideological. Adaptation is a consequence of change that happens to work favorably for a population.

However, not all change is positive or adaptive, and not all cultures are equally well equipped for making the necessary adjustments in a timely fashion. In a stable society, change may occur gently and gradually, without altering in any fundamental way the culture's underlying structures, as was the case in much of North America before the European invasion several centuries ago. Sometimes, though, the pace of change may increase dramatically, to the point of destabilizing or even wrecking a cultural system. The modern world is full of examples of such radical changes, from the disintegration of the Soviet Union to the utter devastation of many indigenous communities in the Amazon caused by state efforts to develop Indian homelands and capitalize on the vast rainforest's natural resources.

The causes of change are many, including accidental discoveries, deliberate attempts to solve a perceived problem, and interaction with other people who introduce—or force—new ideas or tools or ways of life. Change imposed upon one group by another continues in much of the world today as culture contact intensifies between societies unequal in power. Among those who have the power to drive and direct change in their favor, it is typically referred to as "progress." But progress is a relative term that implies improvement *as defined* by the people who profit or otherwise benefit from the changes set into motion. In other words, progress is in the eye of the beholder.

MECHANISMS OF CHANGE

Anthropologists are not only interested in the structures of cultures as systems of adaptation, which help us understand how a population maintains itself in a certain habitat, but also in explaining processes of culture change. Some of the major mechanisms involved in culture change are innovation, diffusion, and cultural loss. These types of change are typically voluntary and are not imposed on a population by outside forces.

Innovation

The ultimate source of all culture change is innovation: any new idea, method, or device that gains widespread acceptance in society. **Primary innovation** is the creation, invention, or discovery, by chance, of a completely new idea, method, or device. A **secondary innovation** is a deliberate application or modification of an existing idea, method, or device.

An example of a primary innovation is the discovery that firing clay makes it permanently hard. Presumably, accidental firing of clay occurred frequently in ancient cooking fires—but a chance occurrence is of no account unless someone perceives an application of it. This perception took place about 25,000 years ago, when people began making figurines of fired clay. However, it was not until some time between 9,000 and 8,500 years ago that people recognized a highly practical application of fired clay and began using it to make pottery containers and cooking vessels.

The accidental discoveries responsible for primary innovations are not generated by environmental change or some other need, nor are they necessarily adaptive. They are, however, given structure by the cultural context. Thus, the outcome of the discovery of fired clay by migratory food foragers 25,000 years ago was very

> **primary innovation** The creation, invention, or chance discovery of a completely new idea, method, or device.
>
> **secondary innovation** A new and deliberate application or modification of an existing idea, method, or device.

A Hopi Indian woman firing pottery vessels. The earliest discovery that firing clay vessels makes them more durable took place in Asia, probably when clay-lined basins next to cooking fires were accidentally fired. Later, a similar innovation took place in the Americas.

© Stephen Trimble

different from what it was when discovered later by more sedentary farmers in Southwest Asia, where it set off a cultural chain reaction as one invention led to another. Indeed, given particular sets of cultural goals, values, and knowledge, certain innovations are nearly inevitable.

Although an innovation must be reasonably consistent with a society's needs, values, and goals in order to gain acceptance, it takes more than this. Force of custom or habit tends to obstruct ready acceptance of the new or unfamiliar, for people typically stick with what they are used to rather than adopt something strange that requires adjustment on their part.

Obviously, an innovation is not assured of acceptance simply because it is notably better than the thing, method, or idea it might replace. Much may depend on the prestige of the innovator and potential adopters. If the innovator's prestige is high, this will help gain more general acceptance for the innovation. If it is low, acceptance is less likely, unless the innovator can attract a sponsor who has high prestige.

Diffusion

The spread of certain ideas, customs, or practices from one culture to another is known as **diffusion.** So common is cross-cultural borrowing that North American anthropologist Ralph Linton suggested that it accounts for as much as 90 percent of any culture's content. People are creative about their borrowing, however, picking and choosing from multiple possibilities and sources. Usually their selections are limited to those compatible with the existing culture. In Guatemala in the 1960s, for example, Maya Indians, who then (as now) made up more than half of that country's population, would adopt Western ways if the practical advantage of what they adopted was self-evident and did not conflict with deeply rooted traditional values and customs. The use of metal hoes, shovels, and machetes became standard early on, for they are superior to stone tools and yet compatible with the cultivation of corn in the traditional way by men using hand tools.

Yet, certain other modern practices that might seem advantageous to the Maya were resisted if they were perceived to be in conflict with Indian tradition. Pursuing these practices could make one a social outcast. This happened to a young farmer who tried his hand at growing vegetables to sell, using chemical fertilizers and pesticides to grow cash crops not eaten by the Maya and having market value only in the city. Following this line of work, he found he could not secure a "good"

woman for a wife—a "good" woman (in his cultural context) being one who has never had sex with another man and is hard-working, skilled at domestic chores, and willing to attend to her husband's needs. However, after abandoning his unorthodox ways, he gained acceptance in his community as a "real" man—one who provides for his household by working steadily at farming and making charcoal in the traditional ways. No longer conspicuous as someone different from other local men, he married well within a short time.[1]

An awareness of the extent of cultural borrowing can be eye opening. Take, for example, the numerous things that people all around the globe have borrowed from American Indians. Domestic plants developed ("invented") by the Indians—potatoes, avocados, beans, squash, tomatoes, peanuts, manioc, chili peppers, chocolate, sweet potatoes, and last but not least corn or maize, to name a few—furnish a major portion of the world's food supply. In fact, American Indians are recognized as primary contributors to the world's varied cuisine and credited with developing the largest array of nutritious foods.[2] These borrowings are so thoroughly integrated into contemporary societies across the globe that few people are aware of their source.

Despite the obvious importance of diffusion, an innovation from another culture probably faces more obstacles when it comes to being accepted than does one that is "homegrown" simply because it is foreign. In the United States, for example, this is one reason why people have been so reluctant to abandon the cumbersome English system of weights and measures for the far more logical metric system. While all other countries in the world have essentially converted to metric, in the United States the switchover is still less than about 50 percent. Hence, ethnocentrism may act as a barrier to cultural borrowing.

Cultural Loss

Most often people look at culture change as an accumulation of innovations. Frequently, however, the acceptance of a new innovation results in **cultural loss**—the abandonment of an existing practice or trait. For example, in ancient times chariots and carts were used widely in northern Africa and southwestern Asia, but wheeled

---

diffusion The spread of certain ideas, customs, or practices from one culture to another.

cultural loss The abandonment of an existing practice or trait.

---

[1]Reina, R. E. (1966). *The law of the saints* (pp. 65–68). Indianapolis: Bobbs-Merrill.

[2]Weatherford, J. (1988). *Indian givers: How the Indians of the Americas transformed the New World* (p. 115). New York: Ballantine.

vehicles virtually disappeared from Morocco to Afghanistan about 1,500 years ago. They were replaced by camels, not because of some reversion to the past but because camels used as pack animals worked better. The old Roman empire roads had deteriorated, and these sturdy animals traveled well with or without roads. Their endurance, longevity, and ability to ford rivers and traverse rough ground made pack camels admirably suited for the region. Plus, they were economical in terms of labor: A wagon required a man for every two draft animals, but a single person could manage up to six pack camels.

Often overlooked is another facet of losing apparently useful traits: loss without replacement. An example of this is the historical absence of boats among the indigenous inhabitants of the Canary Islands, a group of small islands isolated off North Africa's Atlantic coast. The ancestors of these people must have had boats, for without them they could never have transported themselves and their domestic livestock to the islands in the first place. Later, without boats, they had no way to communicate between islands or with the mainland. This loss of something useful came about due to the islands' lack of stone suitable for making polished stone axes, which in turn limited the islanders' carpentry.[3]

REPRESSIVE CHANGE

Innovation, diffusion, and cultural loss all may take place among peoples who are free to decide for themselves what changes they will or will not accept. Not always, however, do people have the liberty to make their own choices. Frequently, changes they would not willingly make have been forced upon them by some other group, usually in the course of conquest and colonialism. A direct outcome in many cases is repressive culture change, which anthropologists call acculturation. The most radical form of repressive change is ethnocide.

Acculturation and Ethnocide

Acculturation is the massive culture change that occurs in a society when it experiences intensive firsthand contact with a more powerful society. It always involves an element of force, either directly, as in conquests, or indirectly, as in the implicit or explicit threat that force will be used if people refuse to make the demanded

> **acculturation** Massive culture changes that people are forced to make as a consequence of intensive firsthand contact between their own group and another, often more powerful, society.

changes. Other variables include degree of cultural difference; circumstances, intensity, frequency, and hostility of contact; relative status of the agents of contact; who is dominant and who is submissive; and whether the nature of the flow is reciprocal or nonreciprocal. *Acculturation* and *diffusion* are not equivalent terms; one culture can borrow from another without being in the least acculturated.

In the course of cultural contact, any one of a number of things may happen. Merger or fusion occurs when two cultures lose their separate identities and form a single culture, as historically expressed by the melting pot ideology of English-speaking, Protestant Euramerican culture in the United States. Sometimes, though, one of the cultures loses its autonomy but retains its identity as a subculture in the form of a caste, class, or ethnic group. This is typical of conquest or slavery situations, and the United States has examples of this in spite of its melting pot ideology—we need look no further than the nearest American Indian reservation. In virtually all parts of the world today, people are faced with the tragedy of forced removal from their traditional homelands, as entire communities are uprooted to make way for hydroelectric projects, grazing lands for cattle, mining operations, or highway construction. In Brazil's rush to develop the vast Amazon rainforest, for instance, entire indigenous communities have been relocated to "national parks," where resources are inadequate for the number of people and where former enemies are often forced to live in close proximity.

Ethnocide, the violent eradication of an ethnic group's collective identity as a distinctive nation, occurs when a dominant society deliberately sets out to destroy another people's cultural heritage. This may take place when a powerful nation aggressively expands its territorial control by annexing neighboring peoples and their territories, incorporating the conquered groups as subjects. A policy of ethnocide typically includes forbidding a subjugated nation's ancestral language, criminalizing their traditional customs, destroying their religion and demolishing sacred places and practices, breaking up their social organizations, and dispossessing or removing the survivors from their homelands—in essence, stopping short of physical extermination while removing all traces of their unique culture.

One tragic current example is Tibet, which could not defend itself against an invasion by the Chinese communist army in 1950. The Chinese government then initiated its ethnocidal policies by means of systematic attacks against traditional Tibetan culture. Seeking to stamp out deeply rooted religious beliefs and prac-

> **ethnocide** The violent eradication of an ethnic group's collective identity as a distinctive nation.

---

[3]Coon, C. S. (1954). *The story of man* (p. 174). New York: Knopf.

tices, it ordered the demolition of most Buddhist temples and monasteries. Following a mass uprising, hundreds of thousands of Tibetans were killed or forced into exile abroad. Seeking to annihilate Tibetan identity, China sought to turn the survivors remaining in their ancestral homeland into political subjects who would culturally identify themselves as Chinese nationals.[4]

Ethnocide may also take place when so many carriers of a culture die that those who manage to survive become refugees, living among peoples of different cultures. Examples of this may be seen in many parts of the world today (Figure 17.1). A particularly well-documented case occurred in Brazil's Amazon basin in 1968, when developers hired killers to wipe out several Indian groups, using arsenic, dynamite, and machine guns from light planes.

Violence continues to be used in Brazil as a means of dealing with indigenous peoples. For example, according to conservative estimates, at least 1,500 Yanomami Indians died in the 1980s, many the victims

of deliberate massacres, as cattle ranchers and gold miners poured into northern Brazil. By 1990, 70 percent of Yanomami land in Brazil had been illegally expropriated; fish supplies were poisoned by mercury contamination of rivers; and malaria, venereal disease, and tuberculosis were running rampant. The Yanomami were dying at the rate of 10 percent a year, and their fertility had dropped to near zero. Many villages were left with no children or old people, and the survivors awaited their fate with a profound terror of extinction.[5]

The typical attitude of Brazilians toward such situations is illustrated by their government's reaction to a diplomatic journey that two Kayapó Indian leaders and an anthropologist made to the United States. They ventured north to speak with World Bank authorities and various government officials in the U.S. Congress and State Department concerning the destruction of their land and way of life caused by internationally financed development projects. All three were charged with violating Brazil's Foreign Sedition Act, which prohibits foreigners from secretly stirring up discontent, resis-

[4]http://www.savetibet.org/tibet/us/proceedings/senatefrmauramoynihan.php. See also Avedon, John F. (1997). *In exile from the land of snows: The definitive account of the Dalai Lama and Tibet since the Chinese conquest.* New York: Harper.

[5]Turner, T. (1991). Major shift in Brazilian Yanomami policy. *Anthropology Newsletter, 32*(5), 1, 46.

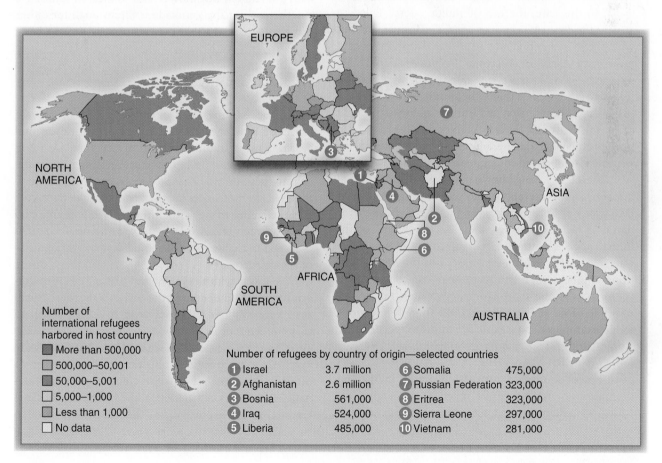

Figure 17.1
Increasing refugee populations, a consequence of conflict between nationalities living in multinational states, have become a burden and source of instability in the states to which they have fled.

tance, or revolt against the government in power. This charge and other relevant atrocities provoked international outrage, which in turn prompted Brazilian authorities to recommend policy changes that could favorably impact the country's indigenous peoples. However, whether their recommendations will be sufficient to effect positive change, or will even be acted upon fully, remains to be seen.

Genocide

The Brazilian Indian case just cited raises the issue of **genocide**—the physical extermination of one people by another, either as a deliberate act or as the unforeseen outcome of activities carried out by one people with little regard for their impact on others. Genocide, like ethnocide, is not new in the world. In North America, for example, European newcomers massacred numerous Indian communities from the 1500s up until the last one at Wounded Knee, South Dakota, in 1890.

Of course, such acts were by no means restricted to North America. One of the most famous 19th-century acts of genocide was the extermination of the indigenous inhabitants of Tasmania, a large island just south of Australia. In this case, the use of military force failed to achieve the complete elimination of the Tasmanians, but what the military could not achieve, a British Protestant missionary George Augustus Robinson could. He rounded up the surviving natives and brought them to his mission station. Once there, the deadly combination of psychological depression and European disease brought about the demise of the last full-blooded Tasmanians in time for Robinson to retire to Britain and contemplate the horrible if unintended consequences of his actions.

The most widely known act of genocide in recent history was the attempt of the Nazis during World War II to wipe out European Jews and Roma (Gypsies) in the name of racial superiority and "improvement" of the human species. Unfortunately, the common practice of referring to this as "*the* Holocaust"—as if it were something unique, or at least exceptional—tends to blind us to the fact that this thoroughly monstrous act is but one example of an all-too-common phenomenon. Among many examples of mass murder in more recent years, Khmer Rouge soldiers in Cambodia killed 1.7 million fellow citizens in the 1970s. In the following decade, government-sponsored terrorism against indigenous communities in Guatemala reached its height, and Saddam Hussein's government used poison gas against the Kurdish ethnic minority in northern Iraq. In the 1990s, more than half a million Tutsi people were slaughtered by their Hutu neighbors in the African country of Rwanda, and today a genocidal campaign is waged against the non-Arab black peoples in the Darfur desert region of western Sudan. Estimates vary, but during the 20th century, as many as 83 million people died of genocide and tyranny.[6]

If such ugly practices are ever to end, we must gain a better understanding of what is behind them. Anthropologists are actively engaged in this, carrying out cross-cultural as well as specific case studies. One finding to emerge is the regularity with which religious, economic, and political interests are allied in cases of genocide. In Tasmania, for example, British wool growers wanted indigenous peoples off the island so that they could have it for their sheep. The government advanced their interests through its military campaigns against the natives, but it was the British missionary work that finally secured Tasmania for the commercial wool interests.

It is important to reiterate that genocide is not always a deliberate act. It can occur as the unforeseen outcome of activities carried out with little regard for their impact on other peoples. For the people whose lives are snuffed out, however, it makes no difference whether or not the genocide is intentional, for either way they face the same deadly result.

Directed Change

The most extreme cases of acculturation occur as a result of military conquest or massive invasion and breaking up of traditional political structures by dominant newcomers who know or care nothing about the culture they control. The indigenous people—unable to resist effectively changes imposed on them and obstructed in carrying out many of their own social, religious, and economic activities—may be forced into new practices that tend to isolate individuals and destroy the integrity of their societies.

So it was with the Ju/'hoansi of Namibia in southern Africa. Rounded up in the early 1960s, these Bushmen were confined to a reservation in Tsumkwe where they could not possibly provide for their own needs. The government supplied them with rations, but these were insufficient to meet basic nutritional needs. In poor health and prevented from developing meaningful alternatives to traditional activities, the Ju/'hoansi became embittered and depressed, and their death rate came to

---

genocide The physical extermination of one people by another, often in the name of progress, either as a deliberate act or as the accidental outcome of activities carried out by one people with little regard for their impact on others.

[6]White, M. (2001). *Historical atlas of the twentieth century.* http://users.erols.com/mwhite28/20centry.htm; see also Van Den Berghe, P. (1992). The modern state: Nation builder or nation killer? *International Journal of Group Tensions, 22*(3), 198.

Two of many examples of attempted genocide in the 20th century: Hitler's Germany against Jews and Gypsies in the 1930s and the 1940s; and Hutus against Tutsis in Rwanda, as in this 1994 massacre.

© Bettmann/Corbis

© Scully/Getty Images

exceed the birthrate. Within the next few years, however, surviving Ju/'hoansi began to take matters into their own hands. They returned to water holes in their traditional homeland, where, assisted by anthropologists and others concerned with their welfare, they are trying to sustain themselves by raising livestock. Whether this will succeed or not remains to be seen, as there are still many obstacles to success.

One byproduct of colonial dealings with indigenous peoples has been the growth of *applied anthropology*, defined in Chapter 1 as the use of anthropological techniques and knowledge for the purpose of solving practical problems. For example, in the United States, the Bureau of American Ethnology was founded in 1876 to gather reliable data the government might use to formulate Indian policies. At the time, anthropologists were convinced of the practicality of their discipline, and many who did ethnographic work among Indians devoted a great deal of time, energy, and even money to assisting their informants, whose interests were frequently threatened from outside.

In the 20th century, the scope and intent of applied anthropology as a form of social engineering expanded.

In the first part of that century, the applied work of Franz Boas—who almost single-handedly trained an entire generation of anthropologists in the United States—proved instrumental in reforming the country's immigration policies. With impressive statistical data based on comparative skull measurements, this German Jewish immigrant challenged popular race theories of the day. He demonstrated that theories privileging non-Jewish immigrants from western Europe and discriminating against Jews and others deemed undesirable as newcomers in the United States were based not on fact but on deeply rooted racial prejudice.

In the 1930s, anthropologists with clearly pragmatic objectives did a number of studies in industrial and other institutional settings in the United States. With World War II came increased involvement at colonial administration beyond U.S. borders, especially in the Pacific, by American officers trained in anthropology. The rapid postwar recovery of Japan was due in no small measure to the influence of anthropologists in structuring the U.S. occupation. Anthropologists continue to play an active role today in administering U.S. trust territories in the Pacific.

All too often, however, states and other powerful institutions directly intervening in the affairs of different ethnic groups or foreign societies fail to seek professional advice from anthropologists who possess relevant cross-cultural expertise and deeper insights. Such failures have contributed to a host of avoidable errors in planning and executing nation-building programs in ethnically divided countries such as Iraq and Afghanistan, both of which are now devastated by war and violence.

Today, applied anthropologists are in growing demand in the field of international development because of their specialized knowledge of social structure, value systems, and the functional interrelatedness of cultures targeted for development. Those working in this arena face a particular challenge: As anthropologists, they are bound to respect other peoples' dignity and cultural integrity, yet they are asked for advice on how to change certain aspects of those cultures. If the request comes from the people themselves, that is one thing, but more often than not, it comes from outsiders. Supposedly, the proposed change is for the good of the targeted population, yet members of that community do not always see it that way. Just how far applied anthropologists should go in advising outsiders how to manipulate people—especially those without the power to resist—to embrace changes proposed for them is a serious ethical question.

In direct response to such critical questions concerning the application and benefits of anthropological research, an alternative type of practical anthropology has emerged during the last half century. Known by a variety of names—including action anthropology and committed, engaged, involved, and advocacy anthropology—this involves community-based research and action in collaboration and solidarity with indigenous societies, ethnic minorities, and other besieged or repressed groups. In sum, the practical application of anthropology is thriving today as never before.

REACTIONS TO REPRESSIVE CHANGE

The reactions of indigenous peoples to the changes outsiders have thrust upon them have varied considerably. Some have responded by moving to the nearest available forest, desert, or other remote places in hopes of being left alone. In Brazil, a number of communities once located near the coast took this option a few hundred years ago and were successful until the great push to develop the Amazon forest began in the 1960s. Others, like many Indians of North America, took up arms to fight back but were ultimately forced to sign treaties and surrender much of their ancestral lands, after which they were

reduced to an impoverished underclass in their own land. Today, they continue to fight to retain their identities as distinct peoples through nonmilitary means and seek to regain control over natural resources on their lands.

In addition, ethnic groups may try to hold on to their distinctive identities by maintaining cultural boundaries such as holding on to traditional language, festive ceremonies, customary dress, ritual songs and dances, unique food, and so on. Indeed, in opposing modernization, people often seek cultural protection and emotional comfort in the force of **tradition**—customary ideas and practices passed on from generation to generation, which in a modernizing society may form an obstacle to new ways of doing things.

When people are able to hold on to some of their traditions in the face of powerful outside domination, the result may be **syncretism**—a blending of indigenous and foreign traits to form a new system. A fine illustration of this is the game of cricket as played by the Trobriand Islanders of Melanesia, some of whose practices we looked at in earlier chapters. When Trobrianders were under British rule, missionaries introduced them to this rather reserved British game to replace the erotic dancing and open sexuality that normally followed the yam harvests. Traditionally, this was the season when chiefs sought to spread their fame by hosting nights of dancing, providing food for the hundreds of young married people who participated. For several months, there would be night after night of provocative dancing, accompanied by chanting and shouting full of sexual innuendo, each night ending as couples disappeared into the bush together.

Since no chief wished to be outdone by any other (being outdone brought into question the strength of one's magic), the dancing had a strong competitive element, and fighting sometimes erupted. To the British Protestant missionaries, cricket seemed a good way to end all of this in a way that would encourage conformity to "civilized" comportment in dress, religion, and sportsmanship. The Trobrianders, however, were determined to "rubbish" (throw out) the British rules of the game. They did this by turning it into the same kind of distinctly Trobriand event that their thrilling dance competitions had once been.

Making cricket their own, Trobrianders added battle dress and battle magic and incorporated erotic dancing into the festivities. Instead of inviting dancers each night, chiefs now arrange games of cricket. Pitching has been modified from the British style to one

tradition Customary ideas and practices passed on from generation to generation, which in a modernizing society may form an obstacle to new ways of doing things.
syncretism In acculturation, the blending of indigenous and foreign traits to form a new system.

Indigenous peoples have reacted to colonialism in many different ways. When British missionaries pressed Trobriand Islanders of Melanesia to celebrate yam harvests with a game of cricket rather than traditional erotic dances, Trobrianders responded by transforming the staid British sport into an exuberant event that featured sexual chants and dances between innings.

© Jerry Leach

closer to their old way of throwing a spear. Following the game, they hold massive feasts, where wealth is displayed to enhance their prestige.

Cricket, in its altered form, has been made to serve traditional systems of prestige and exchange. Neither primitive nor passively accepted in its original form, Trobriand cricket was thoughtfully and creatively adapted into a sophisticated activity reflecting the importance of basic indigenous cultural premises. Exuberance and pride are displayed by everyone associated with the game, and the players are as much concerned with conveying the full meaning of who they are as with scoring well. From the sensual dressing in preparation for the game to the team chanting of songs full of sexual metaphors to erotic chorus-line dancing between the innings, it is clear that each participant is playing for his own importance, for the fame of his team, and for the hundreds of attractive young women who usually watch the game.

Revitalization Movements

Another common reaction to repressive change is revitalization. As noted in Chapter 16, revitalization movements are efforts toward radical cultural reforms in response to widespread social disruption and collective feelings of anxiety and despair. When primary ties of culture, social relationships, and activities are broken and meaningless activity is imposed by outside forces, individuals and groups characteristically react with a rejection of newly introduced cultural elements, reclamation of historical roots and traditional identity, as well as spiritual imagination.

In the United States, revitalization movements have occurred often—whenever significant segments of the population have found their conditions in life to be at odds with the values of the American Dream. For example, the 1960s saw the emergence of revitalization movements among the young of middle-class and even upper-class families. In their case, the professed cultural values of peace, equality, and individual freedom were seen to be at odds with the realities of persistent war, poverty, and constraints on individual action imposed by a variety of impersonal institutions. Youths countered these realities by advocating free love, joining hippie communes, celebrating new forms of rock and folk music, using mind-altering drugs, challenging authority, growing their hair long, and wearing unconventional clothes.

Clearly, when value systems get out of step with existing realities, for whatever reason, a condition of cultural crisis is likely to build up that may breed some forms of reactive movement. Not all suppressed, conquered, or colonized people eventually rebel against established authority, although why they do not is still a debated issue. When they do, however, cultural resistance may take one of several forms, all of which are varieties of revitalization movements. Some of these revitalization movements take on a revolutionary character, as did the Taliban in Afghanistan.

REBELLION AND REVOLUTION

When the scale of discontent within a society reaches a certain level, the possibilities are high for **rebellion**—organized armed resistance to an established government or authority in power. For instance, there have been many peasant rebellions around the world in the course

rebellion Organized armed resistance to an established government or authority in power.

of history. Often, such rebellions are triggered by repressive regimes imposing new taxes on the already struggling small farmers unable to feed their families under such unacceptable levels of exploitation.

One current example is the ongoing Zapatista Maya Indian uprising in southern Mexico, which began in the mid-1990s. This rebellion involves thousands of poor Indian farmers whose livelihoods have been threatened by the changes imposed on them and whose human rights under the Mexican constitution have never been fully implemented.

In contrast to rebellions, which have rather limited objectives, revolutions involve a more radical turnover. When the level of discontent is very high, it may lead to a **revolution**—a radical change in a society or culture. In the political arena, revolution involves the forced overthrow of an old government and the establishment of a completely new one.

Such was the case when Muslim fundamentalists in Iran toppled the imperial regime of the shah in 1979 and replaced him with Ayatollah Khomeini, a high-ranking Shiite Muslim religious leader. Returning to his homeland from exile, and becoming Iran's new leader, he instituted a new social and political order.

The question of why revolutions erupt, as well as why they frequently fail to live up to the expectations of the people initiating them, is unsolved. It is clear, however, that the colonial policies of countries such as Britain, France, Spain, Portugal, and the United States during the 19th and early 20th centuries have created a worldwide situation in which revolution is nearly inevitable. Despite the political independence most colonies have gained since World War II, more powerful countries continue to exploit many of these "underdeveloped" countries for their natural resources and cheap labor, causing a deep resentment of rulers beholden to foreign powers. Further discontent has been caused as governing elites in newly independent states try to assert their control over peoples living within their boundaries. By virtue of a common ancestry, possession of distinct cultures, persistent occupation of their own territories, and traditions of self-determination, the peoples they aim to control identify themselves as distinct nations and refuse to recognize the legitimacy of what they regard as a foreign government.

Thus, in many a former colony, large numbers of people have taken up arms to resist annexation and absorption by imposed state governments run by people of other nationalities. As they attempt to make their multi-ethnic states into unified countries, ruling elites of one nationality set about stripping the peoples of other

nations within their states of their lands, resources, and particular cultural identities. The phenomenon is so common that it led Belgian sociologist Pierre van den Berghe to label what modern states refer to as "nation building" as, in fact, "nation killing."[7]

One of the most important facts of our time is that the vast majority of the distinct peoples of the world have never consented to rule by the governments of states within which they find themselves living.[8] In many a newly emerged country, such peoples feel they have no other option than to fight. Of the hundreds of armed conflicts in the world today, almost all are in the economically poor countries of Africa, Asia, Central and South America, many of which were at one time under European colonial domination (Figure 17.2). Of these wars, the majority are between the state and one or more nations or ethnic groups within the state's borders who are seeking to maintain or regain control of their personal lives, communities, lands, and resources in the face of what they regard as repression or subjugation by a foreign power.[9]

Revolutions do not always accomplish what they set out to do. One of the stated goals of the 1949 Chinese communist revolution, for example, was to liberate women from the oppression of a strongly patriarchal society in which a woman owed lifelong obedience to some male relative—first her father, later her husband and, after his death, her oldest son. Although changes were (and continue to be) made, the transformation overall has been frustrated by the cultural lens through which the revolutionaries viewed their work. A tradition of deeply rooted patriarchy extending back at least 2,200 years is not easily overcome and has influenced many of the decisions made by communist China's leaders since the revolution.

In many parts of rural China today, as in the past, a woman's life is still largely determined by her relationship to a man, be it her father, husband, or son, rather than by her own efforts or failures. What's more, many rural women face official local policies that identify their primary roles as wives and mothers. When they do work outside the house, it is generally at jobs with low pay, low status, and no benefits. Indeed, the 1990s saw a major outbreak of the abduction and sale of women from rural areas as brides and workers. Women's no-wage home labor (and low-wage outside labor) for their husbands' households have been essential to China's economic expansion, which relies on the allocation of labor by the heads of patrilineal households.[10]

---

revolution Radical change in a society or culture. In the political arena, it involves the forced overthrow of an old government and establishment of a completely new one.

[7]van den Berghe, P. (1992). The modern state: Nation builder or nation killer? *International Journal of Group Tensions, 22*(3), 191–207.
[8]Nietschmann, B. (1987). The third world war. *Cultural Survival Quarterly, 11*(3), 3.
[9]Nietschmann, p. 7.
[10]Gates, H. (1996) Buying brides in China—again. *Anthropology Today, 12*(4), 10.

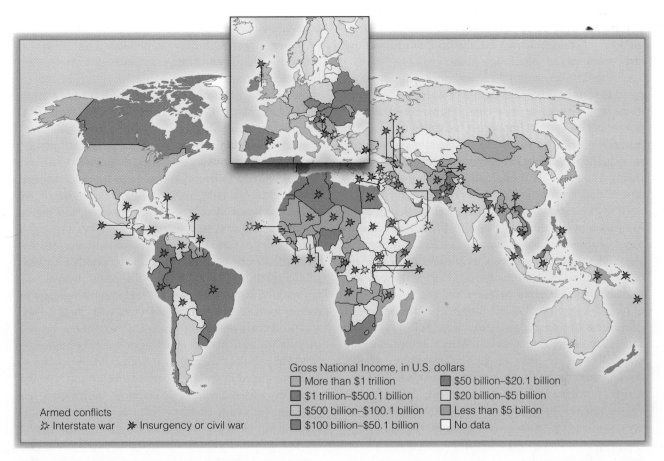

Figure 17.2
Armed conflict in the 1990s was concentrated among the world's poor countries, as is true today.

This situation shows that the undermining of revolutionary goals, if it occurs, is not necessarily by political opponents. Rather, it may be a consequence of the revolutionaries' own traditional cultural background. In rural China, as long as women marry out and their labor is controlled by male heads of families, women will be seen as something of a commodity.

It should be understood that revolution is a relatively recent phenomenon, occurring only during the past 5,000 years or so. The reason is that political rebellion requires a centralized political authority to rebel against, and states did not exist before 5,000 years ago. Obviously, then, in kin-ordered societies organized as tribes and bands, without a centralized government, there could be no rebellion or political revolution.

MODERNIZATION

One of the most frequently used terms to describe social and cultural changes as they are occurring today

> **modernization** The process of political and socioeconomic change, whereby developing societies acquire some of the cultural characteristics of Western industrial societies.

is **modernization.** This is most clearly defined as an all-encompassing and global process of political and socioeconomic change, whereby developing societies acquire some of the cultural characteristics common to Western industrial societies.

Derived from the Latin word *modo* ("just now"), modernization literally refers to something "in the present time." The dominant idea behind this concept is that "becoming modern" is becoming like North American and other industrial societies, with the very clear implication that not to do so is to be stuck in the past—backward, inferior, and needing to be improved. It is unfortunate that the term *modernization* continues to be so widely used. Since we seem to be stuck with it, the best we can do at the moment is to recognize its problematic one-sidedness, even as we continue to use it.

The process of modernization may be best understood as consisting of four subprocesses, of which one is *technological development*. In the course of modernization, traditional knowledge and techniques give way to the application of scientific knowledge and techniques borrowed mainly from the industrialized West.

Another subprocess is *agricultural development*, represented by a shift in emphasis from subsistence farming to commercial farming. Instead of raising crops and livestock for their own use, people turn with growing frequency to the production of cash crops, with increased reliance on a cash economy and on global markets for selling farm products and purchasing goods.

A third subprocess is *industrialization,* with a greater emphasis placed on material forms of energy—especially fossil fuels—to drive machines. Human and animal power becomes less important, as do handicrafts in general. The fourth subprocess is *urbanization,* marked particularly by population movements from rural settlements into cities. Although all four subprocesses are interrelated, there is no fixed order of appearance.

As modernization proceeds, other changes are likely to follow. In the political realm, political parties and some sort of electoral apparatus frequently appear, along with the development of an administrative bureaucracy. In formal education, institutional learning opportunities expand, literacy increases, and an indigenous educated elite develops. Religion becomes less important in many areas of thought and behavior as traditional beliefs and practices are undermined. Many traditional rights and duties connected with kinship are altered, if not eliminated, especially where distant relatives are concerned. Finally, where social stratification is a factor, social mobility increases as ascribed status becomes less important and personal achievement counts for more.

Modernization and Self-Determination

In the 1960s Saami reindeer herders in Scandinavia (such as the man featured in the chapter opening photo) eagerly adopted snowmobiles, expecting that the new technology would make herding physically easier and economically more advantageous. The choice to modernize was essentially theirs, but for many it backfired. As snowmobile technology replaced traditional skills,

the ability of the Saami (historically also known as Lapps) to creatively survive on their own diminished, and their dependency on the outside world grew. Given the high cost of buying, maintaining, and fueling the machines, they faced a sharp rise in their need for cash. To obtain money, men began going outside

their communities for wage labor more than just occasionally, as had previously been the case.

One might argue that dependency on the larger economy and the need for cash are prices worth paying for an improved system of reindeer herding. However, snowmobiles contributed in a significant way to a disastrous decline in reindeer herding in some Saami communities, such as the Skolt Lapps of northern Finland. Traditionally Skolt men tended the animals, moving about on wooden skis and associating closely with the herds—intensively from November to January and periodically from January to April. But once snowmobiles were introduced, the old familiar, prolonged, and largely peaceful relationship between herder and beast changed into a noisy, traumatic one. The humans reindeer encountered came speeding out of the woods on noisy, smelly machines that invariably chased the animals, often for long distances. Instead of helping the reindeer in their winter food quest, aiding does with their calves, and protecting the herd from predators, men appeared periodically, either to slaughter or castrate the animals.

The reindeer became wary of people, resulting in de-domestication, with reindeer scattering and running off to less accessible areas. In addition, snowmobile harassment seemed to adversely affect birthing and the survival of calves. Within a decade the average size of the family herd among the Skolts had dropped from fifty to twelve—a number that is not economically viable.

This is a classic illustration that change, even when initiated by a community on its own volition, is not always advantageous. The financial cost of mechanized herding and the decline in domesticated herd size have led many to abandon herding altogether. Now, the majority of men are no longer herders at all. This constitutes a serious economic problem, since few local subsistence alternatives are available.[11]

In contrast to the Saami, the Shuar Indians of Ecuador's tropical forest deliberately avoided modernization until they felt that they had no other option if they were to fend off the same outside forces that elsewhere in the Amazon Basin have destroyed whole societies. Traditionally organized in small autonomous groups, which engaged in constant feuding, the Shuar (historically

[11]Pelto, P. J. (1973). *The snowmobile revolution: Technology and social change in the Arctic.* Menlo Park, CA: Cummings.

better known as Jivaro) survived on a mixed subsistence strategy of foraging and gardening. In 1964, threatened with the loss of their land base as more and more Ecuadoran colonists intruded into their territory, leaders from the many, widely scattered Shuar communities came together and founded a fully independent ethnic organization—the Shuar Federation—to take control over their own future.

Recognized by Ecuador's government, albeit reluctantly, the federation is officially dedicated to promotion of the social, economic, and moral advancement of the growing Shuar population, and to coordinating development with official governmental agencies. Since its founding, the federation has secured title to more than 96,000 hectares of communal land; established a cattle herd of more than 15,000 head as the people's primary source of income; taken control of their own education, using their own language and mostly Shuar teachers; and established their own bilingual radio station and a bilingual newspaper.

Obviously, all of this has transformed daily life among the Shuar, but they have been able to maintain a variety of distinctive cultural markers, including their language, communal land tenure, cooperative production

and distribution, a basically egalitarian economy, and kin-based communities that retain maximum autonomy. Thus, for all the changes, they feel they are still Shuar and distinct from other Ecuadorans.[12]

The Shuar case shows that indigenous peoples are capable of taking control of their own destinies even in the face of intense outside pressures, *if* allowed to do so. Unfortunately, until recently, few have had that option. Prior to European invasions of the Amazon rainforest, more than 700 distinct ethnic groups inhabited this vast region. By 1900 in Brazil, the number was down to 270, and today something like 180 remain.[13] Many of these survivors find themselves in situations not unlike that of the Yanomami, described earlier in this chapter. Nevertheless, some are showing resourcefulness in resisting the outside forces of destruction arrayed against them. Some receive help from anthropologists, as discussed in this chapter's Anthropology Applied feature.

---

[12]Bodley, J. H. (1990). *Victims of progress* (3rd ed., pp. 160–162). Mountain View, CA: Mayfield.

[13]*Cultural Survival Quarterly* (1991), *14*(4), 38.

Anthropology Applied

Development Anthropology and Dams

Over a 35-year career in scholarly and applied work, Michael M. Horowitz, president and executive director of the Institute for Development Anthropology (IDA) and Distinguished Professor of Anthropology at the State University of New York at Binghamton, has made pioneering contributions to applied anthropology. His work has focused on

achieving equitable economic growth, environmental sustainability, conflict resolution, and participatory government in the former colonial world.

Since co-founding IDA in 1976, Horowitz has been its principal leader. He has played a key role in bringing anthropology forward as an applied science in international development

organizations such as the World Bank, the United Nations Fund for Women, and the US Agency for International Development (USAID), as well as nongovernmental organizations (NGOs) such as Oxfam and the International Union for the Conservation of Nature. He has mentored several generations of young scholars and professionals—paying

[continued]

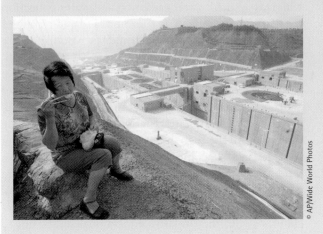

© AP/Wide World Photos

A local woman eats her breakfast overlooking the ship locks of China's Three Gorges hydroelectric dam on the Yangtze River. Under construction since 1992 and due for completion in 2009, the dam has been controversial since its inception, raising concerns among environmentalists around the world, not to mention among peasant farmers living downstream. If completed, the dam will result in the largest forced displacement of people in the world's history. Close to 2 million people must be relocated to make way for its 365-mile-long reservoir, and bitter complaints abound among those who have already been moved. Unlike the dam described in this Anthropology Applied box, not one social scientist was consulted in the planning and assessment phase of Three Gorges Dam.

[continued]

particular attention to those from developing countries—encouraging the application of anthropology's comparative and holistic methodologies and theories to empower low-income majorities in the so-called underdeveloped world.

Horowitz's work with pastoralists and floodplain dwellers has had substantial positive impact on the well-being of small producers and small landholders in developing countries. A clear example of this is the impact of his work on the lives and livelihoods of people living downstream of a hydropower dam in West Africa. Beginning in the 1980s, he and his IDA team carried out rigorous anthropological research along the Senegal River, which flows through Mali, Senegal, and Mauritania. Their study showed that traditional, pre-dam, flood-recession farming yielded better results than irrigated agriculture and was better for the environment.

This finding influenced decisions made by these countries and affiliated NGOs to manage the system with a controlled release from the Manatali Dam in Mali in order to reproduce as nearly as possible the pre-dam flow system. Horowitz's long-term field research demonstrated that seasonal flooding would provide economic, environmental, and sociocultural benefits for nearly a million small producers.

Recognized by national governments, NGOs, and development funding agencies, the work of Horowitz and his IDA colleagues on the Senegal River Basin Monitoring Activity (SRBMA) was a breakthrough in the concepts of resettlement and river management, and it continues to influence development policy. Prior to IDA's work in West Africa, no hydropower dam had ever been managed with a controlled flood. Since then, IDA has been asked to help apply the SRMBA model to other parts of the world, including the lower Zambezi River in Mozambique and the Mekong River in Laos, Cambodia, and Vietnam. *(Adapted from W. Young (Ed.). (2000). Kimball Award winner.* Anthropology News, *41(8), 29, with update based on personal communication with IDA, November 2003.)* ■ ■ ■

Globalization in the "Underdeveloped" World

Throughout the so-called underdeveloped world, in Africa, Asia, South and Central America, and elsewhere, whole countries are in the throes of radical political and economic change and overall cultural transformation. In fact, new inventions and major advances in industrial production, mass transportation, and communication and information technologies are transforming societies in Europe and North America as well. This worldwide process of accelerated modernization in which all parts of the earth are becoming interconnected in one vast interrelated and all-encompassing system is known as globalization—as earlier defined in Chapter 1.

All around the globe we are witnessing the removal of economic activities—or at least their control—from the family and community setting. And we are seeing the altered structure of the family in the face of the changing labor market: the increased reliance of young children on parents alone for affection, instead of on the extended family; the decline of general parental authority; schools replacing the family as the primary educational unit; old people spending their last days in nursing homes rather than with family members; and many other changes.

In traditional societies, these changes are now happening very fast, without the time to adjust gradually. Changes that took generations to accomplish in Europe and North America are attempted within the span of a single generation in developing countries. In the process they frequently face the erosion of a number of dearly held values they had no intention of giving up. Anthropologists doing fieldwork in distant communities throughout the world have witnessed how these traditional cultures have been affected, and often destroyed, by powerful global forces.

Commonly, the burden of modernization falls most heavily on women. For example, the commercialization of agriculture often involves land reforms that overlook or ignore women's traditional land rights. This reduces their control of and access to resources at the same time that mechanization of food production and processing drastically reduces their opportunities for employment. As a consequence, women are confined more and more to traditional domestic tasks, which, as commercial production becomes peoples' dominant concern, are increasingly downgraded in value.

Moreover, the domestic workload tends to increase, because men are less available to help out, while tasks such as fuel gathering and water collection are made more difficult as common land and resources come to be privately owned and as woodlands are reserved for commercial exploitation. To top it all off, the growing of nonfood crops such as cotton and sisal or luxury crops such as tea, coffee, and cacao (source of chocolate) for the world market makes households vulnerable to wide price fluctuations. As a result, people cannot afford the high-quality diet subsistence farming provided and become malnourished. In short, with modernization, women frequently find themselves in an increasingly inferior position. As their workload increases, the value assigned to the work they do declines, as does their relative educational status, not to mention their health and nutrition.

Globalization: Must It Be Painful?

Most anthropologists see the radical changes that affect traditional non-Western peoples caught up in the modern technological world as an ordeal. Yet, the more common attitude in the industrial West has been that modernization is both inevitable and good— that however disagreeable the "medicine" may be, it is worth it for the "backward" people to become just like people in the West. (For a serious look at the consequences of these changes, see the Biocultural Connection below.)

This Western view has little to do with the cold political and economic realities of the contemporary world. It overlooks the stark fact that the standard of middle- and upper-class living in the Western world is based on a rate of consumption of nonrenewable resources whereby a small fraction of the world's population uses the vast majority of these precious resources. The imbalance continues, suggesting that it is impossible for most peoples of the world to achieve a material standard of living at all comparable to that of many people in Western countries in the near future. At the very least, the peoples of the industrial and postindustrial West would have to cut drastically their unrelenting and often wasteful consumption of resources. So far, few have shown a willingness to seriously adjust their standard of living in order to do this.

Countless people around the world today have been led to aspire to a material standard of living like

Biocultural Connection
Studying the Emergence of New Diseases

Ever since the Neolithic, humans have had to cope with a host of new diseases that began as a consequence of changes in human behavior. Recently, this has become a renewed source of concern following the resurgence of infectious diseases and spread of a host of new and lethal diseases.[a]

All told, more than thirty diseases new to medicine have emerged in the past 25 years, of which perhaps the best known is AIDS, which has become the fourth most common killer among infectious diseases, with 5.8 million people infected in 1998 alone.[b] But there are others—like Ebola hemorrhagic fever, which causes victims to bleed to death; hemorrhagic fevers like dengue fever, Lassa fever, and hantavirus; invasive Streptococcus A, which consumes the victims' flesh; Legionnaire's disease; and Lyme disease.

What has sparked the appearance and spread of these new diseases remains a mystery, but one theory is that some are the result of human activities. In particular, the intrusion of people into new ecological settings, such as rainforests, along with construction of roads allows viruses and other infectious microbes to spread rapidly to large numbers of people. It is now generally accepted that the HIV virus responsible for AIDS transferred to humans from chimpanzees in the forests of the Democratic Republic of Congo as a consequence of hunting and butchering these animals for food. For the first 30 years, few people were affected; it was not until people began congregating in cities like Kinshasa that conditions were ripe for an epidemic.

To gain a better understanding of the interplay between ecological disturbance and the emergence of new diseases, U.S. medical anthropologist Carol Jenkins obtained a grant from the MacArthur Foundation in 1993. From her base at the Papua New Guinea Institute of Medical Research, she is tracking the health of local people in the wake of a massive logging operation. From her work should come a better understanding of how disease organisms spread from animal hosts to humans.

Since most of the "new" viruses that have suddenly afflicted humans are in fact old ones that have been present in animals like monkeys (monkey pox), rodents (hantavirus), deer (Lyme disease), and insects (West Nile virus), it appears that something new has enabled them to jump from their animal hosts to humans.

A recent example comes from the Democratic Republic of Congo. Here civil war created a situation where villagers in the central part of the country were faced with starvation. Their response was to increase the hunting of animals, including monkeys, squirrels, and rats that carry a disease called monkey pox. Related to smallpox, the disease transfers easily to humans, resulting in the largest outbreak of this disease ever seen among humans. What makes this outbreak even more serious is an apparently new strain of the infection, enabling it to spread from person to person, instead of only from an animal host.[c]

Large-scale habitat disturbance is an obvious candidate for such disease transfers, but this needs to be confirmed and the process understood. So far, it is hard to make more than a circumstantial case, by looking back after a disease outbreak. The work of Jenkins and her team is unique in that she was able to get baseline health data on local people before their environment was disturbed. Thus, she is in a position to follow events as they unfold.

It will be some time before conclusions can be drawn from Jenkins's study. Its importance is obvious; in an era of globalization, as air travel allows tropical diseases to spread worldwide, we need a fuller understanding of how viruses interact with their hosts if we are to devise effective preventive and therapeutic strategies to deal with them. ■ ■ ■

[a]Gibbons, A. (1993). Where are new diseases born? *Science, 261,* 680–681.
[b]Balter, M. (1998). On world AIDS day, a shadow looms over southern Africa. *Science, 282,* 1,790.
[c]Cohen, J. (1997). Is an old virus up to new tricks? *Science, 277,* 312–313.

that enjoyed by the middle class and well-to-do in many industrialized and postindustrialized countries, even as the gap between the rich and the poor continues to widen. Every year, many millions of people slide below the poverty level.[14] This has led to the development of what U.S. anthropologist Paul Magnarella called a new "culture of discontent" in which aspirations far exceed the bounds of local opportunities.

---

[14]Kurth, P. (1998, October 14). Capitol crimes. *Seven Days*, 7.

No longer satisfied with traditional values and often unable to sustain themselves in the rural backlands, people all over the world are moving to the large cities to find a better life. All too often they live out their days in poor, congested, and disease-ridden slums while attempting to achieve what is usually beyond their reach. Unfortunately, despite rosy predictions about a better future, hundreds of millions of people in our world remain trapped in a wretched reality, struggling against poverty, hunger, poor health and other dangers.

Chapter Summary

■ Although cultures may be remarkably stable, culture change is characteristic of all cultures to a greater or lesser degree. Change is often caused by accidents, including the unexpected outcome of particular actions or events. Another cause is people's deliberate attempt to solve some perceived problem. Finally, change may be forced upon one group in the course of especially intense contact between two societies. Adaptation and progress are consequences rather than causes of change, although not all changes are necessarily adaptive. *Progress* is a relative term, meaning different things to different cultural groups.

■ The mechanisms involved in culture change are innovation, diffusion, cultural loss, and acculturation. The ultimate source of culture change is innovation: any new idea, method, or device that gains widespread acceptance in society. A primary innovation is the creation, invention, or discovery of a new idea, method, or device—such as the discovery that firing clay makes it permanently hard. A secondary innovation is a new application or modification of an existing idea, method, or device—for example, modeling clay into familiar forms to be fired by known techniques. Primary innovations may prompt rapid culture change and stimulate other inventions. An innovation's chance of being accepted depends partly, but not entirely, on its perceived superiority to the method or object it replaces. Its acceptance may also be connected with the prestige of the innovator.

■ Diffusion is the borrowing of a cultural element from one society by another. Cultural loss involves the abandonment of some trait or practice with or without replacement. Anthropologists have given considerable attention to acculturation: massive culture changes that people are forced to make as a consequence of intensive, firsthand contact between their own group and a more powerful society.

■ Applied anthropology—the application of anthropological insights and methods to solving practical problems—arose as anthropologists sought to provide colonial administrators with a better understanding of native cultures, often to control

them better, sometimes to avoid serious disruption of them. An alternative type of practical anthropology has emerged during the last half century. Known under a variety of different names, including action anthropology, it involves community-based research and action in collaboration and solidarity with indigenous societies, ethnic minorities, and other besieged or repressed groups.

■ Reactions of indigenous peoples to imposed changes vary considerably. Some have retreated to inaccessible places in hopes of being left alone, while some others have lapsed into apathy. Some, like the Trobriand Islanders, have reasserted their traditional culture's values by modifying foreign practices to conform to indigenous values, a phenomenon known as syncretism.

■ If a culture's values get widely out of step with reality, the situation may give rise to revitalization movements—collective efforts for radical cultural reform in response to widespread social disruption and collective feelings of anxiety and despair. Some revitalization movements try to speed up the acculturation process to get more of the benefits expected from the dominant culture. Others try to reconstitute a bygone but still remembered way of life. In other cases, a repressed group may try to introduce a new social order based on its ideology.

■ When the scale of discontent within a society reaches a certain level, the possibilities are high for rebellion—organized armed resistance to an established government or authority in power. And if the level of dissatisfaction rises even higher, it may lead to revolution—a radical change in a society or culture. In the political arena, revolution refers to the forced overthrow of an old government and the establishment of a new one.

■ Modernization refers to an all-encompassing and global process of political and socioeconomic change, whereby developing societies acquire some of the cultural characteristics common to Western industrial societies. The process consists of four subprocesses: technological development, agricultural development, industrialization, and urbanization.

Other changes follow in the areas of political organization, education, religion, and social organization.

■ Traditional peoples do not always react in the same way to modernization, and the results are mixed. The Skolt Lapps, a group of Saami reindeer herders in Finland, welcomed snowmobile technology in hopes of easing their labor and increasing economic advantages. Instead, they lost the security afforded by their traditional way of life. In Ecuador, the Shuar Indians modernized to escape the destruction visited upon many other Amazonian peoples. So far they have been successful, and others are mobilizing their resources in attempts to achieve similar success. Nevertheless, formidable forces are still arrayed against such cultures, and on a worldwide basis, it is a painful fact that modernization has often led to deterioration rather than improvement of peoples' quality of life.

Questions for Reflection

1. A people's ability to change their culture has always been a key requirement for long-term human survival. However, globalization radically challenges us to adjust at an ever-faster pace. Considering your own situation, can you identify any powerful outside force such as a government agency or large corporation that has caused changes for your own family, community, or neighborhood? Do you feel that these changes are good for everyone?

2. What are some of the driving forces of culture change in the world today? Which groups are benefiting the most from free markets all across the globe?

3. On a regular basis, the news media are reporting about violent uprisings or rebellion and armed conflicts that result in death and destruction. Why do you think many people feel the need to fight?

4. When societies become involved in the modernizing process, all levels of their cultural systems are affected by these changes. Do you think that people are always aware of the long-term consequences of the changes they themselves may have welcomed? Can you come up with any examples of unforeseen changes in your own community or neighborhood?

Key Terms

primary innovation	genocide
secondary innovation	tradition
diffusion	syncretism
cultural loss	rebellion
acculturation	revolution
ethnocide	modernization

Multimedia Review Tools

Make the Grade in Anthropology with ThomsonNOW

Thomson NOW! This powerful online study tool provides you with a *personalized study plan* based on your responses to a diagnostic pretest. Once you have mastered the material with the help of interactive learning tools, an integrated e-book, and more, you can take a post-test to confirm you are ready to move on to the next chapter. To get started with ThomsonNOW, check the card packaged with your book for the access code. Then go to http://www.thomsonedu.com to create an account through 1pass™. If there is no card in your book, go to http://www.thomsonedu.com to purchase an access code.

Companion Website and Anthropology Resource Center

Go to http://anthropology.wadsworth.com to reach the companion website for your text. This offers many study aids, including self quizzes for each chapter and a practice final exam, as well as links to anthropology websites and information on the latest theories and discoveries in the field.

Also, check out the Anthropology Resource Center for a wealth of learning materials that include interactive maps, video exercises, simulations, and breaking news in anthropology. Be sure to explore InfoTrac College Edition®, your online library that offers full-length articles from thousands of scholarly and popular publications. To reach the Anthropology Resource Center and InfoTrac College Edition, check the card packaged with your book for the access code. Then go to http://www.thomsonedu.com to create an account through 1pass™. If there is no card in your book, go to http://www.thomsonedu.com to purchase an access code.

© Luis Marden/INGS Image Collectic

CHALLENGE ISSUE

Throughout today's world, countries and communities face the challenge of dealing with a flood of economic and political refugees fleeing for survival. One major driving force is poverty and the ever-widening economic gap between destitute and otherwise troubled countries and wealthy states primarily in western Europe and North America. Another force is fear—the desperate need to escape the political turmoil and violent repression in states where a dominant ethnic or religious group is trampling the human rights of minorities who are trying to retain their own natural resources, national identities, and cultural traditions.

18

Global Challenges, Local Responses, and the Role of Anthropology

Anthropology is superficially described by those who know little about it as an exotic discipline interested mainly in what happened long ago and far away. The most common stereotype is that anthropologists devote all of their attention to digging up the past and describing the last surviving tribal peoples with traditional ways of life. Yet, as noted earlier in this book, neither archaeologists nor paleoanthropologists (the anthropologists most devoted to looking into the past) limit their interests to ancient times, nor do ethnographers (who focus on contemporary cultures) overlook the ways and workings of industrial and postindustrial societies. Indeed, anthropologists are interested in the entire range of human cultures past and present—in their similarities and differences and in the multiple ways they influence one another.

Moreover, many anthropologists have a special concern with the future and the changes it may bring. They wonder what today's globalizing processes will create and what will be transformed, disrupted, or damaged beyond repair. As we saw in the preceding chapter, when traditional peoples are exposed to intense contact with technologically empowered Western peoples, their cultures typically change with unprecedented speed, often for the worse, becoming both less supportive and less adaptive. Since globalization seems unstoppable, we are compelled to ask: How can the thousands of different cultures, developed in the course of centuries if not millennia, deal successfully with the multiple challenges hurled at them?

THE CULTURAL FUTURE OF HUMANITY

To comprehend anthropology's role in understanding and solving problems in times to come, we must look at flaws frequently seen in publications and planning efforts focused on the future. First of all, rarely do futurist writers or planners look more than about 50 years ahead, and more often than not the trends they project are those of recent history. This predisposes people to think that a trend that seems acceptable today will always be so. The danger of this assumption is neatly captured in anthropologist George Cowgill's comment: "It is worth recalling the story of the person who leaped from a very tall building and on being asked how things were going as he passed the 20th floor replied 'Fine, so far.'"[1]

A second flaw typical in futurist projections is a tendency to treat subjects in isolation, without reference to pertinent trends outside an expert's field of competence. For example, agricultural planning is often based on the assumption that a certain amount of water is available for irrigation, whether or not urban planners or others have designs upon that same water. Thus, people may be counting on natural resources in the future that will not, in fact, be available.

This brings us to a third flaw common among futurists: The tendency to project the hopes and expectations of one's own social group or culture into the future interferes with the scientific objectivity necessary to see and address emerging problems. A recent example is the war in Iraq, where the hopes and expectations of the planners blinded them to the problems that would emerge.

Against this background, anthropology's contribution to our understanding of the future is clear. With their holistic and integrative perspective, anthropologists are specialists at seeing how parts fit together into a larger whole. With their comparative and long-term historical perspective, they can place short-term trends in deeper and wider perspective. With more than 100 years of cross-cultural research behind them—based on ancient archaeological finds, linguistic information, biological data, as well as participant observation within living cultures—anthropologists can recognize culture-bound assertions when they encounter them. Last but not least, they are familiar with alternative ways of dealing with a wide variety of problems.

Global Culture

Human populations have always been on the move. But today, more people travel faster and farther than ever before due to modern means of transportation (Figure 18.1). Moreover, revolutions in communication technology—from print media to telegraph and telephone to radio, television, satellites, and the Internet—make it possible to exchange more information with more people faster and over greater distances. Obviously, this global flow of humans, their products, and their ideas plays a major role in culture change.

A popular belief since the mid-1900s has been that the future world will see the development of a single homogeneous world culture. This idea is based largely on the observation that technological developments in communication, transportation, and trade are causing peoples of the world to increasingly watch the same television programs, read the same newspapers, eat the same foods, wear the same types of clothes, and communicate via satellites and the Internet. Also of note, at least 175 million people (2.5 percent of the world's population) now live outside their countries of birth—not as refugees but as migrants who earn their living in one country while being citizens in another. The continuation of such trends, so this thinking goes, would mean that North Americans who travel in the year 2100 to Afghanistan, Botswana, Colombia, or Denmark would find the local inhabitants living in a manner identical or similar to theirs. Yet, looking at ethnic conflicts around the world, we must ask if this prediction is likely to be accurate.

Is the World Coming Together or Coming Apart?

Certainly it is striking, the extent to which such items as Western-style clothing, bicycles, cars, cameras, computers, and soft drinks have spread to virtually all parts of the world. And many countries—Japan, for example—appear to have gone a long way toward becoming Westernized. Moreover, looking back over the past 5,000 years of human history, we see that political units have tended to become larger, more all-encompassing and fewer in number. The logical outcome of this trend would be a further reduction of autonomous political units into a single one taking in the entire globe.

Informed by comparative historical and cross-cultural research, anthropologists call attention to something that all large states throughout time have had in common: a tendency to come apart. Not only have the great empires of the past, without exception, broken up into numbers of smaller independent states, but states in virtually all parts of the world today show this same tendency to fragment, usually along major geographic and ethnic divisions.

---

[1]Cowgill, G. L. (1980). Letter, *Science, 210,* 1,305.

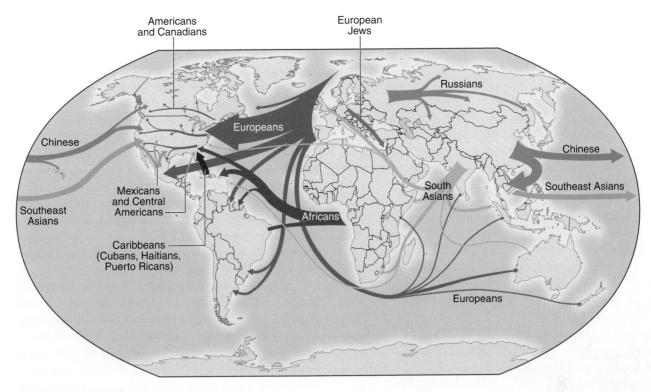

***Figure 18.1* World Migrations**
Migration has had and continues to have a significant effect on world social geography, contributing to culture change and development, to the diffusion of ideas and innovations, and to the complex mixture of people and cultures found in the world today. Internal migration occurs within the boundaries of a country; external migration is movement from one country or region to another. Over the last 50 years, the most important migrations in the world have been internal, largely the rural-to-urban migration that has been responsible for the recent rise of global urbanization. Prior to the mid-20th century, three types of external migration were most important: voluntary, most often in search of better conditions and opportunities; involuntary or forced, involving people who have been driven from their homelands by war, political unrest, or environmental disasters, or transported as slaves or prisoners; and imposed, not entirely forced but made advisable by the circumstances.
Source: From *Student Atlas of Anthropology* by John Allen and Audrey Shalinksy, p. 73. Copyright © 2003 by the McGraw-Hill Companies, Inc. All rights reserved. Reprinted by permission of McGraw-Hill/Dushkin Publishing.

The threat of political collapse is ever-present in multi-ethnic states, especially when these countries are large, difficult to travel in, and lack major unifying cultural forces such as a common national language. Such has been the case, for instance, with Afghanistan. This vast, mountainous country is inhabited by several major ethnic groups, including the Pashtun who live mainly in the south, and Tajik, Uzbek, Hazara, and Turkmen who live mainly in the north. Although the Pashtun are greatest in number and most dominant in the past 200 years, they were never able to successfully impose their political will on the other ethnic groups who maintain a great deal of independence, nor did they succeed in making their own native tongue, Pashto, the country's national language.

The tendency of multi-ethnic states to break apart has been especially noteworthy since the end of the Cold War between the United States and the former Soviet Union around 1990. For example, 1991 saw the

dramatic breakup of the Soviet Union into about a dozen independent republics—Russia, Armenia, Kazakhstan, and Ukraine, among others. In 1992 Czechoslovakia split into the Czech and the Slovak republics. That same year the Republic of Yugoslavia began splintering into what are now five independent states in the Balkan Mountains.

The splintering tendency of multi-ethnic states can also be seen in separatist movements such as that of French-speaking peoples in Canada; Basques in Spain; Tibetans in China; the Karen in Burma (Myanmar); Tamils in Sri Lanka; Kurds in Turkey, Iran, and Iraq, and so on—this list is far from exhaustive. Nor is the United States immune, as can be seen in Native American attempts to secure greater political self-determination on their reservations.

All of these examples involve peoples who see themselves as members of distinct nations by virtue of their birth and their cultural and territorial heritage—nations over whom peoples of some other ethnic background have tried to assert political control. An estimated 5,000 such national groups exist in the world today, as opposed to a mere 191 states formally admitted as members of the United Nations (up from fewer than fifty in the 1940s).[2] Although some of these ethnic groups are small in population and area—100 or so people living on a few acres—many others are quite large. The Karen people inhabiting southern Burma (Myanmar), for example, number some 4.5 to 5 million, exceeding the population of nearly half of the countries in the world.

The reactions of such groups to forced annexation and domination by state regimes controlled by people of other nations range all the way from the nonviolence of Scottish and Welsh nationalism to bloody fights for national independence by the Irish, Algerians, Vietnamese, or Tamil Tigers. Many struggles for independence have been going on for years. Today, about 35 million people in almost half of the world's countries are either internally displaced or have crossed international borders as refugees. Some 12 million of these unfortunates have been forced outside their countries, most of them suffering in makeshift camps where they cannot make a living.

In some cases, a large proportion of an ethnic group's entire population finds itself forced to abandon their homes and flee for their lives. For instance, although long ignored by the Western media, some 4 million Dinka, Nuer, and dozens of other African peoples in central and southern Sudan are currently either internally displaced or refugees.

It is possible that we are reaching a point where the tendency for political units to increase in size while decreasing in number is being canceled out by the tendency for such units to fragment into a greater number of smaller ones. Despite these examples, there are also a few instances of reunification. Best known among these is the 1990 reunification of Germany, divided since the end of World War II as East and West Germany, into one large federal republic. Another notable exception is the recent integration of European countries into the European Union—however hindered by mutual distrust.

Global Culture: A Good Idea or Not?

The idea of a shared global culture may have a degree of popular appeal, in that it might diminish chances for the kinds of misunderstandings and conflicting viewpoints that so often in the past few hundred years have led to violent clashes and even full-scale wars. Anthropologists greet this prognosis with skepticism, though, suspecting that distinctive worldviews will persist as they have for

hundreds of years, even in the face of massive changes. Indeed, one might argue that the chance for conflicting viewpoints actually increases, given the intensified interactions among people in the world today.

Some have argued that perhaps a generalized world culture would be desirable in the future, because some traditional cultures may be too specialized to adjust to a changed environment. For instance, when Amazonian Indians pursuing traditional ways of life that are well adapted to South America's tropical rainforest are confronted with sudden, radical changes brought on by foreign invaders, their long-established cultures often collapse. The reason for this, it is argued, is that the forest dwellers' traditions and political and social organizations are not adapted to modern ways and that they are naturally destined to give way to the new.

A problem with this argument is that, far from being unable to adapt, such traditional peoples have been robbed repeatedly of the opportunity to work out their own adaptations based on their own agendas. Their demise is caused not by laws of nature but rather by the political and economic choices of the powerful, fueled by arrogance, intolerance, and greed, along with a willingness to invade and exploit lands already owned and long inhabited by indigenous people. A key point to be made here is that in the globalization process economically and technologically empowered people have defined others—indeed, whole societies—as inferior, subservient, irrelevant, and not entitled to human rights, including self-determination.

Ethnic Resurgence

Despite the worldwide adoption of such products as blue jeans, sunglasses, Coca-Cola, and the Big Mac, and despite ever-growing pressures on traditional cultures to disappear, it is clear that cultural differences are still with us in the world today. In fact, resistance to many aspects of globalization is growing in many parts of the world. We see evidence of this in examples already noted, as well as in repeated public protests around the globe against policies of the Geneva-based World Trade Organization. In addition, Greenpeace and a host of less radical environmental groups can be found demonstrating worldwide against such practices as French nuclear testing in the Pacific or Japanese commercial whaling. Other examples include symbolic attacks by small farmers in France against corporate control, genetically modified crops, industrial agriculture, and McDonald's fast-food outlets. Resistance to globalization is also evident in political movements in Bolivia and Venezuela, as well as Muslim fundamentalist movements in Algeria and Egypt. The remarkable recent revival of shamanism in former communist Mongolia is yet another example,

---

[2]*Cultural Survival Quarterly* (1991), *15*(4), 38.

as is the increasing political activism of many other indigenous peoples from every corner of the world.

North Americans and Europeans often have difficulty adjusting to the fact that not everyone wants to be just like they are. In the United States, for example, children are taught to believe that the "American way of life" is one to which all other peoples aspire. Although it is true that many peoples from poor countries across the world seek to improve their living conditions and enjoy the fruits of freedom, such aspirations should not be confused with wanting to become "American." Moreover, in the globalizing world dominated by the United States, Japan, and a handful of European capitalist states today, whole countries that once valued Western ways are now drawing the line or even turning against many Western ideas, trends, and practices.

One striking case of such a cultural reaction was that of a group of Muslim religious fundamentalists in Afghanistan known as the Taliban (the Pashto word for "students," specifically of Islam). After helping to force the Russian army out of their country and ending the subsequent civil war, they rose to power in the 1990s and imposed a radical version of traditional Islamic law

© Zahid Hussein/Reuters

Sometimes resistance to modernization takes the form of cultural traditionalism and religious fundamentalism, as in Afghanistan during recent decades. This reactionary practice is evident in this family's clothing, the mother's veil, and the father's beard.

(Shariah) in an effort to create an Islamic republic based on strict religious values. A somewhat similar, though less radical, reaction against modernity is taking place in the United States, which, in recent years has elected "born-again" and other fundamentalist politicians dedicated to creating a national culture based on what they see as traditional Christian values.[3]

Cultural Pluralism

If a single homogenous global culture is not necessarily the wave of the future, what is? Some predict a world in which ethnic groups will become more nationalistic in response to globalization, each group stressing its unique cultural heritage and emphasizing differences with neighboring groups. But not all ethnic groups organize themselves politically as distinctive nations with their own state. In fact, it has been common for two or more neighboring ethnic groups or nations to draw together in a loose political union while maintaining their particular cultural identities. However, because such pluralistic societies lack a common cultural identity and heritage, and often do not share the same language or religion, political relationships between them can be fraught with tension. When feelings of ethnonationalism are not far from the surface, political pressure may build up and result in separation and independence.

One way of curbing divisive pressures in pluralistic or multi-ethnic societies is the adoption of a collective policy based on mutual respect and tolerance for cultural differences. Known as **multiculturalism,** such an official policy or doctrine asserts the value of different cultures co-existing within a country and stresses the reciprocal responsibility of all citizens to accept the rights of others to freely express their views and values. In contrast to state policies in which a dominant ethnic group uses its power to impose its own culture as the national standard on other groups within the same state, forcing them to assimilate, multiculturalism involves a public policy for managing a society's cultural diversity. Examples of long-established multiculturalism may be seen in states such as Switzerland (where German-, French-, Italian-, and Romansh-speaking peoples co-exist under the same government) and Canada

multiculturalism Public policy for managing cultural diversity in a multi-ethnic society, officially stressing mutual respect and tolerance for cultural differences within a country's borders.

[3]Marsella, J. (1982). Pulling it together: Discussion and comments. In S. Pastner & W. A. Haviland (Eds.), *Confronting the creationists* (pp. 79–80). *Northeastern Anthropological Association, Occasional Proceedings,* 1.

(where French- and English-speaking Canadians, as well as dozens of indigenous nations live side by side).

Although cultural pluralism is still more common than multiculturalism, several multi-ethnic countries have recently changed their official melting pot ideology and associated policies of assimilation. One example of a country that is moving toward multiculturalism is the United States, which now has over 120 different ethnic groups within its borders (in addition to hundreds of federally recognized American Indian groups). Another is Australia, now counting over 100 ethnic groups and with eighty languages spoken within its territorial boundaries. Similar changes are also under way in many European countries where millions of foreign immigrants have settled during the past few decades. Such changes are not easy, and often engender protests along the way. In many pluralistic societies, however, governments lack the ideological commitment or political capacity to successfully structure a national cultural system.

We cannot ignore the fact that, historically, what has been called "nation building" in all parts of the world almost always involves attempts to destroy the cultures of peoples whose nationalities differ from those controlling the governments in those countries.[4] During the last two decades of the 20th century, states were borrowing more money to fight peoples within their own boundaries than for all other programs combined. Nearly all state debt in Africa and nearly half of all other debt in "underdeveloped" countries comes from the cost of weapons purchased by states to fight their own citizens.[5] The more divergent cultural traditions are, the more difficult it is to make pluralism work.

That said, states as political constructs are products of human imagination, and nothing prevents us from imagining in ways that are more tolerant of cultural pluralism or multiculturalism. For example, consider once again Switzerland, where multiculturalism has worked out to the satisfaction of all four ethnic groups. In this confederation of small states (cantons), a political tradition of direct democracy is combined with a political organization that does not interfere with the country's regional, linguistic, and religious differences.

Obviously, replicating such a success in other political arenas will take a good deal of work, but at least the international community recognizes the concept of *group* rights. Even though it often fails to act on it, the United Nations General Assembly in its 1966 Covenant of Human Rights states unequivocally

> In those states in which ethnic, religious or linguistic minorities exist, persons belonging

to such minorities shall not be denied the rights, in community with the other members of their group, to enjoy their own culture, to profess and practice their own religion or to use their own language.[6]

Education has a key role to play in making this acknowledged right a reality. This includes the sort of advocacy work that many anthropologists do on behalf of indigenous peoples.

During the 1970s the world's indigenous peoples began to organize self-determination power movements, culminating in the formation of the World

Rigoberta Menchú, a Maya woman who won the Nobel Peace Prize in 1992 for her activism on behalf of indigenous rights. Receiving this honor in 1992 had particular political significance, because it was the year of the Columbian quincentennial in which people in Europe and the Americas commemorated Columbus' pioneering journey across the Atlantic ocean—a journey that had devastating consequences for American Indians. The prize focused international attention on the ongoing repression of indigenous peoples in Guatemala and helped pave the way to peace accords in late December 1996.

---

[4]van den Berghe, P. (1992). The modern state: Nation builder or nation killer? *International Journal of Group Tensions, 22*(3), 194–198.
[5]*Cultural Survival Quarterly* (1991). *15*(4), 38.

[6]Quoted in Bodley, J. H. (1990). *Victims of progress* (3rd ed., p. 99). Mountain View, CA: Mayfield.

Council of Indigenous Peoples in 1975. This group now has official status as a nongovernmental organization of the United Nations, which allows it to present the cases of indigenous peoples before the world community. Leaders of this movement see their own societies as community based, egalitarian, and close to nature, and they are intent upon keeping them that way.

In 1993, representatives of some 124 indigenous groups and organizations agreed to a draft Declaration of the Rights of Indigenous Peoples that had taken a decade to produce. Presented to the UN General Assembly, it contains some 150 articles urging respect for indigenous cultural heritages, calling for recognition of indigenous land titles and rights of self-determination, and demanding an end to all forms of oppression and discrimination as a principle of international law. So far, this draft document is largely symbolic. It remains under consideration by the UN, which to date has agreed upon only a handful of its articles. Whether it will be adopted remains to be seen.

Ethnocentrism and Cultural Pluralism

The major problem associated with cultural pluralism has to do with ethnocentrism—the belief that the ways of one's own culture are the only proper ones. To function effectively, we may expect a society to embrace at least a degree of ethnocentrism. Such national self-satisfaction provides individuals with ethnic pride and a loyalty to their cultural traditions, from which they derive psychological support and a firm social bond to their group. In societies where one's self-identification derives from the group, the idea that one's own customary ideas and practices are ideal is essential to a sense of personal worth.

As illustrated again and again in this book, the problem with ethnocentrism is that it is all too easy to take it as a charter for condemning other cultures as inferior and to denigrate and exploit them for the benefit of one's own. Although this does not have to be the result, when it is, unrest, hostility, and violence commonly result.

In the world today, powerful governments frequently operate on the basis of the political idea that no group has the right to stand in the way of "the greater good for the greater number." This concept is commonly used to justify the expropriation of natural resources in regions traditionally occupied by subsistence farmers, pastoral nomads, or food foragers—without any respect for the rights, concerns, or wishes of these peoples. But is it truly the greater good for the greater number? A look at the rise of global corporations helps to answer this question.

The Rise of Global Corporations

The resistance of the world to political integration might seem to be offset to some extent by the rise and ongoing growth of global corporations. Because these cut across the international boundaries between states, they are a force for worldwide integration despite the political, linguistic, religious, and other cultural differences that separate people.

Global corporations, rare before the latter half of the 20th century, now are a far-reaching economic and political force in the world. Modern-day business giants such as General Electric, Shell, and Toyota are actually clusters of several corporations joined by ties of common ownership and responsive to a common management strategy. Usually tightly controlled by a head office in one country, these enterprises organize and integrate production across the international boundaries of different countries for interests formulated in corporate boardrooms, irrespective of whether these are consistent with the interests of people in the countries where they operate. These megacorporations are the products of the technological revolution, for without sophisticated data-processing equipment and electronic communication, they could not keep adequate track of their worldwide operations.

Though typically thought of as responding impersonally to outside market forces, large corporations are in fact controlled by an increasingly smaller number of wealthy capitalists who benefit directly from their operations. Yet, unlike political leaders, the world's largest individual stockholders and most powerful directors are known to few people. For that matter, most people cannot even name the world's major global corporations, which include Wal-Mart, Shell, ExxonMobil, British Petroleum, General Motors, DaimlerChrysler, Toyota, General Electric, and Citigroup (Figure 18.2). Each of these business giants currently generates annual revenues above $120 billion, and one of them—Wal-Mart—is near the $250 billion mark.[7]

So great is the power of large businesses operating all across the globe that they increasingly thwart the wishes of national governments or international organizations such as the United Nations, Red Cross, International Court of Justice, or the World Council of Churches. Because the information these corporations process is kept from flowing in a meaningful way to the population at large, or even to lower levels within the organization, it becomes difficult for governments to get the information they need for informed policy decisions. It took years for the U.S. Congress to extract the information it needed from tobacco companies to decide what to do about tobacco legislation—and it is nearly as slow-going today getting energy and media companies to provide data needed for regulatory purposes.

Beyond this, the global corporations have repeatedly shown they can overrule foreign policy decisions.

---

[7]Forbes International 500 List.

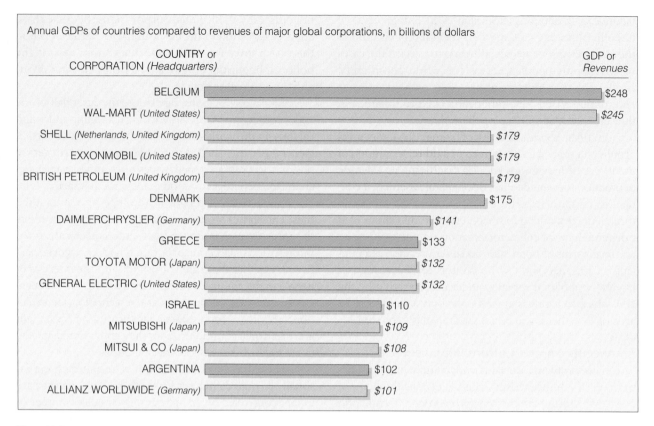

Figure 18.2
In today's consumer-driven world, it is not uncommon for the yearly revenues of large multinational corporations to equal and even exceed the total value of all goods and services produced within a country per year, known as a country's gross domestic product (GDP). This graph shows the annual GDPs of selected countries alongside the annual revenues of leading global corporations (Note: GDP says nothing about the unequal distribution of wealth within a country.)
Source: Based on 2002 figures posted on www.forbes.com and www.worldbank.org.

While some might see this as a hopeful signal for getting beyond national vices and rivalries, it raises the unsettling issue of whether or not the global arena should be controlled by immensely large and powerful private corporations interested only in financial profits. According to one market research organization,

> Today, the top 100 companies control 33 percent of the world's assets, but employ only one percent of the world's workforce. General Motors is larger than Denmark, Wal-Mart bigger than South Africa. The mega-corporations roam freely around the globe, lobbying legislators, bankrolling elections and playing governments off against each other to get the best deals. Their private hands control the bulk of the world's news and information flows.[8]

If the ability of global corporations to ignore the wishes of sovereign governments is cause for concern, so is their ability to act in concert with such governments. Here, in fact, is where their worst excesses have occurred. One example took place in Brazil, where the situation is hardly unique but is especially well documented. After a 1964 military coup in that country, a partnership emerged between the new government, which was anxious to proceed as rapidly as possible with development of the Amazon rainforest, and a number of global corporations and international lending institutions. (The corporations included ALCOA, Borden, Union Carbide, Swift-Armour, and Volkswagen, among others, and the lending institutions included the Export-Import Bank, the Inter-American Development Bank, and the World Bank.[9])

To help bring about what they liked to call the Brazilian miracle, these allies initiated new road construction projects and introduced inappropriate

---

[8]www.adbusters.org. Accessed January 10, 2003. See also Hertz, N. (2001). *The silent takeover: Global capitalism and the death of democracy* (p. 43). New York: Arrow Books.

[9]Davis, S. H. (1982). *Victims of the miracle.* Cambridge, England: Cambridge University Press.

technology and ecologically unsound practices into the region, converting vast woodlands into semi-desert. Far more shocking, however, has been the practice of uprooting whole human societies because they were seen as obstacles to economic growth.

Eager to alleviate acute land shortages in the country's impoverished northeastern region, but unwilling to break up the huge rural estates owned by a powerful elite and embark on much-needed land reform, government officials launched massive resettlement schemes. They lured millions of Brazilian peasants to the Amazon to clear the forest and settle as farmers in territories traditionally owned and long inhabited by many different indigenous nations. Soon, however, it became obvious that few of these newcomers could adequately support their families, so tens of thousands turned to gold mining. This, in turn, resulted in poisoning the rivers with mercury, creating serious health problems.

Bad as this was for these poor peasants, the disease, death, and human suffering that such schemes and policies unleashed upon the native Indians can only be described as massive. Entire indigenous groups have been (and are still being) destroyed with a thoroughness not achieved even by the communist dictator Stalin during his "Great Terror" in the Soviet Union of the 1930s or the Nazis in World War II. Were it not so well documented, it would be beyond belief.

In their never-ending search for cheap labor, multinational corporations have returned to a practice once seen in the textile mills of 19th-century Britain and New England, but now on a much larger scale. More than ever before, they have come to favor women for low-skilled assembly jobs. In so-called underdeveloped countries, as subsistence farming gives way to mechanized agriculture for production of crops for export,

women are less able to contribute to their families' survival. Together with the devaluation of domestic work, this places pressure on women to seek jobs outside the household to contribute to its support. Since most women in these countries do not have the time or resources to get an education or to develop special job skills, only low-paying jobs are open to them.

Corporate officials, for their part, assume female workers are strictly temporary, and high turnover means that wages can be kept low. Unmarried women are especially favored for employment, for it is assumed that they are free from family responsibilities until they marry, whereupon they will leave the labor force. Thus, the increasing importance of the multinationals in developing countries is contributing to the emergence of a marked gender-segregated division of labor. On top of their housework, women hold low-paying jobs that require little skill; altogether, they may work as many as 15 hours a day. Higher-paying jobs, or at least those that require special skills, are generally held by men, whose workday may be shorter since they do not have additional domestic tasks to perform. Men who lack special skills—and many do—are often doomed to lives of unemployment.

In recent years, the power of corporations has become all the greater through media expansion. Over the past two decades, a global commercial media system has developed, dominated by a few megacorporations, most based in the United States. Having control of television and other media, as well as the advertising industry, gives global corporations such as GE and Disney enormous influence on the ideas and behavior of hundreds of millions of ordinary people across the world in ways they little suspect and can hardly imagine.

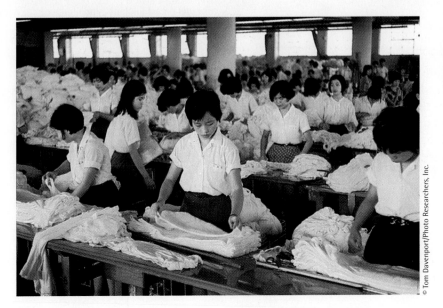

In so-called underdeveloped countries, women have become a source of cheap labor for large corporations, as subsistence farming has given way to mechanized agriculture. Unable to contribute to their families' well-being in any other way, they have no choice but to take on menial jobs for low wages.

© Tom Davenport/Photo Researchers, Inc.

Consider, for example, the powerful marketing messages that shape cultural standards concerning the ideal human body. The widespread nature of this concern is evident in the highly popular U.S. television program *Extreme Makeover*, featuring a few individuals chosen from many thousands of applicants to have their dream come true—to change their looks in an effort to lead better lives. They receive free plastic surgery and other radical cosmetic procedures in exchange for undergoing the knife on camera and allowing the details of their makeover to be broadcast on international television. The following Original Study offers details on what has become a lucrative cosmetic surgery industry.

Original Study

Standardizing the Body: The Question of Choice

The question of choice is central to the story of how medicine and business generate controlling processes in the shaping of women's bodies. Images of the body appear natural within their specific cultural milieus. For example, breast implants are not seen as odd within the cultural milieu of the United States, and female circumcision and infibulation (also known as female genital mutilation or FGM) are not considered odd among people from the Sudan and several other African countries. However, many feminist writers differenti- ate FGM from breast implantation by arguing that North American women *choose* to have breast implants whereas in Africa women are presumably subject to indoctrination since they experience circumcision as young girls.

One of the most heated debates arising from the public health concern over breast implants is whether the re- cipients are freely situated—that is, whether their decision is voluntary or whether control is disguised as free will.

An informed response to the free choice argument requires knowing how the beauty-industrial complex works. Toward this end, corporate accountabil- ity researcher Linda Coco carried out fieldwork in multiple sites, gaining in- sights into the inner workings of a multibillion-dollar industry that seg- ments the female body and manufac- tures commodities of and for the body.

Coco's research shows how some women get caught in the official beauty ideology, and in the case of sili- cone-gel breast implants some hun- dreds of thousands of women have been ensnared. But who gets caught and when are important to an under- standing of the ecology of power. The average age of a woman having breast implantation is 36 years, and she has an

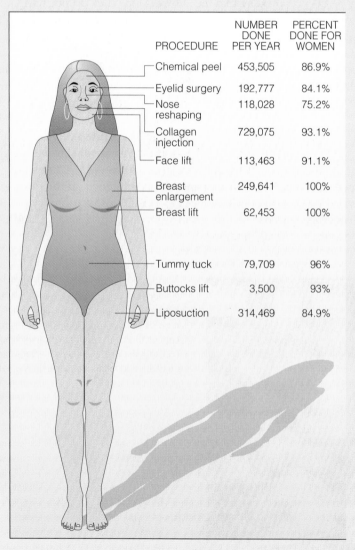

PROCEDURE	NUMBER DONE PER YEAR	PERCENT DONE FOR WOMEN
Chemical peel	453,505	86.9%
Eyelid surgery	192,777	84.1%
Nose reshaping	118,028	75.2%
Collagen injection	729,075	93.1%
Face lift	113,463	91.1%
Breast enlargement	249,641	100%
Breast lift	62,453	100%
Tummy tuck	79,709	96%
Buttocks lift	3,500	93%
Liposuction	314,469	84.9%

Figure 18.3
Cosmetic surgical and nonsurgical procedures in the United States (2002) and the percentage carried out for women. In 2002 there were more than 1.4 million cosmetic surgeries done in the United States at a cost of about $5.4 billion, and nearly 4.7 million nonsurgi- cal procedures (chemical peels, collagen injections, and so on) at a cost of over $2.3 billion. From 1997 to 2002, the number of cosmetic procedures performed increased 228 percent.

average of two children. She is the beauty industry's insecure consumer recast as a patient with an illness the industry defines as hypertrophy (small breasts).

Coco quotes a past president of the American Society of Plastic and Reconstructive Surgery (ASPRS): "There is substantial and enlarging medical knowledge to the effect that these deformities (small breasts) are really a disease which result in the patient's feelings of inadequacies, lack of self-confidence, distortion of body image, and a total lack of well-being due to a lack of self-perceived femininity. . . . Enlargement . . . is therefore . . . necessary to ensure the quality of life for the patient." In other words, cosmetic surgery is necessary to the patient's psychological health.

The plastic surgeon regards the construction of the official breast as art, the aim being to reform the female body according to the ideals of classic Western art. One surgeon pioneering procedures for correcting "deformity" took as his ideal female figure that of ancient Greek statues, which he carefully measured, noticing the exact size and shape of the breasts, their vertical location between the third and seventh ribs, the horizontal between the line of the sternal (breast bone) border and the anterior axillary line, and so forth. In Coco's analysis the exercise of the plastic surgeon's technoart recreates a particular static, official breast shape and applies this creation ostensibly to relieve women's mental suffering. The surgeon becomes a psychological healer as well as an artist.

Along with art and psychology, there is, of course, the business of organized plastic surgery, which responds to the demands and opportunities of market economics (Figure 18.3). By the late 1970s and early 1980s there was a glut of plastic surgeons. The ASPRS began to operate like a commercial enterprise instead of a medical society, saturating the media with ads and even providing low-cost financing. The discourse became a sales pitch. Women "seek" breast implants to keep their husbands or their jobs, to attract men, or to become socially acceptable. Coco calls this "patriarchal capitalism" and questions whether this is free choice or "mind colonization."

Understanding "choice" led Coco to an examination of the power both in the doctor–patient relationship and in the control of information. She found that women "were told by the media, plastic surgeons, women's magazines, other women, and the business world that they could enhance their lives by enhancing their bust lines . . . the social imperative for appearance was personalized, psychologized, and normalized." Social surveys indicate that, to the extent that women internalize the social imperative, they feel they are making the decision on their own.

Not surprisingly, women whose surgery resulted in medical complications often came to recognize the external processes of coercive persuasion that had led them to seek implants. In some ways, they resembled former cult members who had been deprogrammed: Their disillusionment caused them to question the system that had encouraged them to make the decision in the first place. The result was a gradual building of protest against the industry, expressed in networks, newsletters, support groups, workshops, and seminars. As have some former cult members, women have brought suit, testified before lawmakers, and challenged in other ways some of the largest corporations and insurance companies in the land.

The choice of implants, they learn, is part of a matrix of controlling processes in which women are subjects. Given the right circumstances it could happen to anyone. In the Sudan, the young girl is told that FGM procedures are done for her and not to her. In the United States the mutilation of natural breasts is also done for the recreation of femininity. Although power is exercised differently in these two cases, Coco notes the similarity: "The operation on the female breast in America holds much of the same social symbolism and expression of cultural mandate as does FGM in Sudan. Thus, the question of why women choose breast augmentation becomes moot."

Breast implantation is now spreading elsewhere, most notably to China. Will it become a functional equivalent to foot-binding in China as part of the competition between patriarchies East and West? Whatever the answer, many social thinkers agree that people are always more vulnerable to intense persuasion during periods of historical dislocation—a break with structures and symbols familiar to the life cycle—in which the media can bring us images and ideas originating in past, contemporary, or even imaginary worlds.

Feminist researchers have sought to crack controlling paradigms such as those that define women's capacities and those that construct a standardized body shape and determine what is beautiful in women. Some of their writings are attempts to free the mind from the beauty constructions of cosmetic industries and fashion magazines. Others relay how the one model of Western beauty is affecting members of ethnic groups who aspire to look the way advertisements say they should. Choice is an illusion, since the restructuring of taste is inextricably linked to shifts in the organization of consumption.
(Adapted from L. Nader (1997). Controlling processes: Tracing the dynamics of power. Current Anthropology, 38, 715–717.) ▪ ▪ ▪

STRUCTURAL POWER IN THE AGE OF GLOBALIZATION

All of the above makes it clear that a new form of expansive international capitalism has emerged since the mid-1900s. Operating under the banner of globalization, it builds on earlier cultural structures of worldwide trade networks, and it is the successor to a system of colonialism in which a handful of powerful, mainly European, capitalist states ruled and exploited foreign nations inhabiting distant territories.

Enormously complex and turbulent, globalization is a dynamically structured process in which individuals, business corporations, and political institutions are actively rearranging and restructuring the social field of force to their own competitive advantage, vying for increasingly scarce natural resources, cheap labor, new commercial markets, and ever-larger profits in a huge political arena spanning the entire globe. Doing this, of course, requires a great deal of power.

As discussed previously, power refers to the ability of individuals or groups to impose their will upon others and make them do things even against their own wants or wishes. Power plays a major role in coordinating and regulating collective behavior toward imposing or maintaining law and order within—and beyond—a particular community or society.

There are different levels of power within societies, as well as among societies. The recently deceased Austrian-American anthropologist Eric Wolf pointed out the importance of understanding a macro level of power that he referred to as **structural power**—power that organizes and orchestrates the systemic interaction within and among societies, directing economic and political forces on the one hand and ideological forces that shape public ideas, values, and beliefs on the other.[10]

The concept of structural power applies not only to regional political organizations such as chiefdoms or states but also captures the complex new cultural formations currently emerging in the globalization process. It focuses attention on the systemic interaction between the global forces directing the world's changing economies and political institutions on the one hand and those that shape public ideas, values, and beliefs on the other.

Joseph Nye, a political scientist, international security specialist, and former Assistant Secretary of Defense in the U.S. government, refers to these two major interacting forces in the worldwide arena as "hard power" and "soft power."[11] **Hard power** is the kind of coercive power that is backed up by economic and military force. **Soft power** is co-optive rather than coercive, pressing others through attraction and persuasion to change their ideas, beliefs, values, and behaviors. Although propaganda is a

form of soft power, the exercise of ideological influence (the global struggle for hearts and minds) also operates through more subtle means, such as foreign aid, international diplomacy, news media, sports, entertainment, museum exhibits, and academic exchanges.

In today's globalization process, the United States has more hard power at its disposal than any of its allies or rivals worldwide. It is the global leader in military spending—about $340 billion per year, followed (despite its pacifist constitution) by Japan ($47 billion), Britain ($36 billion), France ($34 billion), and China ($31 billion). In fact, as the world's dominant superpower, the United States spends more on its armed forces than the next twenty leading countries combined. And although there are about eight other nuclear weapons states (Russia, Britain, France, and China, as well as Israel, India, Pakistan, and probably North Korea, collectively possessing about 30,000 nuclear missiles and bombs), the United States has by far the largest arsenal at its disposal.[12]

In addition to military might, hard power involves the use of economic strength as a political instrument of coercion or intimidation in the global structuring process. Among other things, this means that economic size and productivity, technological capability, and finance capital may be brought to bear on the global market, forcing weaker states to break down trade barriers protecting their workers, natural resources, and local markets.

As the world's largest economy and leading exporter, the United States has long pushed for free trade for its corporations doing business on a global scale. Sometimes it uses military power to impose changes on a foreign political landscape by means of armed interventions or full-scale invasions. Through history, the United States (like several other powerful countries, including Russia, Britain, and France) has engaged in such military interventions around the world. Because of this, many see the United States as an ever-present threat, apt to use overwhelming military force in order to benefit its corporate interests from fruit to fuel, from microchips to automobiles. The corporations, in turn, wield enormous political and financial power over governments and international organizations, including the World Trade Organization, headquartered in Geneva, and global banking institutions such as the International Monetary Fund (IMF) and World Bank, both based in Washington, DC.

Globalization does more than create a worldwide field of force in which megacorporations reap megaprofits. It also wreaks havoc in many traditional cultures and

---

structural power Power that organizes and orchestrates the systemic interaction within and among societies, directing economic and political forces on the one hand and ideological forces that shape public ideas, values, and beliefs on the other.

hard power Coercive power that is backed up by economic and military force.

soft power Pressing others through attraction and persuasion to change their ideas, beliefs, values, and behaviors.

---

[10]Wolf, E. R. (1999). *Envisioning power: Ideologies of dominance and crisis* (p. 5). Berkeley: University of California Press.

[11]Nye, J. (2002). *The paradox of American power: Why the world's only superpower can't go it alone.* New York: Oxford University Press.

[12]Sparks, J. (2003, December 22). The power game. *Newsweek, 142*(25).

September 2003 annual meeting of two global banking institutions: the World Bank and the International Monetary Fund. Both institutions have tremendous structural power, for they direct flows of capital to certain regions of the world—resulting in massive economic change.

© Courtesy of IMF

disrupts long-established social organizations everywhere. By the early 21st century, the global trend of economic inequality is becoming clear: The poor are becoming poorer and the rich are becoming richer. For the many thousands of big winners or have-lots, there are many millions of losers or have-nots.

As home base to more global corporations than any other country, the United States is endeavoring to protect its interests by investing in creating and controlling what it refers to as a *global security environment.* Numerous other countries, unable to afford expensive weapons systems (or blocked from developing or acquiring them), have invested in biological or chemical warfare technology. Still others, including relatively powerless political groups, have resorted to guerilla tactics or terrorism as part of their local, regional, or even global warfare strategies.

In addition to reliance on military and economic hard power in the global quest for dominance and profit, competing states and corporations utilize the ideological persuasion of soft power as transmitted by means of electronic and digital media, communications satellites, and other forms of information and communication technology. One of the major tasks of soft power is to package and sell the general idea of globalization as something positive and progressive (as "freedom," "free" trade, "free" market) and to frame or brand anything that opposes capitalism in negative terms.

One outcome of this complex interaction between hard and soft power in structuring the global arena is the creation of a new collective awareness of worldwide connectivity, making peoples everywhere understand and possibly accept the new cultural order. Considering existing cultural differences, political divisions, and competing economic interests, combined with growing worldwide resistance against superpower domination, the emerging world system is inherently unstable, vulnerable, and unpredictable.

Structural power and its associated concepts of hard and soft power enable us to better understand the wider field of force in which local communities throughout the world are now compelled to operate. To comprehend it is to realize how unequal the distribution of power is in today's global arena.

That said, no matter how effectively a dominant state or corporation combines its hard and soft power, globalization does run into opposition. Pockets of resistance exist within the wealthy industrial and postindustrial states as well as elsewhere in the world. This resistance may manifest itself in the rise of traditionalisms and revitalization movements—efforts to return to life as it was (or how people think it was) before the familiar order became unhinged and people became unsettled. Some of these reactionary movements may take the form of resurgent ethnonationalism or religious fundamentalist movements. Others may find expression in alternative grassroots movements from radical environmental groups to peace groups.

Increasingly, such movements use the Internet to further their causes. While it is true that states and big corporations have expanded their power and influence through electronic communication technologies, it is also true that these same technologies present opportunities to individuals and groups that have traditionally been powerless. They provide a means of distributing information and promoting activities that are distinct from or in opposition to those of the dominant society.

The far-reaching capabilities of modern electronic and digital technologies have led to the creation of a new global media environment that plays a major role in how individuals and even societies view themselves and their place in the world. Together with radio and television, the Internet is now the dominant means of mass communication around the world. Today, the global flow of information made possible by fiber optic cables and communications satellites orbiting the earth is almost entirely digital-electronic and takes place in a new boundless cultural space that Indian anthropologist Arjun Appadurai refers to as a "global mediascape."

PROBLEMS OF STRUCTURAL VIOLENCE

Based on their capacity to harness, direct, and distribute global resources and energy flows, heavily armed states, megacorporations, and very wealthy elites are using their coercive and co-optive powers to structure or rearrange the emerging world system and direct global processes to their own competitive advantage. When such structural power undermines the well-being of others, we may speak of **structural violence**—physical and/or psychological harm (including repression, environmental destruction, poverty, hunger, illness, and premature death) caused by impersonal, exploitative, and unjust social, political, and economic systems.

Clearly, the current structures are positioned in a way that leads to more wealth, power, comfort, and glory for the happy few and little more than poverty, subservience, suffering, and death for multitudes. Every day millions of people around the world face famine, ecological disasters, health problems, political instability, and violence rooted in development programs or profit-making maneuvers directed by powerful states or global corporations.

A useful baseline for identifying structural violence is provided by the Universal Declaration of Human Rights, officially adopted by all members of the United Nations in 1948. Anthropologists played a key role in drafting this important document. The declaration's preamble begins with the statement that "recognition of the inherent dignity and of the equal and inalienable rights of all members of the human family is the foundation of freedom, justice and peace in the world."[13] Generally

---

structural violence Physical and/or psychological harm (including repression, environmental destruction, poverty, hunger, illness, and premature death) caused by impersonal, exploitative, and unjust social, political, and economic systems.

---

[13]www.ccnmtl.columbia.edu/projects/mmt/udhr.

speaking, structural violence concerns the impersonal systemic violation of the human rights of individuals and communities to a healthy, peaceful, and dignified life.

Although human rights abuses are nothing new, globalization has enormously expanded and intensified structural violence. For instance, it is leading to an ever-widening gap between the wealthiest and poorest peoples, the powerful and powerless. In 1960 the average income for the twenty wealthiest countries in the world was fifteen times that of the twenty poorest. Today it is thirty times higher.[14]

More remarkable is the fact that the world's 225 richest individuals have a combined wealth equal to the annual income of the poorest 47 percent of the entire world population. In fact, half of all people in the world get by on less than $2 per day, and more than 1.2 billion people live on just $1 a day. Measuring the gap in another way reveals that the poorest 80 percent of the human population make do with 14 percent of all goods and services in the world, the poorest 20 percent with a mere 1.3 percent. Meanwhile, the richest 20 percent enjoy 86 percent.[15]

Structural violence has countless manifestations in addition to widespread poverty. These range from the cultural destruction already indicated to hunger and obesity, environmental degradation, and emotional discontent, all discussed in the remaining pages of this chapter.

Overpopulation and Poverty

In 1750, 1 billion people lived on earth. Over the next two centuries our numbers climbed to nearly 2.5 billion. And between 1950 and 2000 the world population soared above 6 billion (Figure 18.4). Today, India and China alone have more than 1 billion inhabitants each. Such increases are highly significant because population growth increases the scale of hunger and pollution—and the many problems tied to these two big issues. Although controlling population growth does not by itself make the other problems go away, it is unlikely those other problems can be solved unless population growth is stopped or even reversed.

Despite progress in population control, the number of humans on earth continues to grow overall. Population projections are extremely tricky, given variables such as AIDS, but current projections suggest that

---

[14] www.worldbank.org/poverty. (2003 statistics).
[15]Kurth, P. (1998, October 14). Capital crimes. *Seven Days,* 7; Swaminathan, M. S. (2000). Science in response to basic human needs. *Science, 287,* 425. See also Human Development Report 2002, *Deepening democracy in a fragmented world,* United Nations Development Program.

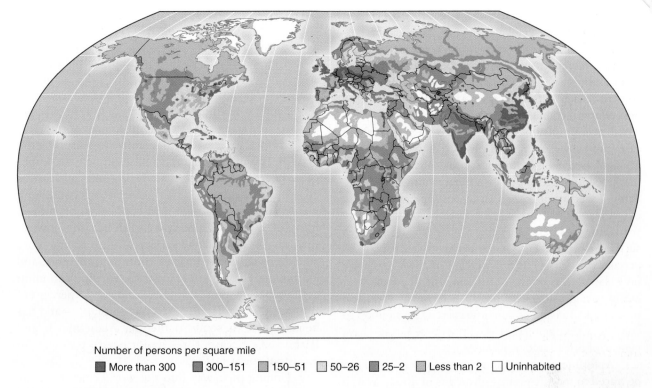

Number of persons per square mile

■ More than 300   ■ 300–151   ■ 150–51   □ 50–26   ■ 25–2   ■ Less than 2   □ Uninhabited

Figure 18.4 **Global Population Density**
Three great concentrations of human population appear on this map—East Asia, South Asia, and Europe—with a fourth, lesser concentration in eastern North America. Population growth is still rapid in South Asia, which is expected to become even more densely populated in the early 21st century. Density in the other three regions is expected to remain about as it now appears due to relatively stable population rates resulting from economic development. The areas of future high-density population, in addition to those already existing, are likely to be Central Africa and Central and South America, where growth rates are well above the world average.
Source: From *Student Atlas of Anthropology* by John Allen and Audrey Shalinksy, p. 72. Copyright © 2003 by the McGraw-Hill Companies, Inc. All rights reserved. Reprinted by permission of McGraw-Hill/Dushkin Publishing.

global population will peak around 2050 at about 9.37 billion people.

The problem's severity becomes clear when it is realized that the present world population of more than 6 billion people can be sustained only by using up nonrenewable resources such as oil, which is like living off income-producing capital. It works for a time, but once the capital is gone, so is the possibility of even having an income to live on.

Hunger and Obesity

As frequently dramatized in media reports, hundreds of millions of people face hunger on a regular basis, leading to a variety of health problems, premature death, and other forms of suffering. Today, over a quarter of the world's countries do not produce enough food to feed their populations and cannot afford to import what is needed. The majority of these countries are in sub-Saharan Africa.

All told, about 1 billion people in the world are undernourished. Some 6 million children aged 5 and under die every year due to hunger, and those who survive often suffer from physical and mental impairment.[16] For the victims of this situation, the effect is violent, even though it was not caused by the deliberate hostile act of a specific individual. The source of the violence may have been the unplanned yet devastatingly real impact of structural power—for instance, through the collapse of local markets due to subsidized foreign imports—and this is what structural violence is all about.

Ironically, while many millions of people in some parts of the world are starving, many millions of others are overeating—quite literally eating themselves to death. In fact, the number of overfed people now exceeds those who are underfed. According to the World Watch Institute in Washington, DC, more than 1.1 billion people worldwide are now overweight. And 300 million of these are obese (but, however difficult to imagine, still often malnourished).

Seriously concerned about the sharp rise in associated health problems (including stroke, diabetes, cancer,

---

[16]Hunger Project 2003; Swaminathan, p. 425.

heart disease), the World Health Organization *sifies* obesity as a global epidemic. Overeating is par*ularly* unhealthy for individuals living in societies where machines have eased the physical burdens of work and other human activities, which helps explain why more than half of the people in some industrial and postindustrial countries are overweight.

However, the obesity epidemic is not due solely to excessive eating and lack of physical activity. A key ingredient is the high sugar and fat content of mass-marketed foods. The problem is spreading and has become a serious concern even in some developing countries. In fact, the highest rates of obesity in the world now exist among Pacific Islanders living in places such as Samoa and Fiji. On the island of Nauru, up to 65 percent of the men and 70 percent of the women are now classified as obese. (That said, not all people who are overweight or obese are so because they eat too much junk food and do too little exercise. In addition to cultural factors, being overweight or obese can also have genetic or other biological causes.)

As for hunger cases, about 10 percent of them can be traced to specific events—droughts or floods, as well as various social, economic, and political disruptions, including warfare. During the 20th century, 44 million people died due to human-made famine.[17] For example, in several sub-Saharan African countries plagued by chronic civil strife, it has been almost impossible to raise and harvest crops, for hoards of refugees and soldiers constantly raid fields, often at gunpoint. Another problem is that millions of acres in Africa, Asia, and Latin America once devoted to subsistence farming have been given over to the raising of cash crops for export. This has enriched members of elite social classes in these parts of the world, while satisfying the appetites of people in the developed countries for coffee, tea, chocolate, bananas, and beef. Those who used to farm the land for their own food needs have been relocated—either to urban areas, where all too often there is no employment for them, or to areas ecologically unsuited for farming.

In Africa, such lands are often occupied seasonally by pastoral nomads, and turning them over to cultivation has reduced pasture available for livestock and led to overgrazing. The increase in cleared land, coupled with overgrazing, has depleted both soil and water, with disastrous consequences to nomad and farmer alike. So it is that more than 250 million people can no longer grow crops on their farms, and 1 billion people in 100 countries are in danger of losing their ability to grow crops.[18]

Pollution

The effects of big agribusiness practices are part of larger problems of environmental degradation in which pollution is tolerated for the sake of higher profits that benefit select individuals and societies (see this chapter's Biocultural Connection). Industrial activities are producing highly toxic substances at unprecedented rates, and factory emissions are poisoning the air. For example, smokestack gases are clearly implicated in acid rain, which is damaging lakes and forests all over northeastern North America. Air containing water vapor with a high acid content is, of course, harmful to the lungs, but the health hazard is greater than this. As ground and surface waters become more acidic, the solubility of lead, cadmium, mercury, and aluminum, all of them toxic, rises sharply. Aluminum contamination alone is high enough on 17 percent of the world's farmland to be toxic to plants—and has been linked to senile dementia, Alzheimer's, and Parkinson's disease, three major health problems in industrial countries.

Finding their way into the world's oceans, toxic substances also create hazards for seafood consumers. For instance, Canadian Inuit face health problems related to eating fish and sea mammals that feed in waters contaminated by industrial chemical waste such as polychlorinated biphenyls (PCBs). Living thousands of miles from the industrial sources poisoning their environment, Inuit women have a right to be alarmed that their breast milk now contains levels of PCBs five to ten times higher than women in southern Canada.[19] Obviously, environmental poisoning affects peoples all across the globe (Figure 18.5).

Added to this is the problem of global warming—the greenhouse effect—caused primarily by the burning of fossil fuels. Although much is unknown about the extent of global warming, scientists now overwhelmingly agree it is real and that it is due to combustion of carbon-based fuels. Experts predict that it will lead to an expansion of the geographical ranges of tropical diseases and increase the incidence of respiratory diseases due to additional smog caused by warmer temperatures. Also, they expect an increase in deaths due to heat waves, as witnessed in the 15,000 deaths attributed to the 2003 heat wave in France.[20]

Unfortunately, public concern about this is minimal, in large part because energy interests sponsor pub-

[17]Hunger Project 2003; White, M. (2001). *Historical atlas of the twentieth century.* http://users.erols.com/mwhite28/20centry.htm.

[18]Godfrey, T. (2000, December 27). Biotech threatening biodiversity. *Burlington Free Press,* 10A.

[19]Inuit Tapiirit Katami. http://www.taprisat.ca/english-text/itk/departments/enviro/ncp.

[20]World Meteorological Organization, quoted in "Increasing heat waves and other health hazards." Accessed December 2003, greenpeaceusa.org/climate/index.fpl/7096/article/907.html.

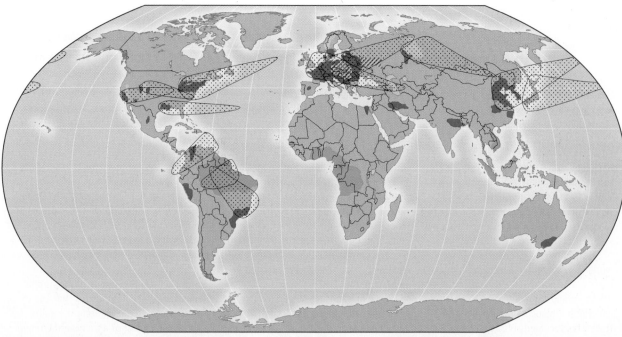

☑ Land areas with significant acid precipitation and atmospheric pollution

■ Land areas with significant atmospheric pollution

☐ Land areas with significant acid precipitation

▨ Land areas of secondary atmospheric pollution

⊡ Air pollution plume: average wind direction and force

(Wind blows in the direction of the tapered end of the air pollution plume and the force of the wind is indicated by the size of the plume.)

Figure 18.5 Global Pollution
Almost all processes of physical geography begin and end with the flows of energy and matter among land, sea, and air. Because of the primacy of the atmosphere in this exchange system, air pollution is potentially one of the most dangerous human modifications in environmental systems. Pollutants such as various oxides of nitrogen or sulfur cause the development of acid precipitation, which damages soil, vegetation, and wildlife. Air pollution in the form of smog is often dangerous for human health. And atmospheric scientists generally agree that the efficiency of the atmosphere in retaining heat—the greenhouse effect—is being enhanced by increased carbon dioxide, methane, and other gases produced by industrial and agricultural activities. The result, they fear, will be a period of global warming that will dramatically alter climates in all parts of the world.
Source: From *Student Atlas of Anthropology* by John Allen and Audrey Shalinksy, p. 132. Copyright © 2003 by the McGraw-Hill Companies, Inc. All rights reserved. Reprinted by permission of McGraw-Hill/Dushkin Publishing.

lic relations campaigns to convince people that global warming is not real—or at least, not a problem—just as tobacco companies once ran campaigns claiming that smoking was not hazardous.

Structural violence also manifests itself in the shift of manufacturing and hazardous waste disposal from developed to developing countries. This trend is encouraged by cheap labor and less stringent safety and environmental regulations, which translate into lower production costs and larger profits for corporations. Typically, a few well-placed officials or business-people in the developing countries benefit financially from these overseas arrangements, while powerless workers are exploited and environmental pollution is expanded. For instance, not long ago the president of Benin in West Africa signed a contract with a European waste company enabling that company to dump toxic and low-grade radioactive waste on the lands of his political opposition.[21] In the United States, both

government and industry have tried to persuade American Indians on reservations that the solution to their severe economic problems lies in allowing disposal of nuclear and other hazardous waste on their lands.

Given a general awareness of the causes and dangers of pollution, why is it that the human species as a whole is not committed to controlling practices that foul its own nest? At least part of the answer lies in philosophical and theological traditions. In Western industrial and postindustrial societies, people accept the biblical assertion (found in the Koran as well) of human dominion over the earth, interpreting that to mean that it is their sacred duty to subdue and control the earth and all its inhabitants. These societies are the biggest contributors to global pollution. For example, on average, one North American consumes hundreds of times the resources of a single African, with all that implies with respect to waste disposal and environmental degradation. Moreover, each person in North America adds, on average, 20 tons of carbon dioxide (a greenhouse

_____

[21]*Cultural Survival Quarterly* (1991).15(4),5.

Biocultural
Connection

Picturing Pesticides

The toxic effects of pesticides have long been known. After all, these compounds are designed to kill bugs. However, documenting the toxic effects of pesticides on humans has been more difficult, as they are subtle—sometimes taking years to become apparent. A further complication is that a particular pesticide may seem safe by itself, but may be quite unsafe in combination with other chemical substances—as is usual in the real world.

Anthropologist Elizabeth Guillette, working in a Yaqui Indian community in Mexico, combined ethnographic observation, biological monitoring of pesticide levels in the blood, and neurobehavioral testing to document the impairment of child development by pesticides.[a] Working with colleagues from the Technological Institute of Sonora in Obregón, Mexico, Guillette compared children and families from two Yaqui communities: one living in farm valleys who were exposed to large doses of pesticides and one living in ranching villages in the foothills nearby.

Guillette documented the frequency of pesticide use among the farming Yaqui to be forty-five times per crop cycle with two crop cycles per year. In the farming valleys she also noted that families tended to use household bug sprays on a daily basis, thus increasing their exposure to toxic pesticides. In the foothill ranches, she found that the only pesticides that the Yaqui were exposed to consisted of DDT sprayed by the government to control malaria. In these communities, indoor bugs were swatted or tolerated.

Pesticide exposure was linked to child health and development through two sets of measures. First, levels of pesticides in the blood of valley children at birth and throughout their childhood were examined and found to be far higher than in the children from the foothills. Further, the presence of pesticides in breast milk of nursing mothers from the valley farms was also documented.

Second, children from the two communities were asked to perform a variety of normal childhood activities, such as jumping, memory games, playing catch, and drawing pictures. The children exposed to high doses of pesticides had significantly less stamina, eye–hand coordination, large motor coordination, and drawing ability compared to the Yaqui children from the foothills. These children exhibited no overt symptoms of pesticide poisoning—instead exhibiting delays and impairment in their neurobehavioral abilities that may be irreversible.

Though Guillette's study was thoroughly embedded in one ethnographic community, she emphasizes that the exposure to pesticides among the Yaqui farmers is typical of agricultural communities globally and has significance for changing human practices regarding the use of pesticides everywhere. ■ ■ ■

[a]Guillette. E. A., et al. (1998). An anthropological approach to the evaluation of preschool children exposed to pesticides in Mexico. *Environmental Health Perspectives, 106* (June), 347.

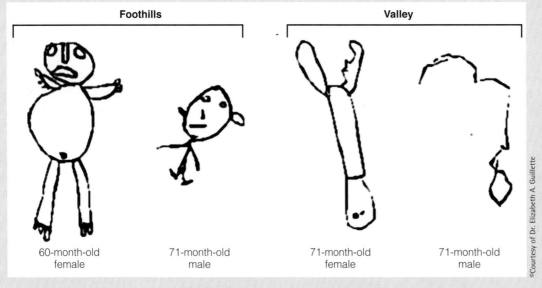

Foothills		Valley	
60-month-old female	71-month-old male	71-month-old female	71-month-old male

©Courtesy of Dr. Elizabeth A. Guillette

Compare the drawings typically done by Yaqui children heavily exposed to pesticides (valley) to those made by Yaqui children living in nearby areas who were relatively unexposed (foothills).

gas) a year to the atmosphere. In "underdeveloped" countries, less than 3 tons per person are emitted.[22] According to botanist Peter Raven, "if everyone lived like Americans, you'd need three planet earths . . . to sustain that level of consumption."[23]

The Culture of Discontent

For the past several decades, the world's poor countries have been sold on the idea they should and actually can enjoy a standard of living comparable to that of the rich countries. Yet, the resources necessary to maintain such a luxurious standard of living are not unlimited. This growing gap between expectations and realizations has led to the creation of a culture of discontent.

The problem involves not just population growth outstripping available natural resources, but also unequal access to decent jobs, housing, sanitation, health care, leisure, and adequate police and fire protection. It is one in which personal disappointments are echoed in a natural environment degraded by overcrowding, pollution, and soil erosion.

This culture of discontent is not limited to people living in poor and overpopulated countries. Because capitalism thrives on growing demands, powerful advertising strategies target people with financial means to purchase more and more luxury goods and services. In the process, even those whose needs are more than met will be made to feel the pinch of discontent and spend their money in pursuit of material dreams.

Some dramatic changes in cultural values and motivations, as well as in social institutions and the types of technologies we employ, are required if humans are going to realize a sustainable future for generations to come. The short-sighted emphasis on consumerism and individual self-interest so characteristic of the world's affluent countries needs to be abandoned in favor of a more balanced social and environmental ethic. These can be created from values still found in many of the world's non-Western cultures. Such values include a worldview that sees humanity as part of the natural world rather than superior to it. Included, too, is a sense of social responsibility that recognizes that no individual, people, or state has the right to expropriate resources at the expense of others. Finally, an awareness is needed of how important supportive ties are for individuals, such as seen in kinship or other associations in the world's traditional societies. Is humanity up to the challenge? And will anthropology play a role in meeting that challenge?

---

[22]Broecker, W. S. (1992, April). Global warming on trial. *Natural History*, 14.
[23]Quoted in Becker, J. (2004, March). *National Geographic*, 90.

CONCLUDING REMARKS

As defined in this book's first chapter, anthropology is the comparative study of humankind everywhere and throughout time. It seeks to produce reliable knowledge about different peoples and cultures, their ideas and behaviors. Since the beginning of the discipline in the mid-1800s, generations of anthropologists have studied our species in all its cultural and biological varieties. In the process, they described in great detail an enormous number of different cultures and biological variations among humans in all parts of the world. They also collected a staggering volume of ethnographic artifacts and used still and motion picture cameras to visually document hundreds of different cultures.

Today, many of the cultures studied by the earliest anthropologists more than a century ago have changed profoundly in response to powerful outside influences and internal dynamics. Others have simply disappeared as a result of deadly epidemics, violent conflicts, acculturation, ethnocide, or even genocide. All too often, the only detailed records we now possess of these altered and vanished cultures are those that some visiting anthropologist was able to document before it was too late.

But, anthropologists do much more than trying to preserve precious information about distinctive peoples and cultures. As chronicled in the pages of this book, they also try to explain why cultures are similar or different, why and how they did or did not change. Moreover, they try to identify the particular knowledge and insights that each culture holds concerning the human condition.

Less apt than other scholarly specialists to see facts and activities as separate and unrelated, anthropologists are trained to understand and explain economic, social, political, ideological, and biological features and processes as parts of dynamic systems by means of theoretical concepts such as structural power and structural violence. Their cross-cultural and comparative historical perspective on local communities in the age of globalization enables them to make key contributions to our understanding of such troubling problems as overpopulation, food shortages, pollution, and widespread discontent in the world. This is evident, for instance, in hiring choices at the World Bank in the wake of a series of ill-conceived and mismanaged development projects that harmed more than helped local populations. Recognizing the value of anthropological knowledge and methods, the bank now employs and contracts dozens of professional anthropologists for projects all across the world. The same is true for other international organizations, as well as some global corporations and state government agencies.

© Reuters/Corbis

© Amnesty International

"Never doubt that a small group of committed people can change the world; indeed it is the only thing that ever has." (Margaret Mead, anthropologist) Many anthropologists do fieldwork that results in information with practical value for the communities in which they do their studies. Not surprisingly, we find anthropologists working for international service organizations such as Oxfam, founded at Oxford University during World War II for famine relief in war-torn Europe. Today, Oxfam offers aid and advocacy worldwide for refugees and others in need. Anthropologists have also long been active in the United Nations Educational, Scientific and Cultural Organization (UNESCO), headquartered in Paris and with offices all over the globe. Founded in 1945, this international forum contributes to peace and security by promoting collaboration among the nations through education, science, and culture. Anthropologists are also participants in international human rights organizations such as Amnesty International, founded in London in 1961 to work on behalf of political prisoners. Active in more than 160 countries, Amnesty now has over 1 million members and is more broadly focused on exposing and ending all violations to the Universal Declaration of Human Rights. In 1977, it won the Nobel Peace Prize. Some anthropologists also work with Doctors Without Borders, another Nobel Peace Prize winner. Founded in Paris in 1971 by a group of medical doctors, it has some 2,000 volunteers serving in over eighty countries.

© AP/Wide World Photos

Some anthropologists go beyond just studying different cultures and reach out to assist besieged groups that are struggling to survive in today's rapidly changing world. In so doing, they seek to put into practice their own knowledge about humankind—knowledge deepened through the comparative perspective of anthropology, which is cross-culturally, historically, and biologically informed.

The idea that anthropological research is fascinating in itself and also has the potential of helping solve practical problems on local and global levels has drawn and continues to draw a unique group of people into the discipline. Most of these individuals are inspired by the old but still valid idea that anthropology must aim to live up to its ideal as the most liberating of the sciences.

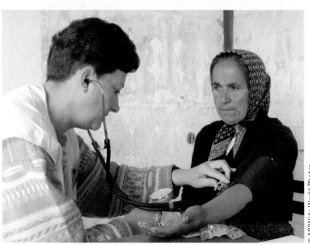

© AP/Wide World Photos

Chapter Summary

■ Anthropologists strive to gain a better understanding of the existing world situation so that decisions affecting humanity's future may be made intelligently. They are especially well suited for this, owing to their experience at seeing things in context, their long-term historical and biocultural perspective, their ability to recognize culture-bound biases, and their familiarity with cultural alternatives.

■ However humanity changes biologically, culture remains the chief means by which humans try to solve their problems of existence. Rapid developments in communication, transportation, and world trade, some believe, are leading people toward a single world culture that could lessen chances for conflict. Most anthropologists are as skeptical of this as they are critical of the way industrial countries tend to treat traditional societies as obsolete.

■ Ethnic tension, common in pluralistic societies, sometimes turns violent, leading to formal separation. To manage cultural diversity within such societies, some countries have adopted multiculturalism, an official public policy of mutual respect and tolerance for cultural differences.

■ Cutting across international boundaries, global corporations are a powerful force for worldwide integration despite the political, linguistic, religious, and other cultural differences that separate people. Their power and wealth, often exceeding that of national governments, has increased dramatically through media expansion. Major players in the globalization process, these megacorporations have enormous influence on the ideas and behavior of hundreds of millions of people worldwide. In pursuit of wealth and power, states and corporations now compete for increasingly scarce natural resources, cheap labor, new commercial markets, and ever-larger profits in a huge political arena spanning the entire globe.

■ Structural power refers to the global forces that direct economic and political institutions and shape public ideas and values. Hard power is backed up by economic and military force, and soft power is ideological persuasion. The world's largest corporations are almost all based in a small group of wealthy and powerful states, which also dominate international trade and finance organizations. Their development projects in poor countries do not always benefit local populations, including indigenous peoples.

■ Globalization provides megaprofits for large corporations but often wreaks havoc in many traditional cultures and disrupts long-established social organizations. By means of soft power, globalization is marketed as positive and progressive for everyone, but the poor are becoming poorer even as the rich get richer. Globalization also engenders worldwide resistance against superpower domination. For this reason, the emerging world system is inherently unstable, vulnerable, and unpredictable.

■ One result of globalization is worldwide and growing structural violence—physical and/or psychological harm (including repression, cultural and environmental destruction, poverty, hunger and obesity, illness, and premature death) caused by impersonal, exploitative, and unjust social, political, and economic systems.

■ Uncontrolled population growth makes all of these problems worse. Due to rising expectations created by the media, coupled with limited opportunities, a culture of discontent is growing.

■ Some dramatic changes in cultural values and motivations, as well as in social institutions and the types of technologies we employ, are required if humans are going to realize a sustainable future for generations to come. The shortsighted emphasis on consumerism and individual self-interest so characteristic of the world's affluent countries needs to be abandoned in favor of a more balanced social and environmental ethic. Trained in what has been called the most liberating of the sciences, anthropologists have a contribution to make in bringing about this shift. They are well versed in the dangers of culture-bound thinking, and they bring a holistic biocultural and comparative historical perspective to the challenge of understanding and balancing the sometimes conflicting needs and desires of local communities in the age of globalization.

Questions for Reflection

1. Throughout today's world, many pluralistic or multi-ethnic countries face the challenge of "nation building." What would it take for a political organization such as the one developed in Switzerland to work as a model for countries in which minorities have been trampled as they attempt to retain their own natural resources, national identities, and cultural traditions?

2. Most of the world's major global corporations are U.S. based, including Wal-Mart, which generates almost $250 billion in annual revenues. Measured in economic terms, this business is bigger than South Africa, inhabited by 45 million people. In what ways might such a megacorporation use its enormous economic power? Could it influence the U.S. government in terms of world trade policies? If so, would the company benefit more from free trade or protectionism?

3. Considering the relationship between structural power and structural violence, does your own lifestyle in terms of buying clothes and food, driving cars, and so on reflect or have an effect on the globalization process?

4. In the high-tech sphere of the global mediascape, television viewers and Internet users are not only consumers of news and entertainment but are also exposed to soft power. Can you think of an example of soft power in your own daily life? And at which point does such influence turn into propaganda or manipulation?

5. The World Health Organization, UNESCO, Oxfam, and Amnesty International are global institutions concerned with structural violence and human rights violations. Confronted

with genocidal conflicts, famines, epidemics, and torture of political prisoners, people active in these organizations try to improve the human condition. Why do you think that an anthropological perspective on such worldwide problems might be of practical use? Can you think of an example?

Key Terms

multiculturalism

structural power

hard power

soft power

structural violence

Multimedia Review Tools

Make the Grade in Anthropology with ThomsonNOW

Thomson™ NOW! This powerful online study tool provides you with a *personalized study plan* based on your responses to a diagnostic pretest. Once you have mastered the material with the help of interactive learning tools, an integrated e-book, and more, you can take a post-test to confirm you are ready to move on to the next chapter. To get started with ThomsonNOW, check the card packaged with your book for the access code. Then go to http://www.thomsonedu.com to create an account through 1pass™. If there is no card in your book, go to http://www.thomsonedu.com to purchase an access code.

Companion Website and Anthropology Resource Center

Go to http://anthropology.wadsworth.com to reach the companion website for your text. This offers many study aids, including self quizzes for each chapter and a practice final exam, as well as links to anthropology websites and information on the latest theories and discoveries in the field.

Also, check out the Anthropology Resource Center for a wealth of learning materials that include interactive maps, video exercises, simulations, and breaking news in anthropology. Be sure to explore InfoTrac College Edition®, your online library that offers full-length articles from thousands of scholarly and popular publications. To reach the Anthropology Resource Center and InfoTrac College Edition, check the card packaged with your book for the access code. Then go to http://www.thomsonedu.com to create an account through 1pass™. If there is no card in your book, go to http://www.thomsonedu.com to purchase an access code.

Glossary

absolute or chronometric dating In archaeology and paleoanthropology, dates for physical and cultural remains materials based on solar years, centuries, or other units of absolute time.

acculturation Massive culture changes that people are forced to make as a consequence of intensive firsthand contact between their own group and another, often more powerful, society.

action theory The theory that self-serving actions by forceful leaders play a role in civilization's emergence.

adaptation A series of beneficial adjustments to the environment.

adjudication Mediation with an unbiased third party making the ultimate decision.

age grade An organized category of people based on age; every individual passes through a series of such categories over his or her lifetime.

age set A formally established group of people born during a certain time span who move through the series of age grade categories together.

agriculture Intensive crop cultivation, employing plows, fertilizers, and/or irrigation.

alleles Alternate forms of a single gene.

anagenesis A sustained directional shift in a population's average characteristics.

analogies In biology, structures possessed by different organisms that are superficially similar due to similar function; without sharing a common developmental pathway or structure.

animatism A belief that nature is enlivened or energized by an impersonal spiritual power or supernatural potency.

animism A belief that nature is enlivened or energized by distinct personalized spirit beings separable from bodies.

anthropoids A subdivision within the primate order that includes New World Monkeys, Old World monkeys, and apes (including humans).

anthropology The study of humankind in all times and places.

applied anthropology The use of anthropological knowledge and methods to solve practical problems, often for a specific client.

arboreal Living in the trees.

archaeology The study of human cultures through the recovery and analysis of material remains and environmental data.

Archaic cultures Term used to refer to Mesolithic cultures in the Americas.

art The creative use of the human imagination to symbolically interpret, express, and enjoy life.

artifact Any object fashioned or altered by humans.

Australopithecus The genus including several species of early bipeds from southern and eastern Africa living between about 4.3 and 1.1 million years ago, one of whom was directly ancestral to humans.

balanced reciprocity A mode of exchange in which the giving and the receiving are specific as to the value of the goods and the time of their delivery.

band A relatively small and loosely organized kin-ordered group that inhabits a specific territory and that may split periodically into smaller extended family groups that are politically independent.

binocular vision Vision with increased depth perception from two eyes set next to each other allowing their visual fields to overlap.

bioarchaeology The archaeological study of human remains emphasizing the preservation of cultural and social processes in the skeleton.

biocultural Focusing on the interaction of biology and culture.

bipedalism A special form of locomotion on two feet found in humans and their ancestors.

brachiation Using the arms to move from branch to branch, with the body hanging suspended beneath the arms.

bride-price Compensation the groom or his family pays to the bride's family upon marriage. Also called bride wealth.

bride service A designated period of time after marriage when the groom works for the bride's family.

Bronze Age In the Old World, the period marked by the production of tools and ornaments of bronze; began about 5,000 years ago in China and Southwest

Asia and about 500 years earlier in Southeast Asia.

cargo cults Spiritual movements (especially noted in Melanesia) in reaction to disruptive contact with Western capitalism, promising resurrection of deceased relatives, destruction or enslavement of white foreigners, and the magical arrival of utopian riches.

carrying capacity The number of people that the available resources can support at a given level of food-getting techniques.

caste A closed social class in which membership is determined by birth and fixed for life.

chiefdom A regional polity in which two or more local groups are organized under a single chief, who is at the head of a ranked hierarchy of people.

chromosomes In the cell nucleus, the structures visible during cellular division containing long strands of DNA combined with a protein.

civilization In anthropology, a type of society marked by the presence of cities, social classes, and the state.

cladogenesis Speciation through a branching mechanism whereby an ancestral population gives rise to two or more descendant populations.

clan An extended unilineal kinship group, often consisting of several lineages, whose members claim common descent from a remote ancestor, usually legendary or mythological.

clines Gradual changes in the frequency of an allele or trait over space.

common-interest associations Associations that result from an act of joining based on sharing particular activities, objectives, values, or beliefs.

community A unit of primate social organization composed of fifty or more individuals who inhabit a large geographical area together.

conjugal family A family established through marriage.

conspicuous consumption The display of wealth for social prestige.

contagious magic Magic based on the principle that things once in contact can influence each other after the contact is broken.

continental drift According to the theory of plate tectonics, the movement of continents embedded in underlying plates on the earth's surface in relation to one another over the history of life on earth.

convergent evolution In cultural evolution, the development of similar cultural adaptations to similar environmental conditions by different peoples with different ancestral cultures.

coprolites Preserved fecal material providing evidence of the diet and health of past organisms.

core values Those values especially promoted by a particular culture.

core vocabularies The most basic and long-lasting words in any language—pronouns, lower numerals, and names for body parts and natural objects.

cross cousin Child of a mother's brother or a father's sister.

cultural adaptation A complex of ideas, activities, and technologies that enable people to survive and even thrive.

cultural anthropology Also known as social or sociocultural anthropology. The study of customary patterns in human behavior, thought, and feelings. It focuses on humans as culture-producing and culture-reproducing creatures.

cultural control Control through beliefs and values deeply internalized in the minds of individuals.

cultural ecology The dynamic interaction of specific cultures with their environments.

cultural evolution Culture change over time (not to be confused with progress).

cultural loss The abandonment of an existing practice or trait.

cultural relativism The thesis that one must suspend judgment of other people's practices in order to understand them in their own cultural terms.

cultural resource management A branch of archaeology that is concerned with survey and/or excavation of archaeological and historical remains threatened by construction or development and policy surrounding protection of cultural resources.

culture A society's shared and socially transmitted ideas, values, and perceptions, which are used to make sense of experience and generate behavior and are reflected in that behavior.

culture-bound Theories about the world and reality based on the assumptions and values of one's own culture

datum point The starting, or reference, point for a grid system.

dependence training Child-rearing practices that foster compliance in the performance of assigned tasks and dependence on the domestic group, rather than reliance on oneself.

descent group Any kinship group with a membership lineally descending from a real historical or fictional common ancestor.

dialects Varying forms of a language that reflect particular regions, occupations, or social classes and that are similar enough to be mutually intelligible.

diffusion The spread of certain ideas, customs, or practices from one culture to another.

diurnal Active during the day and at rest at night.

DNA Deoxyribonucleic acid. The genetic material consisting of a complex molecule whose base structure directs the synthesis of proteins.

domestication An evolutionary process whereby humans modify, either intentionally or unintentionally, the genetic makeup of a population of plants or animals, sometimes to the extent that members of the population are unable to survive and/or reproduce without human assistance.

dominance The ability of one allele for a trait to mask the presence of another allele.

dominance hierarchies An observed ranking system in primate societies ordering individuals from high (alpha) to low standing corresponding to predictable behavioral interactions including domination.

dowry Payment of a woman's inheritance at the time of her marriage, either to her or to her husband.

economic system An organizational arrangement for producing, distributing, and consuming goods.

ecosystem A system, or a functioning whole, composed of both the natural environment and all the organisms living within it.

egalitarian societies Societies in which everyone has about equal rank, access to, and power over basic resources.

empirical Based on observations of the world rather than on intuition or faith.

enculturation The process by which a society's culture is transmitted from one generation to the next and individuals become members of their society.

endocast A cast of the inside of a skull; helps determine the size and shape of the brain.

endogamy Marriage within a particular group or category of individuals.

Eskimo system Kinship reckoning in which the nuclear family is emphasized by specifically identifying the mother, father, brother, and sister, while lumping together all other relatives into broad categories such as uncle, aunt, and cousin. Also referred to as lineal system.

ethnic group People who collectively and publicly identify themselves as a distinct group based on various cultural features such as shared ancestry and common origin, language, customs, and traditional beliefs.

ethnicity This term, rooted in the Greek word *ethnikos* ("nation") and related to *ethnos* ("custom") is the expression of the set of cultural ideas held by an ethnic group.

ethnic psychoses Mental disorders specific to particular ethnic groups.

ethnocentrism The belief that the ways of one's own culture are the only proper ones.

ethnocide The violent eradication of an ethnic group's collective identity as a distinctive nation.

ethnography A detailed description of a particular culture primarily based on fieldwork.

ethnolinguistics A branch of linguistics that studies the relationships between language and culture and how they mutually influence and inform each other.

ethnology The study and analysis of different cultures from a comparative or historical point of view, utilizing ethnographic accounts and developing anthropological theories that help explain why certain important differences or similarities occur among groups.

ethnomusicology The study of a society's music in terms of its cultural setting.

evolution Changes in allele frequencies in populations. Also known as microevolution.

exogamy Marriage outside the group.

extended family Several closely related nuclear families clustered together into a large domestic group.

family Two or more people related by blood, marriage, or adoption. The family may take many forms, ranging from a single parent with one or more children, to a married couple or polygamous.

spouses with offspring, to several generations of parents and their children.

fieldwork The term anthropologists use for on-location research.

fission The splitting of a descent group into two or more new descent groups.

flotation An archeological technique employed to recover very tiny objects by immersion of soil samples in water to separate heavy from light particles.

food foraging Hunting, fishing, and gathering wild plant foods.

forensic anthropology Subfield of applied physical anthropology that specializes in the identification of human skeletal remains for legal purposes.

fossil The preserved remains of plants and animals that lived in the past.

founder effects A particular form of genetic drift deriving from a small founding population not possessing all the alleles present in the original population.

gender The cultural elaborations and meanings assigned to the biological differentiation between the sexes.

gendered speech Distinct male and female speech patterns, which vary across social and cultural settings.

gene flow The introduction of alleles from the gene pool of one population into that of another.

gene pool All the genetic variants possessed by members of a population.

generalized reciprocity A mode of exchange in which the value of the gift is not calculated, nor is the time of repayment specified.

genes Portions of DNA molecules that direct the synthesis of specific proteins.

genetic drift Chance fluctuations of allele frequencies in the gene pool of a population.

genocide The extermination of one people by another, often in the name of progress, either as a deliberate act or as the accidental outcome of activities carried out by one people with little regard for their impact on others.

genome The complete structure sequence of DNA for a species.

genotype The alleles possessed for a particular trait.

genus, genera (pl.) In the system of plant and animal classification, a group of like species.

gesture Facial expressions and bodily postures and motions that convey intended as well as subconscious messages.

globalization Worldwide interconnectedness, evidenced in global movements of natural resources, trade goods, human labor, finance capital, information, and infectious diseases.

glottochronology In linguistics, a method for identifying the approximate time that languages branched off from a common ancestor. It is based on analyzing core vocabularies.

gracile australopithecines Members of the genus *Australopithecus* possessing a more lightly built chewing apparatus; likely had a diet that included more meat than that of the robust australopithecines.

grammar The entire formal structure of a language, including morphology and syntax.

grave goods Items such as utensils, figurines, and personal possessions, symbolically placed in the grave for the deceased person's use in the afterlife.

grid system A system for recording data in three dimensions from an archaeological excavation.

grooming The ritual cleaning of another animal's coat to remove parasites and other matter.

group marriage Marriage in which several men and women have sexual access to one another. Also called co-marriage.

hard power Coercive power that is backed up by economic and military force.

Hawaiian system Kinship reckoning in which all relatives of the same sex and generation are referred to by the same term.

hemoglobin The protein that carries oxygen in the red blood cells.

heterozygous Refers to a chromosome pair that bears different alleles for a single gene.

holistic perspective A fundamental principle of anthropology, that the various parts of human culture and biology must be viewed in the broadest possible context in order to understand their interconnections and interdependence.

Homo erectus "Upright man." A species within the genus *Homo* first appearing just after 2 million years ago in Africa and ultimately spreading throughout the Old World.

Homo habilis "Handy man." The first fossil members of the genus *Homo* appearing 2.5 million years ago, with larger brains and smaller faces than australopithecines.

homologies In biology, structures possessed by two different organisms that arise in similar fashion and pass through similar stages during embryonic development though they may possess different functions.

homozygous Refers to a chromosome pair that bears identical alleles for a single gene.

horticulture Cultivation of crops carried out with simple hand tools such as digging sticks or hoes.

household The basic residential unit where economic production, consumption, inheritance, child rearing, and shelter are organized and carried out.

hydraulic theory The theory that explains civilization's emergence as the result of the construction of elaborate irrigation systems, the functioning of which required full-time managers whose control blossomed into the first governing body and elite social class.

hypothesis A tentative explanation of the relation between certain phenomena.

imitative magic Magic based on the principle that like produces like; sometimes called sympathetic magic.

incest taboo The prohibition of sexual relations between specified individuals, usually parent and child and sibling relations at a minimum.

incorporation In rites of passage, reincorporation of the individual into society in his or her new status.

independence training Child-rearing practices that promote independence, self-reliance, and personal achievement on the part of the child.

informal economy Network of producing and circulating marketable commodities, labor, and services that for various reasons escape government control.

infrastructure The economic foundation of a society, including its subsistence practices, and the tools and other material equipment used to make a living.

intersexuals People born with reproductive organs, genitalia, and/or sex chromosomes that are not exclusively male or female.

Iroquois system Kinship reckoning in which a father and father's brother are referred to by a single term, as are a mother and mother's sister, but a father's sister and mother's brother are given separate terms. Parallel cousins are classified with brothers and sisters, while cross cousins are classified separately but not equated with relatives of some other generation.

kindred An individual's genetically close relatives on the maternal and paternal sides of his or her family.

kinesics A system of notating and analyzing postures, facial expressions, and body motions that convey messages.

kinship A network of relatives within which individuals possess certain mutual rights and obligations.

Kula ring A form of balanced reciprocity that reinforces social relations among the seafaring Trobriand people who inhabit a large ring of islands in the southern Pacific off the eastern coast of Papua New Guinea, and other Melanesians.

lactase An enzyme in the small intestine that enables humans to assimilate lactose.

lactose A sugar that is the primary constituent of fresh milk.

language A system of communication using sounds or gestures that are put together in meaningful ways according to a set of rules.

language family A group of languages descended from a single ancestral language.

law Formal rules of conduct that, when violated, effectuate negative sanctions.

law of independent assortment The Mendelian principle that genes controlling different traits are inherited independently of one another.

law of segregation The Mendelian principle that variants of genes for a particular trait retain their separate identities through the generations.

legend A story about a memorable event or figure handed down by tradition and told as true but without historical evidence.

legitimacy The right of political leaders to govern—to hold, use, and allocate power—based on the values a particular society holds.

leveling mechanism A cultural obligation compelling prosperous members of a community to give away goods, host public feasts, provide free service, or otherwise demonstrate generosity so that no one permanently accumulates significantly more wealth than anyone else.

lineage A unilineal kinship group descended from a known ancestor or founder, who commonly lived about five generations ago, and in which relationships between each member can be exactly stated in genealogical terms.

linguistic anthropology The study of human languages.

linguistic determinism The idea that language to some extent shapes the way in which we view and think about the world around us; sometimes called the Sapir-Whorf hypothesis after its originators Edward Sapir and his student Benjamin Lee Whorf.

linguistic divergence The development of different languages from a single ancestral language.

linguistic nationalism The attempt by ethnic minorities and even countries to proclaim independence by purging their language of foreign terms.

linguistic relativity The idea that distinctions encoded in one language are unique to that language alone.

linguistics The modern scientific study of all aspects of language.

Lower Paleolithic Old Stone Age beginning with the earliest Oldowan tools spanning from about 2.6 million to 250,000 or 200,000 years ago.

macroevolution Evolution above the species level.

mammals The class of vertebrate animals distinguished by bodies covered with fur, self-regulating temperature, and in females milk-producing mammary glands.

market exchange The buying and selling of goods and services, with prices set by rules of supply and demand.

marriage A culturally sanctioned union between two or more people that establishes certain rights and obligations between the people, between them and their children, and between them and their in-laws. Such marriage rights and obligations most often include, but are not limited to, sex, labor, property, child rearing, exchange, and status.

material culture The durable aspects of culture such as tools, structures, and art.

matrilineal descent Descent traced exclusively through the female line to establish group membership.

matrilocal residence A residence pattern in which a married couple lives in the locality associated with the wife's parents.

mediation Settlement of a dispute through negotiation assisted by an unbiased third party.

medical anthropology A specialization in anthropology that brings theoretical and applied approaches from cultural and biological anthropology to the study of human health and disease.

meiosis A kind of cell division that produces the sex cells, each of which has half the number of chromosomes found in other cells of the organism.

Mesoamerica The region encompassing southern Mexico and northern Central America.

Mesolithic The Middle Stone Age of Europe, Asia, and Africa beginning about 12,000 years ago.

microlith A small blade of flint or similar stone, several of which were hafted together in wooden handles to make tools; widespread in the Mesolithic.

middens A refuse or garbage disposal area in an archaeological site.

mitosis A kind of cell division that produces new cells having exactly the same number of chromosome pairs, and hence copies of genes, as the parent cell.

modal personality The body of character traits that occur with the highest frequency in a culturally bounded population.

modernization The process of political and socioeconomic change, whereby developing societies acquire some of the cultural characteristics of Western industrial societies.

moiety Each group that results from a division of a society into two halves on the basis of descent.

molecular anthropology A branch of biological anthropology that uses genetic and biochemical techniques to test hypotheses about human evolution, adaptation, and variation.

money Anything used to make payments for other things (goods or labor) as well as to measure their value; may be special purpose or multipurpose.

monogamy Marriage in which both partners have just one spouse.

morphemes The smallest units of sound that carry a meaning in language. They are distinct from phonemes, which can alter meaning, but have no meaning by themselves.

morphology The study of the patterns or rules of word formation in a language (including such things as rules concerning verb tense, pluralization, and compound words).

Mousterian The tool industry of the Neandertals and their contemporaries of Europe, Southwest Asia, and northern Africa from 125,000 to 40,000 years ago.

multiculturalism Public policy for managing cultural diversity in a multi-ethnic society, officially stressing mutual respect and tolerance for cultural differences within a country's borders.

multiregional hypothesis The hypothesis that modern humans originated through a process of simultaneous local transition from *Homo erectus* to *Homo sapiens* throughout the inhabited world.

mutation Chance alteration of genetic material that produces new variation.

myth A sacred narrative that explains the fundamentals of human existence—where we and everything in our world came from, why we are here, and where we are going.

naming ceremony A special event or ritual to mark the naming of a child.

nation A people who share a collective identity based on a common culture, language, territorial base, and history.

Natufian culture A Mesolithic culture living in the lands that are now Israel, Lebanon, and western Syria, between about 12,500 and 10,200 years ago.

natural selection The evolutionary process through which factors in the environment exert pressure, favoring some individuals over others to produce the next generation.

Neandertals A distinct group within the genus *Homo* inhabiting Europe and Southwest Asia from approximately 125,000 to 30,000 years ago.

negative reciprocity A form of exchange in which the aim is to get something for as little as possible. Neither fair nor balanced, it may involve hard bargaining, manipulation, outright cheating, and even theft.

negotiation The use of direct argument and compromise by the parties to a dispute to arrive voluntarily at a mutually satisfactory agreement.

Neolithic The New Stone Age; prehistoric period beginning about 10,000 years ago in which peoples possessed stone-based technologies and depended on domesticated crops and/or animals.

Neolithic revolution Domestication of plants and animals by peoples with stone-based technologies, beginning about 10,000 years ago and leading to radical transformations in cultural systems.

neolocal residence A pattern in which a married couple establish their household in a location apart from either the husband's or the wife's relatives.

nocturnal Active at night and at rest during the day.

nuclear family A group consisting of one or more parents and dependent offspring, which may include a stepparent, stepsiblings, and adopted children. (Until recently this term referred only to the father/mother/children unit.)

Oldowan The first stone tool industry, beginning between 2.6 and 2.5 million years ago.

opposable Able to bring the thumb or big toe in contact with the tips of the other digits on the same hand or foot in order to grasp objects.

ovulation Moment when an egg released from the ovaries into the womb is receptive for fertilization.

paleoanthropology The study of the origins and predecessors of the present human species.

pantheon The several gods and goddesses of a people.

paralanguage Voice effects that accompany language and convey meaning. These include vocalizations such as giggling, groaning, or sighing, as well as voice qualities such as pitch and tempo.

parallel cousin Child of a father's brother or a mother's sister.

parallel evolution In cultural evolution, the development of similar cultural adaptations to similar environmental conditions by peoples whose ancestral cultures were already somewhat alike.

participant observation In ethnography, the technique of learning a people's culture through social participation and personal observation within the community being studied, as well as interviews and discussion with individual members of the group over an extended period of time.

pastoralism Breeding and managing migratory herds of domesticated grazing animals, such as goats, sheep, cattle, llamas, or camels.

patrilineal descent Descent traced exclusively through the male line to establish group membership.

patrilocal residence A residence pattern in which a married couple lives in the locality associated with the husband's father's relatives.

personality The distinctive way a person thinks, feels, and behaves.

phenotype The observable or testable appearance of an organism that may or may not reflect a particular genotype due to the variable expression of dominant and recessive alleles.

phonemes The smallest units of sound that make a difference in meaning in a language.

phonetics The systematic identification and description of distinctive speech sounds in a language.

phonology The study of language sounds.

phratry A unilineal descent group composed of at least two clans that supposedly share a common ancestry, whether or not they really do.

physical anthropology Also known as biological anthropology. The systematic study of humans as biological organisms.

pluralistic society A society in which two or more ethnic groups or nationalities are politically organized into one territorial state but maintain their cultural differences.

political organization The way power is distributed and embedded in society; the means through which a society creates and maintains social order and reduces social disorder.

polyandry Marriage of a woman to two or more men at one time; a form of polygamy.

polygamy One individual having multiple spouses at the same time; from the Greek word *poly* ("many") and *gamous* ("marriage").

polygenetic inheritance When two or more genes contribute to the phenotypic expression of a single character.

polygyny Marriage of a man to two or more women at the same time; a form of polygamy.

polymerase chain reaction (PCR) A technique for amplifying or creating multiple copies of fragments of DNA so that it can be studied in the laboratory.

polytheism Belief in several gods and/or goddesses (as contrasted with monotheism—belief in one god or goddess).

population In biology, a group of similar individuals that can and do interbreed.

potlatch On the northwest coast of North America, a ceremonial event in which a village chief publicly gives away stockpiled food and other goods that signify wealth.

power The ability of individuals or groups to impose their will upon others and make them do things even against their own wants or wishes.

prehensile Having the ability to grasp.

prehistory A conventional term used to refer to the period of time before the appearance of written records. Does not deny the existence of history, merely of *written* history.

prestige economy Creation of a surplus for the express purpose of gaining prestige through a public display of wealth that is given away as gifts.

priest or priestess A full-time religious specialist formally recognized for his or her role in guiding the religious practices of others and for contacting and influencing supernatural powers.

primary innovation The creation, invention, or chance discovery of a completely new idea, method, or device.

primates The group of mammals that includes lemurs, lorises, tarsiers, monkeys, apes, and humans.

primatology The study of living and fossil primates.

progress The ethnocentric notion that humans are moving forward to a higher, more advanced stage in their development toward perfection.

prosimians A subdivision within the primate order that includes lemurs, lorises, and tarsiers.

proxemics The cross-cultural study of humankind's perception and use of space.

punctuated equilibria A model of macroevolutionary change that suggests evolution occurs via long periods of stability or stasis punctuated by periods of rapid change.

race In biology, the taxonomic category of subspecies that is not applicable to humans because the division of humans into discrete types does not represent the true nature of human biological variation. In some societies race is an important social category.

racism A doctrine of superiority by which one group justifies the dehumanization of others based on their distinctive physical characteristics.

rebellion Organized armed resistance to an established government or authority in power.

recent African origins hypothesis The hypothesis that all modern people are derived from one single population of archaic *H. sapiens* from Africa who migrated out of Africa after 100,000 years ago, replacing all other archaic forms due to their superior cultural capabilities. Also called the Eve or out of Africa hypothesis.

recessive An allele for a trait whose expression is masked by the presence of a dominant allele.

reciprocity The exchange of goods and services, of approximately equal value, between two parties.

redistribution A form of exchange in which goods flow into a central place, where they are sorted, counted, and reallocated.

relative dating In archaeology and paleoanthropology, designating an event, object, or fossil as being older or younger than another.

religion An organized system of ideas about the spiritual sphere or the supernatural, along with associated ceremonial practices by which people try to interpret and/or influence aspects of the universe otherwise beyond their control.

revitalization movements Movements for radical cultural reform in response to widespread social disruption and collective feelings of anxiety and despair.

revolution Radical change in a society or culture. In the political arena, it involves the forced overthrow of an old government and establishment of a completely new one.

rites of passage Rituals that mark important stages in an individual's life cycle, such as birth, marriage, and death.

robust australopithecines Several species within the genus *Australopithecus*, who lived from 2.5 and 1.1 million years ago in eastern and southern Africa; known for the rugged nature of their chewing apparatus (large back teeth, large chewing muscles, and a bony ridge on their skull tops for the insertion of these large muscles).

sanctions Externalized social controls designed to encourage conformity to social norms.

secondary innovation A new and deliberate application or modification of an existing idea, method, or device.

self-awareness The ability to identify oneself as an individual, to reflect on oneself, and to evaluate oneself.

separation In rites of passage, the ritual removal of the individual from society.

serial monogamy A marriage form in which a man or a woman marries or lives with a series of partners in succession.

shaman A person who enters an altered state of consciousness—at will—to contact and utilize an ordinarily hidden reality in order to acquire knowledge, power, and to help others.

sickle-cell anemia An inherited form of anemia caused by a mutation in the hemoglobin protein that causes the red blood cells to assume a sickle shape.

signals Instinctive sounds or gestures that have a natural or self-evident meaning.

social class A category of individuals who enjoy equal or nearly equal prestige according to the system of evaluation.

social control External control through open coercion.

social structure The rule-governed relationships—with all their rights and obligations—that hold members of a society together. This includes households, families, associations, and power relations, including politics.

society An organized group or groups of interdependent people who generally share a common territory, language, and culture and who act together for collective survival and well-being.

sociolinguistics The study of the relationship between language and society through examining how social categories influence the use and interpretation of distinctive styles of speech.

soft power Pressing others through attraction and persuasion to change their ideas, beliefs, values, and behaviors.

soil marks Stains that show up on the surface of recently plowed fields that reveal an archaeological site.

speciation The process of forming new species.

species The smallest working unit in the system of classification. Among living organisms, species are populations or groups of populations capable of interbreeding and producing fertile viable offspring.

spirituality Concern with the sacred, as distinguished from material matters. In contrast to religion, spirituality is often individual rather than collective and does not require a distinctive format or traditional organization.

state In anthropology, a centralized political system that has the capacity and authority to make laws and use force to maintain social order.

stereoscopic vision Complete three-dimensional vision (or depth perception) from binocular vision and nerve connections that run from each eye to both sides of the brain allowing nerve cells to integrate the images derived from each eye.

stratified Layered; said of archaeological sites where the remains lie in layers, one upon another.

stratified societies Societies in which people are hierarchically divided and ranked into social strata, or layers, and do not share equally in basic resources that support survival, influence, and prestige.

structural power Power that organizes and orchestrates the systemic interaction within and among societies, directing economic and political forces on the one hand and ideological forces that shape public ideas, values, and beliefs on the other.

structural violence Physical and/or psychological harm (including repression, environmental destruction, poverty, hunger, illness, and premature death) caused by impersonal, exploitative, and unjust social, political, and economic systems.

subculture A distinctive set of standards and behavior patterns by which a group within a larger society operates.

superstructure A society's shared sense of identity and worldview. The collective body of ideas, beliefs, and values by which a group of people makes sense of the world—its shape, challenges, and opportunities—and their place in it. This includes religion and national ideology.

swidden farming Also known as slash-and-burn. An extensive form of horticulture in which the natural vegetation is cut, the slash is subsequently burned, and crops are then planted among the ashes.

symbols Signs, sounds, gestures, and other things that are arbitrarily linked to something else and represent it in a meaningful way.

syncretism In acculturation, the blending of indigenous and foreign traits to form a new system.

syntax The patterns or rules for the formation of phrases and sentences in a language.

taxonomy The science of classification.

technology Tools and other material equipment, together with the knowledge of how to make and use them.

theory In science, an explanation of natural phenomena, supported by a reliable body of data.

thrifty genotype Human genotype that permits efficient storage of fat to draw on in times of food shortage and conservation of glucose and nitrogen.

tonality In music, scale systems and their modifications.

tonal language A language in which the sound pitch of a spoken word is an essential part of its pronunciation and meaning.

tool An object used to facilitate some task or activity.

totemism The belief that people are related to particular animals, plants, or natural objects by virtue of descent from common ancestral spirits.

tradition Customary ideas and practices passed on from generation to generation, which in a modernizing society may form an obstacle to new ways of doing things.

transgenders People who cross over or occupy a culturally accepted intermediate position in the binary male–female gender construction.

transhumance A subsistence strategy in which people move their grazing animals from winter pastures in low steppe lands to summer pastures on high plateaus.

transition In rites of passage, isolation of the individual following separation and prior to incorporation into society.

tribe In anthropology, refers to a range of kin-ordered groups that are politically integrated by some unifying factor and whose members share a common ancestry, identity, culture, language, and territory.

unilineal descent Descent that establishes group membership exclusively through either the male or female line.

Upper Paleolithic The last part (40,000 to10,000 years ago) of the Old Stone Age, featuring tool industries characterized by long slim blades and an explosion of creative symbolic forms.

vegeculture The cultivation of domesticated root crops, such as yams and taro.

witchcraft An explanation of events based on the belief that certain individuals possess an innate psychic power capable of causing harm, including sickness and death.

worldview The collective body of ideas that members of a culture generally share concerning the ultimate shape and substance of their reality.

writing system A set of visible or tactile signs used to represent units of language in a systematic way.

Bibliography

Abbot, E. (2001). *A history of celibacy*. Cambridge, MA: Da Capo Press.

Aberle, D. F., Bronfenbrenner, U., Hess, E. H., Miller, D. R., Schneider, D. H., & Spuhler, J. N. (1963). The incest taboo and the mating patterns of animals. *American Anthropologist, 65,* 253–265.

Abu-Lughod, L. (1986). *Veiled sentiments: Honor and poetry in a Bedouin society*. Berkeley: University of California Press.

Adams, R. E. W. (1977). *Prehistoric Mesoamerica*. Boston: Little, Brown.

Adams, R. M. (1966). *The evolution of urban society*. Chicago: Aldine.

Adams, R. M. (2001). Scale and complexity in archaic states. *Latin American Antiquity, 11,* 188.

Adbusters. *www.adbusters.org*. Accessed January 2003.

AIDS Monthly Surveillance Summary (through July 1997). (1997). San Francisco.

Al-Issa, I., & Dennis, W. (Eds.). (1970). *Cross cultural studies of behavior*. New York: Holt, Rinehart and Winston.

Alland, A., Jr. (1970). *Adaptation in cultural evolution: An approach to medical anthropology*. New York: Columbia University Press.

Alland, A., Jr. (1971). *Human diversity*. New York: Columbia University Press.

Allen, J. L., & Shalinsky, A. C. (2004). *Student atlas of anthropology*. New York: McGraw-Hill.

Allen, J. S., & Cheer, S. M. (1996). The non-thrifty genotype. *Current Anthropology, 37,* 831–842.

Alvard, M. S., & Kuznar, L. (2001). Deferred harvest: The transition from hunting to animal husbandry. *American Anthropologist, 103*(2), 295–311.

Amábile-Cuevas, C. F., & Chicurel, M. E. (1993). Horizontal gene transfer. *American Scientist, 81,* 332–341.

Ambrose, S. H. (2001). Paleolithic technology and human evolution. *Science, 291,* 1,748–1,753.

American Anthropological Association. (1998). Statement on "race." www.aaanet.org/stmts/racepp.htmstmts.

Amiran, R. (1965). The beginnings of pottery-making in the Near East. In F. R. Matson (Ed.), *Ceramics and man* (pp. 240–247). Viking Fund Publications, In *Anthropology*, No. 41.

Andrews, L. B., & Nelkin, D. (1996). The bell curve: A statement. *Science, 271,* 13.

Appadurai, A. (1996). *Modernity at large: Cultural dimensions of globalization*. Minneapolis: University of Minnesota Press.

Appenzeller, T. (1998). Art: Evolution or revolution? *Science, 282,* 1,451–1,454.

Armstrong, D. F., Stokoe, W. C., & Wilcox, S. E. (1993). Signs of the origin of syntax. *Current Anthropology, 34,* 349–368.

Ashmore, W. (Ed.). (1981). *Lowland Maya settlement patterns*. Albuquerque: University of New Mexico Press.

Aureli, F., & de Waal, F. B. M. (2000). *Natural conflict resolution*. Berkeley: University of California Press.

Avedon, J. F. (1997). *In exile from the land of snows: The definitive account of the Dalai Lama and Tibet since the Chinese conquest*. New York: Harper.

Bailey, R. C., & Aunger, R. (1989). Net hunters vs. archers: Variation in women's subsistence strategies in the Ituri Forest. *Human Ecology, 17,* 273–297.

Balandier, G. (1971). *Political anthropology*. New York: Pantheon.

Balikci, A. (1970). *The Netsilik Eskimo*. Garden City, NY: Natural History Press.

Balter, M. (1998). On world AIDS day, a shadow looms over southern Africa. *Science, 282,* 1,790.

Balter, M. (1998). Why settle down? The mystery of communities. *Science, 282,* 1,442–1,444;

Balter, M. (1999). A long season puts Çatalhöyük in context. *Science, 286,* 890–891.

Balter, M. (2001). Did plaster hold Neolithic society together? *Science, 294,* 2,278–2,281.

Balter, M. (2001). In search of the first Europeans. *Science, 291,* 1,724.

Banton, M. (1968). Voluntary association: Anthropological aspects. In *International encyclopedia of the social sciences* (Vol. 16, pp. 357–362). New York: Macmillan.

Barber, B. (1957). *Social stratification*. New York: Harcourt.

Barham, L. S. (1998). Possible early pigment use in South-Central Africa. *Current Anthropology, 39,* 703–710.

Barnard, A. (1995). Monboddo's *Orang Outang* and the definition of man. In R. Corbey & B. Theunissen (Eds.), *Ape, man, apeman: Changing views since 1600* (pp. 71–85). Leiden: Department of Prehistory, Leiden University.

Barnett, H. (1953). *Innovation: The basis of cultural change*. New York: McGraw-Hill.

Barnouw, V. (1985). *Culture and personality* (4th ed.). Homewood, IL: Dorsey Press.

Barr, R. G. (1997, October). The crying game. *Natural History*, 47.

Barth, F. (1961). *Nomads of South Persia: The Basseri tribe of the Khamseh confederacy*. Boston: Little, Brown (series in anthropology).

Barth, F. (1962). Nomadism in the mountain and plateau areas of South West Asia. *The problems of the arid zone* (pp. 341–355). Paris: UNESCO.

Bar-Yosef, O. (1986), The walls of Jericho: An alternative interpretation. *Current Anthropology, 27,* 160.

Bar-Yosef, O., Vandermeesch, B., Arensburg, B., Belfer-Cohen, A., Goldberg, P., Laville, H., Meignen, L., Rak, Y., Speth, J. D., Tchernov, E., Tillier, A-M., & Weiner, S. (1992). The excavations in Kebara Cave, Mt. Carmel. *Current Anthropology, 33,* 497–550.

Bascom, W. (1969). *The Yoruba of southwestern Nigeria*. New York: Holt, Rinehart and Winston.

Bates, D. G. (2001). *Human adaptive strategies: Ecology, culture, and politics* (2nd ed.). Boston: Allyn & Bacon.

Bates, D. G., & Plog, F. (1991). *Human adaptive strategies*. New York: McGraw-Hill.

Beals, A. R. (1972). Gopalpur: *A South Indian village*. New York: Holt, Rinehart and Winston.

Beattie, J. (1964). *Other cultures: Aims, methods and achievements*. New York: Free Press.

Becker, J. (2004, March). *National Geographic, 90.*

Bednarik, R. G. (1995). Concept-mediated marking in the Lower Paleolithic. *Current Anthropology, 36,* 606.

Behrensmeyer, A. K., Todd, N. E., Potts, R., & McBrinn, G. E. (1997). Late Pliocene faunal turnover in the Turkana basin, Kenya, and Ethiopia. *Science, 278,* 1,589–1,594.

Beidelman, T. O. (Ed.). (1971). *The transition of culture: Essays to E. E. Evans-Pritchard.* London: Tavistock.

Bell, D. (1997). Defining marriage and legitimacy. *Current Anthropology, 38,* 241.

Belshaw, C. S. (1958). The significance of modern cults in Melanesian development. In W. Lessa & E. Z. Vogt (Eds.), *Reader in comparative religion: An anthropological approach.* New York: Harper & Row.

Benedict, R. (1959). *Patterns of culture.* New York: New American Library.

Bennett, J. W. (1964). Myth, theory, and value in cultural anthropology. In E. W. Caint & G. T. Bowles (Eds.), *Fact and theory in social science.* Syracuse, NY: Syracuse University Press.

Berdan, F. F. (1982). *The Aztecs of Central Mexico.* New York: Holt, Rinehart and Winston.

Bermúdez de Castro, J. M., Arsuaga, J. L., Cabonell, E., Rosas, A., Martinez, I., & Mosquera, M. (1997). A hominid from the lower Pleistocene of Atapuerca, Spain: Possible ancestor to Neandertals and modern humans. *Science, 276,* 1,392–1,395.

Bernal, I. (1969). *The Olmec world.* Berkeley: University of California Press.

Bernard, H. R. (2002). *Research methods in anthropology: Qualitative and quantitative approaches* (3rd ed.). Walnut Creek, CA: Altamira Press.

Bernard, H. R., & Sibley, W. E. (1975). *Anthropology and jobs.* Washington, DC: American Anthropological Association.

Bernardi, B. (1985) *Age class systems: Social institutions and policies based on age.* New York: Cambridge University Press.

Berra, T. M. (1990). *Evolution and the myth of creationism.* Stanford, CA: Stanford University Press.

Berreman, G. D. (1968). Caste: The concept of caste. *International Encyclopedia of the Social Sciences* (Vol. 2, pp. 333–338). New York: Macmillan.

Bicchieri, M. G. (Ed.). (1972). *Hunters and gatherers today: A socioeconomic study of eleven such cultures in the twentieth century.* New York: Holt, Rinehart and Winston.

Binford, L. R. (1972). *An archaeological perspective.* New York: Seminar Press.

Binford, L. R., & Chuan, K. H. (1985). Taphonomy at a distance: Zhoukoudian, the cave home of Beijing man? *Current Anthropology, 26,* 413–442.

Birdsell, J. H. (1977). The recalibration of a paradigm for the first peopling of Greater Australia. In J. Allen, J. Golson, & R. Jones (Eds.), *Sunda and Sahul: Prehistoric studies in Southeast Asia, Melanesia, and Australia* (pp. 113–167). New York: Academic Press.

Blackless, M., et al. (2000). How sexually dimorphic are we? Review and synthesis. *American Journal of Human Biology, 12,* 151–166.

Blakey, M. (2003). *African Burial Ground Project.* Department of Anthropology, College of William & Mary.

Blumberg, R. L. (1991). *Gender, family, and the economy: The triple overlap.* Newbury Park, CA: Sage.

Blumer, M. A., & Byrne, R. (1991). The ecological genetics and domestication and the origins of agriculture. *Current Anthropology, 32,* 30.

Boas, F. (1962). *Primitive art.* Gloucester, MA: Peter Smith.

Boas, F. (1966). *Race, language and culture.* New York: Free Press.

Bodley, J. H. (1985). *Anthropology and contemporary human problems* (2nd ed.). Palo Alto, CA: Mayfield.

Bodley, J. H. (1990). *Victims of progress* (3rd ed.). Mountain View, CA: Mayfield.

Bodley, J. H. (1998). *Victims of progress* (4th ed.). San Francisco: McGraw-Hill.

Bodley, J. H. (2000). *Anthropology and contemporary human problems* (4th ed.). Palo Alto, CA: Mayfield.

Boehm, C. (2000). The evolution of moral communities. *School of American Research, 2000 Annual Report,* 7.

Bohannan, P. (Ed.). (1967). *Law and warfare: Studies in the anthropology of conflict.* Garden City, NY: Natural History Press.

Bohannan, P., & Dalton, G. (Eds.). (1962). *Markets in Africa.* Evanston, IL: Northwestern University Press.

Bohannan, P., & Middleton, J. (Eds.). (1968). *Kinship and social organization.* Garden City, NY: Natural History Press (American Museum Source Books in Anthropology).

Bohannan, P., & Middleton, J. (Eds.). (1968). *Marriage, family, and residence.* Garden City, NY: Natural History Press (American Museum Source Books in Anthropology).

Bolinger, D. (1968). *Aspects of language.* New York: Harcourt.

Bongaarts, J. (1998). Demographic consequences of declining fertility. *Science, 182,* 419.

Bonvillain, N. (2000). *Language, culture, and communication: The meaning of messages* (3rd ed.). Upper Saddle River, NJ: Prentice-Hall.

Bordes, F. (1972). *A tale of two caves.* New York: Harper & Row.

Bornstein, M. H. (1975). The influence of visual perception on culture. *American Anthropologist, 77*(4), 774–798.

Brace, C. L. (1981). Tales of the phylogenetic woods: The evolution and significance of phylogenetic trees. *American Journal of Physical Anthropology, 56,* 411–429.

Brace, C. L. (1997). Cro-Magnons R us? *Anthropology Newsletter, 38*(8), 1, 4.

Brace, C. L. (2000). *Evolution in an anthropological view* (p. 341). Walnut Creek, CA: Altamira.

Brace, C. L., Nelson, H., & Korn, N. (1979). *Atlas of human evolution* (2nd ed.). New York: Holt, Rinehart and Winston.

Bradfield, R. M. (1998). *A natural history of associations* (2nd ed.). New York: International Universities Press.

Bradford, P. V., & Blume, H. (1992). *Ota Benga: The pygmy in the zoo.* New York: St. Martin's Press.

Braidwood, R. J. (1960). The agricultural revolution. *Scientific American, 203,* 130–141.

Braidwood, R. J. (1975). *Prehistoric men* (8th ed.). Glenview, IL: Scott, Foresman.

Brain, C. K. (1968). Who killed the Swartkrans ape-men? *South African Museums Association Bulletin, 9,* 127–139.

Brain, C. K. (1969). The contribution of Namib Desert Hottentots to an understanding of australopithecine bone accumulations. *Scientific Papers of the Namib Desert Research Station,* 13.

Branda, R. F., & Eatoil, J. W. (1978). Skin color and photolysis: An evolutionary hypothesis. *Science, 201,* 625–626.

Brettell, C. B., & Sargent, C. F. (Eds.). (2000). *Gender in cross-cultural perspective* (3rd ed.). Upper Saddle River, NJ: Prentice-Hall.

Brew, J. O. (1968). *One hundred years of anthropology.* Cambridge, MA: Harvard University Press.

Broecker, W. S. (1992, April). Global warming on trial. *Natural History,* 14.

Brothwell, D. R., & Higgs, E. (Eds.). (1969). *Science in archaeology* (Rev. ed.). London: Thames & Hudson.

Brown, B., Walker, A., Ward, C. V., & Leakey, R. E. (1993). New *Australopithecus boisei* calvaria from East Lake Turkana, Kenya. *American Journal of Physical Anthropology, 91,* 137–159.

Brown, D. E. (1991). *Human universals.* New York: McGraw-Hill.

Brown, P., et al. (2004). A new small-bodied hominin from the Late Pleistocene of Flores, Indonesia. *Nature, 431,* 1,055–1,061.

Brues, A. M. (1977). *People and races.* New York: Macmillan.

Brunet, M., et al. (2002). A new hominid from the Upper Miocene of Chad, Central Africa. *Nature, 418,* 145–151.

Burling, R. (1969). Linguistics and ethnographic description. *American Anthropologist, 71,* 817–827.

Burling, R. (1970). *Man's many voices: Language in its cultural context.* New York: Holt, Rinehart and Winston.

Burling, R. (1993). Primate calls, human language, and nonverbal communication. *Current Anthropology, 34,* 25–53.

Butzer, K. (1971). *Environment and anthropology: An ecological approach to prehistory* (2nd ed.). Chicago: Aldine.

Byers, D. S. (Ed.). (1967). *The prehistory of the Tehuacan Valley: Vol. 1. Environment and subsistence.* Austin: University of Texas Press.

Cachel, S. (1997). Dietary shifts and the European Upper Paleolithic transition. *Current Anthropology, 38,* 590.

Calloway, C. (1997). Introduction: Surviving the Dark Ages. In C. G. Calloway (Ed.), *After King Philip's war: Presence and persistence in Indian New England* (pp. 1–28). Hanover, NH: University Press of New England.

Campbell, B. G., & Loy, J. D. (1995). *Humankind emerging* (7th ed.). New York: HarperCollins.

Carmack, R. (1983). Indians and the Guatemalan revolution. *Cultural Survival Quarterly, 7*(3), 52–54.

Carneiro, R. L. (1970). A theory of the origin of the state. *Science, 169,* 733–738.

Caroulis, J. (1996). Food for thought. *Pennsylvania Gazette, 95*(3), 16.

Carpenter, E. (1973). *Eskimo realities.* New York: Holt, Rinehart and Winston.

Carroll, J. B. (Ed.). (1956). *Language, thought and reality: Selected writings of Benjamin Lee Whorf.* Cambridge, MA: MIT Press.

Cartmill, M. (1998). The gift of gab. *Discover 19*(11), 64.

Cashdan, E. (1989). Hunters and gatherers: Economic behavior in bands. In S. Plattner (Ed.), *Economic anthropology* (pp. 21–48). Stanford, CA: Stanford University Press.

Catford, J. C. (1988). *A practical introduction to phonetics.* Oxford, England: Clarendon Press.

Cavalli-Sforza, L. L. (1977). *Elements of human genetics.* Menlo Park, CA: W. A. Benjamin.

Cavallo, J. A. (1990, February). Cat in the human cradle. *Natural History,* 54–60.

Centers for Disease Control. (1997). *Centers for Disease Control Semi-Annual AIDS Report* (through June 1996). Atlanta, GA.

Chagnon, N. A. (1988). *Yanomamo: The fierce people* (3rd ed.). New York: Holt, Rinehart and Winston.

Chagnon, N. A., & Irons, W. (Eds.). (1979). *Evolutionary biology and human social behavior.* North Scituate, MA: Duxbury Press.

Chan, J. W. C., & Vernon, P. E. (1988). Individual differences among the peoples of China. In J. W. Berry (Ed.), *Human abilities in cultural context* (pp. 340–357). Cambridge, England: Cambridge University Press.

Chang, K. C. (Ed.). (1968). *Settlement archaeology.* Palo Alto, CA: National Press.

Chapple, E. D. (1970). *Cultural and biological man: Explorations in behavioral anthropology.* New York: Holt, Rinehart and Winston.

Chase, C. (1998). Hermaphrodites with attitude. *Gay and Lesbian Quarterly, 4*(2), 189–211.

Chatty, D. (1996). *Mobile pastoralists: Development planning and social change in Oman.* New York: Columbia University Press.

Chicurel, M. (2001). Can organisms speed their own evolution? *Science, 292,* 1,824–1,827.

Childe, V. G. (1951). *Man makes himself.* New York: New American Library. (orig.1936).

Childe, V. G. (1954). *What happened in history.* Baltimore: Penguin.

Cigno, A. (1994). *Economics of the family.* New York: Oxford University Press.

Ciochon, R. L., & Fleagle, J. G. (Eds.). (1987). *Primate evolution and human origins.* Hawthorne, NY: Aldine.

Ciochon, R. L., & Fleagle, J. G. (1993). *The human evolution source book.* Englewood Cliffs, NJ: Prentice-Hall.

Clark, E. E. (1966). *Indian legends of the Pacific Northwest.* Berkeley: University of California Press.

Clark, G. (1967). *The Stone Age hunters.* New York: McGraw-Hill.

Clark, G. (1972). *Starr Carr: A case study in bioarchaeology.* Reading, MA: Addison-Wesley.

Clark, G. A. (1997). Neandertal genetics. *Science, 277,* 1,024.

Clark, G. A. (2002). Neandertal archaeology: Implications for our origins. *American Anthropologist, 104*(1), 50–67.

Clark, J. G. D. (1962). *Prehistoric Europe: The economic basis.* Stanford, CA: Stanford University Press.

Clark, W. E. L. (1960). *The antecedents of man.* Chicago: Quadrangle Books.

Clark, W. E. L. (1966). *History of the primates* (5th ed.). Chicago: University of Chicago Press.

Clark, W. E. L. (1967). *Man-apes or ape-men? The story of discoveries in Africa.* New York: Holt, Rinehart and Winston.

Clarke, R. J. (1998). First ever discovery of a well preserved skull and associated skeleton of *Australopithecus. South African Journal of Science, 94,* 460–464.

Clarke, R. J., & Tobias, P. V. (1995). Sterkfontein member 2 foot bones of the oldest South African hominid. *Science, 269,* 521–524.

Clay, J. W. (1987). Genocide in the age of enlightenment. *Cultural Survival Quarterly 12*(3).

Clay, J. W. (1996). What's a nation? In W. A. Haviland & R. J. Gordon (Eds.), *Talking about people* (2nd ed., pp. 188–189). Mountain View, CA: Mayfield.

Clough, S. B., & Cole, C. W. (1952). *Economic history of Europe* (3rd ed.). Lexington, MA: Heath.

Codere, H. (1950). *Fighting with property.* Seattle: University of Washington Press (American Ethnological Society, Monograph 18).

Coe, S. D. (1994). *America's first cuisines.* Austin: University of Texas Press.

Coe, W. R. (1967). *Tikal: A handbook of the ancient Maya ruins.* Philadelphia: University of Pennsylvania Museum.

Coe, W. R., & Haviland, W. A. (1982). *Introduction to the archaeology of Tikal.* Philadelphia: University Museum.

Cohen, J. (1997). Is an old virus up to new tricks? *Science, 277,* 312–313.

Cohen, M. L. (1967). Variations in complexity among Chinese family groups: The impact of modernization. *Transactions of the New York Academy of Sciences, 295,* 638–647.

Cohen, M. N. (1977). *The food crisis in prehistory.* New Haven, CT: Yale University Press.

Cohen, M. N. (1995). Anthropology and race: The bell curve phenomenon. *General Anthropology, 2*(1), 1–4.

Cohen, M. N., & Armelagos, G. J. (1984). *Paleopathology at the origins of agriculture.* Orlando: Academic Press.

Cohen, R., & Middleton, J. (Eds.). (1967). *Comparative political systems.* Garden City, NY: Natural History Press.

Cohen, Y. (1968). *Man in adaptation: The cultural present.* Chicago: Aldine.

Colburn, T., Dumanoski, D., & Myers, J. P. (1996). Hormonal sabotage. *Natural History, 3,* 45–46.

Cole, S. (1975). *Leakey's luck: The life of Louis Seymour Bazett Leakey. 1903–1972.* New York: Harcourt Brace Jovanovich.

Collier, J., Rosaldo, M. Z., & Yanagisako, S. (1982). Is there a family? New anthropological views. In B. Thorne & M. Yalom (Eds.), *Rethinking the family: Some feminist questions* (pp. 25–39). New York: Longman.

Collier, J. F., & Yanagisako, S. J. (Eds.). (1987). *Gender and kinship: Essays toward a unified analysis.* Stanford, CA: Stanford University Press.

Connelly, J. C. (1979). Hopi social organization. In A. Ortiz (Ed.), *Handbook of North American Indians, Vol. 9, Southwest* (pp. 539–553). Washington, DC: Smithsonian Institution.

Conner, M. (1996). The archaeology of contemporary mass graves. *SAA Bulletin, 14*(4), 6, 31.

Conroy, G. C. (1997). *Reconstructing human origins: A modern synthesis* (p. 427). New York: Norton.

Coon, C. S. (1954). *The story of man.* New York: Knopf.

Coon, C. S., Garn, S. N., & Birdsell, J. (1950). *Races: A study of the problems of race formation in man.* Springfield, IL: Charles C Thomas.

Cooper, A., Poinar, H. N., Pääbo, S., Radovci, C. J., Debènath, A., Caparros, M., Barroso-Ruiz, C., Bertranpetit, J., Nielsen-March, C., Hedges, R. E. M., & Sykes, B. (1997). Neanderthal genetics. *Science, 277,* 1,021–1,024.

Coppa, A., et al. (2006). Early Neolithic tradition of dentistry. *Nature, 440,* 755–756.

Coppens, Y., Howell, F. C., Isaac, G. L., & Leakey, R. E. F. (Eds.). (1976). *Earliest man and environments in the Lake Rudolf Basin: Stratigraphy, paleoecology, and evolution.* Chicago: University of Chicago Press.

Corbey, R. (1995). Introduction: Missing links, or the ape's place in nature. In R. Corbey & B. Theunissen (Eds.), *Ape, man, apeman: Changing views since 1600* (p. 1). Leiden: Department of Prehistory, Leiden University.

Cornwell, T. (1995, November 10). Skeleton staff. *Times Higher Education,* p. 20.

Corruccini, R. S. (1992). Metrical reconsideration of the Skhul IV and IX and Border Cave I crania in the context of modern human origins. *American Journal of Physical Anthropology, 87,* 433–445.

Cottrell, L. (1963). *The lost pharaohs.* New York: Grosset & Dunlap.

Courlander, H. (1971). *The fourth world of the Hopis.* New York: Crown.

Court says same-sex marriage is a right. (2004, February 5). *San Francisco Chronicle.*

Cowgill, G. L. (1980). Letter, *Science, 210,* 1,305.

Cowgill, G. L. (1997). State and society at Teotihuacan, Mexico. *Annual Review of Anthropology, 26,* 129–161.

Cox, O. C. (1959). *Caste, class, and race: A study in dynamics.* New York: Monthly Review Press.

Crane, L. B., Yeager, E., & Whitman, R. L. (1981). *An introduction to linguistics.* Boston: Little, Brown.

Cretney, S. (2003). *Family law in the twentieth century: A history.* New York: Oxford University Press.

Crocker, W. A., & Crocker, J. (1994). *The Canela, bonding through kinship, ritual, and sex.* Fort Worth, TX: Harcourt Brace.

Culbert, T. P. (Ed.). (1973). *The Classic Maya collapse.* Albuquerque: University of New Mexico Press.

Culotta, E. (1992). A new take on anthropoid origins, *Science, 256,* 1,516–1,517.

Culotta, E. (1995). Asian hominids grow older. *Science, 270,* 1,116–1,117.

Culotta, E. (1995). New finds rekindle debate over anthropoid origins. *Science, 268,* 1,851.

Culotta, E. (1995). New hominid crowds the field. *Science, 269,* 918.

Culotta, E., & Koshland, D. E., Jr. (1994). DNA repair works its way to the top. *Science, 266,* 1,926.

Cultural Survival Quarterly. (1991), *15*(4), 5.

Cultural Survival Quarterly. (1991). *15*(4), 38.

Current population survey. (2002). U.S. Census Bureau.

Dalton, G. (Ed.). (1967). *Tribal and peasant economics: Readings in economic anthropology.* Garden City, NY: Natural History Press.

Daniel, G. (1970). *The first civilizations: The archaeology of their origins.* New York: Apollo Editions.

Dalton, G. (1971). *Traditional tribal and peasant economics: An introductory survey of economic anthropology.* Reading, MA: Addison-Wesley.

Daniel, G. (1975). *A hundred and fifty years of archaeology.* (2nd ed.) London: Duckworth.

Darwin, C. (1936). *The descent of man and selection in relation to sex.* New York: Random House (Modern Library). (orig. 1871).

Darwin, C. (1967). *On the origin of species.* New York: Atheneum. (orig. 1859). Davenport, W. (1959). Linear descent and descent groups. *American Anthropologist, 61,* 557–573.

Davis, S. H. (1982). *Victims of the miracle.* Cambridge, England: Cambridge University Press.

Death and disorder in Guatemala. (1983).*Cultural Survival Quarterly, 7*(1).

DeBeer, Sir G. R. (1964). *Atlas of evolution.* London: Nelson.

Deetz, J. (1967). *Invitation to archaeology.* New York: Doubleday.

Deevy, E. S., Jr. (1960). The human population. *Scientific American, 203,* 194–204.

de Laguna, F. (1977). *Voyage to Greenland: A personal initiation into anthropology.* New York: Norton.

De Mott, B. (1990). *The imperial middle: Why Americans can't think straight about class.* New York: Morrow.

de Pelliam, A., & Burton, F. D. (1976). More on predatory behavior in non-human primates. *Current Anthropology, 17*(3).

d'Errico, F., Zilhão, J., Julien, M., Baffier, D., & Pelegrin, J. (1998). Neandertal acculturation in Western Europe? *Current Anthropology, 39,* 521.

Dettwyler, K. A. (1994). *Dancing skeletons: Life and death in West Africa.* Prospect Heights, IL: Waveland Press.

Dettwyler, K. A. (1997, October). When to wean. *Natural History,* 49.

Devereux, G. (1963). Institutionalized homosexuality of the Mohave Indians. In H. M. Ruitenbeck (Ed.), *The problem of homosexuality in modern society.* New York: Dutton.

DeVore, I. (Ed.). (1965). *Primate behavior: Field studies of monkeys and apes.* New York: Holt, Rinehart and Winston.

de Waal, A. (1994). Genocide in Rwanda. *Anthropology Today, 10*(3), 1–2.

de Waal, F. (1996). *Good natured: The origins of right and wrong in humans and other animals.* Cambridge, MA: Harvard University Press.

de Waal, F. B. M. (2000). Primates—A natural heritage of conflict resolution. *Science, 28,* 586–590.

de Waal, F. B. M. (2001). *The ape and the sushi master.* New York: Basic Books.

de Waal, F. B. M. (2001). Sing the song of evolution. *Natural History, 110* (8), 77.

de Waal, F. B. M., & Johanowicz, D. L. (1993). Modification of reconciliation behavior through social experience: An experiment with two macaque species. *Child Development, 64,* 897–908.

de Waal, F., Kano, T., & Parish, A. R. (1998). Comments. *Current Anthropology, 39,* 408, 410, 413.

Diamond, J. (1994). How Africa became black. *Discover, 15*(2), 72–81.

Diamond, J. (1994). Race without color. *Discover, 15*(11), 83–89.

Diamond, J. (1997). *Guns, germs, and steel.* New York: Norton.

Diamond, J. (1998). Ants, crops, and history. *Science, 281,* 1,974–1,975.

Dissanayake, E. (2000). Birth of the arts. *Natural History, 109*(10), 89.

Dixon, J. E., Cann, J. R., & Renfrew, C. (1968). Obsidian and the origins of trade, *Scientific American, 218,* 38–46.

Dobyns, H. F., Doughty, P. L., & Lasswell, H. D. (Eds.). (1971). *Peasants, power, and applied social change.* London: Sage.

Dobzhansky, T. (1962). *Mankind evolving.* New Haven, CT: Yale University Press.

Doist, R. (1997). Molecular evolution and scientific inquiry, misperceived. *American Scientist, 85,* 475.

Domestic violence against women and girls. (2000, June). *Innocenti Digest,* 6 (p. 4). Florence: United Nations Children's Fund, Innocenti Research Center.

Dozier, E. (1970). *The Pueblo Indians of North America.* New York: Holt, Rinehart and Winston.

Draper, P. (1975). !Kung women: Contrasts in sexual egalitarianism in foraging and sedentary contexts. In R. Reiter (Ed.), *Toward an anthropology of women* (pp. 77–109). New York: Monthly Review Press.

Driver, H. (1964). *Indians of North America.* Chicago: University of Chicago Press.

Dubois, C. (1944). *The people of Alor.* Minneapolis: University of Minnesota Press.

Dubos, R. (1968). *So human an animal.* New York: Scribner.

Dumurat-Dreger, A. (1998, May/June). "Ambiguous sex" or ambivalent medicine? *The Hastings Center Report, 28*(3), 2,435 (posted on the Intersex Society of North America website: www.isna.org).

Duncan, A. S., Kappelman, J., & Shapiro, L. J. (1994). Metasophalangeal joint function and positional behavior in *Australopithecus afarensis. American Journal of Physical Anthropology, 93,* 67–81.

Dundes, A. (1980). *Interpreting folklore.* Bloomington: Indiana University Press.

Durant, J. C. (2000, April 23). Everybody into the gene pool. *New York Times Book Review,* p. 11.

Duranti, A. (2001). Linguistic anthropology: History, ideas, and issues. In A. Duranti (Ed.), *Linguistic anthropology: A reader* (pp. 1–38). Oxford: Blackwell.

Durkheim, E. (1964). *The division of labor in society.* New York: Free Press.

Durkheim, E. (1965). *The elementary forms of the religious life.* New York: Free Press.

duToit, B. M. (1991). *Human sexuality: Crosscultural readings.* New York: McGraw- Hill.

Eastman, C. M. (1990). *Aspects of language and culture* (2nd ed.). Novato, CA: Chandler & Sharp.

Eaton, S. B, Konner, M., & Shostak, M. (1988). Stone-agers in the fast lane: Chronic degenerative diseases in evolutionary perspective. *American Journal of Medicine, 84*(4), 739–749.

Edey, M. A., & Johannson, D. (1989). *Blueprints: Solving the mystery of evolution.* Boston: Little, Brown.

Edwards, J. (Ed.). (1999). *Technologies of procreation: Kinship in the age of assisted conception.* New York: Routledge (distributed by St. Martin's Press).

Edwards, S. W. (1978). Nonutilitarian activities on the Lower Paleolithic: A look at the two kinds of evidence. *Current Anthropology. 19*(l), 135–137.

Egan, T. (1999, February 28). The persistence of polygamy. *New York Times Magazine,* p. 52.

Eggan, F. (1954). Social anthropology and the method of controlled comparison. *American Anthropologist, 56,* 743–763.

Eiseley, L. (1958). *Darwin's century: Evolution and the men who discovered it.* New York: Doubleday.

Eisenstadt, S. N. (1956). *From generation to generation: Age groups and social structure.* New York: Free Press.

Elkin, A. P. (1964). *The Australian aborigines.* Garden City, NY: Doubleday/ Anchor Books.

Ellison, P. T. (1990). Human ovarian function and reproductive ecology: New hypotheses. *American Anthropologist, 92,* 933–952.

Ember, C. R., & Ember, M. (1985). *Cultural anthropology* (4th ed.). Englewood Cliffs, NJ: Prentice-Hall.

Ember, C. R., & Ember, M. (1996). What have we learned from cross-cultural research? *General Anthropology, 2*(2), 5.

Enard, W., et al. (2002). Molecular evolution of FOXP2, a gene involved in speech and language. *Nature, 418,* 869–872.

Erasmus, C. J. (1950). Patolli, Pachisi, and the limitation of possibilities. *Southwestern Journal of Anthropology, 6,* 369–381.

Erasmus, C. J., & Smith, W. (1967). Cultural anthropology in the United States since 1900. *Southwestern Journal of Anthropology, 23,* 11–40.

Erickson, P. A. & Murphy, L. D. (2003). *A history of anthropological theory* (2nd ed.). Peterborough, Ontario: Broadview Press.

Errington, F. K., & Gewertz, D. B. (2001). *Cultural alternatives and a feminist anthropology: An analysis of culturally constructed gender interests in Papua New Guinea.* Cambridge, England, and New York: Cambridge University Press.

Ervin-Tripp, S. (1973). *Language acquisition and communicative choice.* Stanford, CA: Stanford University Press.

Esber, G. S., Jr. (1987). Designing Apache houses with Apaches. In R. M. Wulff & S. J. Fiske (Eds.), *Anthropological praxis: Translating knowledge into action* (pp. 187–196). Boulder, CO: Westview Press.

Evans, W. (1968). *Communication in the animal world.* New York: Crowell.

Evans-Pritchard, E. E. (1937). *Witchcraft, oracles and magic among the Azande.* London: Oxford University Press.

Evans-Pritchard, E. E. (1968). *The Nuer: A description of the modes of livelihood and political institutions of a Nilotic people.* London: Oxford University Press.

Fagan, B. M. (1995*). People of the earth* (8th ed.). New York: HarperCollins.

Fagan, B. M. (1995). The quest for the past. In L. L. Hasten (Ed.), *Annual Editions 95/96, Archaeology* (p. 10). Guilford, CT: Dushkin.

Fagan, B. M. (1999). *Archaeology: A brief introduction* (7th ed.). New York: Longman.

Fagan, B. M. (2000). *Ancient lives: An introduction to archaeology.* (pp. 125–133). Englewood Cliffs, NJ: Prentice-Hall.

Falk, D. (1975). Comparative anatomy of the larynx in man and the chimpanzee: Implications for language in Neanderthal. *American Journal of Physical Anthropology, 43*(1), 123–132.

Falk, D. (1989). Ape-like endocast of "Ape Man Taung." *American Journal of Physical Anthropology, 80*, 335–339.

Falk, D. (1993). A good brain is hard to cool. *Natural History, 102*(8), 65.

Falk, D. (1993). Hominid paleoneurology. In R. L. Ciochon & J. G. Fleagle (Eds.), *The human evolution source book.* Englewood Cliffs, NJ: Prentice-Hall.

Falk, D., et al. (2005). The brain of LB1, *Homo floresiensis. Science, 308*, 242–245.

Farmer, P. (1992). *AIDS and accusation: Haiti and the geography of blame.* Berkeley: University of California Press.

Farnell, B. (1995). *Do you see what I mean? Plains Indian sign talk and the embodiment of action.* Austin: University of Texas Press.

Fausto-Sterling, A. (1993, March/April). The five sexes: Why male and female are not enough. *The Sciences, 33*(2), 20–24.

Fausto-Sterling, A. (2000, July/August). The five sexes revisited. *The Sciences, 40*(4), 19–24.

Fausto-Sterling, A. (2003, August 2). Personal email communication.

Feder, K. L. (1999). *Frauds, myths, and mysteries* (3rd ed.). Mountain View, CA: Mayfield.

Federoff, N. E., & Nowak, R. M. (1997). Man and his dog. *Science, 278*, 305.

Fedigan, L. M. (1986). The changing role of women in models of human evolution. *Annual Review of Anthropology, 15*, 25–56.

Female genital mutilation. (2000). Fact sheet no. 241. World Health Organization.

Fernandez-Carriba, S., & Loeches, A. (2001). Fruit smearing by captive chimpanzees: A newly observed food-processing behavior. *Current Anthropology, 42*, 143–147.

Ferrie, H. (1997). An interview with C. Loring Brace. *Current Anthropology, 38*, 851–869.

Finkler, K. (2000). *Experiencing the new genetics: Family and kinship on the medical frontier.* Philadelphia: University of Pennsylvania Press.

The First Americans, ca. 20,000 b.c. (1998). *Discover, 19*(6), 24.

Firth, R. (1952). *Elements of social organization.* London: Watts.

Firth, R. (1957). *Man and culture: An evaluation of Bronislaw Malinowski.* London: Routledge.

Firth, R. (Ed.). (1967). *Themes in economic anthropology.* London: Tavistock.

Fisher, R., & Ury, W. L. (1991). *Getting to yes: Negotiating agreement without giving in* (2nd ed.). Boston: Houghton Mifflin.

Flannery, K. V. (1973). The origins of agriculture. In B. J. Siegel, A. R. Beals, & S. A. Tyler (Eds.), *Annual Review of Anthropology* (Vol. 2, pp. 271–310). Palo Alto, CA: Annual Reviews.

Flannery, K. V. (Ed.). (1976). *The Mesoamerican village.* New York: Seminar Press.

Folger, T. (1993). The naked and the bipedal. *Discover, 14*(11), 34–35.

Forbes, J. D. (1964). *The Indian in America's past.* Englewood Cliffs, NJ: Prentice-Hall.

Forbes International 500 List. (2003).

Forde, C. D. (1955). The Nupe. In D. Forde (Ed.), *Peoples of the Niger-Benue confluence.* London: International African Institute (Ethnographic Survey of Africa. Western Africa, part 10).

Forde, C. D. (1968). Double descent among the Yakô. In P. Bohannan & J. Middleton (Eds.), *Kinship and social organization* (pp. 179–191). Garden City, NY: Natural History Press.

Fortes, M. (1950). Kinship and marriage among the Ashanti. In A. R. Radcliffe-Brown & C. D. Forde (Eds.), *African systems of kinship and marriage.* London: Oxford University Press.

Fortes, M. (1969). *Kinship and the social order: The legacy of Lewis Henry Morgan.* Chicago: Aldine.

Fortes, M., & Evans-Pritchard, E. E. (Eds.). (1962). *African political systems.* London: Oxford University Press. (orig.1940).

Fossey, D. (1983). *Gorillas in the mist.* Burlington, MA: Houghton Mifflin.

Foster, G. M. (1955). Peasant society and the image of the limited good. *American Anthropologist, 67*, 293–315.

Fox, R. (1967). *Kinship and marriage in an anthropological perspective.* Baltimore: Penguin.

Fox, R. (1968). *Encounter with anthropology.* New York: Dell.

Frake, C. O. (1992). Lessons of the Mayan sky. In A. F. Aveni (Ed.), *The sky in Mayan literature* (pp. 274–291). New York: Oxford University Press.

Frankfort, H. (1968). *The birth of civilization in the Near East.* New York: Barnes & Noble.

Fraser, D. (1962). *Primitive art.* New York: Doubleday.

Fraser, D. (Ed.). (1966). *The many faces of primitive art: A critical anthology.* Englewood Cliffs, NJ: Prentice-Hall.

Frayer, D. W. (1981). Body size, weapon use, and natural selection in the European Upper Paleolithic and Mesolithic. *American Anthropologist, 83*, 57–73.

Frazer, Sir J. G. (1961 reissue). *The new golden bough.* New York: Doubleday, Anchor Books.

Freeman, J. D. (1960). The Iban of western Borneo. In G. P. Murdock (Ed.), *Social* structure in Southeast Asia. Chicago: Quadrangle Books.

Freeman, L. G. (1992). *Ambrona and Torralba: New evidence and interpretation.* Paper presented at the 91st Annual Meeting, American Anthropological Association.

Fried, M. (1960). On the evolution of social stratification and the state. In S. Diamond (Ed.), *Culture in history: Essays in honor of Paul Radin.* New York: Columbia University Press.

Fried, M. (1967). *The evolution of political society: An essay in political anthropology.* New York: Random House.

Fried, M. (1972). *The study of anthropology.* New York: Crowell.

Fried, M., Harris, M., & Murphy, R. (1968). *War: The anthropology of armed conflict and aggression.* Garden City, NY: Natural History Press.

Friedl, E. (1975). *Women and men: An anthropologist's view.* New York: Holt, Rinehart and Winston.

Friedman, J. (Ed.). (2003). *Globalization, the state, and violence.* Walnut Creek, CA: Altamira Press.

Fritz, G. J. (1994). Are the first American farmers getting younger? *Current Anthropology, 35,* 305–309.

Frye, D. P. (2000). Conflict management in cross-cultural perspective. In F. Aureli & F. B. M. de Waal, *Natural conflict resolution* (pp. 334–351). Berkeley: University of California Press.

Frye, M. (1983). Sexism. In *The politics of reality* (pp. 17–40). New York: Crossing Press.

Furst, P. T. (1976). *Hallucinogens and culture* (p. 7). Novato, CA: Chandler & Sharp.

Gamble, C. (1986). *The Paleolithic settlement of Europe.* Cambridge: Cambridge University Press.

Gardner, R. A., Gardner, B. T., & Van Cantfort, T. E. (Eds.). (1989). *Teaching sign language to chimpanzees.* Albany: State University of New York Press.

Gamst, F. C., & Norbeck, E. (1976). *Ideas of culture: Sources and uses.* New York: Holt, Rinehart and Winston.

Garn, S. M. (1970). *Human races* (3rd ed.). Springfield, IL: Charles C. Thomas.

Gates, H. (1996). Buying brides in China—again. *Anthropology Today, 12*(4), 10.

Gebo, D. L., Dagosto, D., Beard, K. C., & Tao, Q. (2001). Middle Eocene primate tarsals from China: Implica-

tions for haplorhine evolution. *American Journal of Physical Anthropology, 116,* 83–107.

Geertz, C. (1963). *Agricultural involution: The process of ecological change in Indonesia.* Berkeley: University of California Press.

Geertz, C. (1965). The impact of the concept of culture on the concept of man. In J. R. Platt (Ed.), *New views of man.* Chicago: University of Chicago Press.

Geertz, C. (1984). Distinguished lecture: Antirelativism. *American Anthropologist, 86,* 263–278.

Gelb, I. J. (1952). *A study of writing.* London: Routledge.

Gell, A. (1988). Technology and magic. *Anthropology Today, 4*(2), 6–9.

Gellner, E. (1969). *Saints of the atlas.* Chicago: University of Chicago Press (The Nature of Human Society Series).

Gibbons, A. (1992). Mitochondrial Eve: Wounded, but not yet dead. *Science, 257,* 873–875.

Gibbons, A. (1993). Where are new diseases born? *Science, 261,* 680–681.

Gibbons, A. (1996). Did Neandertals lose an evolutionary "arms" race? *Science, 272,* 1,586–1,587.

Gibbons, A. (1997). Ideas on human origins evolve at anthropology gathering. *Science, 276,* 535–536.

Gibbons, A. (1997). A new face for human ancestors. *Science, 276,* 1,331–1,333.

Gibbons, A. (1998). Ancient island tools suggest *Homo erectus* was a seafarer. *Science, 279,* 1,635.

Gibbons, A. (2001). The riddle of coexistence. *Science, 291,* 1,726.

Gibbons, A. (2001). Studying humans— and their cousins and parasites. *Science, 292,* 627.

Gibbons, A., & Culotta, E. (1997). Miocene primates go ape. *Science, 276,* 355–356.

Gibbs, J. L., Jr. (1965). The Kpelle of Liberia. In J. L. Gibbs, Jr. (Ed.), *Peoples of Africa* (pp. 216–218). New York: Holt, Rinehart and Winston.

Giddens, A. (1990). *The consequences of modernity.* Stanford, CA: Stanford University Press.

Ginsburg, F. D., Abu-Lughod, L., & Larkin, B. (Eds.). (2002). *Media worlds: Anthropology on new terrain.* Berkeley: University of California Press.

Gleason, H. A., Jr. (1966). *An introduction to descriptive linguistics* (Rev. ed.). New York: Holt, Rinehart and Winston.

Gledhill. J. (2000). *Power and its disguises: Anthropological perspectives on politics* (2nd ed.). Boulder, CO: Pluto Press.

Gluckman, M. (1955). *The judicial process among the Barotse of Northern Rhodesia.* New York: Free Press.

Goddard, V. (1993). Child labor in Naples. In W. A. Haviland & R. J. Gordon (Eds.), *Talking about people* (pp. 105–109). Mountain View, CA: Mayfield.

Godfrey, T. (2000, December 27). Biotech threatening biodiversity. *Burlington Free Press,* p.10A.

Godlier, M. (1971). Salt currency and the circulation of commodities among the Baruya of New Guinea. In G. Dalton (Ed.), *Studies in economic anthropology.* Washington, DC: American Anthropological Association (Anthropological Studies No. 7).

Golden, M., Birns, B., Bridger, W., & Moss, A. (1971). Social–class differentiation in cognitive development among black preschool children. *Child Development, 42,* 37–45.

Goodall, J. (1986). *The chimpanzees of Gombe: Patterns of behavior.* Cambridge, MA: Belknap Press.

Goodall, J. (1990). *Through a window: My thirty years with the chimpanzees of Gombe.* Boston: Houghton Mifflin.

Goodall, J. (2000). *Reason for hope: A spiritual journey.* New York: Warner Books.

Goode, W. (1963). *World revolution and family patterns.* New York: Free Press.

Goodenough, W. (1956). Residence rules. *Southwestern Journal of Anthropology, 12,* 22–37.

Goodenough, W. (1961). Comment on cultural evolution. *Daedalus, 90,* 521–528.

Goodenough, W. (Ed.). (1964). *Explorations in cultural anthropology: Essays in honor of George Murdock.* New York: McGraw–Hill.

Goodenough, W. (1965). Rethinking status and role: Toward a general model of the cultural organization of social relationships. In M. Benton (Ed.), *The relevance of models for social anthropology.* New York: Praeger (ASA Monographs l).

Goodenough, W. (1970). *Description and comparison in cultural anthropology.* Chicago: Aldine.

Goodenough, W. H. (1990). Evolution of the human capacity for beliefs. *American Anthropologist, 92,* 601.

Goodman, A., & Armelagos, G. J. (1985). Death and disease at Dr. Dickson's mounds. *Natural History, 94*(9), 12–18.

Goodman, M. E. (1967). *The individual and culture.* Homewood, IL: Dorsey Press.

Goody, J. (1969). *Comparative studies in kinship.* Stanford, CA: Stanford University Press.

Goody, J. (Ed.). (1972). *Developmental cycle in domestic groups.* New York: Cambridge University Press (Papers in Social Anthropology, No. 1).

Goody, J. (1976). *Production and reproduction: A comparative study of the domestic domain.* Cambridge: Cambridge University Press.

Goody, J. (1983). *The development of the family and marriage in Europe.* Cambridge, MA: Cambridge University Press.

Gordon, R. J. (1992). *The Bushman myth: The making of a Namibian underclass.* Boulder, CO: Westview Press.

Gordon, R. J., & Megitt, M. J. (1985). *Law and order in the New Guinea highlands.* Hanover, NH: University Press of New England.

Gorman, E. M. (1989). The AIDS epidemic in San Francisco: Epidemiological and anthropological perspectives. In A. Podolefsky & P. J. Brown (Eds.), *Applying anthropology, An introductory reader.* Mountain View, CA: Mayfield.

Gould, S. J. (1983). *Hen's teeth and horses' toes.* New York: Norton.

Gould, S. J. (1985). *The flamingo's smile: Reflections in natural history.* New York: Norton.

Gould, S. J. (1986). Of kiwi eggs and the Liberty Bell. *Natural History, 95,* 20–29.

Gould, S. J. (1989). *Wonderful life.* New York: Norton.

Gould, S. J. (1991). *Bully for brontosaurus.* New York: Norton.

Gould, S. J. (1994). The geometer of race. *Discover, 15*(11), 65–69.

Gould, S. J. (1996). *Full house: The spread of excellence from Plato to Darwin* (pp. 176–195). New York: Harmony Books.

Gould, S. J. (1996). *The mismeasure of man* (Rev. ed.). New York: Norton.

Gould, S. J. (1997). *Questioning the millennium.* New York: Crown.

Gould, S. J. (2000). The narthex of San Marco and the pangenetic paradigm. *Natural History 109*(6), 29.

Gould, S. J. (2000). What does the dreaded "E" word mean anyway? *Natural History, 109*(1), 34–36.

Graburn, N. H. (1969). *Eskimos without igloos: Social and economic development in Sugluk.* Boston: Little, Brown.

Graburn, N. H. (1971). *Readings in kinship and social structure.* New York: Harper & Row.

Graham, S. B. (1979). Biology and human social behavior: A response to Van den Berghe and Barash. *American Anthropologist, 81*(2), 357–360.

Graves, P. (1991). New models and metaphors for the Neanderthal debate. *Current Anthropology, 32*(5), 513–543.

Gray, P. M., et al. (2001). The music of nature and the nature of music. *Science, 291,* 52.

Green, E. C. (1987). The planning of health education strategies in Swaziland, and the integration of modern and traditional health sectors in Swaziland. In R. M. Wulff & S. J. Fiske (Eds.), *Anthropological praxis: Translating knowledge into action* (pp. 15–25, 87–97). Boulder, CO: Westview Press.

Greenberg, J. H. (1968). *Anthropological linguistics: An introduction.* New York: Random House.

Grine, F. E. (1993). Australopithecine taxonomy and phylogeny: Historical background and recent interpretation. In R. L. Ciochon & J. G. Fleagle (Eds.), *The human evolution source book,* Englewood Cliffs, NJ: Prentice-Hall.

Grün, R., & Thorne, A. (1997). Dating the Ngandong humans, *Science, 276,* 1,575.

Guillette. E. A., et al. (1998, June). An anthropological approach to the evaluation of preschool children exposed to pesticides in Mexico. *Environmental Health Perspectives, 106,* 347.

Gulliver, P. (1968). Age differentiation. In *International encyclopedia of the social sciences* (Vol. 1, pp. 157–162). New York: Macmillan.

Guthrie, S. (1993). *Faces in the clouds: A new theory of religions.* New York: Oxford University Press.

Gutin, J. A. (1995). Do Kenya tools root birth of modern thought in Africa? *Science, 270,* 1,118–1,119.

Haeri, N. (1997). The reproduction of symbolic capital: Language, state, and class in Egypt. *Current Anthropology, 38,* 795–816.

Hafkin, N., & Bay, E. (Eds.). (1976). *Women in Africa.* Stanford, CA: Stanford University Press.

Hager, L. (1989). The evolution of sex differences in the hominid bony pelvis. Ph.D. dissertation, University of California, Berkeley.

Hall, E. T. (1959). *The silent language.* Garden City, NY: Anchor Press / Doubleday.

Hall, E. T., & Hall, M. R. (1986). The sounds of silence. In E. Angeloni (Ed.), *Anthropology 86/87* (pp. 65–70). Guilford, CT: Dushkin.

Hall, K. R. L., & DeVore, I. (1965). Baboon social behavior. In I. DeVore (Ed.), *Primate behavior.* New York: Holt, Rinehart and Winston.

Hallowell, A. I. (1955). *Culture and experience.* Philadelphia: University of Pennsylvania Press.

Halperin, R. H. (1994). *Cultural economies: Past and present.* Austin: University of Texas Press.

Halverson, J. (1989). Review of Altimira Revisited and other essays on early art. *American Antiquity, 54,* 883.

Hamblin, D. J., & the Editors of Time-Life. (1973). *The first cities.* New York: Time-Life.

Hamburg, D. A., & McGown, E. R. (Eds.). (1979). *The great apes.* Menlo Park, CA: Cummings.

Hammond, D. (1972). *Associations.* Reading, MA: Addison-Wesley.

Hannah, J. L. (1988). *Dance, sex, and gender.* Chicago: University of Chicago Press.

Harlow, H. F. (1962). Social deprivation in monkeys. *Scientific American, 206,* 1–10.

Harner, M. (1980). *The way of the shaman: A guide to power and healing.* San Francisco: Harper & Row.

Harpending, J. H., & Harpending, H. C. (1995). Ancient differences in population can mimic a recent African origin of modern humans. *Current Anthropology, 36,* 667–674.

Harris, M. (1965). The cultural ecology of India's sacred cattle. *Current Anthropology, 7,* 51–66.

Harris, M. (1968). *The rise of anthropological theory: A history of theories of culture.* New York: Crowell.

Harrison, G. G. (1975). Primary adult lactase deficiency: A problem in anthropological genetics. *American Anthropologist, 77,* 815–819.

Hart, C. W., Pilling, A. R., & Goodale, J. (1988). *Tiwi of North Australia* (3rd ed.). New York: Holt, Rinehart and Winston.

Hart, D., & Sussman, R. W. (2005). *Man the hunted: Primates, predators, and hu-*

man evolution. Boulder, CO: Westview Press.

Hartwig, W. C., & Doneski, K. (1998). Evolution of the Hominid hand and toolmaking behavior. *American Journal of Physical Anthropology, 106,* 401–402.

Hatch, E. (1983). *Culture and morality: The relativity of values in anthropology.* New York: Columbia University Press.

Hatcher, E. P. (1985). *Art as culture, an introduction to the anthropology of art.* New York: University Press of America.

Haviland, W. (1967). Stature at Tikal, Guatemala: Implications for ancient Maya, demography, and social organization. *American Antiquity, 32,* 316–325.

Haviland, W. (1970). Tikal, Guatemala and Mesoamerican urbanism. *World Archaeology, 2,* 186–198.

Haviland, W. A. (1972). A new look at Classic Maya social organization at Tikal. *Ceramica de Cultura Maya, 8,* 1–16.

Haviland, W. A. (1974). Farming, seafaring and bilocal residence on the coast of Maine. *Man in the Northeast, 6,* 31–44.

Haviland, W. A. (1975). The ancient Maya and the evolution of urban society. *University of Northern Colorado Museum of Anthropology,* Miscellaneous Series, 37.

Haviland, W. A. (1997). Cleansing young minds, or what should we be doing in introductory anthropology? In C. P Kottak, J. J. White, R. H. Furlow, & P. C. Rice (Eds.), *The teaching of anthropology: Problems, issues, and decisions* (p. 35). Mountain View, CA: Mayfield.

Haviland, W. A. (1997). The rise and fall of sexual inequality: Death and gender at Tikal, Guatemala. *Ancient Mesoamerica, 8,* 1–12.

Haviland, W. A. (2002). Settlement, society, and demography at Tikal. In J. Sabloff (Ed.), *Tikal.* Santa Fe: School of American Research.

Haviland, W. A. (2003). *Tikal, Guatemala: A Maya way to urbanism.* Paper prepared for 3rd INAH/Penn State Conference on Mesoamerican Urbanism.

Haviland, W. A., et al. (1985). *Excavations in small residential groups of Tikal: Groups 4F-1 and 4F-2.* Philadelphia: University Museum.

Haviland, W. A., & Moholy-Nagy, H. (1992). Distinguishing the high and mighty from the hoi polloi at Tikal, Guatemala. In A. F. Chase & D. Z. Chase (Eds.), *Mesoamerican elites: An archaeological assessment.* Norman: Oklahoma University Press.

Haviland, W. A., & Power, M. W. (1994). *The original Vermonters* (2nd ed.). Hanover, NH: University Press of New England.

Hawkes, K., O'Connell, J. F., & Blurton-Jones, N. G. (1997). Hadza women's time allocation, offspring, provisioning, and the evolution of long post-menopausal life spans. *Current Anthropology, 38,* 551–577.

Hays, H. R. (1965). *From ape to angel: An informal history of social anthropology.* New York: Knopf.

Heichel, G. (1976). Agricultural production and energy resources. *American Scientist, 64.*

Heilbroner, R. L. (1972). *The making of economic society* (4th ed.). Englewood Cliffs, NJ: Prentice-Hall.

Heilbroner, R. L., & Thurow, L. C. (1981). *The economic problem* (6th ed.). Englewood Cliffs, NJ: Prentice-Hall.

Helm, J. (1962). The ecological approach in anthropology. *American Journal of Sociology, 67,* 630–649.

Henry, D. O., et al. (2004). Human behavioral organization in the Middle Paleolithic: Were Neandertals different? *American Anthropologist, 107*(1), 17–31.

Henry, J. (1965). *Culture against man.* New York: Vintage Books.

Henry, J. (1966). The metaphysic of youth, beauty, and romantic love. In S. Farber & R. Wilson (Eds.), *The challenge of women.* New York: Basic Books.

Henry, J. (1974). A theory for an anthropological analysis of American culture. In J. G. Jorgensen & M. Truzzi (Eds.), *Anthropology and American life.* Englewood Cliffs, NJ: Prentice-Hall.

Herdt, G. H. (1993). Semen transactions in Sambia culture. In D. N. Suggs & A. W. Mirade (Eds.), *Culture and human sexuality* (pp. 298–327). Pacific Grove, CA: Brooks/Cole.

Herskovits, M. J. (1952). *Economic anthropology: A study in comparative economics* (2nd ed.). New York: Knopf.

Herskovits, M. J. (1964). *Cultural dynamics.* New York: Knopf.

Hertz, N. (2001). *The silent takeover: Global capitalism and the death of democracy.* New York: Arrow Books.

Hewes, G. W. (1973). Primate communication and the gestural origin of language. *Current Anthropology, 14,* 5–24.

Himmelfarb, E. J. (2000). First alphabet found in Egypt. *Archaeology, 53*(1).

Hodgen, M. (1964). *Early anthropology in the sixteenth and seventeenth centuries.*

Philadelphia: University of Pennsylvania Press.

Hoebel, E. A. (1954). *The law of primitive man: A study in comparative legal dynamics.* Cambridge, MA: Harvard University Press.

Hoebel, E. A. (1958). *Man in the primitive world: An introduction to anthropology.* New York: McGraw-Hill.

Hoebel, E. A. (1960). *The Cheyennes: Indians of the Great Plains.* New York: Holt, Rinehart and Winston.

Hoebel, E. A. (1972). *Anthropology: The study of man* (4th ed.). New York: McGraw-Hill.

Holden, C. (1983). Simon and Kahn versus Global 2000. *Science, 221,* 342.

Holden, C. (1996). Missing link for Miocene apes. *Science, 271,* 151.

Holden, C. (1998). No last word on language origins. *Science, 282,* 1,455–1,458.

Holden, C. (1999). Ancient child burial uncovered in Portugal. *Science, 283,* 169.

Hole, F. (1966). Investigating the origins of Mesopotamian civilization. *Science, 153,* 605–611.

Hole, F., & Heizer, R. F. (1969). *An introduction to prehistoric archeology.* New York: Holt, Rinehart and Winston.

Holloway, R. L. (1980). The O. H. 7 (Olduvai Gorge, Tanzania) hominid partial brain endocast revisited. *American Journal of Physical Anthropology, 53,* 267–274.

Holloway, R. L. (1981). The Indonesian *Homo erectus* brain endocast revisited. *American Journal of Physical Anthropology, 55,* 503–521.

Holloway, R. L. (1981). Volumetric and asymmetry determinations on recent hominid endocasts: Spy I and II, Djebel Jhroud 1, and the Salb *Homo erectus* specimens, with some notes on Neanderthal brain size. *American Journal of Physical Anthropology, 55,* 385–393.

Holloway, R. L., & de LaCoste-Lareymondie, M. C. (1982). Brain endocast asymmetry in pongids and hominids: Some preliminary findings on the paleontology of cerebral dominance. *American Journal of Physical Anthropology, 58,* 101–110.

Holmes, L. D. (2000). Paradise bent (film review). *American Anthropologist, 102*(3), 604–605.

Hostetler, J., & Huntington, G. (1971). *Children in Amish society.* New York: Holt, Rinehart and Winston.

Houle, A. (1999). The origin of platyrrhines: An evaluation of the Antarctic scenario and the floating island model. *American Journal of Physical Anthropology, 109,* 554–556.

Howell, F. C. (1970). *Early man.* New York: Time-Life.

Hsiaotung, F. (1939). *Peasant life in China.* London: Kegan, Paul, Trench, & Truber.

Hsu, F. L. (1961). *Psychological anthropology: Approaches to culture and personality.* Homewood, IL: Dorsey Press.

Hsu, F. L. K. (1979). The cultural problems of the cultural anthropologist. *American Anthropologist, 81,* 517–532.

Hubert, H., & Mauss, M. (1964). *Sacrifice.* Chicago: University of Chicago Press.

Human development report. (2002). *Deepening democracy in a fragmented world.* United Nations Development Program.

Hunger Project. (2003). www.thp.org.

Hunt, R. C. (Ed.). (1967). *Personalities and cultures: Readings in psychological anthropology.* Garden City, NY: Natural History Press.

Hymes, D. (1964). *Language in culture and society: A reader in linguistics and anthropology.* New York: Harper & Row.

Hymes, D. (Ed.). (1972). *Reinventing anthropology.* New York: Pantheon.

Inda, J. X., & Rosaldo, R. (Eds.). (2001). *The anthropology of globalization: A reader.* Malden, MA, and Oxford: Blackwell.

Ingmanson, E. J. (1998). Comment. *Current Anthropology, 39,* 409.

Inkeles, A., Hanfmann, E., & Beier, H. (1961). Modal personality and adjustment to the Soviet socio-political system. In B. Kaplan (Ed.), *Studying personality cross culturally.* New York: Harper & Row.

Inkeles, A., & Levinson, D. J. (1954). National character: The study of modal personality and socio-cultural systems. In G. Lindzey (Ed.), *Handbook of social psychology.* Reading, MA: Addison-Wesley.

Interview with Laura Nader. *California Monthly.* November 2000.

Inuit Tapiirit Katami. http://www.taprisat.ca/english-text/itk/departments/enviro/ncp.

Ireland, E. (1991). Neither warriors nor victims, the wauja peacefully organize to defend their land. *Cultural Survival Quarterly, 15*(1), 54–59.

Iroquois constitution. Available at http://www.law.ou.edu/hist/iroquois.html.

Irvine, M. (1999, November 24). Mom-and-pop houses grow rare. *Burlington Free Press.*

Italy-Germany verbal war hots up. (2003, July 9). *Deccan Herald.* (Bangalore, India).

It's the law: Child labor protection. (1997, November/December). *Peace and Justice News,* p. 11.

Jacobs, S. E. (1994). Native American two-spirits. *Anthropology Newsletter, 35*(8), 7.

Jacoby, R., & Glauberman, N. (Eds.). (1995). *The Bell Curve debate.* New York: Random House.

Jennings, F. (1976). *The invasion of America.* New York: Norton.

Jennings, J. D. (1974). *Prehistory of North America* (2nd ed.). New York: McGraw-Hill.

Johanson, D., & Shreeve, J. (1989). *Lucy's child: The discovery of a human ancestor.* New York: Avon.

Johanson, D. C., & Edey, M. (1981). *Lucy, the beginnings of humankind.* New York: Simon & Schuster.

Johanson, D. C., & White, T. D. (1979). A systematic assessment of early African hominids. *Science, 203,* 321–330.

John, V. (1971). Whose is the failure? In C. L. Brace, G. R. Gamble, & J. T. Bond (Eds.), *Race and intelligence.* Washington, DC: American Anthropological Association (Anthropological Studies No. 8).

Johnson, A. (1989). Horticulturalists: Economic behavior in tribes. In S. Plattner (Ed.), *Economic anthropology* (pp. 49–77). Stanford, CA: Stanford University Press.

Johnson, A. W., & Earle, T. (1987). *The evolution of human societies, from foraging group to agrarian state.* Stanford, CA: Stanford University Press.

Johnson, D. (1996). Polygamists emerge from secrecy, seeking not just peace but respect. In W. A. Haviland & R. J. Gordon (Eds.), *Talking about people* (2nd ed., pp. 129–131). Mountain View, CA: Mayfield.

Jolly, A. (1985). *The evolution of primate behavior* (2nd ed.). New York: Macmillan.

Jolly, A. (1991). Thinking like a vervet. *Science, 251,* 574.

Jolly, C. J. (1970). The seed eaters: A new model of hominid differentiation based on a baboon analogy. *Man, 5,* 5–26.

Jolly, C. J., & Plog, F. (1986). *Physical anthropology and archaeology* (4th ed.). New York: Knopf.

Jones, S., Martin, R., & Pilbeam, D. (1992). *Cambridge encyclopedia of human evolution.* New York: Cambridge University Press.

Jopling, C. F. (1971). *Art and aesthetics in primitive societies: A critical anthology.* New York: Dutton.

Jorgensen, J. (1972). *The sun dance religion.* Chicago: University of Chicago Press.

Joukowsky, M. A. (1980). *A complete field manual of archeology: Tools and techniques of field work for archaeologists.* Englewood Cliffs, NJ: Prentice-Hall.

Joyce, C. (1991). *Witnesses from the grave: The stories bones tell.* Boston: Little, Brown and Company.

Kahn, H., & Wiener, A. J. (1967). *The year 2000.* New York: Macmillan.

Kaiser, J. (1994). A new theory of insect wing origins takes off. *Science, 266,* 363.

Kalwet, H. (1988). *Dreamtime and inner space: The world of the shaman.* New York: Random House.

Kaplan, D. (1972). *Culture theory.* Englewood Cliffs, NJ: Prentice-Hall (Foundations of Modern Anthropology).

Kaplan, D. (2000). The darker side of the original affluent society. *Journal of Anthropological Research, 53*(3), 301–324.

Karavani, I., & Smith, F. H. (2000). More on the Neanderthal problem: The Vindija case. *Current Anthropology, 41,* 839.

Kardiner, A. (1939). *The individual and his society: The psycho-dynamics of primitive social organization.* New York: Columbia University Press.

Kardiner, A., & Preble, E. (1961). *They studied men.* New York: Mentor.

Kay, R. F., Fleagle, J. G., & Simons, E. L. (1981). A revision of the Oligocene apes of the Fayum Province, Egypt. *American Journal of Physical Anthropology, 55,* 293–322.

Kay, R. F., Ross, C., & Williams, B. A. (1997). Anthropoid origins. *Science, 275,* 797–804.

Kay, R. F., Theweissen, J. G. M., & Yoder, A. D. (1992). Cranial anatomy of *Ignacius graybullianus* and the affinities of the plesiadapiformes. *American Journal of Physical Anthropology, 89*(4), 477–498.

Keen, B. (1971). *The Aztec image in western thought* (p. 13). New Brunswick, NJ: Rutgers University Press.

Kehoe, A. (2000). *Shamans and religion: An anthropological exploration in critical thinking.* Prospect Heights, IL: Waveland Press.

Kenyon, K. (1957). *Digging up Jericho.* London: Ben.

Kerri, J. N. (1976). Studying voluntary associations as adaptive mechanisms: A review of anthropological perspectives. *Current Anthropology, 17*(1).

Kessler, E. (1975). *Women.* New York: Holt, Rinehart and Winston.

Key, M. R. (1975). *Paralanguage and kinesics: Nonverbal communication.* Metuchen, NJ: Scarecrow Press.

Kirkpatrick, R. C. (2000). The evolution of human homosexual behavior. *Current Anthropology, 41,* 384.

Klass, M. (1995). *Ordered universes: Approaches to the anthropology of religion.* Boulder, CO: Westview Press.

Klass, M., & Weisgrau, M. (Eds.). (1999). *Across the boundaries of belief: Contemporary issues in the anthropology of religion.* Boulder, CO: Westview Press.

Kleinman, A. (1976). Concepts and a model for the comparison of medical systems as cultural systems. *Social Science and Medicine, 12*(2B), 85–95.

Kluckhohn, C. (1970). *Mirror for man.* Greenwich, CT: Fawcett.

Kluckhohn, C. (1994). Navajo witchcraft. *Papers of the Peabody Museum of American Archaeology and Ethnology, 22*(2).

Knauft, B. (1991). Violence and sociality in human evolution. *Current Anthropology, 32,* 391–409.

Koch, G. (1997). Songs, land rights, and archives in Australia. *Cultural Survival Quarterly, 20*(4).

Konner, M., & Worthman, C. (1980). Nursing frequency, gonadal function, and birth spacing among !Kung hunter-gatherers. *Science, 207,* 788–791.

Koufos, G. (1993). Mandible of *Ouranopithecus macedoniensis* (hominidae: primates) from a new late Miocene locality in Macedonia (Greece). *American Journal of Physical Anthropology, 91,* 225–234.

Krader, L. (1968). *Formation of the state.* Englewood Cliffs, NJ: Prentice-Hall (Foundation of Modern Anthropology).

Krajick, K. (1998). Greenfarming by the Incas? *Science, 281,* 323.

Kramer, P. A. (1998). The costs of human locomotion: Maternal investment in child transport. *American Journal of Physical Anthropology, 107,* 71–85.

Kraybill, D. B. (2001). *The riddle of Amish culture.* Baltimore: Johns Hopkins University Press.

Kroeber, A. (1958). Totem and taboo: An ethnologic psycho-analysis. In W. Lessa & E. Z. Vogt (Eds.), *Reader in comparative religion: An anthropological approach.* New York: Harper & Row.

Kroeber, A. L. (1939). Cultural and natural areas of native North America. *American Archaeology and Ethnology* (Vol. 38). Berkeley: University of California Press.

Kroeber, A. L. (1963). *Anthropology: Cultural processes and patterns.* New York: Harcourt.

Kroeber, A. L., & Kluckhohn, C. (1952). *Culture: A critical review of concepts and definitions.* Cambridge, MA: Harvard University Press (*Papers of the Peabody Museum of American Archaeology and Ethnology, 47*).

Kruger, J., et al. (2005). *Journal of Personality and Social Psychology, 89*(6), 925–936.

Kuhn, T. (1968). *The structure of scientific revolutions.* Chicago: University of Chicago Press (International Encyclopedia of Unified Science, 2[27]).

Kummer, H. (1971). *Primate societies: Group techniques of ecological adaptation.* Chicago: Aldine.

Kunzig, R. (1999). A tale of two obsessed archaeologists, one ancient city and nagging doubts about whether science can ever hope to reveal the past. *Discover, 20*(5), 84–92.

Kuper, H. (1965). The Swazi of Swaziland. In J. L. Gibbs (Ed.), *Peoples of Africa* (pp. 479–511). New York: Holt, Rinehart and Winston.

Kurth, P. (1998, October 14). Capital crimes. *Seven Days, 7.*

Kurtz, D. V. (2001). *Political anthropology: Paradigms and power.* Boulder, CO: Westview Press.

Kushner, G. (1969). *Anthropology of complex societies.* Stanford, CA: Stanford University Press.

La Barre, W. (1945). Some observations of character structure in the Orient: The Japanese. *Psychiatry, 8.*

LaFont, S. (Ed.). (2003). *Constructing sexualities: Readings in sexuality, gender, and culture.* Upper Saddle River, NJ: Prentice-Hall.

Lai, C. S. L., et al. (2001). A forkhead-domain gene is mutated in severe speech and language disorder. *Nature, 413,* 519–523.

Lakoff, R. T. (2004). *Language and woman's place,* Mary Bucholtz (Ed.). New York: Oxford University Press.

Lampl, M., Velhuis, J. D., & Johnson, M. L. (1992). Saltation and statsis: A model of human growth. *Science, 258*(5083), 801–803.

Lancaster, J. B. (1975). *Primate behavior and the emergence of human culture.* New York: Holt, Rinehart and Winston.

Landau, M. (1991). *Narratives of human evolution.* New Haven, CT: Yale University Press.

Landes, R. (1982). Comment. *Current Anthropology, 23,* 401.

Langan, P., & Harlow, C. (1994). *Child rape victims, 1992.* Washington, DC: Bureau of Justice Statistics, U.S. Department of Justice.

Lanning, E. P. (1967). *Peru before the Incas.* Englewood Cliffs, NJ: Prentice-Hall.

Lanternari, V. (1963). *The religions of the oppressed.* New York: Mentor.

Lasker, G. W., & Tyzzer, R. (1982). *Physical anthropology* (3rd ed.) New York: Holt, Rinehart and Winston.

Laughlin, W. S., & Osborne, R. H. (Eds.). (1967). *Human variation and origins.* San Francisco: Freeman.

Laurel, K. (1990). In the company of witches. *Natural History, 92.*

Lawler, A. (2001). Writing gets a rewrite. *Science, 292,* 2,419.

Layton, R. (1991). *The anthropology of art* (2nd ed.). Cambridge: Cambridge University Press.

Leach, E. (1961). *Rethinking anthropology.* London: Athione Press.

Leach, E. (1962). The determinants of differential cross-cousin marriage. *Man, 62,* 238.

Leach, E. (1962). On certain unconsidered aspects of double descent systems. *Man, 214,* 13–34.

Leach, E. (1965). *Political systems of highland Burma.* Boston: Beacon Press.

Leach, E. (1982). *Social anthropology.* Glasgow: Fontana Paperbacks.

Leacock, E. (1981). *Myths of male dominance: Collected articles on women cross culturally.* New York: Monthly Review Press.

Leacock, E. (1981). Women's status in egalitarian society: Implications for social evolution. In *Myths of male dominance: Collected articles on women cross culturally.* New York: Monthly Review Press.

Leakey, L. S. B. (1965). *Olduvai Gorge, 1951–1961* (Vol. 1). London: Cambridge University Press.

Leakey, L. S. B. (1967). Development of aggression as a factor in early man and prehuman evolution. In C. Clements & D. Lundsley (Eds.), *Aggression and defense*. Los Angeles: University of California Press.

Leakey, L.S. B., Tobias, P. B., & Napier, J. R., (1964). A new species of the genus *Homo* from Olduvai Gorge. *Nature, 202*, 7–9.

Leakey, M. G., Spoor, F., Brown, F. H., Gathogo, P. N., Kiare, C., Leakey, L. N., & McDougal, I. (2001). New hominin genus from eastern Africa shows diverse middle Pliocene lineages. *Nature, 410*, 433–440.

Leakey, M. D. (1971). *Olduvai Gorge: Excavations in Beds I and II. 1960–1963*. London and New York: Cambridge University Press.

Leap, W. L. (1987). Tribally controlled culture change: The Northern Ute language revival project. In R. M. Wulff & S. J. Fiske (Eds.), *Anthropological praxis: Translating knowledge into action* (pp. 197–211). Boulder, CO: Westview Press.

Leavitt, G. C. (1990). Sociobiological explanations of incest avoidance: A critical review of evidential claims. *American Anthropologist, 92*, 982.

Leclerc-Madlala, S. (2002). Bodies and politics: Healing rituals in the democratic South Africa. In V. Faure (Ed.), *Les cahiers de 'l'IFAS*, No. 2. Johannesburg: The French Institute.

Lee, R. (1993). *The Dobe Ju/hoansi*. Ft. Worth, TX: Harcourt Brace.

Lee, R. B., & Daly, R. H. (1999). *The Cambridge encyclopedia of hunters and gatherers*. New York: Cambridge University Press.

Lee, R. B., & DeVore, I. (Eds.). (1968). *Man the hunter*. Chicago: Aldine.

Leeds, A., & Vayda, A. P. (Eds.). (1965). *Man, culture and animals: The role of animals in human ecological adjustments*. Washington, DC: American Association for the Advancement of Science.

Lees, R. (1953). The basis of glottochronology. *Language, 29*, 113–127.

Legros, D. (1997). Comment. *Current Anthropology, 38*, 617.

Lehman, E. C., Jr. (2002). Women's path into the ministry. *Pulpit & Pew Research Reports, 1*(Fall), 4.

Lehmann, A. C., & Myers, J. E. (Eds.). (1993). *Magic, witchcraft and religion: An anthropological study of the supernatural* (3rd ed.). Mountain View, CA: Mayfield.

Lehmann, W. P. (1973). *Historical linguistics, An introduction* (2nd ed.). New York: Holt, Rinehart and Winston.

Leigh, S. R., & Park, P. B. (1998). Evolution of human growth prolongation. *American Journal of Physical Anthropology, 107*, 331–350.

Leinhardt, G. (1964). *Social anthropology*. London: Oxford University Press.

LeMay, M. (1975). The language capability of Neanderthal man. *American Journal of Physical Anthropology, 43*(1), 9–14.

Lenski, G. (1966). *Power and privilege: A theory of social stratification*. New York: McGraw-Hill.

Leroi-Gourhan, A. (1968). The evolution of Paleolithic art. *Scientific American, 218*, 58ff.

Lestel, D. (1998). How chimpanzees have domesticated humans. *Anthropology Today, 12*(3).

Lett, J. (1987). *The human enterprise: A critical introduction to anthropological theory*. Boulder, CO: Westview Press.

Levine, N. E., & Silk, J. B. (1997). Why polyandry fails. *Current Anthropology, 38*, 375–398.

Levine, R. (1973). *Culture, behavior and personality*. Chicago: Aldine.

Lévi-Strauss, C. (1963). The sorcerer and his magic. In *Structural anthropology*. New York: Basic Books.

Lewellen, T. C. (2002). *The anthropology of globalization: Cultural anthropology enters the 21st century*. Westport, CT: Greenwood Publishing Group/Bergin & Garvey.

Lewin, R. (1983). Is the orangutan a living fossil? *Science, 222*, 1,223.

Lewin, R. (1985). Tooth enamel tells a complex story. *Science, 228*, 707.

Lewin, R. (1986). New fossil upsets human family" *Science, 233*, 720–721.

Lewin, R. (1987). Debate over emergence of human tooth pattern. *Science, 235*, 749.

Lewin, R. (1987). The earliest "humans" were more like apes. *Science, 236*, 1,062–1,063.

Lewin, R. (1987). Four legs bad, two legs good. *Science, 235*, 969.

Lewin, R. (1987). Why is ape tool use so confusing? *Science, 236*, 776–777.

Lewin, R. (1988). Molecular clocks turn a quarter century. *Science, 235*, 969–971.

Lewin, R. (1993). Paleolithic paint job. *Discover, 14*(7), 64–70.

Lewis, I. M. (1965). Problems in the comparative study of unilineal descent. In M. Banton (Ed.), *The relevance of models for social organization* (A.S.A. Monograph No. 1). London: Tavistock.

Lewis, I. M. (1976). *Social anthropology in perspective*. Harmondsworth, England: Penguin.

Lewis-Williams, J. D. (1990). *Discovering southern African rock art*. Cape Town and Johannesburg: David Philip.

Lewis-Williams, J. D., & Dowson, T. A. (1988). Signs of all times: Entoptic phenomena in Upper Paleolithic art. *Current Anthropology, 29*, 201–245.

Lewis-Williams, J. D., & Dowson, T. A. (1993). On vision and power in the Neolithic: Evidence from the decorated monuments. *Current Anthropology, 34*, 55–65.

Lewis-Williams, J. D., Dowson, T. A., & Deacon, J. (1993). Rock art and changing perceptions of Southern Africa's past: Ezeljagdspoort reviewed. *Antiquity, 67*, 273–291.

Lewontin, R. C. (1972). The apportionment of human diversity. In T. Dobzhansky, et al. (Eds.), *Evolutionary biology* (pp. 381–398). New York: Plenum Press.

Lewontin, R. C., Rose, S., & Kamin, L. J. (1984). *Not in our genes*. New York: Pantheon.

Li, X., Harbottle, G., Zhang, J., & Wang, C. (2003).The earliest writing? Sign use in the seventh millennium BC at Jiahu, Henan Province, China. *Antiquity, 77*, 31–44.

Lindenbaum, S. (1978). *Kuru sorcery: Disease and danger in the New Guinea highlands*. New York: McGraw-Hill.

Little, K. (1964). The role of voluntary associations in West African urbanization. In P. van den Berghe (Ed.), *Africa: Social problems of change and conflict*. San Francisco: Chandler.

Livingstone, F. B. (1973). The distribution of abnormal hemoglobin genes and their significance for human evolution. In C. Loring Brace & J. Metress (Eds.), *Man in evolutionary perspective*. New York: Wiley.

Lloyd, C. B. (Ed.). (2005). *Growing up global: The changing transitions to adulthood in developing countries* (pp. 450–453). Washington, DC: National Academies Press, Committee on Population, National Research Council and Institute of Medicine of the National Academies.

Lock, M. (2001). *Twice dead: Organ transplants and the reinvention of death*. Berkeley: University of California Press.

Louckey, J., & Carlsen, R. (1991). Massacre in Santiago Atitlán. *Cultural Survival Quarterly, 15*(3), 70.

Lorenzo, C., Carretero, J. M., Arsuaga, J. L., Gracia, A., & Martinez, I. (1998). Intrapopulational body size variation and cranial capacity variation in middle Pleistocene humans: The Sima de los Huesos sample (Sierra de Atapuerca, Spain). *American Journal of Physical Anthropology, 106,* 19–33.

Lounsbury, F. (1964). The structural analysis of kinship semantics. In H. G. Lunt (Ed.), *Proceedings of the Ninth International Congress of Linguists.* The Hague: Mouton.

Lovejoy, C. O. (1981). Origin of man. *Science, 211*(4480), 341–350.

Lowenstein, J. M. (1992, December). Genetic surprises. *Discover 13,* 82–88.

Lowie, R. H. (1948). *Social organization.* New York: Holt, Rinehart and Winston.

Lowie, R. H. (1956). *Crow Indians.* New York: Holt, Rinehart and Winston. (orig. 1935).

Lowie, R. H. (1966). *Culture and ethnology.* New York: Basic Books.

Lucy, J. A. (1997). Linguistic relativity. *Annual Review of Anthropology, 26,* 291–312.

Lustig-Arecco, V. (1975). *Technology strategies for survival.* New York: Holt, Rinehart and Winston.

MacCormack, C. P. (1977). Biological events and cultural control. *Signs, 3,* 93–100.

MacLarnon, A. M., & Hewitt, G. P. (1999). The evolution of human speech: The role of enhanced breathing control. *American Journal of Physical Anthropology, 109,* 341–363.

MacNeish, R. S. (1992). *The origins of agriculture and settled life.* Norman: University of Oklahoma Press.

Mair, L. (1969). *Witchcraft.* New York: McGraw-Hill.

Mair, L. (1971). *Marriage.* Baltimore: Penguin.

Malefijt, A. de W. (1969). *Religion and culture: An introduction to anthropology of religion.* London: Macmillan.

Malefijt, A. de W. (1974). *Images of man.* New York: Knopf.

Malinowski, B. (1922). *Argonauts of the western Pacific.* London: Routledge & Kegan Paul.

Malinowski, B. (1945). *The dynamics of culture change.* New Haven, CT: Yale University Press.

Malinowski, B. (1951). *Crime and custom in savage society* (p. 55). London: Routledge.

Mann, A., Lampl, M, & Monge, J. (1990). Patterns of ontogeny in human evolution: Evidence from dental development. *Yearbook of Physical Anthropology, 33,* 111–150.

Mann, C. C. (2000). Misconduct alleged in Yanomamo studies. *Science, 289, 2,* 253.

Mann, C. C. (2002).The real dirt on rainforest fertility. *Science, 297,* 920–923.

Marcus, J., & Flannery, K. V. (1996). *Zapotec civilization: How urban society evolved in Mexico's Oaxaca Valley.* New York: Thames & Hudson.

Marks, J. (1995). *Human biodiversity: Genes, race and history.* Hawthorne, NY: Aldine.

Marks, J. (2000, May 12). 98% alike (what our similarity to apes tells us about our understanding of genetics). *Chronicle of Higher Education,* p. B7.

Marks, J. (2002). *What it means to be 98 percent chimpanzee: Apes, people, and their genes.* Berkeley: University of California Press.

Marsella, J. (1982). Pulling it together: Discussion and comments. In S. Pastner & W. A. Haviland (Eds.), *Confronting the creationists* (pp. 79–80). *Northeastern Anthropological Association, Occasional Proceedings, 1.*

Marshack, A. (1972). *The roots of civilization: A study in prehistoric cognition; the origins of art, symbol and notation.* New York: McGraw-Hill.

Marshack, A. (1976). Some implications of the Paleolithic symbolic evidence for the origin of language. *Current Anthropology, 17*(2), 274–282.

Marshack, A. (1989). *Evolution of the human capacity: The symbolic evidence. Yearbook of physical anthropology* (Vol. 32, pp. 1–34). New York: Alan R. Liss.

Marshall, L. (1961). Sharing, talking and giving: Relief of social tensions among !Kung bushmen. *Africa, 31,* 231–249.

Marshall, M. (1990). Two tales from the Trukese taproom. In P. R. DeVita (Ed.), *The humbled anthropologist* (pp. 12–17). Belmont, CA: Wadsworth.

Martin, E. (1994). *Flexible bodies: Tracking immunity in American culture—from the days of polio to the age of AIDS.* Boston: Beacon Press.

Martin, E. (1999). Flexible survivors. *Anthropology News, 40*(6), 5–7.

Martorell, R. (1988). Body size, adaptation, and function. *Human Organization* Vol. 48(1). *GDP,* 335–347.

Mascia-Lees, F. E., & Black, N. J. (2000). *Gender and anthropology.* Prospect Heights, IL: Waveland Press.

Mason, J. A. (1957). *The ancient civilizations of Peru.* Baltimore: Penguin.

Matson, F. R. (Ed.). (1965). *Ceramics and man.* New York: Viking Fund Publications in Anthropology, No. 41.

Maybury-Lewis, D. (1960). Parallel descent and the Apinaye anomaly. *Southwestern Journal of Anthropology, 16,* 191–216.

Maybury-Lewis, D. (1984). The prospects for plural societies. *1982 Proceedings of the American Ethnological Society.*

Maybury-Lewis, D. (1993, fall). A new world dilemma: The Indian question in the Americas. *Symbols,* 17–23.

Maybury-Lewis, D. (2001). *Indigenous peoples, ethnic groups, and the state.* (2nd ed.). Boston: Allyn & Bacon.

McCorriston, J., & Hole, F. (1991). The ecology of seasonal stress and the origins of agriculture in the Near East. *American Anthropologist, 93,* 46–69.

McDermott, L. (1996). Self-representation in Upper Paleolithic female figurines. *Current Anthropology, 37,* 227–276.

McFee, M. (1972). *Modern Blackfeet: Montanans on a reservation.* New York: Holt, Rinehart and Winston.

McGrew, W. C. (2000). Dental care in chimps. *Science, 288,* 1,747.

McHale, J. (1969). *The future of the future.* New York: Braziller.

McHenry, H. (1975). Fossils and the mosaic nature of human evolution. *Science, 190,* 424–431.

McHenry, H. M. (1992). Body size and proportions in early hominids. *American Journal of Physical Anthropology, 87,* 407–431.

McKenna, J. (1999). Co-sleeping and SIDS. In W. Trevathan, E. O. Smith, & J. J. McKenna (Eds.), *Evolutionary medicine.* London: Oxford University Press.

McKenna, J. J. (2002, September-October). Breastfeeding and bedsharing. *Mothering,* 28–37.

Mead, M. (1928). *Coming of age in Samoa.* New York: Morrow.

Mead, M. (1950). *Sex and temperament in three primitive societies.* New York: New American Library. (orig. 1935).

Mead, M. (1963). *Sex and temperament in three primitive societies* (3rd ed). New York: Morrow. (orig.1935).

Mead, M. (1970). *Culture and commitment.* Garden City, NY: Natural History Press, Universe Books.

Medicine, B. (1994). Gender. In M. B. Davis (Ed.), *Native America in the twentieth century*. New York: Garland.

Melaart, J. (1967). *Çatalhöyük: A Neolithic town in Anatolia*. London: Thames and Hudson.

Mellars, P. (1989). Major issues in the emergence of modern humans. *Current Anthropology, 30*, 356–357.

Meltzer, D., Fowler, D., & Sabloff, J. (Eds.). (1986). *American archaeology: Past & future*. Washington, DC: Smithsonian Institution Press.

Merin, Y. (2002). *Equality for same-sex couples: The legal recognition of gay partnerships in Europe and the United States*. Chicago: University of Chicago Press.

Merrell, D. J. (1962). *Evolution and genetics: The modern theory of genetics*. New York: Holt, Rinehart and Winston.

Merriam, A. P. (1964). *The anthropology of music*. Chicago: Northwestern University Press.

Michaels, J. W. (1973). *Dating methods in archaeology*. New York: Seminar Press.

Middleton, J. (Ed.). (1970). *From child to adult: Studies in the anthropology of education*. Garden City, NY: Natural History Press (American Museum Source Books in Anthropology).

Miles, H. L. W. (1993). Language and the orangutan: The "old person" of the forest. In P. Cavalieri & P. Singer (Eds.), *The great ape project* (pp. 45–50). New York: St. Martin's Press.

Miller, J. M. A. (2000). Craniofacial variation in *Homo habilis*: An analysis of the evidence for multiple species. *American Journal of Physical Anthropology, 112*, 122.

Millon, R. (1973). *Urbanization of Teotihuacán, Mexico: Vol. 1, Part 1. The Teotihuacán map*. Austin: University of Texas Press.

Mintz, S. (1996). A taste of history. In W. A. Haviland & R. J. Gordon (Eds.), *Talking about people* (2nd ed., pp. 81–82). Mountain View, CA: Mayfield.

Minugh-Purvis, N. (1992). The inhabitants of Ice Age Europe. *Expedition, 34*(3), 23–36.

Mitchell, W. E. (1973, December). A new weapon stirs up old ghosts. *Natural History*, 77–84.

Mitchell, W. E. (1978). *Mishpokhe: A study of New York City Jewish family clubs*. The Hague: Mouton.

Molnar, S. (1992). *Human variation: Races, types and ethnic groups* (3rd ed.). Englewood Cliffs, NJ: Prentice-Hall.

Monaghan, L., Hinton, L., & Kephart, R. (1997). Can't teach a dog to be a cat? The dialogue on ebonics. *Anthropology Newsletter, 38*(3), 1, 8, 9.

Montagu, A. (1964). *The concept of race*. London: Macmillan.

Montagu, A. (1964). *Man's most dangerous myth: The fallacy of race* (4th ed.) New York: World Publishing.

Montagu, A. (1975). *Race and IQ*. New York: Oxford University Press.

Morgan, L. H. (1877). *Ancient society*. New York: World Publishing.

Morse, D., et al. (1979). *Gestures: Their origins and distribution*. New York: Stein & Day.

Moscati, S. (1962). *The face of the ancient orient*. New York: Doubleday.

Mullings, L. (1989). Gender and the application of anthropological knowledge to public policy in the United States. In S. Morgan (Ed.), *Gender and anthropology* (pp. 360–381). Washington, DC: American Anthropological Association.

Murdock, G. (1960). Cognatic forms of social organization. In G. P. Murdock (Ed.), *Social structure in Southeast Asia* (pp. 1–14). Chicago: Quadrangle Books.

Murdock, G. P. (1965). *Social structure*. New York: Free Press.

Murdock, G. P. (1971). How culture changes. In H. L. Shapiro (Ed.), *Man, culture and society* (2nd ed.) New York: Oxford University Press.

Murphy, R. (1971). *The dialectics of social life: Alarms and excursions in anthropological theory*. New York: Basic Books.

Murphy, R., & Kasdan, L. (1959). The structure of parallel cousin marriage. *American Anthropologist, 61*, 17–29.

Mydens, S. (2001, August 12). He's not hairy, he's my brother. *New York Times*, sec. 4, p. 5.

Myrdal, G. (1974). Challenge to affluence: The emergence of an "under-class." In J. G. Jorgensen & M. Truzzi (Eds.), *Anthropology and American life*. Englewood Cliffs, NJ: Prentice-Hall.

Nader, L. (Ed.). (1965). The ethnography of law, part II. *American Anthropologist, 67*(6).

Nader, L. (Ed.). (1969). *Law in culture and society*. Chicago: Aldine.

Nader, L. (1981, December). [Interview for Coast Telecourses, Inc.]. Los Angeles.

Nader, L. (Ed.). (1996). *Naked science: Anthropological inquiry into boundaries, power, and knowledge*. New York: Routledge.

Nader, L. (1997). Controlling processes: Tracing the dynamics of power. *Current Anthropology, 38*, 715–717.

Nader, L. (2002). *The life of the law: Anthropological projects*. Berkeley: University of California Press.

Nader, L., & Todd, Jr., H. F. (1978). *The disputing process: Law in ten societies*. New York: Columbia University Press.

Nanda, S. (1990). *Neither man nor woman: The hijras of India*. Belmont, CA: Wadsworth.

Nanda, S. (1992). Arranging a marriage in India. In P. R. De Vita (Ed.), *The naked anthropologist* (pp. 139–143). Belmont, CA: Wadsworth.

Naroll, R. (1973). Holocultural theory tests. In R. Naroll & F. Naroll (Eds.), *Main currents in cultural anthropology*. New York: Appleton.

Natadecha-Sponsal, P. (1993). The young, the rich and the famous: Individualism as an American cultural value. In P. R. DeVita & J. D. Armstrong (Eds.), *Distant mirrors: America as a foreign culture* (pp. 46–53). Belmont, CA: Wadsworth.

Needham, R. (Ed.). (1971). *Rethinking kinship and marriage*. London: Tavistock.

Needham, R. (1972). *Belief, language and experience*. Chicago: University of Chicago Press.

Neer, R. M. (1975). The evolutionary significance of vitamin D, skin pigment, and ultraviolet light. *American Journal of Physical Anthropology, 43*, 409–416.

Netting, R. M., Wilk, R. R., & Arnould, E. J. (Eds.). (1984). *Households: Comparative and historical studies of the domestic group*. Berkeley: University of California Press.

Nettl, B. (1956). *Music in primitive culture*. Cambridge, MA: Harvard University Press.

Newman, P. L. (1965). *Knowing the Gururumba*. New York: Holt, Rinehart and Winston.

Nietschmann, B. (1987). The third world war. *Cultural Survival Quarterly, 11*(3), 1–16.

Norbeck, E., Price-Williams, D., & McCord, W. (Eds.). (1968). *The study of personality: An interdisciplinary appraisal*. New York: Holt, Rinehart and Winston.

Normile, D. (1998). Habitat seen as playing larger role in shaping behavior. *Science, 279,* 1,454.

Nunney, L. (1998). Are we selfish, are we nice, or are we nice because we are selfish? *Science, 281,* 1,619.

Nye, E. I., & Berardo, F. M. (1975). *The family: Its structure and interaction.* New York: Macmillan.

Nye, J. (2002). *The paradox of American power: Why the world's only superpower can't go it alone.* New York: Oxford University Press.

Oakley, K. P. (1964). *Man the tool-maker.* Chicago: University of Chicago Press.

O'Barr, W. M., & Conley, J. M. (1993). When a juror watches a lawyer. In W. A. Haviland & R. J. Gordon (Eds.), *Talking about people* (2nd. ed., pp. 42–45). Mountain View, CA: Mayfield.

Obler, R. S. (1982). Is the female husband a man? Woman/woman marriage among the Nandi of Kenya. *Ethnology, 19,* 69–88.

Offiong, D. (1985). Witchcraft among the Ibibio of Nigeria. In A. C. Lehmann & J. E. Myers (Eds.), *Magic, witchcraft, and religion* (pp. 152–165). Palo Alto, CA: Mayfield.

Okonjo, K. (1976). The dual-sex political system in operation: Igbo women and community politics in midwestern Nigeria. In N. Hafkin & E. Bay (Eds.), *Women in Africa.* Stanford, CA: Stanford University Press.

Olszewki, D. I. (1991). Comment. *Current Anthropology, 32,* 43.

Ong, A. (1999). *Flexible citizenship: The cultural logics of transnationality.* Durham, NC: Duke University Press.

Ortiz, A. (1969). *The Tewa world.* Chicago: The University of Chicago Press.

Oswalt, W. H. (1970). *Understanding our culture.* New York: Holt, Rinehart and Winston.

Oswalt, W. H. (1972). *Habitat and technology.* New York: Holt, Rinehart and Winston.

Oswalt, W. H. (1972). *Other peoples other customs: World ethnography and its history.* New York: Holt, Rinehart and Winston.

Otten, C. M. (1971). *Anthropology and art: Readings in cross-cultural aesthetics.* Garden City, NY: Natural History Press.

Ottenberg, P. (1965). The Afikpo Ibo of eastern Nigeria. In J. L. Gibbs (Ed.), *Peoples of Africa.* New York: Holt, Rinehart and Winston.

Ottenheimer, Martin. (1996). *Forbidden relatives: The American myth of cousin marriage.* Chicago: University of Illinois Press.

Otterbein, K. F. (1971). *The evolution of war.* New Haven, CT: HRAF Press.

Pandian, J. (1991). *Culture, religion, and the sacred self: A critical introduction to the anthropological study of religion.* Englewood Cliffs, NJ: Prentice-Hall.

Parker, R. G. (1991). *Bodies, pleasures, and passions: Sexual culture in contemporary Brazil.* Boston: Beacon Press.

Parker, S., & Parker, H. (1979). The myth of male superiority: Rise and demise. *American Anthropologist, 81*(2), 289–309.

Parkin, R. (1997). *Kinship: An introduction to basic concepts.* Cambridge, MA: Blackwell.

Parnell, R. (1999). Gorilla exposé. *Natural History, 108*(8), 43.

Partridge, W. (Ed.). (1984). *Training manual in development anthropology.* Washington, DC: American Anthropological Association.

Pastner, S., & Haviland, W. A. (Eds.). (1982). Confronting the creationists. *Northeastern Anthropological Association Occasional Proceedings, I.*

Patterson, F., & Linden, E. (1981). *The education of Koko.* New York: Holt, Rinehart and Winston.

Patterson, T. C. (1981). *Archeology: The evolution of ancient societies.* Englewood Cliffs, NJ: Prentice-Hall.

Peacock, J. L. (2002). *The anthropological lens: Harsh light, soft focus.* (2nd ed.). New York: Cambridge University Press.

Pease, T. (2000). Taking the third side. *Andover Bulletin* (Spring).

Pelliam, A. de, & Burton, F. D. (1976). More on predatory behavior in nonhuman primates. *Current Anthropology, 17*(3), 512–513.

Pelto, G. H., Goodman, A. H., & Dufour, D. L. (Eds.). (2000). *Nutritional anthropology: Biocultural perspectives on food and nutrition.* Mountain View, CA: Mayfield,

Pelto, P. J. (1973). *The snowmobile revolution: Technology and social change in the Arctic.* Menlo Park, CA: Cummings.

Penniman, T. K. (1965). *A hundred years of anthropology.* London: Duckworth.

Pennisi, E. (1999). Genetic study shakes up out of Africa theory. *Science, 283,* 1,828.

Peters, C. R. (1979). Toward an ecological model of African Plio-Pleistocene hominid adaptations. *American Anthropologist, 81*(2), 261–278.

Petersen J. B., Neuves, E., & Heckenberger, M. J. (2001). Gift from the past: *Terra preta* and prehistoric American occupation in Amazonia. In C. McEwan and C. Barreo (Eds.) *Unknown Amazon* (pp. 86–105). London: British Museum Press.

Peterson, F. L. (1962). *Ancient Mexico, An introduction to the pre-Hispanic cultures.* New York: Capricorn Books.

Pfeiffer, J. E. (1977). *The emergence of society.* New York: McGraw-Hill.

Pfeiffer, J. E. (1978). *The emergence of man.* New York: Harper & Row.

Pfeiffer, J. E. (1985). *The creative explosion.* Ithaca, NY: Cornell University Press.

Piddocke, S. (1965). The potlatch system of the southern Kwakiutl: A new perspective. *Southwestern Journal of Anthropology, 21,* 244–264.

Piggott, S. (1965). *Ancient Europe.* Chicago: Aldine.

Pilbeam, D. (1987). Rethinking human origins. In *Primate evolution and human origins.* Hawthorne, NY: Aldine.

Pilbeam, D., & Gould, S. J. (1974). Size and scaling in human evolution. *Science, 186,* 892–901.

Pimentel, D. (1991). Response. *Science, 252,* 358.

Pimentel, D., Hurd, L. E., Bellotti, A. C., Forster, M. J., Oka, I. N., Sholes, O. D., & Whitman, R. J. (1973). Food production and the energy crisis. *Science, 182.*

Piperno, D. R., & Fritz, G. J. (1994). On the emergence of agriculture in the new world. *Current Anthropology, 35,* 637–643.

Pitts, V. (2003). *In the flesh: The cultural politics of body modification.* New York: Palgrave Macmillan.

Plane, A. M. (1996). Putting a face on colonization: Factionalism and gender politics in the life history of Awashunkes, the "Squaw Sachem" of Saconnet. In R. S. Grumet (Ed.), *Northeastern Indian Lives, 1632–1816* (pp.140–175). Amherst: University of Massachusetts Press.

Plattner, S. (1989). Markets and market places. In S. Plattner (Ed.), *Economic anthropology.* Stanford, CA: Stanford University Press.

Podolefsky, A., & Brown, P. J. (Eds.). (1989). *Applying anthropology, an introductory reader.* Mountain View, CA: Mayfield.

Pohl, M. E. D., Pope, K. O., & von Nagy, C. (2002). Olmec origins of Mesoamerican writing, *Science, 298,* 1,984–1,987.

Polanyi, K. (1968). The economy as instituted process. In E. E. LeClair, Jr., & H. K. Schneider (Eds.), *Economic anthropology: Readings in theory and analysis* (pp. 127–138). New York: Holt, Rinehart and Winston.

Pollan, M. (2001). *The botany of desire: A plant's-eye view of the world.* New York: Random House.

Pope, G. (1989, October). Bamboo and human evolution. *Natural History, 98,* 48–57.

Pope, G. G. (1992). Craniofacial evidence for the origin of modern humans in China. *Yearbook of Physical Anthropology, 35,* 243–298.

Pospisil, L. (1963). *The Kapauku Papuans of west New Guinea.* New York: Holt, Rinehart and Winston.

Pospisil, L. (1971). *Anthropology of law: A comparative theory.* New York: Harper & Row.

Power, M. G. (1995). Gombe revisited: Are chimpanzees violent and hierarchical in the free state? *General Anthropology, 2*(1), 5–9.

Premack, A. J., & Premack, D. (1972). Teaching language to an ape. *Scientific American, 277*(4), 92–99.

Price, T. D., & Feinman, G. M. (Eds.). (1995). *Foundations of social inequality.* New York: Plenum.

Pringle, H. (1997). Ice Age communities may be earliest known net hunters. *Science, 277,* 1,203–1,204.

Pringle, H. (1998). The slow birth of agriculture. *Science, 282,* 1,449.

Prins, A. H. J. (1953). *East African class systems.* Groningen, the Netherlands: J. B. Wolters.

Prins, H. E. L. (1996). *The Mi'kmaq: Resistance, accommodation, and cultural survival.* Belmont, CA: Wadsworth/Holt, Rinehart and Winston.

Prins, H. E. L. (2002). Visual media and the primitivist perplex: Colonial fantasies, indigenous imagination, and advocacy in North America. In F. D. Ginsburg et al., *Media worlds: Anthropology on new terrain* (pp. 58–74). Berkeley: University of California Press.

Puleston, D. E. (1983). *The settlement survey of Tikal.* Philadelphia: University Museum.

Radcliffe-Brown, A. R. (1931). Social organization of Australian tribes. *Oceana Monographs, 1,* 29.

Radcliffe-Brown, A. R., & Forde, C. D. (Eds.). (1950). *African systems of kinship and marriage.* London: Oxford University Press.

Radin, P. (1923). The Winnebago tribe. In *37th annual report of the Bureau of American Ethnology, 1915–1916* (pp. 33–550). Washington, DC: Government Printing Office.

Rappaport, R. A. (1969). Ritual regulation of environmental relations among a New Guinea people. In A. P Vayda (Ed.), *Environment and cultural behavior* (pp. 181–201). Garden City, NY Natural History Press.

Rappaport, R. A. (1984). *Pigs for the ancestors* New Haven, CT: Yale University Press.

Rappaport, R. A. (1994). Commentary. *Anthropology Newsletters, 35*(6), 76.

Rappaport, R. A. (1999). *Holiness and humanity: Ritual in the making of religious life.* New York: Cambridge University Press.

Rathje, W. L. (1974). The garbage project: A new way of looking at the problems of archaeology. *Archaeology, 27,* 236–241.

Rathje, W. L. (1993). Rubbish! In W. A. Haviland & R. J. Gordon (Eds.), *Talking about people: Readings in contemporary cultural anthropology.* Mountain View, CA: Mayfield.

Read-Martin, C. E., & Read, D. W. (1975). Australopithecine scavenging and human evolution: An approach from faunal analysis. *Current Anthropology, 16*(3), 359–368.

Recent demographic developments in Europe—2000. Council of Europe.

Recer, P. (1998, February 16). Apes shown to communicate in the wild. *Burlington Free Press,* p. 12A.

Redfield, R., Linton, R., & Herskovits, M. J. (1936). Memorandum of the study of acculturation. *American Anthropologist, 38,* 149–152.

Redman, C. L. (1978). *The rise of civilization: From early farmers to urban society in the ancient Near East.* San Francisco: Freeman.

Reid, J. J., Schiffer, M. B., & Rathje, W. L. (1975). Behavioral archaeology: Four strategies. *American Anthropologist, 77,* 864–869.

Reina, R. E. (1966). *The law of the saints.* Indianapolis: Bobbs-Merrill.

Reiter, R. (Ed.). (1975). *Toward an anthropology of women.* New York: Monthly Review Press.

Relethford, J. H. (2001). Absence of regional affinities of Neandertal DNA with living humans does not reject multiregional evolution. *American Journal of Physical Anthropology, 115,* 95–98.

Relethford, J. H., & Harpending, H. C. (1994). Craniometric variation, genetic theory, and modern human origins. *American Journal of Physical Anthropology, 95,* 249–270.

Renfrew, C. (1973). *Before civilization: The radiocarbon revolution and prehistoric Europe.* London: Jonathan Cape.

Reynolds, V. (1994). Primates in the field, primates in the lab. *Anthropology Today, 10*(2), 4.

Rice, D. S., & Prudence, M. (1984). Lessons from the Maya. *Latin American Research Review, 19*(3), 7–34.

Rice, P. (2000). Paleoanthropology 2000—part 1. *General Anthropology, 7*(1), 11.

Richmond, B. G., Fleagle, J. K., & Swisher III, C. C. (1998). First Hominoid elbow from the Miocene of Ethiopia and the evolution of the Catarrhine elbow. *American Journal of Physical Anthropology, 105,* 257–277.

Ridley, M. (1999). *Genome: The autobiography of a species in 23 chapters.* New York: HarperCollins.

Rightmire, G. P. (1990). *The evolution of Homo erectus: Comparative anatomical studies of an extinct human species.* Cambridge: Cambridge University Press.

Rightmire, G. P. (1998). Evidence from facial morphology for similarity of Asian and African representatives of Homo erectus. *American Journal of Physical Anthropology, 106,* 61–85.

Rindos, D. (1984). *The origins of agriculture: An evolutionary perspective.* Orlando: Academic Press.

Rogers, J. (1994). Levels of the genealogical hierarchy and the problem of hominoid phylogeny. *American Journal of Physical Anthropology, 94,* 81–88.

Romer, A. S. (1945). *Vertebrate paleontology.* Chicago: University of Chicago Press.

Rosas, A., & Bermdez de Castro, J. M. (1998). On the taxonomic affinities of the Dmanisi mandible (Georgia). *American Journal of Physical Anthropology, 107,* 145–162.

Roscoe, P. B. (1995). The perils of "positivism" in cultural anthropology. *American Anthropologist, 97,* 497.

Roscoe, W. (1991). *Zuni man-woman.* Albuquerque: University of New Mexico Press.

Rowe, T. (1988). New issues for phylogenetics. *Science, 239,* 1,183–1,184.

Ruhlen, M. (1994). *The origin of language: Tracing the evolution of the mother tongue.* New York: Wiley.

Ruvdo, M. (1994). Molecular evolutionary processes and conflicting gene trees: The hominoid case. *American Journal of Physical Anthropology, 94,* 89–113.

Sabloff, J. A. (1989). *The cities of ancient Mexico.* New York: Thomas & Hudson.

Sabloff, J. A., & Lambert-Karlovsky, C. C. (1973). *Ancient civilization and trade.* Albuquerque: University of New Mexico Press.

Sabloff, J. A., & Lambert-Karlovsky, C. C. (Eds.). (1974). *The rise and fall of civilizations, modern archaeological approaches to ancient cultures.* Menlo Park, CA: Cummings.

Sahlins, M. (1961). The segmentary lineage: An organization of predatory expansion. *American Anthropologist, 63,* 322–343.

Sahlins, M. (1968). *Tribesmen.* Englewood Cliffs, NJ: Prentice-Hall (Foundations of Modern Anthropology).

Sahlins, M. (1972). *Stone age economics.* Chicago: Aldine.

Salthe, S. N. (1972). *Evolutionary biology.* New York: Holt, Rinehart and Winston.

Sanday, P. R. (1975). On the causes of IQ differences between groups and implications for social policy. In M. F. A. Montagu (Ed.), *Race and IQ* (pp. 232–238). New York: Oxford.

Sanday, P. R. (1981). *Female power and male dominance: On the origins of sexual inequality.* Cambridge, England: Cambridge University Press.

Sanday, P. R. (2002). *Women at the center: Life in a modern matriarchy.* Ithaca: Cornell University Press.

Sangree, W. H. (1965). The Bantu Tiriki of western Kenya. In J. L. Gibbs, Jr. (Ed.), *Peoples of Africa* (pp. 69–72). New York: Holt, Rinehart and Winston.

Sanjek R. (1990). On ethnographic validity. In R. Sanjek (Ed.), *Field notes.* Ithaca, New York: Cornell University Press.

Sapir, E. (1921). *Language.* New York: Harcourt.

Scaglion, R. (1987). Contemporary law development in Papua New Guinea. In R. M. Wulff & S. J. Fiske (Eds.), *Anthropological praxis: Translating knowledge into action.* Boulder, CO: Westview Press.

Scarr-Salapatek, S. (1971). Unknowns in the IQ equation. *Science, 174,* 1,223–1,228.

Schaller, G. B. (1971). *The year of the gorilla.* New York: Ballantine.

Scheflen, A. E. (1972). *Body language and the social order.* Englewood Cliffs, NJ: Prentice-Hall.

Schepartz, L.A. (1993). Language and human origins. *Yearbook of Physical Anthropology, 36,* 91–126.

Scheper-Hughes, N. (1979). *Saints, scholars and schizophrenics.* Berkeley: University of California Press.

Schlegel, A. (1977). Male and female in Hopi thought and action. In A. Schlegel (Ed.), *Sexual stratification* (pp. 245–269). New York: Columbia University Press.

Schrire, C. (Ed.). (1984). *Past and present in hunter-gatherer studies.* Orlando, FL: Academic Press.

Schusky, E. L. (1975). *Variation in kinship.* New York: Holt, Rinehart and Winston.

Schusky, E. L. (1983). *Manual for kinship analysis* (2nd ed.). Lanham, MD: University Press of America.

Schuster, C., & Edmund Carpenter, E. (1996). *Patterns that connect: Social symbolism in ancient and tribal art.* New York: Abrams.

Schwartz, J. H. (1984). Hominoid evolution: A review and a reassessment. *Current Anthropology, 25*(5), 655–672.

Scupin, R. (Ed.). (2000). *Religion and culture: An anthropological focus.* Upper Saddle River, NJ: Prentice-Hall.

Sellen, D. W., & Mace, R. (1997). Fertility and mode of subsistence: A phylogenetic analysis. *Current Anthropology, 38,* 886.

Semenov, S. A. (1964). *Prehistoric technology.* New York: Barnes & Noble.

Sen, G., & Grown, C. (1987). *Development, crisis, and alternative visions: Third World women's perspectives.* New York: Monthly Review Press.

Senut, B., et al. (2001). First hominid from the Miocene (Lukeino formation, Kenya). *C. R. Academy of Science, Paris, 332,* 137–144.

Seyfarth, R. M., et al. (1980). Monkey responses to three different alarm calls: Evidence for predator classification and semantic communication. *Science, 210,* 801–803.

Seymour, D. Z. (1986). Black children, black speech. In P. Escholz, A. Rosa & V. Clark (Eds.), *Language awareness* (4th ed.). New York: St. Martin's Press.

Shapiro, H. (Ed.). (1971). *Man, culture and society* (2nd. ed.). New York: Oxford University Press.

Sharer, R. J., & Ashmore, W. (1993). *Archaeology: Discovering our past* (2nd ed.). Palo Alto, CA: Mayfield.

Shaw, D. G. (1984). A light at the end of the tunnel: Anthropological contributions toward global competence. *Anthropology Newsletter, 25,* 16.

Shearer, R. R., & Gould, S. J. (1999), Of two minds and one nature. *Science 286,* 1093.

Sheets, P. (1993). Dawn of a new Stone Age in eye surgery. In R. J. Sharer & W. Ashmore, *Archaeology: Discovering our past* (2nd ed.). Palo Alto, CA: Mayfield.

Shimkin, D. B., Tax, S., & Morrison, J. W. (Eds.). (1978). *Anthropology for the future.* Urbana: Department of Anthropology, University of Illinois, Research Report No. 4.

Shinnie, M. (1970). *Ancient African kingdoms.* New York: New American Library.

Shipman, P. (1981). *Life history of a fossil: An introduction to taphonomy and paleoecology.* Cambridge, MA: Harvard University Press.

Shore, B. (1996). *Culture in mind: Meaning, construction, and cultural cognition.* New York: Oxford University Press.

Shostak, M. (1983). *Nisa: The life and words of a !Kung woman.* New York: Vintage.

Shreeve, J. (1994). "Lucy," crucial early human ancestor, finally gets a head. *Science, 264,* 34–35.

Shreeve, J. (1994). Terms of estrangement. *Discover, 15*(11), 60.

Shreeve, J. (1995). *The Neandertal enigma: Solving the mystery of modern human origins.* New York: William Morrow.

Shuey, A. M. (1966). *The testing of Negro intelligence.* New York: Social Science Press.

Sillen, A., & Brain, C. K. (1990). Old flame. *Natural History, 4,* 6–10.

Simons, E. L. (1972). *Primate evolution.* New York: Macmillan.

Simons, E. L. (1989) Human origins. *Science 245,* 1,349.

Simons, E. L. (1995). Skulls and anterior teeth of Catopithecus (primates: anthropoidea) from the Eocene and anthropoid origins. *Science, 268,* 1,885–1,888.

Simons, E. L., Rasmussen, D. T., & Gebo, D. L. (1987). A new species of Propliopithecus from the Fayum, Egypt. *American Journal of Physical Anthropology, 73,* 139–147.

Simpson, G. G. (1949). *The meaning of evolution.* New Haven, CT: Yale University Press.

Simpson, S. (1995, April). Whispers from the ice. *Alaska,* 23–28.

Sjoberg, G. (1960). *The preindustrial city.* New York: Free Press.

Skelton, R. R., McHenry, H. M., & Drawhorn, G. M. (1986). Phylogenetic analysis of early hominids. *Current Anthropology, 27,* 21–43.

Skolnick, A., & Skolnick, J. (Eds.). (2001). *Family in transition* (11th ed.). Boston: Allyn &Bacon.

Slobin, D. I. (1971). *Psycholinguistics.* Glenview, IL: Scott, Foresman.

Small, M. F. (1997). Making connections. *American Scientist, 85,* 503.

Smith, B. D. (1977). Archaeological inference and inductive confirmation. *American Anthropologist, 79*(3), 598–617.

Smith, B. H. (1994). Patterns of dental development in Homo, Australopithecus, Pan, and gorilla. *American Journal of Physical Anthropology, 94,* 307–325.

Smith, F. H., & Raynard, G. C.. (1980). Evolution of the supraorbital region in Upper Pleistocene fossil hominids from South-Central Europe. *American Journal of Physical Anthropology, 53,* 589–610.

Smith, P. E. L. (1976). *Food production and its consequences* (2nd ed.). Menlo Park, CA: Cummings.

Smith, R. (1970). Social stratification in the Caribbean. In L. Plotnicov & A. Tudin (Eds.), *Essays in comparative social stratification.* Pittsburgh: University of Pittsburgh Press.

Smuts, B. (1987). What are friends for? *Natural History. 96*(2), 36–44.

Snowden, C. T. (1990). Language capabilities of nonhuman animals. *Yearbook of Physical Anthropology, 33,* 215–243.

Sparks, J. (2003, December 22). The power game. *Newsweek, 142*(25).

Speck, F. G. (1920). Penobscot shamanism. *Memoirs of the American Anthropological Association, 6,* 239–288.

Speck, F. G. (1935). Penobscot tales and religious beliefs. *Journal of American Folk-Lore, 48*(187), 1–107.

Speck, F. G. (1970). *Penobscot man: The life history of a forest tribe in Maine.* New York: Octagon Books.

Spencer, F., & Smith, F. H. (1981). The significance of Ales Hrdlicka's "Neanderthal phase of man": A historical and current assessment. *American Journal of Physical Anthropology, 56,* 435–459.

Spencer, H. (1896). *Principles of sociology.* New York: Appleton.

Spencer, R. F. (1984). North Alaska Coast Eskimo. In D. Damas (Ed.), *Arctic* (Vol. 5): *Handbook of North American Indians* (pp. 320–337). Washington, DC: Smithsonian Institution.

Spiro, M. E. (1966). Religion: Problems of definition and explanation. In M. Banton (Ed.), *Anthropological approaches to the study of religion* (A.S.A. Monographs). London: Tavistock.

Spradley, J. P. (1979). *The ethnographic interview.* New York: Holt, Rinehart and Winston.

Spradley, J. P. (1980). *Participant observation.* New York: Holt, Rinehart and Winston.

Squires, S. (1997). The market research and product industry discovers anthropology. *Anthropology Newsletter, 38*(4), 31.

Stacey, J. (1990). *Brave new families.* New York: Basic Books.

Stahl, A. B. (1984). Hominid dietary selection before fire. *Current Anthropology, 25,* 151–168.

Stanford, C. B. (1998). The social behavior of chimpanzees and bonobos: Empirical evidence and shifting assumptions. *Current Anthropology, 39,* 399–420.

Stanford, C. B. (2001). *Chimpanzee and red colobus: The ecology of predator and prey.* Cambridge, MA: Harvard University Press.

Stanley, S. M. (1979). *Macroevolution.* San Francisco: Freeman.

Stannard, D. E. (1992). *American holocaust.* Oxford: Oxford University Press.

Stedman, H. H., et al. (2004). Myosin gene mutation correlates with anatomical changes in the human lineage. *Nature, 428,* 415–418.

Steward, J. H. (1972). *Theory of culture change: The methodology of multilinear evolution.* Urbana: University of Illinois Press.

Stiglitz, J. E. (2003). *Globalization and its discontents.* New York: Norton.

Stiles, D. (1979). Early Acheulean and developed Oldowan. *Current Anthropology, 20*(l), 126–129.

Stiles, D. (1992). The hunter-gatherer "revisionist" debate. *Anthropology Today, 8*(2), 13–17.

Stirton, R. A. (1967). *Time, life, and man.* New York: Wiley.

Stocking, G. W., Jr. (1968). *Race, culture and evolution: Essays in the history of anthropology.* New York: Free Press.

Stone, L. (1998). *Kinship and gender: An introduction.* Boulder, CO: Westview Press.

Stone, R. (1995). If the mercury soars, so may health hazards. *Science, 267,* 958.

Straughan, B. (1996). The secrets of ancient Tiwanaku are benefiting today's Bolivia. In W. A. Haviland & R. J. Gordon (Eds.), *Talking about people* (2nd ed., pp. 76–78). Mountain View, CA: Mayfield.

Straus, W. L., & Cave, A. J. E. (1957). Pathology and the posture of Neanderthal man. *Quarterly Review of Biology, 32.*

Stringer, C. B., & McKie, R. (1996). *African exodus: The origins of modern humanity.* London: Jonathan Cape.

Stuart-MacAdam, P., & Dettwyler, K. A. (Eds.). (1995). *Breastfeeding: Biocultural perspectives.* New York: Aldine de Gruyter.

Suarez-Orozoco, M. M., Spindler, G., & Spindler, L. (1994). *The making of psychological anthropology, II.* Fort Worth, TX: Harcourt Brace.

Sullivan, M. (1999). Chimpanzee hunting habit yield clues about early ancestors. *Chronicle of Higher Education.*

Susman, R. L. (1988). Hand of *Paranthropus robustus* from Member 1, Swartkrans: Fossil evidence for tool behavior. *Science, 240,* 781–784.

Swadesh, M. (1959). Linguistics as an instrument of prehistory. *Southwestern Journal of Anthropology, 15,* 20–35.

Swaminathan, M. S. (2000). Science in response to basic human needs. *Science, 287,* 425.

Swartz, M. J., Turner, V. W., & Tuden, A. (1966). *Political anthropology.* Chicago: Aldine.

Swisher III, C. C., Curtis, G. H., Jacob, T., Getty, A. G., Suprijo, A., & Widiasmoro. (1994). Age of the earliest known hominids in Java, Indonesia. *Science, 263,* 1,118–1,121.

Tannen, D. (1990). *You just don't understand: Women and men in conversation.* New York: Morrow.

Tapper, M. (1999). *In the blood: Sickle-cell anemia and the politics of race.* Philadelphia: University of Pennsylvania Press.

Tax, S. (1953). *Penny capitalism: A Guatemalan Indian economy.* Washington, DC:

Smithsonian Institution, Institute of Social Anthropology, Pub. No. 16.

Tax, S. (Ed.). (1962). *Anthropology today: Selections.* Chicago: University of Chicago Press.

Tax, S., Stanley, S., et al. (1975). In honor of Sol Tax. *Current Anthropology. 16,* 507–540.

Taylor, G. (2000). *Castration: Abbreviated history of western manhood.* (pp. 38–44, 252–259). New York: Routledge.

Templeton, A. R. (1994). Eve: Hypothesis compatibility versus hypothesis testing. *American Anthropologist, 96*(1), 141–147.

Templeton, A. R. (1995). The "Eve" hypothesis: A genetic critique and reanalysis. *American Anthropologist, 95*(1), 51–72.

Templeton, A. R. (1996). Gene lineages and human evolution. *Science, 272,* 1,363–1,364.

Thomas, D. H. (1998). *Archaeology* (3rd ed.). Fort Worth, TX: Harcourt Brace.

Thomas, E. M. (1994). *The tribe of the tiger: Cats and their culture* (pp. 109–186). New York: Simon & Schuster.

Thompson, S. (1960). *The folktale.* New York: Holt, Rinehart and Winston.

Thomson, K. S. (1997). Natural selection and evolution's smoking gun. *American Scientist, 85,* 516–518.

Thorne, A. G., & Wolpoff, M. D. H. (1981). Regional continuity in Australasian Pleistocene hominid evolution. *American Journal of Physical Anthropology, 55,* 337–349.

Thornhill, N. (1993). Quoted in W. A. Haviland & R. J. Gordon (Eds.), *Talking about people* (p. 127). Mountain View, CA: Mayfield.

Tiffany, S. (Ed.). (1979). *Women in Africa.* St. Albans, VT: Eden Press.

Tobias, P. V. (1980). The natural history of the heliocoidal occlusal plane and its evolution in early *Homo. American Journal of Physical Anthropology, 53,* 173–187.

Tobias, P. V., & von Konigswald, G. H. R. (1964). A comparison between the Olduvai hominines and those of Java and some implications for hominid phylogeny. *Nature, 204,* 515–518.

Trevor-Roper, H. (1992). Invention of tradition: The Highland tradition of Scotland. In E. Hobsbawm & T. Ranger (Eds.), *The invention of tradition* (Ch. 2). Cambridge: Cambridge University Press.

Trinkaus, E. (1986). The Neanderthals and modern human origins. *Annual Review of Anthropology, 15,* 197.

Trinkaus, E., & Shipman, P. (1992). *The Neandertals: Changing the image of mankind.* New York: Knopf.

Trouillot, M. R. (1996). Culture, color, and politics in Haiti. In S. Gregory & R. Sanjek (Eds.), *Race.* New Brunswick, NJ: Rutgers University Press.

Trouillot, M. R. (2003). *Global transformations: Anthropology and the modern world.* New York: Palgrave Macmillan.

Tuden, A. (1970). Slavery and stratification among the Ila of central Africa. In A. Tuden & L. Plotnicov (Eds.), *Social stratification in Africa.* New York: Free Press.

Tumin, M. M. (1967). *Social stratification: The forms and functions of inequality.* Englewood Cliffs, NJ: Prentice-Hall (Foundations of Modern Sociology).

Turnbull, C. (1983). *Mbuti Pygmies: Change and adaptation.* New York: Holt, Rinehart and Winston.

Turnbull, C. M. (1961). *The forest people.* New York: Simon & Schuster.

Turnbull, C. M. (1983). *The human cycle.* New York: Simon & Schuster.

Turner, T. (1991). Major shift in Brazilian Yanomami policy. *Anthropology Newsletter, 32*(5), 1, 46.

Turner, V. W. (1957). *Schism and continuity in an African society.* Manchester, England: University Press.

Turner, V. W. (1969). *The ritual process.* Chicago: Aldine.

Tylor, E. B. (1871). *Primitive culture: Researches into the development of mythology, philosophy, religion, language, art and customs.* London: Murray.

Tylor, Sir E. B. (1931). Animism. In V. F. Calverton (Ed.), *The making of man: An outline of anthropology.* New York: Modern Library.

Ucko, P. J., & Rosenfeld, A. (1967). *Paleolithic cave art.* New York: McGraw-Hill.

Ucko, P. J., Tringham, R., & Dimbleby, G. W. (Eds.). (1972). *Man, settlement, and urbanism.* London: Duckworth.

Ury, W. L. (1993). *Getting past no: Negotiating your way from confrontation.* New York: Bantam Books.

Ury, W. L. (1999). *Getting to peace: Transforming conflict at home, at work, and in the world.* New York: Viking.

Ury, W. (2002). A global immune system. *Andover Bulletin* (Winter).

Ury, W. L. (Ed.). (2002). *Must we fight? From the battlefield to the schoolyard—A new perspective on violent conflict and its prevention.* Hoboken, NJ: Jossey-Bass.

U.S. Census 2000. www.adherents.com.

U.S. Department of Commerce, Census Bureau. (2000, January).

Valentine, C. A. (1968). *Culture and poverty.* Chicago: University of Chicago Press.

Van Allen, J. (1997). Sitting on a man: Colonialism and the lost political institutions of Igbo women. In R. Grinker & C. Steiner (Eds.), *Perspectives on Africa* (p. 450). Boston: Blackwell Press.

Van den Berghe, P. (1992). The modern state: Nation builder or nation killer? *International Journal of Group Tensions, 22*(3), 191–207.

Van Gennep, A. (1960). *The rites of passage.* Chicago: University of Chicago Press.

Vansina, J. (1965). *Oral tradition: A study in historical methodology* (H. M. Wright, Trans.). Chicago: Aldine.

Van Willigen, J. (1986). *Applied anthropology.* South Hadley, MA: Bergin & Garvey.

Vayda, A. P. (1961). Expansion and warfare among swidden agriculturalists. *American Anthropologist, 63,* 346–358.

Vayda, A. P. (Ed.). (1969). *Environment and cultural behavior: Ecological studies in cultural anthropology.* Garden City: Natural History Press.

Vincent, J. (1979). On the special division of labor, population, and the origins of agriculture. *Current Anthropology, 20*(2), 422–425.

Voget, F. W. (1975). *A history of ethnology.* New York, Holt, Rinehart and Winston.

Vogt, E. Z. (1990). *The Zinacantecos of Mexico: A modern Maya way of life* (2nd ed.). Fort Worth: Holt, Rinehart and Winston.

Wagner, P. L. (1960). *A history of ethnology.* New York: Holt, Rinehart and Winston.

Wallace, A. F. C. (1956). Revitalization movements. *American Anthropologist, 58,* 264–281.

Wallace, A. F. C. (1965). The problem of the psychological validity of componential analysis. *American Anthropologist, Special Publication (Part 2), 67*(5), 229–248.

Wallace, A. F. C. (1966). *Religion: An anthropological view.* New York: Random House.

Wallace, A. F. C. (1970). *Culture and personality* (2nd ed.). New York: Random House.

Wallace, E., & Hoebel, E. A. (1952). *The Comanches*. Norman: University of Oklahoma Press.

Ward, C. V., Walker, A., Teaford, M. F., & Odhiambo, I. (1993). Partial skeleton of Proconsul nyanzae from Mfangano Island, Kenya. *American Journal of Physical Anthropology, 90*, 77–111.

Wardhaugh, R. (1972). *Introduction to linguistics*. New York: McGraw-Hill.

Washburn, S. L., & Moore, R. (1980). *Ape into human: A study of human evolution* (2nd ed.). Boston: Little, Brown.

Weatherford, J. (1988). *Indian givers: How the Indians of the Americas transformed the world*. New York: Ballantine.

Weaver, M. P. (1972). *The Aztecs, Maya and their predecessors*. New York: Seminar Press.

Weiner, A. B. (1977). Review of Trobriand cricket: An ingenious response to colonialism. *American Anthropologist, 79*, 506.

Weiner, A. B. (1988). *The Trobrianders of Papua New Guinea*. New York: Holt, Rinehart and Winston.

Weiner, J. S. (1955). *The Piltdown forgery*. Oxford: Oxford University Press.

Weiner, M. (1966). *Modernization: The dynamics of growth*. New York: Basic Books.

Weiss, M. L., & Mann, A. E. (1990). *Human biology and behavior* (5th ed.). Boston: Little, Brown.

Weitzman, L. J. (1985). *The divorce revolution: The unexpected social and economic consequences for women and children in America*. New York: Free Press.

Werner, D. (1990). *Amazon journey*. Englewood Cliffs, NJ: Prentice-Hall.

Wernick, R., & the Editors of Time-Life. (1973). *The monument builders*. New York: Time-Life.

Westermarck, E. A. (1926). *A short history of marriage*. New York: Macmillan.

Wheeler, P. (1993). Human ancestors walked tall, stayed cool. *Natural History, 102*(8), 65–66.

Whelehan, P. (1985). Review of incest, a biosocial view. *American Anthropologist, 87*, 678.

White, D. R. (1988). Rethinking polygyny: Co-wives, codes, and cultural systems. *Current Anthropology, 29*, 529–572.

White, E., Brown, D., & the Editors of Time-Life. (1973). *The first men*. New York: Time-Life.

White, L. (1949). *The science of culture: A study of man and civilization*. New York: Farrar, Strauss.

White, L. (1959). *The evolution of culture: The development of civilization to the fall of Rome*. New York: McGraw-Hill.

White, M. (2001). *Historical atlas of the twentieth century*. http://users.erols .com/mwhite28/20centry.htm.

White, P. (1976). *The past is human* (2nd ed.). New York: Maplinger.

White, R. (1992). The earliest images: Ice Age "art" in Europe. *Expedition, 34*(3), 37–51.

White, T., Asfaw, B., Degusta, D., Gilbert, H., Richards, G., Suwa, G., Howell, F. C. (2003). Pleistocene *Homo sapiens* from the Middle Awash, Ethiopia. *Nature, 423*, 742–747.

White, T. D. (1979). Evolutionary implications of Pliocene hominid footprints. *Science, 208*, 175–176.

White, T. D. (2003). Early hominids—diversity or distortion? *Science, 299*, 1,994–1,997.

White, T. D., & Toth, N. (2000). Cutmarks on a Plio-Pleistocene hominid from Sterkfontein, South Africa. *American Journal of Physical Anthropology, 111*, 579–584.

Whitehead, B. D. & Popenoe, D. (2004). *The state of our unions: The social health of marriage in America 2004*. Rutgers, NJ: Rutgers University National Marriage Project.

Whitehead, N., & Ferguson, R. B. (Eds.). (1992). *War in the tribal zone*. Santa Fe: School of American Research Press.

Whitehead, N. L., & Ferguson, R. B. (1993, November). Deceptive stereotypes about tribal warfare. *Chronicle of Higher Education*, p. A48.

Whiting, B. B. (Ed.). (1963). *Six cultures: Studies of child rearing*. New York: Wiley.

Whiting, J. W. M., & Child, I. L. (1953). *Child training and personality: A cross-cultural study*. New Haven, CT: Yale University Press.

Whiting, J. W. M., Sodergem, J. A., & Stigler, S. M. (1982). Winter temperature as a constraint to the migration of preindustrial peoples. *American Anthropologist, 84*, 289.

Wilk, R. R. (1996). *Economics and cultures: An introduction to economic anthropology*. Boulder, CO: Westview Press.

Willey, G. R. (1966). *An introduction to American archaeology: Vol. 1. North America*. Englewood Cliffs, NJ: Prentice-Hall.

Willey, G. R. (1971). *An introduction to American archaeology, Vol. 2: South America*. Englewood Cliffs, NJ: Prentice-Hall.

Williams, A. M. (1996). *Sex, drugs, and HIV: A sociocultural analysis of two, groups of gay and bisexual male substance users who practice unprotected sex*. Unpublished manuscript.

Williamson, R. K. (1995). The blessed curse: Spirituality and sexual difference as viewed by Euro-American and Native American cultures. *The College News, 18*(4).

Wills, C. (1994). The skin we're in. *Discover, 15*(11), 79.

Wilson, A. K., & Sarich, V. M. (1969). A molecular time scale for human evolution. *Proceedings of the National Academy of Science, 63*, 1,089–1,093.

Wingert, P. (1965). *Primitive art: Its tradition and styles*. New York: World.

Winick, C. (Ed.). (1970). *Dictionary of anthropology*. Totowa, NJ: Littlefield, Adams.

Wirsing, R. L. (1985). The health of traditional societies and the effects of acculturation. *Current Anthropology, 26*(3), 303–322.

Wittfogel, K. A. (1957). *Oriental despotism, a comparative study of total power*. New Haven, CT: Yale University Press.

Wolf, E. R. (1959). *Sons of the shaking earth*. Chicago: University of Chicago Press.

Wolf, E. R. (1966). *Peasants*. Englewood Cliffs, NJ: Prentice-Hall.

Wolf, E. R. (1982). *Europe and the people without history*. Berkeley: University of California Press.

Wolf, E. R. (1999). *Envisioning power: Ideologies of dominance and crisis*. Berkeley: University of California Press.

Wolf, M. (1972). *Women and the family in rural Taiwan*. Stanford, CA: Stanford University Press.

Wolf, M. (1985). *Revolution postponed: Women in contemporary China*. Stanford, CA: Stanford University Press.

Wolpoff, M. H. (1977). Review of earliest man in the Lake Rudolf Basin. *American Anthropologist, 79*, 708-711.

Wolpoff, M. H. (1982). *Ramapithecus* and hominid origins. *Current Anthropology, 23*, 501–522.

Wolpoff, M. H. (1993). Evolution in *Homo erectus*: The question of stasis. In R. L.

Ciochon & J. G. Fleagle (Eds.), *The human evolution source book*. Englewood Cliffs, NJ: Prentice-Hall.

Wolpoff, M. H. (1993). Multiregional evolution: The fossil alternative to Eden. In R. L. Ciochon & J. G. Fleagle (Eds.), *The human evolution source book*. Englewood Cliffs, NJ: Prentice-Hall.

Wolpoff, M. (1996). *Australopithecus:* A new look at an old ancestor. *General Anthropology, 3*(1), 2.

Wolpoff, M., & Caspari, R. (1997). *Race and human evolution*. New York: Simon & Schuster.

Wolpoff, M. H., Wu, X. Z. & Thorne, A. G. (1984). Modern *Homo sapiens* origins: A general theory of hominid evolution involving fossil evidence from east Asia. In F. H. Smith and F. Spencer (Eds.), *The origins of modern humans* (pp. 411–483). New York: Alan R. Liss.

Womack, M. (1994). Program 5: *Psychological anthropology. Faces of culture*. Fountain Valley, CA: Coast Telecourses, Inc.

Wong, K. (1998, January). Ancestral quandary: Neanderthals not our ancestors? Not so fast. *Scientific American,* 30–32.

Wood, B., & Aiello, L. C. (1998). Taxonomic and functional implications of mandibular scaling in early hominines. *American Journal of Physical Anthropology, 105,* 523–538.

Wood, B., Wood, C., & Konigsberg, L. (1994). *Paranthropus boisei:* An example of evolutionary stasis? *American Journal of Physical Anthropology, 95,* 117–136.

Woodward, V. (1992). *Human heredity and society*. St. Paul, MN: West.

Woolfson, P. (1972). Language, thought, and culture. In V. P. Clark, P. A. Escholz, & A. F. Rosa (Eds.), *Language*. New York: St. Martin's Press.

World Bank. (1982). *Tribal peoples and economic development*. Washington, DC: World Bank.

World Bank. (2003). www.worldbank.org /poverty. Accessed January 2003.

World Health Organization. http://www.who.int/about /definition/en/.

World Meteorological Organization. (2003). Increasing heat waves and other health hazards. greenpeaceusa.org/climate /index.fpl/7096/article/907.html. Accessed December 2003.

Worsley, P. (1959). Cargo cults. *Scientific American, 200* (May), 117–128.

Wrangham, R., & Peterson, D. (1996). *Demonic males*. Boston: Houghton Mifflin.

Wright, R. (1984). Towards a new Indian policy in Brazil. *Cultural Survival Quarterly 8*(1).

Wright, R. M. (1997). Violence on Indian day in Brazil 1997: Symbol of the past and future. *Cultural Survival Quarterly, 21* (2), 47–49.

Wulff, R. M., & Fiske, S. J. (1987). *Anthropological praxis: Translating knowledge into action*. Boulder, CO: Westview Press.

Yip, M. (2002). *Tone*. New York: Cambridge University Press.

Young, A. (1981). The creation of medical knowledge: Some problems in interpretation. *Social Science and Medicine, 17,*1,205–1,211.

Young, W. (Ed.). (2000). Kimball award winner. *Anthropology News, 41*(8), 29.

Zeder, M. A., & Hesse, B. (2000). The initial domestication of goats (*Capra hircus*) in the Zagros Mountains 10,000 years ago. *Science, 287,* 2,254–2,257.

Zilhão, J. (2000). Fate of the Neandertals. *Archaeology, 53*(4), 30.

Zimmer, C. (1999). New date for the dawn of dream time. *Science, 284,* 1,243.

Zohary, D., & Hopf, M. (1993). *Domestication of plants in the Old World* (2nd ed.). Oxford: Clarenden Press.

Photo Credits

Chapter 1 Opener Page 2: ©Sandi Fellman; Page 4: ©Documentary Educational Resources; Page 6: ©1998 Jim Leachman; Page 8: ©Susan Meiselas/Magnum Photos; Page 14: ©Kerry Cullinan; Page 17: ©Gordon Gahnan/National Geographic Image Collection.

Chapter 2 Opener Page 20: ©Chris Benton; Page 26: ©Biophoto Associates/Photo Researchers, Inc.; Page 31: *X-Men*©2000 Twentieth Century Fox. All rights reserved.; Page 34: ©Meckers/Ottowa/Photo Researchers, Inc.

Chapter 3 Opener Page 38: ©Jodi Cobb/National Geographic Image Collection; Page 41: McGuire/Anthro-Photo; Page 42: ©Irven DeVore/Anthro-Photo; Page 45 top: Dani/Jeske/Animals Animals-Earth Scenes – All rights reserved; Page 45 bottom: ©Michael Dick/Animals Animals-Earth Scenes – All rights reserved; Page 46: Courtesy of Dana Walrath; Page 47: ©Peter Drowne/Color-Pic, Inc.; Page 49: ©Amy Parish/Anthro-Photo. Page 53: ©Martha Harvey/Peter Arnold, Inc.

Chapter 4 Opener Page 58: ©Javier Trueba/Madrid Scientific Films; Page 61: ©AP/Wide World Photos; Page 64: Courtesy of Dana Walrath; Page 65: ©Mike Andrews/Ancient Art & Architecture Collection; Page 66: ©William A. Haviland; Page 67: ©William A Haviland; Page 68: From: *Tikal, A Handbook of the Ancient Maya Ruins* by William R. Coe. University of Pennsylvania Museum, 1967; Page 69: ©2001 David L. Brill/Brill Atlanta.

Chapter 5 Opener Page 74: ©AP/Wide World Photos; Page 77: ©Oliver Meckes/Photo Researchers, Inc.; Page 81 left: ©David L. Brill by permission of Owen Lovejoy; Page 81 right: ©1985 David L. Brill; Page 82: ©1999 David L. Brill; Page 85: ©Antoine Devouard/REA Agency/Redux Pictures; Page 86 left and right: ©William A. Haviland; Page 88 left and right: ©David L. Brill; Page 91: ©Erich Lessing/Art Resource, NY.

Chapter 6 Opener Page 96: ©Erich Lessing/Art Resource, NY; Page 100: Illustration by W. C. Galinat. Reprinted with permission from W. C. Galinat, "The origin of maize: grain of humanity." Economic Botany Vol 49, pp 3-12, Fig. 1A-C, copyright 1995, The New York Botanical Garden; Page 109: ©Ankara

Archeological Museum/Ara Guler, Istanbul; Page 111: ©Alan H. Goodman, Hampshire College.

Chapter 7 Opener Page116: ©Susan Zheng/UNEP/Peter Arnold, Inc.; Page 120: ©William A. Haviland; Page 122: ©Rolox Awards for Enterprise, Susan Gray; Page 123: The University Museum, University of Pennsylvania; Page 124: ©Robert Holmes/Corbis; Page 125: ©Anita de Laguna Haviland; Page 127: Courtesy of Tavid Bingham.

Chapter 8 Opener Page 132: ©White Packert/Iconica/Getty Images; Page 136 top: ©Laurance Dutton/Getty Images; Page 136 bottom: Photo by R. R. Grinker; Page 137: ©Scott Nelson/Getty Images; Page 143: ©Susan Van Etten/PhotoEdit – All rights reserved; Page 144: ©Gusto/Photo Researchers.

Chapter 9 Opener Page 148: ©David Wells/The Image Works; Page 151: ©David Young-Wolff/PhotoEdit – All rights reserved; Page 153: ©Dennis McDonald/PhotoEdit – All rights reserved; Page 157: ©David Tejada/Getty Images; Page 159: ©Alec Duncan.

Chapter 10 Opener Page 164: ©Yavuz Arslan/Peter Arnold; Page 167: ©Lyn Miles, Ph.D/Chantek Foundation; Page 177 left: ©John Chellmann/Animals Animals; Page 177 right: © Julia Klee/Corbis.

Chapter 11 Opener Page 182: ©Danny Lehman/Corbis; Page 185 left: ©1991 Richard Lord; Page 185 right: ©David Young-Wolff/PhotoEdit – All rights reserved; Page 191: ©Napoleon Chagnon/Anthro-Photo; Page 197: Photography Hugh Heartshorne, Copyright ©Re Angle Pictures.

Chapter 12 Opener Page 202: ©1991 Richard Lord; Page 206: ©Nathan Benn/Corbis; Page 208: ©Reinhold Loeffler; Page 211: ©Irven DeVore/Anthro-Photo; Page 213 left and right: ©Anthony Bannister/ABPL; Page 215: ©Stan Washburn/Anthro-Photo; Page 219: ©1998 Richard Lord.

Chapter 13 Opener Page 224: ©Richard T. Nowitz/Corbis; Page 226 left: ©Lisa Krantz/The Image Works; Page 226 right: Catherine Kamaow/Corbis; Page 231 left: ©AP/Wide World Photos; Page 231 right: ©Lauren Goodsmith/The Image Works; Page 236: ©Momatiuk/Eastcott/Woodfin Camp

& Associates, Inc.; Page 239: ©John Eastcott/Eve Monatiuk/The Image Works.

Chapter 14 Opener Page 244: ©Wally Turnbull; Page 248: Arizona State Museum, University of Arizona. Helga Teiwes, Photographer; Page 249: ©David Sanipass; Page 253: John Vereist/National Archives of Canada; Page 257: ©Bruce Davidson/Nature Picture Library; Page 259: ©Chris Trotman/New Sport/Corbis; Page 260 left: ©Charles and Josette Lenars/Corbis; Page 260 right: ©Rob Crandall/The Image Works.

Chapter 15 Opener Page 266: ©AP Photo/Santiago Andrade/Wide World Photos; Page 270: ©George Holton/Photo Researchers, Inc.; Page 274 left: ©Reuters/Corbis; Page 274 right: ©K. Prouse/Pressnet/Topham/The Image Works; Page 277: ©Cunera Buijs; Page 280: ©Jay Dickman; Page 283: ©Napoleon Chagnon/Anthro-Photo.

Chapter 16 Opener Page 288: Photographer: Hester and Hardaway Photographers. The Menil Collection, Houston; Page 291: ©Francesco Campani Photography/photographersdiret.com; Page 294: ©Irven DeVore/Anthro-Photo; Page 299: ©AP/Wide World Photos; Page 302: ©The Cover Story/Corbis; Page 303: Courtesy of the National Museum of the American Indian, Smithsonian Institution. Photo No 4771; Page 304: Courtesy of the Burke Museum of Natural History and Culture. Painting # 1163.

Chapter 17 Opener Page 308: ©Staffan Widstrand/Corbis; Page 310: ©Stephen Trimble; Page 315 bottom: ©Scully/Getty Images; Page 315 top: ©Bettmann/Corbis; Page 317: ©Jerry Leach; Page 321: ©AP/Wide World Photos.

Chapter 18 Opener Page 326: ©Luis Marden/NGS Image Collection; Page 331: ©Zahid Hussein/Reuters; Page 332: ©AP/Wide World Photos; Page 335: ©Tom Davenport/Photo Researchers, Inc.; Page 339: Courtesy of IMF; Page 344: Courtesy of Elizabeth A. Guilette; Page 346 top left: ©Reuters/Corbis; Page 346 top right: Amnesty International; Page 346 center right and bottom right: ©AP/Wide World Photos.

Index

Wolpoff, M., 80, 92
Women. *See* Gender
Woods, Tiger, 138
Woods, William I., 105–106
World Bank, 321, 334, 338, 339
World Council of Churches, 333
World migrations, 329
World Trade Center attacks, 8–9
World Trade Organization (WTO), 330, 338
Worldview, 289–290
 naturalistic worldview, 291
World Watch Institute, 341
Wounded Knee, battle of, 314
Wrangham, Richard, 54, 282

Writing, 180
 development of, 179–180
 in early civilizations, 125
 of Maya, 125, 180
Wulff, R. M., 297–298

X
X chromosome, 26

Y
Yakö society, double descent in, 248
Yanomami society, 191
 ethnocide and, 313–314
 warfare in, 283
Yaqui Indians, 344

Y chromosome, 26
Yes, gesture expressions for, 178
Young, W., 321–322

Z
Zagros Mountains
 animal domestication in, 100
 Bakhtiari people, 208
Zambia, Kabwe skull, 89
Zapatista Maya Indian uprising, 318
Zeder, M. A., 100
Zimmerman, Michael, 63
Zoos, primates in, 55
Zulu culture and AIDS, 14–15
The Zuni Man-Woman (Roscoe), 194